THE PSALMS IN
ISRAEL'S WORSHIP

SIGMUND MOWINCKEL

THE PSALMS IN ISRAEL'S WORSHIP

Translated by

D. R. AP-THOMAS

*Lecturer in Hebrew & Old Testament,
University College of North Wales
Bangor*

In Two Volumes — Volume I

ABINGDON PRESS

new york · nashville

1967

First printed 1962
Reprinted 1967

PRINTED IN GREAT BRITAIN

CONTENTS

Volume I

I, b

Volume II

Translator's Preface

I rejoice that at last one of the really significant works of our day on the biblical psalms is available to a wider circle of readers than could be reached by the original one-volume Norwegian edition. This book however is more than a translation of *Offersang og Sangoffer* as published in 1951 by H. Aschehoug & Co. of Oslo; it gives the reader a fully revised text. One chapter from the original has been dropped because the author felt that it was not fully relevant here; the material in another chapter has been redistributed; less immediately germane excursuses have been arranged as a series of Additional Notes appended to volume II; and most chapters show more or less extensive revision at the hands of the author, the final revisions having been incorporated at the proof stage, so that the present edition may claim to represent the author's latest views. These revisions, but still more the fulfilment of a lecturer's manifold tasks, have delayed the appearance of this book far beyond what had been expected. But the author has never once chided me for my slowness, and I am most grateful to him also for his careful reading of the proofs—which should guarantee that his views are nowhere seriously mis-represented in this volume. Where the author's technical terms seemed to me to carry overtones not present in the conventional English equivalents, I have not hesitated to translate more literally than elegantly.

References to the Old Testament follow the chapter (Psalm) and verse in Hebrew as given in *BH*[3]. (this means, as most will know, that for the psalms in English the verse number must usually be decreased by one). English renderings are based on the author's own Norwegian renderings in most cases. Where the Hebrew text is quoted, transliteration has been used, in spite of some complication in the chapter on metrics; the system used will, it is hoped, be obvious to the Hebraist and not too uncouth to the uninitiated.

I fear that consistency in such matters as abbreviation and form of reference has not entirely been attained, but it is hoped that intelligibility at least has been preserved. In addition to the many scripture references, all the bibliographical references given in the notes—with a few exceptions on account of inaccessibility—have been cross-checked for this edition, and my warmest thanks are due to Professor emeritus H. H. Rowley, who not only placed the splendid resources of his own library at my disposal but most generously helped me to track down and borrow books from other sources also. Wherever an English translation of a work referred to was known to me, a reference thereto has been added if applicable; but it should be pointed out that in some cases published translations are incomplete, consequently—and for the convenience of those possessing the original—the reference to the foreign work has been retained in every case.

In preparing the MS. for the press I have had every co-operation from my typists, Mrs F. G. Hughes and Miss Joan Yates. My friend the Rev. D. J. Williams and my wife, too, have helped me a great deal in checking the final draft of the MS.; in addition to these, I would like to thank the publisher for his continuous interest and readiness to discuss each stage of the work. Père de Vaux and L'école biblique at Jerusalem most graciously allowed me to use the resources of their magnificent library for some final checking while the MS. was in press.

D. R. Ap-Thomas.

Bangor,
October, 1961

Author's Preface to the English Edition

This book originally appeared in Norwegian dress in 1951; it has been revised in certain respects for the present edition. One chapter, which dealt with the use of the psalms in the Church, and which was strongly coloured by having been written during enemy occupation, has been omitted.

Scientifically speaking, the historical viewpoint from which I regard the psalms is that of form history—or, as it may better be termed, type history (*Gattungsgeschichte*)—a method of approach introduced by Hermann Gunkel. But when I began my *Psalmenstudien* I–VI (1921–24) it had become apparent to me that that point of view was not sufficient. In order to understand the psalms in their relationship to the religious life of Israel and of Judaism it is necessary also to use in addition the cult functional approach. They must be viewed and comprehended in their relationship to the congregation's devotional life. The great majority of the psalms which have come down to us do not simply derive, as a matter of form history or literary history, from ancient cult poetry—they are real cult psalms composed for and used in the actual services in the Temple. Private and more personal psalm poetry first occurs in the late Jewish period. In the Psalter such psalms constitute a minority.

The Norwegian edition bore the title *Offersang og Sangoffer*—'Song of sacrifice and Sacrifice of song' or 'Offering song and Song offering'. This was meant to suggest one of the avenues through the history of psalm poetry in the Old Testament. What I mean by that will appear in the chapter entitled 'The Learned Psalmography' (Chap. XVI).

One result of my work in connexion with the psalms—which has even surprised myself—is to see to how great an extent the piety and image of God which grew up within the official cult religion in the Temple at Jerusalem is presupposed by, and not a result of, the activity of the great classical prophets. Within the Christian Church the Psalter has always been the most used and most beloved book of the Old Testament. The biblical psalms have been the *fons et origo* of Christian hymnody, and they have still much to teach us about the real essence of writing hymns for divine service; for they provide a corrective to the often only too subjectively lyrical in more modern religious poetry and song.

The chapter on The Psalms at the Enthronement Festival of Yahweh was delivered as the Dale Lectures at Mansfield College, Oxford in 1953. I frequently think back with joy and gratitude to that occasion.

I would also express my thanks to the translator, Mr D. R. Ap-Thomas for his unwearying patience and care; the work has not been easy. My thanks go likewise to the publisher for his kindness in undertaking to publish the English edition.

SIGMUND MOWINCKEL.

Oslo,
October, 1961

CHAPTER I

The Psalms and the Cult

I

No book of the Old Testament has been read so much throughout the ages as the book of Psalms, 'the Psalms of David' as they are popularly termed.

The sense of the actuality of the prophets has often fluctuated; in evil times, in war, and in great disasters men have felt their significance more easily than under other conditions. But in the psalms the human heart has found its own counterpart at all times, in sorrow and in happiness, as an individual and as a member of God's People.

Hence it is natural that the psalms have been more often examined and interpreted than any other part of the Old Testament. Both the theologian and the historian of literature are interested in this poetry, and desire to know what are the conditions for understanding it, the soil from which it has sprung, the background against which it must be seen. Who are the men who are here pouring out their hearts and in whose words we are still doing the same? When did they live, under what conditions did they strive and suffer, sorrow and rejoice? What have they experienced, and what have they to tell us of their faith and hope, and of the reality on which that faith and hope are founded?

We wish to become acquainted with the psalms as they really were, namely, as real prayers uttered by men of flesh and blood praying in actual situations at a definite period. And with that background we also wish to see what is common and representative in them—that which makes them live to this day.

We must therefore try to understand them historically, on the basis of their own times. But this also means that we must try to find their place and function in the religious life of ancient Israel, or in early Judaism, if a critical historical examination should show that we have both pre-exilic and post-exilic psalms in the Psalter. Incidentally, in my view, this difference in time has not been of any great importance for their real place and function in the religious life of the congregation.

It is against this background of the historical and religio-phenomenological understanding that the real and lasting qualities of the psalms will appear.

What then, is the right view of the psalms? What are they essentially?

Neither the Greek word *psalmós* nor its Hebrew equivalent *mizmōr* necessarily means a cultic song only, but they are mostly used in this sense.

And by the word 'psalm' (Norwegian 'salme' is used also for hymn) we nowadays as a rule mean, in contrast to other spiritual songs, not a religious poem generally, but one which is connected with the worship of the congregation.[1] In any case it means a poem which arises from, or is related to, that experience which is expressed in worship, a worship which expresses the ideas and sentiments of the worshippers and their common attitude to the Godhead; such a poem therefore makes a more or less marked use of language which has already been shaped by worship.

Closer investigation has proved that in all religions, Christianity included, religious poetry has originated in connexion with congregational worship, and has been subordinated to it. Then the question arises: was this also the case in the Israelitic-Jewish religion, and does it thus apply to the poetic pieces collected in the book of Psalms?

It is quite clear that many psalms in the Psalter have been *used* in the cult of the Second Temple. Scholars have often called the Psalter 'the hymnbook of the Second Temple' meaning that it was collected just for this purpose. In this form the thesis is not quite correct: the Psalter may have *become* the cultic hymnbook, but was scarcely made with that end in view. Of the cultic use of many psalms, however, there is much evidence.

2

The title of the book of Psalms in Hebrew is *Tĕhillîm*, which means 'cultic songs of praise'.[2] This tallies with the indications we have that the songs and music of the levitical singers belonged to the solemn religious festivals as well as to daily sacrifices in the Temple. Such evidence is found both in the book of Chronicles and in Ecclesiasticus.[3]

In this connexion we must also draw attention to the technical terms in the psalm headings. Though the meaning of most of them is uncertain, there can be no doubt that many of them refer to liturgical practice in the temple service, some having reference to the cult-ritual acts for which the psalms in question have been used, some to the manner in which they were used, and some with other connexions. (See below, Chap. XXIII.)

In addition to this we have the Rabbinic tradition preserved both in Mishna and Talmud regarding a series of psalms which were used on different occasions in the temple cult.[4] Some of these traditions are supported by the titles in the Hebrew text. Thus we are told that Ps. 92 was used 'on the Sabbath'. No doubt what is referred to is the singing after the

---

[1] The word has received this sense through the usage of the Church. Greek *psalmós*, used in Greek Bible tradition about the Psalter (*psalmói*), in itself has no particularly religious meaning, but is used about a song accompanied on strings, and therefore in G (see note 5 below) as a rule renders Hebrew *mizmōr*, which has the same meaning and an analogous etymology, and may also be used of secular poems.

[2] See Additional Note I.

[3] See for instance 1 Chron. 16; Sir. 50.16ff.; 1 Mac. 4.54.

[4] The sources will be found in Buhl, *Psalmerne*,[2] pp. VIIIf.; Bentzen, *Indledning til Salmerne*, p. 29; likewise in the article on 'Psalms' in *The Jewish Encyclopedia*, X.244.

drink offering at the daily morning sacrifice (*tāmîdh*) in the temple. Notes in the Septuagint (the oldest Greek Bible translation)[5] and in the Mishna and Talmud[6] add information as to the psalms for the other days of the week.[7] Ps. 44.24 belonged to the *tāmîdh* sacrifice also for some time, whether every day or on certain occasions only we do not know. The Maccabean high priest and king, Hyrcanus I (134–104), who probably reformed the service, abolished this rite.[8]

Other psalms were sung at the special 'additional' festival offerings (the Musaf sacrifices) during the seven days of the feast of Tabernacles.[9] The special 'festival psalms', 120–134, were sung at the water-pouring rite on 'the great day of the festival', i.e.' the eighth day of celebration. According to the Targum, the old Aramaic synagogue translation of the Biblical texts, Ps. 81 was sung at the Musaf on new year's day (the feast of trumpets), the first of Tishri (that is September–October). Ps. 47 was also used as a new year hymn. At the feast of Dedication (of the Second Temple) which was instituted during the time of the Maccabees, Ps. 30[10] was sung—as corroborated by its title. The same psalm was used when the first-fruits were presented.[11] The so-called 'Egyptian Hallel', i.e. Pss. 113–118, was sung both at the slaying of the Paschal lamb[12] and at the feast of Tabernacles[13] and according to other sources also at the feast of Weeks (Pentecost) and at the feast of Dedication.[14] A very late source[15] mentions psalms also in connexion with the feast of Dedication, Purim, the first six days of the Passover and the seventh day, at Pentecost, and at the Lamentation on the eighth of Ab.[16] A title in the book of Psalms itself says that Ps. 100 was used at a special sacrifice, 'The Sacrifice of Thanksgiving'.[17] Probably also another of the titles (*Lĕhazkîr*), points to a specific sacrifice, the so-called *'azkārâ* offering.[18] This interpretation is supported by Sir. 38.9, 11.

[5] Hereafter shortened to G (=Graeca); often also shortened to LXX. On the true nature of the Septuagint see now Kahle, *The Cairo Geniza*, pp. 132ff.
[6] Mishna Tamid VII 4; cf. Talm. Bab. Rosh hashshana 30b, 31a; Sopherim XVIII 1.
[7] Ps. 24 on Sundays (G), 48 on Mondays, 82 on Tuesdays, 94 on Wednesdays (G), 81 on Thursdays (L), 93 on Fridays (G).
[8] Mishna Sota IX 10 (47ab); Tosephta to the passage; Sota 48a. cf. B. Jacob in *ZATW* 16, 1896, p. 141.
[9] Pss. 29; 50.16ff.; 94.16ff.; 81.7ff.; 65. See Bab. Sukka 55a; cf. G, for Ps. 29, referring the latter to the eighth day of the festival.—At the musaf-sacrifice on the Sabbath, according to Bab. Rosh hashshana 31a they would sing out of Deut. 32, and at the evening sacrifice Ex. 15 and Num. 21.17ff. See Snaith, *Studies in the Psalter*, p. 47. This, however, probably refers to the synagogue service. See Mowinckel, *Z. isr. Neujahr u. z. Deutung der Thronbesteigungspss.*, pp. 41f.
[10] Talmud. Sopherim XVIII.
[11] Mishna Bikkurim III 4.
[12] Mishna Pesahim V 7; Tosephta Pesahim III 11.
[13] Mishna Sukka IV 1. Cf. Büchler in *ZATW* 20, 1900, pp. 114ff., and the essay of Jacob (note 8 above).
[14] Tosephta Sukka III 2.
[15] Talmud Sopherim XVIII.
[16] Respectively Pss. 30; 7; 135; (according to other Rabbis, 83), 'the Egyptian Hallel' (see ch. XXII 2 j), 29 and 137.
[17] See Lev. 7.12ff.; 22.29; 2 Chron. 33.16.
[18] Pss. 38.1; 70.1; Lev. 2.2, 9, 16; 5.12; 6.8; Num. 5.26; Sir. 38.11; 45.16. Cf. Jacob, *ZATW* 17, 1897, pp. 48ff.

Some scholars have held that these items of information in the tradition do not refer to the service in the Temple, but to that in the synagogue.[19] But that is impossible. The synagogue is on the whole later than the period of biblical psalmody. The earliest mention of a synagogue is found in an inscription from Egypt from a time after 247 B.C. and all the evidence shows its introduction to have been later in Palestine than in the Dispersion. As an institution for worship the synagogue was not created to supplant the temple service, but to gather the congregation for the reading and teaching of the law and for common prayer at the appointed hours. The synagogue service was in ancient times always songless. It is quite another matter that in the course of time portions of psalms came to be used as lessons and prayers at the service in the synagogue. That only happened after the psalms had become 'Holy Scripture', and has nothing to do with hymn singing. We are here concerned with the recital by the synagogue 'recitator' (*miqrē*) who at certain intervals asks the congregation to answer with an 'Amen'! Not before mediaeval times did synagogal poetry and singing come into existence.[20]

The traditional use of the psalms in the temple service is confirmed by the fact that when the Chronicler in 1 Chron. 16 uses quotations from the so-called 'Enthronement Psalms' for the description of a certain cultic occasion, this tallies with the idea of the festival of 'Yahweh's enthronement' and with the ideation of these psalms and the situation from which they in fact must have sprung (see below, Chap. V).

But does (later) cultic use demand cultic origin? No. It is quite possible that poems which were not originally composed for cultic use, may later have been thus applied—as is also the case with so many hymn tunes. There are several instances of this in the hymnbooks of most Protestant denominations. And so it may have been in the Psalter, at least with some psalms.

[19] So for instance Duhm, *Die Psalmen*, p. XXIV; Staerk in *S.A.T.* III 1² p. 88. Quell, *Kult. Probl. d. Pss.* p. 5, also seems to attach little importance to the traditions about the use of psalms in the Temple. Cf. also Jacob in *ZATW* 16, 1896, p. 145 about the information in Sopherim XVIII.

[20] On the age of the synagogues see Hölscher, *Gesch. d. isr. u. jüd. Religion*, pp. 177f.; Schürer, *Gesch. d. jüd. Volkes* II⁴, pp. 497ff. Theological handbooks keep telling us that the synagogues originated during the Exile, that is to say shortly after the carrying off to Babylonia (for instance Wellhausen, *Isr. u. jüd. Gesch.*,⁶ pp. 149f.; 196f.), but this is nowhere justified by the sources, and the idea is as unlikely as it could possibly be. J. Morgenstern's arguments in support of A. Lods' suggestion that the Josianic reformation, 621 B.C., called forth the synagogue ('The Origin of the Synagogue' in *Studi Orientalistici in honore G. Levi della Vida II*, pp. 192ff.) are not convincing—especially not when it is recognized that the basis of Josiah's reform cannot have been Deuteronomy—which is most certainly an early post-exilic book. As to the synagogue in Palestine see for instance Oesterley, *A Fresh Approach*, pp. 153ff. The synagogue originally without singing: see Jacob in *ZATW* 16, 17, 18, 1896–98; Moore, *Judaism* I, pp. 241, 296; III, p. 65. *Reading* (!) parts of the psalms in the synagogue a 'Biblicism': see Oesterley, *op. cit.* pp. 106ff.; Hirsch's article 'Psalms' in *JE* X: the usual psalms were Pss. 105-107 ; 111-114 ; 116-118; 135 ; 136; 146–150. On the later poetry and singing of the synagogues (*piyyutim* and *hizanoth*), see Elbogen, *Jüd. Gottesdienst*, pp. 206ff. What Oesterley says (*op. cit.*, pp. 106ff.) about the singing of psalms in the synagogue is partly hypothesis based on testimonies which actually refer to the temple service, and partly a reference to the use of psalms or psalm verses as *prayers* ('Biblicism', see above).

The possibility cannot be denied. There is at least one psalm whose attested liturgical use, according to the heading, does not correspond to its original purpose: Ps. 30, once used 'at the Dedication of the House', i.e. the temple dedication festival, instituted in 164 B.C., was no doubt composed for a quite different use, being concerned with a single individual, and not with the congregation as a whole. But this does not—even in this case—mean that Ps. 30 was composed for non-cultic use.

The prevalent opinion among both ancient scholars and the older generation of modern critical psalm interpreters has been, that both psalmody as such and our extant psalms originated as private individual lyrics, and only at a later stage were given a secondary use as songs for the temple service. For this opinion they seem not to have felt it necessary to give any proof.

Among modern interpreters, there have always been some, e.g. B. Duhm and Fr. Buhl, who were inclined to admit that this or that psalm was originally composed for liturgical purposes, even if they very seldom made any attempt to find the definite 'liturgical' or cultic situation of the psalm in question; especially in psalms composed wholly of set formulas, as e.g., Ps. 136, they were inclined to see 'merely liturgical compositions'. One has the impression that these interpreters were less interested in a psalm that was made for 'liturgical purpose' only, and that this of itself was a sign of a certain inferiority in such a psalm. In their opinion—so it seems—the good psalms were individual poetry, the poor ones might be made for liturgical (cultic) purpose. But why should only poetically poorer products have been made for the cultic service? Both Christian and 'pagan' cult lyrics offer many examples which demonstrate that even poems of the highest poetical and religious quality have been made for the cultic use of the congregation in question.

3

So we have to look for more scientifically founded criteria for the cultic purpose of psalms. And such criteria can be found.

Even at a first glance there are psalms, apart from those composed of set formulas and more or less clearly liturgical phrases, which must have been composed for some liturgical and ritual purpose, and which at the same time are of high poetical quality and great originality. To give some concrete examples, we have psalms that obviously presuppose, and are made for, a festal procession, such as Pss. 24; 68; 118; 132. They can only be understood in connexion with a vision of the procession itself and its different acts and scenes. The interpreter has to use both the descriptions of such cultic processions and the allusions to them in other Old Testament texts, and his own imagination, to recall a picture of the definite situation from which such a psalm cannot be separated. Only thus is it possible to find the inner connexion between the apparently incoherent stanzas of, e.g., Ps. 68.

Ps. 24 divides into three main parts which were used during the procession on the way to the Temple, before the gates, and when the procession winds in through the gates.

Ps. 118 also starts before the Temple and resounds while the 'procession' (*ḥagh*) marches through 'the Gate of Righteousness' and encircles the altar of burnt-offerings in the temple court.

Ps. 132 is (part of) the text for a dramatically performed procession, where we meet both the reigning king, playing the role of 'David', and his men who have been searching for Yahweh's holy shrine (the ark) and now are bringing it back to its proper place in the sanctuary of Zion. We hear the song of the priests who carry the shrine, the intercession for the anointed descendant of David referring to the merits of his ancestor: 'for thy servant David's sake', and at last the promise in Yahweh's name from the temple prophet to the king, if he keeps Yahweh's commandments.

In other psalms we find allusions to what can only be understood as definite ritual acts.

So the worshipper in Ps. 5.7 says that he has now 'come into Yahweh's house and will worship toward his holy Temple'. In Ps. 66.13 the worshipper comes into Yahweh's house with burnt offerings to keep the vows he has previously made. In Ps. 63.2–4 he comes at the dawn of day to the sanctuary to obtain proof of God's power and his glory and to get help in his distress. In Ps. 26.6f. he draws attention to the fact that he has 'washed his hands in innocency, and compassed God's altar', 'that he may publish with the voice of thanksgiving, and tell of all his wondrous works', i.e., sing the thanksgiving psalm when the prayer has been granted and the distress ended. It is an affirmation of innocence, alluding to the fact that the worshipper has been through the prescribed rites which gained him purgation from sin, and testified that he was now pure and blameless and worthy of help. Ps. 51.9 also alludes to such purification, e.g., the sprinkling with a hyssop wand and holy water, as we know it from the ritual prescriptions for purification and purificatory sacrifices. In v.8 the same psalm probably alludes to previous omens and signs which the priest (or the temple prophet) has interpreted for the suppliant. Ps. 86.17 prays for such a 'token for good'.

Probably it is an augural sacrifice, a sacrifice which accompanies the 'scrying' for the oracular answer, which is alluded to by the rare verb *biqqēr* in Pss. 5.4 and 27.4.

Ps. 84 gives a resounding testimony both to the psalm's inner bonds with the holy place and to its living connexion with the cult:

> How amiable thy dwelling is,
> O Yahweh, Lord of Hosts!
> My soul has (long) been panting, pining
> for the temple courts of Yahweh,
> Now soul and body thrill with joy
> over the living God.

> The bird has found her home at last,
> a nest to lay her young,
> at thine own altars, Lord of hosts,
> my King and my God!

These random samples do not stand isolated. We shall not here anticipate the systematic research into psalm types. At this stage of our inquiry we shall only draw attention to a number of definite allusions which show the close connexion which both psalms and poets had with the Temple on Mount Zion and with its rules and rites.[21] Very often they describe the pious as already in or going towards 'Zion', 'Jerusalem', 'Salem', 'The City', 'the Gates of the Temple', 'Mount Zion', 'the Holy Mount', 'God's Mountain', 'Yahweh's tent', his 'house', 'abode', or 'palace', his 'dwelling place', 'the Place', 'the Sanctuary'. The suppliant stands before God's 'choir', 'before God', and prostrates himself before 'his Holy Shrine' (the ark) which is his 'footstool', or before the 'Throne' 'on the cherubim'. There are allusions to the 'Holy Feasts' and 'Processions' and to the 'walking round about the altar' or the 'city walks', to the cultic dance, and to the 'via sacra'. And now and then the action is performed in such a way as to make it quite clear that the psalm in question belongs to one or other of these particular rites. We have mentioned above, the procession psalm 118 with its allusions to the circumambulation of the altar. We may note 'the procession' to the temple gates in Ps. 24 as well as the walking round about the city walls in Ps. 48. Allusions to the festal processions are also found in Pss. 42.5 and 68.25f.

The 'New Moon and the Full Moon Feasts' are mentioned, and also the 'New Year Festival' (Ps. 81), the latter being alluded to as the beginning of the new 'Time of Grace' (Ps. 65). The suppliants speak of the 'vigils' in the Temple (Isa. 30.29; Ps. 134.1), 'evening offerings', 'the night-(service)'. They present themselves both in 'the beauty of holiness' and in the 'sackcloth' of the penitent. They exhort to adoration the holy ones, 'the priests, Yahweh's servants' and others 'dwelling in Yahweh's house', 'standing in his palace'. Again and again the suppliant declares that he presents himself at the 'altar of Yahweh' and 'prepares' offerings of all kinds: 'sacrifice' (of animals, zebhaḥ), 'sin-offerings' (better: 'sacrifice of purification'), 'meat offerings', 'incense', 'voluntary offerings', 'votive offerings', 'burnt-offerings', 'whole burnt sacrifice', 'fat offerings', 'drink offerings'; 'with bullocks, rams, and he-goats' he will 'meet Yahweh'; he will 'prepare an augural sacrifice' and 'look for Yahweh's answer'. He often alludes not only to the sacrifices[22] but also to many ritual ceremonies connected with them.[23] He testifies that he is 'pure', 'pure both in heart and hands', he 'washes his hands in innocency and walks around the altar' (28.6), or

---

[21] For this section see Quell, *Kult. Probl. d. Pss.*, pp. 149–156, with systematically arranged references to the sources of all these cues and many more.
[22] Pss. 22.27; 20.4; 27.6; 66.13ff.; 116.17, and other places.
[23] Cf. Pss. 51.19; 73.13; 116.13; 118.27.

asks to be 'purified', or 'redeemed', and 'purged with hyssop that he might be clean' (51.9). He asks for a 'blessing' and himself utters both 'blessings' and 'curses'. At times he comes in 'mourning' or 'sackcloth'. He 'kneels' and 'prostrates himself' 'before Yahweh', 'lies on the threshold of God's house', 'stretches out his hands' in 'humble prayer' and 'laments' or 'cries out' his 'praise', and employs all the usual cultic expressions.

He does all this, not when alone in his closet, or in the fields, but in 'the midst of the Great Assembly', in the 'congregation', 'before his brethren', i.e. his fellow believers. In these exercises he feels himself a member of the 'house of Jacob', of 'Israel', of 'the sons of Zion', of 'the flock of Yahweh', as one of 'his chosen', his 'righteous', his 'servants' i.e. worshippers, his 'faithful' or 'devotees'—ḥăsîdhîm, the Hebrew word, might perhaps be translated 'bondmen' or 'covenanters' or 'devotees'[24]—as one of the 'brethren', one of 'the Sons of Yahweh'.[25]

In all ancient cults *song, music and dance* play an important role. So they do in the psalms, and we shall therefore examine this characteristic somewhat more in detail.

There can be no doubt that the psalms were meant to be sung. They contain a number of allusions to singing,[26] and they are often described in the titles[27] as 'songs' (šîr) rendered to music, or as 'hymns' (mizmōr). But it is a very doubtful exegesis for scholars to interpret a number of the titles as directions about the tunes,[28] as was formerly, and is sometimes still, done.

As we shall see below, a song is a quite common feature of the cult. This springs from a universal psychological law. The frequently repeated invocation of the deity,[29] which belongs to the older religions and cults, grows of itself into a rhythmical call, a short invocational song with some kind of melody, be it ever so simple. When a human being is 'moved' by the 'holy' he cries aloud. The cry grows into ecstatic song, a primitive hymn of praise. Hymns belong to the oldest cultic utterance everywhere.[30] The lament also calls for repetition, and grows into entreaty.[31] The same prayer is repeated again and again, and the emotional crescendo and decrescendo between despair and confidence, with the exhalation and inhalation, create a rhythm and a rising and falling tune, however simple.

Even the primitive *ex opere operato* formula is full of awe and ecstasy[32] and grows into a metric chant, which is 'sung'.

[24] Cf. Nelson Glueck, *Das Wort hesed* (BZATW 47).
[25] See the statistics given by Quell, *op. cit.*, pp. 154ff.
[26] The words 'song' (singing) and 'sing' occur 38 times in all in the psalms; zāmar, 'accompany the singing', 43 times. For these and other terms for singing and music and doxology etc. see Jacob in ZATW 17, 1897, pp. 266f., 273, and Quell, *Kult. Probl. d. Pss.*, pp. 152f.
[27] For these two terms see *Ps. St.* IV, pp. 2f. and below, Chap. XXIII 1-2.
[28] Cf. *Ps. St.* IV, pp. 22f. and below, Chap. XXIII no. 2.
[29] See van der Leeuw, *Phänomenologie*, pp. 345, 401f.
[30] *Ibid*, p. 406; Heiler, *Das Gebet*,[4] pp. 157ff.
[31] Hebr. *taḥănûnîm* = entreaty for indulgence and mercy. It is a significant fact that the word is mostly used in the plural.
[32] Cf. what is told of the Australians, that they are often moved to tears, when performing their 'magical' ceremonies, Söderblom, *Gudstrons uppkomst*, pp. 184, 190.

In many languages the word for 'song' originally betokened the power-full ritual word.[33]

In the psalms we constantly hear the poet, and through him the worshipper or the congregation, declaring their intention to 'sing' or 'praise' or 'sing and play' for Yahweh. The poet will recite his hymn 'to psaltery and harp', and so on. The psalm will be a song sung to Yahweh, either in praise and thanksgiving, or with prayer for help and deliverance. In this respect its connexion with the cult is clear enough.

We know nothing about the tunes in Israel's temple cult. But if we are to judge from analogies in more recent oriental music, we may assume that they were quite simple. It is a safe supposition that as the 'period' (the verse) was the proper rhythmic unit, it was also the melodic one. The 'tune' was limited to the single verse, perhaps with a marked rise or fall at the end of the last line in a 'stanza' or 'strophe'.

According to what we know and can conjecture from later times in the East, music was not based on the octave scale. As far as we can judge, the tune was extremely simple, hardly to be called a tune, but more like a sort of recitative.[34]

The first task of the muscial accompaniment was undoubtedly to stress the rhythm, to 'keep time'. We may draw that conclusion both from analogies in the present,[35] and from the old oriental and Israelite instruments of music.[36] The psalms mention the tambourine, the cymbals, the horn, the trumpet, different kinds of lyre (R.V. harp and cithern), flute and castanets.[37]

At all periods all kinds of cult have made use of instrumental music.[38] Like rhythm and tune it is a way of expressing the sense of rapture and sublime abandonment. It is a reaction to the encounter with the holy. By means of the rhythmical sound made by his own voice and the instrument, the individual 'shapes' this reality which affects his inner being, and thereby makes it his own; he objectivizes it and is in turn filled and used by it. Music is an expression of the soul, and affects the soul intensely. As in so many other religions, the rhythmical noisy music of ancient Israel was also used to induce that ecstasy in which the cultic experience culminates, and which is the form and medium of the inspiration in the holy men, the prophets and seers.[39]

[33] This applies for instance to Latin *carmen* as well as to Arabian *sa 'r* and *saj'*, probably also to Hebr. *shir*.
[34] Cf. Eerdmans, *Hebr. Book of Pss.* (*O.T.S.* IV), pp. 51ff. See below, Chap. XV 2.
[35] Besides Eerdmans (n. 34 above), see also Sachsse in *ZDPV* 50.
[36] Gressmann, *Musik und Musikinstrum. im. A.T.*; Bentzen, *Indledn.*, p. 95; Galling, article 'Musik (und Musikinstrumente)' in *BRL* col. 389ff.; Kolari, *Musikinstrumente und ihre Verwendung im A.T.*; R. Follet u. P. Nober, 'Zur altorientalischen Musik', *Biblica* XXXV, 1954, pp. 230ff. Murray in *Verbum Domini* 32, pp. 84ff. Wegner, *Die Musik-instrumente der alten Orients*. For a fuller list of literature see Schürer, *Gesch. d. jüd. Volkes*[4] II, p. 334 n. 83.
[37] Pss. 57.9; 92.4; 149.3; 150.4; 68.26; 71.22; 81.3f; 98.5f; 150.3–5; Ex. 15.20; 2 Sam. 6.5; Jer. 31.4; Neh. 12.27; 1 Chron. 15.16ff.; 2 Chron. 5.12; 20.28; 29.26f.
[38] Van der Leeuw, *Phänomenologie*, p. 431; Heiler, *Das Gebet*,[4] pp. 165f.; for Oriental and Israelite cult, see Oesterley, *A Fresh Approach*, pp. 91ff., 106ff.
[39] 1 Sam. 10.5; 19.24; 2 Kgs. 3.15. See Lindblom, *Profetismen i Israel*, pp. 131f.

It is repeatedly alluded to in the psalms themselves, and expressly told in the Chronicler's description of the divine service and in his account of the temple ritual, that instrumental music had its place in the hymn singing. As is well known, the Temple in Jerusalem had its own guild of singers and musicians (see Chap. XV). When the Chronicler describes the work and the equipment of the temple singers he usually dwells on the musical instruments. The temple music had no independent significance. It was meant to accompany the song, the chanting recitation of prayers and hymns.[40] All the words for 'singing' and 'playing' in the Old Testament really signify the musical expression as a whole, the unity of song and instrumental accompaniment.

As to the point in the service at which, in old times, the song occurred, little is known. One thing is certain, that it was supposed primarily to belong to the sacrificial act.[41] This also applies to the private offering (Ps. 116.17). So we may suppose that also at the private and congregational sin and purification sacrifice those lamentation psalms and prayers which belonged to the ritual were offered together with the sacrifice or in immediate succession to it.

Together with cultic song and music goes the *dance*,[42] which is a common way of expressing the encounter with the holy. The dance is a spontaneous human expression of the sense of rapture, and hence it is regarded and utilized as a means to bring about this rapture and an experience of holy power and the presence of the divine. It is well known that the dance is associated with the fertility cult, because the dance may also be an expression of sexual elation. In the cult it is an expression of, and a means to produce, that feeling of strength which guarantees fertility, victory, success in hunting, and daily bread; it is 'work', 'cult'. At a higher religious level it develops into an expression of the joy at the encounter with the Holy One, an act for the glory of God (2 Sam. 6.20ff). It behoves one to give such visible and boisterous expression of 'the joy before Yahweh'.

Israel too had the cultic dance[43] as a means to produce ecstasy and that fullness of power to which it testified.[44] It was a part of the regular congregational cult, a testimony to the 'joy in Yahweh', and a mark of honour to him. We find both the whirling and leaping dance practised by more or less ecstatic individuals,[45] and the calmer kind, termed cult processions and circumambulation. The cultic festal procession in Israel must not, however, be visualized as anything like a grave and solemn march of the

---

[40] See Schürer, *Gesch. d. jüd. Volkes*[4] II, p. 335.

[41] Ps. 100.1; 2 Chron. 29.26ff.; Sir. 47.9; 50.18f.; Mishna Tamid VII 3. Cf. Schürer, *op. cit.*, pp. 350, 355.

[42] Cf. van der Leeuw, *op. cit.*, pp. 351f.; Oesterley, *Sacred Dance*; Backman, *Religious Dances*; Johs. Pedersen, *Israel, its Life and Culture*, III–IV, pp. 436ff.; Bentzen, *Indledn.*, pp. 98ff.; Heiler, *Das Gebet*[4], p. 159.

[43] Ex. 15.20; 2 Sam. 6.5, 12ff.; Pss. 30.12; 87.7; 149.33; 150.4; Judith 15.13.

[44] Lindblom, *Profetismen* p. 132; cf. index *s.v.* 'Dans'.

[45] 1 Sam. 10.5ff.; 2 Sam. 6.14ff.; cf. the Syrian name of the god *Ba'al marqod*, 'the Baal of the (ecstatic) dance'.

citizens. It has always something of the character of the folk dance. We can see this in Assyrian and Egyptian pictures of cultic processions[46] which display something of the original conception of the procession as a power-increasing and strength-conferring ambulation with holy powerful objects, as e.g., the holy ark of Yahweh. The idea of circling is preserved in the Hebrew word *ḥagh* which means circling, ambulation. In Pss. 48 and 118 the circling of the city wall[47] or the altar is itself the procession and the dance. Of course not all processions had the character of circum-ambulation. The grand procession which served as the enthronement pro-cession of Yahweh held a prominent place at the great feast (see below, Chap. V.7). We may judge from the description of the procession with the ark in the second book of Samuel (ch. 6)—a description which is of course no contemporary 'reportage', but is modelled on the feasts of the writer's own time—that even the procession at the Throne Ascension of Yahweh had something of the elated mood of the dance.

Both music and song belong to the festive dance. When the warriors come home with victory they are met by dancing, singing and playing virgins (Jdg. 11.34; 1 Sam. 18.6), and that is how the legend imagines the people as celebrating and worshipping after the crossing of the Reed Sea (Ex. 15.20), and a festival psalm declares:

We are seeing thy processions, O God,
The processions of my God and my King in the sanctuary,
Singers in front, musicians behind,
Between them girls with tambourines.   (Ps. 68.25.)

The psalms often mention the cultic parade dance, or dance procession, in a way which shows it to have been the characteristic form for the festival cult, and that this was where many of the psalms were used.[48] At the cult place on Mount Zion 'start-up the springs of life of the singers and dancers' (Ps. 87.7).

The cultic dance went on right down to the last days of the Temple. Rabbinic tradition speaks particularly of a torch dance by night at the water pouring ceremony at the feast of Tabernacles: 'It was said that the gladness there was above everything. Pious men danced with torches in their hands and sang songs of joy and praise, while the Levites played all sorts of instruments. The dance drew great crowds of spectators for whom grandstands had been erected. It did not end until the morning at a given sign, when water from the spring of Shiloh was poured over the altar'.[49] This is certainly not the invention of later Jewish times, but a very old tradition.[50]

[46] See illustrations in Bentzen, *Indledn*, pp. 99 and 101.
[47] Cf. Neh. 12.31ff.
[48] Pss. 30.12; 87.7; 149.3; 150.4; Isa. 30.29.
[49] After Bentzen, *Indledn*. pp. 98f.; see Mishna Sukka IV 9, cf. V 5; Talmud Sukka 51a.
[50] Cf. Oesterley, *Sacred Dance*, p. 94.

The testimonies to the connexion of the psalms with the cult and its ceremonies, its sacrifices and lustrations, its song, music and dance are thus both numerous and strong, and certainly not to be found only in such psalms as are composed of 'set liturgical formulas'; the quotations given above are fairly equally dispersed over the whole Psalter.

4

Here one might object: those positive relations to temple and cult may be valid for the personal religion of the psalmists, but do they prove a cultic aim for their poems? They are at least more valid proofs than the unproved supposition of a mere private, individual origin for the psalms—a supposition that in fact is only a traditional prejudice.

It is, in fact, surprising that a cultic interpretation of the psalms has not been suggested long ago.

The traditional Jewish and Christian interpretation, however, took it for granted that the psalms were originally private, individual poetry. They were of course bound by the theory that most of the psalms had been composed by David and some of his supposed contemporaries, such as Asaph, Heman, etc. This exegesis was concerned to discover what events in David's public or private life had occasioned a particular psalm[51]—a point of view that is reflected already in the Massoretic headings of many psalms (see Chap. XV.5). Even the older, critical, historically orientated type of interpretation represented by scholars such as de Wette, Ewald, Wellhausen, Duhm, Buhl, Briggs, etc.,[52] was primarily interested in finding references to contemporary historical events in the psalms, and trying to discover the historical background and the date of the single psalm. In the main, these scholars believed that the psalms had sprung from the life and experiences of individual persons, and sometimes they even tried to find the historical person who had 'written' this or that definite psalm. Wellhausen went so far as to declare that without the prophetic activity and personal experiences of Jeremiah, the psalms would never have been composed.[53]

Smend shared the common presumption, but thought that the poets had spoken in the name of the congregation; in the 'I' of the psalms he found a poetical personification of the Jewish congregation—the theory of the so-called 'collective I'. But even Smend and his followers did not take the next step, to discuss a real cultic destination of the psalms; even to them 'the congregation' meant the pious 'private' lay circles supposed to exist within it, and to which they applied the expressions, the 'ănāwîm, the hăsîdhîm, the ṣaddîqîm, occurring in the psalms.

---

[51] Cf. *Ps. St.* VI, pp. 76–94, particularly pp. 84ff. An example from later times of this method of interpretation is J. S. H. Storjohann, *Kong David, hans liv og salmer*, Kristiania, 1900.
[52] See additional Note II.
[53]. Wellhausen, *Isr. u. jüd. Geschichte*[6] p. 149f.

The more or less conscious presupposition on which these opinions rested, was the interpreters' personal low estimate of cult and liturgy, at which I have hinted above. 'Cult religion' was adjudged bad and primitive religion, and 'liturgical psalms' were poor psalms. The Roman Catholic exegetes might have shown more insight, but they were bound by their dogmatic presupposition of Davidic, Asaphite, etc. authorship—as was also the oldest Protestant exegesis. The modern, critical Protestant interpreters, in fact, had no real understanding of the cult either in Biblical religion or in religion in general. More or less consciously they all shared that contempt of ordered ecclesiastical worship which was common to pietism, revivalist movements, rationalism, and liberalism. Often coming from pietistically influenced circles themselves, they took it for granted that such groups had existed in Judaism as well, and found there the birthplace of psalmody.

In the meantime, the comparative study of religions had brought to the fore the important place of the cult in religion in general. The rediscovery of the old oriental cultures showed biblical scholars that exactly the same was true of the religions of the peoples that surrounded Israel, from whose culture and religion Israel had taken over many important customs and conceptions. Even in Protestant Christianity a better understanding of the value of ordered worship has emerged—although in some circles it is still branded as a 'high church' tendency. This change in the scholarly and spiritual situation has necessarily influenced also the interpretation of the Old Testament and especially of the psalms.

The man who pioneered the way for a new understanding of the psalms, and laid the foundation for a cultic interpretation, was Hermann Gunkel.

By his 'form-critical' or 'form-historical' (*formgeschichtliche*) and 'type-critical' (*gattungsgeschichtliche*) methods he has proved beyond doubt that in Israel also the origin of psalm poetry is to be found in the public cult: the different types of psalms have come into existence in connexion with different cultic situations and acts to which they originally belonged.

By tracing the peculiarities of the different types back to the attested or supposed cultic situations from which they have sprung, light falls both on the type and on its style as a whole, and on all its motifs and its formal peculiarities in their relation to one another. This is very important; Gunkel has by his method laid the foundation for a real historical and literary understanding of psalm poetry. In the following chapter we shall discuss the full content of his discovery.

On the basis of Gunkel's discovery of the cultic origin of the oldest Hebrew psalmody as such, the present author has for decades urged the cultic interpretation of the psalms and tried to show that this includes both a revision of many points in the older critical view of Old Testament religious history and a revaluation of the disparaged 'cult religion' of the Old Testament. The number of adherents to the cultic interpretation has increased, and in some circles there has lately appeared a tendency even to exaggerate the cultic aspect in the interpretation of the Old Testament.[54]

But Gunkel himself thought that the direct cultic connexion was true only with regard to the original, now mostly lost, psalm poetry; the now extant psalms were to be considered as a later evolution, a free, 'private' poetry, unconnected with the cultic situations, but imitating the style and the motifs of the older one. In this case we should have the following evolution of psalm poetry: from the cultic origin to private individual poetry, and back to the cult again.

It must be admitted that it is conceivable and confirmed by historical experience, that cultic poetry can engender a freer, so to speak, 'private' religious poetry, which will, to a great extent, use the old cultic forms and images, but can express more individual and private needs, moods and experiences. Both from Jeremiah and from Deutero-Isaiah[55] we can see that there have been non-cultic imitations of the style of the cultic psalms and that, moreover, in Israel. In later Judaism a religious poetry sprang up, independent of the cult, but to a great extent making use of old forms,[56] frequently enough in a very loose way.

But in the imitations by the prophets there are always sure indications that these poems are, and are intended to be, something other than cult songs, namely prophecies, or prayers springing out of the prophet's consciousness of a personal calling and its problems. Late Jewish psalm poetry moreover betrays its detachment from the cult by many obvious signs, both by an individual personal note, and by a breaking up and mixing of the old typical cultic psalm styles.

This seems to me to be a fairly strong argument against Gunkel's theory that the greater part of the psalms were 'private' imitations of old cult songs.

And what are Gunkel's arguments for this departure from his own sound fundamental position? They are, in fact, just the same as with the older critical school: the asserted incompatibility between the personal religious note in so many of the psalms, and the 'impersonal' character of the 'liturgical formula'. In other words: the newer Protestant lack of understanding of the importance of the cult and of its real essence. If Gunkel and his followers were right at this point, exactly the same argument should be valid against the psalmists' strong dependence on all the conventional forms of the old cultic style.

We shall in a later chapter see that there is no real incompatibility between 'traditionalism' and 'personality' in religious poetry. Here I only want to remark that traditional 'sacred' forms and expressions may often carry a richly personal content. True enough, they can become worn out and petrified by use. But through all the various experiences and emotions associated with them through generations, they may also be able some-

---

[54] See below, Chap. XVIII.2; cf. Chap. XVI.3.
[55] See below, Chap. XVI.
[56] See below, note 28 to Chap. V.

how to store the religious experience of the generations and become symbols and 'ideograms', 'words saturated with experience', as V. Grön- bech calls them, words which only need to be mentioned to release a series of associations, of thoughts, experiences, and emotions. The words convey more than they seemingly contain. The stereotyped phrase may express a personally experienced and genuine religion, both for the poet and for those who use the psalm in worship.

The task which psalm exegesis then has to face, is to try whether a consistent cultic interpretation can be applied to them in a natural way.

Having put this question, our duty is to obtain a right understanding of the meaning of 'cult' in religion, especially in the religion of Israel.

5

What is meant by cult? It has been said that religion appears in three main aspects, as cult, as myth and as ethos. Or, in other terms, as worship, as doctrine, and as behaviour (morals). This does not mean that religion can be split up into three sharply divided 'parts' or 'sections'. The three words signify forms of expression and manifestations, aspects of religion. The whole living content of a religion is present in all three. One and the same phenomenon may be seen from any of these three points of view. But the picture will be different according to which viewpoint we adopt. In the cult both doctrine and morals are expressed, and both draw power and new life from the cult.

The cult is thus a general phenomenon appearing in all religions, even in the most 'anti-cultic' Protestant sects and groups. It is indeed an essen- tial and constitutive feature of a religion, that in which the nature and spiritual structure of a religion is most clearly manifested. It may take many forms, though a closer examination reveals the same main features in all religions. Like everything living, the cult has its history—a necessary evolution which is specific for each individual religion and is structurally determined by that which is peculiar, essential, and central in the religion in question.

Cult or ritual may be defined as the socially established and regulated holy acts and words in which the encounter and communion of the Deity with the congregation is established, developed, and brought to its ulti- mate goal. In other words: a relation in which a religion becomes a vitalizing function as a communion of God and congregation, and of the members of the congregation amongst themselves.

It stands to reason that inside a common field of culture like the ancient East, where all the nations have lived for thousands of years in the closest connexion with one another, in war and peace, at the same cultural level and with their ways of thinking and their sense of reality in common— interchanging hundreds of cultural forms and ideas—many elements and forms of the cult will be the same or similar, being variations of the same basic types. *A priori*, we could expect Israel, which after entering Canaan adopted the material culture of the natives, and therewith also a good deal of its modes of thought and spiritual culture, to have a cult whose basic elements would be the same as those of the neighbouring peoples. That this was so is proved at several points both by texts and archaeological findings.[57] We may be sure that several of these conformities are the result of direct borrowing. In many cases then, where the Old Testament texts contain only casual and vague allusions to a cultic custom or rite, the picture can be successfully completed by analogies from the cults of neighbouring peoples, which throw light on the allusions of the Old Testament. The same holds good where certain allusions in a group of psalms, or the situation to which they refer, seem to point to a cult ritual in connexion with which the group of psalms must be understood. Such conclusions are corroborated by the fact that a similar ritual and cultic situation is to be found among other oriental peoples with whom Israel has been in close connexion. There is no doubt that allusions here and there in the Old Testament and the later Jewish and Rabbinic literature to certain ideas and customs connected with the great annual festival—that of the New Year—are explained and amplified by a comparison with the annual festival of neighbouring peoples (see further, Chap. V).

The picture of the Israelite cult which we may draw from allusions in the sources, and which may throw some light on the psalms and give them their right setting, is conditioned by the extent of our general understanding of the nature and basic elements of the cult. It will, therefore, be better to say a little more about the cult in general, in order to amplify the short definitions given above.[58]

The cult is, as mentioned above, the visible and audible expression of the relation between the congregation and the deity.

It may often look as though the initiative lies with the congregation, on the human side. But seen from the point of view of cult and religion it is rather the other way round: the initiative lies with God. True enough, it is man that 'searches for God', 'seeks God', but he can, and does so, because the deity has first 'revealed himself' and taught man where and when and how to seek him. That is a fundamental idea in all religion, and

---

[57] Cf. R. Dussaud, *Origines Cananéennes du sacrifice Israelite²*; Lods in *RHPhR* 1929, pp. 199ff.; W. F. Albright, *Archaeol. and the Relig. of Isr.*, pp. 70ff., 90ff., 127f., 165 etc.; Cook, *The Relig. of Anc. Palestine in the Light of Archaeology*; Burrows, *What Mean these Stones?* Our knowledge of the conformity has been strengthened and extended through the Ugaritic texts, see Dussaud, *Origines*,² pp. 325ff., cf. Hooke, *Origin of Early Semit. Ritual*, p. 66; the general view of Dussaud has not been seriously invalidated by Gray in *ZATW* 62, 1950, pp. 207ff., even if the specific technical meaning of a term may have changed during the centuries. Gray is not right in concluding from the silence about the sacrificial terms in the Patriarchal tales that the Patriarchs as semi-nomadic immigrants are not representative of the culture of Canaan proper, Gray, however, is right in criticizing Dussaud's theory of the common South-Canaanite ('Negebite') origin of the 'Hebrews' and the Phoenicians. Cf. also Rowley, 'The Meaning of Sacrifice in the O.T.', *BJRL* 33.1. (1950), pp. 74–110.

[58] For the following, see Mowinckel, *Religion und Kultus*, pp. 10ff., with the necessary references to sources and literature.

not least in Israel. The deity represents a reality and a power which is different from the human, and belongs to a sphere termed '*the holy*', he is experienced as something 'different' and 'separate'—which is the original meaning of the word 'holy', 'sacred', in many languages—and imparts powers and effects which are holy. This holy sphere is inaccessible to man in his normal condition; it is 'taboo', and requires certain rules and forms of association, and a 'holy', or 'purified' quality in the person who desires to approach it. It is full of 'power' or *mana*—the Polynesian word which is often used by the science of comparative religion. Through the cult this effective and wonderful 'power' is imparted to the partakers, the congregation or the society. It may well be that at some stage, somewhere, sometime, 'the deity' has been construed quite indefinitely in the form of holy powers or influences, more or less impersonally conceived. But after all, it is not 'something holy', but 'The Holy One'—more or less clearly conceived—to whom the congregation turns in its cult. We can also trace the notion that through the words and acts of the cult, not only the congregation, but the holy forces and powers themselves are increased and fortified. The 'glory and power' of the deity waxes by the cult. But usually the deity is conceived of as the personal will and power that comes to the congregation through the cult, and creates and gives it what it needs, through the sacred acts and words. This is quite evidently the case with the cult in Israel.

At all events it is a mutual relation which is set up and developed in the cult. The acts and words express and produce this mutuality. Hence there are acts and words directed, so to speak, upwards from below, from the congregation to the deity—'sacrificial' acts and words—and also such as are directed downwards from above, from the deity to the congregation—'sacramental' acts and words. But the boundary between them is not sharply defined.

In the cult something happens: a relationship is established and developed which is of vital importance to the congregation, and the acts and words express what happens.

What the congregation wants to achieve through the cult, and what the 'power' from God is to create, is *life*—in the most comprehensive sense of the word, from the fundamental material need: rain, sun, fertility, the continuation of the race, the strength and victory of the tribe, and so on, up to the spiritual, religious and ethical values that are the lifeblood of the society—life for everything that belongs to its 'world'. The Israelites expressed the same idea by the word 'blessing'.[59] Blessing is to be created, increased, and secured through the cult; the office of the priest is to 'bless in Yahweh's name'. Both life and blessing have their ultimate source in the deity.

One of the most important means to increase and secure blessing and life, in Israel also, was the *sacrifice*. Through the changing ages the various

[59] See Pedersen, *Israel* I–II, pp. 182ff.; III–IV, pp. 299ff.

religions have had numerous and changing ideas about that. Such was also the case in Israel. It might be seen as a gift or present to Yahweh, or as a potent, sacramental meal, in which both Yahweh and the congregation take part, where the congregation are guests of Yahweh, and where fellowship and covenant both with him and amongst the members of the congregation are renewed and strengthened. By sanctifying and giving to Yahweh part of the herd or the harvest, the remainder is 'sanctified' and strengthened, and man is given blessing and life. Later the gift point of view is more prominent. The congregation gives to Yahweh a present of beasts and fruits, and in return he blesses them. The mental attitude may be emphasized: it is not the gift in itself Yahweh desires, but the humble or grateful mind of which it is an expression.[60] The sacrifice may also be the means of purification and expiation, ordained by Yahweh in order to have the sin and uncleanness obliterated and forgiven. This may be conceived in a more physical way ('magically'), blood being a 'magic' substance which 'cleanses' and 'redeems'; or in a more spiritual way: the rites purify and create goodwill and forgiveness, when they are enacted in obedience to what Yahweh has ordained.

That life is thus *created* through the cult means salvation from that distress and destruction which would befall, if life were not renewed. For existence is an everlasting war between the forces of life and death, of blessing and curse.[61] 'The world' is worn out if it is not regularly renewed, as anyone can see by the annual course of life and nature. Thus it is the 'fact of salvation' which is actualized in the cult.

This actualization of the fact of salvation is repeated as often as necessary. There are certain climaxes in life, crises when such a renewal is specially needed: all the important transitions, birth, maturity, death, spring, autumn, mid-summer, mid-winter, seed-time, and so on. The cult therefore follows the course of the natural year, and takes shape in ritual festivals, at certain climaxes of life. Some of these have a more private character (birth, marriage, death), others are for the whole society in common: the great annual festivals at sowing time and harvest time, new year and solstice, passing from the dry season to rain, and so on. The main festival of earliest, semi-nomadic Israel, was Passover, at the vernal equinox. It was connected with the breeding of sheep and goats. By that time the lambs were big enough to be sacrificed and eaten; the rains had ceased (it was now a question of the pastures holding out); what little barley and other grain the flock-rearing nomads grew, was ripe. In Canaan the Israelites took over the three agricultural festivals already in force there: the barley harvest festival (*maṣṣôth*, or barley cake feast), which coincided with the Passover; the feast of weeks, or wheat harvest festival, seven weeks later; and the wine and fruit harvest festival or feast of Tabernacles, at the autumnal equinox, before the rains started. The feast

[60] See Pss. 50; 51, and for more details below, Chap. VIII.11; X.2.
[61] Cf. Pedersen, *Israel* I–II, pp. 453ff.

of Tabernacles was the greatest of these, the real 'festival of Yahweh', or 'day of Yahweh'; and it was in olden times celebrated as the new year festival (see Chap. V).

Through the acts and words of the festal cult, laid down in fixed, sacred *ritual*, the reality which is to be created—the renewal of the herd, of the field, of the forces of life, of righteousness, of blessing and life—is portrayed ('acted') in visual and audible form. The actualization takes place through the representation. This does not mean that the representation, the acts and words, are seen as 'magic' which by itself creates life and renewal. It is the 'powers', or the deity, Yahweh, who acts and creates through them; to that extent they are 'sacramental'.

The representation may be *either*, more or less realistic, *or*, more or less symbolic—more often the latter, i.e. the rites stand for something; they symbolize and represent that for which they stand.

Their inner meaning is that the powers of death are overcome by the powers of life, by the Life-giver himself, by Yahweh, the living and life-giving God. Thus they symbolize a *struggle*. In the festival Yahweh comes and *conquers* the evil powers, and establishes 'the world' of his people anew, with 'peace' (*šālôm*), new life and blessing and happiness.

Hence the festival cult invariably has a more or less dramatic character; it is a sacred drama, representing the salvation which takes place. This dramatic character tallies with the fact that the cult is a mutual act on the part of God and of the congregation, with address and answer, action and reaction.

The fact that the cult is a repetition and a renewed creation leads to the view that the salvation which takes place is a *repetition* of a *first salvation* which took place in the dawn of time.

The very fact that the cult is creative led to this first salvation being generally conceived as the first creation of life and blessedness, of the 'land/world' (the Hebrew word *'ereṣ* meaning both). Creation *is* salvation. This idea of the cult at the great festival as a reiteration of the creation is the general one all over the ancient East. Israel, also, was quite familiar with it. But in Israel a new thought was added, the idea that the people itself had been created by the *election* which even for the earliest Israelites was manifested primarily by the Exodus from Egypt and the accompanying miracles, and in the making of the covenant. Ever since then it has been a basic element in Israel's religion that Yahweh acts and manifests himself in the actual history of the people. He is the *God of history* no less than the God of creation. Hence it is especially the historical facts of salvation which are 'remembered', and thereby turned into new effectual reality by Yahweh's presence at the festival. All he formerly did, gave, and secured, he does and gives and secures again when he 'appears' at his festival.

The epic story—or the allusions in the songs of praise—that recites the deeds of salvation which are 'remembered' and repeated at the cultic festival, form its *festal myth*. The myth expresses what happens in the cult, and what once happened for the first time. There is consequently no disagreement between myth and reality. The nucleus of Israel's festal myth was the remembrance of that historic reality: the Exodus, the election, the covenant, the immigration.

In the cult, action and words belong together. The acts—the rites—represent, symbolize, and are agents for what happens. When water from the holy spring Gihon in the valley of Kidron is poured over the altar at the autumnal festival, this signifies that the rainy season will bring rain in plenty. A sacrifice is similarly effective. The sacrificial meal creates and demonstrates community and covenant. The imposition of hands conveys the blessing. The fact that Yahweh, represented by his holy ark, enters the Temple in a solemn procession, means and shows that he now comes as the victorious king, conqueror of all evil powers, of Israel's and his own enemies. The fact that he is there, in his Temple, means that earth is once more firm, in spite of the furious uproar of the primeval ocean; earth is once more created as in the beginning, cf. Ps. 93. It is the rites which symbolize the struggle and victory of the deity that more especially provide the clear stamp of a real cult drama. In the same way, in Egypt, the death of Osiris and the struggle of Horus, his son, against his enemies, and his victory over them, and the resurrection and enthronement of Osiris, are produced in dramatic form, and thus experienced as reality. An analogous case was Marduk's triumph over the dragon of the primeval ocean in Babylon, and, in Assyria, Assur's fight and victory. In Canaan, the content of the cultic drama was Baal's defeat in the fight against Môt (Death), followed by his resurrection and victory over Môt, his ascension to the throne as ruler over gods and men, and the re-creation of the world and of the Temple. In Israel, too, Yahweh's royal entry, the festal procession, had much of this dramatic character, with a representation of Yahweh's fight, victory and accession, as will be demonstrated in Chap. V.

The *words* of the cult seem originally to belong to the acts as interpretation and complement—that also being one side of the cult's dramatic character. The power inherent in the act is also concentrated in the word; the holy word is effective and creative. Word and act co-operate in the creation of reality. We find many instances of this in Israel's cult, both in the old clan and tribal cult as well as in the temple cult of the people.

Before Isaac can communicate the force of his own and his clan's blessing to his son, a ritual meal must be prepared and celebrated—this is the act. Thereby his power is strengthened and the communion deepened. Then he lays his hands on his son's head—the act again—and blesses him—the words (Gen. 27).

When the clan's daughter is to be given in marriage to another house, the clan gathers round her and gives her the blessing which is to make her fruitful and increase the power and glory of her new clan in the days to come. It says:

Our sister, be thou thousands of myriads,
    may thy seed possess the gates of their enemies.
(Gen. 24.60.)

No doubt this took place accompanied by the imposition of hands and other ritual ceremonies.

When the tribe is threatened by a mighty enemy, or arms itself to go to war, a great sacrifice is held, and (as we can read in the legend of Balaam) a curse, which is to break the power of the enemy and lodge defeat in his soul (Num. 22–27), is composed and uttered, to the accompaniment of very specific ceremonies.

Other rites bring us to the temple cult in Jerusalem, to the holy processions with the ark of Yahweh. When the priests lifted the ark to carry it in the procession[62] or in battle (1 Sam. 4) it signified that Yahweh himself on his throne headed his 'hosts'. So they used to lift the ark with a short song calling upon Yahweh himself to march:

Rise up, Yahweh, and let thine enemies be scattered,
    let them that hate thee flee before thee!

and when the army pitched camp, or the procession reached its destination and the ark was put down, the words were:

Take thy seat, Yahweh, among the myriads of Israel.
(Num. 10.35f.)

On the festal days, when the service was over, the high priest concentrated the essence of the whole in an act which was visibly and audibly to convey to the congregation the blessing gained by it. He reached out his hands over the people and pronounced the well known 'Aaronic blessing', 'The Lord bless thee, and keep thee', etc. (Num. 6.22–27.)

Also the older type, the word which explains the act and is intended to increase its effect, was long preserved in the temple service. We see this among other things, from the words accompanying the 'ordeal' which the priest imposed upon the wife suspected of adultery. (Num. 5.19ff.)

In most of these cases the words express what is to happen to the congregation or to an individual member by an act of the deity. They are 'sacramental' words. This applies also to the cultic *oracle*, the augural and future-shaping answer from Yahweh, or his 'directions' or 'guidance' as to what the inquirer should do, e.g. in case of war and in impending danger generally (see further below, Chap. XII). The word may also express the *demand* and direction of the deity addressed to those who come to the place to partake of the blessing of the cult, and thus may become a vehicle for the religion's moral demand on the worshipper, 'the holy law' of the deity and the place (see below, pp. 177ff.).

But the words may also be the congregation's words to the deity (sacrificial words). They then express the congregation's reaction to and acceptance of what happens, as when the appearance of the deity in the pro-

[62] The journeyings through the desert in Num. 10–11ff. are described on the model of a cultic procession; cf. Ps. 132.

cession is greeted with hymns of praise, or the congregation gives thanks for the benefactions received. But they may also contain the congregation's prayer for help, salvation and blessing.

Prayer has not, as such, sprung from the cult, but in all higher cults it gradually takes precedence over everything else. Invocation and prayer are older than any cult, and independent of it. They are the primary expressions of religion.[63] That is why they have their place in the socially regulated intercourse with the divine, and may in the cult both be connected with, and have embodied and displaced, more magically significant and effective words which have their origin in the primitive 'magical' conception of life, which may be the background, but is not the 'origin', of religion. But on the other hand, the prayer may be overgrown by magic and, in a petrified religion and cult, sink down, to become a more or less magically conceived formula. But normally prayer is a petition to a powerful, willing and personally acting God, and is intended consciously to support, underline and express what the acts in their way express and effect. What is performed is accompanied by prayer and praise. It has been thus in all oriental cults, and without doubt also in Israel. The psalms are the actual proof of it.

It appears to be a universal law that the words in the cult take on a rhythmic form. In the rhythmic poetic form the 'force' of the words is more obvious both to perception and to emotion, and is further heightened by the music. The natural form of the cultic prayer is the *psalm*. Hence the large place in the cult which is given to the psalm in all the ancient oriental religions—in India, Iran, Babylonia-Assyria, Egypt, by the Hittites in Asia Minor, and by the Canaanites before the invasion of Israel, not to mention the many later developments during the Hellenistic age, in Manicheism and the Gnostic sects. Christian hymn-writing also grew out of worship, as is seen from the New Testament (cf. 1 Cor. 14.26).

Accordingly we find that psalms—hymns of praise, supplications, thanksgiving psalms, etc.—have in the different religions been connected with almost every one of the above cultic acts and ceremonies. From Babylonia-Assyria, Egypt, the Hittites in Asia Minor, India, etc., we have long series of psalms with indications of the definite cultic performance at which they were to be recited. The Ugaritic texts give strong reason to believe that the same was done by the Canaanites.

From Am. 5.23 must be concluded that hymn-singing at that time was a normal part of the Israelite cult, as well (cf. 6.5, and see below, Chap. XVIII.2).

It is therefore at least a very strongly founded working hypothesis that the biblical psalms are to be interpreted as cultic texts.

If this interpretation can be applied to the psalms individually there is no reason to look for any other explanation. It is the non-cultic character of a psalm which has to be proved, the contrary being the more likely supposition.

[63] Cf. Heiler, *Das Gebet*[4], pp. 157f.

CHAPTER II

The Method of the Cultic Interpretation

I

It follows from what has been said in Chap. I that a cultic interpretation—
and a real understanding—of the psalms means setting each one of them in
relation to the definite cultic act—or the cultic acts—to which it belonged.

All scientific research demands a proper arrangement of material, a
classifying and a grouping, so that the things which belong together may
be seen in their mutual connexions and illuminate one another. But the
principles and criteria of classification must be derived from the material
itself, not from disparate fields or modern interests and points of view. Not
seldom the 'catchwords' for classification have been taken from the loci of
Christian dogmatics, e.g. from the different divine attributes. But the
ancient Israelites did not shape their thoughts to the pattern of Christian
dogmas and morals. Nor can a classification according to the religious
ideas represented in the different psalms be considered satisfactory: we
cannot be sure that the idea which to us seems most prominent was so
for the poet. It is quite unsystematic to group together 'nature psalms',
'creation psalms', 'psalms on the majesty of God', with 'prayer psalms',
'thanksgiving psalms', 'penitential psalms', etc.[1] The creation and the
majesty of God, etc., may well be mentioned both in a 'prayer psalm'
and a 'thanksgiving psalm'; the question is: why, and with what aim?
There is no psalm which does not accept God's majesty and his power to
intervene everywhere and all the time, or which does not acknowledge
him as creator; the question is: why does, e.g., *this* special psalm speak at
greater length and in more detail about creation than is usual in the
psalms? It is misleading to speak of a 'nature psalm', because 'Nature'—
this modern conception—plays no independent part in the psalms at all,
but only occurs as an example of God's creative work. But why do certain
psalms call 'heaven and earth, mountains and oceans, trees and fields,
beasts and birds', etc., to praise the Lord, whilst the regular call to praise
in the psalms is directed to the congregation of Israel, or the like?

All this modern grouping only leads us to ask the poets about things
which interest *us*, but to which *they* often have no answer; instead of trying
to see things from *their* point of view, and asking what is in *their* mind,
e.g. when they appeal to God's omniscience, or call upon nature to praise

[1] See Additional Note III.

Yahweh. The usual interpretations of Pss. 90 and 139 are examples of such a mistaken way of putting the question. We read them as contemplations of the eternity or the omnipresence of God—but that is not what the poems seek to convey. They speak out of a definite situation, and it is in order to make God intervene in this situation that they speak of his eternity and omniscience. We must first listen to the emotion in the psalmist's own heart, and to be able to do that we must try to find the actual situation in which he is placed. Only then can we ask what he— and God through him—has to say to *us* in *our* situation.[2]

A proper classification must try to find the different fundamental types or species of psalms according to their own rules. How can these rules be recognized and described?

This is where Gunkel's 'form-critical' ('form-historical', *formgeschichtliche*) or 'type-critical' (*gattungsgeschichtliche*) method comes in.[3]

Even a superficial consideration shows that, in form and in details of content and structure, the psalms largely fall into a certain number of markedly different groups, which usually show a close conformation in form and matter within each individual group.

A number of psalms, for instance, are immediately recognizable as praises of Yahweh and of his great works and attributes. We soon discover that certain fundamental elements recur in such psalms with great regularity, and that in regard to their structure also the psalms of this group have certain traits in common. Another group consists of prayers and lamentations, in which a 'we' or 'I' voice their distress and beg Yahweh's help. Here too we meet with a number of characteristic details and common formulas both of prayer and lamentation, and with particular motivations for granting the prayer (*Gebetserhörungsmotive*), which in many variations constantly recur. Thus we are here confronted with special 'kinds' or 'types' of psalm whose peculiarities of content and form are amenable to description and explanation, and in which the agreement between form and content can be studied. These conformities cannot be accidental.

The first task is to classify the different forms and styles, thoughts and moods, of the psalms which are more or less distinctly alike in all these respects, and which thus form a special group or 'type' (species), for the moment leaving the dubious cases aside. Thus we become able to give a more or less complete description of the characteristics and peculiarities of every single group or species, each one containing those psalms which

[2] For this statement see Mowinckel, *The Old Testament as Word of God*, pp. 120ff.

[3] Gunkel presented the programme of his investigations in his *Israelitische Literaturgeschichte*; see further the article 'Psalmen' in *RGG*[1] and *RGG*[2]; followed up concretely in *Ausgewählte Psalmen*[4] and in the commentary *Die Psalmen* (in *HKAT*) as well as in Gunkel-Begrich, *Einleitung in die Pss*. Further references in *Einleitung*, p. 20. Even earlier B. Jacob (*ZATW* 17, 1897) and Matthes (*ZATW* 22, 1902), among others, had stood up for the principle of a cultic interpretation of the psalms. Bickel already saw and—without stating any reasons for it—declared that the psalms had been composed with a view to the public worship (*Dichtungen der Hebräer* I, p. VI). But only the historical method of studying form and type has been able to provide a safe basis for this theory.

show a fund of common forms, thoughts and moods. The work may be compared with that of the botanist, who decides the species of the individual plant and its place within the system on the basis of such objective criteria as the form and number of stamens, petals and sepals, and the place of these organs above or below the ovary.

We have to do with fixed style forms, where the similarities between the individual pieces within the group cannot be due to one poet having imitated the other, but to the fixity of a traditional and conventional style.

In a closed cultural orbit, both in a primitive culture and in the ancient high civilizations, the power of tradition and custom over form was much stronger than in modern times, when both an open exchange of cultural values and a much higher appreciation of the individual and his peculiar qualities have broken up the formerly closed and uniform circles of culture. The durability of form, and the power of convention over what is to be thought and said and done in the different constantly recurrent typical situations of life, we Norwegians, for example, until quite recently have had the opportunity of studying in our own remote valleys and communities. The conditions in ancient Israel were very much the same. Thus the hold of style over the poet was very great; from one point of view poetic composition was a thing which might be learned by anyone who cared to familiarize himself with the ideas and forms which custom demanded on typical occasions. Poetry, then, exists in definite traditional types or kinds, each with its own special rules as to content and form.

Content and form belong together. There exists no form without a content, and no content without a form. The psalms are poetry, and poetry is an art, and in art both content and form are determinants. Good art means a work in which there is unity of content and aim on the one hand, and of form and style on the other—where the form serves and adequately expresses the content, makes it living and allows it to appear with its full weight and to exhibit its real character. But especially in a remote culture, the forms are easier to detect, and they are often more fixed and more durable than the content. A form may live, even if the content has become more or less incomprehensible, and the ideas connected with it have changed, or have got a different emphasis. It goes without saying that in the classification of the psalms due attention must be paid to the motifs or themes included in the different form elements and thus recurring in several psalms as characteristic of the group. Essential parts of the content lie concealed in the form elements. Each motif or theme must be followed up in the different psalms and its quality be determined by comparison.

But even so, the fixed forms provide the easiest point of departure, and that is just what Gunkel has seen. So he came to call his method the *formgeschichtliche*, the form-historical, or form-critical method. The term is not quite adequate, and has given rise to misunderstanding. We might better call it the 'type-critical' or 'type-historical' method.

The fixed form elements will usually begin to appear in the opening words of the psalm.[4] Any one could at once classify a piece of writing that began: 'Once upon a time', or 'Dear Friend', or 'We are in receipt of your favour' . . . . In the same way we find that a certain group of psalms, a 'psalm-type', quite regularly starts with 'Praise Yahweh', or 'Let us praise', and so on. Another starts with a mention of Yahweh's name (the 'invocation') and a supplication, 'LORD (i.e. Yahweh), I cry unto thee', and so on.

Just as important as the opening words are the closing ones. Compare 'and they lived happily ever after', or 'Yours faithfully'. In the psalms we very often find that the closing words, in some form or other, re-iterate or correspond to the opening ones.

But even the central portion or main part has its typical elements of form and content. Religious experience and custom had long ago decided what details of content, what thoughts and formulas in the cult were 'right' and 'appropriate' in each type of psalm and situation in the cult. And these forms persist, even where the individual poet does not think consciously of a purpose any longer, or of gaining anything by his prayer. Thus we see that with the exhortation to praise God in the opening words there usually goes an enumeration of Yahweh's great and glorious works, his tĕhillôth. Very often a description of the sorry state and need of the suppliant corresponds to the opening invocation and prayer, and an appeal to the attributes of Yahweh or his deeds which make it likely that help may be given.

The realization of which elements of form normally belong to a certain type not only makes it possible to define the individual psalm and the cultic situation from which it originates, but is also of considerable importance for the exegesis, and for the interpretation of any obscure passage. The problem is frequently solved when we find out to what fundamental type the psalm in question belongs. It is also important when solving the question of how to divide a psalm into stanzas. The form may decide whether a verse belongs to the preceding or to the succeeding part. The determination of type can also answer the question we often meet with in the commentaries as to whether a psalm is a unit or should be divided into two; in the light of form criticism we can tell which subject matter and elements of form regularly belong to, or may belong to, a certain type.

Gunkel also realized that there is a close connexion between the fixed forms and contents on the one hand, and certain typical, more or less regularly recurring situations in the life of the community in question. Each 'literary' type has its special place in life, from which it has sprung.

As hinted above, there are in the life of every society, and especially in a closed cultural orbit, like that of the Hebrews, certain ever recurrent situations where certain things have to be done and certain words to be said. That applies both to what we call secular life, and to the sacred, cultic life. That means that even what we call secular, but important,

[4] For further details see Gunkel-Begrich, *Einleitung*, pp. 25f.

situations in life tend to become hedged by fixed 'rituals'. In his book *Rites de passage*, A. van Gennep has demonstrated this as a very important side of man's culture and cult. In the decisive situations of life, in life's supreme moments, it is necessary that something vital be created and obtained; and the means by which it was to be attained were the efficacious rites and words. As an element in these acts and words art has always found its place, from the cave paintings of the Mousterians to the cultic poetry, song, and music of the higher religions.

Poetry, like all other sorts of art, may have come into existence by the eruptive expression of what filled man's soul, without any other aim and purpose than just to express, to give birth to what demands expression, just because it 'presses on' the soul. But even this is an 'aim', although perhaps an unconscious one; man at once experiences that he has gained something by the expression, and that what he has created is useful to obtain certain results. What he expresses makes an impression on the others. It can and shall be used.

To primitive man art and poetry have their aim and purpose, their 'tendency' in the good sense of the word. The ancient civilizations do not know of poetry which is not 'tendentious'. Even the fairy-tale has its purpose: to entertain, to move, to excite and to release. No ancient oriental could have conceived of 'Art for art's sake'. Art and poetry are individual and personal, but also social. Primitive poetry has its place in definite situations in life, and aims at expressing what then happens and should happen, what is felt and should be felt; what should then be said, because the situation demands a lofty form of expression. Poetry itself was an expression of a sociological function. Certain emotions, thoughts and words were to be expressed so as to bring about a certain result, important for the life of the community, and the form had to be the 'impressive', creating, efficacious form of poetry. At the marriage ceremony the rhythmic blessing was meant to induce fertility in the bride and numerous offspring for the husband and his clan, as in the narrative of the betrothal of Rebekah. Before the battle a curse was flung against the enemy to break his 'luck', put 'bane' and evil 'charms' into his soul, to enable them to stand up to him and drive him away, as in the Balaam story (Num. 22–24). At the holy places, when the council sat and cases were brought forward, the priests gave their directions from Yahweh in traditional forms. Before the battle they and the prophets give oracular answers. When the army comes home, the women sing paeans. At a burial the 'mourning-women' sing their dirge, the *qînâ*. Each of these 'literary categories' has its traditional form and its traditional subject.[5] No chance words were then spoken, but

---

[5] See the survey in Gunkel's fundamental *Israelitische Literatur* (above, note 3). Since then the individual types have been thoroughly examined in a great many special works. For the *tôrâh* or instruction in sacral law and 'oracle of the priest' cf. for instance Alt, *Urspr. d. isr. Rechts*; Begrich, 'Die priesterliche Tora' in *Werden u. Wesen d. A.T.* ed. Hempel, *BZATW* 66, pp. 63ff.; for the funeral wail, Jahnow, *Das hebr. Leichenlied*; for the prophetic oracle, for instance, Mowinckel in *GTMMM* III, pp. 38ff.; cf. Begrich, 'Das priesterliche Heilsorakel', *ZATW* 52, 1934, pp. 81ff.

words of a defined content, worked by a poet or poetess into a poem according to set rules governed by a long tradition. The content was determined by the aim, and the aim, again, was dictated by the situation.

In the same way the situations also determined the form. The form is the one which, in each case, was felt to be the most natural and most suitable means of expressing the word to be said and of reaching the goal to be attained. This consideration consciously or unconsciously decides the choice of the details to be included, the expressions and imagery employed, the fundamental mood, and the composition as a whole into which the details have been fitted.

This general principle must also be applied to the psalms. The classification into different groups, each with its specific peculiarities as to style, form and content, is no subjective arrangement of the material, based on aesthetical considerations and feelings. By taking the fixed forms as a starting point, the form-critical method shows that it is founded on something objective and amenable to control, dependent on external observations, which it classifies, systematizes and explains. In the forms—here taken in the widest sense of the word—some essential information is found. The study of the formal criteria of the different stylistic 'types' shows the way to the different situations in life from which they have sprung. To each of the main psalm types corresponds a definite situation; they have all their definite setting or place in life. It then becomes quite clear that all these situations are cultic situations.

The content and the style of the 'public psalm of lament', such as, e.g. Pss. 44; 74; 79; 80; are just those which can be singled out from the description in 1 Sam. 7 of what was done and said as the Philistines oppressed the Israelites and the latter 'gathered together to Mizpah, and drew water, and poured it out before the LORD, and fasted on that day, and said there, We have sinned against the LORD . . . and the children of Israel said to Samuel, Cease not to cry unto the LORD our God for us, that he will save us out of the hand of the Philistines. And Samuel took a sucking lamb, and offered it for a whole burnt offering unto the LORD: and Samuel cried unto the LORD for Israel'. What, at a similar celebration 'in the time of dearth' (according to Jer. 14), used to be said to Yahweh is, as to content and form and style, in the closest correspondence with the same psalm type. What, according to Isa. 38 or Jonah 2, a man used to say to Yahweh when bringing his thanksgiving gift after being saved from great danger—sickness or the like—has also its close parallels in a definite type of psalm represented by Pss. 32, 116, and others. When the Chronicler describes a cultic celebration of some sort, he often lets the singers sing a hymn of praise which, in all essentials, often even in the wording, has its formal and material parallels in the Psalter.

So Gunkel could confidently draw the conclusion that psalm poetry as such, all the main psalm types with their formal and material characteristics, have sprung from definite cultic situations. Every psalm type as such has been created to serve cultic performances in a definite cultic situation with its own specific aim—hence its typical content, its structure and its formal expression.

With an objective inner logic the cultic situations demand a particular content in a particular form. Within the framework of a divine service of worship nothing is accidental. Everything has its significance and its purpose, which we must try to fathom. All the formal and material peculiarities of a type are explained by that origin and that purpose. To find these definite cultic situations was to Gunkel an integrating part of his form-historical research. So far, he was, in principle, absolutely right, as has been acknowledged by most recent interpreters,[6] and all further investigations of the psalms must be based on the foundation thus laid by him.

2

But, as already mentioned, Gunkel has not drawn the full consequences from his own fundamental discovery. His commentary on the psalms (*Die Psalmen*) and the Gunkel-Begrich 'Introduction to the Psalms' (*Einleitung in die Psalmen*) have gone only half-way. His method led him to see that psalm poetry as such was old in Israel, and that many psalms must be dated to pre-exilic times; but in the main he kept to the opinion ruling at the beginning of this century, that the greater number of extant psalms were post-exilic and came from small, more or less private 'conventicles' of pious laymen—for the existence of which he has given just as little proof as did his predecessors. The majority of extant psalms were in Gunkel's opinion no real cult psalms; they were 'spiritualized' imitations of the old, now mostly lost, cultic psalm poetry. In the many allusions to cultic rites and performances (see above, Chap. I) he would see only metaphors, and in this supposed emancipation from the cult, in the psalmists' 'freedom from the cult religion', he saw just that religious 'progress' which gave the psalms their religious value. The psalms had, so to say, to apologize for their cultic origin. He clung, like most of the older psalm interpreters, to the curious prejudice that direct cultic destination—as 'cult formulas', as they said—was more or less incompatible with deep personal feeling and experience—and the presence of these latter traits in many psalms they of course could not deny.

From this position, however, arose a serious problem which neither Gunkel himself nor his nearest followers perceived, or which, at least, they left unsolved. Both the titles of the psalms and express notes in the Jewish tradition in the Mishna and Talmud show—as we have seen—that several psalms have definitely been used in the temple service. But since we know that Judaism, like all other ancient cult religions, always demanded that everything concerning the cult should rest on old and sacred

[6] See Additional Note IV.

heritage and tradition, and that the cult should be a kind of closed world which no 'profane' influence might enter, it is inconceivable how any younger, private, lay poetry could possibly have made its way into the cult, and even supplanted most of the genuine old ritual poetry.

If the many psalms in which 'the suffering ones' or 'the hapless ones' ('ŏnîyîm, 'anāwîm) complain about their oppressors, originate from the 'suppressed' lower classes in the congregation—as the long prevailing theory of Rahlfs and others would have—how can it then be explained that they later on found their way into the official cult, which was in the hands of the supposed oppressors of the authors, the mighty and wealthy priesthood and the rulers of the congregation? In fact those 'oppressed ones' are the nation of Israel itself, suffering under the oppression of its heathen neighbours or the oriental world empires. Or, to take another instance, if the Korah psalms, Pss. 42–44, as Snaith has tried to demonstrate, originated in the circles which Nehemiah drove out from Jerusalem, and Pss. 50; 73–83 from the Jewish rigorists at that time, can it be conceived that this private polemical poetry has been taken up into the official cult, at a time when its true nature must still have been known to everyone?

To this problem there is only one satisfying answer: the psalms are—with very few exceptions—real cult psalms, made for cultic use.

Another consideration points in the same direction.

We do have a Jewish psalm poetry which came into existence as 'private religious lyrics' without any connexion with the temple cult, and without cultic destination. This psalmody emanated from certain 'pious circles', which really existed in later Judaism, after the days of the predominance of the written law on the one hand, and the Hellenizing influences among the upper classes before and after the Maccabean revolt on the other. It is to be found in the so-called Psalms of Solomon, and the newly found Essenian Hodayoth from the Qumran caves. Owing to the emancipation from the temple cult and the individualistic spirit of the poets concerned, they demonstrate a far-reaching disintegration of the old fixed forms and a mixture of elements from different styles and types not found in the biblical psalms, where in all essentials the old fixed formal and stylistic rules predominate.

What strikes us in the biblical psalms is the uniformity and formality which characterize most of them. One is often so like another that they are difficult to differentiate. The personal, individual element is pushed into the background. Imagery and phraseology are often the stereotyped traditional ones. Rarely is there a clear allusion to the poet's personal situation, rarely anything definite and concrete, almost invariably only what is typical of a whole circle, in the most general terms. This cannot be explained as only the usual lyric dependence on a particular style with its partiality for that in which everybody can join; for even then there can be room for personal variations, as may be seen from the dirge over Saul and Jonathan in 2 Sam. 1.19ff., compared with the usual stereotyped dirge. The set formality of the psalms can only be explained on the basis that they are not primarily meant to be personal effusions, but are, in accordance with their type and origin, ritual lyrics. It is of the nature of the cultic psalm that it cannot express the individual's definite, once-for-all, experiences and emotions. It voices those moods and experiences which have common currency within the cult community. Hence everything which is too concrete and individual is pushed into the background.[7] In its original form the cultic psalm springs from set formulas, suiting all occasions. We meet the same formality to a much higher degree in Babylonian-Assyrian cultic psalms.[8]

This does not imply that the personal element has been cut out, or that type analysis pays no heed to it. We shall return to this point in a special chapter.

But also in another respect Gunkel—and after him many of his followers —went only half-way. He often stuck too much to the mere formal registration and labelling of the single elements of a psalm and did not see clearly enough that his own form-historical method demanded that it be developed into a real *cult-functional method*.

The form may be overrated so as to arrest one's vision and understanding through purely formal limitations, and make one overlook important inner correspondences between psalms which outwardly appear to belong to different groups, but which are governed by the same ideas, and thus prove to belong together, perhaps as psalms for some specific festival.

In course of time an old form may have become the bearer of new contents in a new situation.[9] That also must be taken into consideration.

On the other hand, an alien form may have been used as an effective means of expressing the content. Thus although the prophets often used the psalm-style to underline and emphasize their message; nevertheless their utterances are prophecies and neither hymns nor lamentations. And the psalm-writer may use the form of the 'wisdom-poetry' for his personal expression of the praise of God, or thanksgiving for a blessing received— without his psalm becoming a wisdom or problem poem.

Occasionally we meet with 'compound' psalms, whose different parts use two completely different form types, e.g. hymn of praise plus lamentation, or thanksgiving plus lamentation. In such cases the older critical psalm interpreter often solved the problem by declaring that here two different psalms had been joined together 'by chance'. This was possible when the psalms were still viewed from a purely literary and aesthetic point of view, and one did not raise the question about their background

[7] Cf. my treatise 'Salmeboken' in *NTT* 1927, pp. 153f., where this peculiarity even in Danish and Norwegian psalmography ("hymnology") is briefly commented on.
[8] Cf. Jastrow, *Relig. Babyl. u. Assyr.* II, pp. 10f., 61f., 116; Weber, *Liter. d. Babyl. u. Assyr.*, pp. 116f.
[9] Gunkel is of course fully aware of this, for instance, when he maintains that a new sense has been 'spiritually' assigned to the cultic psalms of illness, so as to change them into individual cult-free prayers. But this theory of a new reading is itself untenable.

in an actual cultic situation. Even Gunkel's interpretation, which on
principle took its point of departure from the latter point, sometimes failed
here and was content to classify and establish the facts instead of explaining
them. An instance of such a failure is his treatment of Pss. 9–10, which
form *one* psalm bound together by 'the alphabetical scheme', that is, each
new stanza starts with another letter, in alphabetical order. The first part
of this, the letters *aleph* to *kaph* (*a–k*) make a hymn; while the second part,
the letters *lamedh* to *taw* (*l–t*), is a lament. Gunkel's explanation is that
when the poet reached *lamedh* he could not, on the spur of the moment,
find any other word starting with an 'l' than *lamma* 'why', and hence he
plunged into the lament style, where the lamenting phrase 'Why hast thou
forsaken me?' and the like, frequently recur, and continued in this
lamentation style! This is a curiously superficial explanation, poorly
corresponding with the firm and conscious style of the poem, and is only
possible because Gunkel with regard to the individual psalms usually
betrays his own cultic principle, maintaining that they are not real
cult psalms, but only 'literary' imitations.[10]

Sometimes Gunkel stressed the formal identity between the psalms of a
definite species at the risk of drawing too narrow limits for the species in
question, thus failing to see an important idea that at least has some inner
connexion with that species. There can be no doubt that Gunkel is wrong in
excluding Ps. 95 from the category of the 'enthronement' psalms 93;
96–99. Ps. 95 has all the characteristics of the others, *plus* something more:
and this plus in fact opens the way to a deeper understanding of the
enthronement psalms, and widens the number of psalms belonging in the
same ideological connexion. We then see that the narrow group of enthronement psalms, in the strictest sense of the word, tells us very little
about religious experience, life and thought in ancient Israel, compared
with the great complex of experiences and ideas that we grasp when we
put the real cult functional question: to which cultic occasion must this
psalm group have belonged, and what has the congregation experienced
and felt on that occasion? The definition 'enthronement psalms' must be
made not only from the formal literary, but also from the cult functional
point of view, and the latter is the more important.

That the psalms belong to the cult will in many cases mean that they
belong to some definite cultic festival cult to the ancient Israelite meant
primarily 'festival'.

But the experience, thought, and mood involved in a particular cultic
festival are generally many-sided, and complex enough to cover the whole
range of religious content and experience. The ritual of a festival service
is in fact a very complex affair with many subdivisions, each intended to
express a certain aspect of the experience and of the 'cultic drama', and

---

[10] A much more organic understanding of the connexion between the two parts of the psalm
is found in Bentzen, *Fortolkning til de gt. lige Salmer, ad loc.*, cf. also Junker in *Revue Biblique* 60,
1953, pp. 161ff. Bentzen is right in his criticism of the present author in *Ps. St.* I 172.

the corresponding religious need and mood. Corresponding to these different aspects are different kinds of style, evolved to express each of them. So to the same festival there may have belonged both plaintive prayers for help in distress and need, and joyous hymns to the living God, thanking him for salvation promised or 'seen' and grasped by the believer in the symbols of the cult. The festival cult involved a number of very different acts and ceremonies. This point Gunkel of course had seen, when he recognized a 'sacramental' element, an oracle of Yahweh, in some psalms, and defined a group of psalms as '(compound) liturgies'. But each festival also has its main idea, with many varying notions and conceptions. This main idea and the conceptions which accompany it will of course characterize most of the appertaining 'words' and psalms. With us, for instance, the main idea of Easter or Whitsun, and the reality of salvation which these festivals express and revive, will in many ways stamp all true Easter or Pentecost hymns, and appear in prayer and confession as well as in hymns of thanks and praise. There is no Christian Easter hymn—of whatever style—that does not in some manner refer to Christ's victorious resurrection and its power and hope. It is not sufficient then, to define a psalm as a lamentation or prayer-psalm, if its main idea suggests in addition a connexion with the idea and experience of a particular festival. This must become perfectly clear, and we shall have understood neither the psalm nor its place in actual life, its cultic situation and its aim, until we have connected it with the festival in question, and with its idea and cultic forms.

In other words, the purely form-historical classification and interpretation of Gunkel, the pure 'examination of types', and grouping of the psalms according to the form categories found by the form critic, has to be enlarged and replaced by proper cult-historical ones. The formal point of view is only a provisional help.

This point of view, then, will lead us to a modified division of the psalms and to another principle of interpretation than that of Gunkel, viz. to the form *and* cult-historical one. If we take this seriously at the same time remembering the old Israelite 'collective' (corporate) view of people and community, as it appears in the cult (see below, Chap. III.1), we shall see that a purely formal classification often has only a relative value. We shall not have reached our goal by, e.g., dividing the 'lamentation-psalms' into 'we-psalms' and 'I-psalms', and imagining that we have in that way reached two really different categories and cultic situations. The I-form in reality includes psalms of two very different cultic types, each with its own cultic and historic background and causation. One of these groups— the so-called public (congregational) lamentations—is objectively and cult historically much more closely related to the 'we-psalms' than it is to the proper 'I-psalms'. There is a series of 'I-psalms' where the 'I' is not the single, private member of the congregation, but the social, political and cultic representative of the people—that is to say, the king. In this case the occasion and the corresponding cultic situation is, as we shall see below, a public matter, not the experience and situation of a single private individual.[11] This leads both to somewhat of a return to older positions in the interpretation of the 'I' in the psalms,[12] and to a view of the so-called 'royal psalms' diverging from Gunkel's (see Chap. III).

In practice the form-critical and the cult-functional method cannot be separated from each other, but must work hand in hand when we arrange the psalms in groups or species, according to such common forms, thoughts and moods as are in accordance with that cultic situation, or that special festival, which is supposed to be the background of the species in question. True enough, the common elements must be the essential ones in the psalms in question; but if a whole coherent complex of ideas is included in the supposed cultic festival, it may well happen that one of the components of this complex is predominant in one psalm, another component in another. Here it will be necessary to bear in mind the old Israelite way of 'thinking in totalities': if one note of a chord is struck, all the others sound in his mind; one important component of a complex of ideas being mentioned, the others are recalled in his consciousness.

The present author has for a good many years in his studies on the psalms endeavoured to apply a really cult-functional interpretation, and to bring out all these features in the psalms and in what we know about the Israelite and Jewish cult which help to prove that the psalms of the Psalter, on the whole, are real cult-psalms and an expression of that experience of God which the cult seeks to further.[13]

The cult-functional method includes the attempt to understand every surviving psalm as a real cult psalm, made for a definite cultic situation. The foundation has been laid by Gunkel's explanation of the cultic origin of the different types. But in trying to trace the consequences for the surviving psalms, we shall find ourselves concerned with more of such situations than he thought, and realize that the connexion between psalm and cult is much closer than he imagined.

To understand a psalm means to see it in the right cultic connexion. This is, in fact, a quite elementary truth. Everybody will agree that a Christian baptismal hymn or a communion hymn acquires full significance only when seen in connexion with the holy act to which it belongs.

---

[11] See Chap. VII.

[12] This applies for instance to the view of the so-called 'collective ego', which has more of truth in it than the purely form-historical school has been willing to admit. It also applies to the view of the political background and the events occasioning the I-laments, which are actually 'national' (royal) psalms, as has been demonstrated especially by Birkeland (*Feinde d. Indiv.*); he shares this interpretation with earlier critical psalm interpreters like de Wette and Fr. Buhl; cf. Bentzen's remark on the book by Birkeland: 'Many of B.'s arguments, when read today, half a dozen years after the appearance of the book, look like a "repristination", a return to earlier criticism' (Bentzen, *Sakrale kongedömme*, p. 39). This is true, as far as it goes, but no real objection. Even earlier critics may sometimes be in the right!

[13] Cf. the summary in my essay in *NTT* 1924, pp. 1ff. As far as some groups of psalms are concerned this point of view has been followed up in my *Ps. St.* I–VI; but the conception in *Ps. St.* I especially is in need of the thorough re-examination carried out in the present book.

From the cult new light falls on the psalms, and from the psalms light falls on new sides of the cult. There is no first and last here. In the actual process of research these two points of view must be kept in a constant reciprocity.

The best proof for the correctness of our method will be when we succeed in explaining the whole extant material in this way. This the following chapters will try to do.

But our method will also afford a possibility of distinguishing between real cult psalms and a 'private' psalmody which partly uses the old styles and forms, but in many ways points to another 'place in life'. There *are*, even in the Psalter, some non-cultic psalms, but they are few.

A true interpretation of the psalms must try to form as complete and vivid a picture as possible of the old Israelite and Jewish cult and its many situations and acts.

3

Apparently we are quite well informed about the cult in Israel. The whole central part of the Pentateuch consists of cultic and ritual laws. But these are mostly to be found in a relatively late form and system, such as the 'Priestly Document' (P), the latest of the Pentateuchal sources, collected in post-exilic, Jewish times. As is shown by a comparison with the allusions in older sources and in the historical books, the view taken of important ritual acts (e.g. of the importance of the sacrifice), has changed and developed; so that it would be a mistake to base our conception of the psalms on the later stages of Israelitic-Jewish cultic development. The psalms are to a very great extent much older, and date from the time of the monarchy (before the exile). Further, the picture which the priestly source gives us of the cult is both one-sided and fragmentary. It presents ritual and other features of the service from the priests' own technical point of view. The laws (priests' agenda) speak of the kind and number of beasts to be sacrificed, and how the priest is to conduct himself in the course of the sacrificial act. We are also told what sacrifices and contributions the lay people are to offer, and the rituals at certain purifications and sacrifices are described from the point of view of the officiating priest. But they never give a living picture of a ritual festival as a whole. We hear practically nothing about the part played by the congregation, e.g. in the great festal processions which, from other sources, we know belonged to it. Nor do they say anything about the words which belonged to the cult, the prayers which were prayed, and the psalms which were sung. But from other sources, e.g. the book of Chronicles, we know that they formed part of the service. Only very rarely do the laws record a cultic prayer (Deut. 21.7–9; 26.1ff.), and we hear very little about hymn singing, even though other sources contain allusions to ritual acts where hymns were sung.[14]

[14] Cf. Am. 5.23; Job 33.27; 2 Sam. 6.5; 1 Kgs. 8.12; 1 Chron. 16.8ff.; 2 Chron. 6.1f.; 6.41f., and other places.

In addition to what is given in the laws, we find, in historical and legendary accounts and in the prophets, more incidental remarks and allusions which may serve to amplify the picture.

But, to a certain extent, the situations can and must be pictured from hints in the psalms themselves. When once we have grasped that each situation creates its own formal language around a definite subject-content, then we are able, from the characteristics of the content and form in a certain group of psalms, to reconstruct the precise cultic occasion which has produced them, and which also supplies their natural explanation. In this way Gunkel and others after him re-discovered important parts of the ancient Israelite cult which were not mentioned in the laws. We shall look more closely at this when treating of the particular types of psalms and their origin.

This process of induction from the types of psalms to the underlying cultic situation of course becomes increasingly convincing as it can be confirmed by analogies from neighbouring oriental civilizations. We must realize that in matters of the framework of the cult, and incidentally, of many of the ideas expressed through it, the partially Canaanized Israelites took as models the temple cults of neighbouring peoples. The Yahweh religion in the period immediately following the immigration (and especially after the blending with the indigenous population had been achieved with the rise of the monarchy), had been deeply influenced by Canaanite religion, that is to say by oriental religion generally. The religious history of Israel in the following period largely consists of a dramatic struggle to expel the obviously syncretistic, and to work out the peculiar historical significances of the Yahweh religion. Israel's cult places were to a great extent the same as those of the ancient Canaanites, and there followed, as a matter of course, the adoption of many Canaanite cultic traditions. The three great annual festivals are characteristic agricultural festivals, which Israel adopted from the natives and adjusted to the religion of Yahweh, giving them a new, historically orientated interpretation. The first of them, the festival of the barley harvest, the *Maṣṣôth* festival, corresponded in time to the old Israelite cattle-breeding festival of Easter (*Pesaḥ*), and could be combined with it. The very Temple in Jerusalem was built according to Canaanite patterns. To worship Yahweh in temples was a novel custom. In Jerusalem, Yahweh was 'identified' with the ancient deities, and inherited their names and titles of honour. There can, for instance, be no doubt that the name El Elyon, 'The Highest God', which in the Old Testament means Yahweh, originally signified the chief god of Jebusite Jerusalem. There are even signs that point to a connexion between the new priestly family to whom David entrusted the Yahweh cult in the Temple—the Zadokites—and the ancient dynasty of priest kings in Jerusalem.[15] Israel had no tradition as to the framing of a temple cult which went back to the period of desert wander-

[15] See below, n. 87 to Chap. V.

ing. That was adopted from outside. Another very important case of influence from oriental cultic ideas and customs will be demonstrated in Chap. V.

Hence it goes without saying that the knowledge of other oriental cult rituals—as Gunkel has already shown[16]—will throw light on much in the cult of Jerusalem, and thereby yield important contributions for a correct location of the psalms in the cult—not least because they so often support the conclusions one can draw from the psalms themselves.

In several respects—e.g. in the way we look at the collective element in many of the 'I-psalms'—our presentation will mean a return to older positions in psalm-interpretation,[17] but in new connexions and in a new light. Such is often the way of science.

In spite of a definite and fundamental cult-historical view we shall, in what follows, resist the one-sided exaggeration of this view which has cropped up in certain quarters lately, where it has even been suggested that all psalms and all details in them allude to cult-mythical happenings and experiences, leaving no room for an historical background or for allusions in any of the psalms to historical events. This can be understood as a reaction against older interpretations which paid no heed to the cultic side, and of each psalm asked first of all, 'what historical occasion is here alluded to, and who can the author of this psalm be?' That is an untenable position; but the reaction goes too far. Even though the lamentation-psalms belong to a cultic situation, there can be no doubt that they have for their background and cause historical events in the life of Israel, such as a definite national catastrophe or defeat in the fight against known enemies. Sometimes this is expressly stated. The duty to take this into account in the interpretation cannot be put aside by speaking slightingly of 'historicism', and the like.

4

A classification of the psalms must—like every understanding of them—be in accord with the 'divisions' in the cult itself, its different occasions, situations and acts.

At the present stage there is only the question of a rough classification, according to the main features.

What main types of divine service were there in ancient Israel and in Judaism? From what points of view can we classify them?

As we have already mentioned, the service is always essentially a communion, a matter that concerns both God and the congregation. To ancient Israel this was a matter of course, in accordance with the 'collective' or 'corporate' view of the relation between the society and the individual (see further, Chap. III). From the human point of view, the

[16] This applies to the whole 'religio-historical school' and was an important point in the scientific programme of the latter.
[17] See note 12 above.

protagonist in the cult, the one in whose name the action and speaking takes place, is the congregation.

But the congregation is also positively interested in the individual members, regardless of the degree in which they represent the whole. There are cultic actions on behalf of the individual, in which he or she is the centre. From our own divine service we may mention baptisms, churchings, weddings and funerals. But here too it is the congregation which is the real actor. The individual is regarded as a member of the congregation. To us, therefore, the natural form of the cultic psalm is the first person plural, 'we'. But the I-form, too, may be the right one, either when the cultic act in question is performed for the sake of the individual, or when he is so representative a person that he appears on behalf of the people, and in such a way that what is done to him is also done to the whole. The last train of ideas is characteristic of ancient religions, including that of ancient Israel.

In the psalms we meet with both the we-form and the I-form. How is this to be explained?

The simplest solution would be to say—like Gunkel and others—that the I-form means there is an individual who is speaking, a Mr So-and-so who is in need of that special cultic act, or a certain person who has composed the psalm or has had it composed to express his personal situation and experience. Only the psalms in the we-form are then congregational psalms proper.

There can be no doubt that this view contains a substantial truth. The psalms may be divided into those which concern the congregation or the people, that is *national* psalms or *congregational* psalms, and such as are connected with the individual's, possibly a private person's, religious and ritual need, that is, *personal* or *individual* psalms.

But the problem is not solved yet. The matter cannot be decided simply on the basis of I- or we-forms. There are also psalms where there is no doubt that the 'I' in question speaks on behalf of a plurality (as in Ps. 118), or where a 'we' appears together with and in the same sense as an 'I' (e.g., Ps. 44). There are also 'I-psalms' where the matter that caused the supplication to Yahweh obviously is a public one, concerning the whole people, and not only a single person (e.g., Ps. 66).

To this may be added that it is only to us moderns that it seems a matter of course that the natural form of plurality should be 'we'. In reality this 'we' presupposes a mental attitude and outlook which is individualizing compared to the old corporate one—a mental attitude proper to each individual person who has begun to be conscious of his own individuality, the congregation being a sum of 'I's (a 'we'). In the religion and common prayer of ancient peoples and civilizations the I-form is the usual and natural one, because there it is the whole and not the individual that is given reality, a 'corporate personality' which may act through a representative personality who 'incorporates' the whole. According to such an attitude it will be natural for the representative of the collective prayer to use the I-form. We see this for instance in Babylonian hymns,[18] and it has persisted through the ages.

An apparent I-psalm therefore may be really a congregational psalm, because the 'I' is the national and cultic representative of the congregation. Below (Chap. III) we shall see that the full appreciation of this fact helped on the study of the so-called royal psalms.

But there are also real I-psalms where the suppliant is the single member of the congregation. They belonged to cultic acts performed on behalf of the individual as a 'private' person—no matter who he was, a king, or a nobody. That Israel had such cultic acts is seen from many of the ritual laws of the Pentateuch.

There is, then, after all, a reality in the distinction between congregational or national psalms, and individual or private psalms. This distinction must be the point of departure in psalm interpretation, even though it is only of relative value, and cannot be carried through in all its details in this chapter.

Another division is that between joy and thanksgiving festivals, and days of penitence. They demand each their own type of prayer and psalm. From these two principles of division spring the *four main types* of psalms in the Psalter, the praises and thanksgivings of the congregation, private (that is, individual) thanksgivings, and besides them both congregational and individual lamentation and prayer psalms.

The praise and thanksgiving psalms of the congregation divide into two kinds: the common praises or hymns, about God's excellence and benefactions in general (Chap. IV), and the special thanksgiving psalms, giving thanks for a particular, just experienced, salvation (Chap. IX). This may be a special historical act of salvation, or one renewed at regular intervals.

In the same way we can distinguish between the common prayer psalms of the congregation (see Chap. VI.5–6) and lamentation and prayer psalms on a special occasion such as a catastrophe or a threatening danger (see Chap. VI.1–3). Within the latter group we can distinguish between real lamentations, when a catastrophe has already taken place, and 'protective psalms' where the event is as yet only a threat (Chap. VI.4). The last-mentioned distinction of course also obtains for the 'I-psalms' which are really royal or congregational psalms (see Chap. VII).

Besides these six or seven important types there are a certain number of less frequent kinds and types of psalms.

In the following chapters an account will be given of the most important kinds of psalm, and the cultic situations to which they belonged. I want to underline again that the foundations for such an investigation were laid by Gunkel, even if I, on many points already hinted at, disagree with his results.

[18] For examples, see Birkeland, *Die Feinde d. Individ.*, pp. 352ff.

5

In this form- and cult-historical investigation of the psalms it is important that *all* the material be taken into account. There are psalms outside the Psalter, and whether these have been composed for the same purpose as the others, or are only literary imitations, they are nevertheless dependent on traditional style and thus contribute to the explanation of the types.

This other material is to be found in several places in the Old Testament and in post-canonical literature. The narrative books, both the historical and the legendary ones, quite frequently let their dramatis personae utter a psalm or a prayer in the psalm style: e.g. Hannah's thanksgiving, king Hezekiah's thanksgiving, Jonah's prayer, Tobiah's and Judith's thanksgiving.[19] Or they may record parts of psalms that were sung at the festivals they describe.[20]

Poems in the style of the dirge, which may be regular cultic lamentations, have come down to us in Lamentations, Chaps. 3 and 5.

In addition to this we have the literary imitations in the book of Job, where Job himself often laments his afflictions in phrases typical of the psalms,[21] and the friends praise God's greatness, power and righteousness in the hymn style.[22]

In the prophets too we find many psalm-like passages. Sometimes the collectors of their prophecies, the later prophet-disciples, have given expression to the song of joy which the congregation is to sing, when once salvation has become a fact.[23] Sometimes they themselves exhorted the congregation to break into praise for the salvation which already sends its rays into the age.[24] More often they used the psalm form as an effective garb for the prophecy. Jeremiah laments on behalf of the people, or lets the people itself lament the disaster as if it had already happened—an effective way of driving the prophecy home. Deutero-Isaiah fashions his salvation prophecy as a hymn to Yahweh who works such great things, or opens his prophecies with such a song of praise. In the style of the 'personal lamentation', Jeremiah laments to Yahweh over the sufferings which the prophetic calling has brought on him, and prays for help.[25]

Wisdom poetry, too, like the proverbial philosophy of Ecclesiasticus, has many touches of the psalm style.[26] The sages felt that they were spiritual guides, *pneumatikoi*, the heirs of prophets and psalm writers. They saw a proof of their inspiration in the very fact that they were able to formulate a worthy prayer to God and to praise him in lofty psalms.[27]

[19] 1 Sam. 2; Isa. 38.9ff.; Jonah 2; Tob. 13; Judith 16. See Chap. XVI.6.
[20] 1 Chron. 16.8ff.; 2 Chron. 6.41f.; Ezra 3.11.
[21] Job 10; 13.23–14.22; 16.6–17.9; 19.7ff., etc. Cf. Mowinckel, *Diktet om Ijôb*, pp. 115ff.
[22] Job 5.9ff.; 9.3–13; 12.13ff.; 26.5ff.; 36.26ff.; 38.4ff. Cf. Mowinckel, *op. cit.* pp. 120ff.
[23] Isa. 12; 25.1ff.; 26.1ff.
[24] Isa. 42.10–12; 49.13; 52.9f., etc.
[25] See Baumgartner, *Klagegedichte des Jeremia*, *BZATW* 32; Mowinckel in *Edda* VI, 1926, pp. 276–304; Gressmann 'Die literarische analyse Deuterojesajas' in *ZATW* 34, 1914, pp. 283ff.
[26] Cf. Baumgartner, 'Die Literar. Gattungen i. d. Weisheit d. Jesus Sirach', *ZATW* 34, 1914, pp. 169ff.
[27] Cf. H. Ludin Jansen, *Spätj. Psalmdichtung*, pp. 55ff. See below, Chap. XVI.1–3.

From late Jewish times we have a collection of psalms called, 'The Psalms of Solomon', which show that the sages were still composing psalms in the old style, though no longer for cultic use.[28]

The old style psalm-poetry of Israel and Judaism reaches right down into the New Testament. We may instance the songs of Zacharias and Mary in St Luke[29] and the hymns in the book of Revelation.[30]

Lastly we find strong elements of psalm poetry—both in style and subject matter—in the prose prayers which are to be found in several places in the Old Testament. This is only natural, for the psalms are prayers, and experience shows that so-called 'free prayer' is to a large extent dependent on the pattern set by the prayers and psalms of public worship.[31]

All these imitations illuminate the various forms of style and individual peculiarities of the psalms.

6

In conclusion it must be mentioned that we have valuable material for comparison in other *ancient oriental psalm poetry*—the Babylonian-Assyrian, the Egyptian, the Canaanite and Hittite—which throws light on the style-forms and types of biblical psalm poetry.

It becomes evident that most of the stylistic and formal elements, and quite a number of details of content in general oriental cult poetry are either the same as the biblical ones, or at least show many great similarities to it. Undoubtedly there is here a great common cult-historical connexion. As the Babylonian-Assyrian psalm poetry is many centuries older than the Israelite, there can be no doubt that the latter has taken over a very great part of its style and form of expression, partly also its ideas and thoughts, from the older religious forms of expression common to the East. This, too, Gunkel has clearly seen, and duly underlined. The special characteristics of Israel's religious poetry developed against a background of general oriental culture. This is all the more probable as the Israelite liturgy to a large extent adopted the older cultic patterns of the East, with Canaan as intermediary.[32]

A thorough comparison between Israelite and other oriental psalm poetry, both from stylistic and cult-historical points of view, as well as from that of the contents, should be of the greatest interest. It would throw light on the types of psalms and their cultic connexion, not only on the biblical ones but also on the others. Such a comparison would also help to draw into a clearer and sharper focus the peculiarities of biblical psalm poetry and religion in relation to that of neighbouring civilizations, and to show what the religion of revelation has made of the foreign material it has adopted in expressing its own peculiar nature. Such a comparative examination has only just begun. (See below, Chap. XXI.)

[28] See Jansen, *op. cit.*, and below, Chap. XVI.6.
[29] Lk. 1.46ff.; 1.67ff., and below, Chap. XVIII.7.
[30] Rev. 4.11; 5.9ff.; 11.17f.; 15.3f.; 19.5f.
[31] Cf. Wendel, *Das freie Laiengebet*, which, however, includes much material belonging to cultic prayers in verse. Ample material for comparison is given by Heiler, *Das Gebet.*[4]
[32] See above, p. 16 with note 57 to Chap. I; and further, below, p. 134 and Additional Note XX.

CHAPTER III

'I' and 'We' in the Psalms
—The Royal Psalms

I

How the corporate view of reality and society in ancient Israel determines the relation between 'we'-psalms and 'I'-psalms has already been mentioned.

The basic reality in human life is, for the Israelite, not the individual, but the community.[1] The individual had his real existence in the tribe. Outside of that he was nothing, a severed member, one without rights, 'whom everyone that findeth him shall slay', as Cain said. But this community was not only an external and judicial one, it was even more a spiritual one. To the Israelite, a species, e.g. an animal species, was not a combination of individuals, an abstraction, or a sum. The species was the original entity, which manifests itself in the single specimen. Likewise with human beings: the tribe—'Israel', 'Moab', etc.—was not looked upon as a sum of individuals who had joined together, or who enjoyed an existence of their own apart from the whole to which they belonged; it was the real entity which manifested itself in each separate member. We might, with Johs. Pedersen, say that 'the individual Moabite is not a section of a number of Moabitic individuals, but a revelation of "Moabite-hood"'. To the Israelite this was the reality, it was in no wise an abstraction. One sees this from the general attitude to the traditional blood revenge. The responsibility lay on all, not so that each one had a part in it, but placing the whole responsibility on each individual. To those who had the grievance, every single member of the manslayer's clan or tribe would at a given moment represent the whole tribe.

We may also see this clearly in the view taken of the founder of the tribe. Each tribe, or group of tribes, has a common ancestor, 'the Great Sheikh' as the Bedouins call him today, and the tribe is named after him. All the historical memories of the tribe, besides all sorts of legends and stories are centered in his person. Traditions about the life and wanderings of the tribe, its social and religious institutions, its borders, rights of possession to wells, and so on, are usually in some way or other connected with the person of the ancestor;[2] he is the one who has experienced and

---

[1] For the following statement cf. Johs. Pedersen, *Israel* I–II, pp. 263ff. and Index *s.v.* Individual, Individualism; Wheeler Robinson in *Werden u. Wesen d. A.T.* (*BZATW* 66), pp. 49ff.; id., *The Group and the Individual.* Cf. also Bräunlich in *Islamica*, 1933, 1–2.

[2] After J. Lindblom, *Israels religion*, pp. 13f.

achieved it all. This is important for the understanding of Israel's patriarchal traditions. The ancestor represents the clan or tribe, and embodies
its life in himself. Quite naturally, therefore, he is often looked upon as
the deity of the tribe—or in other cases he may bear the name of the
tribe. Side by side with such tribe-names as Gad, Asher and Edom we
have the divine names Gad, Ashera and Edom. The character and will of
the ancestor, his 'soul', lives in all his descendants; they all bear his stamp,
are revelations of him and of the sociological unity which he represents.
He is the 'father' of each one.

The tribe is a living corporate personality which to the mind of the
Israelite naturally presented itself as an 'individual'. For him this was not
a conscious artificial act of the imagination, a poetical personification, as
when we speak of 'Mother Norway', or 'Mother England', but the self-
evident way of seeing and thinking. The whole was a greater 'I'. Hence it
came quite naturally to an Israelite story-teller to relate the origin of the
conquest in this way: 'Judah said to his brother Simeon, "Come up with
me into my lot, that we may fight against the Canaanites, and I likewise
will go with thee into thy lot" '.[3] This refers to the *tribes* of Judah and
Simeon, and not to the persons.

In all important situations the paterfamilias, the chief, or the king,
represents the whole. He is not merely a casually chosen 'representative'
in our modern sense of the word. He could not be replaced by anybody
else. He is the 'representative' because the 'soul', the history, the honour,
the vigour and the blessing of the whole are concentrated in him. And,
the other way round, all the others participate dynamically in what he
represents. Because the clan, outwardly as well, constitutes a community,
having not only 'flesh and blood' in common, but nature, blessing, soul
and honour too, everything flows from the one to the other, from the representative to the whole, and vice versa.

Normally a similarity between all the separate members in feeling, will
and thought corresponds to this mode of thinking. To be 'original', someone apart, a 'personality', whose right of existence depended on being
different, would not to the ancient Israelites have appeared as an ideal
or an end to attain, but on the contrary, as a madness, an arrogance,
something abnormal, or, in their own words, an 'unrighteousness' and a
'folly'.

This does not mean that the single member was not conscious of himself
as an individual and a personality. He was; but he found himself, his
'personality' and his 'rightness', in being an ideal expression of what was
common to all, of what was his clan's 'nature' and 'blessing' and 'honour'.
Of course the individual distinguished between himself and the one who
on public occasions 'represented' his clan in its unity; but he identified

---

[3] Jdg. 1.3. Many other references in Smend's paper 'Über das Ich der Psalmen', *ZATW* 8,
1888, pp. 61ff. Balla's explanation, *Das Ich der Psalmen*, pp. 118ff. is here too modernizing and
rationalistic.

himself with him too. They were one in nature and feeling and will. And the representative knew that he carried them all within him, that the honour and blessing and 'peace' of all depended on him, and that what he could win flowed to all by the law of community, and gave to all honour and power.

Within the nation the king is the representative of the whole. Israel is his 'house' and he is its father. The covenant between Yahweh and Israel and between Yahweh and David is one and the same thing.[4]

This unity of the whole and its proper representative becomes particularly clear in the cult. The single person who then steps forward is one with the history of his people from his first ancestor onwards. When the individual Israelite brought the first-fruits to the holy place he said a prayer beginning like this, 'My father was a wandering Aramean' (Deut. 26.5). He is thinking of his progenitor, Jacob. And he goes on, 'The Egyptians afflicted us with burdens and made us to serve with rigour'. The suppliant is identified at the same time both with the progenitor and with the Israelites in Egypt; he is a part of the body everlasting and incorporates it within himself. Likewise, the priest or the king contains the whole and all its members, when he appears as the leader of the cult. He really represents—in the old meaning of the word—the whole people. When he says 'I' it is the whole Israel, who speaks through him and who appears in his person 'in the presence of Yahweh'.

In course of time this old way of thinking has been tempered and modified by a much more individualizing one. The 'we'-form in the mouth of the congregational leader is a proof of that. It proves that the whole is also conscious of being a number of individuals. But all cult is conservative, not least in its forms. Both in its experiences—common experiences binding all together—and in its forms, the old way of thinking lives on.

On this basis it will be seen to be quite natural that the congregation through its cult-representative or representatives appears as a 'corporate personality' speaking in the first person singular, 'I'; and is answered with a 'thou'. The prayer with the first-fruits mentioned above is introduced by a statutory provision beginning thus: 'When thou hast entered the land which Yahweh, thy God, gives thee in possession, and thou hast subjected it' (Deut. 26.1). The ritual legislator is here really speaking to the whole people—the one which was contemporary with Moses, and that which *is* today. The single suppliant is looked upon as if he were the whole people. The commandment and the prayer-rubrics have regard to 'the unity, Israel' and to the single Israelite.

We find the same thing in the Decalogue. 'I am Yahweh, thy God, which have brought thee out of the land of Egypt, out of the house of bondage. Thou shalt have no other gods before me. Thou shalt not make unto thee any graven image . . . .' It is Israel as a whole, and hence the

[4] Cf. Isa. 55.3f. and see Mowinckel, *He That Cometh*, pp. 89, 98ff., 158.

single Israelite also, that is addressed. It is in the public cult of the people that Yahweh alone is to be worshipped. It is in the cult, that is, in the community, that there shall be no graven image. In the following commandments the individual point of view is more prominent, as in prohibiting theft, homicide, adultery, the bearing of false witness, covetousness. When the priest in the cult pronounces the Aaronic blessing (Num. 6.22–27): 'Yahweh bless thee and keep thee', etc., the 'thee' is not primarily the individual Israelite, but the congregation, and only through it the individual member, as it is also expressly stated in the introduction: 'With these words shall you (i.e. the priests) bless the children of Israel' (i.e. the congregation). In the utterances of the prophets we meet with many echoes of such cultic modes of speech.[5]

Thus it would be quite natural to find this mode of speech in the psalms as well. When the historian makes 'Moses and the Israelites' burst into a song of praise for the miraculous crossing of the Reed Lake—no doubt a congregational festive psalm-beginning like this: 'I will sing unto the Lord, for he hath triumphed gloriously. . . .' (Ex. 15.1–2) he no doubt means that it is Israel who here praise their God, the God of their fathers who has just saved them from distress and proved himself a mighty 'man of war'. Moses, or, according to another reading, Miriam (Ex. 15.20f.) is the singer, but cultically they represent Israel with the whole of its history. When the saga-writer lets them say 'I' and 'me' they are not speaking on their own behalf, but on behalf of the congregation. The singer represents the 'corporate, greater I' of the congregation.

Examples of this form of speech may also be found in the Psalter. In Ps. 129 it says:

> 'Cruelly have they harried me from my youth'—
>   may Israel now say,
> 'cruelly have they harried me from my youth,
>   yet they have not crushed me.
> The plowmen plowed upon my back,
>   and long they drew their furrows'.

This 'I' is not a unique exception, nor a casual 'poetic personification' demanding the line 'may Israel now say', in order to be understood, but normal ancient, Israelitic cult style.

It is not surprising therefore that investigators have felt this question of the 'I' and the 'we' in the psalms to be a problem. It was impossible not to see that at times 'I' and 'we' alternate in the same psalm, without apparent reason—as e.g. in Ps. 44. Nor could it be overlooked that many 'I'-psalms really spoke about matters concerning the people and the congregation.

---

[5] See Balla, *op. cit.*, pp. 122ff. But here we are dealing not with 'poetical personifications', as Balla thinks, but with remnants of ancient modes of expression in the cult.

Smend gives the explanation that the 'I' in the psalms is *always* a 'personification of the congregation'.[6] This view is both exaggerated and distorted. There is no question of personification as a form of art. Smend has not been able to see that we are dealing with an ancient Hebrew conception that is bound up with their view of the community and the individual, and with the whole psychology of the Israelite. Nor was he aware of the fact that the representative in the cult spoke on behalf of the whole, and that, so far, the 'I' was a reality even from a modern point of view. In fact the 'I' is very often the king or another cultic representative of the congregation. And there are also many psalms in which the 'I' is really a single individual speaking about strictly personal matters.

But Balla's refutation[7] of Smend and the other supporters of the theory of 'the collective I' (as it was misleadingly termed) goes much too far when he maintains that the only instance of such a mode of speech is presented by Ps. 129. Balla, like Gunkel, has seen that an alternating 'I' and 'we' often means that one person is speaking on behalf of the whole. But he was not aware that there is nevertheless a much more intimate relationship between the individual and the whole than our modern individualizing psychology takes into account; and both Gunkel and Balla are definitely wrong when they deny that many of the 'I-psalms' deal with congregational and national matters. They greatly exaggerate the private, individualistic point of view.

The explanation of the problem is to be found in the ancient conception of 'corporate personality' and in the fact that there is, in the ancient meaning of the word, a *representative* person in the cult speaking on behalf of the congregation. Because he embodies it in himself, he is the congregation, and the congregation is he himself—as we have endeavoured to show above.

But this representative personality in the royal Temple in Jerusalem was the king himself. Our way to full certainty in this matter lies along a path indicated by Gunkel, namely the conviction that there are in the Psalter a number of psalms where the king clearly and definitely stands as protagonist. And this brings us to the royal psalms proper.

2

According to the traditional theological view, most of the psalms should indeed be royal psalms, to the extent that they were supposed to have been composed by king David, and dealt with his relationship to his own and the nation's enemies, and with his difficulties as a king. But in its earlier phase modern scientific study of the psalms tended to deny the presence of any royal figure in the psalms, and it was maintained that they had been largely composed in Jewish times, after the Exile, out of

[6] Smend in *ZATW* 8, 1888, pp. 56ff.
[7] Balla, *Das Ich der Psalmen*.

the private experiences of ordinary people in the joys and sorrows of daily life, and through impulses from certain individual prophets (cf. above, p. 12). About the group of psalms, 93 and 95–99, which has so many traits in common with the sayings of Deutero-Isaiah, the general opinion even of conservative theologians was that they had been composed in imitation of the style and thoughts of Deutero-Isaiah.[8] Where we do meet a royal figure, as in the so-called 'Messianic' psalms, this figure was interpreted as a personification of the people of Israel.[9] Gunkel was the first to re-conceive of the royal psalms as real king psalms, and place this interpretation on a sure scientific foundation.[10] The present author has tried to give the interpretation a broader foundation by connecting the picture of the king drawn in these psalms, not only with the general oriental one, but also with the actual religion and cult of ancient Israel,[11] and this work has been continued by younger investigators.

Now, what do we mean by the expression 'royal psalms'?

These psalms are not a special 'kind' or 'type' (*Gattung*) from the point of view of the history of style or literature or liturgy. They comprise nearly all kinds of psalms, both hymns of praise and lamentations, thanksgivings and prophetic sayings, and several other types. Common to them is the circumstance that the king is in the foreground. He is the one who prays or the one who is spoken of, or who is prayed for. They include Pss. 2; 18; 20; 21; 45; 72; 101; 110; 132; 28; 61; 63; 89; and quite a number of others.

That these psalms concern a real king, a definite individual person, and not a poetical personification of the people or the congregation is quite clear. The congregation talks about him as 'our shield', and intercedes for him.

The supposed prophetic poet could not have let Yahweh say to the people of Israel that he has begotten him 'today'. That will fit only one person who 'today', that is at the moment that the psalm is being sung, becomes what he is—Yahweh's 'son' and king (Ps. 2.7). Israel, on the other hand, became Yahweh's 'son' when Yahweh called him out of Egypt (Hos. 11.1). The congregation is not 'Yahweh's king', as is the king in the psalms, but on the contrary, Yahweh is 'the king of Israel'.

It is also beyond question that the kings in these psalms are Israelite or Judaean kings—not, as older psalm critics sometimes held, foreign kings, the Ptolemaic and Seleucid rulers of the Jews. The king in Ps. 2 reigns in Zion (v. 6), the same is the case with the king in Ps. 110.2 and in Pss. 20.3; 132.15; he is a descendant of David, Pss. 18.51; 89.15; 132.10, 17; his friends are 'the faithful of the land' (101.6); the king's people is

[8] E.g. the psalm commentaries of both Delitzsch and Buhl.
[9] E.g. Wellhausen, Buhl[1], Gray.
[10] Gunkel, 'Die Königspsalmen', *Preuss. Jahrb.* 1914.
[11] Mowinckel, *Kongesalmerne*; *Ps. St. II* pp. 299ff. Neither in the treatise in *Preuss. Jahrb.* nor in *Einleitung*, pp. 140ff. have Gunkel and Begrich realized the extent of the royal psalms and their significance for the understanding of psalm problems; cf. Birkeland, *Feinde des Indiv.*, pp. 144ff.

'Jacob', 'Yahweh's people and heritage', he is 'our'—that is Israel's—'shield' (20.2; 28.8f.; 72.2; 84.10). He is 'the Lord's anointed'. The king in Ps. 20 is a Yahweh-worshipper; he and the people ('we') worship the same god. The king's victory forms the greatness and triumph of Israel. Likewise in Ps. 21, the king 'joys in the strength of Yahweh', 'he trusteth in the Lord', and he lives and reigns 'before the countenance of Yahweh'. In Ps. 45.8 Yahweh is the god of the king. When Yahweh saves the king from distress, in Ps. 28.9, it is at the same time the salvation of the people of Yahweh. In Ps. 63.12 the cause of the king and the Yahweh-worshipper is identical. In Ps. 61.4f. the praying king says that Yahweh has always been a shelter to him, and he will abide in God's tabernacle for ever, that is, in the sanctuary on Zion.

Nor is the alternative explanation possible, which was used to maintain that the psalms belonged to a later time, namely to interpret the king as one of the later Maccabean priest kings. John Hyrcanus (134–104 B.C.) was the first to call himself a king, but at that time the compilation of the Psalter had long since been finished. Nor can the royal psalms allude to any of the earlier Maccabean princes. These were not considered as 'the Lord's anointed', like the king in Pss. 2; 20; 45; 28; 89; 39. Nor were they the sons of kings, like the king in Ps. 72, or David's descendants, like the king in Pss. 18 and 132.

So they must be real Judaean or Israelite kings in these psalms.[12]

We must also make it clear at once that these psalms refer not to a future king, the 'Messiah', but to the reigning king, who is a contemporary of the poet.[13] In Ps. 110 the situation is that the poet-prophet stands before the king, who is sitting on his throne, addresses him as, 'My Lord', and pronounces an oracle from Yahweh. The situation in Ps. 45 is of a similar kind. The king sits by the side of his queen on their wedding day, and the poet recites his ode to them. Ps. 18 is a thanksgiving in which the king thanks Yahweh for the help he has given him on the battlefield, and for the victory he has already won. In Ps. 89 the king laments about the defeat he has suffered in the fight against his enemies, who have pulled down his castles and wasted his land. In Ps. 132 we meet the king as the leader of a religious festival play in remembrance of the time when David brought Yahweh's holy shrine up to Zion, and the king is here playing the part of David. In Ps. 28 he asks for help in sickness; in Pss. 61 and 63 for salvation

[12] The historical interpretation of the royal psalms has actually been accepted not only by such interpreters as accept the cultic principle of interpretation (see above note 6 to Chap. II) but by most modern exegetes. Cf. Cosgrave, 'Recent Studies on the Psalms', *Canadian Soc. of Bibl. St. Bulln.* No. 5, July 1939, pp. 11ff., Barton in *The Haverford Symposium*, pp. 66ff.; Johnson in *O.T. and Modern Study*, Index *s.v.* 'Royal Psalms'.

[13] A detailed refutation of the messianic (and eschatological) interpretation is given by König, *Die Psalmen*, pp. 453ff.; Nötscher (*Die Psalmen*, pp. 4f. and *seriatim* in the interpretation of Pss. 2, 72, 110 and others) represents an intermediate view-point between directly messianic and historical and typological interpretation, which is quite vague and untenable; he shares the fallacy of the 'religio-historical school', that even before the kingdom there existed a messianic theology after the image of which the king of any particular age might be pictured. Further discussion of the often recurring messianic interpretation of this or that psalm is from the point of view of scientific research unnecessary.

from other dangers. In Ps. 63 he is moreover present in the Temple to pray for Yahweh's help. In Ps. 20 allusion is made to the gifts and burnt-offerings which the king has already presented or will present to Yahweh, and the singer points to the fact that he has just learned—through a divine promise in connexion with the sacrificial act—that Yahweh will now help his anointed. Pss. 20; 21; and 72 are intercessions for the king, and invocations of blessings upon him. A Messiah needs no intercession. When it is a question of a Messiah the congregation prays that he may come; but in these psalms the king is already there, and needs the intercession and good wishes of the congregation to be able to fulfil his high vocation.

The kernel of truth in the Messianic interpretation is, as we shall see, that it is ultimately the same common oriental mythologically conceived superhuman king-ideal, which underlies both the psalm-poets' descriptions of the present king in David's city, and the prophets' description of the future king. Historically considered, the idea of the Messiah is derived from the same king-ideal that we have presented in the royal psalms. True enough, there is a great difference between what the poets have made of this traditional king-ideal, and what the prophets have made of it. The poets thought that the ideal was realized, or hoped that it would be realized, in the earthly king, seated before them on the throne. The prophets were not satisfied with anything which the present reality could offer, and looked hopefully forward to a new king, whom God would send 'in his own good time', and who would be the realization of the ideal which the present kings did not appear to fulfil, because it was beyond human power. Thus both the psalmists' and the prophets' conception point beyond themselves, and are only realized in a figure of a totally different kind, in the Messiah Jesus who was both 'King' and 'Son of Man', and the suffering and expiating 'Servant of the Lord'. To this extent the Church is right in taking the king in the royal psalms as a presage of Jesus, the Messiah.[14] But, historically considered, the king in the psalms is not a future figure, but a contemporary one.

The title 'the Lord's anointed' is the actual title of the reigning king of Israel, and is in the Old Testament never used of the Messiah.[15]

Then how are we to explain the fact of the appearance of the king in the psalms?

[14] The typological-Christological interpretation of the king on the basis of a consistent historical exegesis is different. On this question see Coppens in *Ephemerides Theol. Lovanienses* XXXII; *De Messianische verwachting in het Psalmboek.*

[15] See the complete list of passages in Gesenius-Buhl[16] *s.v. Mashiaḥ,* p. 468, item 3. Buhl's remark here: 'where, however, partly at any rate, a collective interpretation about the people of Israel would naturally suggest itself', is false and a remnant of the interpretation which was fashionable before the part played by the king in the psalms was realized. In Judaism the position of the king, and so the anointing, had passed to the high priest, cf. Lev. 4.3, 5, 16; 6.15; therefore the term 'an anointed' (but not '*the* anointed') is used on one occasion of the high priest, Dan. 9.25f. (or: 'the anointed priest'). Sometimes even a prophet was anointed: therefore in later times the patriarchs who were then all considered to be prophets, might in poetical usage be called 'the anointed (of Yahweh)' (in the plural); cf. Ps. 105.15; 1 Chron. 16.22. However, '*the anointed*' or 'the anointed of Yahweh' in O.T. always indicates the reigning king.

The fact that, in a collection like this, which to a considerable extent contains cult psalms, we also find several psalms about the king, is to be explained by the ancient Israelite view of the king and his position in public worship.

3

The conception of the king held in Israel was fundamentally the same as in the rest of the ancient East[16]—quite naturally, since Israel according to the testimony of the Old Testament itself had adopted kingship in direct imitation of the Canaanites (1 Sam. 8.5), who had in turn obtained ideas, forms and etiquette from the great kings of the Nile and the Euphrates-Tigris.[17] Ultimately these ideas go back to the general primitive view of the chief as the powerful 'great-man', 'mana-man', the bearer of some superhuman quality. But we must not forget that the ancient oriental ideology of the great king, the divine sovereign on earth, is a product of civilization, a special development of the primitive thoughts with the absolutist oriental Imperium as a background, where the king's power and legitimacy are supported by the theory that he is the divine representative of the god, called and enthroned by him, and given authority as his deputy among men. Nor may we overlook the very essential difference between, e.g., the Egyptian and the Babylonian-Assyrian view of the king.[18] There never existed a homogeneous 'general oriental king-ideology', to which the view of the king as held by all Eastern peoples conformed in all details—as has been supposed by several modern scholars.[19]

The most important elements in the ancient oriental view of the king are as follows: the king was more or less clearly and consistently looked upon as 'divine'. In Egypt he was held to be a god incarnate, begotten of the queen by the god, who took the guise of the reigning king; he was metaphysically one with all the great gods, who in him reveal themselves on earth, and rule with divine power over the universe. He is a god from birth, and at his death he becomes one with Osiris, the god of death and life, and partakes of the eternal life of the gods.

In Mesopotamia and Asia Minor the king is a man made divine. He is chosen for the kingship by the gods, sometimes from his mother's womb, but sometimes he is even predestined for it from the beginning of time.

[16] See Mowinckel, *He That Cometh*, Chap. III with references to literature. The chief works are Labat, *Le caractère religieux de la royauté assyro-babylonienne*; Frankfort, *Kingship and the Gods*. Cf. also Gadd, *Ideas of Divine Rule in the Ancient East*; Fish, *Some Aspects of Kingship in the Sumerian City and Kingdom of Ur*. Less reliable—on account of his tendency to identify likeness in words with likeness in thought and belief—comes Engnell, *Studies in Divine Kingship in the ancient Near East*. Cf. the critical remarks against the methods of Engnell in Frankfort, *Kingship*, p. 405 n. 1; p. 406 n. 35; p. 408, n. 67, n. 69; and de Langhe in *Bibliotheca Orientalis* X, 1953, pp. 18ff.

[17] This was already acknowledged by Gressmann, when he spoke of the influence of 'court style' on the Messiah picture, see *Ursprung d. isr.-jüd. Eschatologie*, pp. 250ff. For further details Gunkel-Begrich, *Einleitung*, pp. 150ff.

[18] This is rightly emphasized very strongly by Frankfort, *Kingship*, pp. 3ff.

[19] Especially in works by Widengren, Haldar and others. Cf. Mowinckel, *He That Cometh*, Chap. III. The theory of the common uniform 'king ideology' is mostly connected with the idea of a common Oriental 'cult pattern', the king being always supposed to represent the suffering, dying and rising god. See Additional Note XX.

'The Kingship'—i.e. the superhuman endowment and quality and majesty, the 'mana' of the king—'descends from heaven' and fills him from his mother's womb. Or it may be conferred on him, strengthened and preserved by the sacramental rites at his accession, and the annually repeated enthronement of him as king at the new year festival, and by the close union with the deity. This he especially experiences by joining with the mother goddess in the 'sacred (cultic) marriage', a fixed part of the fertility cult in the religions of the East. He is the 'son' of the god, adopted, nursed, reared and educated by the different gods and goddesses. Thus he is endowed with divine faculties and power, and is a 'superman' (Sumerian: *lugal*, 'great man'). He is 'holy' and a partaker of divine qualities, e.g. 'life', 'eternity', 'splendour', 'glory', and so on. He is 'like a god', and using religious terms he can be compared with different gods, with the sun god, the national god and the resurrected fertility god.

The king is thus the representative of the gods on earth, the steward of the god or the gods. Through him they exercise their power and sovereignty, and he is the channel through which blessing and happiness and fertility flow from the gods to men. 'He rises like the sun over humanity'. With the right king, in whom the gods have pleasure, all material and spiritual welfare is secured. Speaking poetically and devotionally, he may be said to create all this for his people.

But he is also man's representative before the gods. In him the people is one. According to the corporate view of those times the people was somehow incorporated in him, and the strength and blessing which he receives from the gods were partaken of by the whole country and people.

This double position of the king as the link between gods and men is expressed and made effective through the cult. He is the high priest—in Egypt he is theoretically the only one—and as a 'governor' he is also 'priest-king'. In the cult he represents the gods before men and men before the gods. In Egypt the main stress is laid on the former capacity, in Mesopotamia and elsewhere on the latter. Through his performance of the effective cult acts the re-creation of life and blessing which is the purpose of the cult is realized. In Egypt in the cultic drama which presents and actualizes the struggle and the victory of the life powers over the powers of death and chaos, and the resurrection of life, the king is the god himself who appears bodily, fighting, conquering, and creating. In Mesopotamia he is the champion and helper of the gods, 'representing' them in that way. At the same time he is the representative of man, who by his intimate connexion with the gods experiences their victory and revival of the 'power' (*mana*) and through the mystical fellowship with his people, the 'congregation', transmits the power to them and to their world. As the representative of the congregation he is the lord of the sacrifice and the intercessor, the vicarious penitent, purified and redeemed on behalf of the whole congregation. At the same time—as a priest and the representative of the gods—he conveys these blessings to the congregation. This is particularly obvious when the king is chosen by the goddess to be her partner in the cultic marriage. By mystical union with the goddess he is filled with the forces of fertility and resurrection, joins in the experience of the resurrected fertility god (Tammuz, etc.), and is charged with divinity, life and blessing, which flow on from him to the congregation (the people).

In Egypt the king does all this because he is the god himself, he himself is the embodiment of all the gods. In Mesopotamia, as the representative of mankind, he experiences it in the cultic mystical union. Regarding Egypt we can speak of a really lasting and essential 'identity' between the king and the different gods which he represents, because he *is* and comprises them all. In Mesopotamia the king may occasionally call himself a god and place the divine ideogram before his name; also sometimes an oath may be taken in the names of the gods and the king. But that is something he has become, and it does not abolish his humanity. In Egypt the king is— as 'the good God', as Horus, Re, Osiris, etc.—the object of direct worship in the cult, not least after his death. In Mesopotamia we may at most speak of sacrifices to the king's statue, which in the temple represents him as his intercessor with the gods. The king's 'name' and 'life' in the image must be maintained by sacrificial gifts. We cannot rightly speak of identity of king and god in Mesopotamia, or the countries influenced by its culture, either essentially or as a result of anything which took place in the cult. Even in the cult he is not really the god himself, although he is in a cultic-mystical way imbued with the god's destiny, experience and revived strength, imparting it in his turn to the society of which he—in like 'mystically-corporate' manner—is the visible manifestation.

As we shall see, some of these most characteristic traits are to be found also in the Israelite view of the king.

But although Israel has adopted a number of ideas, functions and style forms of oriental monarchy, the basic conceptions have been fundamentally altered under the influence of the Yahweh religion. There were certain features in the conception of the king—'the king-ideology'—which were incompatible with the belief in Yahweh, as that belief had been shaped already by the time of David. And the history of Israel may from one point of view be seen as a constant tension between the ancient ideas from the desert and the new Canaanite (general oriental) ones. The old ideal of the chief, or sheikh, stemming from the patriarchal conditions of desert life never died. On the contrary it constantly impressed its stamp on the king ideal; and in spite of certain common fundamental features, the semi-nomadic and Bedouin chief ideal is a different type from the oriental king-god ideal.

It is therefore just as important to point out the features which are characteristic of Israel's view, and find what it is that unites them into one characteristic Israelite king ideal, as it is to point out what is common to Israel and the other peoples' view of the king. The general Eastern 'king-ideology' is only the background, throwing its light on and explaining many single features of the Israelite king idea, not only on those which Israel adopted, but indirectly also on those which are different. It is important also to see what Israel did *not* adopt, but on the contrary rejected as something incompatible with its cult and religion.

Fundamental to the king's position is his relation to Yahweh. The king is Yahweh's anointed, and as such he is endowed with the spirit of Yahweh (1 Sam. 10.6, 9ff.; 11.6f.; 16.13) and with supra-normal faculties and powers (Ps. 89.22; Mic. 5.3; Num. 24.17). He is chosen by Yahweh (1 Sam. 10.24; 16.1ff.; 2 Sam. 7.8; Pss. 45.8; 89.21), adopted and fostered by him (Pss. 2.2; 18.35; 89.27f.). He is the son of Yahweh. The filial relation may be expressed in pure mythopoeic form: 'This day have I begotten thee' (Ps. 2.7). 'I have borne thee from the womb of dawn on the holy mount' (Ps. 110.3.G). He stands in a closer relation than other people to Yahweh. 'Yahweh thy God' is said, referring to his and Israel's God.[20] In a special sense he is 'Yahweh's servant',[21] performing his commissions and enjoying his particular favour. He is endowed with 'eternity' (1 Kgs. 1.31; Pss. 21.5; 72.5) i.e. superhuman life-force, even divinity (Ps. 45.7).[22] His person is sacrosanct ('holy'). It is a mortal sin to lay hands on him (1 Sam. 24.7; 31.4; 2 Sam. 1.14). By the anointing, which was a sacred, cultic act, he becomes 'another man', he has 'another heart' (1 Sam. 10.6, 9), that is, he has obtained a special 'holiness', a superhuman quality. He has obtained those faculties and gifts and powers which he needs to be the rightful king. He is the people's source of strength, its 'breath of life' (Lam. 4.20), 'equal to ten thousand of us' (2 Sam. 18.3), 'Israel's lamp' (2 Sam. 21.7), the bearer of divine forces, without whom Israel cannot live (Hos. 3.4), the protector in whose 'shadow' it lives (Lam. 4.20). He is endowed with an extraordinary quality of success (Pss. 20.5f.; 72.6, 17; 2 Sam. 23.3f.), with victory and glory (Pss. 110.2, 5ff.; 72.9; 45.4–6), with righteousness (Pss. 72.1, 4f., 12–14; 45.7f.; 101), wisdom (2 Sam. 14.7; 1 Kgs. 3.5ff.), and piety (Pss. 20.4; 72.1; 18.21ff.). As the son of the highest god, Yahweh, and his viceroy on earth he is entitled to world sovereignty (Pss. 2.8; 72.8–11; 89.26ff.). This is the style in which he speaks, like one of the great rulers on the Euphrates or the Nile.

The attributes and equipment of the kings and of the kingship show that the prevailing ideas, or at least the ideas which these customs are

[20] See for instance 1 Sam. 25.29; 2 Sam. 14.11; 18.28; 1 Kgs. 1.17, 47. Cf. Birkeland, *Feinde d. Individ.* pp. 125f.; cf. also Eissfeldt in *ZATW* 61, 1945/48, p. 11.

[21] See for instance Pss. 18.1; 36.1; 89.4, 21; 132.10; Hag. 2.23; Zech. 3.8; cf. Jer. 25.9; 27.6; 43.10. For details, v. Baudissin, *Kyrios als Gottesname im Judentum* III, pp. 176ff., 196ff., 524ff., 529ff.; Birkeland, *Feinde d. Individ.*, p. 124; Lindhagen, *The Servant Motif in the O.T.*, pp. 285ff. When used about an individual the term 'Yahweh's servant' always indicates a special relationship between Yahweh and the person in question; cf. Smend in *ZATW* 8, 1888, p. 134. The religious use of the word *'ebhedh* is of course older than the kingdom and it is therefore quite false when Lindhagen thinks that this epithet, when used about Abraham, Moses and others, has been transferred from the 'king ideology'.

[22] Cf. 2 Sam. 14.20. In Ps. 89.28, David is 'Elyon', i.e. (like) the supreme God, among the kings of the earth.

derived from, placed the king beside the deity, high above ordinary people. He sits on Yahweh's throne, at the right hand of Yahweh (Ps. 110.1). The king's throne in Jerusalem symbolizes the world-mountain,[23] the king is figured with horns (1 Sam. 2.10; Pss. 89.18; 132.17; Deut. 33.17), the usual symbol of the gods (Num. 24.8; cf. Ps. 89.24). The diadem also, 'the crown' (2 Sam. 1.10; 2 Kgs. 11.12; Pss. 89.20, 40; 132.18) is a divine symbol (2 Sam. 12.30.G), and it is not unthinkable that similar ideas have been linked with the sceptre (Pss. 110.2; 45.7; 2.9; Mic. 7.14) as a 'divine staff' (cf. Ex. 4.17, 20).[24]

To nearly all these special traits closer or more distant 'parallels' in other Eastern civilizations may be found.[25]

Both in Egypt and in Mesopotamia the king is held to be the son of the deity. In Egypt the case is conceived physically and metaphysically; the king is the product of a physical act of generation by the god incarnate. In Mesopotamia also, where the adoption idea is the prevailing one, the king's filial relationship may be represented in mythical forms, as the result of a divine begetting or as the birth of the new sun god on the unknown mountain of the east.[26] Both in Egypt[27] and in Mesopotamia[28] the god addresses the king with the adoption formula, 'thou art my son'. In Egypt this also includes the literally implied 'I have begotten thee'.[29]

That such expressions, when they are sometimes met with in Israel, are there formed upon alien patterns, is seen, among other things, from the fact that phrases which were originally intended to be taken literally have in Israel been transformed into expressions of adoption: 'Today have I borne you'. This conclusion is obvious from the fact that the expression 'I have borne you' is originally to be imagined as spoken by a female deity. In Israel it is turned into a saying of Yahweh.[30]

When the king in Ps. 18.34 says about Yahweh that 'he teacheth my hands to war, so that I can bend a bow of bronze', this may be illustrated by an Egyptian picture of the God Seth teaching Pharaoh Thutmose to use a bow.[31]

In Egyptian pictures we can also see the king sitting in the place of honour at the right side of the throne of the god, as the poet-prophet says to the king on Mount Zion in Ps. 110.[32] In the same psalm Yahweh places the king's enemies 'under his feet'. To symbolize their submission the king

---

[23] Gressmann, *Urspr. d. Eschatologie*, pp. 257f.; cf. Johs. Pedersen, *Israel* III–IV, pp. 79f.
[24] On the attributes of the kingdom and the enthronement of the king, see Pedersen, *Israel* III–IV, pp. 77ff.
[25] For details see Gunkel-Begrich, *Einleitung*, pp. 150ff.; for the different royal psalms Gunkel, *Die Psalmen* (2; 18; 20; 21; 45; 110, etc.); Mowinckel, *He That Cometh*, Chap. III; Pedersen, *op. cit.*
[26] See Engnell, *Div. Kingship* Topical Index *s.v.* 'son of the god'; Frankfort, *Kingship*, pp. 36ff., 159ff., 299ff.; Labat, *Royauté*, pp. 53ff.; Gunkel, *Die Psalmen*, pp. 6f.
[27] Roeder, *Urkunden*, pp. 158f.
[28] *KB* IV, pp. 4f., 320; Law of Hammurabi ¶ 170f.; Meissner, *Bab. u. Ass.* I, p. 390.
[29] Roeder, *Urk.*, p. 159.
[30] Gunkel, *Die Psalmen*, p. 7.
[31] Erman-Ranke, *Aegypten*,[2] p. 325; Gunkel, *Die Psalmen*, p. 65.
[32] Gunkel, *Die Psalmen*, p. 481.

set his foot upon the neck of his enemies, who prostrated themselves before him.[33] Egyptian pictures show Pharaoh enthroned with his foot on the neck of the vanquished.[34] The foot-kissing (Ps. 2.12, cf. Isa. 49.23) as a sign of subjection and homage was a general oriental custom, known both from Egypt, and Babylonia-Assyria.[35]

When the king in Ps. 2 is 'ideally' promised world sovereignty this is of course not to be explained as realistic political aspiration, but is a religious postulate founded on the belief in Yahweh as the Lord of the world. But this idea has much older prototypes both in Egypt and in Mesopotamia, where it belongs to the fundamental 'king-ideology'; Pharaoh is 'king of the two countries', that is to say the bipartite universe.[36] The gods expressly promise him the sovereignty of all countries and peoples.[37] The Babylonian-Assyrian kings also with divine sanction use the title 'king of the lands', 'king of the universe', 'king of the four quarters of the world'.[38] It is worth noting that when the Israelite psalmist wishes to express the king's universal sovereignty, he does so in images which are formed from the Babylonian point of view, and which originated there. 'He shall rule from sea to sea, from the river to the utmost boundaries of the world' (Pss. 72.8; 89.26). 'From ocean to ocean' is a set Babylonian phrase for the whole of the known world: 'from the upper sea in the West (the Mediterranean) to the lower sea in the East' (the Persian Gulf). 'The streams' are the ocean which, according to the ancient conception of the world, lies like a ring round the earth-disk. 'The river' is here, as everywhere in the Bible, the Euphrates. The first expression mentions the extension of the realm from east to west, the other from its centre on the Euphrates to the 'ocean' or 'the ends of the world' on the periphery.

That the king is the 'life-breath' of the people (Lam. 4.20) is a common Canaanite-Egyptian idea, which we often meet with in the letters to Pharaoh from the vassal princes in the Amarna-letters.[39] To the Egyptians Pharaoh is 'the air of all noses', 'the one by whom one breathes'.[40] As in Israel, the people of Egypt and Babylonia live in the 'shadow' of the king (Jdg. 9.15; Lam. 4.20), that is to say, under his cool and pleasant protection.[41]

[33] Josh. 10.24; cf. 1 Kgs. 5.17; Isa. 51.23. For parallel modes of expression in the Amarna letters see Knudtzon in *VAB* II No. 84.4; No. 141.40.

[34] After Gunkel, *Die Psalmen*, p. 482 with reference to illustration in Riehms, *Bibl. Handwörterbuch* art. 'Krieg'. Cf. Gressmann, *AOB*², Abb. 59.

[35] Gunkel, *Die Psalmen*, p. 8, with reference to Erman-Ranke, *Aegypten*,² p. 82; Jastrow, *Relig. Bab. u. Ass.* I, p. 514; Jensen in *KB* VI, 2, pp. 108f.; Klauber, *Assyr. Beamtentum*, p. 15.

[36] See Frankfort, *Kingship*, pp. 19ff.

[37] Cf. Roeder, *Urkunden*, pp. 158ff.

[38] Labat, *Royauté*, pp. 5f., 10, 13f., 18ff.; Frankfort, *Kingship*, pp. 227, 229f.

[39] E.g. Knudtzon in *VAB* II No. 141.2, 7, 10, 13, 37, 43; 143.15, 17; 144.2, 8.

[40] Roeder, *Urkunden*, p. 74; Grapow, *Bild. Ausdrücke der Aeg.*, p. 122.

[41] In Egypt: Erman, *Literatur der Aeg.*, p. 234; Oppenheim in *BASOR* 107, pp. 7ff.; in Mesopotamia: Frankfort, *Kingship*, p. 304.

In Canaan and Mesopotamia also the king is the special 'servant' of the god, his trusted man who stands in a specially close relation to him.[42]

Just as Yahweh chose David to be 'the shepherd of his people',[43] so 'shepherd' is a standing attribute of the king in Mesopotamia. It is his calling to 'tend the black-headed' (i.e., men). Hammurabi is 'the beneficent shepherd' (re'u mušallimu),[44] and so likewise in Egypt.[45]

As was the case in Israel (see below, pp. 6of., 63f.), so in Egypt and Mesopotamia the king was also a priest.[46]

In the same way as the king in Ps. 20, the Egyptian and Babylonian-Assyrian monarchs plead their abundant offerings and pious acts.[47] The king's prayer for 'life' and 'length of days for ever and ever' in Ps. 21 often recurs both in Egyptian and Mesopotamian royal inscriptions.[48]

The king's vow in Ps. 101 to rule Yahweh's people wisely, which has obviously belonged to the great annual feast (see below, pp. 65f.), has, both as to style, content and cultic form, a model in the Babylonian king's confession on the day of penitence at the new year festival, that he has kept Marduk's law and reigned well in Babylon.[49]

Finally we may mention the hymns praising the divine king, of which we have at least one example in the Old Testament, in Ps. 45 (see below, pp. 73f.). They occur somewhat more often in Babylonia[50] and very frequently in Egypt.[51]

But phenomenological 'parallels' are liable to be elusive. If an expression, an image, or a particular idea is found in two different places, in two civilizations and religions, it does not follow that they mean the same, even if there is a direct historical borrowing or influence on one side or the other. Each detail obtains its significance from the whole structure in which it has been incorporated, and of which it is a part. It is not first of all a question of proving that this or that Israelite idea is also found in Babylonia or Egypt or has been 'borrowed' from there. The essential question

---

[42] As for Canaan, see Mowinckel in *NTT* 1942, pp. 24ff.; Engnell, *Div. Kingship* Top. Index *s.v.* 'servant of god'. For Mesopotamia cf. Gadd, *Ideas of Div. Rule*, pp. 3, 34. The king often names himself the *wardu*, 'servant', 'slave' of such and such a god; cf. names of kings like Waradsin, 'Sin's servant'.

[43] Ps. 78.71; cf. Jer. 3.15; Ezk. 34.23; 37.24; Mic. 5.3f.; Nah. 3.18; 2 Sam. 5.2; 7.7; for 'bad herdsmen': Isa. 56.11; Jer. 2.8; 22.22; 23.1, 4; 50.6; Ezk. 34.2ff.; Zech. 11.5; a people without a king is like 'sheep which have no shepherd', Num. 27.17; 1 Kgs. 22.17; Zech. 10.2.

[44] Cf. Gadd, *Ideas of Div. Rule*, pp. 38f.; Jastrow, *Relig. Bab. u. Ass.* I, pp. 48f.

[45] See A. Jeremias, *Ausserbiblische Erlösererwartung*, pp. 108ff.; idem, *D. Alt. Test. im Lichte d. alt. Orients*,[4] p. 653.

[46] The king as priest in Egypt: Erman-Ranke, *Aegypten*,[2] p. 73; Erman, *Die Religion der Aegypten*, pp. 186f.; in Mesopotamia: Meissner, *Bab. u. Ass.* I, pp. 49, 63, 67ff.; Jeremias, *Handbuch*, p. 284; Jastrow, *Relig. Bab. u. Assyr.* I, pp. 211, 217, and especially Labat, *Royauté*, pp. 131ff.; Frankfort, *Kingship*, p. 221; Gadd, *Ideas of Div. Rule*, pp. 39f.

[47] Ps. 20.4; cf. Erman, *Lit. d. Aeg.*, p. 379 (E.T., p. 307); Jastrow, *Relig. Bab. u. Ass.* I, p. 409. Cf, Heiler, *Das Gebet*,[4] p. 85.

[48] Ps. 21.5. Egyptian and Mesopotamian examples with references to sources in Gunkel-Begrich, *Einl.*, pp. 162f.

[49] Frankfort, *Kingship*, pp. 319ff.; Labat, *Royauté*, p. 168.

[50] See Engnell, *Div. Kingship*, p. 45 with references to sources.

[51] See Erman, *Lit. d. Aeg.* pp. 35f.; 44f., 179ff., 318ff.

is, what significance has been imparted to it in its new context; what has the religion of Israel made of it?[51a]

In Israel as in Mesopotamia there are two important sides to the idea of the king. He is the representative of the people, incorporating its 'greater I', and he is the representative of the deity and more than a human being—he has something of the 'divine' in him. We must first make clear that in Israel, the oriental type of divine king has never quite been able to supersede the old, more 'democratic' chieftainship of desert days, when the chief was also priest and the bearer of the blessing, and 'father' and 'holy' and yet held his authority by virtue of his corporate identity with the tribe, and not from any special relation to the great gods. The god of the tribe was his 'father', but so was he to the whole tribe. Many ideas and forms were taken over by Israel from the great kingdoms, but they were considerably modified by the old chiefdom ideology.

If we are to realize what the king's divinity meant to Israel, we must find out what the Israelite meant by 'god', and how the Old Testament understands the king's relationship to Yahweh. The Old Testament uses the word 'god' for all sorts of lower 'supernatural' beings, such as the dead soul, the ghost (1 Sam. 28.13) or a 'demon of sickness' (Job 19.22). 'The divine beings', (literally 'the god-sons'), signifies the lower heavenly beings round Yahweh's throne who are sent forth as his messengers,[52] corresponding to the 'angels' in later usage. Even about man the poet may say that Yahweh 'has made him little less than a god' (Ps. 8.6). But it is just such an expression that shows us the essential difference between such a 'god' and Yahweh. What characterizes a 'god' is a superhuman and supernatural power, wisdom and insight. A 'god' is in a special degree a 'holy' being[53] and partakes of all the faculties and attributes of 'holiness' (cf. above, pp. 54f.). The 'godlikeness' of man in Ps. 8 consists above all in his sovereignty and power over all other beings, in his godlike 'honour and glory' compared to them.

Then how do all these 'gods' differ from the only true God, Yahweh, who 'is', who alone has creative and saving power both as to nature and history?[54] We see the answer most clearly in Ps. 82, where Yahweh passes judgment on all other gods. 'Ye are gods, and all of you are children of the most High. But ye shall die like men, and fall like one of the (earthly) princes'. Any other 'god' can die, and this also applies to the 'divine' king, but Yahweh is 'the living God', 'the holy God who does not die' (Hab. 1.12).

Consequently nowhere in the Old Testament do we meet with a 'meta-

[51a] Alt ('Der Königtum in den Reichen Israel und Juda', *Kleine Schriften* II, pp. 116ff. = *VT* I, 1951, pp. 2ff.) has stressed too strongly the lack of adjustment of the ideological and political content of kingship to the old Israelite ideas and ideals. Cf. my review of Alt's book in *ThLZ* 80.4, April 1955, esp. col. 204.

[52] Pss. 29.1; 89.7; Gen. 6.2, 4; Job 1.6; 2.1; 38.7.

[53] Pss. 16.3; 89.6, 8; Deut. 33.3; Zech. 14.5; Job 5.1; 15.15; Dan. 4.5, 6, 10, 15, 20; 5.11; 8.13; Sir. 42.17.

[54] Isa. 41.4; 43.10f.; 48.12; cf. 43.12f.; 44.6.

physical' unity of Yahweh and the king, or a really 'mythological' idea of the king's relation to Yahweh. Clearly and plainly the king's filial relation to Yahweh is based on an adoption (see above, p. 54). His divinity depends on the endowment he has received at his election and anointing and on the power flowing to him through the holy rites of the cult, by Yahweh's free will, and depending on the king's loyalty and obedience towards Yahweh's commandments.[55] The wish that the king may 'live for ever' (see above, p. 53) contains no thought of immortality. It is not David nor the individual king personally but the royal race which is promised eternal life and which shall sit on David's throne for ever.[56] In spite of all, the relation between Yahweh and the king is no kind of equality, but a relation which shows a distinct superiority and subordination. The king is 'Yahweh's servant', his 'slave',[57] in all respects dependent on Yahweh's allegiance and help and power.[58] Compared to Yahweh the king is a 'mortal man', 'a man of the people' (Ps. 89.26), whom Yahweh 'has lifted up and crowned' and 'placed on high'.[59] In spite of all 'divinity' the king is a human being, and there is an enormous distance between man and the real God.[60] Thus it is not wholly without reason that some have spoken of 'oriental court style' in connexion with the royal psalms' expressions about the king.[61] Many a phrase has been borrowed from the general oriental ritual king style without taking over its original sense, and without giving it greater significance than that which agreed with the Yahweh religion's view of the relation between Yahweh and man, even a superman.[62]

There is then no doubt that the Yahweh religion has radically transformed the general oriental idea of the king, and consequently those forms of the cult which are connected with these ideas. Here we must note the increasing criticism of the kingship which developed in Israel.[63] It arose from religious motives and finally led to the kingship being regarded as

[55] Pss. 89.31–33; 18.21–25; 20.4; 132.10; 2 Sam. 7.14f.
[56] 2 Sam. 7.12–16, 19, 26–28; Pss. 89.29–38; 132.11f.; 72.17; Jer. 22.1–5.
[57] Pss. 18.1; 36.1; 89.4, 21; Zech. 3.8 and other places; this expression is even used about pagan kings: Jer. 25.9; 27.6; 43.10. Cf. above, note 42.
[58] Though with somewhat exaggerated one-sidedness, this has been rightly maintained by North in *ZATW* 50, 1932, pp. 8ff.
[59] Ps. 89.20; 2 Sam. 23.1; 7.8; cf. 1 Sam. 15.17; 2 Sam. 7.18f.
[60] Cf. Seierstad, *Die Offenbarungserlebnisse*, pp. 82ff.
[61] Gressmann, *Urspr. d. Eschatologie*, pp. 250ff.
[62] This is even admitted by the investigators who most strongly emphasize the dependence of Israel on common oriental 'cultic patterns' ('ritual patterns'), when they speak of the disintegration of the ritual pattern, see e.g. Hooke in *Myth and Ritual*, p. 6. But they often seem to content themselves with admitting this in general without entering into the details of the question as to what the Israelite author himself in the concrete instance means by the style pattern and the terms he is using. Thus Widengren in his treatise on Ps. 88 finally declares that he would be misunderstood if his opinion were interpreted to the effect that he 'was supposed to look upon the text of Ps. 88 as it has been handed down to us, as a rendering of the original cult text as it was delivered by the king at a point of the ritual when mythically he was supposed to find himself in the underworld'. Cf. also Engnell, *Div. Kingship*, p. 50. An ordinary exegete would be inclined to think that the exegetical problem starts here, and that what really concerns the exegete is to learn what the author of the psalm himself thought about the worshipper and his actual conditions.
[63] Cf. Johs. Pedersen, *Israel* III–IV, pp. 89ff., 97ff.

contrary to Yahweh's sovereignty.[64] Then gradually a new king ideal grew up, placing the main stress on the righteousness and justice of the king, and on his will to help the suffering, the poor and oppressed and to give them their rights, and on the divine wisdom and wonder-working power he is endowed with to do this, to 'reign in Yahweh's strength'. It is by the help of Yahweh, and because the king humbly relies on his allegiance to Yahweh and his loyalty to Yahweh's covenant, that he can do this. It is really Yahweh who does it for him.[65]

That the king in Israel should have been regarded as identical with Yahweh, or in the cult have played Yahweh's part is thus wholly improbable; nor is there any proof whatever that this was ever the case. The polemics of the prophets give us a clue. They never suggest that the king has made himself a god. The book of Ezekiel is probably the prophetical writing which most violently upbraids the historical kings of Judah for their sins. The climax of the attack is where the prophet points to the blasphemy which the kings have committed by placing the king's palace next door to the temple, and even placing the kings' graves there, thus 'fouling the holy name of Yahweh with their idolatry and their corpses'.[66] It is then easy to imagine what Ezekiel would have said if the king had really made himself equal with Yahweh, and comported himself like God and received worship in the cult. In the cult the king sings and dances 'before Yahweh' at the head of the procession, and in the cultic drama he plays the part of David, while Yahweh is represented by his holy shrine, 'the footstool' before the throne, where he sits invisible.[67] Even in Ps. 110 where the king sits on Yahweh's own throne at his right hand, a clear distinction is made between Yahweh and the king.

Nevertheless it is clear that the notions about the nature and essence of the kingship which reach their climax in the idea of the king's divinity, in Israel too were more than a matter of mere form and 'court style'. They expressed a reality in Israel's belief and cult. When the poet, even after the fall of the country and the kingdom, can speak as he does in the book of Lamentations about 'The breath of our nostrils, the anointed of the Lord, of whom we said "Under his shadow we shall live among the nations"' (4.20), this means more than just a lyrical expression of lost glory. It shows what was actually expected of the king, even after bad experiences with real kings, such as Judah had had with the last kings before the fall of the kingdom. The king's close relation to Yahweh, his

---

[64] Judges 8.22f.; 1 Sam. 8, 6ff. A comparison with the original versions—made possible by a traditio-critical investigation—brings out very clearly that we have here a legendary back-dating of the attitudes of a later age. Buber's attempt in *Königtum Gottes* to trace this idea back to the earliest history of Israel is not convincing; B. does not really seem to have an eye for the natural and historical value of the different sources.

[65] Cf. Isa. 9.5f.; 11.1–5; 16.5; Mic. 5.1, 3, 9f.; Jer. 22.15f.; 23.1–8; Zech. 9.9f; Ezk. 22.6; 34; 37.24f.; 49.9f.; Pss. 18.21, 25f., 28; 20.8; 21.8; 72.1f., 12–14; 101; 2 Sam. 23.3.

[66] Ezk. 43.7–9. See likewise *He That Cometh*, p. 61.

[67] 2 Sam. 6.5, 14ff.; cf. Pss. 42.7; 132.1–10. For the throne in the Temple see Isa. 6.1ff.; cf. Johs. Pedersen, *Israel* III–IV, pp. 247ff. H. Schmidt in *Eucharisterion (Gunkel Festschrift)* I, pp. 120ff.

endowment with divine strength, the experience and assurance of this in the festal cult, the king's appearance there as the visible pledge of the existence and permanence of the covenant, were realities for the religious belief and experience of Israel.

This links up with the other side of the king's being and position. Though Yahweh's representative towards the people, he is even more the representative of the people towards Yahweh. Figuratively speaking he is the channel through which the blessings of the deity flow to the people. But he is also the 'corporate representative' through whom the people approaches Yahweh to partake of the blessing. If the empires of the East have occasionally made a divine being of him, the Yahweh religion with its different idea of God has, in spite of it all, put him back in his right place as the first representative of men towards the deity. He has become a real 'mediator', and the religion of Israel developed a tendency to make his human position more and more clearly marked. As we have seen, he became a 'man of the people' (Ps. 89.26) whose duty it is to mediate the blessing of Yahweh to 'his brethren'. All the great deeds ascribed to him depend on his obeying the will of Yahweh and adhering to him (see above, p. 58).

The old corporate way of thinking keeps on asserting itself. As the 'father' and first man of the people the king 'incorporates' it in himself. In the great crises of the people the king *is* the people. Its 'breath of life' and its 'happiness' are in him and depend on him. Its 'blessing' has its earthly source in him. The king and the people are inextricably bound together. His piety and greatness constitute the righteousness and happiness of the people. If the king is godless disaster strikes the whole people. In his person the people approaches God, and through him God speaks to the people. Thus he is also a priest[68] and has prophetic gifts.[69]

Thus it is in the cult that the king's part as a mediator and his divine qualities and near relation to the deity and his position as the incorporating representative of the people, are most obvious. The day of the king's enthronement (his anointing), was a festival laying the foundation for the future of the people. As far as we can see, the king's enthronement was celebrated each year in a feast not only in Egypt, Babylonia, Assyria, and the other Eastern empires[70] but also in Israel. Ps. 132 shows that this annual enthronement of the king was also felt to be a repetition of David's legitimization as Yahweh's king at Zion, and was accompanied by promises to the royal house corresponding to those which at that time were given to David. In the psalms, e.g. at the procession on the great festival

[68] 1 Sam. 13.9; 2 Sam. 6.17; 7.18; 1 Kgs. 8.5; Ps. 110.4. More fully Gunkel, *Die Psalmen*, p. 484.

[69] 2 Sam. 23.1f. Cf. also 1 Kgs. 8, the prayer of Solomon at the consecration of the Temple, when the saga-writer makes him—hypothetically, certainly—predict all the punishments to overtake Israel, even including the carrying away of the people and the diaspora.

[70] See Dürr, *Reichsgründungsfeiern im antiken Orient*; Böhl, *Nieuwejaarsfeest en konigsdag* (*Opera Minora*, pp. 236–281); Johs. Pedersen, *Israel* III–IV, pp. 746ff. For the special part played by the king in the cult see also Johs. Pedersen, *op. cit.* pp. 428f.

days, the intercession for the king had its place (Ps. 84.10; cf. 63.12), corresponding to the prominent part which the king himself took in the procession.

It is, then, a matter of course that the king at important moments should act as the leader of the festal cult, as we hear of David doing when Yahweh's shrine was taken to Jerusalem, and of Solomon at the consecration of the temple. The king has direct access to Yahweh and arranges the details of the service himself.[71] He holds, at least theoretically, the same position in the cult as the high priest held later. He officiates at the sacrifice. He prays on behalf of the people and he pronounces the blessing on the congregation. He also receives the revelation from Yahweh, e.g. by staying over night in the holy place.[72]

He is responsible for the people towards Yahweh. Through the 'righteousness' of the king, fertility of people, cattle and land is secured (cf. Ps. 72.1–7). The righteousness of the king is the righteousness of the people, his sin is the people's sin (2 Sam. 21.1; 24.1ff.). The whole of the book of Kings is written in accordance with this view of the connexion between the king's relation to Yahweh and the fortunes of the people.

When the king appears in the cult in such a way he is more than what we nowadays mean by the word 'representative'. In a mystical way he *is* what he represents. The people acts, receives, and lives in and through him. The ancient idea of the people as a 'greater I', which at important moments is manifested in an individual, comes to the fore here. We may say that the king at the same time both incorporates and represents the people. It is the old Israelite 'collective' and 'corporate' way of thinking which has produced and formulated these ideas. The king receives the promises of blessing and the power of blessing which are to benefit the whole congregation.[73] And in the rites of penance he appears as the vicarious bearer of all the misfortunes and sufferings which have hit the people, and subjects himself to the rites of expiation which have to be performed, and prays for help and salvation.[74]

Whether the king in such a capacity says 'I' or 'we', on behalf of the people, does not matter. The 'I–form' may seem to be the more exact and original, corresponding to the thought of the 'greater I'; the 'we form' being the later and disclosing a more individualizing and differentiating way of thinking: the totality as a sum of independent units.

4

Starting with this view of the king and his place in the cult we can now understand the royal psalms. The king stands at the centre of the religious festivals. And from the power and blessing he there obtains from Yahweh,

[71] 2 Sam. 6; 1 Kgs. 8; 21.9, 12; 2 Kgs. 16.10ff.; Isa. 37.14ff.; 3 Macc. 6.1ff.
[72] 1 Kgs. 3.5ff., and cf. above, note 69 and Ehrlich, *Der Traum im A.T.*, pp. 19ff.
[73] Pss. 132.11–18; 72; cf. 20.8; 21.14; Isa. 55.3.
[74] See Ps. 102, probably a royal psalm, see Birkeland, *Feinde d. Indiv.*, pp. 311f., 328f.

vital force and blessing radiate to the people. There is a great difference between the kingdom of David and the ancient chiefdom of the time of Moses and the Judges, with which Saul was more closely related. The chief as well was a central figure at the old cult festivals. But there he sits—as Saul did—on his own estate or in the local sanctuary; 'his men and his family are gathered around him, their blessing is centred in him'.[75] It was the clan as a whole that met Yahweh and was active in the cult. After David, the king was the master of the cult: he arranged it, and it took place primarily for his sake. He marches in the procession to the 'king's sanctuary'. He provides and presents the offerings. The priests perform the rites on his behalf. The people are spectators. From his blessing, blessings overflow on to the others.

The royal psalms may thus be grouped about the king festivals. Of special importance are the psalms which have belonged to the anointing and enthronement festivals, both because they give so clear a picture of the 'king ideology', and because they throw light on the religious ritual of the festival.[76]

We can see from the descriptions which by chance have come down to us (1 Kgs. 1.33ff.; 2 Kgs. 11) that the festival was divided into two main parts, the anointing in the Temple and the enthronement in the king's palace. Seated on his royal mule[76a] the king is led to the holy place and anointed by the priest. He stands on a high platform or pediment in view of all the people—we hear of that in Egypt too—and the priest anoints him, 'places the diadem, the crown, on his head and gives him the edict (hā'ēdhûth)[77]. It is the same ceremony which is alluded to in Ps. 2: 'I will declare the decree' (ḥōq). According to the Egyptian ritual of enthronement the reference here is to a written document expressing the divine legitimacy of the king, his calling and enthronement by the deity, and the further destiny and 'name' that will thereby be his. The 'decree' or 'edict' is thus a confirmation of the covenant with David. In other words the 'covenant' and the 'crown' constitute Yahweh's gifts to his adopted royal son.[78]

The decree is based on Yahweh's own word, not only on old promises to the ancestor David, but on the expressly renewed promise at each new enthronement. At the installation the prophet also has his place and the prophetic legends generally intimate that it is the prophet who performs the anointing.[79] In any case the seer-priest[80] and later on, the temple

---

[75] Johs. Pedersen, Israel III–IV, p. 429.

[76] For the ritual of anointing and coronation and its reflection in the psalms, see Mowinckel, Ps. St. II, pp. 6ff.; Widengren, Psalm 110 och det sakrala kungadömet i Israel (UUÅ 1941: 7, 1); v. Rad, Das judäische Königsritual, (ThLZ 4, 1947, also in his Gesammelte Studien).

[76a] See Jdg. 5.10; 10.4, and Mowinckel, He That Cometh, p. 176.

[77] 2 Kgs. 11.12. This word is often falsely changed into ḥaṣṣĕ'adhôth 'the bracelets', after 2 Sam. 1.10; so also in GTMMM II, p. 401; but see v. Rad, op. cit., col. 213f.

[78] See Pss. 132.12; 89.40; for this idea cf. also Ps. 105.10.

[79] 1 Sam. 16.1ff.; 1 Kgs. 1.32ff.; 19.15f.; 2 Kgs. 9.6.

[80] This is the picture of Samuel in 1 Sam. 9; cf. Mowinckel, Ps. St. III, pp. 9ff.

prophet[81] proclaims Yahweh's oracle at the anointing; that which gives the anointed one the legitimate foundation of his kingship. In Pss. 2 and 110 and in allusions in Ps. 89.20ff. such enthronement oracles have come down to us, and it is the style and content of such anointment oracles that furnish the material which the tradition used when, in the legend of Nathan, it makes Nathan pronounce such promises to David.[82] The historical core here is that Yahweh's covenant with the king and his 'decree' at the anointing was expressly understood to be a renewal of 'the favours promised faithfully to David' and of the covenant with him.[83]

The fixed contents of these anointment and instalment oracles embraced also the allusion to the king's filial relation to Yahweh by adoption, the promise of everlasting rule for his family and the allusion to the covenant with the progenitor, as well as the promise of sovereignty over the nations and an allusion to the great 'name' in store for the king.[84] The mention of the king's 'name' contains an allusion to the fact that the oracles and 'decree' really contained those names of honour which the deity gave to the king on the day of his anointing, his 'regnal-name' which expressed both his close relation to Yahweh and the promise of the happiness and honour he was to gain for himself and for his people.[85] We know this to be the case in Egypt, and both in the East generally and in Israel the custom prevailed that the king should take a new name at his accession.[86] The divine conferring of royal names of honour is what the prophet is alluding to in the promise to the newborn royal child in Isaiah 9.1ff.[87]

Several of the traditional royal psalms have their place within the framework of the anointment ritual. This applies, e.g. to Ps. 110. It evidently belongs to the moment when the king is led forth to ascend his throne. The king's throne was in the East looked upon as a symbol of the throne of the deity. It is on a throne flanked by winged lions (cherubs), like that of Solomon, that the deity himself sits in Syro-Canaanite pictures. Such a winged lion throne (empty!) stood in the Temple in Jerusalem also, and it was supposed that 'Yahweh who sits upon the cherubim' was seated on it invisibly. When the king as the 'son of Yahweh' seats himself

---

[81] Cf. *Ps. St.* III, pp. 12ff.; A. R. Johnson, *The Cultic Prophet.*

[82] 2 Sam. 7. See *Ps. St.* III, pp. 35f., 110; 'Natanforjettelsen 2 Sam. Kap. 7', *SEÅ* XII, 1947, pp. 220ff.

[83] Isa. 55.3f.; Pss. 132.11ff.; 89.20ff. On the Davidic covenant see Pedersen, *Israel* III–IV, pp. 87ff., 654ff.; on its identity with the covenant with Israel, see Mowinckel, *He That Cometh*, pp. 89, 98ff., 158.

[84] Sonship: Pss. 2.7; 89.27f.; 2 Sam. 7.14. Everlasting kingdom: Pss. 89.29f., 37f.; 110.4; 2 Sam. 7.18; Isa. 55.3; 2 Sam. 23.5. Covenant with David: Pss. 89.31–34; 132.10–12, 17; 2 Sam. 23.5; 7.12–15. In Ps. 110.4 the promise is based on the idea that the house of David is the righteous successor to Melchizedek. Empire: Pss. 2.8–12; 89.26, 28; 132.18; 110.2, 5f.; Isa. 55.4f. Name: 2 Sam. 7.9; Pss. 72.17; 45.18; cf. 1 Kgs. 1.47.

[85] See von Rad's treatise (mentioned above, n. 76), col. 215f.

[86] See 2 Kgs 23.31 (Shallum-Jo'ahaz); 23.34 (Elijakim-Jehoiakim). 2 Sam. 12.24f. probably also has to be interpreted to the effect that David's son Jediah as king took the name Solomon. See Honeyman in *JBL* LXVII, pp. 13ff. For the names of Egyptian kings see Erman-Ranke, *Ägypten,*[2] pp. 58ff.; for Babylonian-Assyrian names see Meissner, *Babyl. u. Assyr.* I, p. 398.

[87] See v. Rad, *op. cit.*, col. 215f.

on his throne, this is a symbolic expression of the fact that he, as Yahweh's appointed governor, sits on the Lord's own throne, i.e. wields sovereign power in the name of Yahweh. That is the background of the oracle in Ps. 110. There reference is made to the holy robe in which the king has been arrayed for the anointing, to the life-giving water from the holy spring—probably the waters of Gihon—with which he has been purified and strengthened, and to the procession from the brook to the king's palace.[88] And at the moment when he ascends the throne, the temple prophet stands forth and proclaims for him in the name of Yahweh that to the king belongs the seat of honour on the right hand of Yahweh, and the priest kingdom 'after the order of Melchizedek'—or, 'for Melchizedek's sake':

> This oracle hath Yahweh for my lord:
> 'Sit thou throned at my right hand,
> Until I shall have made
>   Thine enemies thy footstool' . . .
> Yahweh hath sworn an oath,
>   and never will repent it;
> 'Thou art to be a priest for ever,
>   (a priest) as once Melchizedek was'.

Yahweh shall send the royal sceptre out from Zion, and go at the king's side in the battle,

> And he shall crush the (peoples') kings
>   in the day of his burning wrath.

The union of royal and priestly power was the main characteristic of El Elyon's kings in ancient Jerusalem, whose realm David and Solomon had inherited and maintained as the foundation of their position of power. But the increasing influence of the priests soon threatened the ecclesiastical power of the king. So it was important to have Yahweh's promise of the old right. Apart from this the warrior-ideal is strongly marked in this psalm. By the eternal 'youthful force' which the king—like the Canaanite fertility god *Tal*, 'Dew'—in that day receives from Yahweh, he shall 'strike through' all his enemies.

When the king had mounted the throne, and received the 'king's homage' (*tĕrû'ath melekh*), it is part of the ceremony that he is to make a speech to his people and his vassals. In so doing he points to the legitimate foundation of his sovereignty and to the way he intends to exert it. He produces, so to speak, his 'political programme' of which we also hear in connexion with Rehoboam, 1 Kgs. 12.14. This is the background of Ps. 2. In its form it is the king's first proclamation to his subjects, and it is the

[88] See Widengren, *Psalm* 110.

king himself who speaks.[89] He imagines the following situation: the subdued vassal kings are planning rebellion—a normal situation at practically every new accession in the Eastern empires—but he warns them, it will be in vain,

> for *I* have (now) been set as His king
> upon Zion, His holy hill.

And in proof of this he points to the legitimizing oracle he has just received through the cult prophet: 'I will declare the decree of Yahweh'; and then follows the oracle of appointment ('initiation oracle') verbatim:

> He said to me: 'Thou art my son,
> this day I have begotten thee.
> Ask, and I make thee master of the nations,
> lord over all the ends of the earth.
> Thou canst maul them with an iron mace,
> and shatter them like potter's ware'.

So the kings have nothing else to do but to 'be wise' and submit to Yahweh and his anointed, if they wish to save their lives.

Two things are noticeable in this proclamation. The first is the idea of the world sovereignty of the king of Zion. Ideally he has such a claim because he is the anointed one and Yahweh's governor, and Yahweh is the God of the world. The other point is the basis of the argument for this close relation between Yahweh and the king. He is 'Yahweh's son', adopted by Yahweh 'today'. It is the election, the anointing and the installation which are viewed as an adoption. Thereby the king is, ideally speaking, world-ruler; and all other kings are his vassals, whose duty it is to pay him homage by 'kissing his feet'—the usual sign of homage to the liege sovereign in the East.[90]

In Ps. 101 the new king proclaims his 'charter' before Yahweh and promises to 'behave himself wisely in a perfect way'. This psalm being

---

[89] If we keep to the text of G and H in v. 6, supported by verbatim parallels from the Ugarit texts, we shall avoid the constant unstylish changing of the person speaking, see Hvidberg, *Graad og Latter i det Gamle Testamente*, p. 34 n. 1–2. For the understanding of the presupposed situation in Ps. 2 see my discussion with Bentzen 'Urmenschen u. "Königsideologie"' in *Studia Theologica* II, pp. 87f. (cf. n. 100). Daiches (*Studies in the Pss.*, pp. 27ff.; 38ff.) maintains—though without any real exegetical basis—that *gôyîm* and *lĕ'ummîm* do not indicate 'nations', but something like 'great people' or 'nobles', and that *mĕlākhîm* in Ps. 2 and other places does not mean (foreign) 'kings', but native 'magnates', 'great noblemen', 'governors' and the like; Ps. 2, then, is supposed not to deal with the relationship between the supreme king and the other nations and kings, but to be a warning to the Judaic magnates that they do justice. D.'s concept of Israelite 'ideas' seems rather rationalistic and modernizing. Cf. also Kaminka (*MGWJ* 71, 1927, p. 296), who finds that Ps. 2 belongs to the poetry 'die Israels geistige Sendung glorifiziert' Morgenstern ('NŠQW BR' in *JQR* XXXII, 1941–42, p. 385) thinks that Ps. 2 (like Ps. 48) has for its background the Messianic expectations at the time of Zerubbabel, supposed to have been terminated very abruptly through some catastrophe in the year 485. The hypothesis is unnecessary—as nothing decisive can be said against a pre-exilic dating—and so is his textual conjecture in v. 12.

[90] See Gunkel, *Die Psalmen*, p. 8 (*ad* Ps. 2.12).

I, 5

typologically quite unique and not to be classed under any of the greater types ('Gattungen') we take the opportunity of analysing it here.

It starts as a hymn, but in a personal form: 'I will sing', and then continues as a vow made by the worshipper before Yahweh. The contents of this promise quite obviously prove that the speaker is supposed to be a king; his 'house' is the people and land of Israel, and the promise has for its object that he is going to rule the kingdom according to 'justice' and the 'goodwill of the covenant'.

From the point of view of form-history, elements from hymn and psalm of lament and prayer are here combined to make a new unity: the hymnal (self-) invitation to praise, and the 'promise' in which lament and psalm of prayer usually end. But there must be a special reason for this combination; it must be a consequence of the fact that this psalm—or psalms of this type—had a definite place in the liturgical framework of religious life. What, then, can possibly be the cultic 'place' for such a solemn promise on the part of the king before Yahweh?

It can hardly be anything else than the religious cultic part of the enthronement of the king, in connexion with the ceremonies of anointing, and in that case, before the proclamation to the vassals in Ps. 2. As we have seen above (p. 64, Chap. III.3), there is every reason to presume that the official festival of anointing, at any rate in the later monarchy, would take place in connexion with the new year festival, and that it would be commemorated as an annual festal day in connexion with the latter. No doubt the pattern from the Babylonian enthronement festival has had its influence here, directly or indirectly.

Now we know it to have been one feature of the enthronement of the king in Babylonia, that the king, by way of a confession before the god, would account for the way he had ruled his kingdom. This was a consequence of the fact that the new year festival was a festival of penance and purification, the king had to play the part of a penitent, humbling himself and laying his dignity at the feet of Marduk, to receive it again from his hand.[91] The confession of sins was always part of the penance. But as we shall see, confession of sins and declaration of innocence go together in the Babylonian as well as in the Israelite psalms of penance. It is not difficult to understand that in a ritual, aiming at the re-instatement of the king into his office, the main emphasis would have to be put on the declaration of innocence. From Babylonian and Egyptian sources we know that it was often part of the rituals of penance for the priest to make use of a kind of 'confessionary mirror'; he would ask the penitent: 'hast thou done this, has thou done that?', and so on. And because, as has been said, in such rituals we have a re-instatement, a 'justification' of the person in question, the answer to the question would usually be: 'I have not done this, I have not done that'. Such a 'negative confession of justification' is for instance made by the dead pharaoh, before he is admitted into the

---

[91] See Frankfort, *Kingship*, pp. 318ff.

realm of Osiris.[92] In Babylonia the confession of the king has the same form: 'I have not sinned, thou Lord of the commandments, I have not failed to honour thy divineness, I have not depraved Babylon', and so on.[93]

It is on behalf of the deity that the priest puts his questions. And in putting them he also gives instruction as to the will and the demands of the deity with regard to the king, as to the religious and moral standards and commandments, according to which he is to rule. The instruction of the deity is answered by the 'confession' of the penitent, but also of the king who is to be installed.

The promise of the king on the day of his anointing must be seen against this background. As we shall discuss in detail below in Chap. XII, the king on his festal day is confronted not only by the promises of Yahweh but also by the religious and moral pre-conditions of such a promise: the promise is dependent on his submission to the commandments and laws of Yahweh. And if the official installation of the king was identical with the great new year festival (Chap. V), and was celebrated every year in connexion with the latter, then king as well as people had to face Yahweh's demands at many points during the festal ritual.

The psalm of promise, Ps. 101, is the answer of the king to these demands from Yahweh, the promise made by him on the day of his election and anointing as king of Yahweh's people. It is, so to speak, his religious 'charter'. It is the counterpart of the intercession for the king in Ps. 72, to the effect that Yahweh may give him 'righteousness' and 'judgments' (pp. 65f). And, as already mentioned, we have reason to believe that it was repeated every year as a regular part of the great new year festival, at which the kind used to play such a prominent part. We may even say that it expresses the thanksgiving of the king to Yahweh for his gracious election, for the 'rightness' and 'faithful goodwill' to David and his house, which Yahweh has shown by electing him king of his people.[94] The king promises to repay all this 'rightness' and 'goodwill' on the part of Yahweh by ruling the 'house' of Israel and the 'city of Yahweh' in conformity with them.

Therefore the psalm starts by paying homage full of awe to Yahweh and his goodwill, and naturally this would take the form of a normal hymnic introduction:

> I will sing of goodwill and righteousness
> and play unto Thee, O Yahweh.

And it agrees with the fundamental idea of Israelite religion, that the king is conscious of receiving the 'rightness' and 'goodwill' needed in his high office, and of having to learn it from Yahweh, as we are told in Ps. 72.1;

---

[92] See Galling in *ZATW* 47, 1927, p. 130. That the rituals of the 'Book of the Dead' were originally concerned with the passage of the king into the world of Osiris is evident. Cf. Frankfort, *Kingship*, pp. 110ff.

[93] See Frankfort, *op. cit.*, p. 320.

[94] Cf. Isa. 55.3: *ḥasēdhê dhāwîdh* = 'the covenant promises of mercy to David'.

it is something for which the king must ask God:

> May I get insight in the perfect way—
> when wilt thou come to me?

In this introduction the tone of the hymn and of the psalm of prayer harmonize perfectly.[95]

The king promises to rule Yahweh's people righteously, and according to the covenant, and to exterminate all the wicked, the deceitful and proud, together with the sorcerers, and to surround himself with only true and honest men.

> Mine eyes shall be upon the faithful of the land,
> that they may dwell with me;
> he that walketh in a perfect way,
> he shall be my servant . . .
> Every morning I will destroy
> all the wicked of the land,
> that I may cut off all evil-doers
> from the city of Yahweh.

Such was the ideal; according to the Yahweh religion the king *ought to be* like this. That everyday reality was very often quite different can be seen both in the speeches of the prophets and in many of the historical records.[96]

The ethical strain in the Yahweh religion and its king-ideal is also clearly expressed in Ps. 72 which constitutes the congregation's petition and good wishes for the new king:

> Inspire the king, O God, with thine own justice,
> endow the king's son with thine own equity,
> that he may rule thy people aright,
> and thy poor with just judgment.

It is the lowly and the helpless among the people who are the special object of Yahweh's care: they are *his* poor, and the king's first task is to see that they are not oppressed. The king who does that shall live long, he lives in his race 'as long as sun and moon exist'. The petition becomes a

---

[95] Danell, *Psalm* 139. Danell places Ps. 139 in the context suggested by Solomon's vigil at Gibeon, 1 Kgs. 3.5ff., and thinks that it was used as 'the king's declaration, his profession to Yahweh after his enthronement during the New Year Festival'—i.e. in a cultic situation analogous to that of Ps. 101. Danell has given no tenable argument for this opinion. In Ps. 139 the worshipper is probably a leading person in the congregation but no king; the linguistic Aramaisms cannot be overlooked. The cultic background of the psalm is not an installation, but a casual distress; the psalm is a psalm of lamentation with a broad hymnic introduction, the purpose of which is the assertion of the innocence of the worshipper. What form a king's proclamation may have taken can be seen from Pss. 2 and 101.

[96] See above, pp. 59f. and n.63.

description of the blessings that shall befall the people:

> He shall come down like rain upon the mown grass:
>   as showers that water the earth.
> In his days shall welfare flourish;
>   and abundance of peace so long as the moon endureth.

The hills shall bear peace and happiness, and right order (i.e. welfare and good things) fill the valleys. Then shall his realm reach over the whole earth and 'all kings shall fall down before him: all nations shall serve him'. The most distant kings shall bring tribute:

> For he shall save the forlorn who cry to him,
>   the poor, and him that has no helper;
> he shall pity the poor and needy,
>   and shall save the life of the weak.
> He shall rescue them from outrage and oppression;
>   and precious shall their blood be in his sight.

When 'righteousness' rules the land, material blessings shall flow as a fruit of the king's probity and divine favour—his 'kingly luck' as the ancient Scandinavians would have said, his 'blessedness' the Israelites termed it:

> May the corn be abundant in the land
>   and sprout on the top of the mountains;
> the fruit thereof bloom like Lebanon,
>   and flourish like grass of the earth.

The psalm becomes a formula of blessing which reminds one strongly of the promises of the prophets as it oscillates between blessing and prediction. The officiating priest who recites the psalm, to begin with speaks on behalf of the congregation and in the form of a petition. But he is also the representative of Yahweh and pronounces strong and effective words with a ring of certainty. Through these he, so to speak, conducts Yahweh's own blessing to the king:

> May he be blessed for ever,
>   his name be confirmed as long as the sun.
> All nations envy his bliss,
>   the tribes of the earth hail him as the Blessed.

Before the king marches to war he offers sacrifice to Yahweh in order to gain his help. In the name of the congregation ('we') the officiating priest pronounces the words of blessing which are to bring fortune and victory, whilst they have at the same time also a note of petition. Thus in Ps. 20:

> May Yahweh answer thee on the day of trouble,
>   the name of the God of Jacob protect thee;
> sending thee help from the sanctuary,
>   and reinforcing thee from Zion.
> May he remember all thy offerings,
>   and be pleased with all thy sacrifices!

And having received Yahweh's answer through the oracle, he can with complete assurance proclaim:

> Now do I certainly know
>   that Yahweh grants victory to his anointed;
> he will hear him from his holy heaven
>   with the saving strength of his right hand.

Ps. 21 begins as a thanksgiving for the blessings which Yahweh has already bestowed on the king: protection, the fulfilment of 'his heart's desire', 'blessings of welfare', 'a golden crown on his head', 'length of days for ever and ever', glory, honour and majesty, and 'joy of thine own presence'; all this is the reward for the king because he has trusted in Yahweh. The second part of the psalm is a promise of victory over his enemies, Yahweh's 'answer' through the officiating priest.

> Thine hand will catch all thine enemies
>   thy right hand will crush those that hate thee . . .
> When they intend evil against thee
>   and plot a device, they shall not perform it.
> For thou wilt make them turn their back,
>   aiming thine arrows at their faces . . .

The situation seems to be similar to that in the previous psalm.

Ps. 89 is a lament, attributed to the king on a day of penance and prayer after lost battles. It starts in hymnal form with praise of Yahweh's mercy and faithfulness, his mighty power which he proved in the victory over the monsters of the primeval sea and in the creation, and of his previous 'deeds of righteousness', his victorious help for Israel and its king throughout the ages. Then the king mentions Yahweh's covenant with David and his promises never to forsake his seed; he may indeed chastise them 'if they forsake his law and walk not in his commandments', but he has sworn never to fail them:

> His seed shall endure for ever,
>   and his throne as the sun before me.
> It shall be established for ever as the moon,
>   as the faithful witness in heaven.

However—here starts the lament—Yahweh has now 'cast off and

abhorred' his anointed, the reigning king, and 'profaned his crown to the ground':

> Thou hast broken down all his walls
> and laid his strongholds in ruin . . .
> thou hast also turned the edge of his sword,
> and hast not made him to stand in the battle.

And at last the prayer: 'How long, Yahweh?'

> Remember, Yahweh, the taunts thrown at thy servants,
> how I do bear in my bosom the insults of the tribes,
> how thine enemies, Yahweh, have insulted,
> insulted the heels of thine anointed.

The last line hints at the flight of the defeated king.

But the king may also have reason to celebrate a festival of thanksgiving, and let psalms of thanks be sung after a victory gained and deliverance from death in the battle. Such a royal psalm of thanks is Ps. 18 with its grandiose description of how the king was already in the jaws of death, surrounded by enemies on every side. He saw himself swallowed up by 'the breakers of Death' and 'the floods of (the land of) Destruction'. Then in his distress he called upon the Lord, and Yahweh revealed himself as when he went to fight against chaos and the primeval sea:

> Then the earth shook and trembled,
> the foundations of the heavens moved . . .
> He rode forth in his cherub [chariot], flying,
> and swooped with the wings of the wind . . .
> And from heaven Yahweh thundered,
> the Most High gave his voice.
> Yea, he sent out his arrows and scattered them,
> he shot out his lightnings, and discomfited them.
> The bed of the ocean then appeared,
> the earth's foundations were laid bare,
> at thy threatening menace, Yahweh,
> at the blast of thy nostrils' breath.
> He stretched from on high and took me,
> he drew me out of great flood;
> he freed me from my foes so strong,
> from haters far too strong for me . . . .

Thus did Yahweh save him and reward him 'according to his righteousness and the cleanness of his hands', 'his faithfulness to the covenant and his perfection', and the psalm now gives thanks for this help. In the following stanzas he returns to the description of the danger and of the deliverance in the same grandiose style, this time without mythological

images, so that one clearly sees that it is a question of war and political
enemies.

> Thou gavest me the shield of thy salvation,
>   thy granting my prayer made me strong.
> Thou enlargedst my steps under me
>   and my ankles did not slip.
> I chased my foes and overtook them,
>   I did not turn till they were killed,
> I smote them through, that they could not rise,
>   they fell under my feet.

Thus the king has again been able to secure ascendancy over his enemies:

> Thou deliveredst me from the rage of nations,
>   thou rescuedst me from violent foes,
> thou liftedst me up above mine enemies
>   and madest me the head of (foreign) peoples.

> Peoples whom I do not know, become my servants,
>   once they hear of me they render homage,
> strangers yield feigned obedience to me,
>   come trembling out of their hiding places . . . .

> And therefore now I thank thee, Yahweh,
>   sing praises to thy name before the nations,
> to him who hath given his king great victories
>   and showed loving kindness to his anointed,
>   to David and to his seed for ever.

It has long been known that this psalm of thanks, both in its construction
and its details and the whole conception and description of events, has
many analogies with the hymn with which Pharaoh Ramses II celebrated
the god Amon in Thebes, after his escape from a critical situation in the
battle against the Hittites at Kadesh in the Orontes valley.[97] Of all the
psalms this is the one which has the most Egyptian style, and reminds
one most directly of hymns to the 'god' Pharaoh, with their highflown
descriptions of his majesty's overwhelming victories over all the wretched
and wicked 'foreign' nations—poetical descriptions which are not always
in accordance with the historical results of the 'victories'. One suspects
the composer of Ps. 18 of having studied the poetical art of Egypt, and
that he too lays more stress on grandiose description and ebullient enthusiasm than on actual facts.

That the king's wedding with a foreign princess was a religious act to be
celebrated with cultic ceremony goes without saying. And the ritual words
of blessing and good wishes for bride and bridegroom which belonged to
the common man's wedding in the times of the patriarchs and the semi-

---

[97] Translation in Erman, *Lit. d. Aegypter*, pp. 329ff. (E.T., pp. 26off.).

nomadic state, were surely still more in place at a royal wedding. It is therefore not surprising to find a royal wedding-hymn in the book of Psalms —Ps. 45. The psalmist stands forth as an inspired proclaimer of power-filled, effectual words of blessing:

> My heart bubbles over with luck-bringing words,
>> I recite my (powerful) poem to the king,
>>> my tongue is like the pen of a quick writer.

It is characteristically oriental that he says little about the bride, but much more about the king:

> Kings' daughters are among thy 'jewels',
>> at thy right hand stands the queen in gold of Ophir ...
> The king's daughter is all glory,
>> her clothing (decorated with) corals set in gold,
>>> in broidered work she is led unto the king.
> Behind her come virgins, her companions,
>> they are brought unto thee with gladness and rejoicing,
>>> they are led and they enter the king's palace.

The poet has also a word to say to her, a word of counsel from an experienced sage:

> Listen, O daughter, and bend thine ear:
>> forget thine own folk and thy father's house,
>>> then will the king desire thy beauty.
> For he is thy lord, render homage to him.
> Then the Tyrian traders shall come with gifts,
>> the richest of the nations shall seek thy favour.

Behind the commonplace sentiments of the counsel there is also a suggestion of the Israelite temple poet's recollections of the evils ensuing for the faithful when a foreign princess like Jezebel was unwilling to forget her father's house, seeing it as her duty to introduce the cult of Baal among Yahweh's people: that must not happen again.

But the greater part of the poem takes the shape of a hymnal description of the king himself:

> Thou art fairer than all the mortals;
>> charm is playing on thy lips
>>> because God hath blessed thee for ever.

The poet describes him as the bold warrior whose 'right hand shall teach him deeds of dread', who 'rides forth prosperously' in his war chariot, and whose 'arrows are sharp in the heart of his enemies'; he is addressed as a god; his sceptre is a 'sceptre of right'; 'thou lovest righteousness and hatest wickedness'; therefore Yahweh has elected him among all his brethren and 'anointed him with the oil of gladness'.

Here too there are marked analogies with other royal hymns of the East, particularly with those of Egypt; but by contrast, in Egypt we often meet with hymns of praise to the divine king, who upholds the world order, creates and secures life and fertility, defends his people against all his enemies, 'rises' (as the sun) over the earth, etc.[98] Ps. 45 is the only example in the whole of Israelite psalm poetry of a true hymn to the king.[99] As regards form it remains within the framework of those effectual words of blessing pronounced according to Yahweh's commission which from the beginning had a place in Israelite cult and ritual, and which had a natural tendency to become a laudatory and promising description of the honour and fortune which will befall the one blest.

It is obvious when we consider this conception of the king—his significance as the people's source of blessing and centre of power, and his place in the cult—that all that concerned him and his house also concerned the people; nothing which happened to him was a purely private affair. The people had the greatest interest in all that concerned him. Everything must be done from the point of view of the official cult to support him as the centre of blessing and prevent anything from happening which might injure his 'soul' and his royal strength and fortune. All misfortunes and dangers which demand divine help become occasions for cultic activities. In case of sickness, sacrifices and prayers were offered up for him along with the ritual purifications which also were necesary. Ps. 28 is, in all probability, a psalm referring to the king's sickness, although it may be uncertain whether this psalm was originally made for this definite occasion or whether an older psalm has been adapted. The suppliant presents himself as 'Yahweh's anointed', and it is suggested that Yahweh by saving his anointed would manifest himself as the 'saving strength' of his people. Hence the petition for the recovery of the king, and the confidence expressed in it, concludes as a prayer to 'save thy people and bless thine inheritance'.

We also learn that when the king has recovered from sickness a thanksgiving is celebrated and a psalm sung, as recorded of king Hezekiah. The hymn of thanks sung on that occasion is preserved in Isa. 38.9ff. At all events the psalm belongs to a cultic thanksgiving festival.[100]

These royal psalms, as we have seen, have arisen out of the prevailing concept of the ideal king which was fundamentally the same throughout the whole of the East—a view of the king which was in no wise primitive, and which differs considerably from the old view of the chief, and which yet has its roots far back in primitive ideas of the powerful 'mana'-being. These royal psalms had their fixed place in the national religious service,

[98] See Erman, *Lit. d. Aegypter*, p. 320 (E.T., p. 256); *ANET*, pp. 373f.
[99] It is worth considering whether the original text of Ps. 21.14 may not have been speaking of the king instead of Yahweh. See note in *BHK³* ad loc.
[100] See Begrich, *Der Psalm des Hiskia*. De Boer (*OTS IX*) comes to the same conclusion.

and expressed the generally accepted ideal of the king. They contain therefore no realistic description of the individual historical king and his particular situation. They present the royal ideal, the typical king as he exists in religious theory and in the people's mind and imagination, and as he should be when he appears before God in the cult. The psalms presuppose and describe typical, constantly recurring situations, e.g. the situation at the death of the old king who is represented as a universal king. Before the enthronement of his successor, the vassals might be preparing insurrection (Ps. 2)[100a] or the enemies have overrun the country (Ps. 89), but the deity arises to save his royal son (Ps. 18), etc.

That traits from the old myths here blend in as poetical elements in the picture is quite possible; thus when distress is seen as an actual descent into the realms of death, as in Ps. 18, this goes back finally to accounts of the death of the vegetation god (see below, Chap. VII.5); but one cannot conclude from this that the king here appears in the form and role of the god. The royal psalms give us the idealized portrait of the king even in the normal kingly situations where the king is identical with his people. We see the king as he should be according to the view obtaining in the circle of the psalmist—and, we may add, in the leading religious circles.

But one must also add: it is not simply a copy of the general oriental king-ideal and king-pattern that we find here.

The foregoing short review of some of the prominent royal psalms has again and again given us occasion to point out special Israelite variations and accentuations of the king ideal, and these modifications are the result of the influence of Israel's own particular religion on the borrowed style. As stated above, both in Babylonia and in Egypt the direct 'hymn to the king', who is more or less clearly described and praised as a god, is quite common,[101] but of this type of poem we have only one actual example in the book of Psalms—the wedding psalm, Ps. 45. With this exception the hymn is in Israel reserved for Yahweh himself. And even Ps. 45 is no purely royal hymn; the glorifying description is rooted in the word of blessing which generally takes the form of a description of the glory and fortune which it calls forth for the one blest. It is Yahweh's glorious gift to the king that the psalmist is painting; for it is Yahweh who has provided him with this grace, power and glory. But thus has Yahweh in his wonderful mercy equipped all mankind, says the poet in Ps. 8.

And just because the royal psalms describe the ideal in the light of

---

[100a] It therefore seems like conceding too much to the extreme exponents of a common oriental god-king-ideology in Israel, when Bentzen in his *Sakrale Kongedømme* is willing to accept that the situation given in Ps. 2 as the background of the enthronement of the new king has been taken over from the conception of the rebellion of the powers of chaos against the god. The situation of Ps. 2 was regularly repeated at the death of practically every Assyrian king. See note 89.

[101] See Steindorff and Seele, *When Egypt Ruled the East*, p. 83; Erman-Ranke, *Aegypten*,[2] pp. 72, 76, 466, 469, 471, 473. On Sumerian royal hymns see Kramer, *Sumerian Mythology*, p. 13; see also Zimmern, *König Lipit-Ištar*, pp. 3ff. We often meet with loud echoes of royal hymns in the I-form in the introductions to the Assyrian epigraphs of kings; cf. Mowinckel, *Statholderen Nehemia*, pp. 140ff.; 'Die vorderasiatischen Königs—und Fürsteninschriften' in *Eucharisterion* I, (*Festschrift Gunkel*), pp. 297ff.

religion, it is not without justification that later Judaism has given them a Messianic interpretation, and the Church has taken the psalms' pictures of the king as prophecies of Christ. They sprang from the need for a super-human helper and saviour, the fulfilment of which is Jesus Christ.[102]

5

According to this view of the king and his relation to the deity and to the people and of his position in the divine services, there is no sharp distinction between public and private psalms—those of the congregation, and those of the separate individual. From one point of view the king is a single person who, for instance in a lament, may speak of his ('my') sickness, or of other distress and danger; but still he is something more. It is really the congregation's, the people's fate that is involved when the king, 'our shield', is in distress and danger.

It goes without saying then, that the king played a prominent part at a number of national cultic festivals, as, for instance, on the days of prayer that were arranged before a war or after a defeat (Chap. VI.1) or at a thanksgiving after victory (Chap. IX).

Thus, when in national hymns of thanks or lamentation, as e.g. Pss. 44 and 66, we meet with a narratory 'I', there can be no doubt that this is the king, or at best a high ranking representative of the congregation— the high priest or the provincial governor or the president of the pro-vincial council—who is here speaking on behalf of the community.

The *royal psalms* in this extended sense are thus really *congregational psalms*. This is the grain of truth in Smend's theory about the so-called 'collective I', which simply took the narratory 'I' as a personification of the congregation (see above, pp. 45f.). In this form the theory is in-correct; there are plenty of cases in which the speaker ranges himself, as an individual person, alongside 'his brethren' in 'the great assembly', that is to say, he is plainly not identical with 'the great assembly', i.e. the congregation, but is a single person in the midst of the congregation. But on some occasions he represents all the others and speaks on their behalf and is in so far one with them. In most of these cases this person is the king.

6

What has been said above has really a much wider bearing.

Many of the set phrases and images which recur in the formally pure 'I'-psalms, are of such a nature as to exclude the possibility of their having been connected with any private person; they evidently refer to some king or great chieftain. The frequent war pictures,[103] to begin with, point in this direction. The matter is still plainer when the petitioner speaks of how 'the peoples', 'peoples and kings', 'all the nations', are interested in his

[102] Cf. for this von Rad in *ZATW* 58, 1940–41, pp. 216ff.
[103] See for instance Pss. 3.7; 27.3; 55.22, and many other places.

welfare.[104] It is the royal and divine symbol that the petitioner borrows when he speaks of 'lifting his horn'.[105] Also the near relationship in which many psalms place the petitioner to Yahweh—as e.g. that he is Yahweh's particular 'servant'—go beyond what the private individual in the old times could take it upon himself to say. It was the king—or the priest and the prophet[106]—who stood in such a particular servant relationship to the national god.

All this points to the fact that in Israel, as in Babylonia and Egypt, the psalms—together with the corresponding august cultic dispositions—were originally intended, not for all and sundry, but for the king and the great.[107] The style of the psalms in all these places shows clear traces of the original conditions.

This is really what was originally meant by the heading *lĕdhāwīdh*, which is usually translated 'by David'. In Israel it was in later times undoubtedly taken as an indication of authorship; this is, among other things, seen from the twelve psalms where to this note has been added information as to *when* David composed or sang the psalm in question. But this interpretation is in many cases impossible; for the expression is also found above psalms which must be more recent than the time of David, since, for instance, they refer to the Temple in Jerusalem (Pss. 24; 64, etc.). In Ps. 18 the petitioning king describes himself as the descendant of David, and in Ps. 132 he begs for Yahweh's blessing 'for David's sake'.[108] The linguistically natural translation of *lĕdhāwīdh* is 'for David', cf. the heading in Ps. 102: 'a prayer of the afflicted' (i.e. for the use of someone in such a situation), 'who poureth out his complaint before the Lord'. The psalms were composed for the use of, and were in due time used by 'David'—that is to say, in most cases, by a king of the house of David. Such information was a good recommendation for the psalm; a psalm which helped a man of good fortune, like David, must needs be pleasing to God and effective, a useful prayer. This interpretation of the expression[109] was thought to be confirmed by recent discoveries at Mari, where the word *davidum* was said to occur as the title of a chief or king, used in particular among semi-nomadic tribes.[110]

---

[104] Pss. 7.7, 9; 9.5; 18.50; 56.8; 57.10;.59.9; 138.4.

[105] Ps. 92.11; 1 Sam. 2.1; cf. Pss. 75.5, 11; 148.14; 89.18; 132.17.

[106] See Lindhagen, *The Servant Motif in the O.T.* L. thinks that the use of the epithet is everywhere due to a transfer from the 'king ideology'. But being originally cultic, its connexion with the priest is sure to be older than that with the king.

[107] See Jastrow, *Relig. Babyl. u. Assyr.* II, pp. 106f., 117; Meissner, *Babyl.-assyr. Literatur*, pp. 37ff.; *Ps. St.* VI, p. 74.

[108] For details see *Ps. St.* VI, pp. 2ff.

[109] See *Ps. St.* VI, pp. 72ff. Eerdmans likewise arrived at this conception of *lĕdhāwīdh*, see *Hebr. Book of Pss.* (*OTS* IV), pp. 36ff.

[110] See Dossin in *Syria* XIX, 1938, pp. 109f.; Bentzen, *Sakrale kongedömme*, pp. 54f. [But Tadmor in JNES XVII, 1958, pp. 129ff., refutes this suggestion.] In Ugarit the king 'sealing a contract in which he participates, or one that he witnesses and so guarantees, does not seal in his own name, but in that of the founder of the dynasty'. 'This practice had already been noticed in the neighbouring city of Alalakh' (N. Nougayrol in *Academie des Inscriptions et Belles-Lettres*, see *Manchester Guardian*, April 18th, 1952, p. 5).

In later times the expression was taken to refer to the author, and naturally to David himself; a notion which in its turn led to the descriptions of situations contained in the headings of several psalms, which have been deduced—as a rule not very convincingly—from the contents of the psalm itself (see below, Chap. XVI.5).

We must consequently look upon many of the 'I-psalms' as really royal psalms, and therefore psalms of the people and the congregation. In numerous other cases however it is very difficult to decide definitely what they are, the reason being that the description of the Psalmist's situation and of his enemies is usually couched in such general and in part stereotyped imagery that it is far from easy—at times impossible—to judge whether it is a question of national or private need and trouble. We shall return to this later (see Chaps. VII, VIII.5, 6).

The view that the narratory 'I' in the psalms mainly represents the king is supported by the fact that this has been proved to be the case in Babylonian-Assyrian (and Egyptian) psalms. There too the elaborate cultic ceremonies with hymn singing, etc. were originally intended for the king and his family and high officials, and the style and imagery of the psalms are completely coloured by this intention. Many of the preserved texts give the name of the king for whom they have been composed or by whom they have been used; others have come down in several versions, of which one mentions the name of one king, another that of a different one. In some copies we read: 'I, N. N. the son of N. N.'. This suggests that these royal psalms might at a later stage be used by or for other persons in connexion with cleansing from sin or sickness or some other evil. In other words, it would seem that a democratization of the cult and the religion had taken place.[111]

7

There is every indication that such a democratization—and individualization—of religion did take place in Israel. Yahweh has gradually become, not only the god of the whole people as in the earliest time, and the god of kings, chiefs, priests, and prophets—as official and cultic representatives of the whole—but the god of the common man and woman as well. This, of course, does not imply that Yahweh was not also from the first the god of the common member of the tribe and the people. Abraham's servant prays to the god of his master Abraham (Gen. 24.12) and Samuel's mother approaches Yahweh with a prayer regarding so private a matter as that of being granted a son (1 Sam. 3). But in the official religion during the monarchy it was the king and the great officials and the cultic ministrants who stood in a particularly near relation to Yahweh and acted as intermediaries between him and the common people. To them the layman generally applied, begging for their intercession, if he wished to obtain

[111] See Additional Note V.

some favour from Yahweh.[112] But a change gradually came about. Whereas in the remoter times the layman spoke to the king and the other great men, or to special men of religion like priests and prophets, of Yahweh, as 'thy God',[113] he can in later times speak of 'our' or 'my' God.[114] The thought gradually gains ground that Yahweh especially cares for the lowly, the widow and the fatherless and the stranger, who have no other help.[115] An important part in this 'individualization' of religion was without doubt played by the personal prayer life of the great prophets with their prayers both intercessory[116] and personal;[117] in at least some measure this life of prayer would be adopted by their disciples and adherents. This fact has been of importance for the Jewish conception of the relation between Yahweh and the individual.

With this development the old royal psalms of the temple service took on a new meaning.

The Temple in Jerusalem was, to begin with, what we might call a royal chapel, a 'royal sanctuary' (Am. 7.10). It is most probable—considering, among other things, the prophets' dislike of pretentious cultic and ritual ceremonies—that in Israel, ritual acts that took place on behalf of a common individual were of a much simpler kind. As a rule they were probably enacted in the local sanctuary, or still more simply in the village. Here the ritual no doubt had a much more ancient and less elaborate form than in the temple rites of Jerusalem, a fact which can be faintly discerned behind the cultic and ritual legislation of the Priestly Code. The local rites took over many forms from older Canaanite and other oriental cults.

A decisive epoch in the history of the temple cult of Jerusalem was introduced with the restoration of the Jewish congregation after the fall of the kingdom. The cult was restored in the old forms, according to old rules and ritual, as is evident from the wealth of old tradition and material which became included in the ritual laws of the priestly code, and also from late psalms in which the old style has been faithfully followed. But the central figure itself—the king and his house—has gon . His place has been taken over by the high priest, partly also by the governor. The Temple becomes a place of pilgrimage and worship[118] for Jews and proselytes from many lands, who come with their purely personal needs and submit themselves to the prescribed rules of the place. The private individual becomes a more important member of the congregation than he had ever been as a member of the corporate national body; his participation or non-participation now depends much more upon himself. Far more than

[112] Gen. 20.7; Ex. 14.5; 15.25; 17.4; 32.11ff.; Num. 11.2; 21.7; 1 Sam. 2.25; Isa. 37.4; Jer. 42.1ff.; 37.3ff.
[113] Ps. 89.27; 2 Sam. 24.3; 14.11, 17; 1 Kgs. 18.10.
[114] Neh. 1.6, 11; 2.8, 12, 18; 5.19; 13.14, 22, 29, 31; Ezra 7.6, 28; 9.6; Sir. 51.1f.; Tob. 3.14; 13.13; Judith 9.4; 16.2; Esth. 13.15 (G).
[115] See for instance 1 Sam. 2.5, 7f.; Pss. 10.14, 18; 18.28; 68.6f.; 113.6f.; Prov. 15.25; Deut. 10.17f.; 24.17f.
[116] Am. 7.2, 5; Jer. 17.16; 11.14; 14.11.
[117] Isa. 8.17; Jer. 11.18f.; 12.1ff.; 15.10ff.; 17.17ff.; 18.18ff.; 20.7ff.
[118] Isa. 56.7; 60.7 (GTMMM III); cf. 1 Kgs. 8.31ff., 41ff.

before Yahweh becomes the god of the individual person. What previously only a priest or a prophet or a king might say to Yahweh is adopted by the common man. The elaborate ritual which in Jerusalem was originally designed for the cleansing of the king or the high officials from their sin and sickness, was in the ritual rules of Leviticus made applicable to any Jew—though occasionally with a certain distinction between rich and poor (see e.g. Lev. 5.7ff.). The book of Job contains direct evidence that the common man and woman in Jewish times presented themselves in the Temple in sickness and distress, and after recovery and other mercies received, in order to offer the various sacrifices and have the appropriate psalm sung.[119] We see the same in Ps. 107, which recounts the different categories of members of the congregation who have made their vows in distress and are now bearing forth offerings and singing psalms of thanksgiving (see Chap. X.3).

It is therefore quite possible—nay, probable—that use was made in ritual acts of texts and psalms which were originally composed for the king, and that furthermore new psalms were composed in the same style, but now for the use of Everyman. The fixity of the stylistic tradition and poetical language led to the old expressions—originally connected with the king—being taken over and continued even where new hymns were composed. This is a further reason for caution when seeking to distinguish between congregational and personal psalms.

[119] Job 33.24–25; cf. Duhm, *Das Buch Hiob*, p. 162. It is interesting to notice that Duhm is here actually anticipating Gunkel's cultic psalm interpretation and that he has seen the connexion between the thanksgiving psalm and the ritual thank-offering. Only it is a pity that so little of this is to be found in Duhm's own psalm commentary.

CHAPTER IV

The Hymn of Praise

The first of the main types to be described is the hymn or song of praise.[1] The Psalter contains many examples of this kind, e.g. Pss. 8; 19; 29; 33; 46; 47; 48; 76; 104; 135; 136; 145–150, which are all typical. To these we may add the three fragments of a hymn of praise which are now embedded in the book of Amos, as 4.12f., 13; 5.8f.; 9.5f.[1a]

I

The core of the hymn of praise is the consciousness of the poet and congregation that they are standing face to face with the Lord himself, meeting the almighty, holy and merciful God in his own place, and worshipping him with praise and adoration. He is in their midst, and they are his chosen people, who owe him everything. Therefore they now meet him, with awe and trembling because he is the Holy One, but also with a sure trust, love, jubilation and overflowing enthusiasm, while remembering all the great and glorious things that he has done. From the encounter with the Holy One, from the reverence and trust, the gratitude, joy and enthusiasm, the song of praise thus rises to the Lord of Hosts, to express what the congregation is seeing and feeling, and to increase his glory in the world. This is the fountain-head from which all the characteristic features of the hymn, too, all its elements of matter and form, must be conceived as taking their rise.[1b]

The hymn opens with the exhortation to sing unto the Lord, to praise,

---

[1] See Gunkel-Begrich, *Einleitung*, pp. 32–94, as also for the sources and evidences of the characteristic individual features of the hymn style; Gunkel gives fairly complete statistics, but Westermann's painstaking analysis (*Das Loben Gottes im A.T.*) does not give much of importance beyond Gunkel.

[1a] These verses have no connexion whatever, either syntactically or logically, with the context of the sayings of Amos; they obviously belong to the same set and are fragments of a 'psalm' in which each stanza ended with the refrain 'Yahweh, the God of Hosts is his name'. The collectors of the book of Amos have inserted a stanza or two in such places as speak of Yahweh's appearing for judgement with the intention of underlining His majesty and power. Cf. *GTMMM* III, pp. 634f.; H. Schmidt, *D. Mythos vom wiederkehrenden König*, p. 29; *Thronfahrt Jahwes*, p. 22.

[1b] Westermann's idea (*Das Loben Gottes im A.T.*) that the origin of the hymn of praise is to be found in some vague urge to praise God for the experience of His interference in history is gainsaid by the fact that this type is found in all religions, even those in which the thought of God's work and witness in history has no place. And when W. considers this urge to be the 'Sitz im Leben' of the hymn of praise, he at any rate gives to this term another meaning, quite different from the one ascribed to it by Gunkel and form-critical and cult-historical research. That the hymn of praise has its setting in the cult cannot be denied, see below, p. 136. The religio-psychological problem is a different question.

82   THE PSALMS IN ISRAEL'S WORSHIP

thank, exalt and bless him, to fall down and worship him, to proclaim him, to 'clap your hands and shout unto God', etc.—usually in the imperative plural.[2] It is in fact the precentor's exhortation to the choir which re-echoes in this 'introit'.[3] Occasionally the exhortation is inclusive: 'O come, let us sing',[4] or still more personally: 'I will praise the Lord', and similar expressions. The 'I' may originally have meant the leader of the choir or the cultic act, the spokesman of the congregation. But it was also appropriate to express the poet's personal and emotional relation to his theme, his identification of himself with what he had to say.[5] The introit may be repeated before every new subdivision or stanza of the hymn, and is reflected in the responsory 'Hallelujah'.

Then those to whom the exhortation is directed are mentioned, generally in some expression or other referring to the congregation: Yahweh's servants (i.e. worshippers), Jacob's or Zion's sons, Yahweh's faithful, 'the righteous', 'they that fear the Lord', etc., that is: Israel as a cultic congregation.[6] At times it is even, with poetic enthusiasm, directed to the whole earth, to all that lives, to peoples and kings and princes,[7] heaven and earth, woods and rocks and sea,[8] even to the heavenly powers ('sons of God'),[9] or to the dead.[10] The personal note in the exhortation finds its complete realization when it is directed to the poet's own 'soul'.[11]

In the exhortation Yahweh's name is always mentioned.[12] To this is sometimes added a series of laudatory (hymnal) attributes: 'The most High', 'Israel's God', or 'King' or 'Creator', 'our King', 'our Defence', etc.[13] This may be varied in such a way that the poet exhorts his hearers to praise 'the name of the Lord',[14] his glory, his power, his deeds, and great works, his wonders, his mercy and faithfulness, in a word, his great and glorious qualities.[15] In such wise is the theme and the aim of the hymn set forth.

---

[2] See references in Gunkel-Begrich, *Einl.*, p. 33. Instances: Pss. 33.3; 96.1, 2; 98.1;– 113.1; 117.1; — 32.2 (thanksgiving psalm); 105.1; 106.1; — 99.5, 9; — 96.2; 134.1f.; — 29.2b; —47.2; 81.2; 100.1 (*hārī'û* indicates the shout of homage *těrū'ā*); 33.1; 81.2; 98.4.

[3] Cf. Pss. 118.2–4; 134.1; 135.19f.

[4] Pss. 95.1, 2; 11.24; 79.13 ('promise' within a psalm of lamentation, see Chap. VI. 3); 115.18, etc.; see Gunkel-Begrich, *Einl.*, p. 34.

[5] Ps. 111.1; Ex. 15.1; Pss. 9.2f.; 104.33; 22.23, etc.; see Gunkel-Begrich, *Einl.*, p. 38.

[6] Pss. 113.1; 134.1; 135.1; — 105.6; 149.2; — 145.10; 149.5; — 33.1; — 22.24, etc.; see Gunkel-Begrich, *Einl.* pp. 35f. For the sense of the terms, 'the righteous', 'the godly', etc., see below, pp. 242ff.

[7] Pss. 33.8; 96.1, 9; 98.4; 100.1; 145.21; 150.6; — 22.28; 96.7; 47.2; 68.33; 138.4; 148.11; see Gunkel-Begrich, *Einl.*, p. 36.

[8] Ps. 96.11f.; cf. Isa. 44.23 (prophetic imitation of the style).

[9] Pss. 29.1; 103.20ff. (thanksgiving psalm in hymnic style); 148.2.

[10] Ps. 22.30 (rd. *kol-yěshēnê 'ereṣ*; hymnic 'promise', see n. 4).

[11] Pss. 104.1; 146.1; cf. 103.1 (a thanksgiving psalm). See Gunkel-Begrich, *Einl.*, p. 39.

[12] For instance Ps. 27.6 (hymnic introduction to a psalm of lamentation, see below, IV. 4); 33.1; 66.1; 81.2; 95.1; 96.1, etc.; see Gunkel-Begrich, *Einl.*, p. 40.

[13] Pss. 9.5 (hymnic introduction, see IV. 4); 92.2 (thanksgiving psalm); 150.1; — 71.22 (hymnic thanksgiving in a psalm of lamentation); 81.2; 149.2; — 47.7; 66.8; 81.2; 95.1; 144.1 (hymnic introduction), and other places; see Gunkel-Begrich, *Einl.*, p. 40.

[14] Pss. 9.3 (see n. 13); 22.23 (see n. 10); 29.2; 92.2; 96.2; 113.1; 135.1, etc.

[15] Pss. 9.12 (see n. 13); 71.8, 18 (see n. 13); 89.2 (hymnic introduction to a lament); 92.3; 96.2, 3; 145.4, 10, 11, 12; 150.2 and other places, see Gunkel-Begrich, *Einl.*, p. 41.

Frequently the mode which the praise is to take is also indicated: 'with harp', 'with the psaltery and an instrument of ten strings', 'with dance', etc.[16] All the significant elements of the introit to the hymn are found together in Ps. 149.1–3.

> Sing unto Yahweh a new song,
>   his praise in the congregation of covenanters!
> Let Israel rejoice in his creator,
>   the sons of Zion be joyful in their King!
> Let them dance in praise of his name,
>   make melody to him with timbrel and lyre!

It is interesting to see how many variations the poets have been able to produce by combining these traditional elements in different ways, and how rich and varied the traditional hymn-style has thus become. The whole of Ps. 150 is, from the point of view of form, just one richly varied introit; praise is implicit throughout the very exhortation itself.

The theme is then further developed in the main body of the hymn. It generally begins with the ground for the exhortation, introduced by a 'for', 'because', e.g. Praise the Lord, 'for he is good'.[17] In this short motivatory section the whole hymn is contained as in a nutshell. The oldest hymns were, it seems, constant repetitions of the reasoned exhortation to praise and jubilation, such as: Praise the Lord, 'for his kindness endureth for ever'. The germinal cell of the hymn is just this again and again repeated jubilant mention of Yahweh's deeds and qualities, such as the short reverential cry of joy that recurs like a refrain in the Greek Dionysos-hymn: 'Worthy bull!'[18] The main body of the hymn gradually grew by the addition of further motivations with more and more praiseworthy works and qualities (těhillôth). Beside the motivated main clause the appositional nouns or participles[19] which we usually translate by relative clauses—'(he) who does so and so'—or explanatory relative sentences are often used.[20]

This interplay between repetition and accretion is clearly demonstrated in Ps. 136, where the first part of each period consists of a praising participle in apposition to 'Yahweh', and the second part of the reiterated motivation, 'for his kindness endureth for ever'.

In consequence of this development the main body of the hymn usually consists of a series of short sentences each of which mentions some praiseworthy deed or quality. Yahweh is as a rule the subject in these sen-

---

[16] Pss. 33.1; 149.2f.; 150.3–5, etc.

[17] Ps. 135.3; Ex. 15.21; cf. Ps. 13.6 (hymnic 'promise', see n. 4).

[18] Cf. Heiler, *Das Gebet*,[4] pp. 160f. Cf. the short paean of victory of the Ama-zulus, consisting of two constantly repeated lines, see Blessing-Dahle in *Festschrift Meinhof*.

[19] See Gunkel-Begrich, *Einl.*, pp. 43f., 33ff.—See, for instance, Pss. 18.2; 65.6; 89.8 (see n. 15); — 9.12 (see n. 13); 103.3–5 (see n. 9); 114.8; 136.3–7; 147.8, 9, 14–17, and other places.

[20] For instance Pss. 46.9; 66.20; 124.6 (public thanksgiving psalm, see Chap. IX); 135.8; 136.23; cf. Gen. 24.27; 1 Sam. 25.32, 39. See Gunkel-Begrich, *Einl.*, pp. 43f.

tences,[21] but sometimes it is his name, his arm, his right hand, or one of his qualities or works: his voice, his word, his dominion, his honour and glory, his mercy, his throne.[22]

These short sentences generally speak of Yahweh's qualities, his permanent divine attributes; consequently they mostly have the form of appositions, relative clauses and nominal clauses. Besides these we have sentences that describe what he is regularly or repeatedly doing, with the verb in the participle, perfect or imperfect. E.g. 'Yahweh looks from heaven, beholding all mankind: from his abode he scans all the inhabitants of the earth' (33.17f.). 'Yahweh sets the captives free, Yahweh gives the blind their sight, Yahweh raises those who are bowed down, Yahweh preserves poor foreigners, the widow and the orphan He relieves' (146. 7-9).[22a]

A prominent place in the hymns of praise, however, is taken by such sentences as speak of Yahweh's special deeds in history—and to the minds of the ancient Israelites even creation, the victory over the primeval monsters, belongs to history. Such sentences have the form of statements (narrative clauses), with the verb in the perfect, imperfect, narrative imperfect, or consecutive imperfect. Examples: 'for He spoke, and (things) came into existence, He commanded, and it appeared' (33.9). 'The world and the fullness thereof, thou hast founded them, the north and the south, thou hast created them' (89.11f.). 'Yahweh hath chosen Jacob to be his, and Israel as his prized possession' (135.4).[23] Besides such short examples we also find longer descriptions, as e.g. in Ps. 104.6ff.:

> Once the primordial ocean covered (the earth),
>> the waters rose over the mountains:
> but they retired by thy rebuke,
>> scared at the sound of thy thunder . . .
> never to pass thine appointed bounds,
>> never to cover the earth again.

[21] As a rule in 3rd person: 24.1f.; 29; 33.1-2; 46; 47; 81.2-6; 95.1-7; 96; 98; 100; 103; 105; 111; 113; 117; 134; 146; 147; 148; 149; 150;. Very seldom in the 2nd person throughout the whole psalm: 8; 65; 139.1-18; cf. Isa. 25.1-5. More often a mixture of 3rd and 2nd person: 9.6-13; 48; 66.1-12; 67; 68; 76; 77.14; 84; 89.2f., 6-19; 92; 97; 99; 104; 135; 145; Ex. 15. See Gunkel-Begrich, *Einl.*, p. 47.

[22] His name: Pss. 8.2; 9.3; 75.2; 76.2; 96.2; 102.13; 111.9; 113.3; 135.3, 13; 148.13. His arm or hand: 48.11; 49.14; Ex. 15.6. His voice: Ps. 29. His words: 12.7; 18.31; 33.4. His testimonies (i.e. promises): 93.5. His commandments: 19.8ff. His eyes: 11.4; 33.18; 34.16; 66.7. His face: 34.17. His plans and thoughts: 33.11; 92.6. His deeds: 33.9; 66.3; 86.8; 92.6; 104.24; 111.2, 3, 7. His wonders: 9.2; 96.3. His ways: 18.31; 25.10; 77.14; Deut. 32.4. His judgments; Pss. 36.7; 48.12; 97.8; 105.7. His dominion and empire; 103.19; 45.13. His throne: 11.4; 93.2. His highness and glory: 8.2; 68.35; 138.5; 145.3; 148.13. His *tĕhillôth* (praises): 48.11; 111.10. His 'mercy and grace and slowness to anger': 103.8; 145.8. His goodness and faithfulness: 31.20; 36.6, 8; 57.11; 63.4; 86.13; 89.3, 15; 100.5; 103.11, 17; 136. His justice (i.e. his saving activity): 36.7; 111.3. His wisdom: 147.5.

[22a] Other instances: Pss. 5.13; 9.9; 11.4-6; 25.8f.; 29.3, 5f.,·8; 33.5, 7, 10; 36.7; 68.7, 20, 36; 84.12; 90.3, 5; 97.10; 103.6, 9f., 13f.; 111.5; 135.6, 14; 138.6; 145.14, 16, 19f.; 147.6, 11, 18; 148.14.

[23] Further examples: Ex. 15.2, 21; Pss. 16.7; 22.25; 24.2; 28.6; 31.22; 52.11; 54.9; 59.17; 66.20; 86.13; 92.5; 95.5; 100.3; 102.26; 103.19; 111.4, 6, 9; 147.13; 1 Sam. 2.8c. See Gunkel-Begrich, *Einl.*, pp. 51f.

Cf. also the description of the crossing of the Jordan in Ps. 114, or the struggle against the primordial dragon in Ps. 74.13–17—in itself a national public psalm of lamentation, but with hymnal motivations of the prayer.[23a]

At times there may also occur the more sentimental, admiring, rhetorical questions: 'Who is like Yahweh?' or an exclamation,[24] or the indicative statement,[25] 'There is no one holy as Yahweh, no rock like our God'. The last form may also become a juxtaposition of Yahweh and other deities: 'For all the gods of the nations are idols: but Yahweh made the heavens'.[26]

It may be due to later developments that hymns occasionally give a more graphic and epic description of one of Yahweh's great works— particularly of the creation, as in Pss. 8; 29; and 104—or of one of his qualities, for instance his superiority over all cosmic and terrestrial enemies. In such cases where the epic-mythical tendency comes to the fore, it presents Yahweh's superiority in the guise of one great mythico-historical victory over all enemies at once, as in Pss. 46; 48; and 76. This is particularly in evidence in the epiphany and enthronement psalms (see below, Chap. V).

But in this epic-mythical form there remains also an original trait from the cultic experience: the hymn concentrates on the praise of that particular act of salvation which Yahweh has now come to the festival to renew; and the description of this circumstance is introduced as an epic strain in the song. At this point, the brief, enumerative style with the independent quasi-detached single sentences is replaced by a broader, more graphic description.

There thus arise *two main types* of hymns: first, the more general one which simply enumerates or points out God's lasting qualities and glorious deeds, a form which may suit any cultic occasions, both daily and festal; secondly, the more special one, which more fully depicts one particular feature of divine activity, a single fundamental act of salvation, a single situation in his both self-assertive and protective struggle. The second type appears to belong to one particular kind of cultic festival, and celebrates Yahweh for the salvation, or the great work, which is to be remembered. Hymns of this type are e.g. Pss. 46; 48; 76; 114.

A representative sample of the first type is Ps. 136:

> O give thanks unto Yahweh, for he is good:
>> for his kindness endureth for ever . . .
> to him who alone doeth wonders,
> to him whose wisdom made the heavens,
> to him who stretched out the earth above the waters,
> to him who made the great lights . . .

[23a] Further examples: Pss. 31.8f.; 44.3f.; 66.10–12; 71.19f.; 77.16–21; 80.9–12; 89.11–13; 99.6–8; 135.9–12; 148.5f.; see Gunkel-Begrich, *Einl.*, p. 52. Several of these psalms are psalms of lamentation with hymnic 'motivations of the prayer' (see below, Chap. VI. 3).

[24] For instance Pss. 8.2, 10; 36.8; 66.3; 92.6; 104.24; 106.2; 113.5; Ex. 15.11. See Gunkel-Begrich, *Einl.*, p. 54f.

[25] 1 Sam. 2.2; Deut. 33.26; Ps. 86.8; see Gunkel-Begrich, *Einl.*, p. 55. On the psalm Deut. 33.2–5, 26–29 see Mowinckel, *Der Achtundsechzigste Psalm*, pp. 75ff. and below, Chap. V, n. 136.

[26] Pss. 96.5; 146.5ff.; Gunkel-Begrich, *Einl.*, pp. 55f.

> to him who killed Egypt's firstborn,
> and brought out Israel from among them . . .
> to him who divided the Reed Lake in sunder
> and made Israel to pass through it . . .
> who giveth food to all flesh!
> o give thanks to the God of heaven!

Each line is here marked by the antiphonic 'for his kindness endureth for ever', two choirs—or a choir-master and a choir—alternately singing a line.

Another typical sample of the appositional style may be found in the book of Amos, in the fragments of a hymn of praise about Yahweh as creator and ruler of the universe: He

> who formed the mountains and created the winds,
> who reveals to man what is in His mind,
> who made the dawn and the darkness,
> who marches over the heights of the earth . . .
> who made the Pleiades and Orion . . .
> who turns the darkness into dawn
> and darkens the day into night,
> who calls upon the waters of the sea
> and pours them out on the surface of the earth.

The other type is more varied and often employs the traditional forms in a free manner. The introductory exhortation may be lacking, and the psalm may open with a revering and glorifying exclamation:

> O Yahweh our Lord, how excellent
> is thy name in all the earth (Ps. 8.2.)

Or with a statement:

> In Judah has God made himself known
> his name is great in Israel (Ps. 76.2.)

> Great is Yahweh, and greatly to be praised
> in the city of our God (Ps. 48.2.)

> God is shelter and stronghold for us,
> as a help in trouble he is always found (Ps. 46.2.)

The praise itself, the principal part of the hymn, may take the form of a series of declarations of confidence, with more or less detailed and graphic reference to the relevant acts of salvation. Thus, for instance, in Ps. 46, which goes on as follows:

Therefore will we not fear, though the earth be removed,
 though the mountains move in the midst of the sea.
May the sea roar and its water be troubled,
 may the mountains shake by its haughtiness:
Yahweh the Almighty[27] is with us;
 the God of Jacob is our refuge. (Ps. 46.3-4.)

Following this reference to the victory over the primeval sea is a mention of the wondrous 'river of God' which is now safeguarding and sanctifying Jerusalem; further, we hear of the Lord's presence in his Temple—the victory over all the peoples of the earth which his coming wil¹ secure, the subjugation of all evil powers, and the peace which he establishes on earth. The psalm ends with Yahweh calling his enemies to submission and declaring that he alone is God:

Be still and know that I am God,
 high over the nations, high over the earth. (v. 10.)

The final refrain sums up the conclusion and repeats once more the chief subject of the psalm: the people's unshakable trust in the only, almighty God, who has again shown that he 'is with us'. Higher praise than the confession that it builds its whole existence on this trust, the congregation cannot give.

At times these special festal hymns may contain an almost epic description of the divine act of deliverance which is praised, as for instance the account of 'the king's' advance on Jerusalem in Ps. 48, and of the annihilation of the enemies on the appearance of Yahweh. See also the description in Ps. 114 of how the sea fled and the Jordan was driven back, and 'the mountains leaped like rams', when Yahweh led Israel out of Egypt and made a covenant with her on Mount Sinai, and the poet's ironical triumphant question: 'What ails thee, sea, that thus thou fleest? Thou Jordan, that thou makest way?' Or the description of Yahweh's victory over the nations in Ps. 76.2-7.

The praising clauses may be varied by an exhortation to the congregation to come and see the great work which the Lord has now accomplished:

Come and see the deeds of Yahweh . . .
 who maketh wars to cease unto the ends of the earth,
breaking the bow and snapping the spear
 and burning the shields in the fire. (Ps. 46.9-10.)

Or, by a statement:

As we have heard, we now have seen
 in the city of our God. (Ps. 48.9.)

---

[27] For this interpretation of *yhwh ṣĕbā 'ôth* see Eissfeldt, 'Jahwe Zebaoth' in *Miscellanea Academ. Berolin.*, 1950, pp. 126ff. Maag ('Jahwäs Heerscharen' in *Köhler-Festschrift*, p. 50) sees in *ṣĕbā'ôth* 'die depotenzierten mythischen Naturmächte Kanaans'.

In the background we find everywhere the traditional elements and forms of the hymn; but the composition itself is very far from following any set pattern or schedule.

The subject of the hymn of praise is, as already mentioned, Yahweh's glorious qualities and his great works, both those which he regularly repeats in nature—including the creation, which at an early stage became a main subject of the hymn of praise—and his great deeds in history, especially in the history of Israel. Particularly in later psalm-poetry, which is influenced by the wisdom-poetry and its didactic, admonitory tendency (see below, Chap. XVII), the wonderful works of Yahweh in ancient times, the election at the time of Moses and at the occupation of Canaan, became a favourite subject, as in Pss. 78 and 105; here there is a marked admonitory strain.

But Yahweh may also be praised more indirectly, by exalting all that belongs to him: his Temple, his holy city, and the blessings which flow from that place where the fountain of life is and where strength is to be found.

> Blessed are they that dwell in thy house:
>   they shall ever be praising thee.
> Blessed the man whose strength is through thee,
>   in whose heart are the paved ways . . .
> They are the stronger as they go
>   till they see the God in Zion.   (Ps. 84.5, 6, 8.)

And of Zion it is said:

> The singers like the dancers (are praising thee):
>   'All my springs are in thee'.   (Ps. 87.7.)

But beneath the praise of the hymn lingers something of the old idea that Yahweh in the festal cult repeats his great works and acts of deliverance; the congregation praises him for what they have themselves experienced; the particular great deed that he has come to the festival to perform again becomes an important subject for the praise. This is particularly clear in the epiphany hymns (see below, pp. 92, 94f.).

The song of praise endeavours to glorify Yahweh to the utmost, to increase his power and renown. Joy, enthusiasm and adoration are its dominant moods. They refer to God himself, not to the needs of man; hence the hymn rarely ends with a prayer (see below, p. 89). Man falls down in worship of the only God, the Holy One.[28] From this, however, faith gains new power. The hymn of praise 'gives power' to Yahweh (Ps. 29.1), but it also provides the congregation with new strength and faith.[29] In the first beginnings of the hymn the naïve idea of flattering the

[28] Cf. also Eissfeldt, ' "Mein Gott" im A.T.', *ZATW* 61, 1945–48, p. 11.
[29] Ps. 84.8. Cf. Ex. 15.2; Isa. 12.2.

deity, of 'smoothing the face of Yahweh' and mollifying him, no doubt played a part; but the deepest motif is the adoration of the Holy One, the experiencing of him as the 'terrible' and the 'glorious', he that humbles and raises up, that 'abases and exalts'.

The hymns of praise express the consciousness of standing before Yahweh personally and of experiencing him as he really is. At the festivals—and particularly at the harvest and new year festival, the chief annual festival (see Chap. V), all Yahweh's great deeds and acts of deliverance were recalled; then the coming of Yahweh and his 'salvation' was experienced; it is the eventuating God, the God who 'reveals himself' and 'saves', to whom the festal hymn is addressed. He, indeed, proves 'terrible' to all enemies, both his own and those of Israel, but is full of kindness and faithfulness and 'saving justice' towards his loyal folk. The hymn greets him as he returns at the festal service to abide with his people and work all his wonders anew. Hence trust becomes one of the dominant moods of the hymn.

Occasionally the hymn closes with a brief wish or *prayer* for the future prosperity of the congregation (Pss. 29.11; 104.31f.; 135.19), or of the poet himself (Pss. 19.14f.; 138.8). As a rule it is couched in general terms. Stylistically this is a relic from the mixed, less pure types of older times (see below, pp. 95f.), rather than evidence of a later mixture of styles. But this kind of conclusion does express a deep and original religious need: to give up oneself and one's cause to such a glorious and mighty God, and to know oneself safe in his care. We find it in some of the most characteristic and personal hymns, e.g. Pss. 84; 104; 125. We meet, in Israel, too, with a phenomenon which is very common in the cultic songs of Babylonia and Assyria, in which a fully formed hymn of praise is used as an introduction to a lament or a petition. A good instance is Pss. 9–10, really one psalm. It is natural that the trust here comes markedly into prominence beside the praise, as is also the case in Pss. 90 and 139. In the same way a psalm of thanksgiving and trust may be used as introduction to a psalm of petition, as in Pss. 27 and 40.

The hymn was recited to the playing of stringed intruments, cymbals and the flute, to which there is frequent reference (see Ps. 150 and above, pp. 8ff.). It often goes together with the cultic dance as we have seen above. Both accompaniments are common in the most widely differing religions,[30] and distinctly belong to the cult.[31]

On the whole the hymn clearly shows its place of origin to be the holy place, to which there is frequent reference. The hymn belongs to the cultic festival[31a] where the people gathers and experiences the Lord's presence and the repetition of all his great works, and remembers what he has done

[30] Cf. Heiler, *Das Gebet*,[4] pp. 159f.
[31] Cf. Oesterley, *The Sacred Dance*.
[31a] Allusions to the holy place and the Temple: Pss. 65.2; 76.3; 84.3, 5; 87.7; 95.2, 6; 100.2, 4; 134.1; 135.2; 138.2; cf. 48.2f.; 89.13. Hymn singing at the sacrifice: Amos 5.21–23; Ps. 96.8; cf. 1 Chron. 23.30f.; 2 Chron. 23.18; 29.27f.; 1 Macc. 4.52ff.

and constantly does. Later on it was also used in the daily service which was gradually evolved in the great temples.[32] Particularly in connexion with the daily morning sacrifices—as generally with sacrificial acts— hymns were sung.[33] But also with the processions to the Temple or round the altar there was singing, as we see from Pss. 24 and 118. Still later on perhaps also the pilgrim crowds sang, when they marched in through the gates of Jerusalem.[34]

In the official congregational service of Israel, the hymn of praise always had a prominent place. To praise God was more and more regarded as a main feature of the cult; its aim and intention was to 'give to God the glory'. The collectors of the book of Psalms looked upon all psalm recital as praise of the Lord and his works, his righteousness, faithfulness, and loving kindness; they accordingly gave to the whole book of Psalms the title: 'Hymns of praise' (těhillîm).

2

It was not unusual to praise Yahweh in a more indirect way by a more detailed laudation of separate benefits which he had bestowed on his people: the Temple, the holy city, etc.[35] In this way there arose several varieties of the hymn of praise.

In the first place must be mentioned the so-called 'Zion-hymns' (as Gunkel called them, using an expression from Ps. 137.3). Instances are Pss. 48; 84; 87 and 122. The type is never unmixed; the 'Zion-hymn' is a motif among others, interchanging with the direct praise of Yahweh. For, of course, it is God himself to whom these hymns give the glory; it is because *he* is there and reveals himself and does his beneficial works of victory and deliverance that 'glorious things can be spoken of Zion'. The most characteristic Zion-hymn is Ps. 87. A special place is taken by Ps. 122 with its deeply personal tone and its free treatment of motifs from other types of poetry, namely, the pilgrim song and the benediction.

Another variety is the hymn to the Law of the Lord, e.g. Ps. 19B. To later Judaism the law appeared as Yahweh's greatest benefaction to his people, as is also expressly said by one of the psalm poets (Ps. 147.20). Through the law Yahweh bestows his blessings on the people and on the individual; Ps. 119, which is intended as a petition, is largely a hymn to the law.[35a]

It is characteristic of the composer of Ps. 19 and his attitude to the law that he has chosen to associate his praise with an evidently very old hymn to the Creator and to the sun; and has used the latter as an introduction to his poem. The thought is clear: in the same way as the sun is the most

[32] Ps. 89.17; 1 Chron. 9.33; Sir. 47.8.
[33] Ps. 100.1; Am. 5.22f.; Sir. 47.8.
[34] This may perhaps be concluded from Ps. 122.1. See, however, below, Chap XVI. 2, p. 311.
[35] Even in Egypt we find this 'indirect' hymn, eulogies of the sanctuary, the royal crown, and so on. See Erman, *Lit. d. Aegypt.*, pp. 337ff., 365ff. (E.T., pp. 270ff.; 295ff.)
[35a] See Mowinckel 'Loven og de 8 termini i Sl. 119', *NTT* 61, 1961, pp. 95ff.

glorious gift of the Creator to his creatures, as regards their physical and material life—no life without sun—thus is the law, with regard to their spiritual life, the 'wisdom' without which a man can neither lead a worthy life nor enjoy it. As the sun illuminates the world from one end to the other, so the law illuminates man both religiously and morally. As nothing is 'hidden' from the rays of the sun, so the law is 'a light to the mind', so that even the 'simplest' becomes 'wise' and can distinguish between right and wrong.[36] For the law of the Lord is not merely statutes, arbitrary regulations, commandments which might have been otherwise: it is a revelation, full of grace, of that fundamental law of all existence which lies in the plan of creation, which must be followed if one is not to collide with the basic laws of life and perish; God's moral and religious law is—to use a modern term—as essentially 'biological' law as the 'natural' laws of physics and chemistry. Hence it is a special mercy that God has revealed this law of life to Israel—'which he has not done to any other people'.

Meditation also hit upon the hymn as its most natural mode of expression. Thus the introductory part of Ps. 90 has become a song of praise to God's everlastingness as a background to a prayer for mercy towards short-lived man:

> Lord, thou has been our dwelling place,
>   in all generations art thou, O God;
> Before the mountains were brought forth,
>   before the earth bore and the continent brought forth.[37]
>
> Thou turnest man back to the dust,
>   and sayest: 'Return, ye children of men'.
> For a thousand years when they are past
>   are but as yesterday unto thee.   (Ps. 90.2–4.)

In the introductory part of Ps. 139 the poet dwells on God's inscrutable wisdom, his omniscience and omnipresence, in dogmatic parlance, and describes it in terms of praise and adoration, borrowed from the thoughts and language of the hymn of praise:

> Yahweh, thou dost explore me throughout,
>   (thou knowest me and all within me) :[38]
> Thou knowest me, my sitting and rising,
>   my very thoughts thou readest from afar.
>
> Thou measurest my path and my lying down,
>   and thou attendest to all my ways.
> For the word is not yet on my tongue—
>   thou, Yahweh, knowest it altogether.

[36] For details on Ps. 19 see Additional Note XL.
[37] On the idea of 'Mother Earth', who has borne the mountains, as well as living beings, see my paper in *Lehmannfestskrift*, 1927, pp. 130ff. MT vocalization *wattĕhôlēl* (passive) is correct; the subject of the clause is *'ereṣ wĕthēbhēl*.
[38] As the psalm is written in regular stanzas, a 'colon' is missed after v.1, the remnant of which is *'attâ* in v.2.

Thou besettest me behind and before,
and layest thy hand upon me (ever).
(Thy) insight is too wonderful for me,
too high—I cannot comprehend it.

Whither should I go from thy spirit,
whither should I flee from thy presence?
If I climb up to heaven, thou art there,
if I make my bed in She'ol, thou art there.

If I could take the wings of the dawn,
and dwell on the other side of the ocean,
Even there thy hand should hold me,
thy right hand take me even there . . .

For thou, thou hast made my reins,
thou hast woven me in my mother's womb,
I praise thee, Yahweh, for thou art awful
and wonderful, thy works are wonders.

Thou knowest my soul even since that time,
my bone-structure was not hid from thee
At the time when I was made in secret,
and wrought in the depths of the earth.

Thine eyes did see all my days,
and in thy book they all were written.
The days were found (and destined for me)
while yet there was not one of them.   (Ps.139.1–10, 13–16.)

In Babylonian–Assyrian psalm poetry we frequently meet with a variety of the hymn, which we might term the *I-hymn*: the god comes forth and tells his name and reveals his character in hymnal form, enumerating his mighty deeds and his divine qualities. This form, of course, arises from the idea of the self-revelation or 'epiphany' of the deity.[39] The book of Psalms contains no such hymn; but that it was known and used also in Israel in connexion with the epiphany of Yahweh, is evident, from, among other things, the hymnal expressions in the self-presentation of Yahweh in a psalm like 81.7–11; cf. Ps. 50.7b. We see it also from the poet's and prophet's imitation of this hymnal form; the whole of Yahweh's speech in the book of Job, chaps. 38ff., is a grand 'I-hymn'; Deutero-Isaiah, too, every now and then lets Yahweh present himself in like manner to his people in order to stir up their faith in his power and will to save them.

[39] For details see below Chap. V.3, 8, pp. 109ff. and 140f. The 'I-hymn' may be found also in the Egyptian-Hellenistic religion; see, for instance, the rendering of the Isis-hymn from Kyme by Schubart in *AO*, XXXV, 2, p. 27. There is also an echo of this mode of composition in the royal inscriptions with their introductory 'I am' and their self-praising enumeration of the great achievements of the king; cf. Mowinckel in (*Gunkel Festschrift*) *Eucharisterion* I[*FRLANT* 36], pp. 278ff.

In this way Deutero-Isaiah emphasizes the position of Yahweh as the only God, the creator of the world and the governor of history and the absolute superior of all strange gods.

The hymn has also been used as an expression of the *individual man's worship* of Yahweh, the Exalted, the Almighty, good and merciful. Such a poem is the 'alphabetic' hymn, Ps. 145.

The creation hymn, Ps. 104, has the same form. It starts with a 'Bless the Lord, O my soul' (i.e. with a song of praise), and ends in a similarly personal manner:

> I will sing unto Yahweh as long as I live,
>> touch the strings to my God while I have my being—
> May then my recital be sweet unto him,
>> that I may have my joy in Yahweh. (Ps. 104.33–34.)

Also in the hymn to the law, Ps. 19, the poet concludes with a reference to his poem, and a wish that it may incline Yahweh to mercy.

It has been supposed that this I-form is more recent than the We-form,[40] but this is disproved by the fact that the I-form practically holds the field in both Babylonian and Ugaritic hymn poetry. From the point of view of style the I-form is really just a variation of that I-form which is implied in the introductory exhortation to praise the Lord: it is the poet-singer himself who in the capacity of choir-master and reciter, exhorts the choir to join in the praises with antiphonies and shouts of homage; the poet imagines himself as precentor and choir-master. This does not prevent there being something consciously personal in the occasional use of this form in Israelite psalm poetry; the very fact that it is so rarely used shows that it has such an intention: the poet desires to give expression to his personal religion and to come under the eye of the deity, whom he worships, and upon whom he knows himself to be wholly dependent.

In other cases the I-form is due to the fact that the psalm in question is not really a congregational hymn, but a personal song of thanksgiving (see Chap. X). In Ps. 103 it is a single individual who makes use of a hymn and its general terms, to express his thanks for the help that he has received from God in sickness and distress—in other words, it is a psalm of thanksgiving in the style of the hymn of praise.

This personal stamp, then, does not imply that the psalm was not meant for cultic use. The poet knows that the whole congregation can and will join in. The composer of Ps. 104, as well, speaks on behalf of the cultic congregation. That is the reason for concluding with the wish for the destruction of the 'sinners', the 'ungodly', all Yahweh's and Israel's enemies, who do not acknowledge the Lord.

---

[40] Gunkel-Begrich, *Einl.*, p. 92; cf. Baumgartner 'Ugaritische Probleme u. i. Trageweite f.d. A. T.', *ThZ* III, p. 94.

3

Is it possible to connect the different individual hymns with definite festivals? This is not always easy, but in certain cases it can be done.

In Judaism the Exodus from Egypt was particularly associated with the *Passover*. This association existed even in early times. As we know, the Passover was the chief religious festival of the semi-nomads before the Entry into Canaan, and there is every reason to believe that it is a true historical tradition which—already in the most ancient records—connects the Exodus with the Passover.

It is, then, natural to conclude that the hymns which dwell on the Exodus belong to this festival. But in the period immediately after the Occupation the Passover seems to have played a less important role, and there is much that suggests that the recollection of the Exodus and the making of the covenant in earlier times was connected with the harvest and new year festival as well (see Chap. V.6).

That many hymns belong to the harvest thanksgiving which, after the settlement and down to a late period, was the main festival, stands to reason. The feast of Tabernacles, held from the fifteenth to the twenty-first of the seventh—in older times the eighth—month,[41] at the beginning of the rainy season, was for long, purely and simply 'the feast of Yahweh'. This feast was distinguished by Yahweh 'appearing', 'making himself known', revealing himself, and being personally present in the midst of his chosen people, visible to the opened eye of faith, and to the outward eye as well, through his visible symbol, the ark of the covenant. There the congregation gathered 'before the face of Yahweh' and 'he came to them and blessed them' (cf. Ex. 20.24). This happened at all festivals, but especially at 'the feast of Yahweh'. The harvest festival was, above all, the feast of Yahweh's *Epiphany*, to use the Greek expression for the same idea, later adopted by the Church.[42] Psalms which speak of Yahweh having manifested himself in Judah (76.1) or having 'shined out of Zion' (50.2) belong to this festival, or have at least sprung from this group of ideas and present the thoughts and experiences which originally belonged to it. The feast of harvest and tabernacles was above all a festival of harvest home, with special reference to the olives;[43] it was therefore also termed 'the feast of ingathering' or 'feast of harvesting' (*hagh hā'āsîph, hagh haqqāṣîr* Ex. 34.22; 23.16). Thanks were then given for the year's crops, and they were made available for human use by sacrifices and

---

[41] This may be concluded from 1 Kgs. 12.32.

[42] See Pfister, art. 'Epiphanie' in Pauly-Wissowa, *Real. Encyclop. d. Class. Altertumswiss.* Supplementband IV, cols. 277ff. The term is used rather comprehensively of any 'appearance' of a deity, whether in the myth or in the oracle or in dreams or through powerful deeds, etc., but especially indicates the appearance and presence and powerful revelation of the god at the cultic festival; whether literally 'visible' to the senses, or visible in symbols or in the experience of faith, is of little importance. The Greeks often looked upon the epiphany day of the god as the 'festival of his birth', where they experienced that marked appearance of which the myth relates.

[43] See Albright in *BASOR* 92, 1943, p. 22, n. 30.

ceremonies. On the same occasion the foundation of the blessing for the new year was also laid; efficacious rites were intended to ensure rain and fertility and new life; the 'coming' and 'appearance' of Yahweh at the feast was a promise of a good 'year of grace'. Prayers in which this fertility aspect of the feast appears are preserved in Deut. 26. 1–15. And there were certainly also psalms giving expression to the same feature. To this festival belong hymns of thanksgiving for the harvest of the year, like Pss. 65 and 67—probably also such psalms as dwell, not only on the appearing of Yahweh, but also on the work of salvation which he has thereby repeated, e.g. Pss. 29; 76 and several others.

Ps. 81 is a new year psalm. In early times the harvest feast (Tabernacles) was also the new year festival; in later Judaism a specific new year's *day* was established, namely, the first day of the seventh month (*Tishri*). To this day belonged the new year psalms proper. But the feast of Tabernacles always retained a strong impress of the new year festival and of the thoughts and ideas associated with it, namely the epiphany of Yahweh, the creation, the 'turning of fortune', and its fixing, i.e. the determining (*šāphaṭ* in the original sense of 'determining', 'establishing', 'fixing')[44] of that which was to happen in the coming year, the renewal of the covenant, and the re-living of memories from the Exodus. We shall examine this many-sided festival further in the next chapter.

4

The hymn of praise has also left its mark on other psalm types. It is not unusual for the psalm of petition or lament to commence with a laudatory introduction, which to us moderns may appear quite independent of the following lament and prayer. See Pss. 9–10; 27; 40; and compare also 90 and 139, which have been mentioned above.

That here it is not a case of a fortuitous collocation or coupling of two independent poems—as some scholars have been inclined to think[45]— but of deliberate composition on the part of the poet is proved, i.a. by Ps. 9–10, which is linked together by the 'alphabetic' scheme formed by the initial letters in each line.

The laudatory introduction has a double purpose, or perhaps rather, a double root. Firstly it is a primary expression of one aspect of the fundamental feeling in the person who is approaching the deity: the attraction, enthusiasm, confidence of him or her who 'knows God'. But then it is also the expression of a more naïvely utilitarian attitude: the suppliant

---

[44] Cf. the original meaning of the Old Norse *døma*, Ags. *dôman* = express an opinion, a decision, determine, establish, fix.

[45] So, for instance, Duhm, *Die Psalmen*, both as regards the psalms mentioned and many others. Even Gunkel treats Ps. 27 as two quite independent poems, and his explanation of 'the context' in Pss. 9–10 (see above, p. 32) is most superficial, just as he does not display any really organic understanding of the idea and intention of Pss. 90 and 139. On the unity of Ps. 27 see Birkeland, 'Die Einheitlichkeit von Ps. 27', *ZATW* 51, 1933, pp. 216ff.

tries to gain Yahweh's favour and induce him to grant the following petition; it belongs to the 'motivation of the prayer' (see below, Chap. VI.3),
appealing to Yahweh's sense of honour, and his obligations in regard to
the petitioner's trust in him; or, as in Ps. 90, the appeal may be to the pity
which the Eternal must feel for mortals; or, as in Ps. 139, to his complete
knowledge of the petitioner's life and thoughts.

Looking at it from the point of view of the form alone, the opinion has
often been expressed that this composite type was a secondary development: the pure hymn of praise was here supposed to have influenced other
types, or to have been subjected to their influence.[46] But this is not correct.

Both the element of prayer which we occasionally find in the hymn of
praise proper, and a comparison with the hymns of the other oriental
nations, and with the ritual songs of primitive peoples prove that the
hymn as a pure type has been brought about by the development of a
single element in the preceding, more complicated prayer songs.[47] The
oldest ritual songs are properly prayers which are introduced by, or framed
and interwoven with, laudatory elements. These latter have a practical
aim in that they are to help to make the deity favourably disposed towards
the suppliant. But they have also, as mentioned, another, purely religious
root. The praise of God's greatness and glory, goodness and care is the
immediate reaction of the soul to all this; it emerges spontaneously from
the encounter with the Holy One, inconceivable and yet revealed, who at
the same time isolates himself and attracts, who excites reverence and fear,
but also enthusiasm, joy and gratitude. Because this response is so essential
an element in religion generally, ritual prayer tends to produce a special
form for this aspect of the approach to the deity: the *hymn of praise*, from
which the other elements—the lament, the prayer, the persuasion, supplication—are suppressed or even eliminated, to form their own type of
prayer psalm, the psalm of lament and petition.

The blend of praise and prayer is thus a survival from an older stage.
In Babylonian and Assyrian psalm poetry it is almost the rule.[48] That the
praise should be used to support the prayer corresponds to a more primitive
and naïve stage of religion; it is the higher stage and purer state of religion
which feels the praise and the adoration as a, so to speak, independent
and necessary religious act, and which adores and praises God for his own
sake without selfish motives.

Actually it is a common law of evolution that the unmixed, simple
forms are later than the composite and undifferentiated ones; in the
history of art also, 'pure' forms are often later than the 'mixed' and undifferentiated ones. 'Mixture of styles' may often be a misleading expression when applied to those types which have grown spontaneously and are
therefore many-sided; that there may also come about a really secondary

---

[46] This is the opinion of Gunkel, see *Einl.*, pp. 84f., cf. 92f.
[47] See Heiler, *Das Gebet*,[4] pp. 157ff.
[48] See Cumming, *Accadian Hymns of Praise*, who has also seen from this standpoint that the
puristic style belongs to a later, distinctly Israelite phase of development.

mixture of originally pure styles is a circumstance that we shall return to later (Chap. XIV.3). The oldest and most characteristic, the most artistically superior and poetically powerful hymns in the Old Testament— e.g. Jdg. 5; Pss. 8; 19A; 68—are those that are most difficult to subject to the general rule of style described above. The great poet is often heedless of conventional rules.

But there are also instances where we can rightly speak of literary influence from the laudatory style. The laudatory form has been used both by other poets and by the prophets to express their views of God and their relation to him. In the book of Job the three friends are constantly proclaiming in hymnal terms God's power and justice and peerlessness and the duty of man to subject himself to his judgments; and they instance, as a proof of his might and power, creation and the struggle with chaos and his judgment of the ungodly. Passages like Job 9.3–13; 12.13–25; 25.2–6; 26.5–14 are, both with regard to style and to content, pure hymns. When Deutero-Isaiah proclaims the shortly forthcoming salvation with his 'Thus saith Yahweh', he frequently adds to this introductory formula a series of hymnic elements, painting God's power and faithfulness, which are to convince the Jews that it is Yahweh and he alone that rules the world, and that he both can and will save his people. Occasionally the prophet is carried away by his enthusiasm so as to give expression to his personal joy and gladness in ecstatic hymnal exclamations.[49]

5

It is particularly in the hymns of praise that we meet with that conception, or perhaps better, that picture of Yahweh as he lived in Israel's consciousness. Thus it will be well to look more closely at the conception of God which is to be found in the psalms.[50] In the hymns of praise we find all the elements of the complete picture. In these Yahweh is praised, thanked and adored for those qualities to which the laments and prayer psalms appeal.

It is really surprising to see how homogeneous the picture of the divine is in the psalms. The inner tension of the historical 'development' in Israel's religion and its conception of God, is little felt in the book of Psalms. The struggle against the Canaanite element is only faintly reflected. Nor is it the contribution of the prophets that we find here. The Yahweh of the main stock of psalms is absolutely superior to all other gods and powers, the only one worthy of the name 'God'. But he is not the only one; the other gods are there as realities, partly as his adversaries whom he conquers and triumphs over and then annihilates, partly as his

[49] See Koehler, *Deuterojesaja*, pp. 120ff.; cf. *GTMMM* III, pp. 52f., 190.
[50] For the following cf. Gunkel-Begrich, *Einl.*, pp. 71ff.; T. H. Robinson in *The Psalmists*, ed. Simpson, pp. 23ff.; P. Synave in art. 'Psaumes' in *Dict. Theol. Catholique*, Paris, 1936, XIII, col. 1115ff. (highly systematizing, according to dogmatic categories).

heavenly 'council', his servants, who pay homage to him, and who, either jubilantly or in fear and trepidation, do as he tells them. It is not the mono-theism of the later prophets, and even less the abstract intellectual mono-theism of Greek philosophy, that we meet with in the psalms. In a way it is the pre-prophetic Yahweh we find here, as he appeared to the experience and belief of those circles which gradually came to put their spiritual and intellectual stamp on the official cult in Jerusalem. In that way it provides one of the main grounds for the appearance and work of the major pro-phets. But the activities of the prophets assisted in at least touching up the image of Yahweh presented in the psalms. We shall in later chapters see how the Yahweh of the psalms has, so to speak, defined his relation to the other gods, and how the prophetic institution and the particularly Israelite prophetic movement had their connexion both with the cult and with the psalm poetry; and we may at once state that a not inconsiderable part of the psalm poetry chronologically follows the great classical pro-phecies, the work of the prophets both of judgment and of restoration, and that certain features of the latter may also be seen in the psalms. There *are* also psalms which are marked by the spirit of early Judaism and its whole conception of God after the full victory of monotheistic thought (115.1ff.; 135.15ff.; 96.6; 97.7). But in these younger psalms it is not the struggle against Canaanite influences which we face; it is the spirit of self-conscious Judaism, feeling its superiority over the stupid polytheism of the surrounding 'idolaters'. On the whole the psalms speak about the Yahweh of the cult of Jerusalem, as he had come to be conceived already before the time of Amos and Isaiah, etc. It means that without the religious development here attained, the appearance and spiritual type of the later prophets would have been unthinkable.

What we can see clearly from the psalms is what Yahweh became in the conception, thought and experience of believers, as a result of the collision between the historic Israel and the Canaanites, and the religio-historical victory of the historic Yahweh, over the gods of Canaan. The people, the *cultic congregation* which stands behind the psalms, is the historical Israel, the result of that full amalgamation of Israel and the natives which reached its final stage with the reign of David and Solomon. The religion behind the psalms is the one that developed as a result of the work of David when he introduced the Yahweh cult as the cult of the royal house and the realm in Jerusalem, founded on both the historical traditions of Israel and the inheritance from the pre-Israelite cult of 'El-'Elyôn, 'The Supreme God' in Jerusalem. It is the 'God of the fathers', the God of the election and the covenant and the historic revelation, whom we here meet, he who has chosen Israel as his people and demonstrated by great historical deeds, in real historical experiences, that he is the one 'who is' (Ex. 3.14). He is active and powerful, and acts in real events. He is superior to all other gods, and orders other peoples' fates as he thinks good to attain his aims for his chosen people. He is the God whose 'rights' and 'laws' go back to the practice and tradition of the time of Kadesh and Sinai, the mighty historical God of the time of the desert wandering and the invasion.

But he is also the God of Canaan, the promised land, the settled country and the kingdom, who has seated himself on the seat of Baal and El-Elyon and the Lord of Heaven. The Yahweh of the psalms and of the cult of Jerusalem is the God who has taken over everything of value, everything great and elevated in the whole previous religious development, all the ideas of the divine, and all the higher religious feelings among the people whose culture Israel took over. But then we must immediately qualify this by adding: in so far as this culture could be united with the religion of the times of Moses and the settlement and with the historical traditions about Yahweh. The Yahweh of the psalms is the God both of creation and the life-force, of the rain and the sun, of fertility and expanding life, of war and justice, and law and order; in a nutshell: for Israel, he is the God of the 'world'. But he is also the god who represents the opposition to and negation of all those features in the conception of the deity in the neighbouring countries, which made the god into a nature god, a vegetation and fertility god, a representative of the changes in nature beyond good and evil, a dying and rising god of fertility and sexuality. The Yahweh of the psalms has no female partner. Nor is he one with the life and force of nature. He is above it and controls it and gives his blessings through it; or keeps them back, according to his own will, which again means: according to the attitude which his people shows towards his holiness, and his will and his 'right'. If there is reason to believe that in Jerusalem, at the time of David and Solomon, Yahweh still had a more 'syncretistic' and 'Canaanite' or 'Baalized' stamp than the texts of the Old Testament now give direct proof of, this has certainly been much modified in the picture now presented by the psalms, where it can be traced only in figures of speech and poetical embellishments.

If it be the case that some psalms are remnants of recast Canaanite ones as e.g. the description of the sun as the youthful 'hero' and the 'bridegroom' in the picture of the sun in Ps. 19, this has in the extant Israelite version become purely poetical imagery, used as testimony to Yahweh's absolute dominion over sun and stars, heaven and earth. If it be the case that in the time of David and Solomon there still existed cultic images of Yahweh after Canaanite patterns, and that for instance his holy shrine, 'the ark', might have contained such an image,[51] there are in any case no traces of this in the psalms other than traditional pictorial expressions like 'seeing the countenance of the Lord', 'seeing his beauty' etc. If it be the case, once more, that the image of the fertility goddess Asherah, which king Asa removed from the Temple at Jerusalem (1 Kgs. 15.13) was intended to represent Yahweh's female partner, then the view of Yahweh contained in the psalms must on the whole belong to a later time.

[51] Cf. Gressmann, *Die Lade Jahves*, pp. 17ff.; Mowinckel in *RHPhR* IX, 1929, pp. 197ff.

It is the view of God which we find in the psalms which led to exactly that kind of cleansing of the Temple that Asa undertook, and this conception itself has been further developed and fixed through such acts of reformation. The Yahweh of the psalms is the Yahweh who, following the 'Yahwistic' tradition and reaction in the religious history of Israel, has taken from the gods of Canaan all that was worth taking, and who has rid himself of all that could keep him down on their level and make him into just one among the crowd of deities. More than anything else the conception of Yahweh in the psalms bears testimony to the high religious level, the purity and promise of further growth 'in the true line' of the religious history of Israel, and renders historically explicable the fact that it was against the background of this so often unjustly criticized cult religion that the major prophets were able to arise and become instruments for further progress in the history of revelation.[52]

Even though the psalms may know of other gods, Yahweh is after all, the only one who is *the* god, God, comprising all the perfection of divinity (cf. Ps. 50.1)—that which is expressed in the plural form *'Elōhîm*, an abstract plural summing up what makes for divine majesty. It is in perfect agreement with the conception of God in the psalms that Deutero-Isaiah repeatedly hears the Lord say: 'I am He', and in this evidently finds the original sense of the name 'Yahweh'. Yahweh is from everlasting to everlasting,[53] the eternal One who has been before all things and whose years are without end, 'the first and the last' in the words of the second Isaiah. He is the Holy One,[54] raised above the earth,[55] who is unique, powerful and dangerous, but also 'the Holy One of Israel'[56] 'the strong one of Jacob,[57] and sure defence of his people. The two chief aspects of holiness: the awe-inspiring and dangerous on the one hand, and the gloriously attractive and confidence-inspiring on the other,[58] are both included in the idea of God as expressed in the psalms.

He is the one that inspires fear,[59] the majestic and glorious,[60] the most

---

[52] See below, Chap. VIII. 11 (II.18) and Chap. XII. 7 (II.68). That the cultic religion of the psalms is independent of the prophets and older than classical prophecy, roughly speaking, has been realized by Weiser as well, 'Theophanie in d. Pss. u. im Festkult' *Bertholetfestschrift*, p. 526.

[53] Pss. 9.8; 10.16; 29.10; 66.7; 90.1ff.; 93.2; 102.13, 26–28; 103.17; 104.31; 135.13; 145.13; 146.10. The following section after Gunkel, *Einl.*, pp. 71ff.

[54] Pss. 22.4; 89.19; 99.5, 9; 105.3; 111.9.

[55] Pss. 46.11; 97.9; .99.2; 113.4.

[56] Pss. 71.22; 78.41; 89.19; Sir. 50.17. Even in Ps. 22.4 some genitive such as 'Jacob's' is likely to have been dropped after 'Holy'—according to the necessities of the metre. See further Isa. 1.4; 5.19, 24; 10.17, 20; 12.6; 17.7; 41.14, 16, 20; 43.3 and other places; here as in so many other cases the ideas and language of the cultic psalms have been adopted by the prophets.

[57] *'abbîr yiśrā'ēl* Ps. 132.2, 5, cf. Gen. 49.24; Isa. 1.24; 49.26; 60.16. Actually the 'bull' of Israel is a term which has probably been adopted from Canaanitish religion. There Baal is the 'bull', *ibr* in the Ugaritic texts, the hump-backed bull, the bison; see Gordon, *Ugaritic Handbook* II, p. 151, Text 75.30–32, and Anat is the 'cow', see Albright, *Archaeology and the Religion of Israel*, pp. 84ff. In Israel, from being an expression for the fertility of nature, it has become an indication of power.

[58] Cf. Otto, *Das Heilige: mysterium tremendum et fascinosum*. (E.T. *The Idea of the Holy*.)

[59] Pss. 42.3; 66.3; 76.5 (Theod., T); 76.13; 89.8; 96.4; 99.3; 111.9.

[60] Pss. 8.2; 57.6, 12; 66.2; 96.6; 104.31; 108.6; 111.3; 113.4; 145.5; 148.13.

wise,[61] the wonderful,[62] great in deeds and thoughts,[63] the omniscient who searches and knows everything (Ps. 139). And yet he is the caring and loving, the faithful and merciful Lord of his people, and the preserver of all his creatures.[64] All these qualities are attributed to Yahweh by the poets, not as abstract philosophical 'categories' fitting systematically into one another, but as something demonstrated in action by a personal God of whom they have themselves had experience in their national history, in the wonders of nature, and in their own lives.

Yahweh is the peerless one, with whom no other gods can be compared.[65] He is 'the God of gods'[66] and 'King of the gods'.[67] He is 'enthroned in heaven',[68] but all the same near; he 'becomes manifest', 'lets himself be found' in his temple[69] where he 'dwells'[70] and helps those that dwell 'in the low places'.[71] First and last he is the only one, who 'alone' is God, and 'alone' has created all things.[72]

A theme which constantly recurs is that of the creation, in which Yahweh has demonstrated his omnipotence, his wisdom and his loving kindness.[73] We shall in the following chapter see how the psalms look at this, and what it means for their piety. That he is the creator also means that he is the mighty Lord of nature, who 'hath done whatsoever he hath pleased' (Pss. 115.3; 136.6), who governs the whole course of nature, the stars and the rain, the thunder and lightning, and who created growth and fruitfulness and opens his hand and satisfies all that lives, upholds all his creatures, gives them the breath of life, and renews the surface of the earth.[74] 'The Lord killeth and maketh alive', he bringeth down to the grave, and bringeth up, maketh poor and enricheth.[75] In everything man is dependent on his lovingkindness and care.

Yahweh reveals himself especially in all that is striking and extraordinary in nature—in the storm, thunder and lightning, fire and earthquake.[76] Here he reveals his awful majesty, his merciful care and his flaming wrath when he comes to judge his enemies. His mighty 'voice', which once subdued the primeval sea, and which yet rings out in the

[61] Pss. 40.6; 104.24; 139.17.
[62] Pss 77.12; 139.14.
[63] Pss. 77.13; 92.6; 104.24; 111.2; 135.5; 145.3; 150.2.
[64] For instance, Pss. 103.11–13; 36.6–8; 89.2f., 6.
[65] Ex. 15.11; 1 Sam. 2.2; Pss. 18.32; 35.10; 71.19; 74.14; 86.8; 89.7, 9; 113.5; 135.5.
[66] Pss. 84.8 (voc. 'el 'ĕlōhîm); 50.1; cf. Josh. 22.22; Dan. 11.36.
[67] Pss. 95.3; 136.2.
[68] Pss. 103.19; 113.5f.; 11.4; 14.2; 33.13f.
[69] Pss. 46.2; 76.2f.; 50.1f.; 53.3; 66.7; 138.6.
[70] Ps. 135.21; cf. 24.3; 15.1.
[71] Pss. 113.5; 11.4.
[72] Pss. 72.18; 83.19; 86.10; 136.4; Deut. 32.12; Sir. 18.1f.
[73] Pss. 33; 104; 115.15; 121.2; 134.3.
[74] Ps. 8.4; Am. 5.8; Pss. 147.8; 76.10–12; 67; 147.8, 16f.; 104.27–30; 145.15f.; 139.13ff.; cf. Job 9.6.
[75] 1 Sam. 2.4–6; Pss. 75.8; 107.35ff.; 113.7ff.; 146.9; 147.6; cf. Job 5.11ff.; 12. 17ff.; 36.5ff.
[76] Judges 5.4f.; Pss. 18.8ff.; 68.34; 97.2ff.; 135.7.

thunder, works both destructive and creative miracles in the earth, as described in Ps. 29.

That these thoughts clothe themselves in the imagery of myth is a matter of course; this means only that the poets are speaking the language proper to religious views of nature and reality. He covers himself with light as a garment, the clouds are his chariot, the winds and lightning his messengers.[77] 'He looketh on the earth and it trembleth: he toucheth the hills, and they smoke' (Gunkel; Ps. 104.32). 'The hills melt like wax at the presence of the Lord' (Ps. 97.5). The mythic forms in which the conception of creation appears will be further treated below, in Chap. V.8.

The psalms dwell frequently on Yahweh's acts in history, in the life of Israel from the election and the Exodus onwards,[78] and on his dominion over all kingdoms and nations.[79] This thought, too, gets its particular formulation in the experience and belief of the festal cult, as we shall see later (Chap. V.8).

As Creator, King and Lord of the Covenant, Yahweh is the almighty; and mankind, and particularly his chosen people, owe him absolute obedience.[80] Life and death depend on him. He is the giver of all good gifts. But he may also hide his face. All the same, God does not appear as an arbitrary tyrant. When we see him in his wrath it is because man has in some way sinned against him and awakened his anger. It is then a question of discovering the transgression and of making expiation. Then Israel may reckon on the bestowal of his grace again.

For the main characteristic of Israel's faith in God as seen in the psalms is that this almighty Lord God and Lord is *Israel's* particular God. He has, through a special historical act in the course of actual history, selected this people, and made his covenant with it—that is the foundation of the creed of Israel. This covenant the psalmist is able to claim on his own behalf and on that of the people, through this old 'historical credo'—to speak in the terms of G. von Rad[81]—has been varied in many ways in the cult poetry. The Lord's revelation to his people is determined by his mercy or faithfulness, his 'lovingkindness'—or whatever word one uses to translate *ḥesedh*,[82] that most important element in the Israelitic conception of God. This lovingkindness he has shown throughout the history of the people, and therefore they can point to his 'lovingkindnesses' to the fathers and expect similar ones towards themselves. The psalmists too know that Yahweh is merciful and gracious, slow to anger, and plenteous in active love, 'a God who forgives sins'.[83] They often speak of his love and faithful-

---

[77] Gunkel, *Einl.*, pp. 73f. with references to Ps. 104.2-4. See likewise Pss. 18.8ff.; 68.7.

[78] Pss. 105; 114; Ex. 15.2ff.; Pss. 22.5f.; 44.2-4; 66.6; 77.16ff.; 80.9ff; 99.6ff.; 103.7f.; 111.4, 6, 9; 119.138; 135.8ff.; 136.10ff.; 147.19.

[79] Pss. 2; 46; 48; 75; 7.8; 44.3; 59.9; 47.10; 99.1; 118.10ff.; 135.8-12.

[80] Cf. T. H. Robinson in *The Psalmists*, ed. Simpson, pp. 32ff.

[81] G. von Rad, *Das formgeschichtliche Problem des Hexateuchs*, BWANT 78, pp. 3ff., 8ff.

[82] Cf. Glueck, *Das Wort hesed*; cf. J. Pedersen, *Israel* I–II, pp. 309f.; A. R. Johnson, 'Hesed and Hasid' in Mowinckel Festschrift (*Interpretationes ad V.T. Pertinentes*, pp. 100ff.

[83] Pss. 86.5; 103.8ff.; 99.8.

ness towards Israel, towards the 'righteous', the 'brethren of the Covenant' (*ḥasîdhîm*),[84] and not least of his pity toward all those that are oppressed and suffering.[85] The psalms appeal to this pity and mercy.[86] These can be equated with his power and honour; for if he allows his people to perish, the other nations will believe that he is unable to carry out his promise and protect his chosen, and that other gods are stronger than he (Pss. 42.4; 79.10; 115.2).

This confident and warm, emotionally tuned relation of the worshipper(s) to Yahweh often finds its expression in the phrase 'our God', or 'my God' when a single person is speaking on behalf of the congregation or of himself. The phrase may be a more or less unaccented formula, antagonism against other gods not being intended; but the confident consciousness of the close relationship to Yahweh always lies implicit in the word.[86a] But his mercies have their conditions. Against sinners he rises in all his wrath. If a sinner—whether the whole people or an individual—is to have hope of divine forgiveness, he must confess his sins, humble himself and do penance.[87] His mercies are dependent on Israel's obeying and serving him, keeping his laws and commandments,[88] the content of which is, in a word, 'the right', 'what is correct and just' (*ṣedheq, ṣĕdhāqâ*). Yahweh is a god who 'loves righteousness' and 'has established right order and righteousness in Jacob', 'the foundation of whose throne is righteousness and justice.'[89] Only he who has clean hands and a pure heart may dwell on his holy hill (Pss. 24.4; 15). The worshipper in the psalms always appeals to the justice of Yahweh for help against his enemies.

But here there is one point in which we notice a difference between the psalms and the prophets of doom. The word which is rendered 'justice', 'judgment' or 'righteousness'—*ṣĕdhāqâ* or *ṣedheq* is not in the first place a moral concept in our sense of the word. It signifies Yahweh's 'right doing' and is based on the covenant. It is one with his lovingkindness (*ḥesedh*) and faithfulness (Ps. 89.2f., 6, 9). Yahweh's 'righteousness' is his power and will to maintain himself, and his covenant, and his promise to obtain the 'right' conditions for his people. In the first place it is used of his positive saving action for the benefit of Israel.[90] Even when the idea of his just government, which rewards and punishes according to deserts, plays a part, the emphasis is laid on the fact of his saving his people.[91] That is exactly why the prophets of doom rarely, if ever, speak of Yahweh's *ṣĕdhāqâ*. In their eyes the Lord is essentially just and righteous, when he

[84] Pss. 33.18; 34.16, 20, 22; 68.36; 97.10; 100.3; 103.8ff.; 135.3f.; 145.10; 148.14; cf. Jer. 14.8; Mic. 7.18; Nah. 1.3, 7f. See below, pp. 174ff.
[85] Pss. 34.19; 68.6f.; 103.6; 107.41; 113.7ff.; 145.14, 19; 146.7ff.; 147.3, 6; 1 Sam. 2.8; cf. Job 5.11.
[86] See below, Chap. VI. 3; VII. 4 (pp. 195, 229ff.).
[86a] See Eissfeldt in *ZATW* 61, pp. 3ff. See, however, n. 12 to Chap XVI.
[87] Pss. 32; 65.4; 103.9f.; Sir. 17.29.
[88] Pss. 81.9ff.; 95.7ff.; 50. For details, see Chap. V. 6, p. 130f.
[89] Pss. 99.4; 76.3; 97.2.
[90] Cf. Leivestad, *Guds straffende rettferdighet*, pp. 21f.
[91] *Ibid.*, pp. 40ff.

upholds the ethical law of his own being by punishing his sinful people.[92] Here the prophets of doom rise above the view which is most prevalent in the psalms.

This, however, does not mean that the ethical element is missing in the conception of God presented by the psalms. On the contrary, 'Yahweh loves those who hate evil', or in another reading: 'Those who love Yahweh hate evil' (Ps. 97.10, cf. 11.5). It is on account of the unjust and immoral government of the other gods on the earth that Yahweh pronounces judgment on them (Ps. 82). To the psalmists it is a sign of Yahweh's righteousness that he helps suffering Israel, whom evil-minded enemies have subjugated. They implore his help against 'deceit' and 'falsehood', 'lies', and 'violence'.

It is implicit in the nature and function of the psalms as cultic psalms that they have no particular reason to enlarge on the ethical aspect of the image of God. All the same, the idea of Yahweh as the maintainer of justice frequently appears. In comparison with their enemies Israel are the 'righteous' ones and it is 'right' that Yahweh should both secure for his people its rights and provide just recompense for the deeds of man.[93] Against injustice Yahweh must interfere.

Here the ideas of justice and injustice are yet, as already mentioned, in part nationally coloured, and this again influences the conception of Yahweh's justice. The psalms hardly get beyond the stage that God's righteousness is proved in the first place by his saving Israel—even though this salvation gradually acquires a deeper content than the politico-nationalistic. But there are also attempts at a more ethical individualistic conception of Yahweh's righteousness. In some of the later psalms—as Pss. 1; 91; 112; 128; 34; 37—we find the thought of just individual recompense: Yahweh rewards or punishes the individual according to his acts and attitude to Yahweh's commandments. But also in the older psalms we see the ethical projecting itself into the ritual, and determining the type of piety, and thence the conception of God. When it is a question of formulating conditions for those who can be allowed a part in the blessing and 'salvation' of the sanctuary, moral demands are stressed besides the ritual and the purely religious ones; see Pss. 15; 24; 50. In Ps. 50 we see that Yahweh watches over righteousness in Israel not only by seeing to it that Israel wins her 'right' in the struggle with her outward enemies, but also by ensuring that injustice does not get the upper hand within the nation.[94] It is obedience to the simple moral commandments that Yahweh here demands from both the individual and the congregation as a whole; the congregation too has to show moral discipline. But this psalm evidently belongs to the later period and has been influenced by the

[92] *Ibid.*, pp. 118ff.
[93] Pss. 11.5ff.; 33.5; 66.7; 89.15; 92.10ff.; 97.2, 10; 98.9; 99.4; 103.6; 111.5; 145.20; 146.9; 147.6.
[94] Leivestad, *op. cit.*, p. 57.

teachings of the prophets of doom. 'The people' is here obviously the small Jewish congregation.

And it is just this psalm that bears witness to that rationalization of the conception of God which always takes place when the ethical aspect comes to the fore. It then forces the mythopoeic view of Yahweh into the background. It is true that Ps. 50 still has some of the old colours in its description of Yahweh's theophany: 'From Zion the God of gods is flashing . . . in front of him devouring fire, encircling him a mighty storm'. But this Yahweh is principally the Lord who 'will take no bullock out of thy house, nor he-goats out of thy folds', and who 'will not eat the flesh of bulls nor drink the blood of goats'. It is by right moral behaviour and by proper discipline that the congregation will honour him.

It is a rich and varied picture of Yahweh that the psalms show us. It has practically all the single features of the prophets' conception of God. But it lacks the ethical passion which characterizes the Yahweh of the prophets, which even leads him to crush his own people, so that justice may prevail. Hence the God of the psalms is not yet the universal God. Yahweh is the God of the world, but he *uses* his universal power as the God of Israel. In practice no wider circle is envisaged, as a rule, than the worshipping cultic congregation; nevertheless there are still some elements which do bespeak the God of the universe.

CHAPTER V

Psalms at the Enthronement Festival of Yahweh

I

The fact that the 'Epiphany psalms', mentioned above in Chap. IV, are connected, at least ideologically, with the harvest festival, is evident from the close relationship between their underlying mood and ideas and those of the so-called *enthronement psalms*. That these psalms are connected with the harvest and new year festival, the present author has tried to show in his *Psalmen-Studien II*, and we shall take up the question further below.

Characteristic of this group is that they salute Yahweh as the king, who has just ascended his royal throne to wield his royal power. The situation envisaged in the poet's imagination, is Yahweh's ascent to the throne and the acclamation of Yahweh as king; the psalm is meant as the song of praise which is to meet Yahweh on his 'epiphany', his appearance as the new, victorious king. Hence the name: enthronement psalms.

This applies, in the first place, to Pss. 47; 93; 96; 97; 98; 99. But Ps. 95, as well, belongs in its first part to the same type, even though it be not purely a hymn, but also contains other important liturgical items. A clear parallel with 95 is 81, with the same construction and the same poetical (and liturgical) vision. This fact indicates that Yahweh's enthronement is ideologically and in the religious consciousness of the Israelites connected with other complexes of ideas and liturgical situations.

It cannot, therefore, be our task solely to give a description of the forms and contents of the enthronement psalms in the narrow sense from the point of view of *Gattungsforschung* and the history of literature, but we must also seek to find the cultic situation which lies behind them, and to give a picture of this in all its ideological and liturgical complexity. Then, granted that there *is* such a cultic situation, Ps. 95 shows that it contained other ideas and liturgical situations besides the idea of the enthronement alone. And that is only what is implicit in the nature of the matter and of the cult. In the cultic festival the whole orchestra of the life and experience of the religion can be heard playing. No single psalm type nor any unbalanced typological treatment can reveal the whole content of the cultic festival. The fact that the second part of Ps. 95 expresses an idea other than the mere enthronement, and that the psalm, from the point of view of *Gattungsforschung* is a 'liturgical composition', gives no right to exclude it from the group of the enthronement psalms and from the scope of our investigation, as Gunkel, and more recently Kraus, have done. This means that we are at once forced outside the narrow circle of the enthrone-ment hymns proper. Among other things the above mentioned epiphany psalms will be seen to have close ideological and liturgical connexions with the ideology and the cultic situation of the enthronement hymns of praise.

But first we must see how far we can advance through a consideration of these latter alone.

2

The characteristic phrase in the enthronement psalms proper—one which often appears in the introduction—is 'Yahweh has become King', *Yahweh mālakh* (93.1; 97.1; 47.8; 96.10). It is not a lasting condition that the poet describes with this expression, and the older translation 'The Lord reigneth' is misleading.[1]

The poet's vision is of something new and important which has just taken place: Yahweh has now become king; hence the new song of joy and praise to be sung. What the poets have seen in their imagination, and describe or allude to, is an event and an act which was linked with an enthronement, Yahweh's ascent of the throne. They see and describe it, of course, in the forms and the colours of the myth; but this mythical event is none the less a real event to them. The myth is the genuine form of the religious conception. We shall see later on how the conception of Yahweh's *becoming* king is related to his eternal kingship.

Other expressions, as well, proclaim his reign[2] or rule ('judgment').[3] The picture seen by the poets is that of a great celebration which they present with the same features as that of the enthronement of a terrestrial monarch,[4] only on a magnified mythical scale and with unearthly splen-dour. Yahweh himself 'comes' (98.9), 'makes himself known' (98.2), 'goes up' (47.6) in solemn procession to his palace, the Temple, seats him-self on his throne (93.2; 97.2; 99.1) and receives his people's acclamation as king (*tĕrû'â*, 47.2). 'Yahweh has become King' is just such a cry of acclamation as 'Absalom has become king!', 'Jehu has become king!' (2 Sam. 15.10; 2 Kgs. 9.13). Before beginning his rule, or in immediate connexion with his enthronement, he performs great deeds (47.4f.; 93.2ff.; 96.10; 97.2ff.; 98.1ff.).

Not only of Israel but of the whole earth, has Yahweh become king. The songs exhort all peoples to acclaim him (47.1, 8ff.; 96.1, 3ff.; 97.1, 6, 9; 98.3f.); all other gods tremble before him and worship him (95.3; 96.4; 97.7, 9; 99.2f.).

---

[1] On the grammatical and ideological meaning of the expression see Additional Note VI.
[2] Pss. 47.3; 95.3; 97.6; 99.4.
[3] Pss. 46.10; 96.7, 13; 97.8, 10–12; 98.9; 99.4.
[4] Cf. 1 Kgs. 1; 2 Kgs. 11.12; 2 Sam. 15.10ff. Cf. *Ps.St.* II, pp. 8ff.; Gunkel-Begrich, *Einl.*, p. 97. See also G. von Rad in *ThLz.*, 1947, col. 211ff.

This universalistic idea is connected with the conception of those psalms regarding the great deed on which the kingdom of Yahweh is founded, namely, the Creation (93.1b; 95.3–5; 96.5), therefore all created things are exhorted to praise him (96.11f.; 97.6a; 98.7f.). As often in the psalmists and the prophets[5] the creation is pictured as a victorious struggle with the primeval dragon or the primeval sea (93.3f.) and its monsters. We have here a mythical conception of creation which may be termed the Primeval Struggle Myth or the Fight with the Dragon Myth, which is alluded to in the mention of the 'victory' (98.1ff.).

The victory of Yahweh is also a catastrophe for all the *other gods*; they are now confounded, stricken with terror (96.7; 97.7; 99.3f.); Yahweh's victory is also a victory over them. But together with the other gods, stand the heathen: them, too, has Yahweh conquered with his coming (47.7f.; 97.7, 10; 99.1). More pointed mention—with reference to history —is made of the Lord's victory over the nations of Egypt and Canaan (47.4f.).

Occasionally the idea of Yahweh's struggle and victory is combined with that of an act of *judgment*: the Lord comes to judge his enemies, either the gods or the whole earth (97.7f.; 98.9; 99.4). But this is not, as a rule, clearly worked out as a concrete judicial act with regular indictment and verdict (a 'forensic act'). For 'to judge' is in Hebrew just as much to rule, or to account for one's enemies in battle, or to save one's friends, as to pronounce judgment; the last is only one of many ways of 'judging'. As a rule, it means setting conditions on earth in the right order; that is the meaning of Yahweh's 'judgment' as a king. But there was also the determination of events for the following year, which, for instance, both the Babylonians and the Jewish tradition in the Mishna speak of as one of the deity's deeds on mounting the throne, and which both refer to the new year festival.

Besides the Creation, and the fight and victory which it represented, there is also mentioned an historical foundation for the Kingdom of Yahweh, namely, *the creation of Israel*, as the Lord's chosen people, *the election* as it was manifested in the Exodus from Egypt, the miracle of the Reed Lake, the revelation of Kadesh and Sinai with the making of the *Covenant*.[6] The sea where the Egyptians perished becomes the primeval sea (cf. Ex. 15.5, 8), Egypt is turned into 'Rahab', the primeval dragon.[7] Some poets declare expressly that it was on the occasion of the Exodus and the making of the covenant that Yahweh became king;[8] in that case the kingship is usually limited to Israel, whereas it is, as a rule, universal

---

[5] Pss. 74.12ff.; 89.10ff.; 104.5ff., 25f.; 44.20; 65.7f.; 18.16ff.; 46.4; 68.31; Isa. 51.9f.; Jer. 51.34, 36, 42; 50.2f.; Am. 9.2f.; Hab. 3.8; Job 9.13; 26.12f; 7.12; 38.8ff.; Ezk. 29.3ff.; 32.2ff. Cf. Gunkel, *Schöpfung und Chaos*, pp. 29ff.

[6] Cf. the term 'our maker', Ps. 95.6f. with vv. 7bff.; 100.3; 99; cf. 97.2–6.

[7] Cf. Isa. 30.7; 51.9; Pss. 87.4; 89.11.

[8] Ps. 114.1f.; Deut. 33.2–5.

in the enthronement psalms. This historical basis of Yahweh's becoming king is alluded to in Ps. 99.

In the poet's imagination this enthronement of Yahweh is an event which has just taken place, and the hymn of praise is sung to acclaim the new king. The enthronement psalms are principally hymns of praise with the usual character of such hymns, and with the free variations occasioned by their special theme: the enthronement and the great deed on which it is based together with the results for the whole earth. The main points are: the exhortation to praise, the mention of Yahweh's glorious presence and of the excellent deeds he has just performed or is about to perform:

> Yahweh has become King! Let earth rejoice;
>   let the many shores be glad thereof.
> Clouds and darkness are round about him;
>   equity and justice are the fundament of his throne.
> Fire blazes in front of him
>   and burns his enemies round about.
> His lightnings illumined the world;
>   till earth shivered at the sight.
> The mountains melted just like wax
>   before the Lord of all the earth. (Ps. 97.1–5.)

> Shout the homage-cry before the King,
>   with bugle and with cornet ...,
> Before Lord Yahweh, for he hath come
>   to reign upon the earth;
> To rule the world with righteousness,
>   the peoples with equity. (Ps. 98.6, 9.)

3

How are these psalms to be interpreted? What are the poets alluding to, and what is it they seek to bring out in their description of the 'enthronement' of Yahweh?

The most prominent feature of these psalms is, as we have seen, their actuality and contemporaneous character. There can be no doubt that the situation into which the poets have projected themselves, which forms the basis of their vision, and which they want the singer and the listeners to take part in, is this: that the people—the congregation—is now actually standing in the presence of the new king to salute him as the victorious king who has ousted his competitors and seated himself on the throne, has established his kingdom and inaugurated a beneficial reign over this people and the whole earth. In whatever way one may explain the circumstance that Yahweh, the Lord, who has through all time been God and

Ruler, can also be pictured as having just succeeded to the throne, there can be no doubt that it is the latter fact which the poets wish to convey: they see before them, and praise—and let the congregation praise—Yahweh as the king who has *now* taken over his realm.

In the Old Testament we also meet with the idea that Yahweh *is* the king of Israel.[9] 'The King' was in the East a very common title and name for the god of the country, or of the town. Marduk of the Babylonians, Asshur of the Assyrians, the Ammonite Milkom, the Tyrian Melkart, the Ugaritic Ba'al and many others—all were 'the King'. It was natural for the Israelites to conceive of Yahweh in the same way. But how is this idea related to the conception that he has at a certain moment *become* King? One might reason as follows: he became king when he chose Israel as his people; and certain psalms suggest this, as we have seen above. But this is evidently not the general idea of the enthronement psalms. As a rule, it is not an historical but a 'cosmic', 'mythical' act of salvation which is conceived of as the foundation of the kingship—in the first place, as mentioned, the Creation in its various aspects. How is this to be understood? What does it mean that the poet and the congregation, who are in these psalms acclaiming Yahweh, are, so to speak, contemporaries of the Creation?

Attempts have been made to interpret them historically, in connexion with some particular historical event, in which Yahweh had clearly proved himself king, e.g. the fall of the Chaldean kingdom and the return of the first 'Diaspora Jews' to Zion.[10] But this does not explain the universal, world-embracing character of these psalms. And why are there no definite references to actual historical events? Psalms like 46 and 48 are quasi-historical, but events like those described—the nations' attack on Jerusalem, and their rout and destruction there—never happened in actual history. And how to explain from an historical view-point the fact that Creation and the fight with the primeval dragon form the foundation of the kingdom? and how the part played by Nature in the exhortation to praise? The historical interpretation is as impracticable in the case of the enthronement psalms as in that of Pss. 46 and 48. They are not actual and historical, but 'mythical', unearthly events, to which the enthronement psalms refer;[11] when there occasionally is a reference to something 'historical' as in Pss. 99; 97 and 95 (and 81), it is a matter of happenings in the remote past.

Others have tried to interpret them eschatologically: the poet and the congregation sing in advance the poem regarding the final salvation, when Yahweh shall annihilate the power of evil and deliver his people and

---

[9] Isa. 6.5; 41.21; 43.15; 44.6; Pss. 5.3; 44.5; 74.12; 84.4; 24.7, 9 and other places.
[10] As eminent representatives of this interpretation may be mentioned Ewald, Cheyne, Baethgen, Wellhausen, Buhl, Davison. Even Olshausen gives a time-historial interpretation, but has realized more clearly than the above-mentioned the liturgical character of these psalms. In addition see *Ps.St.* II, pp. 10-13.
[11] Pss. 93.2ff.; 95.4f.; 96.10. Cf. 24.2; 29.3, 10; 100.3; 149.2.

establish the eschatological kingdom of God, when he wholly and absolutely shall become king and be recognized as such by the whole world.[12] True enough, these ideas are also to be found as elements in the restoration hope and in eschatology; the psalmists, however, did not get them from those sources, but vice versa, as we shall shortly see. When, for instance, Deutero-Isaiah describes the coming salvation as the enthronement day of a cosmic Yahweh,[13] he speaks in the psalm style, showing that these ideas belong to *psalm* poetry. And when the prophets at times break out in such 'anticipatory' salvation songs—as an expressive form of prophecy, and in certainty and joy regarding its arrival—it is always in some way suggested that they are speaking of a future matter: 'On that day ye shall sing and say' (cf. Isa. 12.1, 3f.; 25.9; 27.2; Jer. 31.6). The connexion in which the prophets' lyrical outburst is found proves that it is intended as a spectacular version of the prophecy itself, of which it is a portion.[14] In a separate individual psalm, on the other hand, there is no such 'connexion' indicating that it is to be applied to the future. The only thing that might suggest an eschatological character would be the content, which frequently tallies with eschatological ideas.[15] But the truth of the matter is, as we shall see later on, that eschatology here has drawn its ideas from the same source as the enthronement psalms, and has reinterpreted these ideas in its own way. As a matter of fact there are no properly 'eschatological' psalms in the whole collection.[16]

Everything contained in the enthronement psalms, then, gives the strongest impression of belonging to the actual present. It is not only in their imagination that the poets have witnessed Yahweh's arrival and ascent of the throne as a present event (which by its nature might belong either to the past or to the future); no, they refer to something objective and experienced outside themselves, but with which they have been contemporaneous. That which they are witnessing: that the Lord after certain acts 'goes up' and seats himself on the throne and is acclaimed as having taken the name of the king, is an act which already to the poet's vision is a 'myth', and might easily have been presented in the epic form of the myth. But it is noticeable that the poets never *describe* this enthronement as such; they merely refer to it in hymnal form as something real and well known, and which the audience also can understand. They do not need to describe it; they merely rejoice that it has now taken place. If it had been an image of the future, present only in their imagination, they could not have expected their audience to have understood what they were

---

[12] Cf. Additional Note VII.

[13] See *Ps.St.* II, pp. 190ff.; 238ff.; 251ff.; 256ff.; 273ff.; 282ff.; 292ff.; *GTMMM* III, pp. 188f.

[14] With this, Gunkel's reply (*Einl.*, p. 81) to my own and H. Schmidt's objections to his eschatological interpretation loses its force.

[15] This is certainly admitted by Gunkel, *Einl.*, p. 80. However, as he is likewise forced to admit that the same conceptions also belong in places outside eschatology, namely in an (earlier) cultic enthronement festival (see below, n. 21), his objections lose their validity.

[16] See Additional Note VIII.

talking about; we should then have expected them to describe what they saw and tell their listeners that this many-sided and portentous enthronement was now taking place, or was going to happen. The picture of the enthronement is thus not simply a poetical conception which the authors have received individually and which they put before their listeners to make them also experience the event. They take it for granted that the series of events referred to is well known beforehand to those who are to hear or sing the psalm; they refer to a (mythical) conception which they share with a large group. The enthronement of Yahweh must to them have been an event which could be both presented and alluded to, because the group knew that it had now taken place. As we have seen, this event is connected both with the Creation of the world and with the Exodus from Egypt.

But at the same time, it is in these psalms presented as something belonging to the living present, something which all who hear or sing the psalm themselves have taken part in and are experiencing at the time, something on which the singing congregation's whole happiness and well-being—their salvation—would depend, and which they are at the moment praising and celebrating. 'O sing unto the Lord, for he is come, he is come!' it says in the enthronement hymn 98.9; and in another psalm, which belongs in fact to the same ideological group, the congregation declares: 'As we have heard, so we have seen' (48.9). But it is, on the other hand, true that there is something in these psalms that points beyond the moment; they also express a hope and a certainty regarding the future, beyond human and political calculations. We shall come back to this later. But the essential point about these psalms is the rejoicing about something recently experienced.

We must ask: *where* are the historico-mythical 'acts of salvation' that are at the same time described as belonging both to the past and the present, and experienced as belonging to the present, with results decisive for the future? From all we know of religious life in its manifestations and especially in the more ancient 'primitive' civilizations, the answer can only be this: it is where religion and religious life unfold in a common experience and realization of 'the real' in all its creative and existential wealth and concrete presence, that is, in the congregational temple cult. In other words the only interpretation which is satisfactory both for the actual and the future, the historical and the cosmic, together with the primeval element (the Creation) in these psalms, and which at the same time tallies with the general view of the psalms which has been presented in the foregoing, is the *cultic* one.[17] That is to say, these psalms presuppose and, from their very nature have sprung from and belong to, a festival, which has, at least from one point of view, been celebrated as a festival of the enthronement of Yahweh.[18] At this festival the congregation has

---

[17] See Additional Note IX.   [18] See Additional Note X.

most vividly experienced the personal coming of the Lord to save his people—his epiphany.[19] In the cultic festival, past, present and future are welded into one. It is an experience of this sort that lies behind the enthronement psalms, and which they express.[20] In fact, this cultic interpretation is the only one that can provide any support for the kernel of truth in Gunkel's eschatological interpretation.[21]

Let us recall what was said above about the essence of the cult. All cult is, from one point of view—as we have seen[22]—repetition, renewed experience of the fundamental facts of life and existence. It was a repetition, which to the ancient peoples did not mean simply 'in memory of', but a positive reality, in the same way as this notion still lives in the Easter greeting of the Orthodox Church: 'Christ is verily arisen!' That means, *now*, as it also rings in our Christmas and Easter hymns: 'Our Saviour has been born *to-day*;' 'Arisen is our Lord, the Christ . . . who *Friday* died the bitter death' . . ., 'Three women went *this morning* forth . . .', and so on.[23]

To the ancients this renewed experience was still more real than it is to us; it was an actual repetition of the event. In the cult the creative and saving events took place again and again, in regular recurrence. Life is a constant struggle between good and evil powers, between 'blessing', and 'curse', between 'life' and 'death'. In this struggle the powers of good must be renewed and strengthened, otherwise the world would perish. This renewal takes place in the cult. At the festival the deity is called, and comes; through the cult, strength and blessing are drawn into human life; a wall is built against the powers of evil, and impurity and sin are washed away. Thus life, 'the World', is created anew. The bond made with the deity in the harvest festival causes the rains to return, so that the curse of drought and death is overcome, dormant nature revives and life awakens, to the benefit of mankind (cf. Ps. 65). In the language and spirit of the Yahweh religion: then the Lord comes and brings all this along with him, vanquishes the powers of evil—including (on principle) the enemies of his chosen people, for whom he 'maketh all things new'.

At the 'enthronement festival'—as we may preliminarily call it—ancient Israel witnessed Yahweh's arrival as king, when he literally founded his kingdom. They acclaimed and celebrated him as conqueror, creator, king of the whole earth, reformer of the people and its fortunes, as the king of Israel who repeats the acts of deliverance from Egypt and the Reed Lake, and who, by his mere coming, has set the world aright again and crushed every onslaught that the enemies might make on his

---

[19] See above, p. 94 and n. 42 to Chap. IV. That the idea of theophany is really connected with the cult and with an actual, regular, 'to all eternity' repeated cultic experience has also been realized by Weiser, who gives further reasons for it, *Festschrift für Bertholet*, pp. 513ff.

[20] See Additional Note XI.

[21] See below, Chap. V. 10, 11 and Additional Note XII.

[22] See above, Chap. I, pp. 15ff., cf. Mowinckel, *Religion und Kultus*, pp. 10ff.

[23] *M.B. Landstads Kirkesalmebok*, revised and added to, Nos. 114, 349.

I, 8

city and his people—though all the kings of the earth were to combine and to conspire together.

To the interpretation that the enthronement psalms on a special festival state that Yahweh has become king, it is not a valid objection to say that Yahweh had, according to the Israelite view, always been king.[24] The latter statement is correct enough. The Old Testament often declares that the Lord is king, 'King for ever', etc.;[25] he is Israel's king, king in Zion, but sometimes also king over all the earth. The notion that the god is the king (*melekh*, *'ādhōn*) of the city or of the land and people, is no original Israelite idea: in the wilderness, a king was unknown to the nomad tribes. The ancient Semitic conception of the deity is that he is the 'father' of the tribe or of the people, and he is therefore often identified with the tribal progenitor.[26]

The conception of the deity as king was taken over by the Israelites from the Canaanites,[27] who had received it from the great kingdoms on the Euphrates and Tigris and Nile,[28] where it had been developed as early as ancient Sumerian times.[29] When Israel was gathered into one state, and acquired its chief national holy place in Jerusalem, Yahweh was looked upon as the king of Zion. There is every reason to believe that the conception of Yahweh as the king of the township derives from the supreme Canaanite deity in Jerusalem, El Elyon, whom Yahweh succeeded, and whose throne and realm he won, with David's conquest of the city and introduction of the worship of Yahweh as the official cult of the kingdom; this becomes still clearer in the new 'royal temple' of Solomon. That the royal title was linked with the pre-Israelite god on Zion, is seen, from the name Melchizedek, i.e. *malkî ṣedheq*—'the god Ṣedeq is my king'.[30]

It naturally followed that Yahweh gradually came to be regarded as king of the land and people of Israel, and, in religious lyrical poetry, as 'the King of all the earth', an idea which in the prophets acquired a practical religious content. He is the world-ruler who uses all nations and kingdoms as his instruments. For as long as Israel has existed as a nation—such was at least the general conception in the time of the kings—Yahweh has been its king (Num. 23.11; Deut. 33.5; Ps. 114); it was also declared that since the creation of the world he has been its universal ruler (cf. Mic. 4.13; Zech. 4.14).

But this did not prevent the view that Yahweh at a certain point of

[24] Thus, for instance, Eissfeldt, Eerdmans and others (see n. 21). This is in fact the only 'positive' argument of Eerdmans against the idea of the enthronement festival.

[25] All the authoritative passages attaching the epithet of *melekh* to Yahweh have been gathered by Eissfeldt, op. cit., p. 89.

[26] See v. Baudissin, *Adonis u. Esmun*, pp. 39ff.

[27] Von Gall, 'Über die Herkunft der Bezeichnung Jahwes als König', in *Wellhausenfestschrift,* pp. 147ff. See further Additional Note XIII.

[28] On this general oriental background of the ideas of the kingship of the god, see Eissfeldt in *ZATW* 46, 1928.

[29] Cf. Gadd, *Ideas of Divine Rule in the Ancient East*; Frankfort, *Kingship*.

[30] See von Gall in *Wellhausenfestschrift*, pp. 155f.

time *became* the king of Israel, i.e. at the election, at the Exodus from Egypt (Ps. 114.1f.), or at the making of the covenant on Mount Sinai (Deut. 33.5). That Yahweh *became* king is bound up with the fundamental fact of salvation in the life of the people.

But in the cult the fact of salvation is re-experienced as a new and actual reality. Yahweh is ever anew witnessed as 'coming', 'revealing himself', and doing works of salvation on earth. The Israelite idea of God was not static but dynamic. Israel did not regard the Lord principally as sitting in calm possession and execution of his divine power,[31] but as one who rises and seizes the power, and wields it in mighty works. And this is as a rule concretely pictured; from the 'mythical' side this is seen epically and dramatically: at a certain time Yahweh *became* king. To the Israelite way of thinking there is no contradiction between this and that he is king for ever; such a contradistinction is modern and rationalistic. This particularly applies to the cult, as it re-experiences as a new reality the fundamental fact of salvation. From the modern point of view we should in such cases say that he has *again* become king, seized the royal power, or the like; the Israelite might have said the same, if his language had distinguished between the 'permansive' and the 'inchoative' act or event— but that is exactly what it does not do.[32] And in the cultic experience the whole attention is concentrated on that which is again witnessed as something actual; it is there conceived as something happening at that moment. The Lord, Yahweh, becomes king, he shows himself as king, and performs kingly deeds, and in the graphic conception and presentation of the cult this is all gathered up in the definite picture of his royal entry and arrival, invisibly mounted on the cherub-borne throne.

Exactly the same logically undeveloped mode of conception obtained in the Babylonian religion. There also Anu, or Enlil, or Marduk, or Ashur, *is* king; but the sources prove that the cultic feast celebrated him as the one *now becoming* king; the new year festival marked his enthronement. So also in Israel.

In the rites and psalms belonging to the festival of the enthronement of Yahweh this idea was mirrored, or, rather, presented, expressed, and experienced. A main event was evidently the great festal procession, the victorious coronation entry of the Lord, to which reference is made in Ps. 47.6. It must have had a strongly dramatic character,[33] with playing, singing and dancing.[34] The personal presence of Yahweh in the festive procession was most probably symbolized by his holy shrine (the ark). Both Ps. 24 and Ps. 132 were probably connected with this procession; but our hypothesis is valid even without these witnesses.

---

[31] As it finds expression for instance in the oriental statues of gods, which also present the god standing or enthroned, with the royal tiara and the royal staff and the like.

[32] See Birkeland, *Grunnriss*, p. 23. (Grammar ¶ 613).

[33] Pss. 68.25ff.; 132; 24. On the connexion of these psalms with the cultic enthronement of Yahweh, see below.

[34] Cf. 2 Sam. 6.5, 12–16; Pss. 42.5; 149.3; 150.4.

It is this appearance and enthronement day of Yahweh which originally was called 'the day of the Lord', 'the day of the feast of Yahweh'.[35]

4

Before taking up the question of the feast day to which Yahweh's enthronement festival may belong, we shall discuss the age of the enthronement psalms. In point of principle this question has two aspects: (a) How old is this form of poetry in itself, the type as such? and (b) How old are the actual enthronement psalms still extant?

Interpreters have always been aware of the close relationship between the enthronement psalms and Deutero-Isaiah, with regard to substance as well as phraseology. For contemporary interpreters it seems almost too obvious that they are dependent on Deutero-Isaiah. Even Gunkel (followed by Kraus) maintains this, though it actually does not agree with his fundamental view of the psalm types; for he admits that Jeremiah imitated the style of the psalms of lamentation and not vice versa, and that Deutero-Isaiah elsewhere imitated the forms and ideas of the hymns. When Gunkel therefore makes the enthronement psalms an exception to his principle, it is as a result of his insistence on the eschatological interpretation. Snaith has taken up the idea of dependence upon Deutero-Isaiah as an argument against tracing them to a pre-exilic new year festival, and tries to prove this by means of long lists of passages showing conformity between the psalms and Deutero-Isaiah.[36] But Johnson is perfectly right in saying that 'such a list may prove to be a two-edged sword, and that as a result quite the opposite conclusion is possible'.[37]

The fundamental question, however, is not concerned with the date of individual enthronement psalms, but with this type (*Gattung*) of psalm as such. A methodical comparison based on the history of forms and ideas provides clear evidence that instead of the now prevalent tendency to attribute to these psalms a dependence on Deutero-Isaiah, exactly the opposite is true. In the same way that Jeremiah is dependent on the traditional style of the psalms of lamentation with their particular elements of form and substance, and as Deutero-Isaiah himself takes up the forms

[35] Hos. 7.5; 2.15; 9.5.—That the 'day' of Yahweh originally indicated the day of his festival becomes quite obvious from Am. 5.17ff., which does not refer to an eschatological day of Yahweh (as supposed by Gunkel, Gressmann, Sellin, Dürr and many others), but where the 'day' is clearly and distinctly imagined as a festival day, see v. Gall, *Basileia*, pp. 25f. Akkadian *umu ili* is the 'festival day of the god'. But in Akkadian already the term has to a certain degree become detached from the cult, indicating in general a day when the god reveals himself in all his power in order to help his worshippers; thus for instance the term 'the day of (the god) Nusku' is used in prayers, see Hölscher, *Urspr. d. jüd. Eschat.*, p. 13. But the idea of 'revelation', 'epiphany', was also originally attached to the cult, see Weinreich in *HBKLA, Ergänzungsbd.*; this also applies to the typical epiphany formula 'I am . . .', see Norden; *Agnostos Theos*, pp. 207ff., 215ff.; Gressmann in *ZATW* 34, 1914, pp. 288ff. The epiphany psalm 50 (see *hôphîa'* v.2) according to tradition belongs to the festival of harvest and tabernacles.

[36] See Snaith, *Studies in the Psalter*, pp. 66ff.—Feuillet, too, champions the dependence on Deutero-Isaiah and the post-exilic date of the enthronement psalms (*Nouv. Revue Theol.*, 73), but without new arguments.

[37] *The O.T. and Modern Study*, ed. H. H. Rowley, p. 194.

and ideas of the hymn, so too is he dependent on the ideology and style of the enthronement psalms. That is to say, he has consciously imitated and used them as a pregnant expression of the message he is bringing.[38] The enthronement psalm as a special cultic type (*Gattung*) therefore is older than Deutero-Isaiah, and must consequently have existed even in the cult at the pre-exilic temple.

This agrees with the fact that other psalms which are closely related to the enthronement psalms as regards ideology and cultic situation, such as Pss. 132; 84; 68; 24, without doubt belong to pre-exilic times. We shall discuss the relationship of these psalms to the enthronement festival more closely below.

This fact does not exclude the possibility that *some* specimens handed down to us of this type, may be later, even post-exilic. From the history of form and cult, however, there is nothing to indicate that the so-called Exile marks any important line of distinction. After the restoration, about 520 B.C., the ancient temple service was certainly as far as possible restored with the old forms and according to traditions still alive both in the levitical families who had been carried away, and among those left behind who even during the 'period of exile' had maintained some kind of cult among the ruins of the Temple (cf. Jer. 41.5). And I feel convinced that it will not be possible to give cogent *proof* of the post-exilic origin of any one of the enthronement psalms. One might be tempted to take the reference to the 'commandments and laws' of Yahweh in Ps. 99 as an expression of the particular spirit of Judaism, namely 'legalism', but we find the same term for the revealed will of Yahweh even in the definitely pre-exilic royal thanksgiving psalm (Ps. 18.23). It is worth noticing that in Ps. 99, Moses like Aaron is included among those 'that call upon the name of Yahweh'. To 'call upon the name of Yahweh', *qārā'* (*bě*)*šēm Yhwh*, is a term used of cultic supplication, especially by the one who is performing the cult, a task in the first instance belonging to the priest (cf. Joel 2.17). So even Samuel is here considered to be a priest, and this agrees with the earlier tradition, where he is a priestly 'seer' (*rō'eh*), whereas the later tradition describes him as a 'prophet'. A divergent version of the Meribah tradition, earlier than the one in the Pentateuch, is presupposed in Ps. 81.[39] The reference to 'Yahweh's footstool', i.e. the ark, in v. 5 may also be taken to indicate a pre-exilic origin of Ps. 99. Ps. 93, too, may well be of pre-exilic origin.[40]

In favour of a post-exilic dating of the enthronement psalms Eissfeldt has urged that in no unquestionably pre-exilic passage is the kingship of Yahweh ever mentioned in connexion with creation,[41] so that this idea

[38] See *Ps.St.* II, pp. 195ff. That Ps. 93 is older than Deutero-Isaiah is maintained by Helen Jefferson in *JBL* LXXI, 1951, pp. 155ff.

[39] See Bentzen, *Salmerne, ad. loc.*

[40] See Jefferson in *JBL* LXXI, 1951, pp. 155ff. Whether Deutero-Isaiah has known this definite psalm or not, is of minor importance since the psalm-type as such undoubtedly is older than he.

[41] See Eissfeldt in *ZATW* 46, 1928, p. 103. Repeated by Kraus, *Die Königsherrschaft Gottes im A.T.*, p. 131.

must have been derived from Deutero-Isaiah. This is completely false. We find it—and moreover in a highly mythological version—in Pss. 74.12ff., and 89.10ff.; in the latter passage the word *melekh* is not used, but 'ruler' (*mōšēl*); but on the other hand we have here the 'homage-cry to the king' (*těrū'â*) as the characteristic mode of homage to Yahweh (v. 16). Doubt remains whether Ps. 89 must be dated from pre-exilic times; in this lament 'the Anointed', i.e. the king, utters the lamentation. And Ps. 74 may with just as much probability be referred to one of the great disasters during the later monarchy, to 598 or 587, as to an unknown conquest and spoliation of the Temple in post-exilic times—the age of the Maccabees is out of the question from reasons based on the history of the canon. So Deutero-Isaiah cannot possibly have a prior claim on the idea of creation as the basis of Yahweh's kingship. In fact he is here dependent on earlier tradition and style, and here, as in many other cases, he has simply drawn on the thoughts and style of the cultic psalms. The idea of creation as the great achievement of Yahweh and the idea of his kingship are both indigenous in the cultic lyrics; that is where the two ideas have been knit together, and that is where Deutero-Isaiah has found thought content as well as thought forms.

So, though one or another enthronement psalm may be of post-exilic origin, it is of no consequence for the problem as to the age of the type as such and of the cultic festival presupposed. In fact Deutero-Isaiah is a witness to the existence of the enthronement psalm type in pre-exilic days. And should this type of psalm presuppose a corresponding cultic 'enthronement festival', then such a festival must have existed in pre-exilic times. The following pages will make apparent so many features of the festival which are so closely connected with Israel's national existence as an independent state, and with the Davidic dynasty, that there can be no further doubt as to its pre-exilic origin.

5

No particular day named after the feast of Yahweh's enthronement is expressly mentioned in the texts. But the enthronement idea may, as shown above, have been only one of many ideas underlying the cultic festival which must be presupposed as the background of the enthronement psalms. This festival is likely to have been one of the well-known great festivals of the year. Let us try to find out which festival it was.

Yahweh's enthronement day is the day when he 'comes' (96.13; 98.9) and 'makes himself known' (98.2), reveals himself and his 'salvation' and his will (93.5; 99.7), when he repeats the theophany of Mount Sinai (97.3ff.; 99.7f.) and renews the election (47.5) of Israel, and the covenant with his people (95.6ff.; 99.6ff.). The mighty 'deed of salvation' upon which his kingdom is founded is the Creation, which is alluded to in a rather mythic guise (93.3f.). His coming means the renewal of the life of nature—this being the reason why the poets exhort heaven and earth and sea, field and stream, trees and mountains, to rejoice at the coming of the king. All these ideas will be dealt with at length below. The festival is, then, a festival of the epiphany of Yahweh[41a] in the literal meaning of this word. As just mentioned, there is reason to think that it—or one of its days—was called 'the day of Yahweh', i.e. the day of his cultic coming and revelation as king (Hos. 7.5); this day was the *yôm ḥagh yhwh*, 'the day of Yahweh's (special) feast' (Hos. 9.5).

Among the three great festivals of the year there was one which in ancient times was considered as '*the* (special) feast of Yahweh', or simply 'the feast', *heḥāgh*, and this was the 'Harvest festival' or 'feast of Tabernacles' in the autumn (Ex. 23.16; 34.22). It closed the agricultural year and opened the new one, which in ancient Canaan began with the rainy season and the awakening of the whole creation to new life (see above, p. 94). In somewhat later times[42] it was celebrated throughout eight days at full moon in the month of Tishri which, according to the Babylonian calendar used by the Jews from the Exile, was reckoned as the seventh. But there is reason to believe that in older times it was celebrated one month later, in the old month of Ethanim (the eighth month), i.e. October/November.[43] The olive harvest lasts this long,[44] and then the rainy season begins. To this festival belongs, without doubt, the public thanksgiving psalm (Ps. 65) with its allusions to the rain that the new 'year of goodness' has brought to the land. Cf. Zech. 14.17, for the connexion between the feast of Tabernacles and the coming of the rain. In Zech. 14.16–19 we are told expressly that this feast is the feast of Yahweh Sèba'oth as king.

Ps. 65 shows that this festival in older times, too, had regard to the annual revival of life. And it also shows that its 'cult myth' was that of Creation (and of the fight with the primeval dragon), and all that was connected with it. To the mind that sees the cult as a reality which liberates new forces and recreates life, this idea of the new year ceremony as

---

[41a] See above, Chap. IV. 3, p. 93.

[42] Mentioned for the first time in the law about the feasts of the Lord, Lev. 23.33ff., in the book of Ezekiel 45.25 and by P in Nu. 28.11ff. (The chronological relation between these three passages is disputed; I consider Lev. 23.33ff. the oldest.) That the feast started on the day when the moon was at her full is also seen from 1 Kgs. 12.33, where the critical remark about Jeroboam does not refer to the day, but to the month. 1 Kgs. 12.26–33 is handed down to us as written by the Deuteronomistic author, but is no doubt based on older material, in the last instance dating from the official annals of Jerusalem. Vv. 28, 30b and 32a at any rate are derived from the sources used by the author.

[43] Notice that the critical remark in 1 Kgs. 12.33, 'which he had devised of his own heart', is not mentioned in the note about the source of v. 32a. Apart from v. 33 there is no reason to refer the words 'like unto the ḥagh of Jerusalem' only to the date; the most natural interpretation is to refer it both to date and month. If so we here find testified that in earlier times even in Jerusalem the harvest feast (he-ḥāgh) was celebrated in the eighth month, that is to say in the month of Bul, not as was later the case, in the 'seventh' Ethanim. Nor is Jeroboam, when he wanted to introduce a festival in competition with that of Jerusalem, very likely to have chosen a date one month later than the latter; then we have far better reason to suppose that the festival of Jerusalem was later advanced one month in order to forestall Bethel. The choice of the month Ethanim would then probably indicate the desire to attach the feast to the time of the autumnal equinox.

[44] See the references above, Chap. IV, n. 43, p. 94.

a world-creation feast would come quite naturally. It is well known that in later Judaism the new year time in autumn was considered as the time of the renewal of the Creation. To the same harvest festival also belongs the thanksgiving psalm (Ps. 67), with the idea of Yahweh's 'ruling' (*šāphaṭ*) the nations of the earth and the consequent blessing of the year as the result of this 'just rule'. The idea of the election and the covenant is alluded to in Ps. 65.5. There is absolutely no reason to reject the tradition in Mishna Sukka IV.5 that Ps. 118 belonged to the feast of Tabernacles. It is a procession psalm and alludes to 'the day' of the feast (v. 24), to the procession up to and around the altar, and to the green branches with which the altar was covered 'up to its horns', or, as read in Sukka IV.5, 'so that their tops bent over the altar'. The psalm alludes also to the Hosanna-cry of the procession, and to the light of the torches in the torch dance on the first night of the feast, giving the rites a symbolic interpretation: 'Yahweh is our God who has brought us light' (v. 27).

It is also quite clear that already in pre-exilic times the harvest festival was also that of the new year. Originally there was probably no specific single day that was considered to be new year's day, as was the case in later Jewish times. The whole seven to eight days of autumn or harvest festival (*ḥagh hā'āsîph, ḥagh haqqāṣîr*) may in older times have been celebrated as the new year's feast; it was expressly stated that the 'feast of ingathering' was to take place 'at the year's end', 'at the turn of the year' (*bithĕqûphath haššānâ*, 'when the year has completed its round'), 'in the beginning of the year' (*bĕṣē'th haššānâ* Ex. 34.22; 23.16).[45] It is not rare in the time-reckoning of ancient nations to find that a rather indefinite 'New Year's Tide' precedes the later definite 'New Year's Day', or that several annual new year festivals were celebrated, whenever one arrived at an important new departure in the round of life and nature. This happened both in Egypt and in Babylonia.[46] The idea is connected with the general conception of the need for special initiating and inaugurating 'transition-rites' at all the important new departures in the life of society and of the individual.[47] The important thing to remember here is that in Israel the harvest thanksgiving was a new year festival. In Jewish times the harvest festival was divided into three parts, following close upon one another: the new year feast or 'the memorial of blowing of trumpets', on Tishri 1st; the feast of the atonement, on the 10th, and the feast of tabernacles on Tishri 15th to 21st; the items of the general festival being to a certain extent distributed between these three.[48] Remembering the invariable

---

[45] See Wellhausen, *Prolegomena*³ A, Chap. 3, pp. 109ff. (E.T., pp. 108ff.). The festival of harvest and tabernacles always retained this character of new year even after a definite new year day, *rō'š haššānâ*, 1st of Tishri, had come into being; see Volz, *Das Neujahrsfest Jahwes*, pp. 7ff.; Mowinckel, *Ps.St.* II, pp. 94ff. See Additional Note XIV.

[46] Cf. van der Leeuw, *Phänomenologie*, ¶ 56.2, p. 368 (E.T., p. 391); Nilsson, *Primitive Time-Reckoning*, pp. 267ff.; Frankfort, *Kingship*, pp. 103f., 313f.; Mowinckel, *Zum isr. Neujahr*, p. 18.

[47] Cf. van Gennep, *Les rites de passage.*

[48] Lev. 23.23–36.—In *HUCA* I, III and X Morgenstern has tried to penetrate into the question as to when and how this division took place.

conservatism of cults we find no reason to doubt that many of the ideas and ceremonies which are connected with the opening day of the year in later Judaism are largely derived from the older, more comprehensive celebration of harvest and new year, the feast of tabernacles.[49] All over the East these ideas have been connected with the new year cult, the greatest of all the annual celebrations.[50]

Our thesis then will be that even on the basis of the special group of 'enthronement psalms' in the form-critical sense, we shall be able to prove that the enthronement festival of Yahweh, presupposed by them, could not be a separate, as yet unknown festival, but must have been the old festival of harvest and new year, the 'feast of tabernacles'. We have not here a newly discovered festival, not referred to elsewhere in the Old Testament, but a hitherto unheeded aspect of the well-known and frequently mentioned feast of tabernacles in its character of new year festival.[51]

We have already seen that the enthronement festival of Yahweh and the feast of tabernacles and of New Year have in common the idea of Yahweh's 'appearance' and 'epiphany', of the renewal of nature and creation, of the repeated 'work of salvation' to be performed by him, and of Yahweh's universal dominion over the earth (cf. Ps. 65).

In addition there are further reasons. Jewish tradition affirms the enthronement psalm (Ps. 47), to be a new year psalm. There can be no reason to doubt that this liturgical usage corresponds with the original meaning of the psalm, particularly since the great procession which it implies is known to have been the usual oriental new year's rite. The Mishna tradition of course, refers to the later special new year's day on the 1st of Tishri, which dates back to earlier Judaic times and is a result of the independent development of a single aspect of an original festal complex of several days. The new thing about this new year day is that it has become a single day in advance of the main festival; its substance is derived from the earlier festal complex.

According to tradition as well as the explicit testimony of the psalm itself, Ps. 81 is also a new year psalm. But Ps. 81, both with regard to logical structure—the different items contained in it—and the cultic situation making up its background, is an exact parallel to the enthronement psalm (Ps. 95). In common with Ps. 95 it has the conception of Yahweh's appearance and the revelation of his nature ('name') and will—the epiphany concept—also the renewal of the covenant, and an admoni-

---

[49] For details see below in the text, pp. 135ff.

[50] Cf. Wensinck in *Act. Or.* I, pp. 158ff.; *id., Arabic New Year*.

[51] That this is the meaning of the expression 'Enthronement festival' has been made perfectly clear already in *Ps.St.* II. Nevertheless, the objection has been made again and again (e.g. by Gunkel, *Einl.*, pp. 105f., Kraus, *Königsherrschaft Gottes*, pp. 21f., and lastly by McCullough in *A Stubborn Faith*, pp. 53ff.) that no such 'new feast' is known or mentioned in the O.T. The answer to this is simply—as the present author again and again has pointed out—that the feast of tabernacles, the old harvest and new year feast, is mentioned and hinted at very often in the O.T., as is well known to every Bible reader. An unfair objection does not become fair by being repeated (cf. below, n. 60).

tion to faithfulness thereto, with a reference to the fate of the Fathers. Ps. 50 follows the same train of ideas. If we may take for granted that Ps. 81 not only reflects a situation in the imagination of the poet, but a real cultic situation of dramatic character—and there is no reason to doubt this—then this psalm must belong to the same festal complex as Pss. 95 and 47, that is to say, to the complex of harvest and new year festival. But along with Pss. 47f and 95 must also go the whole group of enthronement psalms, properly so called; their cultic situation cannot be distinguished from that of Ps. 95, the first part of which is obviously an enthronement psalm.

To what has been said, may be added a series of other observations. Just as the harvest feast was 'Yahweh's festival', so new year's day on the 1st of Tishri was the special festal day of Yahweh: 'this day is sacred to our Lord' (Neh. 8.10).

New year's day is the day for the 'sounding of horns' (*yôm haśśôphār*), a rite characteristic of the festal enthronement procession of Yahweh (Pss. 47.6; 98.6; cf. 81.4). It is also called the 'day for the cry of homage', *yôm hattĕrû'â*; the cry of homage (*tĕrû'â*) is at the same time characteristic of the psalms and of the day of enthronement (47.2, 6; 98.6); the cry of homage means 'royal homage', 'homage to the king' (*tĕrû'ath melekh*) for Yahweh; when this cry is heard in Israel it is evidence that 'Yahweh her God is with her' (Num. 23.21).[52]

These proofs and indications are supported by the Jewish tradition in the Mishnah. Here new year's day is looked upon as the day of creation, just as the feast of tabernacles, as well as the enthronement psalms, have a special connexion with creation. 'This day is the origin of thy works'.[53] It is also the day when Yahweh 'judgeth', i.e. decides all that is going to happen in the year to come, determines the fate of states and land, of mankind and of the crops of the earth.[54] To the lessons read in the synagogues first of all belong the so-called 'Malkiyoth', i.e. passages from the Scriptures speaking of Yahweh as a king, and the so-called 'Zikronoth', Scripture passages telling that Yahweh 'remembers' his creation.[55] We shall return to this in more detail below, and see that in fact many other psalms are closely related to the substance and cultic situation of the 'enthronement festival' and that they thus throw a new light on both.

The objection might be raised that the traditions of the Mishna are too late to prove anything with regard to Old Testament times.[56] But as long as the thought of creation is undoubtedly to be found in a psalm for the feast of tabernacles, like 65 (which beyond doubt also refers to the turn of the year), the connexion between the idea of creation and that of

[52] The parallelism shows that *melekh* in Nu. 23.21 can be nobody else than Yahweh himself.
[53] See Fiebig, *Rosch ha-schana*, pp. 45, 48f., 53f.
[54] Fiebig, *ibid.*, pp. 41ff., 77.
[55] Fiebig, *ibid.*, pp. 53ff. See *Ps.St.* II, p. 82.
[56] So for instance both Pap and Snaith; see also Johnson in *The O.T. and Modern Study*, pp. 193, 195.

the time of new year has been proved, even with regard to the Old Testament. Nor can the tradition of the Mishna about the connexion between new year's day and the kingship (and enthronement) of Yahweh be quite fortuitous; nor is it likely to be due to foreign influence, at a time when official Judaism tended more and more to isolate itself from anything extraneous. The ideas must have some relevance to an earlier Jewish conception of new year's day or the festal complex of new year. In fact, these very ideas play the leading role in the new year psalm (Ps. 47), which can on no account be dated later than early Jewish times.[57] Another fact is that several rites in the feast of Tabernacles, which are only mentioned in the Mishna, are much older and are actually referred to in the Old Testament.[58]

In the light of all these evidences and indications, increased emphasis must be laid on the fact that the ideas of the appearance and enthronement of the god and of the repeated creation and renewal of life were connected with the new year festivals in the whole of the surrounding orient. It is a fact that Israel's cult has not escaped strong influence from oriental cultic customs and ideas, with Canaan as the nearest and natural connecting link.

On the basis of a cultic interpretation of the enthronement psalms we may therefore state that they take for granted the existence of a corresponding festal day,[59] characterized by the same ideas, and that this festival had the feature of a new year festival.[60] In earlier times the new year festival in Jerusalem was the chief festival of the year, the feast of Tabernacles and of harvest; later, at any rate in earlier post-exilic time, a separate new year's day, rō'š haššānâ (Ezk. 40.1), detached itself and assumed a great many ideas that had hitherto been connected with the wider new year festival. This did not make the latter lose its old character, on the contrary it remained still very much alive in rites as well as psalms till the fall of the Temple, and was even known to the tradition of the Mishna. Amongst these conceptions was that of the kingship of Yahweh based on the creation and renewal of life. So, what has so far been called

[57] Snaith and Aalen deny that the idea of creation is found in the enthronement psalms. See, however, Additional Note XV.

[58] The festival of light (with the dance with torches) is referred to in Ps. 118.27, and so is the dance-like procession (ḥagh); the whole psalm has been sung at such a procession. The same thing applies to the crowning of the altar with garlands of green branches. Isa. 12.3 refers to the ceremony with pouring of water. Worth noticing also is that Isa. 12 and Ps. 118 are almost identical as to substance and partly even phraseology, just as Isa. 12.4–6 stands quite in line with the 'enthronement psalms' as to style, tone and ideas. In fact there is every reason to suppose that the two psalm quotations in Isa. 12 are derived from psalms belonging to the festival of tabernacles (new year) and enthronement. If we bear in mind the religio-phenomenological connexion of the said rites with the primeval 'primitive' rites of fertility, rain and life-revival, it is quite out of the question that they should be late Jewish innovations in the temple cult.

[59] On two new attempts to find another cultic situation behind the enthronement psalms, see Additional Note XVI.

[60] See above, n. 45.

'the enthronement festival of Yahweh' is, historically speaking, actually another aspect of the harvest and new year festival itself.

The question then is, whether the enthronement psalms belong to the detached new year's day or to the new year festival of the older complex. Did the very idea of enthronement, with the ceremonies attached to it, above all the great royal procession, in later time still belong to the festival of the older complex, or has it then been attached to the detached new year's day alone?

Ps. 81 mentions a special new year's day at the new moon besides 'the feast' (*haggēnû*), i.e. of harvest and Tabernacles, at full moon. It contains clear references to the 'cry of homage' and the 'sounding of horns', characteristic of new year's day, the 1st of Tishri, the 'day for sounding horns', the 'day for cries of homage'.[61] But side by side with the 'day of new moon' we are here told of 'the full moon on our feast day'.[62] It is therefore not easy to decide for which of these two days the psalm was composed. But the text at least shows that the author was fully aware that the two feasts belonged to the same set, that they were based on the same ideas, and distinguished in part by the same customs. Nor does the psalm deny that the detached new year's day received its content and rites from the earlier feast of Tabernacles.

The special new year's day is first mentioned in Ezk. 40.1, and for those who hold that the book of Ezekiel is written by Ezekiel himself, the question ought to be settled. The day is mentioned there in a perfectly matter-of-course way, as something well known and not as a piece of news. But even to those who, like the present author, consider the book to be a work of Ezekiel's disciples some time after the return (the restoration), its evidence is not without importance.

But even if we should abide by the impossibility of proving that a new year's day on the 1st of Tishri was pre-exilic, and that the 'enthronement festival' of the monarchy was part of, or an aspect of, the seven days' complex of harvest and new year, the question yet remains whether among the seven (or eight) days of the feast one particular day might stand out as the day of Yahweh's enthronement, to which the enthronement psalms would belong,[63] as was the case with the Babylonian feast of new year and enthronement.[64] If so, it would be natural to think of the seventh day, 'the last day, that great day of the feast', and to suppose that Yahweh's royal entry would take place on that day. In support of this hypothesis we might plead that the Mishna and Talmud refer the procession psalm (Ps. 118), to the seventh day of the feast. The 'last day' is likely to be the seventh; the eighth being considered a supplement to the seven days of the feast proper.

---

[61] See *hārî'û* = 'cry *tĕrû'â*' = 'cry out' (cf. Humbert, *La 'Terou'a'*, pp. 39ff.); 'blow the trumpets on the day when the moon is at her full'.

[62] *bakkese' yôm ḥaggēnû*. See Additional Note XVI.

[63] See above, n. 45.

[64] See Frankfort, *Kingship*, pp. 318ff.

If it be true that the enthronement idea is a pre-exilic aspect of the feast of harvest and Tabernacles, then we have to ask how old this connexion may be. How far back into pre-exilic times can we trace the concept of Yahweh's 'appearance' and epiphany at the harvest feast as a royal entry and an enthronement? Here we need to remember that the feast itself, the chief feast of the year, marking the end of the old year and the beginning of the new, had been adopted from the Canaanites. The ground for this statement is, quite simply, its nature as an agrarian festival. Its basic idea is connected with the cultivation of the earth, and this fact is clearly brought out by its ancient fertility rites, the green branches and the ceremony of water drawing. It was celebrated in Ugarit before the invasion of the Israelites,[65] and by the Canaanites at Shechem at the time of Abimelech (Jdg. 9.27). There is no reason to doubt that the Jebusites in Jerusalem, too, used to celebrate a similar harvest and new year feast. That the festival itself was adopted by the Israelites even before the monarchy will be seen from Jdg. 21 and 1 Sam. 1f.[66]

Everything seems to suggest that the Canaanites already celebrated the festival as an enthronement festival for the god as king. For Ugarit the texts give ample evidence. The resurrection of Baal (and his victorious fight against Môt) ends with his sitting down on the throne, receiving the homage of his people, and building his temple. Therefore it is very likely that the El Elyon feast in the Jebusite Jerusalem was celebrated as an enthronement festival.

On the other hand, the concept of Yahweh as a king would hardly be adopted by the Israelites until they themselves had got a king, and, with him, an obvious occasion to bestow on Yahweh this highest title of honour.

How early Yahweh came to be looked upon as a king in Jerusalem, it is impossible to tell with any certainty on the basis of the few and fragmentary texts handed down to us from earlier times.[67] But at any rate we know that Solomon had furnished the Temple with an (empty) cherub's throne, which was certainly understood to be the throne of Yahweh.[68] In the very old Ps. 110 Yahweh is the king, sitting on his throne and offering to his 'son', the earthly king, the seat of honour at his right side. In the likewise very old Ps. 68 the worshipper calls Yahweh 'his king and his god'. Therefore we have every reason to believe that the rich temple cult in Jerusalem, highly influenced as it was from Canaan, would also very early have adopted and given expression to the idea of Yahweh's royal entry and enthronement—and if so, it would naturally attach it to the chief festival of the year, 'Yahweh's festival'.

---

[65] See Hvidberg, *Graad og Latter*; Kapelrud in *NTT*, 1940, pp. 38ff.

[66] See Judges 21.19; 1 Sam. 1.3, 7, 20f. (the words *wayĕhî lithĕqûphôth hayyāmîm* v. 20 have to be placed before v. 21, see *BHK³*).

[67] See Additional Note XVII.

[68] See H. Schmidt, *Lade und Cherubenthron*, *Gunkelfestschrift*; Johs. Pedersen, Israel III–IV, pp. 246ff.; a little differently, Bellas in *Theologia*, 1930.

There is still another aspect of the feast of harvest and Tabernacles, to which the enthronement psalms refer. In Ps. 93.5 we read:

> Thy testimonies are very sure,
> holiness becomes thine house,
> O Yahweh, unto endless time.

In connexion with Yahweh's victory over the powers of chaos, and his enthronement we hear that his temple has now received the 'holiness' belonging to it. 'Holiness' is the numinous quality, which the Temple must have in order to be an abode worthy of Yahweh, and 'effective' for the purpose at which the cult there is aimed. The opposite is 'profaneness', in this connexion the same thing as 'impurity'. The 'holiness' which the Temple now possesses, is not (only) a consequence of Yahweh's entry into it; according to the conception of the Old Testament, certain cultic measures are required in order to consecrate and cleanse it from impurity; cf. Ex. 19. That is the idea behind the great annual 'day of purification'; even if the form in which we find it in Lev. 16, as a separate *yôm kippûrîm*, five days before the feast of Tabernacles, represents a later system, there can be no doubt that something like it, some re-inauguration, re-consecration of the Temple must have belonged to the preparations for the feast of Tabernacles even in earlier times.[69] This was the case with the Babylonian new year festival. Let us here anticipate slightly by pointing out that the festal hymn preserved for us in Ex. 15, but originally no doubt belonging to the cult, makes the description of the great achievement of Yahweh culminate with the story of the foundation of the Temple, where Yahweh is now enthroned as king:

> A sanctuary thy hands have formed, O Yahweh;
> now Yahweh is king for evermore.

That the Temple has been re-consecrated implies therefore that the whole cultic system is again fully effective as of old. There is a reference to this in Ps. 99 whose true meaning is exactly given in Moffatt's somewhat free translation:[70]

> His priests have still a Moses and an Aaron,
> his worshippers have still a Samuel,
> and Yahweh answers when they call to him,
> still, through the cloudy pillar, speaks to them.

---

[69] In this connexion it may be of interest to point out that the law of Lev. 16 gives the impression of containing different strata; cf. Messel in *ZATW* 27, 1907, pp. 1ff., who claims to have found 3 different strata of laws in the chapter. The original connexion between the festival of tabernacles and new year and that of *Kippurîm* is also maintained with detailed arguments by Bellas in *Theologia*, 1930.

[70] The correct interpretation is given by Buhl, *Psalmerne*; in the second edition he adds a reference to Boehmer, *ZATW* 26, 1906, pp. 156ff.

A re-consecration is a repetition of the first consecration; it is an all but obvious conclusion that it would take place on the anniversary of the original consecration—or, to put it the other way about, from the traditional date of consecration and purification we may deduce that the original consecration must have been performed on that day. This was the line of argument followed in Israel as well. Therefore the first book of Kings (8.1ff.)—in this case probably with the annals of the kingdom for its source—tells us that Solomon consecrated his new Temple 'at the feast in the month Ethanim' (which means the feast of harvest and Tabernacles), and there is no reason to doubt that this is historically correct. The new year feast has been chosen as the feast of the consecration of the Temple! In this connexion it is important that in 1 Kgs. 8 the central act of the temple consecration consists in the ark being brought in a procession into the sanctuary as a symbol of the personal presence of Yahweh. The festal act of 1 Kgs. 8 is described as a repetition of the one in 2 Sam. 6. In this way a connexion has again been established between the enthronement psalms and the new year festival.[71]

The later tradition as it has been handed down to us in the book of Chronicles, traces this connexion to the age of David. When the Chronicler (1.16) in his version of 2 Sam. 6 relates that on the transference of the ark of Yahweh to Jerusalem, a hymn was sung which was composed of passages from the enthronement psalms (Pss. 96 and 97), and other closely related psalms, this cannot be free imagination on his part. There can be hardly any doubt that he conventionalizes his records of the age of David from the actual customs of the festal cult of his own day, in other words, he had a certain day in his mind as a model, the festal day to which the enthronement psalms belonged. Then, we must ask, does not the earlier tradition in 2 Sam. 6 also mean that the transference of the ark, and with it the official inauguration by David of the Yahweh cult in Jerusalem, took place in connexion with the festival of the year, the harvest feast? And as we are able to infer with all likelihood from the Ugaritic texts that the connexion between this festival and the victorious entry of the deity was traditional in Palestine even before the invasion of Israel, and as we consider the purposeful religious politics of David: to fuse the El Elyon cult into the cult of Yahweh and thus make it Israelite, it would be rather strange if he had not seized this opportunity of putting the stamp of Yahwism on this originally Canaanite festival. Even before the time of David it had become the chief festival of the Israelites, being celebrated as such in Shiloh (see above), the centre with which the ark had formerly been associated.

The idea of the purification and re-consecration of the Temple also involves—as can be seen from the law in Lev. 16 about the great day of purification—the idea of atonement for, and forgiveness of, all sins which in the course of the year may have covered people and land with guilt and

[71] See Additional Note XVIII.

impurity. The royal epiphany of Yahweh also means that he shall gracefully forgive the sins of his people. There is even a reference to this in the
enthronement psalm (Ps. 99). As at the time of Moses and Aaron and
Samuel—and in conformity with the intentions of the psalmist, it is safe
to add, ever after in the history of the people—so through the enthronement of Yahweh it has again become evident that

> thou has been a forgiving God to them,
> hast (not) taken vengeance on their deeds. (v. 8)

Even the earthly king would grant an amnesty on the day of his enthronement (1 Kgs. 1.51ff.; 2 Kgs. 25.57ff.; cf. 1 Sam. 11.12ff.).

Even here the enthronement psalms are in accordance with the thoughts
of Judaism on the religious meaning of the new year. It is a well-known
circumstance, which, for instance, finds expression in the prayer Abinu
Malkenu, that to the new year feast belongs the idea that God shall then
forgive the sins of his people, so that they may have a new start as 'new
creatures'.[71a]

In 2 Sam. 6, as well as in 1 Kgs. 8, the king himself, David, or Solomon
respectively, officiates as chief priest, performing the most important cultic
actions with his own hand. This is in full agreement with the ancient
Israelite view of the king as 'Yahweh's anointed', his 'son', his viceroy on
earth.[72] It results from the nature of the case, that the earthly king would
be a central figure in the cult of the new year festival. Of course this will
not be brought out by the enthronement psalms, properly so called, in
which the personal presence and kingship of Yahweh himself is celebrated.
But there are other evidences of the close connexion between the religious
aspect of kingship and the chief festival of the year.

First of all we shall draw attention to the term: 'in the beginning of
the reign of N.N.' (rē'šîth mamlekheth N.N.) Jer. 26.1. As can be seen from
the Akkadian rēš šárruti ša N.N., this is not simply an indefinite dating, but
a technical term with a definite intention. In Akkadian it indicates the
interval between the death of the old king and the actual assumption of
power on the part of his successor and the official sacral installation of the
latter at the following new year festival; this installation of the king was
celebrated over again every year at the same time with solemn cultic
ceremonies. There can be no doubt that the Hebrew term has been
directly adopted and translated from the Akkadian. So there is every
reason to believe that the phrase has the same technical meaning, though
possibly with the difference that it came to indicate especially the very
climax of the period: its solemn termination with the sacral installation of
the king. Jer. 26 shows that at (the end of) the rēšîth mamlekheth of the
king, a great cultic festival would take place. Everything seems to indicate
that this festival was the chief one of the year, the feast of tabernacles and

---

[71a] Cf. Sjöberg in StTh IV, 1951, p. 57.
[72] See my book He that Cometh, Chap. III.2, and above, Chap. III.2-4.

new year. The speech made on that occasion by Jeremiah (see Jer. 7) takes as its starting-point precisely the main thoughts of the festival: the complete confidence of the people in the promises of Yahweh with regard to the existence and importance of the Temple. The basis of this becomes still clearer and the idea still more distinct if we consider it against the background of the thought in Ps. 93.5: the faith in the trustworthy promises, guaranteed by the re-consecrated Temple.

Here Ps. 132 may be brought in. It belongs without any doubt to a dramatic festal procession, Yahweh's entry into his palace, where homage is paid to him at his footstool, that is to say, with himself sitting on his throne. But the procession at the same time celebrates the remembrance of, and calls to life the transference of, the ark to Jerusalem and the inauguration of the cult of Yahweh in Jerusalem, i.e. the situation in 2 Sam. 6; and the king here literally plays the part of David. The festival, to which the psalm belongs, is here again proved to be celebrated as a repetition of the succession to kingship, by the grace of Yahweh, of a scion of the house of David; the very favour and the very blessings once secured to David and re-echoed in Ps. 88.20ff. and 2 Sam. 7, are now secured to the reigning king. We can hardly doubt that this episode had its place within the framework of the new year festival. As we shall see, below, there are other things to indicate that Ps. 132 belongs here. And attention must be drawn to the fact that the connexion between the festival of temple consecration and the covenant of David is explicitly mentioned in Solomon's prayer at the consecration of the Temple, 1 Kgs. 8.16.[73]

Together with 2 Sam. 6 and 1 Kgs. 8, Ps. 132 shows, then, that in the religious and cultic conceptions and arrangements the repetition of the covenant of David was connected with the inauguration of the cult of Yahweh in Jerusalem. In the festal complex, including the commemoration of the erection of the Temple and the annual re-consecration of it, 'David', the king, played a central role, both as the 'son' and representative of the deity, and as the 'father' and representative of the people. The king's person is a visible token of God's merciful and strong presence in the midst of his people—a thought and a 'prophecy' which becomes a higher reality in Christ the king, the son of God, and his presence in the midst of his own, both when two or three are gathered in his name, and when the congregation commemorate his work in church festivals.

Now we may sum up the result of this preliminary research based on the rather confined group of true enthronement psalms with occasional references to other texts.

From the very principle of cultic interpretation it is plain that a 'feast of Yahweh's enthronement' must have existed, the main foci of which must have been Yahweh's enthronement and his kingship, based on his victory over the powers of chaos and the primeval ocean, and the creation, repetition and re-experience of these 'facts of salvation' in and through the

[73] Kraus has rightly drawn attention to this, op. cit., p. 43.

festival, and further, the renewal of the historical 'savation': the election, the deliverance from Egypt, and the making of the covenant. The most prominent act of this festival was the great procession with its dramatic and symbolic character, the personal presence of Yahweh being symbolized by the ark.

This feast was originally one aspect of the old agricultural feast of harvest and new year, probably characteristic of a certain day in the festal complex, possibly the seventh; later on, great parts of its complex of ideas were passed on to the new special new year's day, the 1st of Tishri. The enthronement aspect of the feast of new year and Tabernacles can be traced back to the monarchic period.

Another aspect of the festal complex of harvest and new year was its nature as a repeated festival for the consecration of the Temple, commemorating the inauguration of the cult of Yahweh in Jerusalem; to the feast for the consecration of the Temple was attached an annual purification of the same.

The feast for the consecration of the Temple also had the character of a renewal of the covenant with David and the royal house; this idea is naturally linked up with the idea of a renewal of the covenant on Mount Sinai, completed by the covenant with David. Therefore the offspring of David, the king of Israel, would also play an important role in the rites and conceptions of the festal complex.

6

The whole of the harvest festival as an agricultural feast is of course not a legacy from the time in the desert but, as mentioned above, was taken over from the Canaanites after the settlement; and in the same way the conception of the deity as a king, and the annual celebration of his accession and enthronement are of Canaanite origin.

The ancient Canaanite harvest festival was a religious nature feast closely connected with agriculture and fertility religion. It was a question of calling the forces of nature to life again after the time of drought. The changes of the natural year were a manifestation of divine power. The life of nature was one with the life of the deity, his death and triumphant resurrection, which was communicated to the congregation. Life in general, the earth, the whole world, plants, animals and man were created anew with the awakening of the god. It was this that should be ensured by the potent rites of the cultic feast. This was effected through the representation and realization of the process in a dramatic-symbolical form. To ask which is the primary cause, the creative rites, or the recuperative powers of the divinities, is to put a modern, rationalistic question that is here out of place; each is linked with the others; the rites are sacred and divine and established by the deity to create and ensure life and blessing. To higher vision the deity itself would surely be 'the source of life'.

This original nature and fertility cult has left many traces in the old Israelite harvest festival, right down to the latest times—but charged with a new sense and significance. We may mention such things as the tabernacles (Lev. 23.40ff.), and processions round the altar with green branches and fruits (Ps. 118.27), which to the comparative history of religions appear not as originally a thanksgiving, but as an awakening and force-transferring ceremony.[74] The holy power is also to be transferred to the altar to sanctify it, so that it may radiate blessing—as is suggested in the formula which according to the Mishna was pronounced before the altar when the solemn procession touch it with their branches.[75] The same holds good with regard to the water pouring ceremony which is mentioned in the Mishna and referred to in Isa. 12.3; the ceremony was originally intended to secure rain and water for the coming year.[76] During the feast of Tabernacles the water was fetched every day in a solemn procession from the holy spring, Gihon, and poured over the altar. The rabbis were probably still aware of the connexion between this rite and the approaching period of rains;[77] the water is to procure 'salvation', i.e. peace and prosperity—hence the 'well of salvation'. A corresponding significance originally pertained to the wine-offering which was poured over the altar with a view to obtaining a rich vintage. The ritual lighting of a fire, the torch-dance and the light festival,[78] which are mentioned in late Jewish times and may be referred to in Ps. 118.27a, are also a reminiscence of an ancient sun and light ceremony.[79]

In Israel all these ancient rites were gradually reinterpreted as symbolical expressions of the prayer to Yahweh to come and create life and fertility and peace and salvation ('light');[80] but some of the old ideas shine through, right down to late Jewish times, and appear clearly when the presentation of tithes and first-fruits is connected with the festival (Deut. 26.1ff.; Am. 4.4f.). This presentation was, moreover, no mere thanksgiving rite; it was also a prayer for blessings on land and people (cf. Deut. 26.15).

This harvest and new year festival already in ancient times lasted for several days; we hear of this in the days of the Judges, as regards the temple in Shiloh, and in those of Amos regarding Bethel (1 Sam. 1.19; Am. 4.4f.). In Jerusalem it covered seven-plus-one days (Deut. 16.15; Lev. 23.34ff.). Already in Shiloh it was a *ḥagh*, its chief characteristic

---

[74] Cf. Nilsson, *Primit. Religion*, pp. 31, 33ff. Frazer, *Golden Bough* (1 vol.), pp. 118ff.

[75] *yōphṭ lēkhā hammizbēaḥ*, Bab. Sukka IV, 5; see *Ps.St.* V, pp. 25ff.

[76] Bab. Sukka IV, 5.—The pouring of water as a new year custom also occurs with the Persians and the Syrians, see Feuchtwang in *MGWJ* 1911, p. 60; likewise in Burma, see Bastian, *Völker d. öst Asiens* II, pp. 254f. (after Volz, op. cit., p. 57, n. 60); in the light of comparative anthropology: Patai, *Man and Temple*, pp. 24ff.

[77] Bab. Rosh hasshana 16a; Bab. Ta 'anit 2a.

[78] Cf. Hos. 9.4 and see Bab. Sukka IV, 9f., 48a, b, where the original idea is still alive; see Volz, op. cit., pp. 37, 59.

[79] Cf. Volz, op. cit., pp. 26ff.; Nilsson, op. cit., pp. 31f.; Frazer, op. cit., pp. 78ff., 609ff., 643ff., 647f.

[80] For 'light' as a symbol for life, happiness and salvation see Aalen, op. cit., pp. 63ff., 70f.

being the great dance-like procession. From all later custom in Jerusalem, as we see it in Ps. 132 and are able to judge it from the account of the festal procession in 2 Sam. 6, and from the ancient cultic verse, Num. 10.35,[81] we may safely conclude that already in Shiloh the centre of the procession was formed by the visible symbol of the personal presence of the Lord, his holy ark or shrine, from which the divine power radiated; the ark in Jerusalem was, according to official opinion, identical with that in Shiloh[82] which was associated with Moses himself.

But with Yahweh's shrine was linked the view of Yahweh as king. 'Yahweh Sebaoth who is enthroned on the cherubim' is the name he carries when he is represented by the ark (1 Sam. 4.4); but the meaning of the name is 'he that sits on the cherub throne', the sides and arm-rests of which are formed by two winged cherubim; the king on the throne is 'throned on cherubim'.

The conception of the god as king is, as before mentioned, older than Israel. But it is not only this general form of the idea which Israel has received from the Canaanites, it is the same with its cultic and epic expression of the enthronement of the god. In the religious texts from the town of Ugarit (Ras Shamra) in Phoenicia, the feast of the rains—the harvest and new year festival—signifies the revival and resurrection of the god Baal or Aleyan Baal, who, having conquered death (*Môt*), seats himself on the throne and is proclaimed king of gods and men. Together with the enthronement of the god goes the building and consecration of his temple.[83]

These performances were apparently common to the whole of Canaan, and not restricted to Ugarit. That they have been of importance for the development of the cult of Yahweh in Jerusalem cannot be doubted. We know that the god who in pre-Israelite times was worshipped in Jerusalem as the highest god was El Elyon, in our bible translated as 'the most high God' (Gen. 14.18ff.). Inscriptions prove that El Elyon was widely worshipped in Canaan and Syria.[84] The name is the same as the Ugaritic Aleyan. But the name El Elyon, and with it undoubtedly also features both of the cult and the concept, were in Israel transferred to Yahweh—it is Yahweh who is 'the most high god'. Other deities in pre-Israelite days worshipped in Jerusalem were Melekh (the King), Shalem (the Covenant) and Ṣedeq (Justice);[85] they were probably already in the pre-Israelite age

[81] See Additional Note XIX.
[82] See 2 Sam. 6 together with 1 Sam. 4–6, and Additional Note XIX.
[83] See Hvidberg, *Graad og Latter*; Mowinckel in *NTT* 1939, pp. 16ff.; Kapelrud in *NTT* 1940, pp. 38ff., particularly pp. 44ff.; Engnell, *Div. Kingship*, pp. 97ff.
[84] See for instance the Sujin inscription, Bauer *AfO* VIII, the translation p. 11; cf. *A.N.E.T.*, p. 504; cf. also Johnson in *The Labyrinth*, pp. 81ff.
[85] Cf. the names of the kings of Jerusalem: Adonizedeq = 'Zedeq is (my) lord' and Malkizedeq = 'Zedeq is (my) king', or, 'Zedeq is (the god) Adon', 'Zedeq is (the god) Melek'. Probably it is the name of the god Shalem that makes up the last part of Jerusalem, cf. the local name Jeru'el, 2 Chron. 20.16.—For Shalem in Ugarit see Bauer in *ZATW* 51, 1933, p. 99, W. F. Albright, *A.R.I.*, pp. 73, 79. For Zedeq (Ṣydeq) see Baudissin, *Adonis u. Esmun*, pp. 247f. and Index, ibid.

at least to a certain degree conceived as manifestations of El Elyon. El Elyon was also the sun god, whose rays at daybreak puts the evil powers to flight, and who overthrows the haughty who would occupy his throne (cf. Ps. 46.6; Isa. 14.12–15). In Israel Yahweh himself became both 'King' and 'Justice'. His temple was built as a temple of the sun with its opening towards the east, so that the sun at the equinoxes shone straight through the open gates in towards 'the Holy of Holies', where 'He would dwell in the thick darkness', according to Solomon's inaugural prayer.

Already in pre-Israelite times there were, without doubt, connected with El Elyon and Melekh and Sedeq certain notions as to how it came to pass that the god *became* 'the Most High', *became* 'the King', and the wielder of 'Justice'—a word which also means 'the royal power' and 'fortune'— and of 'the peace of the covenant'. It behoves 'the Most High God' and 'the King' to provide rain and fertility and crops, and also to protect the 'power', 'peace' and 'fortune' of his people. All this the Israelites transferred to the desert war-god Yahweh, who already before Moses was the god of law and justice, of the peace of the covenant, of markets and the roads.[86] A transference of this kind is quite natural, and in keeping with the character of a revealed religion. In these ideas from patriarchal times the Israelites found ready prepared just those conceptions which could serve as links to the highest vision of Yahweh as the god both of the chosen people and of the whole world. This transition becomes still more easily comprehensible if, as certain things indicate, David's new priest in Jerusalem, Zadok, was descended from the ancient race of priest kings, of whom Melchizedek was a representative.[87] David and his successors were professedly 'priests' after the order of Melchizedek ('for the sake of Melchizedek'), as we hear in Ps. 110.

When Yahweh, in the thought and belief of the Israelites, subjected also the countryside and its agriculture, and became Lord (*baʿal*) and king of the land, and the giver of growth and fruitfulness, the ideas connected with the agricultural and harvesting feasts were also transferred to him. It is well known that all the great annual feasts—excepting that of the passover—were originally connected with agriculture, and taken over from the Canaanites.

[86] Cf. the name 'En mishpāṭ—'the fountain of justice (or judgment)'—for Yahweh's holy fountain at Kadesh. Kadesh was the specific cult place of Yahweh already before the tribes of Israel came to Goshen, and was also their first goal when they left Egypt; here the holy mountain Sinai-Horeb was situated, see Mowinckel in Norsk Geogr. Tidsskrift IX, pp. 21ff., J. Gray in *VT*, IV, 1954, pp. 148ff.; Engnell's doubt as to the connexion between Yahweh and Kadesh (*Gml. Testm.*, I, p. 265, in which by the way he gives a rather inaccurate statement of my opinion) is groundless. In the stories of the Exodus this connexion is evident. When Engnell (and Nyberg) suppose the 'original' deity of Kadesh to be the goddess of the same name, this is nothing but mere conjecture. It might be observed that the *name* of the goddess Kadesh must be secondary as compared to the name of the sanctuary, just as the name of the god Bethel is secondary as compared to the local name; and Babylonian Ea, originally indicating the temple, is secondary as the name of the god; the real name of the god is Enki. The name of the goddess Kadesh has probably been shortened from something like Baʿalat Kadesh.

[87] See Mowinckel, *Ezra d. Skriftlaerde*, p. 109, n. 2; Hall in Peake, *The People and the Book*, p. 11; Bentzen, *Stud. o. d. zadok. Praesteskabs Hist.*, pp. 10f.; Rowley in *JBL* LVIII, 1939, pp. 113ff. and in *Festschrift für Bertholet*, pp. 461ff.

It is important that, in the Canaanite temples also, the appearance of the god before the rainy period was celebrated as a royal enthronement festival, at which Baal's death and resurrection, his struggle and victory, ascent of the throne, 'holy marriage', and also the foundation of his temple, which was both his house and symbolically the whole world, and from which blessing should flow, were all dramatically presented and followed by the congregation as a creative reality filling them, too, with the divine forces of blessing, life, and fertility. Together with this transfer or imitation of a Canaanite agricultural feast, and its conversion to a feast of Yahweh, the Israelites took over and Yahwistically reformed the ideas of the enthronement of the deity, of the royal character of the feast, and of the restoration of life in nature as the result of king Yahweh's victory over his enemies.

But it is also important to note that the king-god festival of the Canaanites was, in fact, only a particular version of a general cultic pattern obtaining throughout ancient oriental civilization, its fundamental features being traceable in most of the religions and cultic systems, although naturally stamped by different national and religious characteristics.[88] In several places the cult found its climax in an annual festival, which more or less clearly and completely contained the representation of the death and resurrection of the god, of the creation-myth, the god's fight with and victory over his enemies, his holy marriage and triumphant entry as king. It is principally from Babylonia and Assyria that we have our certain knowledge of these facts. Here was celebrated, in all the larger cultic centres—mostly in the spring, but in some places in the autumn—a new year festival which may be considered as the enthronement festival of the god—Anu, Enlil, Marduk, Asshur, etc.—at which all the features mentioned were in evidence, and at which hymns were sung which acclaimed the god as creator and king, and described the blessing that his victory and reign would bring to his land and people, and to the whole earth.[89] In a similar way the enthronement of Osiris and Horus was celebrated in Egypt.[90]

This idea of the arrival of the life-creating and renewing god as a king mounting the throne, culminating in a great festal procession then faced the Israelites from all quarters, as soon as they had settled in Canaan and started to adapt their cult to settled agricultural and urban conditions.

When the rains came and renewed their 'world' or 'country'—the Hebrew 'ereṣ has both meanings—the Israelites saw in this a sign that Yahweh himself had come to visit his people and had conquered the powers of chaos and death, and seated himself on the throne and re-established his kingdom, bringing peace and prosperity to his people.

[88] See Additional Note XX.
[89] Cf. Zimmern, AO XXXV, 3; Babyl. Neujahrsfest I and II; Pallis, Babyl. Akitu Festival; Gadd in Myth and Ritual, pp. 40ff.
[90] Erman, Aegypt. Relig.,² pp. 62ff.; Ps.St. II, pp. 30ff.; Blackman in Myth and Ritual, pp. 15ff.; cf. Frankfort, Kingship, pp. 181ff.

They then wanted to use the strongest expressions in praise of the Lord and found them in the symbols of the enthronement and the kingdom and the new creation.

In ancient Canaan as well, they spoke of the god's war with, and victory over, the sea and the monsters of the deep. But whether they considered this as an act of *creation* is uncertain; in none of the hitherto known texts does the dragon fight lead to any creation.[91] Baal is on the whole not envisaged as a creator; he is the life-force itself, the god of fertility in field, folk and cattle. It is El, the highest god, who in the Ugarit texts appears as the creator, Baal being identified with the awakening life-force in nature. Yahweh, on the other hand, is the sovereign Lord of the universe, who has conquered chaos and shaped cosmos from it. He is El, Baal and Adon in one, both God and Lord. Yahweh's struggle with chaos and the primeval sea leads to the act of creation.

The same was the case in Babylonia-Assyria, where the annual 're-creation' of life and nature consists in the fields rising from the primeval sea of the spring floods, which inundated the low alluvial plain for miles; there, naturally, the vernal equinox was the time of new year, and there the myth of the primeval sea and the fight with the dragon stood for the story of the creation: Marduk vanquishes Tiamat and creates the world.[92]

Now we find in many places in the Old Testament that in Israel poets and prophets imagined creation as Yahweh's victorious struggle with the primeval sea and its dragon, with Leviathan or Rahab or his 'proud Helpers'.[93] In a much modified and 'rationalized' form the same idea lies at the back of the later story of creation in Gen. 1. No doubt also Canaanite elements now entered into this poetic myth; the Ugarit texts also speak of a dragon, *Lotan* (i.e. Leviathan). But both the strong similarity with corresponding Babylonian religious poetry and the circumstance that it is particularly in the later time of the monarchy (when the connexion with Assyria-Babylonia was lively), that we meet with these ideas in the Old Testament, indicate that it is here a question of Assyrian-Babylonian influence in addition to that of the old Canaanite traditions.

Other features of the enthronement festival point to the same conclusion. First and foremost we may mention the close connexion between the idea of creation and that of the kingship of the deity. In the Babylonian epic of creation, which was the legend and text for the new year's day service, the god Marduk is made king at the council meeting of the gods; and this choice is repeated every year, when they foregather in the 'chamber of fate' in the temple of Marduk. Here fate is 'fixed' for the coming year. The gods 'judge' what the fate of the peoples and the countries is to be, as they 'set fate' ('set that which is determined') for the year.

[91] See Additional Note XXI.
[92] See Additional Note XXII.
[93] Ps. 104.5ff.; Job 38.8ff.; Pss. 74.12ff.; 104.25f.; 89.10f.; Isa. 51.9f.; Job 9.13; 26.12; 7.12; (Ps. 44.20).

The Jewish tradition, too, as we have mentioned, holds that on new year's day, or in the course of the new year festival, Yahweh 'judges' how the new year is to be as to the harvest and the fate of land and people generally.

We may, then, conclude that both ancient Canaanite and Babylonian-Assyrian ideas and customs have contributed elements to the Israelite harvest, new year, and enthronement festival.

In its original form, then, the harvest festival is at the same time a festival of creation and of enthronement. It implies that the 'world' of the congregation is 'created' again, is renewed, and re-constituted a home for mankind, holding fruitfulness and blessing, and secured by the returning deity's apprehended strength and power. This character the feast retained in Israel. We may put it like this, that, when it was a matter of expressing the real religious experience of the festival in the poetical language of the epic myth, then the myth of creation is the original 'legend' of the festival, and this myth includes also that of the enthronement of the god Yahweh: he is made king because of the victory over the enemy, which is implied by the fact of the creation, and because he himself has created his kingdom, the world.

7

In Israel, however, the old, originally Canaanite festival has become something entirely new and *sui generis*. The Yahweh religion has taken over material from many sources. But it has always remoulded this material and made it the bearer of a new spirit.

With regard to the taking over and transforming of the conception of the god's ascension, we must first mention the most important 'negative' new form that Israel gave to it. The conception which was so characteristic of the Canaanite Baal, namely that the defeat, death and resurrection of the god precede his final victory and ascension, was wholly incompatible with Yahweh's essential character.[94] All representations and rites which directly expressed or referred to the death and resurrection of the god therefore had to disappear.

In recent times it has been maintained by several scholars that Israel took over the whole of this 'cultic pattern' more or less unchanged. Some have thought that just as in Canaan, Babylonia-Assyria and other places in the ancient orient, so in Israel, too, the death of the god was dramatically presented in the cult, and the king was regarded as divine, and one with the god; so that when the king in the cultic drama 'died' and 'rose again', he thereby made real the death and resurrection of the god. Through the effective cultic drama the king and the god mutually made each other alive again and gave each other new powers for the new

[94] Cf. Johs. Pedersen, *Israel* III–IV, pp. 441ff., cf. ibid., pp. 458, 466, 484, 737ff., 749; see also *Act. Or.* XVIII, pp. 1ff.; Hvidberg, *Israelitiske religion*, p. 71; Bentzen, *Sakrale kongedømme*, pp. 10ff. and *passim*.

beginning of life.[95] In such a case one could think of it either as a direct taking over of the whole 'cultic pattern' and its ideas, or that it was taken over in a more or less 'disintegrated' form, and in such a way that the customs and rites have only in part retained their original meaning, and have partly been reinterpreted or have disappeared.[96] It has thus been maintained that in the Israelite new year ritual it is not Yahweh himself who suffers, dies and rises again, but that this was transferred to a special fertility god, *Dōd*, who is supposed to have been' split off' from Yahweh, by one of the attributes of Yahweh becoming independent, and he is supposed to have been represented in the cult by the king: *Dōd* linguistically equals 'David', which was also a royal title in Israel.[97]

But this hypothesis, in all its different forms, is untenable. It is of course quite right that the temple cult of Israel to a large degree is based on Canaanite and, in the last resort, general oriental cultic patterns. This appears from what has been said above about the new year festival and is constantly confirmed by new archaeological results and text discoveries.[98] It is something which is self-evident, and also has long been recognized by all Biblical scholars.[99] But it is just as self-evident that this has not taken place without deep changes both of the thought and the cultic forms, due to the peculiarity of the Yahweh religion and its essential difference from the surrounding religions,[100] even though Israel only gradually became conscious of this difference.[101] It is unquestionably right that a fundamental thought both in Babylonian-Assyrian and in Canaanite religion was the death and resurrection of the god, represented as a struggle against the power of death and as the defeat and death of the god, succeeded by his resurrection and victory, the whole presented and experienced as a drama in the cult, a cultic play with actual and real effects.[102] But it is equally clear that Israel itself very early felt that there was a decisive difference between these dying Canaanite gods and Yahweh.

[95] See Johnson in *The Labyrinth*, pp. 71ff., joining Hocart, *Kingship*. Cf. Engnell, *Div. Kingship*, p. 170, n. 4, p. 210; Haldar, *Studies in the book of Nahum*, *passim*. See also n. 97, below.
[96] Cf. above, n. 62 to Chap. III.
[97] Engnell, *Kortfattat bemötande av Prof. Bentzens 'diskusjonsinnlägg' Det Sakrale kongedömme*, a manuscript submitted in connexion with the competition for a professorship in Lund, 1946; cf. H. S. Nyberg's critique thereon in 'Sakkunnigutlätande angående ledigförklarade professorämbetet i exegetisk teologi', published in mimeograph by the University of Lund, 1947, 'Nyberg', p. 15.
[98] See for instance Hooke, *Origins of Early Sem. Ritual*—certainly with a tendency to construct and reckon with too many hypothetical factors—and the summing-up in Albright, *A.R.I.*
[99] See above, n. 57 to Chap. I, and cf. *Ps.St.* II, pp. 200ff.
[100] See references in n. 94 above, and in addition, Baumgartner, *ThZ* III, pp. 98ff.
[101] In spite of justifiable objections to a rigid schematic 'evolutionism', there is a 'development' within historical Yahwism, a development which to a great extent had the nature of a dramatic conflict between the old views of Israel and the religion of the Canaanites; and through which the religion of Israel became conscious of its inherent peculiarities and their potentialities, and expanded them. It is from this 'dramatic' point of view that Hvidberg's *Israelitiske Religions Historie*, for instance, has been written. Cf. also Cook in *The Modern Churchman*, November 1934. To grasp this dramatic history and the line of its development is important even from the point of view of 'revelation history'.
[102] See for instance Hvidberg, *Graad og Latter*; Engnell, *Div. Kingship*, pp. 16ff., 97ff., 143ff., and above, note 95.

While the expression 'the living God' applied to a Canaanite deity meant 'the god who again has become alive' it has, as applied to Yahweh, always meant: The God who always has lived, and always lives, and who, accordingly, everlastingly creates and sustains life.[103] Yahweh is, in the words of the prophet, 'The Holy God who does not die' (Hab. 1.12). That Israel, therefore, should have taken over a complete cult ritual, which implies and exhibits the suffering, death and resurrection of the deity is wholly excluded. Even in the modified form of the 'split-off' vegetation god, who in the person of the king dies and rises again, the theory is unacceptable. In the Old Testament there is no recognizable trace of the cult of such a *Dōd* in Jerusalem. Without doubt the worship of the vegetation god did make its way into many places in Israel, not the least in North Israel,[104] but wherever the Old Testament refers to it, it is in order to condemn it as paganism.[105]

In Canaanite religion—and partly also in Egyptian, but less clearly in Sumero-Babylonian religion—the real thought is that it is the god himself who is renewed in the cult, together with his visible representative, the king. The powerful acts of the cult give to both the god and the king new strength, new blessing, new life, and through his participation in the dramatic rites the king is so to speak (to carry the idea to its extreme) active in creating new life for the god, in order that he in turn should give new life to the fields, the cattle and the people. In Israel, i.e. in the circles who thought and felt in genuinely Israelite fashion, such an idea was unthinkable. For this reason Yahweh was also kept as far away from death and the realm of the dead as possible. Yahweh has nothing to do with the realm of the dead, where he makes no 'wonders'; the dead 'are torn out of his hand', a thought which is emphasized so strongly that logically it enters into opposition to the belief in the omnipotence of Yahweh, and which also led to the strange, unsemitic and non-Hebraic idea that the dead are unclean, and one must have no dealings with them. In Israel the king became, not the one who helps the god to get life and power, but just the reverse, the representative of the whole body of the people, who himself gets all blessing, power and 'life' from Yahweh, because he is Yahweh's 'anointed one', and 'son', who passes on to the people the blessing which he has received from Yahweh through his anointing, and which is renewed for him and the body of the people through the coming of Yahweh in the cult.[106]

This radical exclusion of the thought of the deity's death and resurrection has certainly made the thought of Yahweh's yearly repeated enthronement less logical, but at the same time more deeply religious and realistic.

[103] See v. Baudissin, *Adonis und Esmun*, pp. 450ff.
[104] Reference is made for instance in the Mesha' inscription 1.12 to some Israelite deity Daud or Dod and his cultic equipment. Text to be found in Lidzbarski, *Handbuch d. Nordsem. Epigr.* I, pp. 415f., II, Tafel I, etc.; translation by Gressmann, *A.O.T.B.*[2] p. 441. Differently by Albright in *A.N.E.T.*, 1950, p. 320; cf. Ullendorf in *Docts. from O.T. Times*, p. 198.
[105] Ezk. 9.4; Zech. 12.11. Cf. Baumgartner in *ThZ* III, p. 98.
[106] Cf. Johs. Pedersen, *Israel* III–IV, pp. 84ff.

Yahweh's own power and existence and kingship cannot really be threatened by any enemy; no one equals him either in heaven or on earth or in the underworld.[107] But time and time again the evil powers of existence may threaten his creation and bring his cosmos to the verge of destruction —as may be seen to happen in the droughts of summer, in the hostility of the gentiles against his people, and so on. Then on each occasion Yahweh in battle and victory sustains his honour, saves and restores his creation, secures his 'kingdom' and his people, thus maintaining and proving the kingship which is really his from the beginning of Israel and from eternity. This is what happens at his 'epiphany' in the new year festival, when he comes to be 'enthroned', when, after a new victory and a new creation, he sits again on his world-wide throne.

But on the positive side, too, something new was added to the ideological content of the festival in Israel. This derived partly from the contrast between Yahweh and the local deities of nature and fertility, and partly from the historical influence on Israelite religion of their experience of Yahweh in a decisive historical hour, which resulted in the making of Israel. From this experience emerged a vision, of which the prophets gradually became the greatest exponents: Yahweh works and reveals himself in living history.

On the whole this historical character is a really fundamental feature in the religion of Israel. That Israel had experienced Yahweh in history, and that the prophets ever more clearly continued to see him there, and to interpret real history as the truest revelation of him, or, in theological terms, that God actually 'revealed' himself to his witnesses and to his people through reality itself, that the facts of revealed history are his 'words', properly so called, receiving their full meaning through the historical person who was at the same time the 'Word'—this is what has made Israelite religion something essentially different from the 'natural' religions and 'nature-religions' of the Near East.[108] The aphorism about man as distinct from animals: 'man has no nature, he has only a history', eminently fits the religion of Israel.

This also means that in Yahwism the cult has been made into history, and history has been drawn into the cult. The reality re-experienced through the cult is no longer first and foremost the cyclical course and renewal of nature, but the historical 'facts of salvation'.

The facts of salvation, 'recalled' and repeated by means of the festival, were removed from the sphere of natural religion (fertility and so on) to the world of historical reality.[109] Creation itself was no longer considered an undatable phenomenon, but a mighty mythico-historical action taking place on a definite occasion, later 'recalled' and kept up ('renewed', 'preserved', in the language of dogmatics) through the coming of Yahweh

[107] Ps. 86.6–8; Isa. 43.11; 44.6; 45.5, 6, 14, 18, 21, 22; 46.9.
[108] On this cf. Elliger, *Bedeutung d. Gesch. Israels f. d. Kirche*; see also Birkeland in *SEÅ* XIII, pp. 44f.
[109] See Additional Note XXIII.

at the festival, and through his miracles there. And side by side with the creation and the re-creation of nature through the festival we have the recollection of the deliverance from Egypt, of the miracle at the Reed Lake and of the Covenant of Kadesh-Sinai and the victory over the natives after the settlement, in short *the election*. These were the elements brought to the fore as the true work of a king and the true saving action of Yahweh, cf. the words of the poet in Ex. 15.18; these are the happenings 'recalled' at the festival and 'repeated' there; for the coming and enthronement of Yahweh again guarantee that the election is still valid, and that the 'right' and supremacy (*ṣedeq*) over all enemies thus secured for as long as he shall keep the commandments of Yahweh, were again promised and confirmed to Israel.

From what has been said above (pp. 138f.) we are entitled to conclude that in all probability the enthronement idea has been combined with the 'feast of Yahweh' (*ḥagh* YHWH) in Jerusalem from the very time of the first institution of his cult there. Maybe the idea of Yahweh as king was admitted into Israelite religion even before that time, and if so, presumably at the temple of Shiloh, where the 'Ark of Yahweh Ṣeba'oth' was the central cultic symbol. But we have no clear indications of the enthronement ideas in such early times.[109a]

It goes without saying that not all the ideas connected with the Jerusalem feast of Yahweh's epiphany were taken over at once. The adaptation of the Canaanite ideas to the spirit of the Yahweh religion must have taken time; of course a gradual development of ideas and cult forms has taken place. To this extent our picture of the festival in this chapter is an 'idealized' picture which may not have been fully realized at any particular point of time. A long history has been telescoped in our description. But the main ideas and rites have certainly been the same throughout all the pre-exilic period, and perhaps even much later.

8

As already mentioned, every cultic festival has its festal 'myth', i.e. the tale or 'message' about the 'saving', existential reality, which is being realized through the festival. Such a myth need not be fashioned as an elaborate epic tale, nor even have poetic form; it may be nothing more than a more or less fixed complex of religious concepts about what is taking place, and referred to by the festal songs in more or less detail. So the festival of Yahweh's enthronement naturally had a festal myth,

[109a] A. Alt, 'Gedanken über das Königtum Jahwes', *Kleine Schriften* I, pp. 345ff., has tried to find pointers for dating the idea of Yahweh's kingdom back to the period of the 'Judges' and has drawn attention to many of the points dealt with above (pp. 177ff., and other places). But I can neither subscribe to his early dating of the J-saga, nor to his concluding from the existence of the idea of the *bĕnê 'ĕlohîm* in Gen. 6.1ff., the existence of the idea of Yahweh as king. Alt is right, however, in thinking that these ideas have been combined later on, as we can see from 1 Kgs. 22 and Job 1f.

expressing the prevailing ideas concerning what happened at the coming of Yahweh, what was the basis of his enthronement, and what it led to.

But before passing on, and trying to give a picture of the myths behind the festival, we must first explain why we have to draw on material beyond the range of actual 'enthronement psalms' in the strict form-critical sense of the words. Gunkel identifies the picture given by this specific group of psalms with the picture of the cultic situation underlying it, without always realizing that this situation may be, and often is, only part of a greater liturgical whole. So far as the enthronement psalms are concerned, he is content to give a description of the enthronement as the imagination of the poet pictured it, and he does not make any attempt to describe the content of the festival as a whole; he even rejects any endeavour to justify such attempts.[110] But every cultic festival reflects many sides of life; in it the basic fact of 'salvation' in all its complexity becomes experienced reality. The enthronement festival was the chief festival of the year, *the* feast of Yahweh at his personal 'coming' in the hour of deepest danger and need, and with all the 'salvation' and bliss which this coming includes, so that all the fundamental experiences, emotions and ideas of religion must have met together here.

It is certain therefore that at such a feast not only songs of praise or 'coronation hymns' in the definite form-critical meaning of the word were sung, but that all the emotions and overtones of religion as comprehended in this total experience would have to find expression, from lamentations and prayers of distress 'out of the depths', to rejoicing at the coming of the saviour-god with victory and salvation are as prophesied. To limit our picture of the festival to what may be deduced from a single, though typical, form-historically defined group of psalms, cannot be methodologically correct. It is therefore impossible to draw a hard-and-fast line between psalms of enthronement and other psalms that belong to the new year festival and reflect its ideology.

But we also have to take into account that ideas of enthronement had an influence, too, on other psalms belonging to the 'enthronement festival', and not only on the 'coronation hymns' in the specific sense; just as the chief idea, the real 'message' and 'experience' of Christmas and Easter have had an influence on all hymns belonging to the Christian celebration of these festivals, regardless of the literary type and style of the individual hymns, whether they be hymns of petition or praise. When we are dealing with the 'enthronement festival' as an aspect of a more extensive festival—the epiphany feast of Yahweh—we must therefore also have recourse to such psalms as contain some of the main ideas of the enthronement hymns, and give expression to such distinctive aspects as the idea of Yahweh's epiphany for (renewed) creation, his kingship, his kingly victory over the demons of chaos and primordial ocean, and particularly so if

---

[110] Gunkel-Begrich, *Einl.*, p. 104.—Krauss (op. cit.) follows Gunkel in his formalistic limitation of the material.

these and other features from the enthronement psalms are found combined in one psalm. The other possibility, to which Gunkel draws attention, that there may also have existed other festivals of Advent, is of lesser
importance, as long as we *know* that this Advent feast was pre-eminently
the feast of harvest and new year together with the enthronement of
Yahweh.

The most important of these other psalms are Pss. 46; 48; 75; 76; 81;
24; but there are others, which will be taken into account in the following
paragraphs.[111]

As already mentioned, the fundamental thought in the festal experience
and the festal myth is that Yahweh is coming (96.13; 98.9) and 'revealing
himself', 'becoming revealed' and 'making himself known',[112] appearing
as the one he really is, manifesting his works and his will. This is not
a mere idea, it is reality, visibly expressed through the symbols and
rites of the feast and the emotional reactions of the congregation to its
experiences. The festival, in short, is the *festal epiphany* of Yahweh.

> Yahweh hath 'made known' his salvation,
>   hath 'revealed' his saving victory. (98.2.)
>
> God is within her citadels,
>   hath 'made himself known' as a defence. (48.4.)
>
> God hath 'made himself known' in Judah,
>   his 'name' is great in Israel.
> In Salem is now his pavilion,
>   In Zion his abode. (76.2f.)

This idea was current in the orient generally, and was originally understood quite literally as a cultic reality. In Babylonia as well as in Egypt
it was considered to be a climax in the festival, when the idol was carried
out and the curtain drawn aside, so that the congregation might 'behold
the face of the god', 'see the god in his beauty' or 'grace'. Such terms
were also adopted in Israelite religion (cf. Ps. 27.4), but there they were
taken in a spiritualized sense about the way *faith* 'beholds'. But even in
Israel this 'beholding' was attached to a visible symbol, namely to the
holy ark of Yahweh, which to all appearance was a focal point in the
festal procession at the enthronement (Ps. 132; cf. 2 Sam. 6).

In the festal experience it is first of all through his works, his 'saving
works' (*tĕšû'ôth, ṣĕdhāqôth*) that Yahweh reveals himself, manifesting to all
the world who and what he is. They are the 'message' of the festival.
The term 'glad tidings' (*bŝrt*) was already used in Ugarit about the
announcement that Baal had again become alive,[113] and in the same
terms the cultic festival announced to Israel the appearance of Yahweh

---

[111] On the pertinent material, see Additional Note XXIV.
[112] Ps. 98.2: *hôdhîa', gillâ*. Cf. also *nôdha'*, Pss. 48.4; 76.2; *hôphîa'*, Ps. 50.2.
[113] See Mowinckel in *NTT*, 1931, pp. 205ff.

as king and his enthronement (Ps. 96.2, cf. Isa. 52.7). But—and we shall return to this below—he also reveals his true being by revealing his will, through his laws and the commandments of his Covenant.

The epiphany of Yahweh is described with all the traditional features which, according to the usual oriental conception, belong to a theophany. Yahweh reveals himself with thunder and lightning (Pss. 97.2ff.; 29.3, 7ff.), with storm (29.5; 48.8), earthquake (29.6, 8; 46.7; 97.4), clothed in his wonderful armour, to which belongs also the girdle of strength (93.1). Against his enemies he raises his frightening and miracle-working voice into a war-cry (46.7; 29.3ff.; 76.7), manifesting his flaming majesty (48.6); the poison cup is ready to be drunk by his enemies.[114] The metaphors belong to the usual style of the theophany, indeed they are so conventional that they are used where no definite enemies are mentioned. They serve to depict the majesty of the divine revelation, creating in Yahweh's own worshippers awe and confidence, and smiting his enemies with horror. It would be a most rationalistic exegesis to find in such picturings any recollections of particular historical events,[115] just as in themselves they have nothing whatever to do with the eschatological appearance of Yahweh.[116]

If we start out from the power-charged epiphany of Yahweh, a special light is thrown on all ideas about his work as a king.

Even the special hymns of enthronement bring out very clearly that the fundamental myth of the festival is the *myth of creation* (see above, pp. 108f.). Yahweh has become king of the world, because he has created it. And as we have seen, these psalms do not refer to any abstract notion of creation, but to the same mythical and poetical idea which may be glimpsed behind the account of the creation in Gen. 1, but which is much more prominent in other passages of the Old Testament, namely the idea of creation as the victorious struggle of Yahweh against the dragon of the primeval ocean, or against the primeval ocean itself (*tĕhôm*).

In the enthronement psalms proper this rather mythical conception of creation is not very prominent. But in other psalms it is:

---

[114] Cf. Ps. 75.9. That this metaphor in itself has nothing to do with eschatology, even if taken up by the latter, will be seen from its use in Ps. 60.5, a national psalm of lamentation without any trace of eschatological ideas. Cf. *Ps.St.* II, pp. 330f., 339f.

[115] This applies for instance to the theory of Gunkel and Gressmann and Musil based on evidence that Sinai was once a volcano, so that the revelation there had something to do with an eruption. On the peninsula of Sinai there have been no active volcanos in historical times; but Sinai is closely connected with Kadesh on the Sinai peninsula. Of such geographical interpretations of the metaphors of theophany, Johs. Pedersen most rightly says that we may just as well search the map for the hills 'melting like wax at the presence of Yahweh' (Ps. 97.5).

[116] Gunkel, *Einl.*, p. 115, in these metaphors finds evidence proving that the enthronement psalms must be interpreted in an eschatological manner; the idea that Yahweh would appear in the eruption of a volcano and in an earthquake and the like, 'would be a strange thought at a festival'. The objection just shows that Gunkel has not realized the nature of cultic experience. At the epiphany festival all the thoughts connected with the conception of God and of the fundamental idea of the festival are being actualized; the enthronement psalms often emphasize that Yahweh's appearance is 'terrible' (*nôrā'*), Pss. 96.4; (97.9); 99.3, and a main point of the festal myth is that he comes and defeats his enemies.

> Thou, Yahweh, art my king of old,
>   working victorious salvation on the earth.
> Thou didst divide the ocean by thy power
>   and break the Dragon's heads on the waves.
>
> Thou didst crush the heads of Leviathan to pieces,
>   leaving him a prey to the folk of the jackals.
> Thou didst open springs and torrents,
>   thou didst dry up flowing streams.
>
> Thine is the day and thine is the night,
>   thou settest up the sun as light.
> Thou has set all the zones of the earth,
>   thou has made both summer and winter. (Ps. 74.12–17.)

The connexion between the primeval ocean and the dragons (Leviathan, Rahab), and between the victory over them, and creation and the kingship of Yahweh, is here quite evident. We see the same thing in Ps. 89.10–13:

> Thou art ruler, even if the sea rages,
>   as its waves tossed, thou didst still them.
> Thou didst crush Rahab as a profaned carcass
>   and scattered thine enemies by the force of thine arm.
>
> Thine is the heaven, the earth is thine,
>   thou has founded the continent and its fulness.
> The North and the South, thou hast created them,
>   Tabor and Hermon rejoice in thy name.

But sometimes the conception has been toned down to describe a fight against the ocean of chaos alone, which has been allotted its proper place and limits by Yahweh, so that an ordered cosmos has come into existence:

> Thou didst found the earth upon its pillars,
>   that it never more can be shaken.
> The ocean covered it as a garment,
>   the water stood above the mountains:
> but it retired at thy rebuke,
>   and hasted away at the sound of thy thunder;
> having scaled the mountains, it ran down in the valleys
>   to the place which thou hast determined for it;
> a bound hast thou set which it may not pass over,
>   it shall never cover the earth again. (Ps. 104.5–9.)

An echo of this fight is to be heard in the hymns of enthronement:

The earth is now established, shall never be shaken;
   from that time thy throne is established also,
      from all eternity hast thou (established it).

The floods, they lifted up, O Yahweh,
   the floods, they lifted up their voice,
      the floods, they lifted up their thunder.

But high above the roaring billows,
   high above the ocean breakers
      is Yahweh, glorious on high. (Ps. 93.1b–4.)

It has long been acknowledged[117] that this poetical myth of creation has been derived from the Babylonian one, where the god—Marduk, or whichever god was considered the chief god of that district—takes up arms on behalf of the other gods against the rebellious Tiamat (Hebr. *těhôm*), pictured as a female dragon of the primeval ocean. He captures her in his net, blowing his 'wind' into her jaws, cleaving her with his sword, and finally building up heaven and earth out of her body; the annual re-creation of the world, when the fields rise to the surface of the 'primeval ocean' of the spring flood, finds expression in this myth, and is each time made real again through the cultic rites connected with it. In all probability Israel did not take over these conceptions directly, but North Mesopotamian and Canaanite tales provided a connecting link.[118] The name Leviathan for the dragon of the ocean is now known from the Phoenician Ugarit texts, and possibly the name Rahab also has its origin there. And if the conceptions of the enthronement of the god and of the corresponding cultic festival of enthronement are based on a common oriental 'cultic pattern', Yahweh's achievement as a king, being the basis of the conceptions about his enthronement, must needs also—at least partly—be derived from the same sources.

Whether the Israelites before or in the age of Moses looked upon Yahweh as the god of creation, we do not know. But the conception of a supreme god being at the same time the god of creation, was known in Canaan as well as in the civilized countries surrounding it. So it would not be very long before this thought was transferred to Yahweh; Yahweh is El, he is El Elyon; he who comprises all divinity with his power and holiness, and to whom may therefore be attributed the plural Elohim, 'the gods', but according to its meaning a so-called abstract plural = the 'divinity', the 'divine majesty'. The common oriental conception of creation as the basis of the kingship of the god would therefore be a matter of course to the Israelites. We may presume that even in Israel the mythical conception of creation as a fight against *dragons* and against the

---

[117] See Gunkel, *Schöpfung und Chaos*; *Genesis.*[4]
[118] Cf. Albright in *JBL* LVII, 1938, pp. 230ff.; LVIII, 1939, pp. 91ff.; cf. *Studies in Prophecy* (Robinson festschrift), pp. 1ff.

primeval ocean must have belonged to the ideas of the festival of enthronement from the beginning.

But here the special character of Yahwism makes itself felt as a re-
moulding power. The growth of mono-, or heno-theism in Israel generally
is matched step for step in the cultic myths and psalms. In Israel the
universalistic character involved in the very conception of creation and
in the festival of enthronement was more and more emphasized. But at
the same time this God of creation does not become a pale 'power in the
background', standing aloof from the world, as is not infrequently the case
with the deities of creation in other religions;[119] but he remains a personal
God, actively willing, making plans and carrying them out, charged with
the moral energy of a personality, a concrete figure, who has revealed
himself throughout history and again and again appears in this historical
concreteness. Therefore neither the psalmists nor the prophets ever let go
of the mythical way of thinking about the primeval ocean and the dragon;
this myth was admirably fitted to bring out the concrete personal and
dynamic nature of Yahweh and to give an overwhelming impression of the
reality of his power and secure the confidence that 'blessed is the people
whose God is Yahweh'.

That Yahweh (again) creates, means that out of threatening chaos
(*tōhû wābhōhû*), he makes an ordered cosmos, an earth where men can
live (Isa. 45.18). He (again) establishes the 'right order', without which
heaven and earth cannot exist. It is this establishment of the right order
which the Hebrews express by the verb *šāphaṭ* and the noun *mišpāṭ*, usually
translated by 'judge' and 'judgment'. The words express His 'saving
activity', his *ṣedheq* or *ṣĕdhāqâ*, usually translated 'justice'. In the enthronement psalms we often hear of Yahweh's 'judgments', and the word
is used in many connexions and with many nuances of meaning. One of
them is the activity which we moderns express by the juridical term 'judge';
to the Hebrews, however, this juridical activity is only one side of the idea
of *mišpāṭ*. In the enthronement psalms the sense of (re-)establishment of
the right order and the right relation between the nations is generally
included in the word, whatever may be the relations alluded to.

The original comprehensive meaning of the 'judgment' connected with
the coming of Yahweh and the re-creation of the right order is still to be
seen in an idea which in later Judaism is very clearly connected with the
new year festival. In the Mishna we are told that on new year's day
Yahweh 'judges', i.e. determines what is to happen in the coming year,
both in nature and in the history of nations and the lives of individuals.[120]
In other words he lays down fate. This idea has older roots in the old
enthronement festival. In several psalms there are suggestions that at his
coming Yahweh shall 'turn the destiny' (*šûbh šĕbhûth*) of his people.[121] Like

[119] Cf. van der Leeuw, *Phänomenologie*, pp. 142ff. ¶ 18 (E.T., pp. 159ff.).
[120] Tosephta Rosh hasshana I, 13. Cf. *Ps.St.* II, pp. 74ff.
[121] Pss. 85.2; 126.4; 14.7; 53.7. See Additional Note XXVII.

most other ideas from the enthronement festival this expression has been taken up by eschatology, but in itself it is neutral and originally had nothing to do with the eschatological 'change'.[122] It means letting the thing in question return to its original starting-point in order to start afresh, so it is something like putting it in its original proper condition.[123] In the cult it refers to 'turning' things back to the starting-point in connexion with the 'turning' of the new year.[124]

When Yahweh comes he will change the destiny of his people, and the psalms of the festival ask him to do so:

> That those who are sowing now with tears
> may reap with shouts of joy. (126.5.)

Here we have a reference to the crops of the coming year, which are to be safeguarded by the harvest feast. But the thought goes further. The turning of destiny involves all conceivable happiness, in a moral as well as a material sense; when Yahweh shall again let 'his glory dwell in our land', says the harvest festival liturgy (Ps. 85), then:

> Kindness and faithfulness unite,
> right-order and welfare kiss each other;
> faithfulness rises from the earth,
> and kindness will look down from heaven.

> Thus Yahweh gives all that is good,
> Our land is yielding us its fruit;
> right-order marches before God
> and welfare follows in his steps. (85.11–14.)

In later times the thought of the national restoration of Israel would naturally come to the fore, when the psalms prayed for a 'turning of the destiny' (Pss. 14.7; 53.7), and the more so because the prophets of the return had used the term in this sense.

But as we have seen, it actually means the turning of destiny, the new 'laying down of fate', which would take place, when Yahweh would come at the new year's feast and take up the 'rule' over his people, 'judging' her destiny. This is also seen from the fact that even in Babylonia the same idea belonged to the new year festival. There the gods would meet in the 'room of destiny' (ubšukagina) and 'lay down destiny' (šim šimti) for the coming year, both for nations and kingdoms, first of all for Babylon itself, and for all individuals. To the ritual of the festival also belonged a

[122] See Additional Note XXV.
[123] In all probability the term šûbh šĕbhûth is formed on the pattern of Akkad. šim šimti— 'fixation of the fixed', i.e. the fixation of destiny that takes place in the council of gods every year at the new year festival. See Ps.St. II, pp. 74ff.
[124] Cf. the expressions 'the turning of the sun'—tĕqûphâ—about the point at which, according to the antique view of the world, the sun would turn in the west and return to its starting point (Ps. 19.7), and 'the turning of the year'—tĕqûphath haššânâ, tĕšûbhath haššânâ—about the transition from the old year to the new (Ex. 34.22). Cf. note 45 above, and Additional Note XIV.

prayer for a 'merciful destiny'.[125] It is most likely that the Israelite expression has been modelled on the Babylonian pattern.

This idea of Yahweh's 'judgment' in its manifold nuances and applications has deeply influenced the other ideas connected with the festival, the different versions of the 'festival myth'.

We find this especially when we look at what the psalms have to tell us about Yahweh's relation to *the other gods*. His appearance is 'a horror to all the gods', these 'nobodies' (*'ĕlîlîm*) prostrating themselves before his face and paying homage to him. When he appears, he does so even as 'king over all gods'.[126] This very term points back to the way the concept of enthronement was expressed in the other oriental religions. In the Ugaritic myth Baal becomes the king of gods after his resurrection and victory over Môt. And in the Babylonian epic of creation and enthronement we are told that when Tiamat, the monster of the primeval ocean, revolted against the gods, none of them ventured to take up the fight, until Marduk offered to do so on condition that the other gods should make him king, and the crown of victory consisted in his being proclaimed king over all gods: *marduk-ma šarru*, 'Marduk has become king'. This implies the idea brought out in plain words by the Israelite psalms of enthronement, that the other gods have been 'put to shame'. But here the relationship between them and Yahweh has become a different one. In true Yahwism the other gods had been Yahweh's enemies ever since the struggles of the immigration and the fights for independence against the natives. The fusion of Israel with the natives after David's reign resulted in the identification of the great gods, El, El Elyon, etc., with Yahweh; they became merged in him; and so, also, the great host of gods and heavenly beings, *bĕnê 'ēlîm*, 'the divine ones', the 'divine beings', came to be looked upon as the servants of Yahweh, his household staff, his body guard and his army, and finally were identified with his 'messengers' or 'deputies', 'the angels'. The other national gods were considered as the governors of Yahweh, installed by him to rule over the other nations.[127]

But in spite of all this wholesale conversion to Yahwism some of the tension between Yahweh and the other gods continued to exist. The unlucky experiences suffered by Israel throughout the greater part of her history with regard to other nations and their oppression of Israel taught her that the rule of their gods, Yahweh's vassals, over the world was most unjust:

> Do ye indeed judge righteously, ye gods,
>   do ye reign over mankind with justice?
> No! evil deeds ye do on 'the earth',
>   your hands weigh up violence in the world,

---

[125] See Zimmern, *AO* XXV, 3, pp. 16f.; *Babyl. Neujahrsfest* II, p. 38.
[126] Pss. 96.4f.; 97.7, 9; 99.2f. (in v. 2 read with 3 Mss. *'ĕlōhîm* instead of *hā'ammîm*).
[127] Deut. 32.8 (G, now corroborated by the Qumran texts). For the 'sons of god', i.e. those of divine family, the divine beings, see Ps. 29.1; Job 1f.; cf. 1 Kgs. 22.20ff.

says the psalmist (58.2f.). And thus in the psalms of enthronement the 'gods' gradually move into the rank of evil enemies, 'put to shame' by Yahweh and 'judged' by him when he 'comes' and sits upon his throne. This actually means: they assume the place in the myth, which once belonged to the demons of the primeval ocean and of chaos; we have a *myth about the fight of gods* side by side with the myth about the dragon fight. The term is not quite adequate, for in the psalms we do not hear of any real fight against the gods. They are struck with horror at the very appearance of Yahweh, and tremblingly throw themselves down, paying homage to him. This also means shame and defeat to all 'image worshippers', who put their confidence in 'nothingnesses'. That is why we are told that the appearance of Yahweh puts all the other gods 'to shame' (Ps. 97.7). 'Shame' means defeat and destruction.[128]

It is the idea of Yahweh's 'judgment' in its more juridical sense which has been applied here to his relations to the other gods. And here too we notice the same exclusive tendency, as in the Israelite versions of the myth about the fight against the powers of chaos (see above, pp. 145f.).

The enthronement psalms often allude to Yahweh's righteous and luck-bringing rule after he has been enthroned. This is what is indicated by the words *mišpāṭ* and *dîn* and the corresponding verbs (96.13; 97.8; 98.9; 48.12), traditionally translated by 'judgment' and 'judge', but which do not merely indicate this judicial ('forensic') activity, but all activity on the part of king and leaders for the purpose of maintaining the balance and 'harmony' and 'peace' of society, and to secure to everybody what according to the covenant is his 'right',[129] i.e. what we would call to 'rule' or 'govern'. Thus when the king displays his 'judgment' and 'righteousness'—*ṣedheq, ṣĕdhāqâ*—it means his power to do the 'right' thing in all senses of the word, and create 'right order', i.e. blessing, peace, good morals and victory for his people—'justifying them' (*hiṣdîq*), i.e. creating for them the right social, moral and religious conditions. In this way Yahweh also is going to 'rule' or 'judge' his people. When the verb is used with Israel for its object, it first of all means: provide and secure, or restore, his happiness and welfare and power and 'peace' and 'salvation'; with the enemies for its object, it means conquering, crushing. Therefore can 'the villages of Judah rejoice over the judgments of Yahweh' (Pss. 48.12; 97.8) in the widest sense of the word 'judgment'.

But the mind might also fasten on the fundamental 'act of judgment' at the coming of Yahweh. And then the forensic aspect of the idea would become more prominent and result in the conception of a solemn act of judgment, at which Yahweh summons his antagonists before his judgment seat and judges them, just as this used to be the first act of government of an earthly king.[130] Ps. 76 suggests that when Yahweh revealed himself in

[128] Cf. Johs. Pedersen, *Israel* I–II, pp. 182ff.
[129] See Johs. Pedersen, *Israel* I–II, pp. 336ff.
[130] 1 Kgs. 1.49ff.; 2.13–38; 2 Kgs. 10.1ff.; 1 Sam. 11.12. Cf. Ps. 2.

Salem, he also 'caused judgment to be heard from heaven'; once he has taken his place on his throne in Salem he has 'arisen to judgment to save all the oppressed ones of the earth' (or of 'the land'). In Ps. 75 he speaks words of severe reproof to all the inhabitants of the earth; he is 'the judge (or ruler) who lowers one and lifts another' (v. 8). And the poet describes how Yahweh is standing with the poison cup in his hand, which all his enemies have to empty. Now that he has come to bind kings and nobles with chains and with fetters of iron (Ps. 149), he is 'executing upon them the judgment written'.[131] We are here dealing with a conception which may be called the *myth of doom*.

This myth also colours Yahweh's relationship to other gods. The poet of Ps. 82 describes how Yahweh 'stands out in the assembly of the gods', sentencing them to death for their unjust rule:

> God stands out in the council of the gods,
>   in the midst of the gods he speaks his judgment:
> How long yet will you rule unjustly,
>   (how long yet) favour the evildoers?
> Uphold the weak, the fatherless,
>   let the forlorn and poor have justice!
> Rescue the weak and the wretched ones,
>   pluck them out of the grip of the wicked!
> They know not, neither will understand;
>   all the foundations of the earth are shaken.
> But now I say: though you are gods,
>   all of you sons of the Most High,
> yet you shall die as men must die,
>   shall perish like the (earthly) princes.

As we have seen, the idea of a council (assembly) of gods belongs to the festival of new year and enthronement. It was in such an assembly of 'sons of gods' and 'saints', i.e. divine beings, that Yahweh once portioned out the nations amongst the 'sons of gods' whom he made governors over them.[132] A markedly Israelitic feature of this psalm, which probably belongs to a comparatively late time, is the close connexion between the idea of judgment and that of Yahweh's universal kingship: when the gods are sentenced it is because of their unjust and immoral rule, their want of 'moral sense' and 'understanding', of proper 'knowledge of God'. An essential feature in the Israelite conception of God, the tendency towards ethical monotheism, is here bound up with the historical way of thinking: iniquity in the history of mankind, of nations and states, is what forces Yahweh to interfere in history and pronounce judgment over the mighty

---

[131] Behind this expression may lie a rite corresponding to that of the Egyptian 'execration texts', see Bentzen in [D]TT, 1929, pp. 6off.

[132] Deut. 32.8f. (voc. *běhanḥîl* and *yaṣṣîbh* with 2 Mss. (Ken.) and Sam., and corroborated by a Qumran fragment, see P. W. Skehan in *BASOR* 136, 1954, pp. 12ff.; read *běnê 'ēl*, cf. G, L); and 33.2f. 'Holy ones' in the O.T. always means divine beings.

of this world, who serve evil and faithless gods. Under the rule of such powers Israel has become 'poor and needy and oppressed'; and this is reflected by the internal condition of the people, so that no justice is to be found either for 'widows or fatherless or common people'. But here we get a glimpse, too, of another essential and markedly Israelite feature, to which we shall return in detail below: the future lookingness of the ideas and experiences in the festival of enthronement. The congregation knows that even at the coming of Yahweh this judgment has been laid down, so to speak, only 'in principle'; it has not yet appeared in the visible reality of experience. Therefore this message closes with prayer on the part of the congregation that this may r.ow happen:

> Up, O God, rule thou the earth,
> for to thee belong all the nations!

Yahweh gives judgment as 'ruler', as king. From being an assembly paying homage, as in the Babylonian epic, the assembly of gods has become a judgment hall: the homage-paying vassals, who together with the supreme god 'judged' the fate of the new year, have been changed into unfaithful vassals and have become the accused party, being themselves judged on account of 'crimes against mankind'.[133]

The 'historical' point of view is more prominent in another conception which finds expression in the enthronement psalms: that is, that Yahweh has secured his kingdom and his enthronement by coming and delivering his people and his city from a threatening attack by the united kings and nations of the world (cf. above, p. 109). This conception is to be found in Pss. 46; 48; 75 and 76. Here the idea of Yahweh's historic and ever repeated victory over the 'nations', and the confidence engendered by these experiences and the faith on which they were based, is presented as an epic tale woven around a mythically tinted happening. The 'happening' to which the psalms allude, along with its corresponding 'tale' is an attack on Jerusalem by all the kings and nations of the earth; but just when the distress is at its height Yahweh appears and crushes them all; so the walls of Jerusalem are safe, the 'City of the Great King' stands unshaken. This hardly refers to any single real historical event, as earlier interpreters of the psalms used to think, nor is it meant to be a description of what is going to take place in the 'latter days', in eschatological times. It is described as something just experienced, something the congregation 'itself has seen' (Ps. 48.9). But at the same time it is something it 'has heard of' before. Here, too, the explanation is that there is a reference to the realities of faith being re-experienced as repeated reality in the cult. What has taken place, and always will take place, in faith is presented by the cultic myth as an 'ideal' supra-worldly reality in the epic form of a once-only event. In an 'ideal' and real sense it is repeated whenever Yahweh appears as king, victorious in the festival. It is being ensured to

[133] See Additional Note XXVI.

faith as something that is also going to happen in political and empirical reality, should the 'nations' or any specific nation be so presumptuous as to attack Yahweh's city. Here we have a version of the 'cultic myth' of the festival, which we call the *myth about the fight of nations.*

Even this conception has some of its roots in the myth about the fight against chaos, and in the ancient conception of the state of need and chaos that the world got into before the coming of Yahweh, and from which he comes to deliver it at the last moment, just as the powers of death seem to be victorious. That it is the primeval ocean and the power of chaos which after all loom behind 'the nations', is brought out still more clearly by Ps. 46.2-4, 7f.:

> God is a stronghold and shelter for us,
>   as a helper in trouble always found.
> Therefore we will not fear though the earth be overturned,
>   though the mountains quake in the depths of the sea.
> Let (the ocean) roar, let its billows foam,
>   let the mountains shake under its haughtiness . . .
> The nations raged, the kingdoms were moved,
>   He lifted his voice, and the earth shivered.
> Yahweh, the Lord of Hosts, is with us,
>   the God of Jacob is our fortress.

In Ps. 68, a typical procession psalm for the new year festival—the feast of the 'coming' and 'epiphany' of Yahweh—we also have the identification of the actual and potential enemies of Israel with the chaotic powers. The enemies have now been scattered and destroyed by his mighty 'word' (v. 12).

But at the back of this conception about the repeated attack of the powers of chaos we find actual experiences from the life of nature and of men. For the distress from which Yahweh is coming to deliver man was originally and truly the distress arising because the world had been worn out, destroyed by the deadly powers of drought, and in danger of sinking back again into chaos; thus 'Death'—in Ugaritic mythology, Môt—as a supernatural and demonic being threatens God's world with destruction. This conception we also find in Ps. 68: Yahweh's coming is the salvation from 'the Death' (*māweth*, v. 21). Here the original Canaanite form of the myth, the victory of Baal over Môt is clearly reflected.[133a] The same idea we meet also in Ps. 48.15, Yahweh is our leader against the Death.

This mutation of the chaos myth into a myth about the fight against the nations is the place where the fundamentally historical point of view of Israelite religion breaks in and depicts the distress in a new guise. Israel was constantly experiencing threatened distress of this different kind: the enmity of all the surrounding nations, the 'gentiles' and their kings, constantly planning to destroy Yahweh's people—or, as it is ex-

[133a] See the author's *Der achtundsechsigste Psalm*, p. 48f.

pressed in the royal psalm (Ps. 2), again and again taking counsel against their righteous Lord, Yahweh, and against his Anointed, his vice-gerent on earth. This is the danger and the distress from which Yahweh comes to deliver his people by 'judging' all these enemies in one crushing act. But all the same the mythical way of thinking has always a tendency towards the epic. And in the cult the salvation which is going to be effected in time to come is experienced as concentrated present-day reality. Considering the manner of thinking of Israelite poets and the fullness of the cultic experience, it would be much too abstract to say, for instance, 'now that Yahweh has come we are safe with regard to all eventual enemies who might be expected to attack his city and his people'. To the cultic and mythical way of thinking all these possibilities are concentrated in a single concrete picture: the kings and peoples of the world *have* already taken counsel, and are besieging Yahweh's city; but in its last extremity, at the 'break of day', Yahweh comes, slaying and crushing them all and securing his city to all eternity, for now he himself is there as a victorious king on his throne, therefore it can never be shaken. 'Though the ocean roar and its billows foam—the God of Jacob is our refuge'.

This is the picture drawn for us by Ps. 48.5–8:

> For lo, the kings made a conspiracy,
>   and passed by together.
> They saw—and they were scared with panic
>   and, terrified, they took to flight.
> Fear took hold upon them there
>   like women in travail,
> (as) when the easterly storm breaks down
>   the (biggest) Tarshish-ships.[134]

And therefore the festal psalm (Ps. 76.2–6, see above, p. 142), rejoices over the 'appearance' of Yahweh:

> There (i.e. in Salem) he has broken the arrows of the bow,
>   the shields, and the swords, and all martial weapons.

In this way he 'judges' all his own and Israel's enemies:

> Thou lettest thy sentence be heard from heaven,
>   the earth feared, and was still,
> when God arose to judgment,
>   to save all the oppressed on earth. (76.9f.)

These 'oppressed on earth'—or 'in the land'—are the Israelites themselves.

[134] Read *ka'āsher* and 3. s.f. *těšabbēr*—even if Tarshish also indicates the (earlier) Phoenician name of the town in Sardinia (see Albright in *BASOR* 83, 1941, pp. 21f.), in the O.T. it probably, as Albright also thinks, means Tartessus in Spain. In the expression 'ships of Tarshish' we probably have the proper name, used in the sense of 'distant travellers', 'ocean-farers', not the original appellative sense of 'smelting-boat', 'turret' (*tarshish* = 'smeltery', from Akkad. *rasâsu* = 'melt', see Albright, op. cit.).

Thus has Yahweh hitherto helped his people, not allowing them to be destroyed, in spite of all tribulations and well-deserved chastisements, and thus will he ever help them.

So in the myth of the fight of nations the cosmic and mythical meets with the historically orientated view of the basis of Yahweh's kingship and its consequences to the world.

In the oracles of doom against the enemies of Israel, these latter are always referred to in general terms, not mentioning any particular people— unlike the casual oracles in the psalms of lamentation (see below, Chap. VI.3). It is, however, very possible that a custom of pronouncing a series of oracles against different individual peoples may have developed out of the general oracles at the epiphany feast, and that we have here the 'cultic' background of such oracles as we find in Am. 1–2.[135] If this suggestion is true, we should be inclined to think that such oracles did not belong to the festal ritual proper, but that they mark extempore inspirations and improvisations of the cult prophet, only loosely connected with the festival, and taking place before the crowd, which was eating and drinking and playing in the temple courts.

On the basis of this historical orientation it is understandable that Creation and the rise of Israel should become one: Creation reaches its climax in the rise of Israel, i.e. the *election*, manifesting itself in the escape from Egypt. Egypt becomes the chaotic monster Rahab and the Reed Lake becomes the primeval ocean, Tehom (Isa. 30.7; Ex. 15.48); and just as in the beginning Yahweh 'divided' the waters, so did he also divide the waters of the Reed Lake for his people. Quite logically the thought would also arise that through this 'creative act' on the part of Yahweh, he became king of Israel. In a psalm of epiphany, now forming the frame of the so-called 'blessing of Moses' it says (Deut. 33.2, 4f.):[136]

> From Mount Sinai Yahweh came,
>   from Se'ir he dawned on us,
>   from Paran's range he gleamed out
>   moving from Meribath-Kadesh . . . .

---

[135] See Würthwein's suggestion in *ZATW* 62, 1949–50, pp. 35ff.

[136] Deut. 33.2–5, 26–29 is originally an independent psalm, which the author of the 'Blessing of Moses'—a younger imitator of the 'Blessing of Jacob' in Gen. 49—has used as a framework for his own poem; v. 26 is the direct continuation of v. 5. Ideologically, the psalm belongs to the enthronement feast: note Yahweh's coming from Mount Sinai to his people, his epiphany (*hôphîaʿ*), his becoming King of Israel, his driving over the skies, the byname 'the primeval God', his blessing of the land with dew from heaven, the security of his people under his shelter, cf. Ps. 29.10f. See *GTMMM* I, pp. 421ff.; *Der achtundsechzigste Psalm*, pp. 75ff. The text of vv. 2–5 is very damaged; v. 2 read: *lĕʿammô* (cf. *lānû* G, P, V) for *lāmô*, and *mimmĕribhath qādhesh*; v. 2e is to be connected with 3a; read *ʾēš lappîdhôth* for *ʾēš dath*; 3a read: *ʾaph sĕbhîbhô* (parall. *mîmînô*, v. 2e) *ʿādhath* (or: *qēhal*) *qĕdhôshāw* (athnach *to qedhôshaw*); *lĕyādhô* (so with V) corresponds to *lĕraghlô*; the original text seems to have spoken about heavenly beings (cf. 'His holy ones', in the O.T. always used to indicate supernatural beings) standing 'at his hand', and 'at his foot', cf. Isa. 6.2, but the original wording we can only guess at. V. 4a is a gloss (the idea of Moses and the Torah has no connexion with this stage of the idea of enthronement); v. 5a has its original place before v. 4b.

> The congregation of Jacob became his domain,
>> and he became king in Jeshurun,
> as the chiefs of the people there gathered,
>> and all the clans of Israel.

Jeshurun is an honorific name for Israel. And in another psalm (114.1f.) it says:

> When Israel went out of Egypt,
>> the house of Jacob from the barbarous people,
> Judah became his sacred dominion,
>> Israel his kingly domain.

At that time he apportioned all the other nations among the 'divine ones' ('sons of the gods'), but he kept Israel for himself as his 'part' and his 'heritage' (Deut. 32.8.G). Then it was that he laid the foundation of his true historical 'kingship'.

The festal psalm put in the mouth of Miriam by a later saga writer, and describing the Exodus and the miracle of the Reed Lake and the first settlement in Canaan, ends with a comment on the founding of the sanctuary of Zion, and the proclamation of the kingship of Yahweh (Ex. 15.17f.):

> Thou tookest thy folk and plantedst them in thine own hill,
>> thou madest a shrine for thy dwelling, Yahweh,
> a sanctuary thy hands founded, O Lord:
>> now Yahweh is king for evermore.

What Yahweh has done for Israel in actual history forms the basis of his kingship, and is recalled when in the new year festival he takes his seat on his throne as the victorious king.

But election is bound up with the making of the *covenant*, which is maybe the most important innovation on the basis of the historical orientation of Yahwism. The idea in itself is not new; in ancient Israel all cult was in the nature of a strengthening of the covenant; 'life' just meant covenant. But what was originally thought of was the, so-to-speak, *natural* covenant, made up of family and tribe in connexion with the ancestors and the family god. To Israel after the time of Moses, 'covenant' means the historical covenant which Yahweh in his goodness 'granted' to his elected people. This is a fundamental idea in Israelite religion among the cultic officials as well as among the prophets of doom. At the festival of enthronement, with its 'commemoration' of the election, the idea of a renewal of the covenant would be a leading thought, with explicit reference to what Yahweh had done in history; at the festival he came to renew the covenant he had once made with the people at Kadesh-Sinai.

Through the renewal of the covenant were promised to king and people all the blessing, all the happiness, all the victory they might need in the year to come: a righteous, strong and victorious king, true priests, a pure temple, outer and inner power, a new happiness, a 'turning of the fate', paradisiac fertility, peace, dominion over the neighbouring peoples, victory over enemies, protection against demons and evil powers, and destruction of evil-doers and sinners.[137]

There is a reference to this in Ps. 99.6ff. Now that Yahweh is 'enthroned' on the cherubim and has 'established equity and executed judgment and righteousness in Jacob', the making of the covenant at the time of its foundation in the historical past is repeated:

> His priests have still a Moses and an Aaron,
>   his worshippers have still a Samuel,
> and Yahweh answers when they call to him,
>   Thou Yahweh, our God, Thou answerest them.
> In the cloudy pillar doth he speak to them,
>   when they obey the laws and rules he gave them.
> A forgiving God hast Thou ever been to them,
>   and one who has (not) avenged their evil deeds.

What is meant is this:[138] again there is a Moses, an Aaron, a Samuel, among his people; again he shall answer from the pillar of the cloud, whenever the leaders and intercessors of the people shall cry out to him. The covenant bringing happiness and help and forgiveness of sins to all who keep the commandments of Yahweh has again been established as a result of the enthronement of Yahweh.

That this is a reference to the covenant of Kadesh-Sinai will be seen from such psalms as 95 and 81. The very essence of the covenant is brought out by a stanza like this:

> Let us go in and worship and bow down,
>   kneeling before Yahweh who has made us!
> For he is our God, and we, we are the people
>   which he pastures and shepherds with his hand. (95.6f.)

But these psalms also prove the organic connexion between the idea of a renewal of the covenant and that of epiphany and of the statement of the commandments of the covenant. The first part of Ps. 95 is evidently an enthronement hymn. Now the king, Yahweh, creator of the world and of Israel, has come to take his seat on his throne and receive the homage of his people; in the second part of the psalm it is as a king renewing the covenant—through the mouth of the cultic prophet—that he recalls the

---

[137] For further details see *Ps.St.* II, pp. 150ff.

[138] For the interpretation of Ps. 99 and particularly v. 6, see Buhl, *Psalmerne*[2], pp. 629ff.; *Ps.St.* II, p. 152. Gunkel's interpretation: 'Der zweite Teil nennt die grössten Namen aus der älteren Geschichte, offenbar um zu sagen: sieht, solche Heroen standen in Jahves Diensten!' gives no real connexion between the two parts of the psalm: what would be the point of such a contemplation of the past as past, in a psalm dealing with present day events—much less in an eschatological psalm, as Gunkel makes it? As for the text, v. 8a must be replaced after v. 6b; in v. 8b the negative (*lô'*) is to be inserted.

first making of the covenant and the faithlessness of the people at Meribah and Massah, and warns against breaking the commandments of the covenant. And in the psalm of the new year festival, Ps. 81.11, he reveals himself to the congregation through the ancient 'formula of epiphany',[139] referring to the traditions of the Exodus and of Sinai:

> For I am Yahweh, I am your God
> who brought you out of Egypt's land.

And here, too, we find the reference to the disobedience of the people at the spring of Meribah just after the making of the covenant:

> I tested you at the spring of Meribah:
> 'Open your mouth, and I will fill it'.[140]

The festival of harvest and new year became the festival of the renewal of the historical covenant; and among its 'festal myths' may also be mentioned a *myth about the making of the covenant*, in terms which bring out quite clearly that the word 'myth' may also indicate the religious and cultic conception and formulation of a historical fact.

The covenant of Sinai, according to later Jewish ways of thinking, is itself a renewal of the covenant with the first ancestors, which was fulfilled through the settlement in Canaan. The kingship of Yahweh rests on this coherent historical fact of salvation, and it is all brought to life again through his appearance and epiphany in the festival cult.[141]

Even Yahweh's covenant with David was considered to be a repetition of the covenant of Sinai itself. Therefore the covenant with David is also kept in mind at the festival of harvest and new year, as in Ps. 132.

As already suggested, the *covenant obligations* naturally enter into the thought of the making and renewal of the covenant in Israel, and so have also a place in the festival of the renewal of the covenant. Both Ps. 95 and Ps. 81, like Ps. 99, refer to the commandments and laws given by Yahweh at Kadesh-Sinai, and now repeated and reinforced by him, because both then and later they had been broken by the people. Here we are face to face with another important new development in connexion with the festival, deriving from the special historical nature of Yahwism.

As the ritual of the great annual feast of Jerusalem developed there occurred several points where the traditions about the making of the fundamental covenant and its conditions, the commandments, could link on. One such link was provided by the idea of Yahweh's epiphany. The announcement of Yahweh's epiphany in order to renew the covenant would lead to an emphasis on, and enforcement of, the fundamental

[139] For this formula of 'self-introduction' and its original connexion with the idea of the epiphany of a god, cf. Ed. Norden, *Agnostos Theos*, pp. 191ff., 197ff., 210ff.; Gressmann in *ZATW* 34, 1914, pp. 286 ff.; Mowinckel, *Le Decalogue*, pp. 126f.; Zimmerli in *Geschichte u. AT.*, pp. 179 ff,
[140] The isolated single cola vv. 8b and 11b obviously belong together; if 11b is replaced behind 8b we shall have quite regular stanzas throughout the whole psalm.
[141] See Additional Note XXVII.

commandments on which the covenant rested. In Pss. 95 and 81 we find just this presentation and enforcement. 'Today', Yahweh again admonishes his people, warning them to hear his voice (95.7)—'today', on the day when the covenant is renewed and the commandments announced, as they were at Sinai.[142] And whereas in Ps. 95 Yahweh's warning is against infidelity and grumbling, in Ps. 81.9f. he warns against the transgression of the fundamental commandments themselves:

> Listen, my people, to my warning,
> O Israel, if you would only listen:
> You must allow no foreign god,
> no worship of an outside god.

That these words refer to the very same commandments, which—with greater or smaller variations—were considered to be those of the Sinai covenant and had been formulated in different sets of 'decalogues'[143] is clearly seen from Ps. 81.11, quoted above (p. 157).

This verse is nothing but the traditional introduction to the Ten Commandments. It seems to have been usual to arrange the particular *leges sacrae* applicable to the sanctuary, as well as, later, also the commandments which were considered to be the actual laws of the covenant, as a set of ten (or twelve) commandments; first among these was always the fundamental law of worshipping Yahweh only. By their connexion with the idea of epiphany these collections got the traditional introductory formula referring to the appearance of Yahweh and—because of the historical idea of election and covenant—to the Exodus from Egypt,[144] which was originally considered as the election itself.[145] The influence of this 'decalogical tradition' is also clearly seen in Ps. 15, where the number of commandments making the 'laws of entrance', the 'conditions of admission' to temple and salvation, are precisely ten; this is certainly no mere accident.

The annual renewal of the covenant came to include the idea of commandments in general; not only this, but also of certain specific and definite commandments. We do not imply a recital of written law-books, but the reminder through the cult prophet's mouth of those commandments which at different times were considered to be the fundamental commandments of the covenant. As to which these were, opinions may have differed with changing times, just as have the opinions as to which were the ten fundamental commandments from Mount Sinai. But certain

---

[142] On the Sinai covenant and the Davidic covenant, see Rost in *ThLtz* 72, 1947, col. 129ff.
[143] Ex. 34.14ff.; 20.1ff.; Deut. 5.6ff. See Mowinckel, *Decalogue*, pp. 11ff., 19ff., 36ff.; *ZATW* 55, 1937, pp. 218ff.
[144] See Mowinckel, *Decalogue*, pp. 7ff., 24ff., 125ff. Against Weiser (in *Festschrift für Bertholet*) Bückers, 'Z. Verwertung d. Sinaitradition i.d. Pss.', *Biblica* 32, 1951, pp. 401ff. denies the influence of the Sinai traditions on the psalms and on the cultic festival, without making due allowance, however, for *Ps.St.* II and *Offersang og Sangoffer*, pp. 154ff. (above, pp. 154ff.).
[145] See Galling, *Die Erwählungstraditionen Israels*.

of them always appear to have been included, and foremost the commandment not to have other gods besides Yahweh.

In this rite as well as in the custom of advising the pilgrims and the
partakers of the feast procession about the *leges sacrae* of the holy place
(see below), we have the root of the later custom of the Jewish congregation reciting the law-book, i.e. Deuteronomy, every seventh year at the
feast of Tabernacles.[146]

The *promises* of the epiphany festival are attached, above all, to this
repeated revelation and enforcement of the commandments of the covenant. That a covenant with the deity would be a source of blessing was a
matter of course to the early Hebrews as well as to the Canaanites. But in
the Israel of historical times and in Yahwism it was not just a matter of
course in the same way. A covenant with Yahweh is not a covenant between equals. To Israel it was a historical fact that Yahweh, of his own
free will, had chosen the people in its hour of emergency and made a
covenant with it. This covenant is something 'given' and 'stipulated' by
Yahweh. In the idea of covenant which unfolds in the psalms Yahweh's
sovereign superiority over the people and its king is very prominent. He
always attaches *conditions* to it, namely the commandments of the
covenant.[147] To Yahwistic Israel it was clear that it was not the vitality—the
life power—of gods and men which was being renewed through the festival
—as was the case with the Canaanites—but Yahweh's *promise* and *pledge* of
blessing and power and life. In the liturgies of the festival and in the
psalms reflecting them, such as Pss. 81 and 95 and others, we not only meet
with a warning against breaking the covenant, but also with positive rich
promises to people and king, if they should this time—'today'—keep
Yahweh's commandments better than before:

> Oh that my people would listen to me,
>   that Israel would walk in my ways!
> Then I would soon subdue their foes,
>   and turn my hand against their enemies.
>
> Their haters then would cower before them,
>   their time (of submission) never end.
> But themselves I would feed with the finest wheat,
>   with honey from the rock I would satisfy thee.
>
> (Ps. 81.14–17.)

The blessing that shall ensue to king and people and land, if the king,
and his sons after him, keep the commandments and laws of Yahweh is

[146] In his interesting paper in *ZATW* 62, 1949–50, pp. 44ff., Würthwein in my opinion ante-
dates the cultic rite of reciting the law, and operates too much with the idea of written law texts
in this connexion. This is, however, of no importance to his main thesis. The background of
the message of Amos is not written codes of law, but traditional standards of right and morals
in Israel, and, as Würthwein rightly stresses, among the circles of the temple personnel (in
Jerusalem).

[147] See Galling, op. cit., pp. 5ff.

described in still more detail in Ps. 132, which also belongs to the festival of harvest and new year.

Such cultic promises are echoed by the prophet of re-establishment, Deutero-Isaiah, who describes what is going to happen after the pattern of the festival of enthronement, when he makes Yahweh say to Israel (Isa. 55.3):

> I will make an everlasting covenant with you,
> the favours promised faithfully to David.

Here again the covenant is a renewal of the old one; it is the covenant with David which is to be renewed, but this is in itself the renewal and the crowning of the Sinai-covenant. And even here in the prophet a description has been attached of all the blessings which Israel is going to receive as a free gift: 'corn without money, and wine and milk for nothing'.

Both Pss. 81 and 95 explicitly refer to the grave breach of the covenant of which Israel had been guilty even at Mount Sinai,[148] and warn them against the recurrence of any such thing 'today'. The idea evidently is that such has actually happened much too often; the warning has a present reference, backed up by the sad experience of many generations. The poets know that the future happiness of the people depends on whether it is going to keep the commandments of Yahweh from now on. The fact of the matter is that in the relationship of the people to the commandments of Yahweh they have found the sufficient explanation of its fate. Every year Yahweh renewed the rich promises of his covenant. But when year after year passed and the lot and fate of Israel often seemed to become worse and worse, when none of the expectations and promises of the festival seemed to come true in everyday reality during the ensuing year, then the prophetically inspired authors of the psalms knew the reason, and they did not hide it. It was not because Yahweh could not or would not keep his word. It was due to the *sin* of the people themselves, because in some way or other they always broke the covenant, as they had already done once upon a time at Meribath-Kadesh (Pss. 95.8; 81.8, 11). Like the prophets, the authors of the psalms also had to take up the *problem of theodicy*. In liturgies like Pss. 81 and 95 we indirectly find Yahwism vindicating the justice of God. Yahweh is in the right; we have sinned.

In this cultic *admonition* and rebuke of the transgressions of the people lies the root of the prophetic speech of rebuke and doom. Yahweh's claim to the complete surrender of the people to him as their one and only God,

---

[148] It is strange that they do not allude to the offence with the golden calf, but to the fact that through unbelief and grumbling and disobedience the people 'tempted' Yahweh at Meribah and Massah, Ex. 17.1-7; Num. 20.1-13. This is obviously an earlier tradition than that of the golden calf as the cause of the wanderings in the desert. The earliest traditions about the covenant are attached to Kadesh rather than Sinai, and Meribah or Meribat-Kadesh is the main watering place of these districts, = 'Ain qederāt (see Mowinckel in *Norsk Geografisk Tidsskrift* 9, pp. 21ff., cf. above, n. 86). It is characteristic of the conservatism of the cult that the earlier tradition has been kept up in Pss. 81 and 95, though both of them are comparatively late.

and the inherent ethical approach of the Yahweh religion, resulted in picturing the just judgment of his coming as a judgment not only of their demonic and historical enemies and of the sinners within Israel, but as judgment of *his own people* as well.[149]

The preaching of the great prophets has, in turn, strengthened this idea in the complex of ideas belonging to the festival. This idea of the judgment against Israel is clearly expressed in Ps. 50. According to a tradition in the Mishna this psalm belongs to the feast of Tabernacles, so many of whose old ideas and ancient rites survived even into late times. The psalm itself probably dates from comparatively late times; but its ideo-historical and liturgico-historical connexion with Pss. 81 and 95 and with the idea of the renewal of the covenant against the background of a severe admonition to the people is quite clear. With the enthronement festival Ps. 50 has in common the idea of the epiphany, of the Sinai covenant as the background of what Yahweh is now to say, of his commandments according to the 'decalogical tradition', of his judgment, and of his severe castigation of the sins of the people. The latter is characterized by the verbs *šāphaṭ* and *dîn*, 'judge'. The description of the epiphany is followed by an upbraiding of the congregation because of its laxity towards the sinners and criminals tolerated in its midst. But the idea of judgment is not very prominent here; the congregation is 'lectured' and admonished in prophetic wording, but it is left at that.

In the first instance the historical reference, to which the festal myths bear witness on all points, implies that the idea of Yahweh's kingship is once more limited to *Israel* in practice. But the universalistic feature from the very beginning inherent in the connexion of the idea of enthronement with that of creation could not be obliterated. There came to be a certain tension between the world-wide view involved in the idea of creation—Yahweh as creator and therefore king of the world—together with the prophets' 'practical monotheism' on the one side, and the idea of Yahweh coming to defeat the gentiles and bring 'justice' and salvation to Israel on the other. Side by side with the call for all the world to rejoice over the enthronement of Yahweh, there is an emphasis on the 'shame' this means to the 'nations' and their gods and the idea of the triumph thereby secured to Israel.

But in spite of all this, *Yahweh's universal dominion* nowhere stands out so clearly as in the enthronement psalms, and consequently also his superiority over all other gods. It seems as if the poets cannot help imagining that all the world would rejoice in this just as much as they themselves do. Thus these psalms point forward to the New Testament conception of the 'kingdom' of God, even if the Old Testament limits have not yet

---

[149] This side of the complex of ideas of the feast has also been observed and elaborated by Würthwein in *ZThK* 49, pp. 1ff. In the critical remarks against Würthwein by Hesse in *ZATW* 65, 1953, pp. 45ff., Hesse is right in maintaining that the differences between the ordinary cult prophets and the classic 'great prophets' are not to be blurred; but the first creative impulse came from the ideas of the cult prophets.

been exceeded. The exclusive kingship of Yahweh is not far from true monotheism; the other gods have been completely degraded, not only to the position of servants of Yahweh, but almost to evil beings, defeated by him, as we have seen, at his coming.

We have spoken above of the promises given to the congregation, when Yahweh appeared at the festival, promises certainly pronounced in Yahweh's name by one of the temple prophets officiating at the cult performances (cf. for details, Chap. XII). When Yahweh shall become king and again establish his 'kingdom', his 'kingship', he shall come with rich gifts. Even the earthly kings used to distribute gifts on their festal days (cf. 2 Sam. 6.19), but in the case of the coming of the deity this was something involved in the nature of things. For in the first instance the festival meant a re-awakening to new riches and blessing, and 'salvation' for land and cattle and men; the coming of Yahweh meant the coming of the rainy season, when streams of blessing would again pour over the earth, so that the fields would flow with cream and honey, an expression which is found in the ancient Phoenician cult songs referring to the resurrection and enthronement of Baal.

At Yahweh's festival of enthronement all this receives a more personal touch. The almighty creator is coming to his people, renewing the covenant and securing to them all the 'blessing' which belongs to 'life' and 'peace' and 'salvation'. All the *gifts of the 'kingdom of God'* may indeed be summed up in these words. In fact, to secure all this was the real intention of the festal cult. When Yahweh comes again to the feast from his primeval home in the far south he brings 'abundant rain' with him, and thus restores his suffering people (Ps. 68.8–11). Ps. 65, the thanksgiving psalm of the harvest feast, gives a magnificent picture of all the blessings promised and granted by the new victory over the powers of chaos, the new creation and the coming of the rainy season, in the following outburst of praise:

> who by his might raised up the mountains,
>   being girded with power,
> who stilled the roaring of the sea . . . ,
>   the tumults of its waves,
> so that the dwellers at the ends of the earth
>   were terrified by thy wonders;
> the gates of the morning and evening
>   thou madest to shout with joy.

As the poet is here speaking of the victory over the primordial ocean and of the creation, 'the dwellers at the ends of the earth' are obviously not the 'nations' in the remotest parts of the world—as the glossator in v. 8 thinks—but the demonic powers of the *tĕhōm* around the earth, 'the helpers of Rahab' (Job 9.3), whom Yahweh at that time conquered. This victory Yahweh at the preceding new year feast repeated, and re-established the world 'not as a waste (*tōhû*) but to be inhabited' (Isa.

45.18). The consequence of this 'right order' was the rain, that now yields all the blessings of heaven and earth, for which the congregation at *this* new year feast has to give thanks. The same victory and re-creation are also granted by Yahweh's 'coming' again *this* time, and so the thanksgiving psalm has in mind both the blessings of the year already past, and those to be expected for the year to come:

> Thou has visited now and watered the earth
>   with rains, and greatly enriched her;
> God's river is now full of water;
>   thou hast prepared their corn;
> her ridges hast thou watered well
>   and soaked all her furrows,
> with showers has thou softened her,
>   thou blessest all her growth.
>
> Thou now hast crowned thy year of bliss,
>   for thus hast thou prepared it.
> The ruts of thy carriage wheels flow with fatness,
>   the wilderness overflows,
> the hills are girded with shouts of joy,
>   they shout and sing for joy;
> the meadows now are clothed with flocks,
>   the valleys covered with corn.[150]

But all this blessing and 'salvation' may also be regarded from an ethical point of view, and the mind may dwell on the good social conditions which are to prevail in Yahweh's kingdom, when the fellowship ('loyalty', *ḥesedh*) and faithfulness of the covenant, when justice and right order shall prevail in the land like good angels, while at the same time the 'earth shall give crops' and 'Yahweh give that which is good' as it was described in the quotation above from Ps. 85.

How real and manifold these good gifts of Yahweh were imagined to be will be still more clear to us, if we read the promises of the festal psalms in the light of all the different forms of 'festal myths' discussed in the preceding paragraphs. With Yahweh's victory over the powers of chaos, over primeval ocean and demons—those who 'dwell at the ends (of the earth)' (Ps. 65.9)—'the world is (again) stablished, that it cannot be moved' (Ps. 93.1ff.); chaos and desert have been kept off; the 'river of God', which the mind located high up in the heavens, but which the eyes of faith might also see welling forth from the holy place itself,[151] 'is now

---

[150] As for the text: *hămōn lĕ'ummîm* (v. 8) is a rationalizing gloss to the mythological metaphor, giving the latter a historical application and making the verse-line (stichos, bicolon) too long. V. 10b also makes the line too long, but may be the half-line (hemistich, colon) lacking after v. 12a. Vv. 13b and 14 are of one set; as 14aα and aβ are of one set as parallel cola, both thought-rhyme and metre demand that 14b be placed in front of 14a.

[151] Pss. 46.5; 36.9f.; cf. Ezk. 47.1–12; Isa. 33.21.

full of water' (Ps. 65.10). Yahweh's appearance as king involves a promise; he has renewed the covenant with his people, which in itself guarantees that all such things are going to happen in the coming year of grace and goodwill (Ps. 65.10; Isa. 49.8; 61.2) as faith may expect from the god of the covenant. In Jerusalem the festival was celebrated before the rainy season—and, originally, to cause it; when Yahweh has come, faith knows that blessing and crops and wealth will come also, if king and people but keep the covenant. 'The fate has already been turned' to good things for his people, and the days to come shall prove this.

However, Yahweh's victory over the powers of chaos and death are also transferred to the historical conditions of Israel. His appearance also implies his victory over all the 'nations' and so guarantees that no earthly enemy shall be able to threaten his city or be a match for the people fighting in his power. Yahweh's kingdom is going to be a kingdom of peace, for Israel has already 'been justified'—has got its right granted— and shall have its rights in all conflicts with its enemies. The other nations and their gods have already been judged and 'put to shame'; 'the villages of Judah rejoice over his righteous judgments'. With the coming of Yahweh 'holiness again becometh his house' (93.5); it has again been cleansed and consecrated, and the sources of blessing may again flow from there so that the congregation

> May have their fill of the fatness of thy house
> and drink of thy delicious stream. (Ps. 36.9.)

The poet does not here speak only about what *we* call 'spiritual' goods, but about the 'material' ones as well—and in the first place; these two aspects of reality were still undifferentiated in the minds of the Israelites. The 'holiness' (*qōdheš*) that after the coming of Yahweh again 'becomes his house' (93.5) also includes the sources of the material goods, the 'blessing'. In the Israelite conception of holiness the idea of the 'powerful' is always an important element; as 'the Holy One of Israel' Yahweh shows himself both in destroying the enemies of his people (Deutero-Isaiah) and in punishing his own people (Isaiah) and in re-creating the world. How close to one another the ideas of 'holiness' (taboo) and of 'might' (mana) lay, may be seen in the above mentioned Ps. 65, whose main theme is the renewed fertility of the land:

> we have been satisfied with the good things of thy house,
> with the holiness of thy temple. (v. 5.)

The fertility of the land flows from the source of 'holiness' that now is in the Temple.

But even the *earthly king* of Israel has been renewed and strengthened through the commemoration of his first installation and the repeated promises of Yahweh's coming and covenant: he is going to be the true luck-bringing king, under whose government land and people shall prosper (Ps. 132.11ff.). Israel shall always have true priests and prophets and intercessors (Pss. 99.6f., 132.16), 'her priests are wrapped in salvation', and able to transfer salvation to the rejoicing people. From now on—and on the basis of the entire history of the people—they know that Yahweh is a god who forgives sins, who provides redemption for his people through the religious commandments and rules and the righteous priests he has given them (99.6ff., cf. 93.5). He hears prayers as in days of old, and gives trustworthy oracles and guidance through the revelations received by his temple prophets and priests from the cloudy pillar over his altar (99.7). 'Blessed be the people who has such a god!'

It is a manifold, and to modern feelings perhaps contradictory, picture which is produced by all the versions of 'festal myths' and complexes of ideas attached to them. Nor are they to be systematized. Israel at any rate had not—as had the Hellenes even in Antiquity—arrived at a point when scientific 'mythologists'—we should say, theologians—would try to give a consistent and rationalized epic form to the many apparently contradictory expressions of the religious experience in the cult—the 'myths'—or even try to arrange their ideas in a kind of religio-philosophical system, as for instance Philo of Byblos had tried to do with the Phoenician 'mythology' in his *Sanchuniaton*.

But we may ask whether the thinkers and poets of Israel serving the cult—her *homines religiosi*—ever tried to unite the different variants of the 'festal myth' in separate rounded-off epic versions.

If we realize that the myth is a more or less epic and actualizing conception, and a more or less suggestive tale of the reality 'taking place' and experienced through the cult, then it will be clear that it may, in fact, exist in many versions, right from what may be called its myth seed or myth embryo—the immediate conception at the moment of experience of what 'happens' according to its transcendental and existential meaning—up to the completely formulated and poetically modelled tale of gods, the myth-epic.[152]

When, in the preceding paragraphs, we have been speaking of the different complexes of ideas, such as the 'struggle against chaos' myth, the 'struggle of the nations' myth, the 'judgment myth', the 'myth about the making of the covenant', and so on, we do not necessarily imply that all these myths have existed as rigidly formulated epic tales, whether in verse or prose. Nor need such a tale have been recited at a certain point in the festal liturgies. The original and essential thing is not that the myth is recited, but that it is experienced; it is not told, it is 'acted' and it 'takes place'. That such and such a complex of ideas made up the myth of a festival need mean no more than that the reality expressed by it was reiterated and experienced at the festival. How the reality was to be expressed might, so to speak, be left to the individual. But of course a certain common skeleton is to be found in the more or less realistic or

[152] Cf. Mowinckel, *Religion und Kultus*, pp. 94ff.

symbolical ritual drama, actualizing what was 'taking place'. The myth may exist in the cultic drama and the ritual, and even in the allusions in hymns and prayers to what is 'taking place'.

For the myth to be stabilized in an epic form is a later phase. Its starting-point may have been the explanatory words accompanying the rites: 'this means that the god is doing such and such a thing'; or it may have been the hymns, as they picture the great works of the god, depicted in the rites as 'taking place'.

The development of the myth as epic may come about in different ways. In the first instance it probably happens spontaneously. Some person attached to the cult and acquainted with what is going to 'take place', and possessing the poetic power of 'seeing', and a poet's delight in fabulizing, begins to tell with primeval reality and power about the great happenings here and now, and those 'once upon a time' in the beginning. The wake-night before the great festal day, the intervals between the acts, the day of preparation when the tribes gather and the pilgrims pour in from all quarters, these are all suitable and obvious opportunities for such narrations. The pilgrims to the festival would gather round the narrator, listening and asking and wanting to know more. It would become a custom for such tales to be told. The person with a creative talent would soon find that he could make a profit from it; the audience would be quite willing to spare a gift for an exciting and stimulating bit of saga. What may be called an order of professional saga-tellers would grow into being, attached to the sanctuary in question; or this function would be taken over especially by the wandering 'men of god', the Levites, the seers and nĕbhî'îm, saints and miracle-workers, wandering from one sanctuary to another.

There would be co-operation between the saga-teller and his audience. The interest and the questions would goad the imagination and the delight in telling. Some things would please the audience and be constantly repeated, others would be forgotten. The saga-teller himself would want to hear other versions and new features from other 'wise men'. New features were added and combined with his own repertoire, variants were interwoven and equated; by means of leit-motifs and additions the separate tales were connected into greater series and 'complexes of traditions'. In this way both the religio-mythical and the more 'secular' epic would come to exist, though in antiquity no epic ever became entirely 'secular' and the connexion with the cult and the cult places and with the wandering 'holy men' and minstrels was always more or less recognizable.

The close connexion existing between hymns and cultic drama makes it likely that the epic myth from its start would have had a poetic form and style. All the epic myths known to us from Babylonia as well as from Ugarit are in verse; they are mythical and epic poems. That attempts at earlier stages may sometimes have used plain prose is not to be denied; but we seem justified in maintaining that the true form of the myth was the poetic epic, the cycle of songs; the 'rhapsodist', the 'bard', the 'skald' was at the same time the 'mythologist'. That the myths, for instance about the origin of the world, about creation, about the oldest generations of gods (cosmogony, theogony) are in prose seems to be due to the fact that later 'scientists' used them as material for an extensive historical sketch or some other non-cultic purpose. Thus we have had handed down to us the prose account of the Babylonian creation epic as part of Berossos' 'Babylonian History', and the Phoenician theogony and cosmogony we have as part of Philo's cosmological and philosophical text-book, in which Phoenician traditions are quoted. In much the same way we have the tales of Norse mythology quoted and explained in prose in Snorre's text-book about skaldic art, 'Edda'. There are thus grounds for believing that the same thing happened in Israel.

That poetic accounts of the fight against dragons and chaos, creation, the first man, and so on, existed in Israel at a comparatively early time may be concluded with certainty from the way the psalmists and prophets adopted and imitated such epic pieces.[153] They probably had Canaanite patterns; the Old Testament Leviathan, the dragon of the primeval ocean, corresponds to the dragon Lotan in the mythology of Ugarit. There are also indications that an actual account of creation existed in verse as part of an epic, but without being couched in the form of a fight against dragon and primeval ocean; we seem to find some remnants of such a creation epic in verse underlying the story in Gen. 2-3.[154] And from Ps. 8 we may infer that to the festival also belonged a presentation of creation, which did not have the form of a myth about a fight against dragon and primeval ocean, but was more closely related to the conceptions of Gen. 1.

From the very beginning, however, there was to be found in Israel yet another tradition, which was to become an essential part of the myth, namely the historical tradition about the origin of the people, about Yahweh's miracle at the Exodus and about the making of the covenant. Through the festival Israel very early—perhaps already at the time of David and Solomon—experienced a repetition of the history of her origin. Here the story had become historicized tradition, saga, even before it became a cultic myth. But it was in connexion with the cult that the form and the leading religious ideas were stabilized;[155] and there this history was re-experienced as a real history of salvation, as *mythos*. But in the cult even this tradition became a formula of 'confessions' and of hymns containing versions of the historical traditions,[156] such as the Exodus hymn of Ex. 15.[157] But there are also traces showing that even this traditional material, this 'myth of exodus and settlement and covenant', has been

[153] See Pss. 74.12-17; 89.2-3, 6-17; 104.5-9; Isa. 42.10ff.; 51.9f.; Ezk. 28.11ff.; 29.3f.
[154] See Mowinckel in *ZATW* 53, 1935, pp. 146f.
[155] See v. Rad, *Formgesch. Problem d. Hexateuchs*, pp. 30ff.
[156] v. Rad, op. cit., pp. 3ff., 8ff., is hardly right in saying that the latter type is derived from the former; they are both co-ordinate ritualizings of historical tradition.
[157] See Additional Note XXIV.

made a subject of epic adaptation, an Israelite religious 'national epic'.[158]

If anything becomes a custom in connexion with cult and sanctuary, it naturally develops into a rite. Even the spontaneous and free, or the artistically formed poetical tale about something 'taking place' in some way or other becomes part of the ritual. But the mythical epic may also be composed expressly for the purpose of becoming part of the cultic ritual. This is probably the case with the Babylonian creation epic on seven tablets ending in a hymn to Marduk, in which all his fifty cultic names are specified. But it may also happen in another way, so that the mythic tale first comes to rank as canonical writing, and then it reacts on the cultic liturgy and replaces the earlier freer forms of what is 'taking place'; the tale becomes a cultic 'lesson' ('legend').[159]

Of whether the temple rites of Jerusalem included recitations of such poetic and epic festal myths, and what may have been their form and place in the ritual, we know nothing directly. That the laws in the Pentateuch say nothing about it is of no consequence; for neither do they mention the singing of psalms. But analogies from Babylonia and Egypt, as well as all the allusions in the psalms to the festal myths, make it likely that such epic features would have a part in the festal rituals.

Other things seem to point in the same direction. In so far as the passover festival is concerned, the allusions to the rituals to be found in the Exodus itself contain a piece of information which probably implies that it was part of the ritual to ask questions as to the meaning of the different ceremonies and that these questions were answered by references to the Exodus (Ex. 12.26f.; 13.8). At any rate, later Jewish practice understood it in this way and supposed the answers to be given in the form of a re-narration of the Exodus as we have had it handed down to us in the book of the same name. The fact that these tales contain not a few allusions to, and details from, the festal ritual, proves that in the last instance the form they have is due to the cult. With great certainty we may therefore infer that at a comparatively early time there existed a fairly fixed cultic form of the traditions about the Exodus, forming part of the cult of the passover festival,[160] even if it existed in different versions. This may then permit us to analogize with regard to the other great festivals. But if so, we must remember that we are dealing with versions which are older than, and form the basis of, those which are to be found in the Pentateuch—for instance the story of creation.

Even in Israel the prose versions of the story of creation and of the traditions of exodus and settlement appear as parts of a *saga*, a historical account based on religious and *historical* interests—just like the Baby-

[158] See Mowinckel in *ZATW* 53, 1935, pp. 130ff.

[159] Such was the fate of the 'kerygma', the history of the passion and resurrection in the primitive church: instead of the free 'presentations' and allusions in singing and testimony along with a symbolic dramatic 'realization' in the 'active' liturgy itself, we have the reading of texts from the gospels. Cf. my *Religion und Kultus*, pp. 113f.

[160] See v. Rad, op. cit., pp. 3ff., 18ff., 37ff., and see below, n. 163.

lonian creation story of Berossos. On the whole the reading of 'lessons' seems to have played an inconspicuous part in the temple service, even after Judaism had her Holy Scriptures. The only clear evidence seems to be the reading of the 'law of the covenant' (Deuteronomy) every seven years at the feast of Tabernacles (Deut. 31.10ff.), a custom which obviously originated from the cultic rite of announcing Yahweh's basic commandments as part of the ritual of the covenant (see above, pp. 156f.). Here we may find further evidence that 'Scripture' was replacing the earlier and freer cultic forms. This system also seems to have led to more extensive reading of the 'Law' at the festivals of harvest and new year; at any rate the most natural interpretation of the reading of the law by Ezra at the new year festival, is that it refers to a regular cultic practice, not to the introduction of any new law.[161]

Therefore it is most unlikely that any part of the traditions about early times and the time of the occupation, in the form in which they have been handed down to us in the Pentateuch, should ever have been used in the temple cult as a 'festival legend' in the true sense of the word. This applies, for instance, to the creation tales in Gen. 1 and 2[162] and to the saga about the Exodus in Ex. 1–15.[163] In the form known to us *now*, they are meant to be part of a saga, not a festal myth or legend. But they are derived from earlier forms evidently connected with the festal cult.

9

The enthronement psalms and the other psalms of new year and harvest often allude to different rites and ceremonies belonging to the festal complex; but it is not possible to make a complete picture out of them. We have only a few glimpses.

Here we must recall what was said above of the dramatic character of the cultic festival. The feast is a 'holy drama', where the contents of the festal myths are presented, and thus are embodied and re-experienced as

---

[161] See Mowinckel, *Ezra den skriftlaerde*, pp. 32ff., 72ff.

[162] Humbert's arguments in favour of ascribing Gen. 1 to the new year festival as a 'legend' (*RHPhR* XV, 1935, pp. 1ff.) only suffice to bring out the connexion between the very material of the tradition and the new year festival. Ringgren has also realized this, *SEÅ* XIII, 1948, pp. 9ff. Ringgren's own attempt at showing that Gen. 1 has been formed in conscious protest against a certain (Canaanizing) version of the new year festival, is not convincing. P—like J before him—wanted to write history, and as it was part of the learned and holy tradition that a saga ought to start with the origin of the world (cf. Ehrenzweig in *ZATW* 38, 1919–20, pp. 65f.), both of them had recourse to the material to be found in the cultic tradition, giving it the form and idea of a saga.

[163] Johs. Pedersen has maintained that the saga of the Exodus in Ex. 1–15 is 'a festal legend of the Passover' (*Israel* III–IV, pp. 728ff.,; *ZATW* 52, 1934, pp. 161ff.). If this is to be applied to the form in which it has been handed down to us, it cannot be correct; even if Ex. 1–15 contains many evidences of an earlier connexion between the material of the tradition and the cult, the intention of the form as at present is to be a saga (cf. the preceding note); in fact it has been composed from two literary sources, each of which claims to be a saga—and the argumentation of Pedersen has not been able to impair the force of evidence. See Mowinckel in *StTh* V, 1951, pp. 66ff.

something which is actually creating what is then coming into existence. Only we must not think that this 'presentation' was anything like a modern realistic play. It is just possible that most of the things 'taking place' were presented by means of suggestive symbols. We need to realize the part played by symbols in the cult.[164] The fundamental idea itself, the epiphany of Yahweh as a victorious king, was suggested by carrying the ark in the festal procession. Just as, for instance, the whole of the Christian salvation-drama is presented in the 'holy drama' of the Orthodox Church, so we may very well imagine that the whole of the 'festal myth' described above was in some way or other expressed through dramatic symbols during the seven days' festival of harvest, new year and enthronement.[165]

We have mentioned above the important part played by the festal processions in the ancient cult.[166] Likewise it has been mentioned that, if we are justified in analogizing from corresponding new year and enthronement festivals, for instance in Babylonia, it would probably be on the last day of the seven or eight days of the festal complex—'the last day, that great day of the feast' as it is called in the Gospel of John (7.37)—that the royal entry of Yahweh would take place, the grand procession when the king, Yahweh, was represented by his ark. Now there are many psalms which belonged to the complex of the harvest festival, in which such a procession is taken for granted. We *may* be dealing with different parts of one and the same procession; but there may also be references to several processions on different days of the festival. Therefore it will always be a doubtful undertaking to try to reconstruct the picture of Yahweh's royal entry on the basis of these psalms.

An impressionistic picture of the changing scenes and emotions of the procession is given in Ps. 68, undoubtedly a procession psalm at Yahweh's triumphal entry as king. Other obvious procession psalms are 132, 24, and 118; the two former evidently belong to Yahweh's royal entry itself and, like Ps. 68, allude to the entry of the ark as his visible representative. Whether all these psalms belong to the same procession is more uncertain; they may even reflect the ceremonies of different periods, though certainly the first three, and probably also Ps. 118, date from pre-exilic times.

A 'processional road' always belonged to the cultic processions at the great temples of the orient, a *via sacra*, as it was called by the Romans. Babylon's processional road, Aiburshabu, has been excavated; it was decorated with lions and inscriptions in blue and white faience.[167] But Jerusalem, too, had her *via sacra*; there is a reference to it in Ps. 84.6:

[164] Cf. E. Underhill, *Worship*, p. 20.
[165] Therefore the objection of Kraus does not hold good, when he says (op. cit., p. 23): 'Es muss schon ein kaum vorstellbarer szenischer Aufwand bei der von Mowinckel postulierten dramatischen Aufführung des Festmythus ... angenommen werden, um die Worte und Bilder der Thronbesteigungspsalmen als "Kulterlebnisse" zu verstehen.' It only shows that Kraus has a very vague conception of cult, just as he lacks understanding of the true essence of myth.
[166] See above, Chap. I, pp. 20f.; *Religion und Kultus*, pp. 73ff.
[167] See Weissbach, *AO* V, pp. 26f.; Ravn, *Herodots beskrivelse av Babylon*, pp. 75f. More detailed in Koldewey, *Wiedersteh. Babylon*,[4] pp. 25ff.

> Blessed the man whose strength is in Thee,
> in whose mind are the paved ways!

The 'paved way' (mĕsillâ)—the plural is amplificatory—on which the partakers of the festival have it 'in their hearts' to walk, and on which they intend to walk, is the holy way, on which the procession 'ascend' to the Temple. So the Greek translation is justified in paraphrasing this verse: 'with the "ascension" (i.e. festal procession) in their hearts'. And when, in the spirit, the prophet sees the dispersed Jews returning to Jerusalem with Yahweh at their head, he pictures a mighty procession approaching, and therefore speaks also of the wonderful 'paved way', the 'eschatological' via sacra, which will then be made through the desert:

> and there shall be a paved road
> its name 'The Sacred Way'. (Isa. 35.8.)

On the basis of the story told in 2 Sam. 6 as to how David took Yahweh's ark to Jerusalem, we may guess that the processional way started from a place called the house of Obed-Edom, outside the oldest part of the town, the 'castle of David',[168] and from there it ran on the outside (to the east) of, or through the royal castle and into the temple court through the eastern gate—probably the one also called the water-gate, perhaps because at the ceremony of water drawing the water from the spring Gihon would be carried in this way.[169] Ps. 118.19f. also speaks of a definite gate, the 'Gate of Righteousness' (šaʿârê ṣedḥeq), through which the procession would enter, the 'gate, through which the righteous (i.e. the Israelite congregation), shall enter'. Even the temple and procession gates of Babylonia had such symbolical names: the 'Gate of Allegiance', the 'Gate of Salvation', the 'Gate of Life', etc.[170]

The holy way played a central role in the festival. There would take place the 'pageant of my God and King', as the psalmist would call it—the 'ascension(s)' was the technical term.[171] The royal entry of Yahweh, at which he himself is present, symbolized by his holy 'ark', is the preeminent visible centre of the experiences connected with the enthronement festival:

> God is gone up amid shouts of homage,
> Yahweh (has come) with trumpet blasts.
> Music of praise for God, sing music!
> Music of praise now for our King! (Ps. 47.6f.)

[168] See Mowinckel, Ps.St. II, pp. 128f., giving a more detailed statement.
[169] The water gate is a temple gate, not a gate in the city wall, see Mowinckel in Studier tilegnet Buhl, p. 172. For the city gates of Jerusalem, cf. the article 'Jerusalem' in BRL.
[170] See Zimmern in ZDMG 76, 1922, p. 49, and below, note 191.
[171] This is no doubt the meaning of the psalm heading shîr hammaʿalôth, 'the psalms of ascent, i.e. of the festal procession', see below, Chap. XXIII.3 and Ps.St. IV, p. 3. Vb. ʿālâ 'ascend' is used about the procession in Ps. 47.6.

If we agree that the three psalms 68, 132 and 24 belong to Yahweh's royal entry itself, then it is clear that 132 deals with the preparation for the transport of the ark from some place outside the sanctuary, whereas the first scene of 24 is played before and within the gates of the Temple itself. Ps. 68 seems to reflect the start of the procession, so that its situation partly overlaps that of 132. But Ps. 132 continues after the procession has passed through the gates. With the above reservation (p. 170) we must put the psalms 68, 132 and 24 in this sequence.

As Ps. 68 gives the most vivid general impression of the festival procession, it is best to deal with it first.[172]

That the psalm belongs to a festal procession is quite evident:

> Behold, everyone! the procession (*hălîkhôth*) of Yahweh,
>   the holy procession of my God and King;
> singers in front, musicians behind (them),
>   between, young girls with tambourines. (vv. 25f.)

Then the whole people comes by tribes: Benjamin, Judah, Zebulon, Naphtali, led by their tribal chiefs (vv. 27f.).

The poet speaks in the first person, but he speaks on behalf of the whole festal congregation. He speaks as one who is personally taking part in the procession—as no doubt he is. He gives us the programme of the procession, and describes the impressions made on himself and his fellow worshippers by what happens and what they are now all experiencing: the triumphal entry of Yahweh, their king, into his palace (v. 30), his sanctuary (vv. 18, 36) his 'ascension' to 'the height' (*mārōm*, v. 19)—here the poet uses the technical term '*ālâ* for the procession up to the sanctuary.

The general character of the psalm is hymnal. But the impressionistic character in itself, the changing scenes with the changing emotions—and probably even voices—makes it most natural for us to describe it as a processional cantata. Yahweh is making his entry as king. That he is represented by his visible symbol, the ark, is seen from the introductory version of the ancient 'stanza of breaking camp' (Num. 10.35). He is coming as a victorious king, the festal procession being his rejoicing army. However, he is not only accompanied by his earthly host; in the procession are also his 'thousands upon thousands of chariots', the mythical hosts (v. 18).

Instead of the usual hymnal invitation to praise,[173] the introductory stanza, vv. 2-4, keeps *in medias res* and, in deference to the ancient invitation to 'break up' and start the procession, describes how Yahweh has once

---

[172] As for Ps. 68 the author was long in doubt whether it was a 'casual' song of victory (see Chap. IX.1) or a festal hymn of praise belonging to the enthronement of Yahweh, see *Ps.St.* II, pp. 12, 332; VI, pp. 31, n. 3, 38, n. 9; *Offersang og sangoffer*, pp. 179, 279, here, pp. 182, 226, Years ago now, however, he became convinced that the latter interpretation is the right one (*Offersang*, p. 179, here p. 182), as H. Schmidt has already seen (*Thronfahrt Jahves*, pp. 13ff.), see now *Der achtundsechzigste Psalm*, 1953, with a discussion of Albright's hypothesis in *HUCA* XXIII, 1, 1950, pp. 1ff., and the writer's *Real and Apparent Tricola*, pp. 92ff.

[173] See above, Chap. IV.1, pp. 81f.

more 'risen', scattering his enemies and creating joy and delight in his people, 'the righteous'; what has happened so often before has again become reality. The second stanza, vv. 5–7, goes on with a regular little hymn of praise to Yahweh 'the skyrider', an epithet adopted from Ugarit-Canaan preferentially to indicate Yahweh's coming to fight against the powers of chaos (cf. Ps. 18.11ff.). The congregation is called upon to praise the 'name' of Yahweh, which he has once more made known by his coming to help all those in distress and to destroy 'the rebellious'. In the situation of a festal psalm these general sentences must obviously be applied to Israel and her enemies. The third stanza, vv. 8–11, starts the broader hymnal description of the real theme of the psalm:

> O Yahweh, when thou 'wentest out' before thy people,
>> when thou didst march through the steppes,
> the earth was shaking, the skies were dropping
>> before Yahweh, the God of Israel.
> O Yahweh, thou didst pour out a generous rain,
>> raising up (again) thy weary property;
> thy household is (now) dwelling therein,
>> in thy goodness thou hast raised up the languishing people.

Here we are told how Yahweh personally led his people out of the desert to Canaan, by means of a simple picture, the picture of a triumphal procession. The term 'go forth' ($y\bar{a}\d{s}\bar{a}'$) refers to the start of such a festal procession. The description, however, is not just meant to be an account of the events of the past; this 'act of salvation' is being 'remembered' and thus re-experienced as actual presence; the festal procession of the day is identical with the act of salvation of the past. Even today Yahweh comes, as he did before, from his original dwelling-place in Sinai (v. 18) and enters his 'abode', the Temple (v. 29), accompanied by his delivered people.

The re-experienced act of salvation is not here a mere mythical happening, but the historical experience, the Exodus, the wandering in the desert and the victorious settling in Canaan—just as in the psalm, Ex. 15.2ff. In fact, from the following fourth stanza, vv. 12–15, we see that the act of salvation, which is now re-experienced in the festival, is 'the myth about the victory over the nations'. The festal procession is also 'the mighty host of those bringing the good tidings' of the victory, and tells of 'the fleeing war lords', the slain kings and horses and chariots scattered over the field 'like snow on Black Mountain', and the abundant booty. In the sixth stanza (vv. 20–24) there may be an allusion to a definite people, perhaps Se'ir-Edom as Israel's actual enemy, to whom the myth has been applied (v. 20).

But in the background of this conception we find here too the chaos myth, Yahweh's victory over the primeval chaotic powers. This is not only seen from 'the myriads of chariots' (v. 18) and 'the skyrider' (v. 5), 'that rideth' or, rather, 'driveth on the primeval heaven' (v. 34), but also from the metaphors used in the eighth stanza (vv. 29–32) of 'the nations delighting in war' (v. 31c); 'the beasts of the reeds (or, marshes)', 'the herd of bullocks' are terms for the demonic monsters of chaos, which have been destroyed by Yahweh, and which he is repeatedly asked to destroy by his 'threatening'—the threatening word of power, with which in the beginning he had chased away the primeval ocean (and its monsters) (cf. Ps. 104.7), it is an indication in the same direction when the enemy is characterized as 'those with hairy scalps', *śāʿîr*, a word in which the Israelite must needs hear the by-meaning of 'demoniac' (*śāʿîr*). In v. 21 we are told in plain words that the victory of Yahweh is a victory over, and deliverance from, 'Death', by which here is not meant natural decease, but Death with a capital D, Môt, in Canaanite mythology the adversary of Baʿal, here of Yahweh, in the constantly repeated war between life and death, the Living God and the god of death, Môt. We find the same idea in Ps. 48 (see below, p. 182). That is why the poet can put the triumphal words into the mouth of Yahweh: 'I bring back again from the Dragon— *beshen*[174]—I bring back again from the depths of the Sea' (v. 23). Every year, as we have heard above, Death or 'Prince Sea'—*zebul yam*, as he is named in Ugaritic mythology—seeks to overthrow the land of the living, but every time Yahweh again conquers him, and 'brings back' from his realm.

As in Pss. 46 and 48 (see below) the poet glorifies the sanctuary on the 'mountain of God', the true Olympus (vv. 16f.). And in the eighth stanza (vv. 29–32) the congregation prays that from there (v. 30) Yahweh, who is dwelling there, may 'display thy strength which thou mightily prevailest for us from thy palace' (vv. 29f.), and (again and again) 'rebuke' (Moffatt: check) 'the chaotic powers in the shape of the nations delighting in war' (see above). If it be so, the congregation promises, even kings of the richest and remotest nations, Patros, Egypt and Kush, will bring gifts of gold and silver and other precious metals to this temple and 'stretch out their hands to him'.

In the last, the ninth stanza (vv. 33–35), the hymn of praise, as is often the case, returns to the beginning, and calls all the kingdoms of the earth to praise this mighty God of the heavens, the thunderer, who 'demonstrates his power in the clouds', who is also 'the God of Israel, who bestows power on his people—blessed be He!' This quite corresponds to the enthronement psalms when the cosmic aspect of the festal experience is expressed. To 'what happens' in the cultic drama corresponds what happens in heaven; he that sits enthroned in the Temple is the one who sits enthroned up there, and sends thunder and rain and 'renews the surface of the earth'—and with awe, all kings and peoples ought to recognize that he is at the same time the god of Israel!

Ps. 132 gives us the 'text' of a dramatic procession with Yahweh's ark. It has a markedly historical savour; the procession is here looked upon as

[174] See Albright in *BASOR* 46, 1932, p. 19, n. 16; *HUCA* XXIII, 1, 1950, p. 27.

a repetition of Yahweh's first entry into Jerusalem, when David laid the foundation of the cult of Yahweh there and introduced the holy ark as the centre of the cult and the symbol of the personal presence of Yahweh. That Yahweh's ark, the hub of the old cultic centre of Shiloh, actually did play a part at the institution by David of the cult of Yahweh in Jerusalem is known to us from the tradition in 2 Sam. 6, but it is also a self-evident deduction: David could not have indicated more clearly that his new kingdom was to be based on the traditions of the old Israel. And considering all we know about the way in which cult institutions and the foundation of a kingdom were celebrated in the ancient orient,[175] we may take it for granted that such a ceremony would be repeated as an annual festival; and then everything indicates that the festival of the institution of Temple and cult in Jerusalem was identical with the new year festival, the enthronement festival of Yahweh.[176] For when the Chronicler (2 Chron. 6.41f.) quotes part of this psalm as the festal song at the consecration of the Temple of Solomon in the month of Ethanim, we are justified in taking this as showing how the psalm actually was used, and in concluding that the harvest feast was also considered to be the celebration of the consecration of the Temple; the Temple of the new king was consecrated anew. The psalm proves that the festival of consecration was at the same time the festival of the institution of the cult of Yahweh on Zion under David.

We find a reflection of the ritual of this consecration festival in the description of 2 Sam. 6; of course the saga-writer had no contemporary reports about the festival from the time of David, so he described it on the model of the celebration of his own day.[177] Along with Ps. 132 the description of the saga teller gives us a picture in broad outline of this important part of the festival.

The whole thing has the character of a cultic and historical drama, in which the king, the Anointed, evidently plays the part of David. First we hear the intercessory prayer for 'David'—and so for the whole royal family—that Yahweh may remember the piety of the ancestor who swore never to indulge in sleep or rest till he had found the ark of Yahweh and brought it to its proper place. Here we probably have to imagine that David is waiting to hear from those whom he has sent out to seek for the ark, and that in the meantime the chorus representing the congregation is comforting and strengthening him by this intercession. At this moment

---

[175] See Dürr in *Theol. u. Glaube* 20.
[176] Solomon's consecration of the Temple took place at the 'festival' in the month of Ethanim, the old name for the month of the autumnal equinox Tishri (1 Kgs. 8.2). The central rite was here the procession with Yahweh's ark (8.1ff.), just as at the foundation festival of David (2 Sam. 6). The enthronement psalm 93.5 refers to the consecration of the Temple. Ps. 132 is the dramatic liturgy of the 'procession' at the festival of the foundation of the Temple; the centre is the ark of Yahweh (see above, n. 111). The Chronicler explicitly quotes Ps. 132 as the psalm sung at the festival for the consecration of the Temple under Solomon (2 Chron. 6.41f.). Cf. *Ps.St.* II, pp. 109ff. and above, n. 71, and Additional Note XVIII.
[177] Cf. Additional Note XVI.

a new chorus appears on the 'stage': the men return to say that the ark has been found 'in the precincts of the town of Ephratah', i.e. Kiriath-jearim,[178] whither, according to tradition, it had come from the land of the Philistines; now they are bringing it with them. Let us 'go into his tabernacles—the sanctuary, and (by implication), put the ark in its proper place—and worship at his footstool'; this latter name is that given to the ark itself; in the Temple it stood under the wings of the two giant cherubs, whose outstretched wings span the whole room; on it Yahweh was supposed to be enthroned unseen. Thereupon follows a version of the old 'stanza of breaking up', used when the ark was lifted up and moved forward (Num. 10.35) requesting Yahweh to go at the head of the procession. The priests are referred to as being now clothed in the beauties of holiness and having the proper inner quality, and the people of the covenant shout for joy before their king. Evidently the priests carrying the ark are speaking here. Whether what follows takes place while the ark is still standing in the same place, or a little later, is doubtful; the analogy with 2 Sam. 6.13 rather seems to suggest the latter, and that after having taken six steps they make a halt to offer up a sacrifice for the success of the undertaking. The following prayer for the blessing of Yahweh on 'his anointed', 'for (the ancestor) David's sake', would then be attached to the sacrifice. And as the prayer of vv. 11–18 is answered by a sonorous oracle of bliss to the royal house, to people and country, in the very same style as the royal oracles containing promises to David in Ps. 89.4–5, 20–38 and 2 Sam. 7, and evidently pronounced by one of the temple prophets (cf. Chap. XII.3); it is not unreasonable to imagine that this promise was formulated in connexion with happy auguries from the offering.

An important point strikes us when we compare this festal drama with the corresponding part of the Babylonian new year and enthronement drama.[179] In Babylonia the other gods would go out along with the king and the priests, etc., in a cultic procession to search for and deliver the lost, dead, or imprisoned god. In the cultic drama of Israel it is the king, 'David', who with his army marches out to search for the representative symbol of Yahweh, the holy ark; who finds it, and provides a permanent abode for it on Zion. The search for the god has become part of the *historically* orientated festival for the institution of the Yahweh cult and the erection and consecration of the Temple, Yahweh's 'resting place' or 'home'. This is the true gist of Ps. 132, not for instance the re-instatement of the king. All these national and religious historical memories become merged in the enthronement festival and are repeated through it, becoming a living reality again. Creation, Yahweh's victory over his enemies, is brought to an issue through the creation of his people, i.e. through the

---

[178] Thus Delitzsch in his psalm commentary, pp. 811f., with reference to 1 Chron. 2.50; Kiriath-jearim is a descendant of Hur, who according to 2.19 is a son of (Caleb and) Ephrath.
[179] See Frankfort, *Kingship*, pp. 321ff.

deliverance of the people and the covenant with them, which is again concentrated and renewed through the covenant with the house of David and reaches its climax through the foundation of the Temple and the worship of Yahweh there, an idea also present in the psalm in Ex. 15. Yahweh's victorious and royal entry also includes the entry into the renewed Temple, where from now on he shall 'sit enthroned upon the praises of Israel' (Ps. 22.4).

Ps. 24 gives us another picture of the festival. If Ps. 132 shows us the beginning of the day's procession as it started from a place outside the temple citadel, corresponding to the house of Obed-Edom—where the ark had stood for three months,[180] till David brought it to Zion—then Ps. 24 shows us what happened when the procession reached the temple gate. The psalm falls into three parts: the introductory hymn to the creator and ruler of the world (vv. 1–2), the dialogue between the leader of the procession and the gate-keepers as to who is allowed to enter the sanctuary (the 'conditions of entry'), with the assurance from the side of the pageant (the congregation) that they fulfil the demands (vv. 3–6), and finally the request for the gates to open to the One who is coming, 'the King of glory, Yahweh Zebaoth' (vv. 7–10).

What is of special interest in this connexion is the second scene: the question from the leader of the procession and the answer from the 'gate-keeper', who, in earlier times at any rate, belonged to the higher clergy: in pre-exilic times the 'three keepers of the door' ranked next to the chief priest, and so were second from the top (2 Kgs. 25.18).

This way of asking is no doubt old, and has a natural explanation. The many different sanctuaries, besides having general rules for purification and abstinence and preliminary dues,[181] had also their own special *leges sacrae* or 'laws of the sanctuary', their special rules and special demands as to the qualifications of those to be admitted. The pilgrims, perhaps people from afar, had to put questions about the special rules applying at that sanctuary, what conditions were made, what would be the 'rights' and 'customs' of the deity in that place. In the course of time these natural practices would, as so often happens, develop into a fixed form, a rite: in such and such a way people were to ask, and thus they were to be answered on given occasions, even if everybody knew the answer beforehand.[182] Originally, these laws of the sanctuaries were of an essentially ritual cultic and taboo nature, and concerned with external things; at certain sanctuaries for instance no admittance was granted to women. But certain gross crimes and all sorts of ritual impurity were also reasons for exclusion. It is a remnant of such old prohibitions that in Jerusalem the blind and paralysed were not admitted to the Temple.[183] But gradually the moral

---

[180] 2 Sam. 6.10f. See *Ps.St.* IV, pp. 44f.; *Ps.St.* II, pp. 107ff., 128f.

[181] Cf. 1 Sam. 21.5f., Ex. 19.10, 14f.

[182] Cf. Ex. 12.26f.; 13.8, 14.

[183] 2 Sam. 5.8, which is, in fact, an aetiological explanation of the custom. Later on this taboo was only applied to the admission to priesthood, Lev. 21.18.

commandments became more prominent. In this way religious and moral instruction about the fundamental laws of Yahweh would grow to be a permanent element of the cultic ritual. Such sacred laws are a universal feature at ancient oriental sanctuaries.[184] They may even be cut into a stone or engraved on tablets at the entrance of the temple.[185]

In Israel these commandments, quite naturally, gradually came to be looked upon as commandments of the covenant, and as commandments given by Yahweh at Kadesh or Sinai; the instruction as to the conditions of admittance became merged in the idea of the festival as being a renewal of the covenant and a commemoration of the great works of God and of his commandments, i.e. the fundamental happenings in the life of the people, as we meet them in Pss. 81 and 95; in both cases it is the supposed commandments of Mount Sinai and of Kadesh which are imposed on the congregation at the festival of epiphany.

Here we have a special form or application of Yahweh's demands, which has been called 'laws (*tôrôth*) of entry',[186] i.e. authoritative divine 'instruction' (*tôrâ*) through the priest as to what is demanded from those who are admitted to the sanctuary and cult and the blessing thereof. They may have the form of answers to questions on the part of the congregation, or as in this case, the procession.

In so far as the psalms are texts for the cultic rituals, the commandments of Yahweh and the enforcement of them find a place in psalmography. Ps. 24 gives us an example of this as an element in a larger context. The instruction about 'the conditions of admittance' here becomes part of the dramatically modelled liturgy of the procession at Yahweh's royal entry into his abode (the Temple) after having obtained glory through victory over the powers of chaos, and once more proved himself creator and saviour, and having obtained kingship over the whole earth.

The third element in this logical structure of questions and answers would obviously be a declaration on the part of those who want to attend the cult (the congregation) as to whether they are equal to the demands: I have kept these commandments, I am guiltless of these crimes (taboos). The pattern for this part of the liturgy would then be:

1. Who shall be admitted to the hill of Yahweh?
2. The answer of the priests: he that hath kept such and such rules; he that is of such and such a character.
3. The answer of the procession: we have kept and fulfilled all this.

---

[184] See for instance the texts translated by Sam Wide in *Främ. Relig.-urk.* III, pp. 213f.—The most important collection of classical *leges sacrae* is in Proht and Ziehen, *Leges Graecorum sacrae,* fasc. 1–2. Select pieces in Dittenberger, *Sylloge inscr. Graec.* III, pp. 105ff. See also Helbing, *Auswahl aus gr. Inschr.,* pp. 105–111.

[185] A remnant of this custom is the limestone tablet set up at the entrance to 'the court of Israel' in the Temple of Herod, enforcing the interdict against the access of all non-Jews; one of these tablets has been found in Jerusalem, see Dittenberger, *Orientes Graeci Inscriptiones Selectae* II, 1905, no. 538; Benzinger, *Hebr. Archäologie,*[3] p. 337. The tradition that the ten commandments were written on such tablets is an echo of such a custom.

[186] See Mowinckel, *Decalogue,* pp. 141ff.; *Ps.St.* V, pp. 107ff.; Gunkel-Begrich, *Einl.,* pp. 327ff., 408f., with literary references.

Such an answer may be detailed: I have not committed this and this and this. In Ps. 24 it is summed up shortly in v. 6: 'Such are the men who are in quest of Yahweh, who seek the face of the God of Jacob', i.e. we are confident of fulfilling the demands.[187]

So this part of the cult was developed into a means of religious and moral instruction. Ps. 15 is an independent parallel to the part of Ps. 24 which speaks of the conditions of admittance. Here quite a 'moral catechism' is put before the congregation, telling them what a man must be like, who wants to be 'the guest of Yahweh' and 'eternally blessed'.

We notice that ten conditions are mentioned here. This gives a hint of an important and interesting connexion in the history of liturgy and religion. For here we find the fundamental tendency of Yahwism, the approved tendency to keep aloof from the other religions and to have a moral conception of the essence and will and commandments of Yahweh; we find it conquering, so to speak, and filling the ancient—in itself pre-Yahwistic—pattern of the liturgies of entry. It is the same tendency that find expression in the traditions about the making of the covenant on Mount Sinai and in the commandments of the covenant, Ex. 34 and 20. The custom of announcing the 'sacred laws' of the sanctuary, and the tradition about the making of the covenant and the ancient Yahweh law from Kadesh-Sinai have mutually attracted each other, and in this way the old custom of putting questions as to the laws of admittance was filled with the spirit and essence of Yahwism.

This has been an important factor in the moulding and growth of the tradition about the commandments connected with the making of Yahweh's covenant. The enforcement of the fundamental commandments of the sanctuary, and the fact that these were considered to be derived from the making of the covenant and therefore identical with the law of Yahweh and the commandments of Kadesh and Mount Sinai, together with the tendency of Yahwism to get at the essence of God's demands as a whole, led to a definite tradition about these fundamental commandments, a tradition which—probably in keeping with the ancient practices of sanctuaries—would try to sum up the demands in the shape of ten (sometimes twelve) commandments, 'decalogues', and which we may therefore call the 'decalogical tradition' of Israel. So then, those commandments, which at the time were supposed to be the most important, would make up these ten fundamental commandments. Some of them, of course, would remain constant, e.g. the claim for the exclusive authority of Yahweh, and the rejection of cultic images.

The existing *tôrôth* of entry also belong to the decalogical tradition. The traditional figure 10 in such groupings of the fundamental commandments of the covenant ('the decalogues') is probably derived from the instruction of pilgrims: one commandment for each finger.

[187] On Pss. 15 and 24 cf. also Galling. He understands the context against the same background in *ZATW* 47, 1929, pp. 125ff.

At which of these two points within the ritual of the festival the decalogical tradition first came in is a less important question.[188] The fundamental commandments of the covenant of Mount Sinai encounter the
congregation outside the temple gate, and they are also heard at a climax
of the festal cult, at the renewal of the covenant. Two, by themselves
independent, cultic ideas and customs: the announcement of the conditions of admittance to the sanctuary, and the renewal of the covenant
with its conditions, both receive a new substance of ideas from the historical
tradition in the religion of Israel. And this has probably happened under
mutual influence.

In principle these fundamental religious and moral commandments are
related to the congregation, to 'Israel' collectively, both in Pss. 81 and 95,
and in Pss. 24 and 15. But in the 'liturgy of entry' the commandments
are of such a nature that the challenge must be taken up by the individual,
who is put fact to face with his personal responsibility, both for his own
'blessing' and for the future of the people. Imitations of this mode of
speaking as an expression of the message of the prophets are to be found in
Isa. 33.14–16 and Mic. 6.6–8.

Another procession psalm based on the same ideas and probably also
used at the same festival is Ps. 118. This psalm, too, starts outside the
temple gate and reflects the entry through the 'Gate of Righteousness'.
This is probably the name of an actual gate, very likely the innermost
temple gate,[189] through which only 'the righteous'—the congregation in
a state worthy of the cult—are allowed to enter. It is just possible that
Ps. 24 refers to events taking place outside the outer gate leading to the
precincts of the whole citadel and Temple, whereas Ps. 118 refers to those
taking place before and after the passage through the inner temple gate
proper.[190] The psalm starts with a thanksgiving by the king or the leader
of the congregation on behalf of the people both for the aid Yahweh has
given them in all distress and danger throughout the ages, and because
their enemies have been put to shame, and Israel, though certainly chas-
tised, has not been given over to death, but is now able to rejoice over the
great acts of Yahweh (vv. 1–18). The description of the history of Israel,
so full of distress, is summed up in one concentrated picture: all the nations
compassed her about, but in the name of Yahweh, the king has destroyed
them; here the saga has been conventionalized on the model of the 'myth
about the fight of nations' (see above). Then follows the request to open
the Gate of Righteousness to the righteous, who are now coming (vv.
19–20), followed by a new thanksgiving psalm ending in an allusion to

---

[188] Details about this tangled plexus of ideas connected with the law of Yahweh in the festal
cult, are given in *Ps.St.* V, pp. 107ff.; *Decalogue*, pp. 114–156.—In *Le Decalogue* the present author
had fancied the 'torot d'entré' to be the origin of the promulgation of the commandments at
the renewal of the covenant, but in fact we have to deal with two parallel cultic phenomena
and developments of the Israelitic ritual.

[189] See above, p. 171. If so the gate is not the present 'Golden Gate', the eastern gate to Haram
esh-sherif, as Morgenstern thinks, *HUCA* VI, 1929, pp. 1ff.

[190] Cf. the sketch plan in *BRL* col. 411f.; 'F' indicates the outer gate.

this festal day, created by Yahweh himself (vv. 21–24). The very fact that the congregation was allowed to enter through the Gate of Righteousness was at the same time a corroboration of its righteousness and an imparting of the power of 'righteousness' and happiness.[191] This thanksgiving psalm ends in a prayer of prosperity and happiness (v. 25), to which the priests answer with a blessing from the house of Yahweh on those who are now coming in the name of Yahweh (v. 26). While the procession is marching through the gate another short thanksgiving hymn is sung, with a reference to the 'festival of light' and a call to join in the festal dance up to (and round?) the altar (v. 27). Another thanksgiving hymn accompanies the attendance and finishes the psalm (vv. 28–29).

The 'myth about the fight of nations' has been mentioned above several times. It is the illustration of the idea that the enthronement of Yahweh guarantees victory over the enemies of Israel in the 'mythical' form of a destruction of the 'nations' en bloc outside the walls of Jerusalem. In several psalms this 'fight of the nations' is a central theme, especially in Pss. 46 and 48. Both these psalms refer to the congregation as having 'seen' the 'works' of Yahweh and his 'loving-kindness' (*hesedh*) towards his people (46.9; 48.10):

> Come, behold the works of Yahweh,
>> who endeth the wars all over the world:
> He hath broken the bow and snapped the spear
>> and burned the shields in the fire. (46.9f.)

> What once we heard of, now we have seen
>> within the city of our God:
> that God preserveth it evermore,
>> (it never shall be moved).
> We are now contemplating thy loving-kindness
>> within thy Temple, O God. (48.9f.)

Knowing how thoroughly the cult in ancient times was a 'drama' for the purpose of presenting visibly what faith knew to be happening,[192] and considering the prominent part played by ritual fighting games in the cult of ancient peoples,[193] we can hardly help interpreting the words in the above passages as references to ritual acts, through which was presented in a more or less realistic or symbolical way the victory of Yahweh over the united nations. Perhaps the sword dance, referred to in Ps. 149, had a connexion with this performance. It would be logical, considering the dramatic character of the festival, if these ritual fighting games were to

---

[191] In Babylonia, too, the different temple gates had names indicating the blessing received when entering: 'the gate of grace', 'the gate of salvation', 'the gate of life' and so on. The sick person for instance who is to be cleansed and obtain 'salvation' enters through the 12 gates of the Marduk temple, and for each gate he gets the blessing expressed by the name: 'In the gate of grace he gets grace, in the gate of salvation he sees salvation, in the gate of life, life is given to him.' See Zimmern in *ZDMG* 76, 1922, p. 49, and above, p. 171.

[192] Cf. *Ps.St.* II, pp. 19ff.; the article 'Drama' in *RGG²* I, 2000ff.; *Religion und Kultus*, pp. 73ff.

[193] See for instance *Myth and Ritual*, ed. Hooke, Index *s.v.* 'Combat, ritual'; Engnell, *Div. Kingship*, Topical Index *s.v.* 'Shamfight'.

take place some time *before* the triumphal procession described in the preceding paragraph, since this performance was also followed by a procession, a circumambulation about, or on, the walls of the city, as we can see from Ps. 48.13–15:

> Walk about Zion, go round about her,
>   and count up all her towers;
> mark you well her ramparts now,
>   and scan her citadels,
> that you may tell the age to come
>   that He is Yahweh himself,
> (he is) our God for evermore,
>   he shall guide us against Death.

Probably such a circumabulation was originally supposed to be a consecration of walls and city, by which power was transferred;[194] here it has been 'rationalized': it is meant to assure the congregation that the walls are unshaken, and to strengthen their faith that the city is now safe under the protection of Yahweh.

We can gather from this psalm that the fight of nations had not only earthly and political, but even cosmic dimensions. Behind the idea of Yahweh's coming as a victory over the historical enemies of the people, we find the idea of his coming as a victory over the evil cosmic powers, the dragon of the primeval ocean, the powers of chaos and of death—'Death' itself, or Môt, as the personified adversary of the god in the Canaanite cultic myth was called. The last lines from the quotation above imply this: From now on, the king, Yahweh, will be the guide of his people against 'Death'. All evil powers threatening land and nature and people have been destroyed through the coming and enthronement of Yahweh.[195]

This series of pictures from the rites of the festival gives an indication of their general character and of the unity between the rites and the thoughts and experiences of faith to which they are meant to give expression.

There are also allusions to other ritual festival customs; above (p. 181), we have already mentioned the 'festival of light', the illumination of Temple and city at night during the feast of tabernacles, which is mentioned in the Mishna (Sukka V) and hinted at in Ps. 118.27. Ps. 68 is a procession psalm for this festival, which contains many references, but, unfortunately, mostly to rites unknown to us now.

---

[194] Cf. Neh. 12.27ff., and see Additional Note XIX.

[195] Cf. Johnson in *The Labyrinth*, pp. 94f.—Rowley, *Rediscovery of the O.T.*, pp. 126f., 174, thinks that with such a conception of the creative nature of the cultic drama I must be of the opinion that the ritual had a 'magic' character. That this is not the right interpretation of my opinion ought to become evident from what has been said above of 'the gifts of the kingdom of God', pp. 161ff. That something really 'happens' in the cult does not make it into 'magic'; I doubt the legitimacy of using this notion in the world of religion. If the drama of the Israelite new year festival, as I have sketched it in *Ps.St.* II and in the preceding paragraphs, be 'magic' then the Orthodox, Roman, Anglican and in fact even the Lutheran cult must be 'magic' as well.

10

The enthronement psalms must be understood against the background of this festival, with all the rich experiences contained in it, experiences including past and future in a re-creating present. The psalms of epiphany and enthronement are hymns of praise and prayer which hail Yahweh as the king who has now returned and revealed himself to his people. They express the reactions of the congregation, in jubilant joy and in awe, to the great, constantly repeated and ever new experience. But they are also the congregation's confession of faith in the mighty covenant God, who has again revealed himself to do his work of salvation.[196]

There is every reason to believe that *the true enthronement hymns* in the strictest sense of the term belonged to that day in the festal complex considered to be Yahweh's own particular 'day', the day of his royal entry and triumph. They all take for granted that Yahweh has already gone up to his abode and is sitting on his throne.[197] This explains the calls to pass into his court and appear before him and kneel at his footstool worshipping him[198] and hailing him with the 'shout of royal homage'.[199] All the 'salvation' that finds expression in the festal myths is experienced here and now.[200] The psalms themselves are meant to provide the homage, which the authors call upon the congregation, the king's people, to pay to the king. They claim to be the 'new song' (96.1; 98.1) 'fit' (cf. 65.2) for the newly arrived king at the start of the new year on the re-created earth; they are themselves the songs of homage to the revealed, enthroned King and God, Yahweh.

Their contents may be summed up in the following list.[201] 1. In the usual hymnic introduction they first call for exultant homage to the king, who has now arrived and is sitting on his throne; the invitation contains characteristic peculiarities, connected with the nature and essence of the festival: because Yahweh is king of the world, this invitation is addressed to all nations; because his coming also means re-creation, all nature is called upon to rejoice; because the work performed by him is operative far beyond the borders of Israel, his congregation is called upon to take the message to all nations and make them take part in the homage. 2. As usual in the hymns, the invitation is motivated by short references to the great

---

[196] Cf. Weiser in *Festschrift für Bertholet*, pp. 524f.

[197] Pss. 47.6, 9; 93.2, cf. v. 5b; 96.13; 97.2b, 7b, cf. the description of the epiphany = procession of entry in vv. 3–6; 98.3b, 9b; 99.1.

[198] Pss. 47.2, 7; 96.7–9; 97.12; 98.1a, 4–8; 99.5, 9; cf. 95.1–2, 6–7.

[199] *tĕrû‘ath melekh*, Num. 23.21. Cf. Humbert, *La Terou‘a*, pp. 30ff.

[200] Pss. 47.4f., 10; 93.1c, 5b; 96.3, 6, 10, 13; 97.8, 11f.; 98.1b, 2, 3b, 9. Gunkel (*Einl.*, p. 113) is entirely wrong when he tries to explain this 'actual' character of the psalms mentioned —with the presentation of Yahweh's appearance and salvation as something just having taken place—by supposing that Israel was unable to express the idea of Yahweh's presence in an abstract form and would therefore imagine it to be a lasting state. The actuality is, indeed, the true form of the cultic psalm, which emerges from the cultic experience itself; it is literally meant; the authors do not seek to describe the permanent dwelling of Yahweh in the Temple, but his actual appearance.

[201] Cf. Gunkel-Begrich, *Einl.*, p. 113.

works which Yahweh has performed and which form the basis of his kingship, those 'works of salvation' expressed in the 'festal myth'. There are also occasional references to incidents in the cultic ritual reflecting a 'mythical reality': Yahweh's entry in procession at the head of his people. 3. To this are attached descriptions suggesting the state of things, which will now come about, or in an ideal sense has already come about, with the enthronement of Yahweh, the 'terrible' and 'holy' and 'exalted' and 'glorious one'; his enemies are going to be struck with awe, whereas his people shall rejoice in his righteous and luck-bringing rule.

What has been said above about the heart of the hymn of praise still more applies to the enthronement hymn. This is literally an 'epiphany hymn': now Yahweh has revealed himself as he really is, in all his power and glory, in all his terrible and condemning holiness, in all his saving 'righteousness', and *He* is king of Israel, and Israel is *His* chosen people. Their past and future may rest secure in his covenant faithfulness. For their sake the world has again been created, the powers of death and chaos have been put down, blessing and peace and victory are secured, all wishes and dreams fulfilled. Such another God and king exists nowhere, no people has experienced anything like it, no one can imagine anything higher. This very God is now enthroned as a king in the midst of his people! Should he not be 'enthroned upon the praises of Israel'? Could anything possibly be imagined or composed or said or sung that would be too high for his honour? Whatever the people may have experienced in days past has now become a new reality; 'Rahab' has been destroyed, the covenant renewed, everything now belongs to his people. And the eyes of faith behold him. His hand is full of good things; his Temple is full of holy power. He has been 'revealed in Salem'; we have seen him and all his glorious works, seen them with the eyes of faith, beheld them embodied in the symbols and scenes of the divine service. If the rejoicing at the enthronement of an earthly king would resound, 'so that the earth rent', what then would the shouts of homage be like in honour of King Yahweh! All creation, forests and mountains and valleys and rivers shall clap their hands, hailing him when he comes; his congregation shall fall down before his face in worship; from the newly saved people on the re-created earth the 'new song' shall rise to the King, who is visiting his people and dwelling in their midst. His enemies are trembling with horror, but Jerusalem and the villages of Judah rejoice at his work of righteousness and salvation.

II

But regarding the emotions to which the festal psalms give expression, we are justified in resorting to other psalms also, which have been composed on the basis of ideas drawn from the feast of the epiphany and belong to the complex of harvest and new year in a wider sense. We cannot possibly draw a hard-and-fast line between the 'enthronement festival' and the great festal complex of which it is only one separate aspect.

The experiences contained in the festival made up a spiritual totality and unity. The whole of the religious life in all its aspects and phases was expressed through the festival. Then we realize that not only hymns and thanksgiving psalms but even psalms of prayer and words of promise belong here. Each kind of psalm gives only one aspect of the total sum of experiences and emotions and ideas.

But this also means that the enthronement hymns proper, as is the wont of hymns, as a rule only refer quite briefly to important experiences and ideas which are characteristic of the festival and especially of the whole harvest festival complex. For instance we shall not be able fully to realize the emotions of poet and congregation when, in Ps. 93, creation is mentioned as the basis of kingship, unless we have also realized the actual re-experience of the saving work of creation through the growth and the crops of the blessed year, which is expressed by the authors of harvest festival thanksgiving psalms like 65 or 67. Nor shall we fully understand what the author of Ps. 93 is thinking of when he says that the world is stablished because Yahweh proved himself to be 'mightier' than the waves of the sea, until we have also grasped that aspect of the steadiness of the earth which the author of Pss. 46 or 48 has experienced, and describes by means of the picture of the uproar of the primeval ocean or the assault of all gentile nations on Jerusalem. And vice versa: it is because Yahweh has again appeared as king and has secured the earth against 'the waves of the sea', that Jerusalem may feel sure that even if all the kings and nations of the earth were to conspire against her, Yahweh would destroy them at the very last moment, 'as the east wind breaks the ocean-going ships'.

We have mentioned all this previously, when speaking of the gifts of the festival. But we also need to consider the emotions expressed in the enthronement psalms in the light of all these experiences and promises. If we include all the psalms which, with more or less probability, may be traced to the complex of the new year festival, we shall find that taken together they reflect the whole gamut of religious emotion.

First let us take the joy and rejoicing at the appearance and victory and mighty act of the glorious king. Its basis is the feeling of security at being under the protection of such a king—as clearly expressed in Pss. 46 and 48 and in 95.7; 97.10ff., cf. 125; nothing can, any more, seriously threaten Yahweh's city and people. Even sin will no longer separate them from him, for again he has proved himself to be 'a God who forgives sins' (99.8; 85.3f.; 130.3f.). Therefore gratitude breaks forth, partly in thanksgiving psalms for the good gifts of the passing year (Ps. 65), partly in the admiring contemplation of the work of creation (65.7–9; cf. 8) and the grateful retrospective glance at all the many times past when Yahweh had 'turned the destiny of Israel' (85.2ff.; 126.1ff.), and saved his people from enemies of superior strength (Ps. 124). Hand in hand with gratitude goes love. Quite characteristically, however, it is not the Holy One himself who is described as the object of this love, but outward things, to which his presence was attached and from which his blessing flowed: the cult, the sanctuary, the city where he is now living (122; 84.2ff.). The religious emotion reaches its climax in quiet worship (cf. 95.6; 96.9) without words before the footstool of the One whose nature and name is 'Holy' (99.5).

However, the emotions of the festival have also another pole: fear, or perhaps better, awe. Quite characteristically it is said of Yahweh: 'There is forgiveness with thee, that thou mayest be feared' (130.4). The Holy One not only calls forth ecstatic rejoicings or silent worshipping; he is also the one who frightens, which in an ethical religion means: who demands. At the festival the congregation is reminded of the commandments, the fulfilment of which is the condition of blessing (24.3ff.; 15; 81.9f.; 95.7); and at the renewal of the covenant Yahweh imposes on them obedience to his commandments (95.7ff.; 81.7ff., cf. 132.12). But combined with this, as we have seen (p. 160) was the knowledge that the covenant had constantly been broken, and that this is the reason why the full effect of Yahweh's coming can never eventuate. Grave misgivings mix with joy. Is the turning of the destiny this time going to mean the great turning, which the high hopes of the festival and the prophetic words of the rituals promise? Then the people must clear itself from its sins, just as it and the sanctuary have been cleansed from impurity through the introductory ceremonies of cleansing (the day of expiation). All sinners must needs dread and fear the devouring fire of the Holy One;[202] if anyone would receive forgiveness of his sins he must repent and confess, as we hear in the personal thanksgiving psalm, Ps. 32. Therefore, at this festival is heard the repentant confession of sins on the part of the congregation (130.1ff.). It is connected with the longing for Yahweh to come with forgiveness of sins, happiness and blessing (130.6ff.), with deliverance from all disaster, from sufferings, tormentors and enemies (123; 125). The prayer sometimes rises to stormy impatience, an ardent longing for deliverance as in Ps. 123, found side by side with humble silence in the certainty that with Yahweh is comfort and the satisfaction of all need and all desire, as in Ps. 131.

But beneath all this lies the *expectation* of great things to happen; and so finally we devote some words to that.

12

The festival of harvest and new year looked to both the past and the future; it was a thanksgiving feast for the passing year—being celebrated with delight and rejoicings, when the harvest of wine and olive was safely home, and it was the foundation festival of the coming year.

[202] Cf. Isa. 33.14ff., where we find a new, eschatological reading of the cultic tora of entry in Pss. 24.3–6; 15.

All its different rites stress the future aspect. These rites, which according to the original conception were power-filled, world-renewing, luck- and blessing-bringing, remained as sacramental symbols of the re-creation and blessing Yahweh will bring at his coming. Among such rites may be mentioned the water fetching: from the holy fountain of Gihon the priests would fetch water in solemn procession and pour it on the altar of burnt sacrifice. As can be seen from Jewish popular belief even in New Testament times, this was originally meant to be a powerful means of securing water and rain for the new year.[203] Isa. 12.3 refers to this custom. The festival was also celebrated as a night festival of fire and light with bonfire, illuminations, and torch dancing in the temple court.[204] Like the 'sun-fires' all over the world it was originally meant to re-create and secure sun and light and warmth in the year to come. That the altar was crowned with green branches after the festal procession,[205] and the people lived in 'tabernacles' during the festival,[206] is not only a survival from the stay in the vineyard during the grape-gathering, but is connected with the 'May-branches', the well-known restorative of fertility in nearly all parts of the earth. Even the procession to the Temple and the circumambulation on the walls of the city (Ps. 48.13f.) and around the altar (see above), are originally powerful dramatic cultic customs; they represent the new life and thereby create the same. Looking forward is an essential character-istic of the festival; it can be seen in the psalms in the idea that, from his enthronement onwards, Yahweh will reign as 'eternal king' (Isa. 29.10; Ex. 15.18)—an idea which strictly speaking contradicts the notion of his annual 'coming' and enthronement. But such is the nature of religious experience; the experienced present has 'eternal' importance; and 'eternal' here is not our rationalistic endless temporal line, but rather a quality of value, an eternal present, beyond which our sight does not pass. In other psalms, however, the idea of his 'eternal kingdom' has more of the charac-ter of a rationalized general tenet (145.13), expressing the conviction that he will always protect his people against all evil powers (10.16; 146.10; cf. Jer. 10.10).

The festival is the experience of an all-embracing 'Now' that includes the future—the 'eternal Now'. Therefore the *expectation* of the great thing that is to happen is a fundamental emotion at the festival as well as in the enthronement psalms. 'Yahweh has come to rule the earth', to tend his people and establish justice on earth, and 'Zion is glad and the villages of Judah rejoice because of his judgments' (98.9; 97.8; 48.12). When on his 'day' he renews the covenant and turns destiny, disperses darkness, and lets his 'light be sown for the righteous', he also fulfils whatever his

---

[203] See Billerbeck II, p. 804 n. o. For the ceremonies as a whole see ibid., pp. 799–805; further Moore, *Judaism* II, pp. 44f.; Scheftelowitz, *Alt-Paläst. Bauernglaube*, pp. 93ff.
[204] Cf. Moore, op. cit., II, pp. 46f.
[205] Cf. Ps. 118.26, and see Billerbeck II, pp. 793–799.
[206] Billerbeck II, pp. 774ff.

people, according to tradition, had a right to expect from their righteous, faithful, victorious God, the maintainer of the covenant.

This applies to material blessings as well as to national security and greatness, and to spiritual, religious and moral goods. 'The river of God is full of water', and the rain shall let the corn grow in the valleys and clothe the pastures with little lambs (65.10ff.); 'the streams thereof shall make holy the abode of the Most High' and protect his people against all dangers (46.5), 'He shall subdue the nations under us and provinces under our feet' (47.4); if all the kings on earth were to assemble and march forward together, the very sight of the great king on Mount Zion would suffice to strike them with horror and crush them (48.5ff.). His laws and promises are true and trustworthy; power-filled, protective and blessing-full 'holiness' belongs to his house for evermore (93.5). From now on he will again tend his people (95.7). 'In his hands are the deep places of the earth, and the peaks of the mountains are his also', for he made them all (95.4f.), and now that the waves of the ocean have again been conquered (93.3f.; 46.4; 65.8), so that 'the world is stablished that it cannot be moved', where Yahweh has raised 'his throne' (93.1f.; 29.10), it is a good and safe thing for men, and especially for his people, to live under his protection. His coming will strike with terror all 'idols and them that serve graven images', and the evil shall tremble before his judgment (97.7–10). Now he has laid the foundation of 'salvation and victory'—both these elements are implied in the Hebrew word yĕša'—for Israel, and revealed his self-asserting and covenant-maintaining 'righteousness' and his 'faithfulness' towards his people (98.2f.); from now on he 'preserveth the souls of his saints and delivereth them out of the hand of the wicked' (97.10). He forgives the sins of his people and will hear the prayers, which are sent up by 'his priests' and prophets (99.6ff.). This is all implied in the word 'judge', and that is what Yahweh has now come to do (98.9).

Consequently *prophetic promise* forms part and parcel of the festal liturgies. There are allusions to this in the enthronement psalms, when speaking of the firm promises of Yahweh (93.5). And we find the word of Yahweh, with a particular inversion of the idea, in the enthronement liturgy of Ps. 95 and its parallel Ps. 81, where the promise is conditional upon the faithfulness of the people to the commandments of Yahweh's covenant and thus receives a highly admonitory character. More general and comprehensive promises, in accordance with the expectations just quoted, are to be found in other psalms connected with the festival of harvest and new year or composed on the basis of its ideas and conceptions.[207]

So it is quite easy to understand that whenever the people was in need and danger, it would look forward to the coming 'Yahweh's day', when Yahweh would come and take care of the cause of his people and change darkness into light—as we hear even at the time of Amos (Am. 5.18ff.). In this way the idea of a day of Yahweh with salvation and victory might be

[207] Pss. 46.11; 75.3f.; 82; 85.9ff.; 132.11f.; cf. 50.5ff. For details see Chap. XII.

separated from its cultic basis and, so to speak, start living its own life in the minds of the people as a belief in and a hope for such a Yahweh's 'day of epiphany' to turn the destiny, to restore, avenge and save, whenever Israel was in distress.

13

If we consider the experiences and ideas of the festival of enthronement and new year, we shall be better able to understand the origin of the *hope for re-establishment* and of *eschatology* in Israel—or, rather, from whence this hope derived its conceptions.[208] When attempts have been made to interpret the enthronement psalms as eschatological poems, it has been as a result of the observation that what Yahweh's coming is said to have brought about, or is supposed to bring, in all essentials corresponds to the main items in the prophetic promises of re-establishment and in eschatology.

The strongest reason for the Israelite hope for the future is to be found in the character of revealed religion itself, i.e. in the experience of a God who is so real and so great that he cannot and will not drop his plan and reduce his election and his covenant to mere words. From a historical point of view this hope developed into a conscious hope of re-establishment as a result of the evil destiny of the people and their extinction as an independent kingdom and nation. Then the 'prophecy of re-establishment' took up the idea of the re-establishment of Israel, which became reality in the fullness of time through the New Testament people of God.[209] This hope for the future received its form and a great part of its substance from the experiences and thoughts of the 'day of Yahweh', when he was to appear and become king and establish his kingdom and thus secure justice and a future for his people. Just as the essential notion in Jewish and Christian eschatology has always been the 'kingdom (kingship) of God', so the message about the kingdom was always introduced by some such phrase as: the kingdom of God is at hand! or, in more Old Testament terms, Yahweh has become king, and has come—or shall come—in order to 'judge' on earth. The salvation to come is looked upon as an enthronement day of Yahweh with cosmic dimensions—such in short is the substance of the prophecy of re-establishment and later also of eschatology. That was how Deutero-Isaiah preached it (Isa. 52.7), and he gave the tone to later prophecy. He largely imitates the forms and ideas of the psalms of enthronement and harvest in order to express what was at hand:[210] the victory of Yahweh over all hostile powers and his taking

---

[208] For the following see *Ps.St.* II, Part II.—The connexion between the new year festival and eschatology has also been realized—simultaneously with and independently of *Ps.St.* II— by Wensinck, *Act. Or.* I, 1923, pp. 159ff.
[209] For details see my *He that Cometh*, Chap. V.
[210] See *Ps.St.* II, pp. 49f., 195–199.

possession of the world empire, with the renewal of the covenant with his chosen people and its royal house, and with endless happiness and greatness for his worshippers. It is not, as earlier interpreters of the psalms used to think, the character and style of the enthronement psalms which are modelled on Deutero-Isaiah as a result of poetic concentration on his sayings, but the other way round: prophecy has here, as is so often the case, borrowed forms and expressions from cultic lyrics.[211] In the prophetic descriptions of salvation, accents and motives from the enthronement festival and the feast of Tabernacles are re-echoed, as is clearly seen in Isa. 52.1, 7f.:

> Awake, awake, Jerusalem,
>   put on your bravery,
> put on your finest garment now,
>   O holy city Zion! . . . .
> Look! The herald of good tidings
>   hastening over the hills,
> with glad, good news, with tidings of relief:
>   Your God has now become king!
> Hear, all your watchmen are shouting, hear
>   their joyful triumph cry,
> for they see now Yahweh face to face,
>   returning to Zion again.

'And then the survivors of all the nations which once came against Jerusalem (cf. Ps. 48!) shall "go up" (as in a procession) every year to fall down before king Yahweh Zebaoth, and celebrate the festival of booths. But if any race on earth will not go up to Jerusalem to worship king Yahweh Zebaoth, no rain (the primary natural gift of the festival to land and people) shall fall upon that race' (Zech. 14.16f.).

The Danish poet, Brorson, strikes a truly biblical note when he speaks of the eternal feast of booths by the river of the water of life, the lamb of God being at once host and guest. So was Yahweh on Mount Zion, when the 'river of God ran full of water',[212] the blessing of the new year.

Just because hope for the future and eschatology were conceived after the image of Yahweh's enthronement and the establishment of his kingdom, and described with relevance to psalms and conceptions which considered the enthronement to be a repetition of creation and its original acts of salvation, it became a fundamental motif of eschatology that the last things would be a repetition of the first, a 'turning' back to what originally existed. 'Behold, I shall make the last things like the first', says the early Christian letter of Barnabas.[213] As the earthly king was one of

---

[211] For details *GTMMM* III, pp. 188f.; *Ps.St.* II, pp. 195ff.

[212] Ps. 65.10. For the divine 'river' flowing from the sanctuary and from Heaven, see Hylander in *NTT*, 1931, pp. 1ff.

[213] Epistle of Barnabas 6.13. Cf. *Ps.St.* II, pp. 229f. Gunkel was the first to draw attention to this fundamental motive in his *Schöpfung und Chaos in Urzeit und Endzeit*.

the most important gifts of Yahweh at his 'coming', so in post-exilic and later Judaism the future king, the Messiah, became the most eagerly expected blessing of Yahweh at his last, eschatological coming. To this extent it may be said that the Messianic hope has its root in the cultic festival of Yahweh's epiphany and enthronement.[214]

The forward look of the enthronement psalms and the new year festival, and on the whole the ancient conception of the festival as involving the belief that full 'salvation' was at the door and already in the making, resulted, in turn, in the idea of Israel's full re-establishment being included in the programme of festival and psalms. The future-mindedness made it natural for those in later times, already living in the Jewish hope of re-establishment, to attach the thought of re-establishment to the hopes of the harvest festival.[215] From the experiences and the certainty of the festival the psalmists sometimes, too, look beyond the coming year to the re-establishment of Israel and the eschatological fulfilment, making the latter an object of prayer. In this way—and only in this way—do the psalms obtain an eschatological character.[216] But this happens more in certain psalms for the harvest festival and the feast of Tabernacles, such as Pss. 126 and 85, and in some of the psalms of lamentation and prayer of the congregation (see Chap. VI.5, 6), than in the actual enthronement hymns proper.

In this way the ancient form of the cultic psalm—the praise of the great work of salvation and re-establishment which Yahweh has performed in principle on his coming—also becomes the expression of the expectation and faith of the congregation. Similarly the same thoughts and forms appear in the latest, non-cultic, 'learned' psalmography (Chap. XVI), and in post-canonical legends,[217] not so much as praise for what has already been guaranteed, but as a doxological expression of the faith in the work of salvation, which the Lord certainly will perform as soon as he actually comes. This forward looking witness of faith is given by Sirach in connexion with an admonition to do justice to everyone, because God is a just judge (Sir. 32.24–26). The way the justice of God is referred to, in the usual phrases of the hymns, leads the mind on to the last great day of judgment, when the Lord shall remember his oppressed people and break the tyranny of the unrighteous 'nations', 'plead the cause of his people, giving them victory and joy through his salvation'. Here we find a faint echo of thoughts and forms from the psalms and promises of the enthronement.

[214] See the author's book, *He That Cometh*.
[215] Cf. Volz, *Neujahrsfest Jahwes*, pp. 46f.; Riesenfeld, *Jésus transfig.*, pp. 20ff. Riesenfeld has greatly exaggerated the eschatological element in the feast of tabernacles and the eschatological, symbolic interpretation of the cultic rites; see Kümmel's critique in *Symbl. Bibl. Upsal.* 11, pp. 49ff.
[216] On the question of psalms and eschatology, see Additional Note VIII.
[217] 1 Sam. 2; Jonah 2; Dan. 2.20–24; Tob. 13; Judith 16; Prayer of Manasses (addition to 2 Chron. 33 in G); Dan. 3.26–46 G (prayer of Azariah); Dan. 3.52–90 G (the hymn of thanksgiving sung by the three men in the furnace); for details see Chap. XVI.

The last offshoots of the forms and ideas of the enthronement psalms in their eschatological aspect appear among the young Christian congregations, as expressions both of the experience of the Kingdom that has come with the Messiah Jesus—as in the anthems of praise put in the mouths of Mary and Zacharias—and of the eschatological hope, as expressed in the hymns on the enthronement of the Lord and the Lamb.[218]

[218] For details see below, Chap. XVI, and the author's article in *NTT* 51, 1950, pp. 39ff.

CHAPTER VI

National Psalms of Lamentation

Just as the hymn pre-eminently belongs to the great fixed festivals, as an expression of joy and gratitude and praise, so does the national lament or congregational psalm[1] belong to the days of humiliation and prayer, which were 'proclaimed' on special occasions of crisis, and might be called the 'casual' or *ad hoc* cultic festivals.

I

When war, defeat, imprisonment, epidemics, drought, famine, locusts, and similar public disasters occurred or threatened,[2] a public *fast-day* would be 'proclaimed'.[3] The whole people, great and small, would assemble at the sanctuary. Through different ceremonies the congregation would consecrate themselves; in particular they had to abstain from certain things during the time of humiliation: food and drink, anointing with oil, sexual intercourse and other manifestations of normal life. Humiliation and mourning imply a state of impurity, because disaster, 'curse' has befallen the soul of the person concerned. People would rend their clothes, smite upon their breasts and hips, cut their skins with knives, shave or pluck off hair and beard, put on sackcloth, put dust and ashes on their heads, roll in the dust, fall on their knees or prostrate themselves on the ground, raise their hands in prayer towards the heavens.[4]

The disaster proves that the wrath of Yahweh has been roused because of some sin in the people or their leading men, or at least that Yahweh has not yet roused himself to come to the rescue of his people, now that evil powers or enemies have overtaken them. All these *penitential rites*, originally intended perhaps for the purpose of averting the disaster or protecting against it, and atoning for and cleansing from impurity, in Yahwism became a token of penitence and 'self-humiliation' before Yahweh in order to temper his wrath and rouse his compassion. Other *cultic rites* belonging to the fast-day have the same purpose: sacrifices and the 'pouring out of water before Yahweh' (offering of libation), burning

---

[1] Cf. Gunkel-Begrich, *Einl.*, pp. 177ff.; Widengren, *Accad. and Hebr. Pss. of Lamentation*; Birkeland, *Feinde d. Indiv.*

[2] Deut. 9.18; Josh. 7.6; Jdg. 20.23, 26ff.; 1 Sam. 7.6; 1 Kgs. 8.33ff.; Jer. 2.27; 14.2; Hos. 7.14; Joel 1.13f.; 2 Chron. 20.9.

[3] *qārā*, 1 Kgs. 21.9, 12; Jer. 36.9; Joel 1.14.

[4] Details about rites of penance and fasting with references to sources, in Gunkel-Begrich, *Einl.*, pp. 117–119.

upon the altar, and other measures.[5] From the whole congregation would be heard weeping and loud lamentations and crying, or low, unceasing wailings and sighing.[6]

The prayer of the priest[7] or of some other intercessor, for instance the king, is expressly mentioned. The fasting shall be 'heard' as well as 'seen' (Isa. 58.2f.); the rites come more and more to be interpreted as an emphasizing of the prayer, both when real disaster has actually occurred, and also before some dangerous enterprise, a long journey or some such thing (Ezra 8.21ff.).

That the prayer of humiliation and fasting would in time—at any rate at the larger temples—be moulded on the model of the *psalm* is self evident, and in Israel it may have been so from the very beginning; in Babylonia as well as in Egypt, laments on such occasions are very old.

2

The popular or congregational laments handed down to us belonged to these public fast-days.

Such unquestionably communal or national laments, which are recognizable partly by the use of 'we', partly by the occasion which produced them are Pss. 12; 14; 44; 58; 60; 74; 79; 80; 83; 89; 144; Lam. 5. But actually there are also a great many written in the first person singular which also were occasioned by some public event; we shall return to these below in Chap. VII. And as structure, thought and style are much the same in the 'I-psalms' as in the 'we-psalms', the former, too, will be considered in the following exposé.

From the point of view of style history, the *we-form* is probably later than the *I-form*. This seems obvious from the fact that the style of Israelite psalmody is directly or indirectly derived from Babylonia (see below, Chap. XX.3), and in the Assyro-Babylonian psalms of lamentation such a we-form does not seem to occur; there it is in the I-form that the king represents the people, even in public distress. On the whole this representation through an individual leader, who *is*, or pretends to be, the totality, is the earlier and more primitive idea, as we have seen in Chap. III.1.

So the we-form witnesses to the fact that the people as a fellowship of personal individuals is more prominent in the religion of Israel than in the despotisms of Babylonia and Assyria. It proves, as has been said, that in Israel, there is a *congregation* in the background of the service in a way different from that in Babylonia. Such a self-awareness on the part of the congregation became natural because, as has been mentioned above (Chap. III.6), religion was individualized and became more democratic.

---

[5] 1 Sam. 7.9; Jer. 14.12; Jdg. 20.26; 21.4; 2 Sam. 24.22; Ps. 4.6; also 1 Sam. 7.6; Lam. 2.19; and Num. 17.11ff.

[6] Jdg. 20.23, 26; Mic. 1.8; Jer. 14.12; Isa. 15.2ff.; Hos. 7.14; Isa. 29.4.

[7] Joel 1.13f.; 2.17; 1 Kgs. 8.28ff.; Jer. 7.16; 11.14; 2 Chron. 20.6ff., *et al.*

So far, it might seem more natural to speak first of the laments in the I-form. But since this form may really imply public as well as private occasions of lamentation, and thus two different kinds of psalms—or, in other words, because it partly expresses an old and partly a more modern way of thinking—it will be best to start with the we-psalms. From the point of view of form and style they are the most obvious and at the same time give expression to something characteristically Israelite.

3

Even in the laments there is a close connexion between *form and substance*, which are determined by situations and intentions. The people in its distress comes to the God, whose might and power and loving-kindness and faithfulness to the covenant were praised in the hymns, asking him to help. They know, and have often seen, his benefits; now they have also experienced his wrath, which is weighing heavily on them. He has turned away, he has 'hidden his face', and who can know 'why' and 'how long'. So the aim is to get to speak with him, make him hear and see, 'cry unto him', lay the distress before him, complain how hard it is, describe the horror of it. The people must try to find a way to touch the heart of Yahweh, where he will be susceptible to the prayers of men; they must rouse his compassion, appeal to the faithfulness of his covenant and to his loving-kindness, to his honour and power, so that he 'may again be moved with compassion for us'; they must remove whatever might displease him, ascribe honour and righteousness to him by confessing sins, asking for forgiveness and help, appeasing his wrath, invoking his love. For he is great, and we are small; he can do everything, we can do nothing; nobody else can help, and if he does not save, it will be the end of us, but we confide in him. The lament sprang up on the basis of these spontaneous human and religious thoughts and reactions, it was a call for help to a particular God in a particular situation—wherever it may have found its literary patterns.

Even the first word of the lament contains an *invocation of Yahweh's name*, a turning to God in prayer, with a preceding or following word of prayer in the imperative: 'Hear us!' 'Listen to my voice!' or the like—or right out: 'Give me my right, O Lord' (see below). Israel knows to *whom* she has to turn, among all the many 'gods and holy ones' in the world.

When the name has been mentioned, not infrequently some *hymnal attributes* are added, containing an appeal to the close relationship between Yahweh and his people, to his power and willingness to help, 'O Shepherd of Israel', 'O God of our salvation', 'O Judge of the earth', 'my God'.[8]

Let us give some examples: (*a*) the invocation is immediately followed by a cry for help:

[8] Pss. 83.14; 79.9; 85.5; 80.2, 8, 15; 94.1f., *et al.*

> O Yahweh, keep not thou silence,
> hold not thy peace, and be not still! (83.2.)

(b) To the invocation are added hymnal words, appealing to Yahweh:

> O shepherd of Israel, hear us, thou,
> who leadest Joseph like a flock!
> Thou that thronest upon the cherubs
> shine forth for Ephraim and Manasseh! (80.2.)

or (c) it is immediately followed by the plaintive question:

> O God, why hast thou discarded us for ever,
> why dost thou fume in anger at the flock of thy pasture?
>
>   (74.1)

But the invocation may be missing, and the psalm start with the lament (the description of the conduct of the wicked), as in Ps. 14, or in Ps. 58, where the lament has the form of an accusation in the second person plural, directed against the gods of the oppressors. Or the psalm may start with an elaborate motivation expressing the confidence of the suppliants (see below), as in Ps. 44.

Sometimes this invocation may be developed into a complete hymn of praise, in which the psalm gets a *hymnal introduction*, appealing to the earlier great works of Yahweh and his saving benefactions to his people, calling to mind how he has thereby pledged his honour, and trying thus to make him rise to the rescue.[9] In such cases the hymnal sayings are usually expressed as independent sentences: e.g.

> Age after age, Lord, thou hast been our home,
> from all eternity hast thou been, O God. (90.1.)

Or, and this time entirely hymnal:

> I will always sing of Yahweh's love
> and tell all ages of thy faithfulness. (89.2.)

This cry of supplication indicates the motivation which expresses the real aim of the psalm. This is then followed up in detail in the main part of the psalm, containing *lamentations*, *prayers*, and *motivations of the prayer*. There is no definite sequence; these different items alternate in any order, and often recur several times.

In the true psalms of lamentation the character of the whole is fixed by the *lamentation*. It consists of a longer or shorter *description of the distress*, which is painted in the deepest colours, with regard to both its external and its mental aspect. Israel presents herself as being 'oppressed, distressed, miserable, in need of help'—all these shades of meaning are implied in the Hebrew word '*ānî* or '*ānāw*, generally used here.[10] This description is

---

[9] Pss. 44.2–4; 80.2; 89.2–17; 106.1f.; cf. the 'I-psalms' 9–10; 27; 40.
[10] Pss. 12.6; 74.19–21; cf. 68.11; 76.10; 149.4. Cf. below, pp. 229ff.

in itself aimed at getting the prayer heard: it is intended to rouse the compassion of Yahweh and make him help.

As a rule the national psalms of lamentation are concerned with national and political distress: defeat in war, attack and ravaging by external enemies, who are sometimes named.[11] But we also hear of days of humilitation and fasting with laments for droughts and plagues of locusts, as in Jer. 14 or Joel 1–2.

The background of such a psalm is some definite historical event. The enemies are real and historical; they are the 'nations' who have attacked and invaded Israel (or Judah), and now are oppressing it. In Ps. 83 the names of the enemies are explicitly mentioned: Edom, Moab, the Ishmaelites and the Hagarenes, Gebal, Ammon, Amalek, and the inhabitants of Tyre, and 'Asshur also is joined with them'. The people (or king) complains of the hostility and mockeries of the 'neighbours', i.e. the other Palestinian nations. (See below on the situation in Pss. 44 and 74, and cf. Chap. VII.6.)

As a rule, however, it is not possible to tell which peoples or rulers are intended by 'the enemies' in the psalm in question. The reason is that in ancient Israel, as also in the Akkadian literature, there existed a traditional 'pattern', according to which the 'evil-doers', rĕšāʿîm—the enemies are always rĕšāʿîm—are described. Consequently we have a stereotyped monotony in the description of the enemies, with very few individual traits.[11a]

The distress also has its mental aspect. This is owing to the wrath of Yahweh: his 'anger smokes', he has 'hidden his face' and 'cast off his own people'.—Can such a thing really be possible? Because the distress cannot be understood—'Why, Lord?'—it is increased. Is injustice really going to triumph?—To this bewilderment is added the old Israelite idea that disaster and defeat mean 'shame',[12] which makes the people wince at the sneers of their neighbours.[13] Their mental distress receives a deeper

---

[11] Pss. 60.11; 83.7–9; 137. For the mention of political and national afflictions: 44.10–17, 20, 23–25; 60.3–5, 12; 74.4–11; 79.1–4; 80.5–7, 13f.; 83.3–9; 85.6; 89.39–46; 123.3f.; Lam. 1.9f.; 3.42–51; 5.2–18. Cf. the imitation of the style in the lamentations of the prophets on behalf of the people, Isa. 26.14, 15f.; 33.7–9; 40.27; 49.14; 63.17–19; 64.5f., 9f.; Jer. 10.25; 31.18; Hab. 1.13–16.

Willesen (in *VT* II, 1952, pp. 289ff.) finds as the cultic situation of Ps. 74 (and 79) two cult-dramatical scenes, which were repeated every year, perhaps at the new year festival, the first showing the profanation of the Temple by the powers of chaos, the second the victory of Yahweh and the re-purification of the sanctuary. It is, however, impossible not to see real terrestrial beings in the enemies who are destroying the Temple with axes, hammers and fire; there are no demoniac traits in this description. Willesen also fails to take into due account the role of the hymnic 'motivation of the prayer' in the psalms of lamentation; amongst others, Ps. 89 shows that Yahweh's primordial fight against the powers of chaos is an important motif in ʃthese 'motivations', though even here the enemies are earthly political foes. Cf. below, Additional Note XXXI.

[11a] See Birkeland, *Feinde d. Indiv.*, pp. 59ff.; *The Evildoers in the Pss.*, pp. 23ff. The same observation can be made at the description of the *nābhāl* ('the fool') and the *rāshāʿ* in Proverbs; it is not easy to say in every case to which definite persons or social classes these terms are applied by the wisdom authors.

[12] Ps. 80.17f.; cf. 2 Sam. 19.4f.; Ezk. 36.30; Ps. 40.15f. See Johs. Pedersen, *Israel* I–II, pp. 239ff.

[13] Pss. 44.14ff.; 79.4; 80.7.

religious meaning through the fact that other nations, 'the gentiles', will take it as a proof of Yahweh's powerlessness, and will blaspheme the God of Israel: 'Where is now thy God?'[14] All this tends to intensify the problem involved in the suffering of 'the righteous'—for Israel as a whole are 'the righteous', the people of the covenant, such is the usage of the psalms. The question 'Why?' becomes a big issue, as likewise the impatient 'How long?'.

Looked at in detail, the laments complain of the violence and injustice and abuse of power on the part of the enemies, their faithlessness and arrogance and godlessness—they do not worship Yahweh; the poets take for granted that they ought to do so, accordingly they are 'apostates', 'playing false'; their religion is nothing but 'sorcery'. They are described as completely corrupt people, false, lying, sinners, criminals, 'sorcerers' ("āwen-makers").[15] Compared with them Israel is always right, her enemies are always wrong; even if the congregation may confess their sinfulness before Yahweh (see below), her enemies are persecuting her 'without cause'.

Particularly when disaster has befallen the very Temple of Yahweh there is every reason to describe it in as gloomy colours as possible, in order to appeal to the honour of Yahweh himself. The following description (Ps. 74.3–9) enters into considerable detail:

> Turn thy steps to the long-standing ruins:
>   all has the foe destroyed in the sanctuary!
> Thine enemies roared inside thy festival hall,
>   total destruction have they made therein.
> They have cut down as woodmen bringing home brushwood,
>   brandishing their axes in the thicket of the wood.
> They smashed all the carved work therein,
>   with hatchet and hammer they broke it up;
> They set thy sanctuary ablaze,
>   profaning to the ground the abode of thy name.
> They said to themselves: 'Let us root them out'.
> They burned all houses of God in the land.
> We see no signs concerning us, there is no prophet,
>   and no one among us knows how long.[15a]

The lament may be directed at Yahweh himself, because he has allowed such things to happen: has he really forgotten his covenant with the house of David? e.g.

[14] Pss. 74.10, 18, 22; 79.10, 12. Cf. the I-psalm 42.11.

[15] With more details and references to sources in Birkeland, *Feinde d. Indiv.*, pp. 59–66. For 'āwen see pp. 199f., *Ps.St.* I, pp. 34ff., and Additional Note XXVIII.

[15a] V. 4b, 'they set their signs as signs' yields no sense; 'ôth never means 'emblem' and the conquerors would not set up their own religious or military emblems in a house which they were going to set ablaze; read šāmû šammôth ûmē šammôth bēthôkhāh (cf. Ps. 46.9; Ezk. 23.33; 33.38f.; 35.3). yd' in v. 5 is not 'know', but imperfect of a stem d'y, 'destroy', see Driver in *JBL* LXVIII, 1949, p. 58; rd. yidh'û; pronounce the following words kimēbhî'ê lāmô 'āleh. In v. 6 a verb is missing; rd. hittēthû for wĕ'attâ.

Thou hast abhorred the covenant with thy servant,
  and profaned his crown down to the ground.
Thou hast demolished all his walls,
  his strongholds hast thou laid in ruins;
the passers-by all plunder him,
  he is a butt of all his neighbours.
Thou hast allowed his enemies to triumph,
  giving delight to all his foes;
Thou hast turned back the edge of his sword,
  and hast not upheld him in battle.
His splendid sceptre hast thou broken,
  and cast his throne down to the ground;
the days of his youth hast thou shortened,
  and thou hast covered him with shame. (89.40–46.)

But, as a rule, the lamentations are directed against the enemies of the people.

The *evil and audacious words* of the enemies play a distinct part in the lamentations and the descriptions of the distress. They are not only blasphemies against Yahweh (see above), but also evil plans, and scornful and cursing words against Israel, tending to destroy her honour and paralyse her soul. All such words were considered to be powerful and fatal 'curses',[16] and were even used by the ancients in war, or before a battle, in order to strike the enemy in a way just as effective as the use of sword or spear.[17] That was why, before a war, they would send for the seer or the *nābhī'*, that his powerful words might enervate the enemy, so that the army might defeat him, as we hear for instance in the story about the seer Balaam.[18] In the eyes of those who are the objects of such words, they are naturally looked upon as *evil* curses, unlawful supernatural harmful words and operations, 'sorcery' and 'devilry'. This is what is meant by words like 'guile', 'falsehood', 'delusion', 'mischievous words' and the like, and especially by the word '*āwen*.[19] It indicates the evil 'power', or power used for evil ends, and its effects, and the means of starting it; but also the things and beings filled with this evil 'power'. Above all '*āwen* is used of *words* having such power and such effects. It need not have anything to do with 'sorcerers' and 'magic words' in a technical and, so to speak, professional sense, with people who themselves know that they are practising sorcery, and have established themselves as masters of that art, so to say. According to ancient opinion, *all* words were powerful in

---

[16] Pss. 12.3–5; 44.17; 74.8, 10, 18, 23; 79.10, 12; 80.7; 83.4ff.; and in addition the 'I-psalms'—really 'national psalms'—10.4, 6f.; 42.11; 55.4; 59.8, 13; etc. Cf. n. 17 to Chap. VII and Johs. Pedersen, *Israel* I–II, pp. 437ff.

[17] Pss. 74.8, 23; 83.5, 13; cf. 58.5 (I-psalm).

[18] Num. 22–24; cf. 1 Kgs. 22.11–13; Jdg. 5.12, and see *GTMMM* III, p. 11; Birkeland, *Feinde d. Indiv.*, pp. 62, 73–76.

[19] Pss. 14.4; 125.5; cf. Isa. 29.20; 31.2. Then also in consideration of Chap VII: Pss. 7.15; 10.7; 53.5; 55.4, 11; 56.8; 59.3; 94.23 *et al.* For '*āwen* see Additional Note XXVIII.

proportion to the 'power' of the speaker; evil words, curses, abuse, threats, sneers, evil wishes, 'the evil eye', jealous thoughts, scornful or threatening gestures and looks and symbols—in the eyes of the Israelites and of all other ancient orientals all such things were powerful, and would do harm to the soul and happiness of those against whom they were directed. All the powerful means of the gentile enemies, their plans and threats and sneers, the 'curses' of their prophets and priests, and all their accompanying ceremonies, in short all their religious and cultic measures and acts and words, in the eyes of the Israelites seemed to be sorcery, 'āwen; when used for the gods of the gentiles the word actually means 'demons', 'devils', 'trolls'.[20] What to one person is cultus, to the person on the other side appears as sorcery. Such powerful words on the part of the enemy are 'falsehoods', 'deceitful words', because they call up the 'false', pernicious power in life, 'the curse', draining and laying waste blessing and happiness. But they are also 'falsehoods', because they will make righteous people 'scoundrels', and because, by Yahweh's help, they shall turn out to be unreal and of no effect, injuring only the mischief-maker.

  The psalms complain of such false, mocking 'curses' on the part of their enemies:

> Guile do they speak one to the other
> with flattering lips and double mind, . . .
> They say: 'In our tongues we have our strength,
> our lips are with us, who shall master us?' (12.3, 5.)

The congregation complains of such liars in the service of gentile gods:

> They have in them a venom like a viper's venom,
> like the deaf adder that stops her ear,
> that will not listen to the charmer's voice,
> to the most cunning sorcerer's spell. (58.5f.)
> His mouth is full of curse and deceit,
> under his tongue is oppression and craft. (10.7.)
> They pour forth (curses) from their mouth,
> upon their lips are sharp swords. (59.8.)

The climax of the distress often seems to be the mockery and sneers of enemies and neighbouring nations:

> Thou hast made us the butt of our neighbours,
> a scorn and derision to all around.
> Thou hast made us a byword among the nations,
> a shaking of the head among the peoples.
> All day long the disgrace is before me,
> the shame of it overclouds my face
> at the sound of taunters and scoffers,
> at the sight of the vengeful foe. (44.14–17.)

[20] Isa. 41.29; 66.3; 1 Sam. 15.23; Hos. 10.8; cf. Am. 5.5. In Babylonian-Assyrian texts the political enemies of the king are sometimes called 'evil demons' (devils) see *Ps.St.* I, p. 69.

The *prayer* as a rule is couched in general phrases which constantly recur: 'hear', 'look here', 'arise', 'plead our cause', 'turn our destiny', 'have mercy upon us', 'seek our their wickedness', 'cease from anger', 'do not cast us off for ever', 'forgive our trespasses', 'redeem us', 'help us'.[21]

But after all, of course, form and substance of the prayer depend on the nature of the disaster and of the situation. When defeated and oppressed, the people ask to be rescued from death and distress:

> Do not leave the lives of thy worshippers to destruction,
>> forget not thy poor people for all time. (74.19.)

They pray for the shame to be taken away from them:

> Let not the oppressed be ashamed again,
>> may the weak and wretched have good cause to praise thee!
>>> (74.21.)

And that the people may be raised up again:

> O God of hosts, restore us to power,
>> Let us see the light of thy face, that we may be saved. (80.4.)

And for revenge on their enemies:

> Let the pagans know—and may we see it!—
>> thy vengeance for spilling the blood of thy servants.
> May the moan of the prisoners come before thee,
>> by thy mighty power release those that are in peril of death,
> and render sevenfold unto our neighbours
>> the taunts that they have heaped on thee. (79.10–12.)

Yahweh must not forget how the enemies have mocked at himself and at his people:

> Arise, O God, to vindicate thy cause,
>> remember how the fool scoffs at thee all the day,
> forget not the clamour of thy enemies,
>> the endless din that rises from thy foes. (74.23.)

After the defeat the king prays:

> Remember, O Yahweh, the taunts thrown at thy servants,
>> the insults of the nations we have to bear,
> the taunts of thine own enemies, O Yahweh,
>> taunting the heels of thine anointed. (89.51f.)

'The heels' is a hint at the flight of the king after the battle. May the enemy meet the fate that such 'sorcerers' deserve:

[21] Ps. 80.2; Isa. 37.17.—Pss. 74.20; 80.15; Isa. 37.17; 63.15; 64.8; Lam. 1.9, 11, 20; 2.20; 5.1—Pss. 44.24; 9.20; 10.12; 44.27; 74.22; 82.8; 94.2.—Ps. 72.22.—Pss. 80.2; 94.1.—Pss. 10.12; 74.2–18, 23; 89.48, 51; 106.4; 137.7; Lam. 5.1.—Pss. 80.4, 8, 15, 20; 85.5.—Ps. 126.4.—Ps. 106.4.—Pss. 90.13; 123.3.—Ps. 79.8f.—Pss. 85.8; 80.4, 8, 20.—Pss. 44.27; 79.9, 11; 106.47.

> Shall they not rue it, all these sorcerers,
>   those who devour my people? (14.4)

> Pay them back for the sorcery they have done,
>   let the nations fall by (thine) anger, O God! (56.8.)

The prayer may be fierce, impatient, accusatory:

> Awake, why sleepest thou, O Yahweh?
>   Arise, cast us not off for ever.
> Why dost thou hide thy face before us,
>   forgetting our distress and woe?
> Our soul is bowed down to the dust,
>   our body lies low on the ground.
> Arise and come to our rescue
>   and save us for thy love's sake. (44.24–27.)

As well as prayers couched in the imperative we sometimes come across a *wish* (in the jussive mood, designating desirability):[22] 'may the moanings of the prisoners come before thy presence'; 'may Yahweh cut off all flattering tongues', and so on. This wording is used above all when speaking of the destruction of the enemies. The last example proves that in these 'wishes' we are dealing with terms of cursing and blessing. According to the Hebrew way of thinking something more is involved in such sayings than what we mean by the word 'wish': they are words with operative power. In ritual the operative word is often older than the prayer, and we can see how in the cult in Israel these words in the course of time develop into prayers: the aid of Yahweh is called on by means of the old powerful words. More details about this will be given in Chap. XI.

Prayers and wishes for the destruction of the enemy naturally claim much space in the national psalms of lamentation. Just as natural is that here, particularly, the ancient *formula of cursing* is used: 'may the gentiles be put to shame', 'be destroyed', 'may the culprit go to Sheol' (Hades), 'may Yahweh cut off all flattering lips', and so on.[23] The last is a transition form to actual prayer. In some of the psalms these curses dominate the whole; see, for instance, the detailed curse in Ps. 58.5–10. And see, likewise, the prayer in Ps. 83.14–17, where we only need to omit the reference to Yahweh and replace the imperatives by the subjunctive ('jussive') in order to get the wording of a cursing formula such as, for instance, the king of Moab would have had Balaam speak against Israel.

The aim is to strike at the root of the disaster: the operative evil words and tricks and intrigues of the enemy; and so, by means of the cult and the ritual curses of the psalm (see Chap. XI), the congregation tries to parry the curse words of the enemy. But we are not justified in concluding from this that the psalmists thought that without the will and help of

---

[22] Pss. 9.18a; 12.4; 74.21; 79.10f.; 83.16–19; 90.16f.; 125.5; cf. 104.35.
[23] Pss. 12.4; 74.22f.; 79.6, 12; 83.10–15, 17; cf. 31.18; 35.4, 26; 40.15f.; 56.10; 68.31; 71.13; 86.17; 109.29; cf. also 119.78; 140.10; Jer. 17.18.

Yahweh the word of cursing by itself could deliver them from the enemy; at most we have the lingering remains of the old style. Rather more frequently than the directly cursing word, we find the prayer for Yahweh to slay the enemy by means of his 'ban': *his* operative word, his 'threats' shall destroy them.[24] Even if we find an echo of the old 'magical' formula in many terms, and even if corresponding thoughts *may* at any time be attached to the sacred words of religion, the laments can claim to be true prayers to God, and no magical formulas. Yahweh has to interfere, if the malice of the enemies is to be struck at the root, and brought home to themselves:

> Let the evil of the wicked come to an end,
>   and let the righteous man stand firm!
> For He that trieth hearts and reins
>   is a God who vindicates the right.
>
> My protecting shield is Yahweh himself,
>   who saveth those whose hearts are right;
> yea, Yahweh is a righteous judge,
>   a God indignant every day.
>
> Surely he whets his sword again,
>   he bends his bow and takes aim,
> but his deadly darts and fire-tipped arrows
>   he has made ready against himself.
>
> He's alive with witchcraft, has conceived
>   mischief, and brings forth only deceit;
> he has digged out a pit, and made it deep,
>   but he shall fall into it himself.
>
> His mischief returns on his own head,
>   his violence drops on his own crown.
> But I shall thank Yahweh for his justice,
>   and praise the name of the Most High God. (7.10–18.)

'I shall thank'—i.e., I shall one day have the opportunity of thanking him for the experienced salvation from this particular trouble. The psalms of lamentation trust God to do great things, and expect great things from him. Without him no rituals and 'sacred' words are of any use.

The *prayer for revenge* will often occur in a way which does not agree with the Christian way of thinking.[25] But here we have to remember two things. In the first place, revenge and dread of the joint responsibility of the tribe as against the *gō'ēl* would be the only means of keeping passions in check, and securing a certain legal system in the primitive social conditions under which Israel were living as nomads, and in great measure

---

[24] Cf. the 'I-psalms' (Chap. VII) 52.7; 69.25; 109.15; 139.19.
[25] Ps. 79.10; cf. Nah. 1.2; Pss. 58.11; 91.1; 149.7; 18.48; 106.4.

also after settling down. The request for revenge denotes that the sense of justice is alive, and may not be violated; it is a substitute for the punishment by the society.[26] And in the second place, prayer to the 'God of revenge' must be taken to express the knowledge and the faith that God will not allow justice to be violated. Side by side with the prayer for revenge stands all the time the prayer for God to 'provide justice', to 'still the enemy and the avenger' (Ps. 8.3), to prevent justice from being violated.[27] But even if the scope of the law was confined to Israel, still it was there. And the very fact that the idea of justice is attached to a God, who came gradually to be considered the God of the whole world, guarantees that it will some time break through the national limits—as we can see already in Amos.

Accordingly we find that the prayer against the gentiles takes a more religious turn: 'may they know that thou, Yahweh art God—even thou only' (2 Kgs. 19.19, cf. Ps. 46.11).

The lament as well as the prayer aims to 'smooth the face of Yahweh', i.e. mollify him, and touch Yahweh's heart. This is still more clearly brought out by the motivations of the prayers. In different ways the psalmists try to provide Yahweh with reasons for hearing them and granting their prayer.

We have already seen that the lament involves such a motivation; it seeks to rouse the pity of Yahweh, and thereby make him interfere and help. That is why the distress is painted in sombre colours, while the helplessness of the people and their dependence on Yahweh are called to mind: 'we are brought very low'.[28] When the congregation emphasizes that no one but Yahweh can help them[29] and that nobody else is to be trusted,[30] then the situation is shown to be truly desperate;

> O! help thou us against our foes,
> for men's help is in vain. (Ps. 60.13.)

Especially in the later congregational psalms of lamentation of Jewish times this motive will recur. Thus originally naïve and selfish motives have been deepened into a religious recognition of complete dependence on God.

Rather more in keeping with old Israelite ways of thinking is the appeal to the *honour of Yahweh*. It is directly emphasized that Yahweh's own cause is at stake: '*thy* people', '*thine* inheritance', '*thy* possession', '*thy* congregation', 'the sheep of *thy* pasture', '*thine* anointed', '*thy* sanctuary, '*thine* enemies', and so on.[31] In Pss. 74 and 79 the lament starts with a description of the way Yahweh's Temple has been laid waste; then only do we hear of

---

[26] See Johs. Pedersen, *Israel* I–II, pp. 378ff.; Nyström, *Beduinentum und Jahwismus*, pp. 31ff. cf. 109ff.

[27] Cf. the 'I-psalms' 26.1; 7.7f.; 17.2; 35.1; 43.1, and Hab. 1.12f.

[28] Pss. 79.8; 89.48f.; cf. Isa. 64.7.

[29] Ps. 60.13; cf. Isa. 37.16; Jer. 3.23; 14.22; 2 Chron. 14.10; 20.6; Sir. 33.5 (G).

[30] Ps. 44.7f.; cf. 10.14; 33.20–22; Jer. 14.8; Dan. 9.18; Pss. Solom. 7.6–9; 9.19 (10).

[31] Pss. 74.1f.; 79.9, 13; 83.4; 89.39, 52; cf. 94.5; Isa. 63.18.

the sufferings of the congregation. Yahweh must help for the sake of his name and his honour:

> Help us, O God our saviour,
>   for the glory of thy name.
> Deliver us, purge away our sins
>   for thy name's sake, O God.
> Wherefore should heathen peoples sneer
>   and say: 'Where is thy God?' (79.9f.)

Surely the God who has done such great things in times of old and conferred such blessings on his people,[32] cannot possibly 'sleep' nor 'forget his people'[33] nor, still worse, allow the heathen to blaspheme his name? Shall the gentiles believe that the God of Israel is a powerless, a defeated, an insufficient God?[34]

> How long, O God, is the foe to be scoffing?
>   is the enemy always to blaspheme thee? (74.10.)

> He says to himself: 'God has forgotten,
>   he hides his face and never sees'. (10.11.)

How could Yahweh 'forget the roaring of his enemies' (74.23) and their sneering words? Certainly, he must interfere!

Closely related to the appeal to Yahweh's honour is the *hymnal motive*: in a naïve way the congregation will try to appeal to the grace of Yahweh by 'giving him honour', calling to mind all his great works from the days of creation, Exodus, or covenant, until now. Sometimes this motivation, like the introductory invocation of his name, may extend to quite a hymnal section,[35] as, for instance, the hymnal introduction to Pss. 44, 89, and others (see Chap. IV.5).

But even here the original utilitarian motive has been superseded by a purely religious one; the fear and awe of a mighty and exalted God has been called to life, and makes the psalmist want to approach God with praises; the thought of God's great works inspires confidence in poet and congregation, and makes them dare to approach him in the belief that he will hear their prayers; in the honour and eulogy motifs they find comfort and confidence for themselves.

The appeal to the great benefactions of Yahweh in times past, to his *kindness* ('favour') and 'covenant-mindedness' (*ḥesedh*) and to his 'helpful righteousness' (*ṣedheq*), is not only heard in connexion with the honour motif, but also as comprising an independent motivation for his readiness to hear prayers. How should Yahweh forget his own covenant:

[32] Pss. 44.2-4, 8; 74.2; 80.9-12; 89.50; 125.3; 2 Chron. 20.7; cf. Ps. 115.1; Isa. 63.11-14.
[33] Pss. 44.24f.; 74.19; cf. the 'I-psalm' 10.12.
[34] Pss. 12.5; 74.8, 10, 23; 79.12; 83.3, 5, 13; cf. 94.7; 10.4, 6, 13; 115.2; Isa. 37.17.
[35] Pss. 74.12-17; 77.14ff.; 90.1ff.; cf. the 'I-psalm' 139.1f.

> Remember the community thou didst buy long ago,
>   whom thou didst rescue to be thine own people. (74.2.)

The congregation expects him to be no less 'loyal' (*ḥāsīdh*) and merciful and faithful to the present generation than he used to be to the Fathers,[36] and by this thought their own faith is strengthened.

All these things go to make the basis of the *confidence* of Israel in her God. The congregation trusts in Yahweh's 'loyalty' to his covenant (*ḥesedh*). His faithfulness to the Fathers, his righteousness and the demands of his own honour can alone justify Israel in appealing to all these things. But confidence itself also appears as a separate motivation for hearing prayer, giving us then the 'confidence motif' so often urged by the congregation.

> Thou art the Holy (God of Jacob),
>   enthroned upon the praises of Israel.
> On thee our fathers did rely,
>   relied, and thou didst rescue them.
> They cried to thee, and were delivered,
>   they trusted and were not put to shame. (22.4–6.)

The congregation pleads that it is trusting in Yahweh—so did the Fathers, and they were not put to shame, the present generation must do the same— it is trusting in him who is the only Mighty one and the only Helper;[37] surely Yahweh will not disappoint such confidence!

> Who is my champion against evildoers,
>   who sides with me against such sorcerers?
> If Yahweh had not been my helper,
>   I should soon have dwelt in the silent land.

> If I must say: 'My foot is slipping'—
>   thy goodness, Yahweh, holds me up;
> when fearful thoughts are crowded within me,
>   thy comforts will delight my soul. (94.16–19.)

Thus the motif of confidence develops into a confession of faith, as in the first part of Ps. 44.

But the psalm may also call to mind the *cause of the distress*. Then we are told either that Israel is 'righteous' and has done nothing to outrage Yahweh, or that the wickedness and hate of the enemies are responsible for everything; such is the tone of psalms like 44 and 74. The congregation, 'the righteous' (see below) may plead their *innocence*—'the innocence motivation—and, where this is the case, we may talk of *laments of innocence*.

> All this has come upon us, yet we have
>   not forgotten thee nor failed they covenant. (44.18.)

[36] See n. 32, and Pss. 77.14ff.; 89.18ff.
[37] Ps. 44.7f.; cf. 33.20–22 and the 'I-psalms' 10.14; 13.6; 26.1; 31.7, 15; 55.24; 56.4; 143.8; 16.8; 62.2; Dan. 9.18; Jer. 14.8.

In the earlier national psalms of lamentation this is the most usual attitude. Of the we-psalms mentioned above, only Ps. 79 clearly preserves a different attitude. Even in the I-psalms where an individual is speaking on behalf of the congregation (Chap. VII), we are often assured that he is 'guiltless', 'has not transgressed thy commandments', and that therefore the enemies 'hate him without a cause',[38] or even because of his piety (69.10). So, among others, such psalms as 5; 7; 12; 26.

In this connexion we may be justified in considering a little more closely the term ṣaddîqîm—'*the righteous*'—frequently used in the psalms, and particularly so in contrast to rĕšā'îm, 'the evil-doers', 'the wicked', 'the ungodly.' These two terms have often been taken to indicate two 'parties' or 'tendencies' within the Jewish congregation: the piously obedient to the law, and the ungodly apostates or wordly-minded. And certainly the two terms—especially in the singular—*may* be used to indicate the law-abiding Jew on the one hand, and his wordly-minded and—at any rate in the eyes of the more rigorous party—'apostate' countryman, who has emancipated himself from the law and from the 'tradition of the Fathers' and their conceptions of religion, on the other. Such is the case in the introductory poem to the whole psalter, Ps. 1, and probably also in some other late psalms, belonging to the 'wisdom poetry' (see Chap. XVI), such as Pss. 37 and 73 and others.

But Birkeland has proved beyond all contradiction that the two terms in the psalms do not as a rule indicate two different parties, representing conflicting 'tendencies' within the Jewish congregation, but, oftener than not, point to national antagonisms—which, on account of the way of thinking within the old national religion, would certainly also involve *religious* contrasts between the worshippers of Yahweh and 'the gentiles'. This is evident from a national psalm of lamentation like Ps. 125. Here the congregation first of all expresses its faith that Yahweh will protect those 'who put their confidence in him', 'his people':

> Those who trust in Yahweh are like Mount Zion,
>   the unshakeable, that stands for ever;
> as mountains are round about Jerusalem,
>   so is Yahweh round about his people.

And then the same thought is expressed again with reference to the actual situation of Israel under the supremacy of the gentiles:

> He will not let the sceptre of the wicked
>   rest upon the lot of the righteous,
> lest the righteous put out their hand
>   to do some wickedness.

I.e. Yahweh will prevent 'the ungodly' from having any longer the supremacy over 'the righteous', so that the latter shall not be led astray into

[38] Ps. 86.2; further, 17.3–5; 26.4; 35.7, 19; 59.10; 5.8; 26.6–8; cf. 69.10.

apostasy or heathenism. The prayer that this deliverance may become reality is then added:

> O Yahweh, do good unto those who are good,
> to those who are upright in heart.
> But to those who are wandering crooked ways
> will Yahweh give the sorcerers' fate.

That this alludes to the contrast between Israel and gentiles is confirmed by the final wish, making a kind of refrain to the psalm: 'May Israel prosper!'

The same thing can be seen from Ps. 58. 'The wicked' are 'estranged from the womb'; they stand outside the fellowship of the covenant. In this psalm the lamentation takes the form of an accusation against the strange 'gods', who really ought to be the loyal governors of Yahweh over the nations, over whom he had appointed them to rule (Deut. 32.8), but they were instead ruling with injustice and violence, cf. Ps. 82. The 'strange evil-doers' filling the earth with violence are in the service of these gods.

In the psalms we find other passages, where it is quite obvious that the 'evil-doers', rĕšāʿîm, indicate the gentile enemies and oppressors of Israel.[39] The lamentation in Ps. 58 is caused precisely by the fact that these 'evil-doers' are also oppressing Israel, and the gist of the prayer is that 'the righteous' shall 'see vengeance' and 'wash their feet in the blood of the wicked'. There can be no doubt whatsoever that 'the righteous' in this case indicate Israel as a nation—rĕšāʿîm in the psalms does not signify any single group of men, but all those who act as the enemies of the worshipper. They may be either national enemies or treacherous countrymen or such as practise some sort of witchcraft. But mostly they are the national enemies of Israel, or 'the heathen' oppressors and their helpers within Israel.

The words ṣaddîq and rāšāʿ express the two main notions in the ethical view of life of an Israelite. Ṣaddîq,[40] in our translation of the Bible usually and rather mechanically rendered by 'righteous', actually indicates that a person or a thing is 'right'—is what it ought to be; for instance it may be used of 'fair weights', the 'right way' as distinguished from the wrong way, and so on. The 'right' man is a man who according to the moral concepts of Israel is as he ought to be, the 'ideally normal' man. According to the old Israelite notion with its 'corporate' view of the individual and

---

[39] Pss. 82.2, 4; 28.3. Cf. Birkeland, *Feinde d. Indiv.*, pp. 44f., 59ff. Marschall, *Die 'Gottlosen' des ersten Psalmenbuches*, has seen that rĕshāʿîm is capable of many interpretations, but his definitions of the latter are often erroneous. Much the same must be said of Ridderboos, *De 'Werkers der Ongerechtigheid'*.

[40] For this idea see especially Johs. Pedersen, *Israel* I–II, pp. 260ff.; Leivestad, *Guds straffende rettferdighet*, pp. 9ff. A good, perhaps somewhat too systematized, examination of the ideological content of the terms 'righteous', 'righteousness' is given by van der Weijden in *Die 'Gerechtigkeit' in den Psalmen*, but curiously enough, he does not touch the religio-sociological question, *who* 'the righteous' in the psalms are.

fellowship, he can only be such a man within the fellowship of the covenant, and if he leads the life of a 'normal', 'good' man in mental and
social fellowship with his family and people. It involves the right relationship to the society in which he is living, with its customs and morals, and
'law', and to its god and its religion. As long as he remains within the
fellowship of covenant and cult, and has done nothing to exclude himself
from this fellowship, he is *ṣaddîq*, and belongs to the *ṣaddîqîm*. Through
the cult his being 'right' is confirmed; through it he is cleansed from
eventual trespasses and promised accession to the fellowship of 'the
righteous'. In the Old Testament 'righteousness' does not signify the
highest virtue, but a social and religious relationship; 'righteous' is he who
answers the demands made on him by the fellowship to which he belongs.
A man is either 'righteous', or he is not; there is nothing between.[41] But
the term often involves an inner power as well. To the 'normal' righteousness of such a man also belongs the possession of the power and the will
to 'succeed' in being united with his fellows; the 'right' man is the 'man
of luck', who possesses 'blessing' and the power of good luck. Because of
his covenant with Yahweh, Yahweh makes him 'succeed'; 'whatsoever
he doeth shall prosper'. But it also means that he creates happiness and
the 'right conditions', 'unity' or 'peace' (*šālôm*) in his surroundings; he is
able to uphold himself and those belonging to him; the 'right' person is
also the 'righteous' one. He is 'firm' and 'trustworthy'. That is why, above
all, it is so important that the chief and king should be 'right', should
possess the 'righteousness' that preserves society and vindicates its order,
and sustain and help those in need of it, as it is described, for instance,
in Chaps. 29 and 31 of the poem of Job.

Just because being 'right' was so bound up with the 'fellowship of the
covenant' it was a matter of course to the ancient Israelite that true righteousness could be found only within the covenant, i.e. within the Israelite
fellowship of the covenant. Its members only could be expected to be
'right' and 'righteous'. Obviously a person who had broken away from
the social order would thereby 'make himself an evil-doer' (*rāšā'*), and that
the outcast 'has been made an evil-doer' would in those days go without
saying. And so, 'right' and 'righteous' would be the natural terms for
members of the Israelite covenant fellowship, for Israel itself as a people
and a congregation.

To the religious way of thinking the focal point of being 'right' would
obviously be the right relationship to Yahweh; the 'right' man is he who
does what is 'right in Yahweh's eyes'; 'the righteous' are 'the God-fearing';
but in the psalms this term too nearly always indicates the fellowship of
Yahweh's worshippers, that is to say Israel as contrasted with other
nations that worship 'other gods'. Like all ancient moral notions the
term *ṣaddîq* has of course a religious element; but it is not from the start
specifically religious, nor has it the same meaning as in the nomistic

[41] For details see von Rad in *Festschrift für Bertholet*, pp. 418ff.

I, 14

Judaism of later days. Only after the development of the typical Jewish law-abidingness did 'righteousness' come to indicate a definite behaviour in accordance with the Jewish way of life under the 'Law', such as for instance in Ps. 1. But as has been said, in the psalms the word very seldom has this sense; the psalms represent the earlier, rather more 'inclusive' view of 'righteousness'; after all, 'the righteous' is here a term for Israel as a nation. It gives expression to the naïve self-estimate of the ancients: one's own nation are always the 'right' people; the others are 'strangers' or 'barbarians'. But the word has a full concrete substance as well; it is the most characteristic expression of the old Israelite view of life and morals with its religious undertone.

Closely related to the conception of 'the righteous' in the psalms is that of 'the pious', the *ḥāsîdhîm*, which would be better translated: 'the loyal' or 'the faithful'. In the psalms this term, too, indicates the people and congregation of Israel.[42] This is brought out with perfect clarity in, for instance, the festal psalm for new year, Ps. 149.5ff., where the congregation is rejoicing at the victorious power with which Yahweh's appearance at the festival has filled the people:

> The faithful now exult in glory,
>   and shout for joy here on their benches;
> the praise of God is on their lips,
>   two-edged swords are in their hands;
> to execute vengeance upon the nations
>   and punishment on (all) the peoples,
> to bind their Monarchs with chains,
>   their nobles with iron gyves,
> to execute upon them the written doom—
>   that is the honour of his faithful ones.

What is said here refers to the people as a whole, and not to any 'party'.[43] The traditional translation 'the pious' ('the saints') is misleading; it does not express what the term primarily implies, namely the connexion with the fellowship of the covenant.[44] The term *ḥāsîdh* is closely related to *ṣaddîq*, only that the emotional aspect of the fellowship of the covenant becomes more prominent. The 'right' man has a warm feeling towards his fellow member of the covenant, and 'does *ḥesedh*' towards him, sides with him, takes care of him, and helps him, when in distress; according to the covenant, *ḥesedh* is the proper way of feeling and acting towards one's fellows; the *ḥāsîdh* is a man who feels and acts as a member of the

[42] Pss. 50.5; 79.2; 85.9; 89.20; 97.10; 132.9, 16; 149.1, 5, 9; 145.10. See Birkeland, *Feinde d. Indiv.*, p. 98.
[43] The earlier critical interpretation to the effect that here and elsewhere in the psalms we have the party of 'the pious', the Chasidim, in the Maccabean period, has been decisively refuted by Birkeland, *'Ani und 'anaw in d. Pss; Feinde d. Indiv.*, pp. 94ff.; cf. Additional Note XXIX.
[44] See Nelson Glueck, *Das Wort hesed;* A. R. Johnson in *Interpretationes ... S. Mowinckel ad Septuagenario missae*, pp. 100ff.

covenant, inwardly as well as outwardly. Those who take seriously the way of acting and disposition proper to the brotherhood of the covenant are, '*ḥesedh*-men', true members of the 'brotherhood of the covenant'.

Israel is conscious of being such a people of Yahweh's covenant, just because she exists as a result of Yahweh's elective love and covenant. And this 'righteousness' is fully meant. As a covenant community which stands in the right relationship to Yahweh, and has its righteousness renewed in the cult, Israel knows that she can plead her 'right' in relation to Yahweh; the same is true also of the individual who approaches Yahweh to get his 'right'. The righteousness is based upon Yahweh's cultic and moral demands, and these demands can be fulfilled by a 'right', normal, man—that is the basic assumption in the old Israelite conception of life and of religion, cf. Deut. 30.11–14. The unavoidable failure—'sins of weakness', and 'unwitting sins'—can be remedied in the cult. Therefore as a people Israel are 'the right ones'.[45]

This therefore is what the congregation pleads in her prayers for help in the laments: her members are 'the righteous', 'the fellows of Yahweh's covenant'. Because Israel are the righteous, standing in a relationship of 'devotedness' to Yahweh, Yahweh must help them in his 'favour' (*ḥesedh*).

And so much the more so as their antagonists are 'wicked', 'evil-doers', *rĕšāʿîm*. This word, in our translation of the Bible, is sometimes rendered by 'ungodly' but always means rather 'evil-doer'. What is characteristic of *rāšāʿ*, 'the wicked one', is not that he is an 'atheist', or that he has no religion at all, but that he is not 'right', that he is not a 'normal' man with a normal soul and normal abilities; he is 'crooked' and 'loose' and 'lax' instead of 'right' and 'steadfast'. He does not possess the power of luck, he is one who 'fails' and misses his aim—this gives us roughly the primary sense of the word. He neither feels nor thinks nor acts nor reacts like a 'normal', 'right' man. He is 'bad', a 'fool', intellectually as well as morally. Objectively speaking he is not to be trusted: something in him 'gives way', just like a slack bowstring. He does not acquit himself well in the fellowship of the covenant; he is a danger and a source of misfortune; he is an outsider—and must be one, as he will otherwise bring bad luck upon the fellowship. He is a failure and doomed to fail, and his apparent 'power' is a negative, injurious one, which will finally bring him to his end. His 'fruit' is destruction and death. Later on when hard facts proved that 'the wicked' might and did prosper, while 'the righteous' were defeated, the great moral and religious problem arose, of which Ps. 73 and the poem of Job complain, and on which they ponder. He who in some way or other breaks with the fellowship of the covenant and its customs and laws, 'makes himself an evil-doer', and the fellowship cannot but make him an outsider, and, according to the 'corporate' view of life, he will then have no true existence. Anything may be expected from him.

[45] See Pedersen, *Israel* I–II, pp. 336ff.; Mowinckel, *Diktet om Ijob*, pp. 7ff. Cf. von Rad in *Festschrift für Bertholet*, pp. 418ff.

Whatever he may do is 'wrong'; 'evil-doer' and 'sinner' are synonymous; the imminent 'injurious power' of the evil-doer is 'impurity' and 'sinfulness'.

Of course there are degrees of 'badness', just as there are degrees of 'righteousness' and 'blessing' and 'luck-power'. *Rāšāʿ* may be used of the one who loses a law-suit; in this case he will be the 'wrong man', and his counterpart the 'right man'; to adjudge a man to be 'wrong' was called 'to make him an unrighteous one' (*hiršîaʿ*). If such a man does not take upon himself to pay the penalty, 'atone for his unrighteousness', to his adversary, possibly even do penance before Yahweh, then the 'unrighteousness' will spread in his soul, and he may become quite filled with 'unrighteousness'.

But life also involves the danger for a 'right' man falsely 'to be made unrighteous'. Not only a wrong decision on the part of society may make him an outsider, or an oppressor may take away his 'righteousness' and his 'honour' and make him 'weak' and 'oppressed'—a pariah on the outskirts of society—but demons and evil men may, by means of 'black magic', put 'weakness' and 'impurity' and 'sinfulness' into the soul of an 'honest man', so as to make him lose health and purity and luck-power and honour and normality, and become just as charged with disasters and full of 'curse' as the 'evil-doer' himself. In a later chapter we shall see what society was able to do by way of retrieval in such cases.

'The righteous' of the psalms find themselves in this most paradoxical situation: though they *are* righteous, evil powers have 'made them unrighteous' by robbing them of their 'peace', and hurrying them to destruction. Such a state of things cannot continue; it is existence on the edge of a knife, poised between life and death. Yahweh settles it by interfering, and maintaining and establishing the righteousness of the righteous one.

As time went on and religion in Jewish times became more individualistic and the 'law' of Yahweh the fundamental religious reality, about which the individual had to make up his mind and to which he had to adjust himself, the same thing happened to the notion *rāšāʿ*, that happened to *ṣaddîq*: it came to express a definite view of life and an attitude to life, which alas! was also to be found within the community itself; the 'wicked one', the 'evil-doer' was the man who broke away from the law of Yahweh and from the manners and customs and traditions of the Fathers to imitate the manners and customs of the gentiles, and to join them; 'the publican' in the pay of the gentiles was considered to be the 'sinner' above all others. He is the 'apostate', who in the opinion of the righteous ought to be put outside the fellowship of the covenant, even if political conditions as a rule made it impossible to give effect to this claim. But the pious comforted themselves with the thought that in the end Yahweh was sure to smite the apostates, 'the wicked'. And as the distinguishing mark of the latter was considered to be the disregard of Yahweh's law and the claims of the covenant, the disaster befalling him was consequently looked upon as the just punishment of Yahweh, even if the ancient concept of disaster as the mechanically inevitable 'fruit' was still alive, side by side with the more rationalistic idea of the chastising interference of Yahweh. We find this later, more Jewish than Israelite, conception of 'the wicked' in some of the latest psalms, such as Pss. 37; 49 and 73.

But in the psalms the earlier conception is predominant, and it is in full accordance with it that 'the wicked' as a rule indicate the national and political enemies of Israel, the 'gentile' nations, that have attacked or oppressed her. As indeed all righteousness and 'happiness' was considered to be attached to the 'normal' life in the fellowship of the covenant, and the 'evil-doer' was the person who had made himself or been made an outsider, early Israel would logically conclude or rather immediately feel as a reality that anyone who did not belong to the fellowship of the covenant, i.e. to Israel, must be 'wicked'. To a primitive outlook anybody is wicked if he has an unfriendly disposition towards, or means a danger to, one's own society; in ancient Israel a 'stranger' meant an 'enemy'. That is why the author of Ps. 58.4 says of the oppressors of Israel, worshipping and representing the 'unrighteous' other gods, that

> The wicked are estranged from the womb,
> go astray from their birth and speak (only) lies.

Their religion, like their whole conduct, is a 'falsehood', a deceitful imposture, a 'venom of asps', which, although it may badly hurt 'the righteous', shall yet in the end overtake the wicked themselves.

Such conduct is most hateful to Yahweh. He really must interfere against such 'evil-doers'! Therefore the lament justifies the prayer by pointing out that Israel are the 'righteous members of the covenant', while her enemies are oppressors and 'wicked evil-doers'. Characteristic in this respect is the prayer in Ps. 58.7ff. which follows on the picture of the enemies as venomous asps and beasts of prey, and with the wording of a curse side by side with prayer:

> Break the teeth in their mouth, O God,
> break out the young lions' molars, Yahweh!
> May they vanish like water that runs away,
> be trodden down like grass, and wither!
> Like a snail that melts away into slime,
> an untimely birth, a mole, unseen by the sun!
> May their tents become jungle before they feel it,
> may they be taken by the storm like dust from the threshing floor!
> The right men shall rejoice at seeing vengeance
> and bathe their feet in the blood of the wicked!
> 'Yes', shall men say, 'the right men get their due,
> there is indeed a God who rules on earth'.[46]

[46] For *ḥiṣṣāw kēmô* v. 8 read *kēmô ḥāṣîr*; *ydrk* may be a passive form *yiddārēkhû* or *yĕdhōrēkhû*. V. 9: *nēphal* and *'ēsheth* asyndeton. V. 10 rd. *sukkôthêhem* and *môs miggōren*; *yis'ārennû* imperson.: 'it storms him away'.

Practically all the above mentioned national psalms of lamentation are 'psalms of innocence'. The congregation, the people of Israel, are 'the righteous', 'the covenant minded', Yahweh's (true) 'worshippers', those who 'have never forgotten thee and never proved false to thy covenant'. The enemies are 'deceitful', 'oppressors', 'wicked', 'evil-doers', 'sorcerers', 'fools', 'faithless', 'robbers', 'lions', 'vipers full of venom'. How, then, can Yahweh have 'forgotten' his people, 'hidden his face from them'? How can it be explained that his 'anger is ablaze against them', that he 'has accounted them no better than sheep to be slaughtered', 'discarded them', 'crushed them in anger', 'given them hard times and a cup to drink that has dazed them', 'abjured the covenant with his anointed', 'not upheld him in the battle', 'made them fly from the archers', allowed the foe to 'cut down and burn the vine that he himself has planted', to 'plunder him' and to 'triumph over him'?

But the congregation may also admit that it has sinned, whatever sin it may be that it has committed (Ps. 79.8f.; Lam. 1.18, 20; 3.42); it may admit that Yahweh is right (cf. Ps. 51.6) and thereby do him honour, and make itself as small and miserable as possible; it humbles itself and does penance for its sins. In this way we get a *penitential lament*,[47] dominated by the motives of *penitence*, confession of sins, and humility.[48]

> Remember not against us our fathers' sins!
> May thy compassion hastily meet us—for we are low indeed! . . .
> Do thou deliver us and forgive our sins
> for the sake of thy (holy) name! (79.8, 9b.)

Here the motives of penitence, compassion and honour go together.

Actually in very many psalms the motive of penitence is not dominant. Certainly the feeling of penitence may be there, even if it does not find expression in words and confessions of sin; it is to be found in the penitential rites themselves (see above), which also give expression to an inward feeling of guilt and to the knowledge that the wrath of Yahweh must be appeased, although it may also imply a great deal of primitive, naïve calculation: by making oneself out to be small and miserable, one may rouse the compassion of Yahweh and 'make him great', and thus be restored to his favour. Meekness was no permanent part of the piety of ancient Israel; the main concern of the ancient Israelite was to maintain honour and justice.[49] But very early Yahweh had become so great to the mind of an Israelite that a man could not think of 'maintaining himself' (*hiṣtaddēq*) before him. It is for Yahweh to maintain the 'righteousness' and 'justice' of his people; Job demands from Yahweh that *he* shall

---

[47] Ps. 79; cf. the I-psalms 51; 130; The Prayer of Manasses. The group does not coincide with the traditional group of 'penitential psalms' of the church; most of the latter are not typical penitential psalms. In Bernini's book, *Le preghiere penitenziale*, the approach is more theological and doctrinal than literary.

[48] Pss. 79.8f.; 90.8; cf. the 'I-psalms of lament' (Chap. VII).

[49] Cf. Johs. Pedersen, *Israel* I–II, pp. 363ff.

maintain and prove and restore his 'righteousness'. The very words which the ancient saga-tellers put into the mouth of David show what strict Yahwistic circles considered to be the proper attitude to Yahweh, when he had permitted disaster to strike the righteous one. 'If I shall find favour in the eyes of Yahweh, he will bring me again and show me his face and his habitation: but if he thus say, I have no delight in thee; behold here am I, let him do to me as seemeth good to him'. David also refuses to let Abishai cut down Shimei, who heaped curses on him in his distress: 'If he curseth, it is because Yahweh hath said unto him, "Curse David". Who shall then say, Wherefore hast thou done so?' (2 Sam. 15.25f.; 16.5ff.). The disaster proves that the wrath of Yahweh has been roused over something; then the best thing is to make oneself small and un- noticed 'till his wrath hath passed by'. Therefore it was a wise and pious thing to hold one's peace when struck with disaster.[50] To admit that Yahweh is in the right—even if one does not understand it—means to 'give honour to Yahweh'; then it is to be hoped that he will again see to the miserable one. Therefore it is necessary to 'humble oneself under the mighty hand of God, that he may exalt one in due time'.

During her long and mostly unhappy external history, Israel learnt that Yahweh possessed all power and all rights, and that the very existence of the people was entirely dependent on his grace. She had no other help to fall back upon. The help of man was not to be trusted; all assistance had to come from Yahweh. Comparatively early this note is struck in the psalmography,[51] and it is founded on the historical experiences of Israel ever since the days of the Exodus and the miracle of the Reed Lake. It is part of Yahweh's character to take care of those who are 'helpless', 'in distress', 'lowly'[52]—even this belief is connected with the experiences of the Exodus and of Yahweh's character as the God of ordeals ($mišpāṭ$), and oracles ($tôrâ$), and fair peace (cf. the Treuga Dei) at the ancient cult place Kadesh with the 'Spring of judgement' and the 'Court-well'.[53] The emphasis on humility receives a personal touch and ring from the pro- phets' personal experiences of their complete dependence on God, and of God as absolute holiness and overwhelming majesty.[54] They experienced God as the one who had their minds as well as their bodies in his power, and who overwhelmed them, so that they could but do what he wanted them to, even if it hurt.[55] They also experienced him as the sublimely holy and pure one, so that the knowledge of their own impurity and sin was brought home to them (Isa. 6). And they declared pride to be the real and central sin—that is to say: wanting to be something in oneself, and

---

[50] Ps. 39.3, 10; see below, Chap. VIII.7, II.11.
[51] Pss. 44.7f.; 62.9f. (royal psalm); cf. 118.8f.; 146.3. Cf. the references in n. 30.
[52] Pss. 9.13, 19; 10.17; 18.28; 14.6; 22.25, 27; 34.3, 7; 35.10; 68.11; 69.33; 76.10; 82.3f.; 140.13; 147.6; 149.4; 113.7; 1 Sam. 2.8.
[53] Cf. Mowinckel in *Norsk Geogr. Tidskr.* IX, pp. 21f.
[54] Cf. Mowinckel, *Profeten Jesaja*, pp. 88f., 123f.
[55] Cf. Jer. 20.7ff.; 15.15ff.; Isa. 20.

trusting the wisdom and strength of oneself and of other people.[56] Such piety considers lowliness and humility to be the proper attitude to God. A new *religious ideal of humility* grew into being and became a determining factor in Jewish piety. The terms 'lowly', 'distressed', 'helpless' tend to imply 'religiously humble', which again approaches the sense of 'pious'.[57]

The ideal of humility is in itself of a personal nature. On the one hand the condition of Israel as a nation most of the time was to be 'oppressed' and 'distressed', so that she felt she had a special right to reckon with the aid of him who takes particular care of those in distress; this helped to make the feeling of dependence and lowliness and humility be regarded as the proper attitude of people and of congregation too, an attitude which ought to find expression in public worship. On the other hand, the ideal of humility tended to call forth humility—in actual reality—even with regard to the demands made on Yahweh on behalf of the people, as we can see for instance in Ps. 90; even the congregation must learn not to ask for too great things,[58] but be content to wait humbly, but trustingly, for God, until it should please him to re-establish Israel.

Ps. 123 gives fine expression to this humble feeling of dependence:

> As the eyes of the servants are fixed
>   on the hand of their lord,
> as the maid's eyes are fixed
>   on the hand of her mistress,
> so our eyes look to Yahweh, our God
>   till he take pity on us.
> Take pity on us, Yahweh, take pity,
>   for we have our fill of contempt,
> our souls have more than their fill
>   of the scorns of the proud.

This humility has found its clearest expression in Ps. 131, which is certainly spoken by an individual, but on behalf of the congregation. Therefore the psalm ends by calling upon Israel to 'wait for Yahweh' quietly and humbly, patiently and confidently—salvation shall come about in due season.

But, as we have said: neither the note of penitence nor the ideal of humility is very prominent in the national psalms of lamentation, but they come somewhat more to the fore in the congregation's prayers of Jewish times (see below). In the psalms as a whole it is the motive of innocence which is predominant, not that of penitence. Even if Israel be 'distressed', 'oppressed', she is also 'righteous', 'faithful to the covenant'.

To the prayer is often added as another main item *the vow*. Here is an example, which is admittedly taken from a psalm in the I-form:

[56] Cf. Mowinckel, *Profeten Jesaja*, pp. 104ff.
[57] Cf. Mowinckel, *Jesaja*, p. 98.
[58] Ps 90.17; 126.5f.; 128.5f. Cf. Proverbs 30.8.

> Freehandedly will I sacrifice to thee,
> and confess thy name, that it is good,
> that it has delivered me from all my woes
> and let me triumph over my foes. (54.8f.)

As in this case so in all others also, originally the vow would relate to a thanksgiving sacrifice,[59] or to some other pious work to be performed when Yahweh has rendered aid. A vow in connexion with prayer for help was so usual that the ordinary term for making a vow to the deity (*nāzar*) in Hebrew, as well as in Aramaic, received the sense of praying to the deity, calling upon his help.[60] Perhaps it is no mere accident that in the extant 'we-psalms' the vow is not very prominent, whereas in the 'I-psalms' we find it much oftener; a vow is by its very nature a personal matter. That it also has a place, however, in the national psalms will be seen from the reference in the public thanksgiving psalm (Ps. 66), as well as from the fact that a great many of the I-psalms handed down to us are actually collective psalms in which an individual is speaking on behalf of the congregation.[61]

In connexion with the aim of the psalm even the vow becomes a motivation of the prayer;[62] sometimes the prayer itself suggests that God might give the suppliant a chance of thanking and praising him, that is to say of celebrating with a thanksgiving festival after deliverance from distress.[63] We meet with this development especially in laments (and thanksgiving psalms) in individual form (see Chap. VII), and in the individual psalms, properly so called. We shall return to this below.[64]

As a rule the psalm *ends* by expressing the *confidence of being heard* which is felt by the congregation (or the suppliant). This is not merely a motivation of the prayer, like the declaration of confidence found in the body of the psalm; the confidence is sometimes expressed in such strong language that it gives the effect of a thanksgiving for help already received, as if it were an anticipatory thanksgiving psalm; the style as well as other significant details of the thanksgiving psalm are prominent.[65] An instance of such an expression of confidence may be given:

> Through God we shall do valiantly,
> for He will trample down our foes. (60.14.)

(cf. also 58.11f., quoted above, p. 213.)

This anticipatory confidence and thanksgiving cannot merely be explained psychologically, by saying that through his prayer the suppliant

---

[59] See Ps. 66.13ff., a public thanksgiving psalm (Chap. IX), and cf. Pss. 54.8; 22.26f.
[60] Cf. Ps. 61.6 and see Ginzberg in *Louis Ginzberg Jubilee Volume*, pp. 159ff.
[61] See below, Chap. VII, and for the promise, VII. 4 (pp. 234f.). A detailed treatment of 'the promise' in the O.T. and in Judaism is given by Wendel in *Das israelitische Gelübde*.
[62] Pss. 79.13; 80.19; 144.9f.; cf. 20.6; 21.14 (royal psalms).
[63] Pss. 79.13; 80.19; cf. 51.15–17; 142.8.
[64] See Chaps. VII. 4; VIII. 7; X. 2; cf. VIII. 11.
[65] Pss. 144.12–15; 12.7f.; 60.13f.; 79.13; cf. 58.11f.

has now achieved confidence and assurance. The confidence is based on objective grounds. For the psalms handed down to us show that it was part of the very ritual of the penitential festivals that (the priest or) the temple prophet would promise the suppliant salvation and the granting of his prayer by means of an *oracle* or a *promise* to that effect. A few such promises have been handed down in the texts: Pss. 12.6; 60.8–10; 108.8–10. We shall return to this in a later chapter (Chap. XII.2). From a psalm like Ps. 12 we can also see that it was part of the ritual, that the suppliant after having received the promise should answer by a thanksgiving declaration of confidence, expressing the positive assurance which he had now had imparted to him that his prayer had been heard and that (soon) he would experience its actual realization. The declaration may have the character of an anticipatory thanksgiving psalm in the usual style with perhaps an explicit reference to the promise:

> Those words of Yahweh are precious words,
>   sterling as silver seven times purified.
> Thou Yahweh wilt guard us against evildoing men
>   and ever save us from such a race. (12.7f.)

From its place in this part of the ritual the declaration of assurance was then transferred to the psalm of lamentation where it came to be the usual ending:

> O God, I will sing thee a new song,
>   and play to thee on the ten-stringed lute—
> O thou who makest (thy) kings victorious
>   and (ever) savest thy servant David. (144.9f.)

'David' means here the reigning king of Judah.

To faith, aid was secured and made real as a result of the promise. And so the stylistic and style-historical basis for this feature in the structure of the psalms becomes merged with the purely and wholly religious one: that it is in the nature of prayer to bring forth confidence and assurance that God will help. To what extent this will be the case depends on the willingness and power of the suppliant to resign himself totally into the hands of God and pray with the intention of receiving help for this most important aspect of being heard; a prayer with the qualification that God's will be done and not the suppliant's own, will always be a means of obtaining the peace of heart and the confidence in God's real help, which makes up the assurance of faith. But at this very point Old Testament religion and prayer had narrow limits; they never quite got beyond a personally selfish and nationally this-worldly utilitarianism. Therefore a purely religious and psychological explanation of this standing item in the laments—the confidence of being heard—is not sufficient; the style-historical explanation given above is a fundamental necessity.

Now, if a psalm of lamentation falls into two distinctly separate parts: first, the lament and the prayer, and then a more or less regular thanksgiving or an expression of absolute assurance of being heard, as in Pss. 6; 28; 31; 62, urging something the suppliant has just learnt (62.12; 20.7), the explanation is, that in between the two parts something has happened, on which the assurance is objectively based, namely the promise of salvation uttered by the priest or temple prophet; God's promise, his 'word',[66] is the objective basis of that confidence. As a result of this liturgical pattern it has become usual for the psalm of lamentation to end with an expression of confidence as to being heard, more or less in the style of the anticipatory thanksgiving psalm. The final note of the psalm is one of confidence and thanksgiving, as if the help had already been received.

4

Among the national psalms of lamentation there is a distinction which has to be mentioned. One group of them gives a rather general description of the distress or disaster which the enemy *has* already brought upon land and people and king (Pss. 44; 74; 89). They were no doubt occasioned by a day of prayer and fasting after one or more lost battles, or perhaps the sack of the town. These are the psalms of lamentation proper. With these also belong a series of I–psalms, which apparently are quite personal, but in reality are national (congregational) psalms, such as 9–10; 13; 31; 35; 42–43; 55; 56; 59; 69; 94; 102; 109; 142 (see below, Chap. VII).

Then there are others, which do not contain any description of the distress beyond a reference in general terms to the nature and character of the enemy at large. Consequently they contain a lesser amount of specific complaints or none at all. See Ps. 83, 'the royal psalms', 144 and 20, and others. Evidently they came into existence *before* the distress had become acute, that is to say not as a result of a disaster which had already occurred, but in the middle of, or before some threatening danger. From the story of Naboth and the legend about Samuel as a judge (1 Kgs. 19.14ff.; 1 Sam. 7.5ff.) we can see that days of prayer and fasting with all the cultic acts and words belonging to them were kept when it was announced for instance that the enemy had declared war or was already on the march, or before the king of Israel himself entered upon a military expedition. This other group of psalms belongs to such days of antecedent prayer and fasting. As distinguished from the psalms of lamentation they have therefore been called *protective psalms*:[67] they pray for the protection of Yahweh against an imminent danger.

But as Israelite mentality as well as the very purpose of the day of prayer and the style tradition of the psalms would tend to have both distress and danger painted with as gloomy colours as possible (cf. 'the

[66] Pss. 12.7; 56.11; cf. 68.12; 107.20.
[67] See Birkeland, *Feinde d. Indiv.*, pp. 104ff.

motive of compassion'), it is not always easy to distinguish between protective psalms and psalms of lamentation properly so called. Indeed, in later times they may have been used indiscriminately.

Beyond this we shall only mention that a whole series of such protective psalms are to be found among the national congregational laments in the I-form; e.g. the 'royal psalms' 28; 61; 63, but also some other I-psalms, e.g. Pss. 3; 5; 7; 11; 26; 27; 36; 52; 54; 57; 62; 64; 71; 77; 86; 139; 140.

The tone of the protective psalms is brighter than that of the psalms of lamentation. Above all, the confidence and assurance of getting help is more prominent in them; in some of them—especially in those which according to their form are individual—it is altogether predominant. Such have been called 'psalms of confidence'. But if we consider the psalms from a cultic point of view and divide them into groups according to their place in life, the 'psalms of confidence' are no separate category, but only a somewhat marked group within the protective psalms.

In these psalms of confidence the original connexion between hymns and psalms of prayer (see above, Chap. IV.1, 4) can still be easily distinguished. When confidence is to be expressed it will naturally be in the form of a rather hymnic eulogy: Yahweh is praised for the aspects of his being and for the works past and present on which the worshipper is building his confidence and faith; and that is just why they have a more personal note and form. A good example is the first part of Ps. 27. But this means that they are approaching the 'thanksgiving psalms' (Chap. X.2) with regard to substance and tone. It is significant that it has been discussed whether the psalms of confidence have been 'derived from' psalms of lamentation and prayer, or from thanksgiving psalms,[68] and whether a pure psalm of confidence like Ps. 23 is to be counted in the main group, 'psalms of prayer', or to be considered a thanksgiving psalm.[69] But this way of putting the question is irrelevant. This 'mixing' of eulogy and thanksgiving and confident prayer is in fact an inheritance from earlier times, when the different kinds of psalms had not yet been distinguished from each other and separately cultivated according to their special uses in the cult. And at the same time it is evidence of the fact that the total religious experience of the Holy One and the religious attitude to the deity are spontaneous and do not distinguish between the different elements of which they are made up.

5

A state of distress might last a long while. If such a thing happened, the result might be that the day of penance was repeated more or less regularly. In this way we may get psalms which do not refer to a single attack on the part of a gentile power, but to the foreign nation or the

---

[68] The former has been maintained by Gunkel, the latter earlier by the present author in Ps.St. I.

[69] See Ps.St. I, p. 126; Birkeland, Feinde d. Indiv., p. 253.

foreign ruler in a general complaint. So for instance Pss. 12; 14; 58; 82; 90; and others. Such psalms may possibly derive from the period of the later monarchy, when Israel (Judah) was for a long time under the supremacy of Assyria or Babylonia. Later on, Judaism had a series of annual days of public penance and fasting in remembrance of the great disasters associated with the fall of the kingdom and the destruction of city and Temple (Zech. 7.5; 8.19). On these occasions they would complain of the permanent distress, of the degradation of Israel and the oppression and dishonour of gentile supremacy and ask for deliverance, revenge and re-establishment. To this category probably belong for instance Pss. 90 and 137.

Such a *regularly repeated psalm of lamentation* borders on the ordinary psalm of prayer (see below).

In the eyes both of the prophets of re-establishment[70] and of pious people, gentile supremacy over God's people would often appear to be the cause of all misery and sin to be found among the people. Thus the prayer for deliverance from foreign supremacy would involve prayer for the salvation and re-establishment of Israel in general, a 'turning of the destiny'.

Such Jewish laments, with prayer for the national, moral and religious re-establishment of Israel, for their rights over their enemies and for an undisturbed and happy future, are—in addition to those above mentioned —Pss. 106; 123; 125; and there are others. Like the ancient psalms of lamentation, Ps. 137 in particular, has the character of a lamentation over an actual enemy (Edom), but apart from this it is an example of the introduction of an original and personally felt feature into the traditional style.

The idea of a *turning of destiny* in some of these psalms connects them with the prayers usually heard at the festival of harvest and new year (the enthronement festival).[71] As in those psalms the congregation is here looking forward into the future, towards the 'completion', and prayer finds rest in the faith in re-establishment, full salvation, the coming of the 'kingdom'. In such psalms, therefore, late Judaism could find an expression of the eschatologically tinctured hope in which she lived. A fine example of such a forward-looking congregational lament, in which an individual is speaking on behalf of the community, as the person whose heart is especially loaded with the sufferings and the pressure of his time (see Chap. VII), is Ps. 102.

6

According to *our* conception of divine service we should have expected *ordinary psalms of prayer*—asking for whatever the congregation at any time might be in need of—to have belonged to the regular festal service from the very beginning, just like hymns of praise. But this does not appear

[70] See *GTMMM* III, p. 24.
[71] See Chap. V (pp. 161ff.; 186f.; 190f.).

to have been the case. The Psalter does not contain many ordinary psalms of prayer, and none of them can be traced back to very early times. As not infrequently happens it seems that here, too, the mind first of all fastened on the special case, that calling for special attention. As far as the regular and daily benefits which the cult aimed at securing are concerned, it seems as if belief in the creative power of cultic acts dominated the field for a long time, either consciously or unconsciously; here, more than anywhere else, the prayer and psalm to a freely creating and gracefully giving God was slow in penetrating. We have thanksgiving psalms for the blessings of the year (see Chap. IX.5) but no real prayer-psalms 'for peace and a happy year'—as the old Norse expression runs. For a long time worshippers seem to have contented themselves with the words of general prayer, with which the festal hymn sometimes ends (see above, Chap. IV.3).

Evidently the psalms of prayer for ordinary use gradually evolved out of the increasing habit of repeating on the regular days of prayer psalms of lamentation composed for specific occasions, and out of the Jewish situation indicated by the custom. Of the psalms mentioned above (p. 221), Ps. 90 and to a certain extent Ps. 82 have this general character, possibly also Ps. 58. Ps. 82 prays for the restoration of justice and for the deliverance of the depressed and the improvement of social conditions, which will be the result of the collapse of the tyranny of pagan gods. Ps. 90 in general terms prays that the congregation may see the great works of Yahweh and experience his favour after the long years of suffering, so that every man may have the benefit of the work of his hands in peace. The backbone of it is the deliverance and re-establishment of Israel; all the other benefits follow on from the prayer for deliverance from foreign tyranny. Therefore these psalms, like the later ones of new year and enthronement, are closely connected with the Jewish hope of future re-establishment. The eyes of poet and congregation are turned towards the future, praying for the fulfilment of Israel's hope, 'the turning of the fate' (šûbh šĕbhûth). In accordance with the Jewish ideal of humility (see above, p. 216), we may also find the prayer expressed as a gentle wish, a sigh from longing hearts:

> O that the salvation of Israel
>   would come from Zion (soon)!
> When Yahweh turneth his people's fate
>   shall Jacob exult for joy. (14.7)

To this extent we may speak of an eschatological element in these psalms also.

Psalms 123; 130 and 131 are also of the same character. An individual ('I') speaks on behalf of the congregation, identifying himself with its distress: he is, in fact, the liturgical representative of the congregation—the chief priest, or somebody similar.

Two psalms of prayer (Pss. 85 and 126) can most naturally be interpreted as prayers for peace and a happy year, and most probably they belonged to the festival of harvest and new year; at any rate they have the idea of a 'turning of the destiny' in common with this festival; for this term originally indicates the 'turning' which every new year means and is expected to involve. Especially in Ps. 126 it is most natural to take the mention of sowing and reaping as referring to real life, and not merely as a metaphor for 'salvation' in general, the hoped-for restoration. Referring both to the experiences of the past and to the realization of its hope for the future the congregation prays:

> Turn, O Yahweh, our fate again,
>   like streams in the dry south;
> let those who are sowing now in tears,
>   reap with shouts of joy! (126.4f.)

Both psalms mentioned justify the prayer for a 'turning' by referring to a particular occasion known to everybody, on which God had turned the destinies of the people; this probably is a reference to the restoration after the Exile.

That these psalms are related to the psalms of lamentation is seen when what lies behind the prayer is described. Strong colours are used as if referring to a state of acute need and distress. Consequently scholars have been apt to interpret these two psalms as *ad hoc* laments and psalms of prayer, intended to be used on a special day of penance and prayer occasioned by threatening drought and a bad year. That is not necessary. The Old Testament mentality and poetry do not distinguish between need and disaster; the need of something is in itself disaster, distress.[72] The enthronement psalms and other new year psalms show that conditions as they regularly are before the coming of the new year and the rainy season were looked upon and described as a state of acute distress; the powers of chaos have already obtained the mastery, and if nothing happens, if Yahweh does not 'come' and interfere, 'the world' and mankind must perish. That is why the prayers for a new and blessed 'year of goodwill' or 'grace' (Isa. 61.2; Ps. 65.12) receive the character of laments, describing in the most gloomy colours what would otherwise happen, and as if it had already occurred.[73] But even in these two psalms the thought

---

[72] Westermann (in *ZATW* 66, 1954, pp. 44ff.) states that 'the lament' becomes much less prominent in later psalms of supplication and finally disappears, or develops into a literary species (Gattung) of its own (as e.g. in Jer. 20.14–18). In the Psalter, however, there are no pure 'psalms of supplication' without an element of 'lament', and Westermann seems not to have seen the 'cult-functional' difference between those two not strongly defined types. Nor does the transmitted source material allow for Westermann's theory that the most ancient way of addressing God in danger and distress consisted in laments only; the 'original' prayer was rather the 'cry for help'.

[73] Cf. here the sense of the words 'āni and 'ānaw, which mean being insignificant, poor, lowly in general; as well as being for the moment broken-hearted, distressed, oppressed, deprived of one's 'right'. See Birkeland, '*Ani und 'Anaw; Feinde d. Indiv.*, pp. 317ff.; and below, p. 229, and Additional Note XXIX.

advances; especially in Ps. 85 it is obvious that what, after all, the author is alluding to is the fulfilment of the Israelite hope of re-establishment, and that is what the congregation is including in its prayer.

7

One special kind of prayer is *intercession*.[74] Such, too, has its place in an ordered public worship. This is especially so with regard to the intercession for 'those having authority from God amongst us', i.e. for the person on whom the welfare of people and congregation depends more than on anyone else, above all the king, who in Israel was at the same time the representative of God before the people and of the people before God (see Chap. III. 1–2). Ps. 72 is just such a congregational intercession for the king on the day of his anointing, wishing him all the luck-power and righteousness and piety needed for him to be a king after Yahweh's heart and in conformity with the prevailing ideal of kingship. Ps. 21 belongs rather to the festivities at the annual celebration of the day of anointing and enthronement; it starts with a 'motive of confidence', in the style of the thanksgiving psalms, bringing to mind all the previous blessings which Yahweh has bestowed on the king, and the good wishes for the king end in a prayer for Yahweh to be with the king with his powerful works, so that the congregation in the future also may be able to praise his great works. The first part of Ps. 20 is an intercession for the king before a war or a battle, with a prayer for the victory and renown of his people ('we'); the second part expresses an assurance of being heard in the shape of an anticipatory thanksgiving psalm, and ends by summing up everything in a prayer for help 'to-day'.

Ps. 20, as well as Ps. 21, is partly addressed to the king himself, and in these psalms, as well as in Ps 72, the intercession is distinguished by piling up words of blessing (see Chap. XI); an evidence of the religious and style-historical connexion between the prayer and the word of blessing, which is the cultic origin of the intercession.

In the opinion of the ancient Israelites there was no great difference between the blessing word and the intercessory prayer. They are both to some degree efficacious words, creating what they are expressing. There are also close connexions between such words and the prophetic word, which is also a word filled with creative power. These stylistic and material connexions point, as we shall see later on, to an important element in the old Israelite cult, namely the role of the cult prophet as the intercessor on behalf of the congregation and the king.

---

[74] On intercession in the O.T. see Eichrodt, *Theologie d. A.T.* II–III, pp. 121ff.; for Jeremiah: Hertzberg, *Prophet und Gott*, pp. 146ff.; cf. also F. Hesse, *Die Fürbitte im A.T.* None of these authors are sufficiently aware of the part played by intercessory prayers in the cult; the view of de Boer in OTS III is more correct.

CHAPTER VII

National Psalms of Lamentation in the I-Form

I

Among the national and congregational psalms of lamentation mentioned in the preceding chapter (p. 194) there are several in which 'I' and 'we' alternate (see 44.5, 16; 74.12; 83.14; 123.1; 60.11). In two of them, Pss. 89 and 144, the lament is put into the mouth of one—in Ps. 89 occasionally referring to himself in the third person singular—who is no doubt the king of the people; 'the Anointed' is what he calls himself in 89.39; and in 144.10 he identifies himself with 'David', thus actually indicating that he is a descendant of David, cf. the 'seed of David' used of the worshipper himself in 18.51. There can be no doubt whatsoever that the distress complained of in Ps. 89 is of a national and political nature: enemies have demolished all the walls of David's descendant and laid his fortresses in ruins and cast his crown into the dust and overthrown his throne. In Ps. 144, too, the king is surrounded by foreign invaders and liars and threatened by 'the sword of evil'.

So, evidently, the national lament may have an individual and personal form. As we have seen, the king acts as the representative and the incorporation of the people: the cause of the people is his cause, and vice versa (see Chap. III).

It would hardly be correct to say that here the national psalm of lamentation has been influenced by the form of the individual lament. The fact is rather that here we still find the earliest form, in this case having two roots: first the collective way of thinking of the ancients, which would look upon the plurality as a totality, a person; and then the official royal style, which would be more interested in the king himself than in what he represented. This has been discussed in detail in Chap. III.3.

The question then presents itself whether other apparent I-laments also may not in fact be royal laments, speaking of national and political disasters and dangers. The answer to that question is in the affirmative. It must be emphasized in this connexion that we are not dealing with possible royal psalms in which the distress is private and personal, for instance illness; such poems belong rather to the true individual psalms of lamentation.

2

Psalm 20 is certainly a national psalm of intercession for the king before he goes to war (see Chap. VI.7), with a very pronounced 'assurance of being heard', behind which lies the explicit promise of the cultic leader (v. 7). So it must belong to the 'protective psalms' (Chap. VI.4).

In Ps. 63 also it is the king who prays; and he does so in a strain of confidence; as yet the emergency is only just on the horizon. Early in the morning the king appears in the Temple to offer up sacrifices and prayers for help against the threatening enemies. Ps. 61, too, must be understood in a similar way, as a prayer accompanying the offerings before the battle, far away from that capital and Temple which the king hopes to see again before long.

Accordingly we must be prepared to find that other I-laments, and particularly such as use martial terms and metaphors (cf. Chap. III.7), are actually national psalms of lamentation speaking of national and political conflicts,[1] the speaker being the king of the people or one of the leading men of the congregation, such as the High Priest, or the governor, or the chairman of the council (the 'prince' of Ezk. 45).[1a]

This explanation readily suggests itself, for instance, in psalms in which Yahweh is called upon to interfere against the 'peoples' or the 'nations' (as in 7.7f.; 56.8; 59.4, 6, 9) or in which there is an emphasis on Yahweh's power as lord and judge of the earth and of the peoples,[2] or on his being God and lord of Jacob, or Israel, as for instance in 22.4f. Or again, the psalm may indicate that the salvation of the worshipper is to have world-wide consequences: all the world shall call it to mind, and all tribes shall come and fall prostrate before the face of Yahweh (22.28). Or the psalm may describe the relationship in which the worshipper stands to Yahweh as being so intimate that it goes beyond what in ancient Israel would be said of a common man, and actually refers back to the old conceptions of the close relationship of the king to the national god. Thus, when the worshipper describes Yahweh as his accoucheur and foster-father (22.10f.), this is a feature belonging to the 'king ideology' of Babylonia as well as of Israel.[3]

---

[1] See Chap. III. 1, and cf. for this problem about congregational psalms in the I-form, Smend, 'Über das Ich der Psalmen', *ZATW* 8, 1888; Buhl, *Psalmerne*,[2] pp. XXXVIff.; Linder, 'Indiv. och kollet. pss.', *Kristendomen och vår tid*, 1928, pp. 45ff.; and now especially Birkeland, *Feinde d. Indiv.*, pp. 114ff. Gunkel was in fact on the right track when, following Balla, he observed on Ps. 44.9, 15 that the singular in this 'we-psalm' alludes to 'the person of the leader and intercessor' (*Die Psalmen*, p. 185). What has prevented both Balla and Gunkel from a full understanding of the phenomenon is (a) their lack of a distinct cultic approach, and (b) the mechanical distinction between I-psalms and we-psalms. It is therefore obviously a step backwards when Westermann in his rather formalistic and not very fruitful paper in *ZATW* 66, 1954, adheres to this merely formal distinction without discussing in principle the textual facts pointed out by the present author in *Ps.St.* and in this chapter (*Offersang og Sangoffer*, pp. 227ff.), and by Birkeland in *Feinde des Individuums*. The weakness of Westermann's position is seen from the fact that without any grounds he declares the vv. 16–17 of Ps. 44 to be 'a fragment of an individual psalm of lamentation'; nor does he make any attempt to deal with the undoubted identity of the 'I' and 'we' in Ps. 89. What we do learn from Westermann's paper is that we can attain no further results if we restrict ourselves to Gunkel's one-sided, formal use of the form-typological point of view ('Gattungsforschung').

[1a] See Chap. III. 6–7.

[2] Ps. 9.6–13, 16–20. See also Ps. 59.14; cf. 58.12; 57.10–12; 94.2, 5, 7, 14 and the evidently congregational psalm 82.8.

[3] See Labat, *Royauté*, pp. 5ff.; Engnell, *Div. Kingship*, p. 16, n. 7, and above, p. 54.

Among such psalms Ps. 94 has a first section which in no respect differs from the complaints and prayers of the national laments, whether it has for its background a single disaster (defeat and occupation) or some more lasting subjection under alien rule, abetted by internal traitors (v. 8). The individual ('I') appearing in the second part and complaining of (the same) distress must then be the representative of the congregation on the day of penance, most likely the king.

Similarly Ps. 102. In the first part (vv. 2–12), the speaker laments over his miserable state of disaster, in the same style and phraseology as a king defeated by his enemies, or a sick person seeking cleansing and health by the ritual ceremonies of the Temple. The second part (vv. 13–18), however, shows that the real point and purpose of the psalm is the prayer for the deliverance and restitution of Jerusalem and Israel, the state of which is described as a permanent oppression by the (heathen) 'nations'. The worshipper prays on behalf of his people, and describes himself as, so to say, suffering on behalf of Jerusalem and Israel. Certain allusions to the ideology of the new year festival (vv. 13f.) seem to indicate that the psalm belonged to this festival, among the prayers for Israel's restitution (see above, pp. 219f.).

Ps. 77 is really also a national psalm of lamentation; the whole people has been struck by disaster; the poet's motivation of his prayer is a reference to the benefits conferred on the people by Yahweh in days of old. The speaker is the representative of the people, whose own disaster is identical with the one which has befallen his people, the congregation of Israel.

Many other psalms make the same point: Pss. 7; 9–10; 54; 42–43; 3; 27 and others.

Several of these psalms are 'protective psalms' ('psalms of confidence'; see Chap. VI.4), not psalms of lamentation properly so called; as yet the emergency is but a threatening danger. That is why we get no such descriptions of the demeanour of the enemy as for instance in Pss. 44 and 74, where the description indeed leaves no doubt that here we have to do with political conflicts and enemies.[4]

3

Some psalms complain of *evil tongues and words*, and more definitely of *false charges* and *mendacious accusations* from 'lying lips' and 'deceitful lips', 'violent lips', and so on:

> They are devising deceitful words,
>> and widening their mouth against me. (35.20b, 21a.)

> False witnesses are risen up against me,
>> breathing out violence (upon me). (27.12.)

[4] See above, pp. 197ff. and below, ¶ 6, pp. 241ff. That in these psalms we are dealing first and foremost with national and political enemies and antagonisms, so that to this extent the earlier exegetes were on the right track, has been proved by Birkeland (*Feinde d. Indiv.*), even if he somewhat exaggerates his point of view. See also Additional Note Chap. XXVIII.

The last line refers to the magical blowing of the sorcerer.

> Malicious witnesses have risen up,
> charging me with crimes I know nought of. (35.11.)

We have seen above (Chap. VI.3) that even in the purely national laments, in which the disaster is war and defeat, the evil and injurious 'lying words' play an important part. Words are active instruments of disaster. But the 'lying words' may also contain specific references.

Side by side with complaints of the evil curses and soul-impairing and 'demoniacal' injurious words and sneers and intrigues we hear of evil-minded slanders and false charges (27.2, 12; 35.11). In other psalms Yahweh is called upon to help against the adversary in some lawsuit, or to judge righteously in such a case (35.23f.; 43.1; 7.9; 26.1; 54.3). Or the worshipper rejects an imagined or real accusation (7.4). Besides this, too, the same psalm may speak about the danger of war and hostility on the part of whole 'nations' (7.8; 27.3; 35.1f.; 69.51).

Here again it is the king or the leader of the people who is praying.[5] We know that during the greater part of her existence Israel-Judah was under alien rule; we know also that such a vassal king or governor was always exposed to more or less justifiable (or unjustifiable) accusations before his lord on the part of other, envious neighbouring vassals (as we are told by the governor Nehemiah (6.5–8), or on the part of suspicious superior officials (as we are told about the period after the first return from the Exile (Ezra 4.5ff.; 5.5ff.)), or on the part of subordinates aspiring to a ruler's position. Even the supreme lord himself might find reason for suspicion, and threaten to send an investigating commission or a punitive expedition. The Amarna letters, containing communications from the vassals of the Egyptian king in Syria and Palestine in the fifteenth and fourteenth centuries B.C., give examples of this. Every now and then such a vassal king would be summoned before the supreme king, and this might easily result in deprivation of office and imprisonment; but as in the instance of Manasseh, we see that there might also be hope of pardon (2 Chron. 33.10ff.). Something of the same kind is recorded about Pharaoh Psamthek's father Neku, who was a kinglet in the delta of the Nile, and an Assyrian vassal.[6]

In such disaster and danger the king or governor of Judah does what Manasseh did: humbles himself, and turns to Yahweh with the usual rites of fasting and penance and with psalms. He protests his innocence and prays for help against the mendacious accusations and false lips of deceitful

---

[5] H. Schmidt, *Gebet des Angeklagten*, has tried to prove that we have in these psalms private individuals who have been accused before the authorities of Israel and who are now in ritual forms praying to Yahweh for an acquitting oracle, perhaps by successfully passing some sort of 'ordeal'. Schmidt's hypothesis has been accepted by Bentzen (*Indledning til de gml. t.-lige Salmer; Fortolkning til Salmerne*), Leslie (*The Psalms Translated and Interpreted*) and others. But Birkeland (op. cit.) provides clear evidence that we have here national problems and relations with foreign rulers. See also *GTMMM* IV, introductory remarks on Pss. 7; 26; 35; 54 and others.

[6] Rassam-Cyl. I, 90ff., II, 8ff. See Streck, *Assurbanipal*, pp. 11f., 15f., cf. pp. CCLXXVIIf.

enemies. When the protective psalms speak of 'lying words' and 'lying enemies' they may in many cases refer to enemies of this kind.

These national psalms in the I-form, as well as the real individual psalms to be discussed in the following chapter, have frequently been interpreted as giving evidence of religious and social antagonisms and party disputes inside Israel or the Jewish congregation itself. Above all, this conception has been attached to the terms 'the oppressed' ('suffering', 'poor', Hebr. '$\bar{a}n\hat{i}$ and '$\bar{a}n\bar{a}w$), often occuring in these psalms,[7] and taken to indicate the socially inferior and oppressed 'tendency' or 'party' of the pious within the congregation; the enemies in these psalms, the 'ungodly' (the 'wicked' —$r\check{e}\check{s}\bar{a}'\hat{i}m$) were then supposed to indicate the wordly and well-to-do upper class or a movement that did not take the law too seriously, and would oppress the 'poor', pious people.[8]

This interpretation has proved to be false.[9] Neither religious and social party disputes, nor any 'class struggle', form the background of these psalms, but national-religious antagonisms and external political events. The 'oppressed', or 'humble'—the above mentioned Hebrew may mean either—are no party nor class, but Israel, or her representative men in times of emergency 'oppressed' by external enemies, 'helpless' in their own power, 'in need of help', and 'humbly' hoping for the interference of Yahweh. That the external enemy may in some cases be supported by traitors inside Israel itself, and that 'the enemies', 'the ungodly', and so on, may sometimes include even some Israelite 'quislings', is another matter, and does not alter the general picture of these psalms.

4

Between the national I-laments and the normal national psalms of lamentation ('we'-psalms) the only essential difference of form and content is that which results from substituting the first person singular. Structure and substance are the same: *the invocation*, generally one of the first words of the psalm,[10] and as a rule without any hymnal amplification,[11] but often with additional words emphasizing the relationship of the worshipper to Yahweh: 'my God', 'the God of Israel', and so on;[12] then *the complaint*[13] about the distress, not forgetting its mental aspect, described by means

---

[7] Complete statistics in Birkeland '*Ani und 'Anaw*, p. 1.
[8] See Additional Note XXIX.
[9] See n.8.
[10] Pss. 3.2; 5.2; 7.2; 13.2; 16.1; 17.1; 28.1; 35.1 and other places. Later in the psalm: 42.2; 120.2; Isa. 38.14.—A second invocation at the beginning of a new section: 3.4, 8; 5.9, 11; 7.4, 7; 13.4; 17.6, 13; 43.1; 69.4, 7; 71.13, 17; 77.12; 86.12, 14, etc.—Repeated at the end: 3.8; 43.4.—At other places within the psalm: 4.9; 5.13; 17.18; 27.11; 54.7; 59.13; 69.30; 71.4f., 14f.; 140.8f. and many other places. Cf. Chap. VI. 3. (Statistics after Gunkel).
[11] Such a hymnal addition is found in Jer. 17.12ff.; Prayer of Manasses.
[12] Pss. 3.8; 7.2, 4; 13.4; 16.1; 17.1; 30.9; 35.23; 43.4; 59.12; 86.4f., 8, 15; 69.7, etc.
[13] Pss. 3.2–5; 5.10; 10.1–11; 13.1–3; 27.10; 22.2f., 7–9, 15–19; 31.10–14; 42.2–4, 7–12; 43.2; 54.5; 55.4–6, 10–12, 13–15, 19–22; 56.3; 57.5; 59.4, 7f.; 64.4–7; 69.1b–5, 8–13, 20–22; 102.4–12, 24f., etc.

of many different metaphors,[14] and about the enemies,[15] about mockery and sneers,[16] about evil words and sorcery on the part of ungodly and deceitful enemies and about contemptuous malevolent rejoicing on the part of neighbours and former friends;[17] in addition questions as to 'why?' or 'how long?';[18] next, the *prayers for help*,[19] supported by *motivations of the prayer* (Chap. VI.3); the 'motive of confidence' is particularly prominent, and in many forms;[20] side by side with it may occur 'hymnal motives',[21] 'motives of compassion', such as the brevity and troubles of human life,[22] the 'motive of honour',[23] of 'innocence',[24] and of 'penitence', with confession of sins;[25] finally the *promise* of sacrifice,[26] and expression of thanksgiving,[27] and the *assurance* that the prayer will be heard[28] with more or less marked anticipatory thanksgiving,[29] and reference to the predictions of the priest or temple prophet.[30]

A few examples may serve to illustrate these different elements. *The invocation* and the *complaint*, especially of deceit and treachery, are brought out by this introductory stanza:

> Help, Yahweh! for loyalty (*ḥesedh*) is no more,
> fidelity has vanished now from mankind.
> They speak falsity one to the other,
> with flattering lips and double minds.   (12.2f.)

---

[14] Pss. 42.5; 31.10; 13.3; 40.13, 18; 42.6, 12; 43.5; 102.1.

[15] Pss. 3.2f., 8; 5.9; 7.2f., 6f., 13–17; 13.3, 5; 17.4–14; 27.2f., 6, 11f.; 35.1–8, 11–21, 24–26; 40.15f.; 55.4, 13, 19–22, 24 and many other places, even in the 'account of the distress' in the thanksgiving psalms, for instance 27.2f.

[16] Pss. 22.7f.; 27.11; 31.12, 19, 21; 35.16, 19, 21; 40.16; 42.10f.; 43.2; 54.7; 55.13; 69.10, 20; 109.25; 142.5. Cf. Job 17.2; 19.14f.

[17] Pss. 3.3; 22.9; 35.21, 25; 40.16; 41.6, 9; 42.4, 11; 64.6f.; 71.11. Cf. Jer. 11.19; 17.5; 18.18; 20.10. See above, Chap VI.3 and n. 16 and 19, and for details, Chap. VIII. 2, 4.

[18] Pss. 4.3; 10.1, 13; 22.2; 42.10; 43.2.

[19] Pss. 4.2; 5.2f., 9, 11; 7.2, 7, 9; 13.4; 16.1; 17.1ff., 6–9, 13f., and many other places; complete statistics in Gunkel-Begrich, *Einl.*, p. 218, n. 7, and for the different kinds of prayers ibid., pp. 219ff. Cf. above, Chap. VI.3.

[20] Pss. 13.6; 16.1f.; 26.1; 31.7, 15; 55.24; 56.4; 57.2; 62.2.—Pss. 5.5; 23.4; 27.1; 56.5, 12; 59.9, 11.—Pss. 7.2; 11.1; 16.1; 31.2; 42.2; 57.2; 59.10; 61.5; 63.2; 71.1; 130.6; 143.6.—Pss. 3.4; 31.4; 22.10; 71.5; 42.3, 9; 27.1, 9; 22.5f.; 70.6; 102.15–23; 143.5, etc. For details, Gunkel-Begrich, *Einl.*, pp. 232–236.

[21] Pss. 7.11; 22.4; 25.6, 8–10, 14; 31.4; 86.5, 8.

[22] Pss. 89.48; 109.23; cf. the psalms of illness, 6.6; 30.10; 39.5.

[23] Pss. 10.13; 69.8, 10; cf. Jer. 15.15.

[24] 5.5–8; 7.4f.; 17.3–5; 26.4–8; 35.7, 19; 59.4; 69.10. Cf. the psalm of illness, 38.21.

[25] Pss. 25.11; 40.13; 69.6; prayer of Manasses, vv. 6f. Cf. Ps. 51.5–7, and the psalm of illness, 39.9f., 28. See Chap. VI.3.

[26] Pss. 27.6; 54.8; 56.13; 61.9.

[27] Pss. 27.6; 54.8; 61.9.—Pss. 7.18; 13.6; 22.23ff.; 26.12; 27.6; 28.6f.; 31.8f.; 35.9f., 27f.; 42.6; 43.4f.; 52.11; 54.8; 56.13f.; 57.8f.; 59.17; 63.3, 6; 69.31ff.; 71.8, 14–16; 86.12ff.; 109.30; 119.171f., 175; 140.14; 142.8; 144.9. Cf. 51.15f.; 119.7 and the psalm of illness, 39.9f., 28. See Chap. VI.3.

[28] Pss. 3.8; 5.13; 7.11–14; 13.6; 16.10f.; 26.12; 27.13; 36.13; 52.10; 55.24; 56.10–12; 57.7; cf. the psalm of illness, 6.8–11. See Chap. VI.3.

[29] Pss. 22.24ff.; 56.14; 69.34ff.

[30] Pss. 56.10; 140.13.

The worshipper complains of *suffering* and *distress*:

> I am wearied with crying, my throat is dried,
> > mine eyes are weak with waiting for my God. (69.4.)

and of threatening *enemies*:

> For strangers are risen up against me,
> > oppressors are seeking now my life. (54.4.)

or of the *sorcery* and *deceit* of his enemies:

> He's pregnant with witchcraft, alive with malice
> > (against me)—but shall bring forth deception;
> a deep pit he has digged out—
> > and shall tumble into his own pitfall. (7.15f.)

> He is sprinkling witchcraft over me,
> > and sets upon me furiously. (55.4b.)

and of *mockery* and *sneers*:

> I chasten my soul with fasting—
> > they only jeer at me;
> I wear sack-cloth as my garment—
> > and have become their byword;
> they that sit in the gate talk of me;
> > I have become the beer-drinkers' song. (69.11–13.)

In all this need and trouble the sufferer *prays for help*:

> O Yahweh, listen to my words,
> > consider my recital,
> hearken unto my cry for help,
> > O thou, my King and God! (5.2f.)

> O Yahweh, my God, I trust in thee;
> > deliver me from all my pursuers,
> lest he tear me like a lion,
> > devouring me with none to rescue! (7.2f.)

The worshipper pleads *grounds for granting his prayer*. Not only a description of his wretchedness and need, but also, and not infrequently, his *confidence in Yahweh*:

> In Yahweh do I take my refuge.
> > How dare you say, then, to my soul:
> 'Flee to the mountains like a bird,
> > for wicked men have bent their bow'. (11.1f.)

For Yahweh would take care of the helpless:

> For thou beholdest toil and grief,
> > thou seest the helpless and fatherless;
> he leaves his case in thine hands,
> > thou art his helper, thou (alone). (10.14.)

Therefore the worshipper appeals to his *compassion*:

> But I am a worm, and not a man,
>   derided by men, by my relatives despised. . . .
> My soul is now poured out like water
>   and all my bones are out of joint;
> my heart has now become like wax,
>   is melted here within my breast;
> dry as a potsherd is my throat,
>   my tongue is cleaving to my jaws.
> I can count every bone in my body,
>   (my foes) are gloating over me.
> They've laid me down in the dust of death,
>   and bound my hands and feet (with grave-cloths);
> They are dividing my clothes among them,
>   Are casting lots for (all) my garments.
>   (22.7, 15, 16a, 18, 16b, 17b, 19.)

He *does penance and confesses his sins*, as Yahweh would demand from the trespasser:

> O God, thou knowest my sinful folly,
>   No fault of mine is hid from thee. (69.6.)

So far the suffering has been deserved:

> My transgressions have overtaken me,
>   I cannot bear them any more.
> They are more than the hairs of my head,
>   and my heart has failed me now. (40.13.)

And so he must *ask God's forgiveness*, and do penance:

> O Yahweh, for the sake of thy name,
>   pardon my guilt, for it is great! (25.11.)

But more often the suppliant feels guiltless in relationship to his enemies, and pleads his *innocence* as the ground of the prayer:

> O Yahweh, my God, if I have done it,
>   if there be iniquity in my hands,
> if I have rewarded evil to my ally,
>   if I have plundered my foe for no cause. (7.4f.)

> Trying my heart, searching me out in the night,
>   testing me—thou shalt find no shameful deed.
> My mouth did not trespass at the (wrong) deeds of men,
>   the words of thy lips I have (always) heeded.
> In the paths of the robber [I never walked,
>   on the roads of the wicked I never wandered];
> my footsteps have steadfastly followed thy track,
>   they have never faltered [on thy paths]. (17.3–5.)

And in any case it will *add to the honour of Yahweh*, if he shows that he is
going to help his faithful servant, who trusts him and depends on him:

> For thou art my rock, thou art my castle,
>   [where I can hide myself]
> and, Yahweh, for the sake of thy name,
>   Thou wilt lead me and guide me—Thou! (31.4.)

> It is for thy sake that I suffer taunts,
>   that shame now covers my face. . . .
> Zeal for thy house has eaten me up,
>   taunts against thee fall upon me. (69.8, 10.)

Here also we meet the question '*Wherefore?*':

> Wherefore shall the wicked disdain God,
>   thinking that thou wilt never punish? (10.13.)

The confident appeal to the honour and faithfulness of Yahweh sometimes
takes the form of a hymn (cf. above, Chaps. IV.3; VI.3):

> But Yahweh is within his sacred palace,
>   Yahweh is enthroned in the heavens,
> his eyes behold [the whole earth],
>   his glance tests all mankind. (11.4.)

> My shield that covers [me] is God,
>   who saveth the upright heart;
> God is a judge who maintaineth the right,
>   indignant every day. (7.11f.)

> Thou, Lord, art kind, and ready to forgive,
>   rich in love to all who call on thee. . . .
> There is no God like thee, O Lord,
>   there are no deeds like thy deeds.
> All nations shall come and bow down before thee,
>   glorifying thy name, O Lord.
> For thou art great, thou workest wonders,
>   thou, only thou, art God. (86.5, 8–10.)

As in psalms in the we-form the *vow* originally referred to a thanksgiving
sacrifice:[31]

> I will offer sacrifices of joy within his shrine,
>   and sing praises unto Yahweh. (27.6.)

But in the psalms before us it generally has reference to a thanksgiving
feast with thanksgiving psalm and hymns 'in the midst of the congregation'. In fact, the thanksgiving sacrifice is involved in this vow as a
matter of course; we can see this, for instance, from the reference to it in
the vow of a thanksgiving song in Ps. 22.23ff. But the psalmists stand for

[31] See above, n. 26.

an estimate of the various elements of the cult, different from that of the priests; they rank the hymn above the sacrifice and the other elements of the cult: they consider the thanksgiving psalm better than the sacrifice, indeed it is the essential part of the sacrifice, the real sacrifice. That is why this element is emphasized in the promise:[32]

> I will give thee thanks in the great congregation,
>   I will praise thee in the throng of worshippers;
> and all day long my tongue shall talk
>   of thy justice and thy praiseworthiness. (35.18, 28.)

> I will praise thee, Yahweh, for evermore,
>   because thou has showed (kindness to me),
> I will proclaim thy name, how good it is,
>   in the presence of the men of thy covenant. (52.11.)

Trusting all these reasons ('motivations') why Yahweh should grant the prayer, the worshipper's *assurance of being heard* is a standing part of the psalm of lamentation:

> Surely I believe that I shall see
>   the goodness of Yahweh, in the land of the living. (27.13.)

> I lay me down and sleep (secure),
>   I waken, for Yahweh doth uphold me;
> I fear not an army of (many) myriads
>   ranged against me all around me . . . .
> For thou breakest the cheekbone of all mine enemies,
>   and crushest the teeth of the wicked (foes).
> It is Yahweh's to bring salvation,
>   Thy blessing is upon thy people. (3.6–9.)

Sometimes there is a reference to the *oracle* on which the assurance rests:

> Blessed be Yahweh, because he has heard
>   my voice of supplication!
> Yahweh is my strength and shield,
>   my heart is trusting him. (28.6f.)

> Then shall mine enemies turn their backs.
>   This is what I know: that God is for me.
> Through God I then shall praise the word,
>   through Yahweh I shall praise his word. (56.10f.)

The statement of assurance not infrequently is expressed as an assurance that the worshipper will soon have reason to sing a thanksgiving psalm

---

[32] See above, n. 27.

to Yahweh in the congregation. While 'the violence of the wicked shall drop on his own head',

> I shall have to thank Yahweh for his salvation,
> and sing praise to the name of the Lord most high.
>
> (7.18.)

Here the promise is included in a more indirect form:

> So I shall praise thee on the lute
> for thy loyalty, my God,
> and sing thy praises on the lyre,
> O Holy One of Israel!
>
> My lips shall ring with joyful praise,
> as I sing and play unto thee;
> even the life which thou hast saved
> [shall praise thy grace unto me].   (71.22f.)

But often the poet would sing about his assurance in an *anticipatory thanksgiving psalm*, for with the oracle the prayer is already granted:

> I am under vows to thee, O God,
> I will pay thee my sacrifice of praise.
> For thou hast saved my life from death,
> hast saved my feet from stumbling,
> that I might walk before God's face
> in the brilliant light of life.   (56.13f.)

The difference from the we-laments which may be observed is natural, considering the different points of view: the we-laments look at the distress or danger from the point of view of the people and all the individuals, whereas the I-psalms look at everything from the point of view of the leading person, the king. That is why the former speak much more about the ravaging of land and city and temple, of the lost battles of 'our armies', and as motivation of the prayer will use the promises God had given to the Fathers and the benefits he had bestowed on them, the aid experienced from him in the history of the people. These elements are not completely wanting in the I-psalms either, see for instance 89.41f.; 22.4ff. But particularly important here, as already mentioned, are the complaints resulting from the uncertain position of the vassal king: the complaints of deceit and intrigues and false accusations and such 'violent conduct'. And on the whole, hostility, lying words, curses and sneers are all related to the praying king (leader of the people) himself, as being *his* disaster and as an attack on *him*; the suffering is what he personally feels, *he* is the one to be attacked and sneered at, the disgrace is the loss of honour that he himself has suffered; sometimes it is even emphasized that the success and triumph of the enemies, and his own defeat and disgrace have made him ill (69.21).

But this does not mean any essential difference in the nature of the distress or the enemies; in a whole series of I-psalms the distress, as we have seen, is of a political nature and the enemies are foreign foes and (or) internal traitors. The chief difference is that in the I-psalms we hear more often of attempts to get at the king personally and to remove him from his office, than of real battle tactics. But even where it is a matter of war—in the protective psalms about threatening attacks—everything is related to the king's own person. This royal egocentricity is just as evident in an undoubtedly national lament like Ps. 89, and we find it again in the royal thanksgiving psalm, Ps. 18, where, too, the background is war with its dangers. In short, the characteristic feature of the public I-psalms as distinguished from the we-psalms is the *oriental king-Ego style*, so well known from the old royal inscriptions with their royal I-form: the cause of people and state is looked upon as the personal—so to speak private— cause of the king himself; the whole picture is dominated by the king, so as to make him overshadow the totality he is representing.[33]

Of course this leads to a certain differentiation of detail. Hence the prayer will sometimes have a more personal character, since the very destiny of the people is dependent on the personal relationship of the king to Yahweh (Chap. III). False accusations and intrigues are included in the complaint. The prayer seems to become more fervent: 'I call out to thee', 'I cry', 'I implore thee'.[34] The suppliant calls attention to his personal situation and state of mind.[35] And because the disaster of the people is often occasioned by the sin of the king (the leader), the petition for forgiveness of sins and averting of the punishment will be more prominent.[36] Or the king will plead his personal righteousness and blamelessness.[37] He will also ask for preservation from sin, and for God's guidance to walk righteously.[38] The prayer for help and salvation takes on the form of a prayer for an opportunity of singing psalms of thanksgiving to Yahweh.[39] Even the prayer for the destruction of enemies will sometimes have a more personal nuance.[40]

The *wish form* is more prominent in the prayer than in the pure we-psalms,[41] especially the cursing wish against the enemies.[42] It is significant that in the I-psalms the cursing wish, which is the older form, is

---

[33] Mowinckel, *Statholderen Nehemia*, pp. 124ff.; *Gunkel Festschrift, Eucharisterion* I [*FRLANT* 36], pp. 278ff.

[34] Pss. 5.4; 17.6; 27.8; 28.2; 57.3; 61.3; 63.2; 69.4; 77.2; 102.6; 130.1; 141.1.

[35] Pss. 5.4; 7.2; 17.1; 37.2; 42.2f., 9; 71.1; 77.3.

[36] Ps. 143.2; prayer of Manasses, v. 12; cf. Pss. 25.18; 51.3f., and the psalms of illness, 6.2; 38.2.

[37] Pss. 26.1f., 9; 7.9; 35.24; 43.1. Cf. 139.23f.; Jer. 12.3.

[38] Pss. 5.9; 25.4; 27.10f.; 90.12; 141.3f.; 143.8, 10; cf. 51.12–14.

[39] Pss. 5.12; 20.6; 31.8; 35.9, 28; 40.17; 43.4; 51.10, 16; 52.8; 63.6; 69.7; 71.14–16; 109.30; 142.8.

[40] Pss. 5.11; 7.7, 9; 10.15; 28.4; 35.1, 3; 59.6; 69.24f., 28; 109.6; 143.12. Cf. Jer. 12.3; 15.15; 18.21, 23.

[41] See references in n. 36.

[42] Pss. 7.10; 9.18; 31.18; 34.4, 8, 26; 35.8, 19, 24f.; 40.16; 54.7; 55.16, 24; 56.8, 10; 57.5; 59.13; 63.10f.; 64.9; 69.23, 26, 29; 71.13; 86.17; 109.9ff., 29.

much more frequent than the prayer for the destruction of the enemies; this confirms the conjecture that the I-psalm as a style of writing is older and more original than the we-psalm (see above, p. 194). The fact that Yahweh is not often named as the subject of these wishes for punishment points in the same direction; as a rule the old cursing formula belonging to the idea of the self-active word has been retained.

There is a certain difference, too, with regard to the *motivation of the prayer*;[43] even the latter becomes more personal, when the king himself is in the foreground, and distress and salvation are looked upon as something which in the first place concern him. This applies for instance to a special kind of 'motive of honour'; the suppliant points to the fact that Yahweh will lose a faithful servant, eager to praise him, if he allows him to go under; it is taken for granted that Yahweh wants to be praised and honoured, but the dead, having been 'plucked out of his hand' cannot praise him; in Sheol there are no sounds of praise![44]

> For Sheol does not sing thy praise,
>   Death does not celebrate thee;
> and those who have passed down to the pit
>   have no hope of thy love. (Isa. 38.18.)

So also in the 'private' sickness psalm (Chap. VIII):

> Dost thou work wonders for the dead,
>   do ghosts arise to sing thy praise?
> Do they recount they love in the grave,
>   thy faithfulness in the world below?
> Can thy wonders be known in the land of darkness,
>   thy saving help in the land of oblivion? (88.11–13.)

This note is heard even in a purely congregational psalm:

> The dead, they do not praise Yahweh,
>   nor any who sink to the silent land.
> But we, we will bless Yahweh
>   from this time forth and for evermore. (115.17f.)

As we have seen above (Chap. VI.4), the national psalms of lamentation in the I-form also can be divided into psalms of lamentation proper and *protective psalms*; in fact, the latter type is comparatively frequent. It belongs to the very nature of the protective psalm that the worshipper will emphasize his confidence in Yahweh, that he is not going to fail him when in danger. The accent is more confident because distress is as yet only threatening. This tends to strengthen the personal touch, often found in these psalms; evidently it is easier for the poet to find expressions for it when he is able to identify himself with the individual in whose name the

[43] See notes 20–25 and Chap. VI. 3.
[44] Pss. 115.16f., and the psalms of illness, 6.6; 30.10; 88.11ff.; Isa. 38.18f. Cf. Sir. 17.27f.; Bar. 2.17f.

psalm has been composed.[45] So it is significant that most of the psalms
called 'psalms of confidence' are to be found among the national psalms
in the I-form. We can easily understand this if the suppliant is supposed
to be king of Israel, Yahweh's anointed and 'son', having a particularly
close relationship to the god of the people, and able to rely on 'the everlasting promises of faithfulness to David' and to his offspring.[46] This feature
of warm personal confidence becomes prominent especially in cases where
the prayer part of the psalm is preceded by a hymnal thanksgiving, as in
Pss. 27 and 40. We may quote the first part of Ps. 27, where he who prays
is no doubt a king in the typically bad situation of a vassal king, as described above, pp. 238f.:

> Yahweh is my light and aid;
>   whom should I fear?
> Yahweh is the fortress of my life;
>   whom should I dread?
>
> When wicked men set upon me,
>   with slanders devouring me,
> 'Tis they, my enemies and foes,
>   who stumble to their fall.
>
> Though an host should encamp against me,
>   my heart would have no fear;
> though war should rise against me—still
>   would I be confident.
>
> One thing alone I ask from Yahweh,
>   one thing do I desire . . . ,
> to behold the beauty of Yahweh,
>   and inquire in his palace.
>
> For he hides me in his pavilion
>   whenever trouble comes;
> he shelters me within his tent,
>   takes me up upon his rock.
>
> Then shall my head be lifted up
>   over all my foes around,
> I shall offer sacrifice of joy
>   and sing praises unto Yahweh. (27.1–6.)

The 'inquiry' mentioned in v. 4 is the ritual examination of the omina
in connexion with the festal sacrifices (see below, II.53). To 'behold
the beauty of the god' is an old cultic expression also found in Egypt,

---

[45] We shall see below in Chap. XVII 2, that in a certain sense we have to distinguish between
the author and the pray-er ('the worshipper') of the psalms.
[46] Isa. 55.3; cf. Pss. 89.20ff.; 132.11f.; 18.51.

which originally meant the corporeal vision of the unveiled statue of the god at the festivals, as the highest religious experience. In Yahwism it has become a metaphor for the more spiritual experience of the grace and benevolence of Yahweh manifested especially at the festival of his personal 'epiphany' in the Temple. The verse obviously alludes to the position of the king as the sacral leader of the festal cult; his highest desire is to hold this position with its personal relation to Yahweh also in the future.

5

We shall here draw attention to a particular feature in the description of distress, which in the nature of the case could only occur in the I-psalms, but does so both in the properly national laments and in the authentic individual laments (Chap. VIII), namely the description of the distress not only as a deadly danger but as a real *state of death*.[47] The suppliant finds himself in the underworld (Sheol, Hades), in the 'pit', the 'well':[48]

> For trouble fills my soul to the full,
>> my life draws near unto Sheol;
> I am reckoned among those who sink to the pit,
>> I am like the man who has no strength. . . .
> Thou hast laid me in the lowest pit,
>> in the darkness, in the ocean's deep;
> thy wrath lies heavy upon me
>> and all thy waves overwhelm me. (88.4f., 7f.)

The worshipper feels he is about to be submerged by 'the waters of the underworld', by its 'floods and breakers', he has sunk into the 'mire', 'the sorrows of hell compass him about; the snares of death prevent' him:[49]

> Save me, O God, for the waters have
>> come up unto my throat!
> Now I have sunk deep in the mire
>> where foothold there is none;
> I have fallen into waters deep,
>> and floods sweep over me. (69.2f.)

Nothing worse could happen, for down there Yahweh performs no more miracles, and nobody will have an opportunity there of praising him for his help;[50] if a man has really descended there, he 'shall never again see Yahweh in the land of the living'.[51] Behind this there is the probably

---

[47] Pss. 102.12, 24f.; 109.23; 22.19; 41.6, 9 (psalm of illness); 13.4; 143.7; 51.16.
[48] Ps. 88.4; cf. in the thanksgiving psalms 103.4; 107.20; Jonah 2.7; Isa. 38.10; further Pss. 28.1; 30.10; 69.16; 88.5, 7; 143.7.
[49] Pss. 42.8; 18.5; Jonah 2.4; Pss. 40.3; 69.2f.; 18.6.
[50] Pss. 115.16ff.; 28.1; cf. the psalms of illness 6.6; 30.10; 88.11ff.
[51] Isa. 38.10f.; cf. Pss. 42.8; 130.1; 143.7.

Babylonian conception of the underworld as the depth of the ocean, the primeval ocean under the earth.[52] In keeping with this the sufferer is saved from the danger of death, as Yahweh descends, cleaving the depths of the ocean, stretching out his hand, and drawing him out of the pit, the mire, the foaming waters, and setting his feet upon a rock.[53]

This does not mean that death has actually occurred in our sense of the word. 'Life' to the Israelite means a full and happy life in health and welfare, in the 'light', in the 'land of the living'; 'death' means 'darkness', including any impairment of 'life' in this wide sense.[54] From the Israelite point of view the sick person, or the man who is in danger of death and marked by fear and despair, already carries death about with him, or death has him in its jaws: his soul has left him (cf. 1 Sam. 30.12). Therefore Yahweh must pull him out before it becomes too late. For God can do such a thing, even if according to the ancient faith the realm of the dead lay outside the domain of Yahweh, so that a man who was there, had been 'plucked out of his hand' (88.6; see above, p. 237). We are here dealing with a conception which naturally can only be applied to an individual. Originally it was probably a transfer to the king of the conception of the deity's 'descent into the nether world', of the dying and rising deities of fertility and, in so far, is of foreign origin; we also come across it in Babylonian psalms.[55] It may originally have been transferred to the king as the 'representative incorporation of the people' in the rituals of penitence, and it has as its background the ritual role of the king as the dying and rising partner of the Mother Goddess (cf. above, p. 136). In Israel the conception has been taken over unaware of this original meaning.

Since the thanksgiving psalm (Chap. X) praises Yahweh for having already pulled the unfortunate person out of Sheol, it is evidently no question here of salvation into another life after death, but of deliverance from imminent danger of death into health and happiness and freedom on this earth. According to the Israelite way of thinking, sickness, weakness and dissolution mean 'death', whereas strength and health mean 'life'; 'life' is not mere existence, but full, rich, happy life in 'entirety' and 'welfare' (šālôm).[56] Neither Israel nor early Judaism knew of a faith in any resurrection, nor is such a faith represented in the psalms. Of course the almighty Yahweh *might* every now and then call a dead man back to

---

[52] See Pedersen, *Israel* I–II, pp. 453ff.; *GTMMM* I, p. 351, n. *a* to Deut. 4.18.

[53] Pss. 9.14; 40.2f.; 71.20; 144.7; and cf. the thanksgiving psalm 18.8ff.; Job 33.28; Sir. 51.2ff.

[54] See Johs. Pedersen, *Israel* I–II, pp. 151ff., 179f.; A. R. Johnson, *The Vitality of the Individual*, and *Studies in Prophecy*, ed. H. H. Rowley, pp. 82ff. See also Gierlich, *Der Lichtgedanke in den Psalmen*, a handy collection of material but lacking a sufficient consideration of the cultural background and the ancient Israelite way of thinking; Aalen, *Licht und Finsternis*, pp. 63ff., 70f.

[55] See Sellin, *Zwölfprophetenbuch*,[2] p. 295; Jeremias, *A.T. im Lichte d. A.O.*,[4] pp. 723ff.; v. Baudissin, *Adonis u. Esmun*, p. 409.

[56] Cf. Gunkel-Begrich, *Einl.*, pp. 185ff.; Wheeler Robinson in *The Psalmists*, pp. 57ff.; Birkeland in *SEÅ* XIII, 1948, pp. 43ff.; the same in *StTh* III, pp. 60ff. A. R. Johnson, *The Vitality of the Individual*, pp. 88–107.

life, or give his prophets the power of raising some one from the dead, as we hear in connexion with both Elijah and Elisha. But normally he would do no such thing, and practical religion did not take it into account. The religion of the psalms possesses every qualification for the development of a belief in resurrection, were the 'catalysing' impulse but added, but this came only as a result of the influence of Persian ideas.[57] When the psalms speak of the distressed worshipper as if he were already in the realm of the dead, *we* should call that a 'metaphor'; but to the ancients it meant something more: the concept of the permanent war between the powers of Life and Death, and the faith in the omnipotence of Yahweh, able to deliver a man, even if he was already between the jaws of death.

When a man is struck with disaster or illness, his life literally hangs in the balance. He is alive, and yet he is dead. This is but another expression for the paradoxical position in which the 'righteous one' finds himself when evil powers and impurity have 'made him unrighteous' (see above, pp. 207, 216). It is, so to speak, a matter of split seconds: Yahweh has to interfere immediately and prevent death from making the righteous man unrighteous—for such a thing would be not only logically absurd, but morally and cosmically unmaintainable as well, a break of the covenant and of the very order of the world and its laws instituted by God.

Expressions like those in Pss. 16.10; 17.15; 49.16; 73.23ff. must be understood against this background. Here also the intention is to express assurance that Yahweh will never fail his pious ones, but will save them from mortal peril and deliver them from an evil and sudden death—till they die, some time, 'old and full of days'.[58] That this firm faith deepened and broadened in later Judaism and in the light of Christianity is not our concern here. Ps. 73 shows how near even ancient Israel might approach to it: the bliss of communion with God becomes the highest value, going on beyond life and death.

6

The preceding exposé has proved that in the national psalms of lamentation, as well as in those I-laments which are actually national (congregational), we have real *historical conditions* and happenings; the needs and dangers are disasters which either have already befallen or else threaten people and king from actual, foreign enemies, partly supported by internal traitors—this is so, even if the psalms in most cases use such indefinite, general and conventional terms that we cannot now identify the historical

[57] See the short but excellent statement by Birkeland in *SEÅ* XIII, 1948, and in *StTh* III, pp. 6off. That the psalms of lamentation and thanksgiving know nothing of a faith in resurrection has also been noted by Chr. Barth, though in *Die Errettung vom Tode* he presents his thoughts in a form which is rather unscriptural and too much of the nature of subtle German philosophy, without the proper cultic perspective needed in order to understand the psalms fully (see the review by Kapelrud in *SEÅ* XIII, 1948, pp. 55ff.). De Groot, *De Psalmen*, goes much too far in finding belief in a future life in the psalms.
[58] See Additional Note XXX.

happenings and enemies to which they may refer.[58a] In no less than five 'I-psalms' the enemies are expressly called '(foreign) nations', *gôyîm, 'ammîm, zārîm*.[58b] That we meet the 'nations' as the enemies of the king when he is speaking on behalf of the whole people is only what we should expect.[58c] Other psalms of this type presuppose alien domination.[58d] The sufferer is the butt for the mockeries of the neighbouring peoples in the royal psalm, Ps. 89. 42, 46, 51, as is the whole people in the national psalms of lamentation, Pss. 44.14; 79.4, 12; 80.7. About the reality of the historico-political situation of such psalms there can be no doubt.

It may be seen from the allusions to temple and cult found in some of them[59] that these psalms too had a place in the cultic operations of the Temple, made necessary by distress or threatening danger. But in some cases the psalm was evidently supposed to be recited somewhere far away from capital and Temple, e.g. we hear of the king 'crying from the end of the earth' (61.3); in Pss. 42–43 he turns to Yahweh 'from the land of Jordan and of the Hermonite hills'; perhaps it is meant to be taken literally, when in Ps. 120 the suppliant says that he 'must sojourn as a guest (*gûr*) among archers in the tents of the tribe of Kedar'. Obviously this does not mean that the psalm in question must be a non-cultic poem by a private individual living in exile, as for instance Gunkel holds; even here the worshipper is the representative of the whole people; in Ps. 61.7, he calls himself 'the king' in plain words; in Pss. 42–43 he is looking back on all the times he used to lead the pageant up to the Temple of Yahweh. From a study of such passages we come to the conclusion that during the period of the kings any place might be consecrated as a place of sacrifice for the performance of the necessary cultic acts in wartime— and in these psalms we are dealing with warfare (1 Sam. 14.33f.)—just as the Assyrian kings used to take a transportable altar along with them when making war. That such cultic acts were performed and psalms recited on the battlefield even in late Jewish times may be concluded from one of the Dead Sea Scrolls (IQM), where certain rituals and hymns for cultic field services are found. Certainly the book speaks about the last, eschatological, battle against the Sons of Darkness,[60] but as these are to be found in the historical people, the Kittim, the cultic scenes, too, may have been modelled after the pattern of real customs and rituals, as e.g., those in the wars of the Maccabees.

Quite lately, however, a theory has sprung up, to the effect that in the royal psalms of lamentation we do not have real dangers and sufferings,

[58a] See above, pp. 196f., 226f. with references to Birkeland.

[58b] Pss. 9.9, 18, 20; 10.16; 43.1; 54.5; 56.8 (cf. v. 2); 59.9. Duhm's conjecture: *gē'îm* for *gôyîm* is absolutely groundless; see *i.a.* Birkeland, *The Evildoers*, pp. 12ff.

[58c] See Pss. 18.44f., 48; cf. v. 28 (thanksgiving psalm); 20.8f.; 21.9ff.; 89.51; 144.2, 7, 10.

[58d] E.g. Pss. 12; 14; 58; perhaps 83.

[59] Ps. 20.3f., 7 (the allusion to the oracle of reply); 63.3; 54.8; 3.6 (the incubation); 27.4, 8b–11 (the prayer for an oracle); 27.14 (the promise of the cultic servant). See below, II.20 and references there.

[60] See M. Burrows, *The Dead Sea Scrolls*, pp. 208ff.; Ginsburg in *BASOR* 112, 1948, pp. 19ff.

which have befallen the king; and that the king is not here really suffering, but only 'suffering in the cult', that is to say he is taking part in a cultic 'play' or drama, where he suffers, only to be later exalted. This view is a corollary of the theory mentioned above, that even in Israel the deity was presented in the cult as dying and rising again, and that in the cultic drama the king would play the part of the god, and die and rise along with him; such a performance could also be looked upon as the king's vicarious suffering and death on behalf of the people.[61] This interpretation, it is said, must be applied to the I-psalms discussed in this chapter, as well as to the 'psalms of illness' to be discussed in the next. It is maintained that we have here the adoption of a common Babylonian-Assyrian-Canaanite 'cultic pattern', even if in Israel it has become more or less 'disintegrated' and has therefore partly lost its original meaning.[62]

Accordingly, the 'enemies' of the laments could not be historical and human enemies, but only the mythical and demonic powers of chaos and death, attacking the god-king and defeating him. And the 'metaphor' of the lament, telling of the descent of the distressed one into the nether world and of his sojourn in Sheol, could not be intended to express an actual tangible state of distress and danger, but was to be understood 'literally'—admittedly in a mythical sense—as something experienced in the mythical and cultic 'drama', and so the same kind of 'distress' as is found behind Yahweh's 'appearance' in the enthronement psalms.

We have seen above that the assumption on which this theory was based, does not hold good. In Israel, that is to say in the legitimate Israelite cult of Jerusalem with which we have to deal, Yahweh was never conceived as dying and rising again, so the basis for any ritual, any cultic drama, presenting the king as one who suffers and dies in a cultic and mythical sense, fails. Nor is it very likely that in Israel the king would have appeared in the guise of Yahweh, however much his person may have been deified; the difference between Yahweh and a human being, however great, was too strongly felt for that (see Chap. III.3).

In spite of the central part played by the king in the cult, of which many instances have been given above,[63] the texts do not afford a single clear instance of his taking Yahweh's place in the cult. Even Ps. 110, in which the king receives the seat of honour on the right hand of Yahweh distinguishes clearly between Yahweh and the king. If in the cult the king had actually been made God, it would be most strange that, for instance, Ezekiel, who makes so many accusations against the kings of Judah (Ezk. 17; 19; 34) should not also have accused the king of making himself God; but the worst sacrilege of which Ezekiel can find the kings guilty is their having placed their graves close to the Temple, thus defiling the house of Yahweh (Ezk. 43.7ff.).

[61] See Chap. III, esp. pp. 66ff., and Additional Note XXXI.
[62] See n. 95 to Chap. V, and Additional Note XXXI.
[63] See Chap. III. 3; V. 3, 9; VII. 1–2.

Of course there is some truth in saying that the very picturing of the sufferer as descending into the nether world and sojourning in Sheol, must after all, at any rate partly, be derived from the common oriental, especially Sumerian and Babylonian concepts and myths about the god of vegetation descending thither (see above, p. 75). But to say that one who suffers and is threatened by death 'carries death around with him' and is already 'between the jaws of death', is to use expressions that might be applied to anybody in those circumstances. There is nothing here which is characteristic only of the god of vegetation or of the king taking part in the cult; death and danger of death remain the same thing, whosoever is struck or threatened by them. So there is nothing remarkable about the fact that the condition of the one who is threatened by death is described by means of the same metaphors, whether he be the dying god of vegetation, or a king in the tumult of battle, or any sick person. On the other hand, however, it is but natural that there should be a piling up of drastic descriptions in the myth which describes how the god of life must descend into the domain of death. But then it should also be easy to understand that the authors of the psalms of lamentation, wanting to rouse the compassion of Yahweh by making the distress appear as great and cruel as possible, would preferentially resort to known metaphors from the myth of the descent into the nether world, since this style of writing, like so many others, would spread and be adopted by Hebrew psalmography, that of Canaan possibly acting as the connecting link.[64] Therefore when these descriptions occur in laments and thanksgiving psalms they can never be used to prove the 'cultic descent into the nether world' of the king of Israel.

Another possibility is that parts of old oriental rituals concerned with the sufferings of the king have been taken over by Israel and re-expounded as the vicarious expiatory punishment of the king for the sins of the people. In Babylonia it was part of the festal ritual of new year, that the king was stripped of his regalia and arrayed in penitential clothes and treated by the priest with humiliating rites, such as boxing his ears or striking his cheeks.[65] In itself this rite has probably nothing to do with his sufferings as the representative of the gods, but is an expiatory ceremony on behalf of the whole community before the renewed enthronement of the king at every new year festival. Something like this might have been the case even in Jerusalem; only we have nothing to prove it, and in the royal laments nothing can be found to show that they refer to such sufferings.

On the other hand there are plenty of passages showing that they do speak of real human and historical enemies and real actual sufferings. In the plainly national laments, the 'we-laments', the background of human history is generally quite clear.[66] But even in many of the I-laments,

---

[64] See above, V. 7.
[65] See, for instance, L. Dürr, *Ursprung u. Ausbau*, pp. 135ff.
[66] See above, Chap. VI. 1–2, 3, 4.

the royal laments, the historical and human background is also quite evident. On the whole the enemies are described, as we have seen, in the same terms and metaphors as in the obviously national psalms. The enemies and antagonists of the king and of the leader of the people are 'nations' and no demonic beings;[67] in Ps. 118.6 we are told in plain words that they are 'men'. The sojourn of the suffering person in the realm of the dead, as we have seen, is neither a mythical nor a cultic reality, but a mode of picturing illness and danger of death (Chap. VII.5).

If the king in the laments were to represent the suffering and dying deity, how could he then possibly call to Yahweh for deliverance from the 'realm of the dead', and for help against his enemies? The Jerusalem cult did not allow any other cultic gods within the scope of Yahweh's festival— although at times other gods were worshipped in the Temple of Yahweh. And how could the king in such a case count on the possibility of human help—as he does for instance in Ps. 116.11[68]—if his sufferings were of a mythical cultic character? If we are dealing with a mythical cultic play, how then can the king complain of the enemies that they 'have broken down all his walls, and laid his fortresses in ruins': and how can it be that the 'wayfarers' 'plunder him' and his 'neighbours' 'sneer at him', if his suffering merely means that he has been put in Sheol in the mythical struggle against demons?[69] That here we have quite matter of fact human beings in historical political conditions must be obvious on any sober-minded and unprejudiced interpretation.

Another hypothesis, more in keeping with the essence of Yahwism, has been put forward regarding the king's playing the part of Yahweh.[70] A varying number of royal laments are interpreted as evidence that the king is there acting on behalf of Yahweh in the cultic drama—the 'sham fight' of the cult—presenting Yahweh's struggle and victory over the powers of evil; then the lamentation and the description of the distress refer to the troubles of the king in this drama, until by the aid of Yahweh he defeats all evil powers and in particular wins the victory over all the other nations who are supposed in the cultic drama to attack Jerusalem and Yahweh's anointed. According to this theory we would here have a cultic presentation of the 'myth about the fight of nations', where the king does not act as Yahweh himself, but as Yahweh's representative, his 'son'. That such

[67] It is particularly Birkeland, *Feinde d. Indiv.*, and *Evil-doers in the Pss.*, who has seen and proved this, and so corrected the great one-sidedness from which my statement in *Ps.St.* I was suffering; cf. my discourse as opposer to Birkeland *NTT* 134, pp. 1ff., and above, n. 19 to Chap. VI.

[68] This psalm—which by the way is no 'passion psalm' but a thanksgiving psalm—Engnell (*Div. Kingship*, p. 210, n. 2) would interpret as dealing with 'the king suffering in the cult'. The way Engnell apportions the text to the king (vv. 1-4, 6-14) and the chorus (vv. 5 and 15) conflicts with the obvious stanza division, which shows that v. 5 is closely connected with v. 6, and v. 15 with v. 16. In Ps. 118 we also meet with enemies obviously human, but Johnson (in *The Labyrinth*) would refer this psalm to the apparent sufferings of the king in the cult; see Additional Note XXXI.

[69] Ps. 89.41f. This psalm, too, is interpreted by Johnson (*The Labyrinth*) as referring to the apparent suffering in the cult. See Additional Note XXXI.

[70] This more modest and sympathetic version of the theory of the king as the sufferer in the psalms is represented by Johnson in *The Labyrinth*. See, however, Additional Note XXXI.

a dramatic presentation of the defeat of all the nations outside Jerusalem actually had a place in the old Israelite enthronement festival cult seems fairly certain; Pss. 46 and 48 testify to such a 'ritual sham fight'. We do not know, however, that this ritual fight was presented in the more or less realistic manner found in Egypt and Babylonia; in all probability it was presented by means of symbolic rites, the intrinsic merit of which went far beyond anything the eye could see. Nor is there anything to indicate that in Israel this cultic fight should have been looked upon and presented as a suffering on the part of the king, much less as his cultic death and sojourn in the realm of the dead, and that these laments must be read as the texts for such a cultic drama.

So there is no reason for us to give up the natural interpretation of the sufferings mentioned in the royal laments as real, historical troubles, brought about by actual (as a rule) political, conditions, in which the king is threatened either by hostile neighbouring nations or by a punitive expedition on the part of his foreign lord; some times it may be a genuine case of illness.

7

That a great many psalms of lamentation in the I-form are actually national laments, in which the king or the leader of the people is speaking on behalf of the whole community is confirmed by the fact that this is the undoubted rule in the *Babylonian-Assyrian laments*.[71] There the use of 'we' to indicate the worshipper does not seem to occur,[72] it is everywhere the 'I' of the king who speaks; the psalms are 'royal laments',[73] and very often on a national and political subject.

This point of resemblance is so much the more significant because of the close relationship between the biblical laments and the much older Babylonian-Assyrian laments, in both style and substance (see Chap. XX.3). Therefore the interpretation of the I-laments, which agrees with the use of this style of writing in Babylonian-Assyrian poetry, is likely to be correct: very often in the biblical laments also we do not have the troubles of private individuals, but public distress, with the king as the spokesman of the congregation.

[71] See Birkeland, *Feinde d. Indiv.*, pp. 350–379.
[72] Gunkel-Begrich, *Einl.*, p. 123.
[73] Cf. Gunkel-Begrich, *Einl.*, pp. 124, 127, 128, 129, 132; Jastrow, *Relig. Bab. u. Assyr.* II, pp. 1ff.

THE PSALMS IN
ISRAEL'S WORSHIP

SIGMUND MOWINCKEL

THE PSALMS
IN ISRAEL'S
WORSHIP

Translated by

D. R. AP-THOMAS

*Lecturer in Hebrew & Old Testament,
University College of North Wales
Bangor*

In Two Volumes — Volume II

ABINGDON PRESS

new york · nashville

1967

First printed 1962
Reprinted   1967

PRINTED IN GREAT BRITAIN

CONTENTS

Volume II

The original source of cultic psalm poetry everywhere to be
sought among the cultic personnel, 85—What of the
(greater part of the) extant psalms of Israel and Judah?
85—'The pious', 'the righteous', 'the needy', in the psalms,
86—Were there private pietistic groups in Judaism? 86—
Private psalm singing, 88—The psalms in the synagogue, 88

The temple singers not priests, 90—The psalmists' social
standing, 91—The relationship of singers and psalms to the
temple prophets, 92—The singers as tradents of the psalm
tradition, 94

The titles, 95—Asaph, 96—Heman and Ethan, 96—The sons
of Korah, 97—The historical kernel, 97

The original meaning of the note, 98—The older interpretation on the basis of 'learned' interest, 99—The situations adduced in the titles, 100

CHAPTER VIII

Personal (Private) Psalms of Lamentation

I

The preceding chapter has proved that there exist a great many psalms of lamentation, apparently by, or on behalf of, an individual, which are actually national psalms, general or congregational laments put into the mouth of the king or the leader of the people. The distress is of a historical, national nature, and has befallen the whole community; even where it endangers the personal position of the king (Chap. VII. 3), as for instance in the psalms dealing with false accusations, it is still of such a nature that it will involve consequences for the whole people. Calling these psalms 'individual laments' would be a mis-statement putting the main emphasis on stylistic criteria instead of on actual substance.

The question then arises whether there are true individual laments, that is, *personal (private) laments* in the sense of psalms concerned with the personal, so to speak private state of distress of an individual, and not with general disasters and dangers involving the whole people or the congregation.

Of course by an 'individual' we do not here mean some historical individual whose name would be known to us if we could but get hold of the old 'registers'. Even here the matter has to be considered in the light of the cultic origin and use of the psalms. Here—as in the psalms used by us for instance in connexion with baptisms or wedding ceremonies or burials—we have to do with the individual in general, with 'Everyman', i.e. any individual, high or low, in such a condition that he would need or want to submit to such cultic and ritual acts as his condition might require, including the recitation of a psalm.

Such true individual psalms of lamentation do exist.[1]

2

Among the I-laments there are some at any rate in which the distress in question is *illness*; so for instance in all probability Pss. 6; 30, a thanks-

---

[1] Engnell (*Div. Kingship*, p. 176; *Gamla Test.*, p. 60 ,n. 2) seems to think that the heading *lĕdhāwīdh* 'for David' in the traditional text is a *proof* in each case that the psalm in question belongs to a cultic ritual, in which the king is the leading person; this proof has also been accepted by Riesenfeld, *Resurrect. in Ezek. XXXVIII*, p. 8, n. 2; the said psalm would then belong to the 'national' psalms in the I-form (Chap. VII). This is out of the question, when we consider that in many cases this heading can be proved to have been added in the course of written tradition and as a result of the 'learned' theory that all psalms without any other heading were composed by David; see *Ps.St.* VI, pp. 73ff.; 82ff., and below, n. 52 to Chap. XV.

giving psalm; 32, likewise; 38; 39; 41; 88; possibly also others, such as 28; 22, etc.[2]

Israel came more and more to consider illness as directly caused by Yahweh. Leprosy, especially, was something with which Yahweh would 'smite' a man.[3] Yahweh himself had smitten the firstborn of the Egyptians with plague (Ex. 11.4f.). The reason was that his wrath had been aroused by some sin or other (cf. Gen. 20.17ff.), whether conscious or unconscious. But illness might also be a warning to prevent some sin, or a trial to see if a pious man would measure up to the mark, as in the case of Job. The religious development of Israel tended to refer whatever happened, good as well as evil, to Yahweh (Am. 3.6).

Behind the conception of illness as being *punishment* for sin we find an earlier conception, which looked upon illness—in common with all other disasters—as a direct *outcome* of 'sinfulness'; the disaster was the immanent 'fruit' of sin, its organic and inevitable consequence. Sin was due to an 'unrighteous', 'wrong' ('crooked') soul, and to Israel this would mean a soul without the power (and the will) either to do what was right or to succeed; such a soul was doomed to ruin, its immanent sinfulness would result in disasters not the least of which was illness. This conception is brought out for instance by the speeches of the friends of Job, which are firmly based on this fundamental idea.

But there are also other explanations of illness, just as old. It might be due to supernatural beings, demons or evil spirits, considered partly to be the instruments of Yahweh, partly to be acting of their own accord. Epidemics were due to such an 'angel' (Ps. 78.49; 2 Sam. 24.16; 2 Kgs. 19.35). Another tradition about the firstborn of the Egyptians speaks of the 'Destroyer', going about at night and forcing his way into the houses, except where the door posts were marked with the blood of the passover (Ex. 12.23). 'The Persecutor' (Satan) can smite a man with illness, as we hear of Job (2.7). Demons of death and illness might rise from Sheol and persecute their victims, one of them is called 'the firstborn of death' Job 18.13); other 'terrific beings' ('êmîm) may be sent by Yahweh, too; they live 'in the darkness', in the underworld, where Death reigns as the 'king of terrors'.[4]

But illness may also be due to the 'might' and supernatural 'power'— evil or good—of particular individuals. Just as by means of his immanent

[2] Gunkel considered most of the I-psalms of lament to be psalms of illness, and this view was still more strictly carried through in my *Ps.St.* I. Bentzen ([*D*]*TT*, 1928, pp. 202f.) and Linder (*Kristend. o. vår tid*, 1928, p. 51) have expressed their hesitation. The matter is in a different position after Birkeland's *Feinde d. Indiv.*, as will be seen from the preceding chapter. Birkeland however, goes a little too far in the opposite direction, see *NTT*, 1934, pp. 22ff. See n. 67 to Chap. VII.

[3] Ex. 4.6; Num. 12.9f.; Job 1.11. Cf. 'stroke ("plague") of leprosy', Lev. 13.2f., 9, 20, 25, 27 *et al.*

[4] Lev. 26.16; Ex. 23.27; Deut. 28.22; Hos. 13.14; Job 9.34; 15.20ff.; 18.11; 13.21; 20.25; 33.7; 27.20; 30.15; 33.22; 24.17; 18.14. Cf. Duhm, *Die bösen Geister;* Jirku, *Die Dämonen u. i. Abwehr;* Widengren, *Psalms of Lamentation*, pp. 200ff.; Langton, *Essentials of Demonology*, illustrating the matter by a great many analogies from Arabia, Mesopotamia and Persia.

power and potent words the prophet was supposed to be able to bring on leprosy and other evils (2 Kgs. 5.27), and a priest smite an unfaithful wife with some deadly illness by means of a potent draught with its accompanying curse (Num. 5.21ff.; cf. Ex. 32.20), so there existed also other less legitimate operators, especially women, versed in magic and acting as soothsayers, who were supposed to be able to bring some evil on people, or to cure them of it (Ezk. 13.17ff.). And just as the legitimate representatives of religion might use the potent curse against the enemies of society or other culprits (2 Sam. 3.29; Lev. 5.1; Jdg. 17.1; Ps. 109.17ff.), so there were malicious people, who would use the curse and the 'power of disaster' (Pss. 10.7; 39.13; 37.22; 62.5; Job 31.30) against decent folk.[5] Among such curses were counted all sorts of evil words, calumnies, abusive terms, threatenings, bad wishes, the cultic words of other religions. Together with the potent ceremonies and manipulations, by which they were usually accompanied (Ezk. 13.18, 20; Zech. 5.3), they were all implied in the term 'āwen,[6] 'sorcery'. We need not imagine a special 'class' of 'sorcerers' and 'witches';[7] as in Christendom some centuries ago, there would always be here and there someone who would go in for such things and get paid for them, as for instance among gypsies and such like;[8] but probably still more people were suspected or accused of it, because for some reason or other they were different from others, for instance such poor wretches as were full of complexes and bitterness on account of bodily or mental shortcomings, and had therefore fallen out with their surroundings. 'The evil word', 'the evil eye' and other 'damaging acts' (dibhērê bĕliyya'al) and 'acts of 'āwen' might, in fact, be used by any person against another; the popular mind looked upon the evil word and the evil eye as in themselves potent agents of disaster.

These rather primitive explanations of disaster were adapted to the Yahweh religion by such devices as that Yahweh permitted evil spirits and other men to torment a pious person, as in the case of Job, either in order to try him or to warn him (1.5), or to call his attention to a sin he had committed unwillingly or unknowingly or without paying sufficient attention to it (Job 33.16, 19ff.). Or, on account of some sin, Yahweh might withdraw his protection from the person in question, 'hiding his face from him' (Ps. 30.8), so that evil powers had a chance of stealing upon him. Or Yahweh might simply in his wrath send the evil powers to him as a punishment (1 Sam. 16.14).

As illness was attributed to such 'cursing words' or 'damaging things'

---

[5] Mowinckel in *NTT* 10, 1909, pp. 335ff.; Hölscher, *Die Profeten*, pp. 79, 89ff., 154ff.; Pedersen, *Israel* I–II, pp. 441ff.

[6] See Chap. VI.3, and Additional Note XXVII about the fundamental sense of 'āwen. The *parti pris* objections of Aubert based on the 'distinctive character of the religion of Israel' ('Les Psaumes dans le culte d'Israel', *RThPh* N.S. 15, 1927, pp. 224f.) cannot demolish the concrete evidence for this sense of the word.

[7] This much against Hempel's objections to the interpretation of the 'enemies' in (some of) the psalms as 'sorcerers', *ZDMG* 79, 1925, p. 84 n. 2.

[8] Ex. 22.17; Deut. 18.10; Mal. 3.5; Ezk. 13.19. Cf. Job 30.2–8.

and bound up with some sinfulness, or directly due to sin, it also implied impurity, which called for purification by all sorts of ritual means. Impurity was considered to be dangerous, contagious—not in the modern sense, but in line with the more 'materialistic' view of the ancients, who looked upon sin and unluckiness as something which would be transferred through contact and similar ways. Therefore people would keep away from a sick person, and protect themselves against impurity and danger by means of potent anti-curses, scoffing, and the like. The sick person—like everyone struck by disaster—was considered to be a secret sinner, whom God had unmasked, and over whom his enemies would therefore triumph, whereas his former friends would turn their backs on him.

3

The treatment for such illness would be in accordance with the way of looking at it. Ordinarily only wounds and cuts and ailments with an obviously 'natural' cause would be treated by what we should call natural, even though primitive, medical means, such as squeezing out the matter, bandaging, oils, balsam, plaster, or poultice.[9] And even then religious and cultic measures would probably be resorted to, especially if the illness proved persistent. This simply results from the fact that the view of illness and healing was based on the 'magical' conception of the 'forces' of life and nature, and the 'magical' connexion between all things.[10] This view applied to the sphere of religion, and was brought into relationship with the deity.[11]

If possible the sick person would go up to the Temple, or his relative would do so for him (1 Kgs. 8.37; 2 Sam. 12.16ff.). He would fast, put on sackcloth and cover himself with ashes, and fall prostrate on the ground, and perform all the usual penitential rites (Chap. VI.1), he would pray and vow to bring an offering of thanksgiving (Sir. 38.11). We can see from the law in Lev. 5 that a person, 'bearing his inquity' (Moffat: 'his disaster'), i.e., his punishment, such as illness, would also bring a sin offering, or, more correctly, a sacrifice of cleansing (Lev. 4), or an atoning or trespass offering.

These ceremonies also included purification from the uncleanness caused by the sin and breaking out as illness. In the psalms there are sometimes references to such purification by means of holy water, hyssop, oil, blood, burning, and so on.[12] There is every reason to believe that

---

[9] 2 Kgs. 8.29; 9.14f.; Isa. 1.6; 3.7; Jer. 8.22; 46.11; 2 Kgs. 20.7. See Bertholet, *Kulturgeschichte*, pp. 218ff.; Schürer, *Geschichte* III,³ pp. 294ff. (E.T. II, iii, 151ff.); Miller, *Encyclop. of Bibl. Life*, pp. 334ff. In Egypt: Erman-Ranke, *Aegypten*,² pp. 408ff.; in Babylonia: Meissner, *Babylonien u. Assyrien*, II, pp. 283ff.
[10] See Mowinckel, *Religion und Kultus*, pp. 13ff.
[11] Therefore present-day scholars ought to talk a little less about 'magic' and 'sorcery' in these matters.
[12] Pss. 26.6; 73.13; cf. Deut. 21.4, 6; Ps. 51.9; Isa. 6.6f.

the ceremonial for purification after 'leprosy' (Lev. 14) was originally meant to be an efficacious 'sacramental' purification from the illness itself and the uncleanness which underlay it.[13]

Prayer, too, had its place alongside the offerings and cleansings. The sick person—or somebody else in his place—would pray to Yahweh for healing, confess his sinfulness, or call to mind his pious works. He would call on the compassion of Yahweh, and ask him to withdraw his sentence of death, or neutralize the curses of evil men through his blessing.[14]

Like the psalms of lamentation in general these prayers were real prayers, appealing to a personal, almighty God on the basis of personal faith that he, and he alone, would be able to help. Of course it is impossible to tell with any certainty to what extent the 'pre-logical' conceptions of the self-acting ('magical') power of the rituals survived in popular faith and below the surface of the mind. But as far as the psalmists are concerned we may take for granted that they put the main emphasis on prayer and the personal help of God, and to some extent at any rate looked upon the rites either as sacramental, atoning measures instituted by the deity, or as symbolical expressions of prayer and of the mental disposition of which the prayer was an outcome; this may be inferred from the fact that the psalms so seldom refer to the accompanying rites and ceremonies.

In later times, after the development of a more secular medical art, the sick person would of course not infrequently turn to the physician; but the old ritual treatment remained predominant. Ben Sira sums up what ought to be done in the following three items: pray to the Lord for healing and cease from such sins as may have given cause to the illness; bring offerings of admonition and fat offerings; and then finally: 'send for the physician, for he, too, has been created by the Lord ... and there are cases in which the physician succeeds for he, too, can pray to God to make his diagnosis correct, and the treatment promote recovery' (Sir. 38.9–14).

4

In one section of the individual psalms of lamentation, namely the above mentioned *psalms of illness*, and perhaps others, we have prayers to be used at the cleansings from illness and at sin-offerings and atoning offerings.

We know with certainty that thanksgiving psalms were offered up after the healing of an illness; this we shall discuss in more detail in a later

---

[13] For the view on illness and healing see Lods in *Martifestschrift*, pp. 181ff., Stendahl in *SEÅ* XV, 1950, pp. 5ff. Against the above evidence from the sources, and the evidence in *Ps.St.* I and in Lods, the assertions of Aubert (op. cit., pp. 15f.) that the laws do not explicitly mention illness among the cases in which ritual cleansing and offering should be used, are of no consequence whatever. Moreover, he is not correct; the laws do mention leprosy, and the term 'bear his iniquity', *nāsā' 'awōnô* covers illness too.

[14] For these separate points see: 2 Sam. 12.16; Job 42.8f.—Job 5.8ff.; 8.5ff.; 11.13ff.; 42.8f.; Ps. 107.19, *et al.*—2 Kgs. 20.3.—2 Kgs. 20.1–3.—Ps. 109.22–24, 28.

chapter. But in these others we find references to laments also, uttered during the illness,[15] i.e. in connexion with the other ritual acts.

In Job 33.19ff. we are expressly told that a man overtaken by illness, on performing the cultic acts that belonged to the ritual of cleansing, also 'prays to God' (v. 26). When Elihu here mentions the thanksgiving psalm that the worshipper offers after his restoration to health (v. 29f.), there seems to be no reason to doubt that the ritual prayer at the sacrifice of the sin-offering also took the form of a psalm, i.e. a psalm of lamentation, with allusions to the illness. And when we now find that we have such psalms, with such allusions, there can be no reason against interpreting the above mentioned psalms as belonging to the ritual of cultic healing, and concerned with the distress of a private individual—such as illness must be.[15a]

An important point in these psalms of illness is, what was the connexion between the illness and 'the enemies'?

When several of them complain of *enemies* and illness, we have grounds for supposing that the enemies may be those evil men whom the worshipper, in conformity with the prevailing belief, would accuse of having brought about the illness. Ps. 41 gives a good picture of the way the case was imagined. The sick person suspects the friends, dropping in to see him, of just coming in order to increase his illness and make it fatal (v. 6); they have 'damaging words ('lying words') in their hearts' and 'devise evil things against him'; they find that a 'damaging thing' or a 'damaging word' 'has been poured into him', and sit there 'whispering curses' against him; they 'collect (words of) '*āwen* and go out and recite them'. By these 'words of '*āwen*' and 'lying words' the worshipper may mean their spiteful way of ascertaining that he shall never get up again, but must die (v. 9); such words were in themselves considered to be an efficacious curse, increasing illness and danger of death; but he may also be thinking of other potent and still more direct 'cursing words'. Be this as it may; if he thinks that the illness may be increased and made fatal by such means, this very fact obviously suggests what he imagines to be the origin of it: 'An enemy hath done this' (cf. Matth. 13.28) by means of evil curses and words and arts of '*āwen*. There are occasional allusions to such magic arts, often in metaphors: e.g., making grimaces and pointing fingers at a person, using cords and knots and hoods, blowing and whistling.[16]

In Ps. 6 the certainty of being heard, i.e. of being healed, takes the form of triumphantly asking the '*āwen*-doers, 'mine enemies', to decamp, threatening them with destruction; this strongly suggests that a causative relationship was supposed to exist between enemies and illness; which means that the enemies had brought about the illness, even if maybe it was the sin of the worshipper that enabled them to 'get at' him, so that

---

[15] Pss. 30.9–11; 41.5ff.; Isa. 38.10–14; Ps. 107.19.
[15a] See Additional Note XXXII.
[16] Prov. 6.12ff.; 10.10, (29); Pss. 10.5; 12.6; 27.12; 31.7; Jonah 2.9; Isa. 32.7; 58.9; Ezk. 13.18.

the illness is also looked upon as the chastisement of Yahweh and an outcome of his wrath (v. 2). The same is the case in Ps. 28; the prayer for help, i.e. healing, takes the form of a prayer for the punishment of the false 'evil-doers' and 'āwen-doers who have given pain to the worshipper (vv. 3-5). In Ps. 38 Yahweh's wrath is the underlying cause of the illness, that is to say, his wrath at some sin committed by the worshipper. But the illness is also looked upon as something brought about by those who are seeking an occasion against him and who 'whisper deceitful words and speak mischievous things' against him all the day long (v. 13).

This sense of 'āwen—the operative, evil power, pregnant with disaster, and everything connected with it—and of 'āwen-doers as people who by means of potent curses and other words and magic have brought upon a person impurity, weakness, illness or some other disaster, is probably the original one.[17] But these words are also used, as we have mentioned above (Chap. VI.3) in a wider sense, to express all sorts of disaster brought about by unrighteous and false means, and about those who occasion such 'devilry'; therefore, they may also be used of external enemies. Consequently the words involve a religious and moral judgment on the character and nature of such people and such deeds: they are just as evil and pernicious and sinful and deceitful and hateful to God as 'sorcery' and 'witchcraft'.

These enemies, by whom the illness has been caused, need not always be known to the worshipper. If he is a man in high position, he will always have enemies, known and unknown; and any one of them may be imagined to have used effective cursing words or some other 'deceit' against him, or to have had a 'man of tongues'—one able to utter a powerful word—to do it for them.

Considering what was said above (§2, II.1f.) we would expect to find also allusions to demons as 'enemies' and producers of illness. However, these seem to be rather exceptional in the psalms of lamentation,[18] even though the psalmists no doubt very well know of the belief in demons, and allow for it. Thus we hear of 'the Pestilence going about at night' and of 'the Plague' and of 'the Demon of midday', of 'the Night-terror' and 'the Flying Arrow'; suffering and sick people would fancy themselves persecuted by unknown 'murderers' (mĕmîthîm) and 'slayers' (nēkhîm), such as bring upon people 'plague' (nega', literally 'stroke') and other sorts of evil. It also happens that the worshipper in the laments describes his national or personal enemies in terms also used to denote demons, thus characterizing them as 'devilish' beings, in alliance with evil powers. The enemies are 'lions vomiting out fire, and devouring people'; they are described as wild bulls and dogs and lions—the typical animal form in which Babylonian demons appear. The worshipper calls them 'the killers',

[17] *Ps.St.* I. See above, n. 19 to Chap. VI.
[18] Cf. *Ps.St.* I, pp. 67ff., in which too positive conclusions have been drawn from the references to the demons. The same thing must be said of Nicolsky, *Spuren magischer Formeln*, pp. 17ff.

the same word which is used to indicate the demonic 'murdering angels'.[19] On the whole the line between demons and sorcerers was rather vague in those days. The gods of hostile nations were often considered demons, and their cultic rites 'sorcery' and 'devilry'. Were the enemies to mobilize the operative cursing word against Israel, the latter would imagine that they were engaging all evil powers and crafts against them. And the sick person would think likewise about the enemies who had caused his illness, whether they were thought of as working directly by evil plots, which have so exhausted him as to make him ill, or by secret magic.[19a]

5

Granted that the psalms of illness do complain of enemies who have caused the illness, calling them "āwen-men' or the like, it is of course possible that other psalms also, which do not directly mention the nature of the distress, but do speak of such enemies, may be actually referring to illness. For instance it is just possible that several of the psalms, in which the distress is described as a sojourn in the realm of the dead (Chap. VII.5), are actually meant to be psalms of illness. A sick person feels that he is in the jaws and power of death even more than, for instance, somebody who is threatened by danger of war: see the thanksgiving psalm of king Hezekiah after his recovery from illness in Isa. 38.9ff.

Not infrequently it is quite impossible to decide with any certainty in any specific case, the reason being that the psalms of illness, like other laments, even the national ones against external enemies, were intended for use in the cult, that is: would have to be used over and over again on similar occasions, and by anybody in the position of having to submit to a ritual of fasting and penance with the psalm-singing pertaining thereto. So these psalms have to use sufficiently general wording to be suitable on many similar occasions. They use typical, often set phrases, the actual background of which it is not always easy to discover, for instance, a 'metaphor' such as the descent into Sheol by the person in distress.

6

Several factors indicate that the psalms of illness were originally composed for the use of the *king*. Naturally the illness of the king would be a matter of concern to the whole country. In Ps. 28.8 that is stated in plain words; and if Ps. 22 is a psalm of illness, here too the one who prays is in all probability thought of as a king. In Isa. 38.9ff. we have a thanksgiving psalm after illness which, at least according to tradition, was composed for (by) king Hezekiah, and was certainly used by him.[19b] In later times

[19] Pss. 91.5; 35.15; 57.5; 22.13f., 17; 17.14; Job 33.22. 'The killers' (*mĕmîthîm*) is used of the demons in Akkad. also: *musmitûti*.
    [19a] See Additional Note XXXII.
    [19b] An excellent reconstruction and interpretation of the corrupt text of this psalm has been given by Begrich in *Der Psalm des Hiskia*, on the basis of form criticism. As to the cultic use of the psalm, cf. Mowinckel in *GTMMM* III, pp. 182f.; de Boer in *OTS* IX, pp. 170ff.

similar psalms were used even for the nobles of the royal court, and finally for common people, as can be seen from the heading of Ps. 102.1, even if this actual psalm was originally meant to be spoken by the leader of the whole congregation, praying for the salvation of the whole people (see above, p. 227).

7

On the whole, the structure and the elements of the psalms of illness are the same as those of the other psalms of lamentation in the I-form.[20]

They start with the invocation of Yahweh's name, with or without any emphasizing epithet, such as 'my God', 'my mountain', sometimes even explicitly stating: 'I call to you'.[21] In a single instance (Ps. 41) the lament starts with an introductory hymn which commences by calling the man blessed who shall obtain the favour of God by charity, and goes on to give a description of the merciful help received in return from God in the distress and illness. Here the invocation does not occur until the worshipper is clearly starting on the lament itself (Ps. 41.5). The proper formal introduction is lacking in Ps. 39, where the poet starts with a 'motivation of desert': as the ground for being heard he emphasizes the meritoriousness of his having remained silent, not 'sinning with his tongue', in spite of illness and pain.

The most prominent element, the *lament*, consists of the references to the *illness*,[22] and not least so to its mental aspects.[23] One such typical lament about illness is the following:

> My wounds are foul and festering,
>   thanks to my sinful folly. . . .
> My loins are filled with loathsome pains,
>   there is no soundness in my body;
> I am benumbed and badly bruised,
>   my moans are louder than a lion's roar. . . .
> My heart is throbbing, my strength has left me,
>   and light has gone from mine eyes. (Ps. 38.6, 8, 9, 11.)

The term 'thy terrors' in Ps. 88.17 refers to the *demons of illness*, serving as Yahweh's instruments of punishment (vid. above). More often the

---

[20] Cf. Gunkel-Begrich, *Einl.*, pp. 212ff. In his interpretation of these psalms in *Einl.* ¶ 6 Begrich makes the mistake of not distinguishing between the truly individual psalms and those psalms in which the 'I' is an exponent on behalf of the people, and the distress is of a national and political nature. He looks on all these psalms as psalms of illness, but supposes them to have been composed as private poetry in the conventicle, without any relationship to the cult. Begrich has not quite grasped what effect the ancient Israelites ascribed to the evil word and the evil wish; his interpretation is often too rationalistic and modern. That is why his critique of the one-sidedness of *Ps.St.* I is not very much to the point, see Additional Note XXVIII.

[21] Pss. 6.2; 28.1; 30.9, 11; 38.2; 39.5, 13; 41.5; 88.2.—Pss. 28.1; 88.2.—Pss. 88.3, 10, 14.

[22] Pss. 6.3f.; 28.7; 38.4, 6, 8, 11f., 18; 39.3, 11; 41.4–9; 88.9b, 16f.; (22.15, 16a, 18); cf. 30.3, 7; 32.8f.; Isa. 38.13, 16 (thanksgiving psalms in which a psalm of lamentation is quoted), see below, Chap. X.2.

[23] Pss. 6.4, 8; 39.4; 38.11; Isa. 38.15.

worshipper complains of the evil *enemies*[24] who have caused the illness through their fatal witchcraft, or increased it by evil wishes; their *'damaging words'* are particularly mentioned.[25] Of course the sick person will also complain of the *scorn* and *sneers* of former friends turning in disgust from the unclean supposed sinner.[26] The worshipper complains of being smitten by the *wrath of Yahweh*,[27] and knows that this wrath has been caused by his sins.[28] Ps. 38, quoted above, also says:

> No soundness in my flesh because of thine anger!
> No health in my bones because of my sin!
> For mine iniquities have gone over my head,
>   like a burden much too heavy for me . . .
> I do penance, bowing very deep,
>   all day long I go a-mourning. . . .
> I confess (now) mine iniquity (before thee),
> I sorrow deeply for my sin. (Ps. 38.4, 5, 7, 19.)

In the *prayer*—along with the formulae: 'hear', 'be not silent, deaf', 'do not turn away', and so on[29]—we also find the prayer for *healing*, or, more generally speaking, for deliverance from distress, from death.[30] The sick person prays that Yahweh may be merciful to him and not punish him in his wrath, but deliver him from the consequences of his sin,[31] including of course *forgiveness of the sin*. And he asks for *punishment* and *revenge* on the evil enemies who have caused the illness, and who would otherwise triumph over him.[32]

He appeals to the favour and compassion of Yahweh; he points out how short human life is : is it really going to be cut off prematurely? He points out that he is putting all his confidence in Yahweh; man can trust nobody else to help.[33] The sick person confesses his sinfulness and also points to his penitence. But he emphasizes his 'righteousness' and so pleads his faithfulness to the covenant. Yahweh cannot allow his righteous ones to be 'made unrighteous' and thereby doomed to destruction.[34] The worshipper also points to his piety and his good works, his fervent prayers, and emphasizes that even during the worst pains he has been careful not to sin.[35] This last feature is particularly emphasized in some of the laments of illness: he has been silent 'in order not to sin with his tongue' and has

[24] Pss. 6.8, 9, 11; 38.13, 17; 41.6, 11f. (possibly a thanksgiving psalm with a quotation).
[25] Pss. 38.13; 41.6–9 (thanksgiving psalm with quotation).
[26] Pss. 38.12; 88.9, 19; cf. 41.10 (thanksgiving psalm).
[27] Pss. 6.2f.; 38.2–4; 88.8; cf. 30.6, 8 (thanksgiving psalm).
[28] Pss. 38.19; 39.9, 12; cf. 32.1f., 5 (thanksgiving psalm); 41.5 (ditto).
[29] Pss. 28.2; 39.13; 88.3; cf. 30.11 (thanksgiving psalm).
[30] Pss. 6.3; 39.11; cf. 41.5, 11 (thanksgiving psalm).—6.5; 28.9.—28.1, 3.
[31] Pss 6.3; cf. 30.11; 41.11 (thanksgiving psalms).—6.2; 38.2; 39.11;—39.9, 11.
[32] Pss. 28.4; 41.11f. (thanksgiving psalm).
[33] Pss. 6.5.—6.7f.; 38.17; 88.16.—39.5, 7, 12, 13b, 14.—39.8; 38.16; 28.1; cf. 32.10 (thanksgiving psalm).—39.7, 12.
[34] Pss. 32.5; see notes 28 and 31.—Pss. 38.7; cf. 30.12 (thanksgiving psalm).—Cf. above, pp. 203, 210f., 240f.
[35] Cf. Pss. 41.2, 13.—88.14.—39.2.

given ungodly people no chance of mocking at him for disputing with God (38.14; 29.2ff., 10), and he has not, for instance, resorted to curses against the originator of the disaster, for then he might have had the ill-luck to curse God. But to the minds of pious people silence has an intrinsic value. It is an evidence of the patient humility and confidence which expects all help to come from God; God does not appreciate noisy and obtrusive calls for help, which but too easily may turn into pretensions, and too readily recall the 'roaring' and 'noise' and 'arrogance' of the powers of chaos. Here we have an example of the developing ideal of humility (see above, Chap. VII.3). In Egyptian psalms also we find this same estimation of 'silence'.[36]

By way of contrast with his own demeanour the worshipper emphasizes the wickedness of the enemies as deserving the punishment of God:[37] Yahweh's honour in the world is of concern to him: Yahweh must not let him die and thereby lose a faithful eulogist, for in Sheol he will no more be able to praise Yahweh, as no miracles take place there.[38]

In the still extant psalms of illness we meet with the vow only in indirect references, as in the already mentioned 'motivation of honour' behind which lies the idea that by healing the sick person Yahweh will give him a chance of tendering still more glorious praise. And, usually, the psalm ends in the assurance of being heard, sometimes in the form of an anticipatory thanks-giving psalm (6.9ff.; 28.6ff.). That even here the oracle of the cultic prophet and his promise that Yahweh will hear the prayer and help belonged to the ritual, and at any rate occasionally were placed before the assurance of being heard, can be seen, for instance, from Ps. 6, in which the assurance is expressed as follows:

> Depart from me, all you evildoers (lit. sorcerers),
>   for Yahweh hath heard the voice of my weeping!
> Yahweh hath heard my lamentation,
>   Yahweh hath (now) received my prayer.
> My foes shall all be utterly dismayed,
>   turn (away from me) suddenly ashamed. (Ps. 6.9-11.)

Quite obviously the assurance here rests on an objective basis, some 'precious word from Yahweh'.

As will be seen from this summary, what distinguishes the psalms of illness from the other 'I-psalms' is chiefly the references to the illness and, in connexion with it, to the sin of the worshipper.

8

Considering what has been said above about the Israelite view of the connexion between illness and sin, we can understand that the conscious-ness of sin on the part of the psalmists stands out most clearly in the

[36] Cf. Blackman in *The Psalmists*, pp. 182f.
[37] Pss. 28.3f.; 38.20f., and, on the whole, the 'lament' about the enemies.
[38] Pss. 6.6; 88.11–13; cf. 30.10; Isa. 38.18; see also Chap. VII, n. 44 and 49.

psalms of illness and in the thanksgiving psalms after the restoration to health.[39] So it may be right to say a little more at this point on the psalmists' conception of sin.[40]

We have seen above that the note of penitence is not very strong in the psalms of lamentation. In the manifestly national psalms of lamentation, as well as in those in the I-form, the asseverations of innocence and the consciousness of being 'right' and 'guiltless' are much more prominent. The most marked feature is the consciousness, formulated by the poets on behalf of the congregation as well as of individuals, of belonging to 'the righteous', to 'the fellowship of Yahweh's covenant', and thus having the right to expect his goodwill and help. 'Righteousness' for ancient Israel was certainly an inner quality, namely of normal psychological healthiness and the power of self-assertion and of happiness,[41] but the outcome of it was right behaviour and right actions. The religion of the psalms as well as of all Israel is a religion in which the dangers of moralism and of phariseeism were very close at hand.[42] Sin, too, was an inner quality, namely the abnormality of the soul, weakness and dullness and 'crookedness';[43] but gradually it came to be looked upon as the sinful act. This does not mean, however, that in all essentials sin was *morally* defined; 'sin' also means 'sinfulness', which is a 'state of impurity', like an illness weakening soul as well as body. A person may become sinful without himself knowing it; there are conscious as well as unconscious sins. An uncleanness, having for its cause for instance that a man has happened to touch something that is taboo, such as a corpse or a sick person, also makes him *sinful*, even if he knows nothing about it himself. The 'act' may be a perfectly passive one. The 'evil curses' of an enemy may also make a decent man 'unrighteous' and sinful. In all such cases the sinner will be overtaken by the wrath of Yahweh. That is why the psalms so often pray: 'Punish me not in thine anger' (see for instance 6.2; 90.7f.). Yahweh's reaction to sin and sinfulness is not only determined by moral factors: his 'holiness' is violated by anything that his nature is averse to, and that arouses his anger; but the holiness is often rather in the nature of 'tabooism', at any rate more of an irrationally religious, than of an ethical nature.

Therefore sin is often something the person in question infers from disaster having befallen him; from the disaster of Job, his friends with dogmatic certainty infer that he must be a gross sinner, indeed a hardened sinner, since he is not willing to admit it himself. When an Israelite was

[39] Pss. 25.7, 11, 18; 30.6–8; 32.1ff.; 38.2–6; 39.9; 40.13; 51.3ff.; 65.4; 69.6; 73.2ff.; 78.8–10, 29ff.; 79.5, 8f.; 80.19; 81.12f.; 85.2f.; 90.7f.; 95.8ff.; 99.8; 102.11; 103.3; 106; 107.17; 130.3, 8.
[40] Cf. Wheeler Robinson in *The Psalmists*, pp. 59ff.; P. Synave, 'Psaumes', *Dict. Theol. Cathol.* XIII, col. 1093ff.; Bout, *Het Zondebesef in het Boek der Psalmen.* Cf. however Johs. Pedersen, *Israel* I–II, pp. 411ff. The psalms are in fact founded on the basic Israelite conception of sin with which Pedersen deals, and have in this respect no 'theology' of their own.
[41] Cf. Johs. Pedersen, op. cit., pp. 336ff.
[42] Cf. Wheeler Robinson, op. cit., pp. 53f.
[43] Cf. Johs. Pedersen, op. cit., pp. 411ff.

overtaken by disaster, he must examine himself to see if he can find any divine commandment, any holy usage, any prevailing taboo-customs against which he may have trespassed; his conscience is alarmed and he feels under the wrath of God. But just as often it might well be that he would know of some sin he had committed, whether some neglect of the cult or a crime against one of his fellow-men or against an accepted moral law:

> Well do I know my offences,
> my sin is never out of mind. (Ps. 51.5.)

There is an important difference between biblical and Babylonian psalms; in the latter the worshipper usually asserts that he does not know his sins, and ritual and cultic sins rank first.[44] The Israelite is more realistic and concrete: obviously 'Yahweh has found out his sin and brought his trespasses into the light of his countenance', and so he has to confess and be cleansed from his impurity by means of ritual atonements and receive the promise of God's forgiveness and redress. Forgiveness implies that he has been cleansed and rid of sin by ritual means, and that he knows that the anger of Yahweh has been satisfied, and that Yahweh has again turned his merciful countenance upon him and 'made him righteous' and again admitted him to the 'fellowship of his covenant' (ḥăsîdhîm). However, only the healing fully proves that his sins have been forgiven, and that the suffering and the disasters are going to cease. But through the ritual promise that he shall be cleansed and his prayers be heard, faith grasps forgiveness in advance, as we have seen, and intones the 'anticipatory thanksgiving hymn'.

Confession of sin becomes a religious necessity, not to be avoided even if he has long held back from admitting the sin, as the worshipper of Ps. 32 confesses about himself, and even if it means for him to admit, what Job could not bring himself to admit, that he must have sinned, though not knowing it, and consequently to ask forgiveness of unknown sins (Pss. 19.12; 69.6). Therefore, side by side with the confession of sin, we may find the protestation of innocence (69.5f.).

It is part of old Israelite mentality, and of the way of feeling and thinking in the psalms, that the poet will try to give as strong expression as possible to the confession of sin. If indeed Yahweh demands confession of sin, and appreciates seeing a man humble himself in the dust to prove himself broken and crushed (Pss. 51.19; 34.19), then there is also every reason to emphasize such a response. But there can be no doubt at all that in the psalms we do find evidences of a really deep and spiritualized consciousness of sin. The psalmists agree with the author of the poem of Job that, face to face with God, all creatures are unclean and sinful.

> If thou didst keep strict tally of sins,
> O Lord, who could then stand? (Ps. 130.3, cf. 143.2.)

[44] Cf. Driver, in *The Psalmists*, pp. 136, 170.

The author of Ps. 51 knows that, after all, sin is always sin against God. He also knows that from his very birth he is stained with sin:

> 'Twas stained with sin that I was born.
> Sinful I was conceived in my mother's womb. (51.7.)

This means neither that conception is in itself impure and sinful—which would be an idea absolutely alien to Old Testament ways of thinking—nor that the worshipper was supposed to be the result of an illegitimate, sinful attachment; the saying implies no doctrine of 'original sin'; it is the strongest possible expression on the part of the author of the consciousness that as a weak and frail man he has never been without sin—from his very birth he has given offence in some thing or other. We must consider this against the background of the idea of unconscious sinning, which may happen to anybody at any moment.

It is quite characteristic of the psalms that they do not deal very much with concrete sins. It is the natural result of their being psalms for general use in the cult, that they have to speak in general terms. This actually adds to their value from a present day point of view. They are not too closely bound up with the circumstances of the age and with the specifically Israelite and Jewish way of life; therefore Christians of all ages have been able to use them as adequate expressions of a deepened consciousness of sin.

With a consciousness of sin like the one in Ps. 51 as a background, it is easier for us to understand how the psalmists were led to depreciate the atoning value of external offerings (vid. above). If Yahweh would not be meriful and forgiving, nobody could stand. But for this very reason he will show mercy:

> But there is forgiveness with thee,
> that thou mayest be feared. (Ps. 130.4.)

When God in his mercy forgives sins, the result will be 'fear of God', i.e. religion, the right relationship between God and man.

On the other hand, the old Israelite belief in a so-to-speak inevitable, 'natural' connexion between sin and suffering creates the deepest problem to be faced by Old Testament piety: the problem concerned with the sufferings of a pious person and the justice of God. This problem comes to a head in the poem about Job.[45] How can it be that illness and disaster overtake a person who knows himself to be a righteous man, who has committed no such gross sins as would justify such suffering, and whose moral sense forbids him to take upon himself a confession of sins which does not agree with what he knows to be true? According to the ancient way of thinking a person ought to be able to identify 'righteousness' with health and happiness, and the guarantee was supposed to be Yahweh's

---

[45] Cf. Johs. Pedersen, op. cit., pp. 363ff.; Mowinckel, *Diktet om Ijob*, pp. 1ff.; Lindblom, *Boken om Job*, pp. 98ff.; E. G. Kraeling, *The Book of the Ways of God*, pp. 11ff.

own 'rightness'. How, then, can 'covenant' and a moral world order exist, if Yahweh's 'power of upholding', his 'rightness', does not sustain the harmony of things? Is God perfectly arbitrary? And are piety and righteousness no use, but just like unrighteousness? Are not justice and power the same thing, so that to justice also belongs the power to maintain itself? Job cannot reduce his claim to be 'right' and to have God acknowledge his 'rightness'. To his friends these words seem presumptuous, for they maintain the ancient way of thinking, that rightness and happiness, sinfulness and disaster, are always companions.

In principle the psalmists, too, hold this view. They too knew the problem. For they represent the Israel of Yahweh, 'the righteous', 'the godly', they speak on behalf of those who share Yahweh's covenant and of his anointed and proper king, the Chosen One of Yahweh, and of every 'right' and 'pious' man overtaken by disaster. But they are deeply convinced of the justice of God; only ungodly people may say that God does not actively interfere to reward piety and punish sin (10.11; 53.11). Therefore even to them sufferings become a problem, and the question of God's just retribution, of theodicy, becomes a subject of consideration in some of the later laments and thanksgiving psalms, as for instance 37 and 73. But they remain staunch to the old faith: 'Many sorrows shall be to the wicked', and sudden death: but, 'I have been young and now am old; yet have I not seen the righteous forsaken'.[46] So the sufferings of the pious are something passing, some chastisement or warning, some trial, something caused by wicked men, but something that is going to pass away, as soon as the pious person admits his sins of weakness and ignorance and prays to Yahweh for mercy and help, so that Yahweh shall cease from anger and rise in order to save.[47]

9

It might be an all but obvious conclusion that all psalms in which we find terms for illness or the like, should be 'psalms of illness' to be used by Everyman. We might also be tempted to apply the complaint of 'lying words' and 'deceit' on the part of enemies to wicked men, using 'sorcery' against the worshipper and making him ill. 'Lies' and 'deceit' to the Israelite are not only untruths, objectively speaking, but also everything which lacks good and healthy 'firmness' and consequently is destructive and deadly; the words may therefore be used of evil and magical 'cursing words'—a 'lie' and a 'curse' may be identical.[48]

But the position is that, to the Hebrew, 'illness' and similar words do not cover a medical (pathological) notion so definitely limited as they do to us. A man will call himself 'ill', even when he has been overtaken by

[46] Pss. 32.10; 37.10, 25, 37f.; cf. 25; 32.6f., 10; 34.
[47] Cf. Wheeler Robinson, op. cit., pp. 62ff.
[48] Pss. 10.7; 59.13. See Ps.St. I, pp. 39ff.; Johs. Pedersen, Israel I–II, p. 320.

misfortune and is therefore in low spirits, disheartened and powerless; a blow has been struck at his very honour and vitality. Therefore such words may also refer to the state of sorrow and shame called forth by defeat and disappointed hopes or by fear, and so may be used to express the condition in which the worshipper has been placed, for instance, by the acts of external enemies in time of war, e.g. Ps. 69.21. 'Heal me, O Lord, and I shall be healed', says Jeremiah (17.14); but what he means is: deliver me from the dishonour and the disaster, into which the persecutions of my enemies have plunged me. And we have seen above that the complaints of lying and deceitful tongues in many of the I-psalms refer to political conditions.

We might therefore be tempted to run to the contrary extreme and imagine that all 'I-psalms' actually refer to external national enemies, because many of them undoubtedly do so. Like the psalms of illness, discussed in this chapter, the national I-psalms likewise speak of the evil words of the enemies, working disaster, and describe them as 'sorcerers', injuring the worshipper through their 'deceit'.[48a]

But the fact that psalms complaining of illness were offered in the cult can be seen, for instance, from the thanksgiving psalms treating of healing from illness, and explicitly, quoting the lament prayed by the sick person 'then'.[49] So there can hardly be any doubt that psalms like 6; 38; 39 were real psalms of illness.

We have to admit, however, that it is not always easy to distinguish between a psalm of illness and a psalm in which for instance the king complains of political enemies and their deceitful and noxious 'lying' and 'cursing words'. In fact, the line between the true I-psalms and congregational psalms in the I-form, with the king acting as the exponent of the community, is very vague.

10

Do there exist I-psalms with a purely personal distress, apart from illness, as the cause of the lament and of the visit to the Temple?

It is not easy to anser this question. Apart from the psalms whose background is national and public distress, it is only in the psalms of illness that we find the poets speaking so concretely as to make it possible for us to say anything with sureness about the situation of the worshipper and his particular distress. As a result of this, later interpreters of the psalms have been somewhat inclined to generalize and take all I-psalms as psalms of illness.[50] Gradually it has become evident that this is an exaggeration;

[48a] See Chap. VI.3; VII.3, 4. Stendahl (*SEÅ* XV, 1950) tries to show that the verb *rāphā'* and the psalms where this word is used do not deal with the ordinary healing of individuals, but with the salvation of the congregation, whose distress is described after the pattern of the chaos myth. His arguments do not seem convincing.

[49] Pss. 30.9–11; 32.5; Isa. 38.10ff.; Jonah 2.4f., and see below, Chap. X.2.

[50] This objection may rightly be made to Gunkel's *Die Psalmen*, Gunkel-Begrich, *Einl.*, as well as to my own *Ps.St.* I. See above, n. 2 and 18.

as we have seen, 'illness' is not infrequently a metaphor or a mental consequence of some other kind of distress, such as defeat or political dishonour.

But at any rate the thanksgiving psalms clearly indicate other reasons for a man in distress to turn to Yahweh with prayers (and offerings) and to make vows to him. This also would normally take place in the Temple, 'before Yahweh' (73.17; cf. 32.5); but of course a man might pray and make promises in other places as well, for instance if he got lost in the desert or was in danger at sea (107); naturally in such acute dangers prayer would sometimes, if not always, be a free and spontaneous 'call' to Yahweh for mercy and help, the 'free prayer of a layman'[51] and no regular psalm. It is therefore very possible that psalms may have been written for—and by—people in distress other than illness, even if illness may have been the most frequent reason for the presentation of a lament and the offering up of sacrifices for sin or purification.

The question is simply, whether among the laments and protective psalms handed down to us we can find any for which an altogether private occasion is likely, and in which therefore we do not have a public personage, representing the community during a state of public distress or danger.

If we were to mention any particular psalms, it would be most natural to think of such as 51 and 23. As for Ps. 51, the prayer for a new and clean heart and a right spirit, the prayer not to have the holy spirit taken away, indicates a religious climax in the Psalter; evidently these words, testifying to true personal piety, are written by an individual who has grasped something very essential in the relationship between God and man. However, this does not prove that the reason for his prayer and confession of sin need be of a private nature. The psalm is deeply personal, but for all that may have been written with a view to the public cult and the concerns of the congregation. If we consider it an outcome of entirely private distress, we shall have to declare as is usually done that the two last verses have been added later. But if we want to include these verses, it is certainly more natural to think of a person in a condition much like that of Nehemiah when rebuilding the walls of Jerusalem, and of the hostility to which he was exposed on the part of political antagonists. And on the merits of the case the psalm will then have to be ranked among the public psalms, in which the whole congregation joins with the worshipper, while he officiates as the public religious spokesman of the congregation in a matter concerning them all.

In passing, this question may be raised with regard to several I-psalms. Besides Pss. 51 and 23, may be mentioned Pss. 22 (a psalm of illness?) and 73 (really a thanksgiving psalm, but possibly after an illness). In most of these psalms there are signs to indicate that the worshipper is a representative person, speaking on behalf of the community and suffering the

[51] Cf. Wendel, *Das freie Laiengebet*; see n. 31 to Chap. II.

II, 2

distress which has befallen or is threatening them all. But in many cases it is impossible to say anything certain about it, just because the poets as a rule speak of distress and enemies in such general and conventional terms and metaphors.

Again we have to emphasize that the dividing line between congregational psalms and individual psalms is vague. A purely formal differentiation based on the use of 'I' or 'we', as by Gunkel in his commentary and introduction, does not give us a real understanding of the meaning of the separate psalms or of their place in the cult. A great many I-psalms are quite evidently congregational psalms, in which the 'I' is the official representative of the community. Some of these psalms give evidence of a religion which is quite personally experienced and felt, and of an equally personal reaction to the events that have given occasion for the psalm in question: the poet takes a personal part in the concerns of the congregation, and even wholly identifies himself with the representative of the congregation, for whom he has written his psalm. And then there are also some psalms in which the occasion—the distress—is mentioned in such general wording, and in which the personal character is so prominent, that we cannot help asking ourselves whether the occasion is not here of a quite personal and private nature, and the poet identical with the speaker even to the extent that he himself is the very person who is going to use the psalm in the cult; or we might even question whether maybe this psalm was not originally written without any eye to the cult. The difficulty is that as a rule such questions cannot be answered, just because the occasion is so vaguely described, and because there are no distinct boundary lines or decisive distinguishing marks between these psalms and the other laments in the I-form with a public occasion for their background.

Nor should it be necessary to point out that in the truly individual laments the 'helpless', the 'sufferer', does not represent any 'party' or 'tendency' or 'class'.[52]

II

It has not infrequently been maintained or taken for granted that most of the individual psalms of lamentation had nothing to do with the cult. Even Gunkel, the founder of the form-critical and cult-historical method, held that the I-laments were evidence of an emancipation of religious piety from the cult, expressions of a custom originating within certain circles of pious laymen which had developed the custom of praising Yahweh and singing psalms of prayer to him within these circles. Then the psalms were supposed to be the wholly personal expressions of quite

[52] See Chap. VII.3, and Additional Note XXIX.

personal experiences and feelings on the part of individuals.[53] Both laments as well as thanksgiving psalms were included since they were both thought to testify to the same sort of relationship between psalm and cult. So in what follows we shall discuss also the way in which the thanksgiving psalms themselves treat the thanksgiving psalm as the best offering, a point to which they also refer when speaking of the fulfilment of the vows.

First, we have to emphasize that the whole question falls to be considered from an entirely different point of view, as soon as we admit that a great many I-psalms are actually congregational psalms, in which the representative of the congregation speaks on their behalf about disasters threatening them all. For there is no reason to draw a hard-and-fast line between we-laments and public laments in the I-form; if the former belonged to the cult for public days of penance, there is no reason to deny or doubt that those in the I-form did the same also, for it is in the cult that the king or the governor or the chief priest acts as the spokesman of the congregation and offers up laments and prayers on its behalf. Only individual psalms of illness and other psalms in which it is possible to think of entirely personal distress, can be non-cultic.

But such a 'non-cultic' theory has no sense, as long as even a private individual had to bring his offering to the Temple in order to be cleansed from his illness, as we have seen above, and likewise would probably also bring his thanksgiving offering and sing his thanksgiving psalm there afterwards.

It is also evident that the whole theory about those small circles of lay people of the poorer class being the home of psalmography and psalm singing is not supported by the psalms themselves. It rests on a misinterpretation of the terms 'the sufferers', 'the oppressed' or 'the righteous', etc., and of the enemies in the I–psalms. As has been proved, there are a great many psalms, in which 'the oppressed' and similar terms are used about the people and the congregation of Israel in their relation to the 'pagan' oppressors; they do not refer to the oppressed lower classes, but to Israel herself in her actual condition as 'oppressed', actually suffering under the ravaging or the occupation of enemies or under public disasters. Neither do 'the righteous', 'the godly', 'the pious', 'the members of Yahweh's covenant' (ḥăsîdhîm), and the like indicate any party or any class within the congregation; in the psalms these terms are generally used of the whole congregation as being the 'right' members of Yahweh's covenant in the same sense as 'the great congregation', i.e. the entire congregation gathered at the cult. And it is just as certain that the enemies of a great many I-psalms are not the rich and wordly-minded upper class, but national and political enemies of people or king; the references are not to religious and social antagonisms inside the congregation, but to

[53] This was more or less taken as a matter of course in earlier psalm interpretation, which had not yet discovered the connexion between psalmography and temple service; Barnes, *The Psalms* is one of the latest typical representatives of this tendency. Even Gunkel, who had seen the connexion, still maintains that most psalms are private poetry, see *Einl.*, pp. 175ff.

national and religious ones, to the struggle between Israel, or the congregation, and the pagan enemies and oppressors. In the I-psalms we are not infrequently told that the enemies are 'nations',[54] or, as in the psalms of illness, that they are wicked people whom the sick person suspects of having brought the illness upon him.

So there is no reason to interpret these terms in a different way in the I-psalms, where the national and political background is not so obvious as in the others, nor yet in the psalms of illness. Even here 'the righteous', 'the pious', indicate the whole congregation, just as 'the great congregation' means the cultic congregation.[55] In these psalms, too, there are references to the ritual acts to which they belong: the cleansing by means of holy water and hyssop (51.8), the promise of the oracle (6.10; 26.8), the meal of the thanksgiving offering (22.27; 23.8), the connexion with the Temple (23.6), the distressed person visiting the Temple (73.17). It is from the Temple on Mount Zion that the author of Ps. 50 sees Yahweh 'shining', and it is the 'zeal of Yahweh's house' that has roused the worshipper of Ps. 69 (v. 10).

Gunkel points to the display of personal feelings and experiences so prominent in many of these psalms; this being taken to prove that they have nothing to do with the cult, but must be considered to be entirely private poetry. But to this must be answered that there is no contrast between what is cultic and ritual and what is personally felt and experienced. It is not here a question of either-or; we shall return to this below (Chap. XVII). Even if psalms like 23 or 51 or 42–43 are expressions of personal experiences and feelings and of a quite personal piety, we should not be justified in concluding that the psalms in question were not written to be used in the cult.[56] On the other hand, however, it is right to say that when the poets do use the I-form they seem more easily to bring in the personal relationship to God and the problems raised by this relationship and by life itself, than when using the we-form—even though the poet may be writing in the name of another person, for the use of the leading man of the congregation. That such words were put into his mouth means that a religious climax like the one we meet with in Ps. 51 or Ps. 23, is made a kind of norm for the whole congregation and its individual members; but it does not at all mean that the psalm was not written to be used in the cultic assembly.

One main argument for the conception of the I-psalms as 'cult-free' poetry is that in the laments the promise so seldom speaks of sacrificing

---

[54] Pss. 7.8f.; 9.6, 16, 18, 20; 54.3; 56.8; 59.6.

[55] Pss. 30.5; 31.24; 32.11; 73.1.—22.13f., 26f.; 40.10f.

[56] This erroneous inference is drawn by Gunkel, *Einl.*, pp. 261ff., 279f. That a psalm has been sung somewhere away from the Temple—for instance on the battlefield—is no evidence of non-cultic origin; during the monarchy cultic acts might be performed in any holy place; or any place might for the special occasion be sanctified for an act of sacrifice, see 1 Sam. 14.33f.— That Pss. 42; 43; 55; 61 and 120 were composed 'in the exile' (*Einl.*, p. 262) is a deduction based on erroneous exegesis; the passages prove only that the psalm in question was composed for use somewhere away from Yahweh's city and temple, e.g. for war purposes; see above, Chap. VII. 6.

animals, but much more of the thanksgiving psalm, even emphasizing it as the best kind of offering.

We have already seen (Chap. VI.3) that the reference to the thanksgiving psalm, to be sung by the saved person 'in the great congregation', does not imply that there is no sacrifice; on the contrary it is involved in the promise of a thanksgiving psalm. But without doubt a change has been brought about by the psalmists in the estimation of the different parts of the cult; there is no doubt but that they rank the psalm higher than the offering of animals. We find this in psalms of lamentation as well as in thanksgiving psalms, and it may be right for us to discuss it a little more closely here.

In some psalms (40; 50; 51; 69) this new estimation comes out so distinctly that it is usually interpreted as a condemnation in principle of sacrifice. To this we shall first have to reply that even if it were true, it would not be tantamount to a dissociation from the public worship, or mean that the psalms in question could have no connexion with the cult. For the offering up of animals is only part of the cult, which comprises a great many other and still more essential elements. A cultic religion without any offerings of animals is well known in the synagogue, in Islam, and in Orthodox and Roman Christianity. On the whole, all talk of a 'deliverance from the cult' and of a 'cult-free religion' rests on a misjudgment of the nature of religion as well as of cult. It is altogether misleading to look upon the link between piety and congregational worship in ancient Israel as a kind of fetter or as a lower stage of religion, so that deliverance from it would inevitably mean progress. The prophets may attack the whole cult, because it is performed in a sinful way by a sinful people, obscuring what is just as important a part of religion: the 'loving kindness' towards fellow members of the covenant, righteousness and humble walking with God; but this does not mean any condemnation of the cult as such; they were hardly able to imagine what a 'cult-free' religion would be like. Normally cult and religion belonged to the same set-up; Ps. 51 is evidence of this. This psalm, which refers to the ritual cleansings in the Temple (v. 9), ends by taking a positive stand even towards the offerings as being a normal expression of worship under normal conditions (v. 20f.), for instance when no public disaster proves that the anger of God rests upon the land, so that he does not care about the efforts of men.[57] Therefore when it is said that:

Thou desirest not sacrifice (of peace offering);
 and if I would give a burnt offering, thou wouldst not delight in it.

this saying must be referred to the actual situation and not be given universal validity; the sacrifice does not in itself reconcile God; only the

---

[57] Cf. Hos. 3.4. After the disaster which had befallen the Jewish temple in Elephantine in 410 B.C. the offerings at the sanctuary were suspended, see Sach. Pap. 13495/6 I,21f. (Ungnad, *Aram. Pap. aus Eleph.*, p. 4); translated by Ginsberg in *ANET*, p. 492.

humble penance and the submission to his chastisement, of which it gives evidence, can do that. Therefore the saying must be considered in the light of the following stanza:

> Do good unto Zion in thy benevolence
> and build up Jerusalem's wall (again);
> then wilt thou welcome the due sacrifices,
> and on thine altar shall bullocks be slain. (51.20–21.)

When God has looked in mercy upon the sinner and upon his people, and restored normal relations, then offerings, too, are a normal expression of the grateful homage and honour which the congregation owes to him.

In fact, even those psalms that use the most pungent terms of disparagement about the sacrifices, do not in principle take a stand which distinguishes them from other laments and thanksgiving psalms in the I-form. As has been said, in all of them we are brought face to face with a certain change in the estimate of the different elements of the cult, an alteration about to take place in the conception of what is most important and essential in the cult. The ancients, and certainly the priesthood even far down through the ages, as we can see from the cultic laws of the Priestly Document, certainly put the main emphasis on the sacrifice as the means of winning the goodwill of Yahweh and bringing about atonement and blessing for congregation and individuals (1 Sam. 26.19). The psalmists also knew how to prize sacrifice (see above, Chap. VI.3); but in an increasing degree they give vent to the opinion that it is not the sacrifice of animals, but psalms of penance and thanksgiving, which are most congenial to the right relationship to God and to what he demands from men.

That it is not a question of any condemnation of the sacrifices, much less a 'deliverance from cultic religion', even in the psalms in which the new evaluation is most prominent, is in fact brought out clearly by Ps. 50. Like the others, this psalm testifies to a deepening and spiritualizing, even to some extent to a rationalizing, of cultic religion (cf. 50.9ff.), and in so far bears witness to the progressive line in the revealed religion of the Old Testament. Ps. 50 actually emphasizes that one thing must be done, and the other not left undone. The poet explicitly says that the covenant, the fundamental relationship, to which he urges the people to be faithful, was 'made by sacrifice'. With direct reference to the making of the covenant he makes Yahweh say:

> I am "Yahweh" thy God
> (who brought thee out of the land of Egypt).
> I blame thee not for lack of sacrifice,
> daily thine offerings are set before me.
> But I need no bullock from thy farm,
> no he-goats out of thy folds.

The zeal of the congregation for cultic offerings is not to be reproved, but the Lord needs no offering of animals, he does not 'eat the flesh of bulls nor drink the blood of goats', he is the owner of 'every beast of the forest and the cattle upon a thousand hills'. But he does reprove his people, because zeal for the cultic offerings is coupled with moral laxity and lack of discipline on the part of the congregation, and he is no longer going to be silent about *that*. And then the congregation must call to mind what is the real and true meaning of the offerings: they were meant to be a means of calling on God in distress, and of thanking and praising him when his promises were being fulfilled; they were meant to express a disposition and a proper religious attitude to God. If the congregation call *this* to mind and fulfil their promises in *such* a spirit, then they will be 'honouring God'.

In fact, this is also the attitude of Ps. 51, as mentioned above:

> God's sacrifice is a broken spirit,
> a contrite heart thou wilt not despise.

Sacrifice of itself does not 'reconcile God'—literally: is not what 'God desireth' or 'delighteth in'—it is of no value except as an expression of a real penitence, 'a heart broken with penitence' (Moffatt). Therefore the poet also looks forward to the day when the Lord shall have rebuilt the walls of Jerusalem; then the proper thanksgiving sacrifice shall be offered up on his altar with joy by the spiritually renewed congregation. Ps. 69.31f. explicitly says that the thanksgiving hymn of praise 'shall please the Lord *better than* an ox or bullock that hath horns and' hoofs'; it is nowhere said that he will accept no sacrifice. We must interpret in the same way the doubtful text of Ps. 40.7f., where we are face to face with a change in the evaluation of the different elements of the cult and with a spiritual re-interpretation of the sacrifice, not a condemnation of it. That the sacrifice was still included is everywhere taken for granted, even if it is not often mentioned.

The correctness of this interpretation of the evidence is corroborated by the way the later Jewish rabbis regarded sacrifice. When they speak of penance and the atoning medium instituted by God, the main emphasis is put on the turning away from sin to obedience to the commandments of God; the atoning media of the cult and the sacrifices are seldom mentioned, though everywhere taken for granted as necessary because ordered by God. From the fact that they are rarely mentioned it is not to be concluded that they did not figure here; but the rabbis very well knew that man gives nothing to God through the sacrifice, and that he is not influenced by mere cultic acts as such.[58]

When some psalms particularly emphasize prayer as being more valuable than sacrifice, it is the personal view of the poet which is making itself

[58] Cf. Sjöberg, *Gott und die Sünder*, pp. 221f., 257.

felt, but on the whole they all agree in their basic view of the matter.[59]

There is a certain connexion between this view of sacrifice and the relation of the prophets to the sacrificial cult—namely in so far as the prophets had representatives among the temple personnel (see Chap. XII.1) to whom we owe the psalms (see Chap. XV). But some of the prophets are radicals, preaching judgment on the very way the people regarded religion itself, and consequently on the cult as a whole; the very religion of Israel has been perverted and is therefore condemned by Yahweh. In such a case they lump together sacrifice and prayer and singing of psalms; see Am. 5.21–23; Isa. 1.10–15. But even here in fact there is no question of a condemnation in principle of the cult; as already mentioned, what they condemn is the perverted cult of a sinful people *hic et nunc*, and its superstitious reliance thereon, as if of itself it were an achievement.[60] Here again the prophets can only really be understood in the light of that type of piety that developed on a basis of cultic piety, and which found expression in the psalms.[61]

Several factors may be mentioned as having contributed to this new evaluation of the elements of the cult. It is hardly sufficient to explain it as being the result of the prophetic conception alone; we have here two parallel phenomena, two results of a common tendency in Israel's religion. For as far as the positive aspect is concerned, there is a difference between the views of prophets and psalmists. With the prophets it is the unconditional surrender to God and social morality—'the righteousness' and 'the loving-kindness within the covenant'—which are ranked above sacrifice; with the psalmists it is the thanksgiving psalm and the psalm of penance and the inner disposition these are meant to express. But for some length of time there had been a close connexion between the spheres of temple singers and temple prophets (Chap. XV.3); this fact finds expression in mutual influences on religious ideas and thoughts.

A certain importance attaches to the professional pride of singers and psalmists: they were very conscious of the fact that their own tasks were important and essential elements of the cult. But this proper pride was also backed up by the ancient conviction concerning the true source of inspiration for poet and cultic singer: psalm-singing in its very essence was

[59] The anti-cultic interpretation of these psalms is likewise rejected—from somewhat different motives and text interpretation—by Jacob in *ZATW* 17, 1897, and Matthes, ibid., 22, 1902, pp. 73ff., and most recently again by Schönbächler, *Stellung d. Pss. z. a. t. liches Opferkult.*—That it is a question of 'as well as', and of a development of the cultic act itself, is the result arrived at even by Hulst, *Belijden en loven*, in his investigation of the notion *tôdhâ*. Cf. also Rowley, 'The Meaning of Sacrifice in the O.T.', *BJRL* 33, 1950, and *Expository Times* 56, 1945, pp. 69ff., 305ff.

[60] See *GTMMM* III, pp. 21, 78, and cf. Lattey in *JTS* 42, 1941, pp. 155f.; H. W. Robinson, ibid., 43, 1942, pp. 129ff.; Coleran in *Theol. Studies* V, 4, 1944, pp. 411ff.; Scott, *The Relevance of the Prophets*. Wellhausen and the earlier critics looked upon the prophets as opposed in principle to the cult. This view has been most consistently maintained by Voltz, for instance in his commentary on Jeremiah; he has even traced it back to Moses (*Prophetengestalten*, pp. 55ff.; cf. also his treatise in *ZSTh* 14, pp. 63ff.). Against this modernizing of the prophets see the references in n. 59.

[61] See above, p. 100; details below II.68f.

inspired by the deity.[62] Here the personal convictions of prophet and poet coalesce.

It is also understandable that psalm-singing and psalm-writing were felt to be a much more personal and spiritual profession than that of the priest, who had to perform apparently more mechanical ritual functions. We might call attention to the marked touch of personal experience which, in spite of the traditional conventionalism of style, is so prominent in many of the psalms. We shall return to this below (Chap. XVII, cf. X.4). Where God has been experienced as a personal reality, the desire to praise and thank him will be the immediate outcome of the experience, and become more important than traditional rites. Here psalmists and prophets are at one. The experience of the greatness and supra-worldliness of God lifts him beyond those anthropomorphic ideas[63] which lie behind many parts of the sacrificial cult. God is too great, too holy, too much 'wholly other' for him to need that men should give him food and drink, says Ps. 50.

As to esteeming the thanksgiving psalm above the thanksgiving sacrifice itself, one particular feature from the sacrificial tradition and law may have had some influence. If the prayers of a person in distress had been heard, for instance if he had been healed, a thanksgiving offering was not obligatory, unless he had promised it beforehand ('vowed sacrifice'; Deut. 23.22f.; cf. Lev. 7.16); so it was a perfectly 'voluntary sacrifice'. This may have contributed to the conception that this offering was not so necessary, or at all events a less essential part of the thanksgiving service; one might promise a thanksgiving psalm instead—which, however, normally would include also a thanksgiving offering.

Consequently there is no reason to believe that the authors of laments and thanksgiving psalms—or the psalmists as a whole—would have foregone the aid to holy living rendered by an attachment to the sanctuary and to the set hours and sacred acts of the congregational fellowship. There is no question here of a 'cult-free' religion.[64]

[62] Cf. below, Chap. XXIII. 5; XII and XVI, 3, 4. Details in prefatory remarks to Pss. 49 and 45 in *GTMMM* IV.

[63] Cf. Hempel in *ZATW* 57, 1939, pp. 75ff., and Boman, *Das Hebräische Denken*, pp. 84ff.

[64] Rowley (see above, n. 195 to Chap. V) understands my cultic interpretation of the individual psalms of lamentation as ritual texts for the purification from illness, as if I were attributing 'magical purposes' to the psalms, and as if they were 'a collection of potent spells' (op. cit., p. 126). Criado, *El valor dinamico del nombre divino*, p. 15, n. 53, 53 bis, is of the same opinion. This is a curious misunderstanding. On the contrary, I look upon them as a religious invocation of the merciful and powerful aid of the deity against disasters brought upon the worshipper by evil enemies, amongst other things through the use of 'sorcery' and spells, that is as much as to say: as 'religion' contra 'potent spell'. That the recitation of the psalms was accompanied by rites, to which the Israelite ascribed 'sacramental' operative power, does not alter the fact. If so, even the exorcism of the Roman Church, for instance, and the Holy Communion of the Roman and Lutheran and other Churches must be judged of as 'potent spells'—and Rowley certainly does not want to draw such a conclusion. Even Phillips, *O.T. in the World Church*, p. 136, uses the misleading term 'spells' about such cultic psalms; but he also shows how the psalms, when looked upon as ritual texts, will be spontaneously understood by the oriental, living as he is to this day in the same 'magical' world as the ancient Israelites (see my *Religion und Kultus*, pp. 13ff.).

CHAPTER IX

Public Thanksgiving Psalms

The full range of prayer includes not only doxology in general and prayers for deliverance from distress and danger, but also *thanksgivings for benefits experienced*. This certainly belongs to a more advanced stage, as we can see from the fact that the Hebrew language has no word for 'thank'; it uses words indicating 'praise' (as a rule *hôdhâ*), and 'bless' (*bērēkh*); although the doxology usually included an element of gratitude and thanksgiving.

I

In Israel, a particular *thanksgiving psalm* or *thank-offering psalm* (*tôdhâ*)[1] developed. It corresponds to the occasional psalm of lamentation in distress and danger, and differs from the hymn in that it does not just praise God for his great works in general, nor, so to speak, disinterestedly, for God's own sake, or for the sake of men, as if it were simply overflowing with admiration and adoration of God's own glory, as in the hymn; the *tôdhâ* was composed for some particular occasion, and offers thanks for some particular benefit experienced and bestowed on people or congregation.

For the original thanksgiving psalm is also a congregational psalm, a national psalm expressing experiences common to the community as a whole, and concerned with public affairs.

From the mostly rather late thanksgiving psalms handed down to us, and from references in other places as well, we can see that the occasion was as a rule of a political and military nature: some victory over the enemies of the people. And evidently the thanksgiving psalm has its original pattern in the *song of victory*[2]. Such stanzas or lays of victory might be improvised on the battlefield itself or on the way home, at the home-coming, or when dividing the spoil.[3] Originally they were short stanzas of two lines, repeated indefinitely;[4] out of them grew longer, artistic songs like the Song of Deborah in Jdg. 5. The underlying emotion is that of joy at the great achievement, of pride in the display of power, in the triumph. They contain a description of struggle and victory, of the threatening

---

[1] Hulst (*Beleiden en loven*) thinks that *tôdhâ* originally meant a confession of sin combined with a doxology. The word is, however, never used as a technical term for the confession as such. That the act of confession can be looked at from the view-point of 'giving honour to Yahweh', as in Josh. 7.19; Ezra 10–11—obviously a later use of the expression—is another matter.

[2] Cf. Gen. 4.23f.; 1 Sam. 18.7; Jdg. 5.

[3] Cf. Ex. 15.21; 1 Sam. 18.7; Jdg. 11.34; Isa. 9.2.

[4] With such short, constantly repeated stanzas of victory may be compared the songs of victory of the Zulus, see Blessing-Dahle in *Festschrift Meinhof*, pp. 174ff., 180.

power of the enemy and his defeat, of the eulogies of chiefs and heroes who have espoused the cause of the people.

In these songs of victory a religious element very early made itself felt. The festival at the home-coming would naturally be celebrated at the sanctuary (1 Sam. 15.13), where the people used to celebrate other festivals, with both sacrificial slaughter and feasting, which always had a certain cultic character (1 Sam. 14.31ff.). Besides, Israel was always aware that Yahweh himself was at the head of the army of Israel against her enemies and would smite the enemies with terror and death; her wars were 'the wars of Yahweh' (Num. 21.14), in which 'the heroes came to the help of Yahweh' (Jdg. 5.23). Therefore it is natural that victory would often be described and praised as the great achievement of Yahweh (Exod. 15.21); elements from the hymn permeate the song of victory; and the latter receives a directly doxologizing hymnal introduction and ending, as we can see in the Song of Deborah.

2

The vow contained in the psalms of lamentation (Chap. VI.3) proves that it was usual to hold a thank-offering festival when victory had been won or some danger and distress had been successfully averted.[5] And to the extent that singing became an essential element of the cult in general, the vow would entail a doxology, and the popular thanksgiving song would be part of *the ritual of the thanksgiving festival*; cf. Ps. 66.16ff. Both 'thank-offering' and 'thanksgiving psalm' are called *tôdhâ* in Hebrew.

As such thanksgiving festivals for victory are without doubt as old as Israel, and much older than the kingdom with its personal style, there is reason for us to believe that the oldest thanksgiving psalms had a collective character: the narrator being Israel, or the congregation, whether the plural 'we' was used (68.29), or the 'inclusive I' of the people in the first person singular.

No such old thanksgiving psalms have been preserved. But from fragments to be found incorporated for instance in the Song of Deborah, and from the later thanksgiving psalms, we can discern what the oldest thanksgiving psalm was like with regard to *form and substance*. The underlying emotion was one of rejoicing, with singing, shouting, and instruments playing.[6] We may say that the thanksgiving psalm in its essential feature is an adaptation of the hymn to some individual, specific, divine work of salvation. It seeks to give honour and praise to God for some definite benefit and *thank* him for it. But it has something else in mind as well. It turns to God not only to thank and praise him; it will also witness to his honour before men, and therefore turns to them. The thanksgiving

---

[5] 1 Sam. 15.13; Neh. 12.43; 1 Macc. 4.54; 13.51; Ps. 66.13–15.
[6] Cf. Isa. 12.3, 5f.; 25.9; Ps. 67.5; 68.5, 12, 26; 66.1f., 4.

psalm will *proclaim* the new act of salvation,[7] performed by Yahweh, and call upon men to honour and praise him. The main section is therefore the *tale* of distress and salvation, with an introduction and a final invitation to praise and thanksgiving; hymnal elements addressing Yahweh directly may occur in all three parts. We shall go more into detail about this when speaking of the individual thanksgiving psalms (Chap. X). Sometimes Yahweh's help and victory are described against a background of all his other great achievements in ages past (see Ps. 66.6f.). The psalm may then have a general hymnal introduction, as in 66.1–7.

3

The other extant 'occasional' thanksgiving psalms (for victory) have been influenced by the 'king-Ego' style.[8] Ps. 66 indubitably is such a national thanksgiving psalm, belonging to a thank-offering festival after victory or some similar deliverance from great political distress, which had befallen the whole people. The enemies are 'nations', who have threatened to destroy the worshipper (66.12; cf. 118.10ff.). The connexion with the cultic festival is quite obvious (66.13–15; cf. 118.19f., 26). Throughout the first part it is a 'we', the people, and congregation of Israel, that speaks. But side by side with this an 'I' appears as the centre of the thanksgiving festival and as one who has had to bear in a special sense the distress under which the people has been suffering; the real thanksgiving psalm at the sacrifice is put into the mouth of this individual. There can be no doubt that he is the *leading man of the people*, the king or a corresponding figure among the people.

Ps. 118 resembles Ps. 66; here, too, an 'I' speaks on behalf of the congregation ('we', v. 26f.) and the introductory invitation is addressed to all those who 'fear Yahweh', i.e. the congregation of Israel. But Ps. 118 probably belongs to some regularly repeated congregational festival (see below, §5) and does not refer to any particular victory or salvation. But from its affinity to Ps. 66 we can see how such congregational thanksgiving psalms, with the king as the representative of the people, were fashioned.

Both Ps. 66 and Ps. 118 have a marked liturgical character (see Chap. XIII.2). In Ps. 66 the general hymnal elements have the field all to themselves throughout the first part, vv. 1–12, in which only the last stanza refers to the actual event. In Ps. 118 the real thanksgiving psalm is several times interrupted by references to the festal procession and other cultic ceremonies (vv. 19f., 27), in which probably different voices are heard.

---

[7] In so far Westermann, *Das Loben Gottes in den Psalmen*, is right when he points out that there is a kinship between the hymn of praise and the thanksgiving psalm. But nothing is gained by ignoring that there *is* a stylistic difference, both in composition and in content, between the general hymns of praise and the actual thanksgiving psalms, and that this difference is due to a different setting, a different cultic function.

[8] See Chap. III. 7; VII. 1, 2.

4

Side by side with this mixed form we also find pure royal psalms of thanksgiving. One such psalm, at any rate, has been handed down to us, namely Ps. 18. That the speaker here is a king is said in so many words (v. 51); obviously here we have a salvation from deadly danger in battle (vv. 30f., 35f., 40), when the enemies (vv. 18, 38f., 41, 44, 46, 48) very nearly overpowered him, just as if he were already in Sheol (v. 5f.); this victory resulted in giving the king an expectation of a strong position among 'the nations' (vv. 44f., 48, 59, cf. 28). But in conformity to the usual oriental 'royal I' style[9] the whole battle—that is to say, the account of distress and salvation within the pattern of the thanksgiving psalm —is described as the quite personal concern of the king; we hear neither about his army nor about other human helpers. Yet, according to its substance, the psalm belongs to the public, national thanksgiving psalms. Its form is not due to any imitation of 'private' thanksgiving psalms for the use of an individual, but to a pure cultivation of the king-style as a further development of the earlier national and political thanksgiving psalm with its mixture of collective and individual forms.

Possibly also some other apparently quite individual thanksgiving psalms, like Pss. 92 and 138, must be interpreted in the same way as Ps. 18.

That the royal psalm of thanksgiving as a literary type is older than the congregational thanksgiving psalm is confirmed by parallels known to us from other oriental countries of antiquity. And the latter also prove that its origin is due to these patterns (for details see Chap. XX.4).

5

The earlier 'mixed' form has been developed in the opposite direction also, into pure congregational thanksgiving psalms.

This happened in connexion with the development of another new form, namely the regularly repeated festal thanksgiving psalm, by the side of the ones for special occasions. It is a universal human trait to fasten on the unusual first and only then on what is universal; we are more ready to give thanks for salvation from some particular danger than we are to thank God for blessings and benefits regularly bestowed upon us.

The festival of harvest and new year especially gave occasion for regular thanksgiving psalms. With a feeling of unrest and with grave misgivings, in 'tears', as the poet says (126.6), a Palestinian sows his seed; then he makes promises of sacrifices and thanksgiving to Yahweh, if all goes well. At the harvest festival 'the vows are performed' (65.2; cf. 1 Sam. 1.21); for 'Yahweh in Zion' is a God 'that heareth prayer', and therefore 'praise waiteth for him'. In the background of such feelings and thoughts we may see the weeping and the rejoicing at the death and the

[9] See n. 33 to Chap. VII.

revival of the fertility god and Nature. Two such thanksgiving psalms from the harvest festival have been handed down to us, Pss. 65 and 67. The gratitude is expressed in phrases taken from the hymn. And the miracle that happened, when the rainy season returned, blessing the country so that the seed could be sown, and meadows and hills were covered with corn, and the pastures clothed with flocks of lambs (65.10ff.), is a repetition of the great miracle of the original creation, when Yahweh destroyed the powers of chaos and made the earth a home for men (65.5–7; cf. Isa. 45.18; see above, pp. 162ff.). Therefore the way of Yahweh shall be known upon earth and all the nations shall praise him, exclaims the poet (67.4–6). It is the state of affairs existing before Yahweh's renewed coming at the festival—or in other words: as it would have been, if Yahweh had not come at the festival and once again performed the miracle of salvation—which is here being described as a distress from which the congregation has been saved. The thanksgiving is sometimes combined with a prayer for the future (67.2). The new state of affairs is assured by Yahweh's coming, but it has still to be seen as empirical reality in the days to come; cf. the same attitude of the congregation in Ps. 82.

Later times also produced general festal thanksgiving psalms, having for their subject Yahweh's merciful protection throughout all ages, as it had constantly evidenced itself in the history of the people. Such a festal thanksgiving psalm is Ps. 118, which has still preserved the earlier 'royal I' style (see above). The salvation, the victory, here described is the one that Yahweh has always given his people, so that her many enemies could never get the better of her. As in Pss. 46 and 48 the constant hostility of 'the nations' is combined in one single picture: they have all at the same time 'compassed about' the representative of the people, who is now praying, but by the help of God he has destroyed them; the whole distressful history of Israel and Yahweh's wonderful help are here described in a conventionalized way in a metaphor from 'the myth of the fight against the nations'.[10] This appears in several congregational thanksgiving psalms. In spite of all catastrophes, in spite of the oppressive alien rule still prevailing, the enemies never get the better of Israel (Pss. 124; 149), and finally they will have to withdraw in shame, smitten by the curse of Yahweh (Ps. 129)—here a motive from the laments mingles with the thanksgiving.

In these thanksgiving psalms also it is the quite briefly outlined 'tale' of what has happened, of distress and salvation, which makes up the main section.[11]

[10] See Chap. V. 6.
[11] Cf. for this chapter Gunkel-Begrich, *Einl.*, pp. 311ff.

CHAPTER X

Personal (Private) Thanksgiving Psalms

I

In Israel it had become usual for even ordinary people, who had been delivered from distress and danger, or healed from some illness, or whose prayer had been fulfilled, to present a thank-offering[1] and sing a thanksgiving psalm or have it sung for them; a typical case is mentioned in Job 33.26–28. It was often preceded by a vow promised during the distress; and the laments afford sufficient examples of this[2] 'vowed sacrifice'; but the sacrifice might also be a 'voluntary offering' (Lev. 7.12, 16). To the sacrificial feast with its sacrificial meal the offerer—the 'lord of the offer', *b'l niqê*, as the Babylonian said—would often invite relatives and friends,[3] and then 'they were glad in the sight of Yahweh'; it was also the custom to invite the priest and the poor people of the district;[4] there is a reference to this in Ps. 22.27. On such occasions all these people make up 'the congregation', 'the great assembly', to which laments and thanksgiving psalms refer.[5]

To the ritual of this thank-offering feast belonged also the personal or private thanksgiving psalm, 'the individual thanksgiving psalm'. We can see this from the many passages in the laments promising a song of thanksgiving, in addition to the sacrifice, or without mentioning the latter (Chap. VII.3), and it is confirmed by allusions in the thanksgiving psalms themselves to the sacrifice and other ritual ceremonies.[6]

We know little about the details of the ritual. There are some references in the psalms themselves. The psalm is sung where the sacrificial act is taking place, that is at the sanctuary, in the Temple,[7] before the assembled congregation, 'the god-fearing', 'the righteous', 'the worshippers of Yahweh', and so on.[8] Probably before the sacrificial act itself (116.17ff.; Jonah 2.10), while it was being prepared, the offerer would appear with the 'cup of salvation' in his hand and empty the wine as a drink-offering upon the altar, while calling on the name of Yahweh (116.13); then the song of thanksgiving would follow,[9] either sung by himself or by one of the temple servants—most probably, no doubt, the latter.

[1] 1 Sam. 1.21; Jer. 17.26; Ps. 56.13f.
[2] See Chap. VI. 3; VII. 4; VIII. 7.
[3] Cf. 1 Sam. 16.2f.; 2 Sam. 13.23ff.; 15.11; Prov. 7.14f.; Deut. 12.7.
[4] Cf. Deut. 12.12; 16.11, 14.
[5] Pss. 22.23, 26; 26.12; 35.18; 40.10f.; 68.26; 107.32; 109.30; 116.18; 149.1.
[6] Pss. 26.6; 56.13; 107.22; 116.17f.; 66.13ff.; Jonah 2, 10; Pss. 30, 12; 116.13. Cf. 27.6.
[7] Pss. 26.6; 66.13; 116.19.
[8] Pss 22.24; 30.5; 32.11; 34.10; 66.16; 69.33; 107.32; cf. 118.15. Cf. 34.7, 11. See also n. 5.
[9] See Ps. 66.13f., in which the singer seems to be pointing to the sacrifice he is about to offer up.

To this species of psalm belong Pss. 30; 32; 34; 40.2–11; 73; 92; 103; 116; Isa. 38.9–20⁹ᵃ; Jonah 2.3–10; Job 33.26–28; Sir. 51.1–18; Pss. Solom. 15; 16. To these may be added the two royal psalms of thanksgiving with a national background, Pss. 18 and 138, which with regard to style and structure represent the same original as the others (see Chap. IX.4). Even the small 'anticipatory thanksgiving psalms', which the psalm of lamentation often includes or ends in [10] afford material for the overall picture of this type.

The occasions for a thank-offering with a psalm of thanksgiving were just as numerous as the dangers and tribulations and difficulties of life. We hear of thank-offering feasts upon a happy return from exile and expatriation, of people getting lost and suffering hardships in the desert or being released from prison, of sick people being healed, of such as had been in distress at sea and come safely ashore. Most often the recovery from some illness would afford the occasion.[11]

2

The thanksgiving psalm is a testimony by one who has himself experienced salvation from distress and danger by Yahweh. As already mentioned, it has a twofold object. From one point of view it is meant for the fellow-countrymen present; it is being sung for them and in their hearing, and has the character of a laudatory and narrative *testimony* before them to the saving work God has performed upon the worshipper. But at the same time and first of all it is intended to be a laudatory thanksgiving to God for his salvation; the testimony has the purpose of increasing God's honour in the congregation and in the world. Its content is determined by this twofold object.

As a rule it starts with an *introduction*, in which the aim is expressed: 'I will thank', or some thanksgiving confession: 'I love thee, Yahweh': or, in imitation of the hymn, the call 'Thank!' 'Praise!'. Here Yahweh's name is explicitly mentioned as the one to whom the thanksgiving should be addressed. Typical introductions to a psalm of thanksgiving are the following stanzas:

> I thank thee, Yahweh, with all my heart,
>   I sing thy praise in face of the gods,
>   for thou has listened to the words of my mouth.
>
>   (138.1 (G).)
>
> I will bless Yahweh at all times,
>   his praise shall continually be on my lips. (37.2.)

---

⁹ᵃ On text and interpretation see n. 19b to Chap. VIII.
    [10] Pss. 7.18; 13.6; 22.28–32; 28.6f.; 31.8f., 20–25; 35.9; 57.8–12; 59.17f.; 63.4–6; 71.8, 14–16; 86.12f.; 109.30f.; Jer. 20.13. See pp. 216f., 234f., II.9ff.
    [11] 2 Sam. 15.7f.; Gen. 28.20; 31.13.—Pss. 107.4–32.—30.3f.; 103.3; 116.8ff.; 107.17ff.; Job 33.19ff.; Isa. 38.9.

I will extol thee, Yahweh, for thou hast lifted me up
                                    (i.e. from the pit of Sheol)
    and hast not made my foes to rejoice over me. (30.2.)

With an invitation to thanksgiving:

Sing praises to Yahweh, ye devoted,
    give thanks to his sacred name! (30.5.)

Or by way of confession:

I love Yahweh because he hath heard
    the voice of my supplications. (116.1.)

It is fitting to sing praise to thee,
    Yahweh (who dwellest) in Zion,
and vows shall be paid unto thee,
    O thou who hearest prayer. (65.2–3a.)

Here, in fact, the intention and the note of the whole psalm of thanks-giving is being struck. The psalm is a grateful confession to the 'name' of Yahweh, to his character and work as the faithful almighty God of the covenant. The word usually translated by 'thank' (*hôdhâ*) really means 'confess to'. The worshipper will 'extol his name', make it great in the world, 'give him glory and might', in the real sense of the words. That is also what is included in the expression 'bless Yahweh'. 'To bless' is to impart mental power, and is communicated in gift and greeting (cf. Chap. XI.1). The right way to render thanks for a benefaction is through a 'blessing' in return; 'to bless', therefore, also means to thank and to praise.

Then follows the account of the experience of the worshipper, addressed to the listeners and referring to Yahweh in the third person. Sometimes, and probably in later style, it is addressed to Yahweh himself, and has the character of a thanksgiving prayer, as in Pss. 18.16, 36f.; 30.4f.; 138.3, 7f. The above examples show how the account is attached to the introduction as a statement of the cause: 'I will extol thee, O Lord; *for thou hast lifted me up*'; 'I love Yahweh, *because he hath heard my wailing prayer*'.

Sometimes the account may come first, without any introduction, as in Ps. 40.2–4; Jonah 2.3–8, or it may occupy the whole psalm.

In its complete form the account contains three items, finding its most concentrated expression in Jonah 2.3: (a) 'In mine *affliction*, (b) *I cried* unto Yahweh, (c) *and he heard me*'.

As a rule the account is quite short and only suggestive; often but a few sentences in general wording:

I besought Yahweh and he answered me,
    he delivered me from all my terrors. ...
Here is a poor man whose cry He hath heard,
    and helped him out of all his troubles. (37.5–7.)

On the very day I cried unto thee
   thou answeredst me at once' O Yahweh;
      thou strengthenedst me with strength in my soul. (138.3 (G).)

I was helped, and my body regained strength,
   And with all my heart I thank him. (28.7 (G).)

But sometimes it may become more detailed and enlarge upon the
personal condition of the worshipper. The distress may be described by
means of the same metaphor as was used in the psalms of lamentation:
as a sojourn in the realm of the dead, in Sheol; the distressed person would
'cry from the belly of Sheol':

Thou hadst flung me down in the depths of the sea,
   the floods rolled round me,
and all the breakers and all thy waves
   they swept over me.

Then I thought: 'Now I am flung
   out of thy sight (and mind);
how shall I ever come to see
   thy holy shrine again!'

The waters closed about me,
   and rose up to my throat;
the deeps of old rolled around me,
   and seaweeds wrapped my head.

I sank down to the mountains' roots,
   to the depths of the nether world;
its bars were shut behind me,
   its doors for ever locked.

But thou, thou didst stretch out thine hand
   and tookest me from the dungeon;
thou didst lift up my life from the pit,
   O Yahweh, my God!

When my soul fainted within me
   I called on Yahweh's name,
and my prayers came in unto thee,
   into thine holy shrine. (Jonah 2.4–8.)[12]

In Ps. 18, in which the king gives thanks for having been saved out of
deadly danger in battle, this danger is described by means of the same

[12] As for the text: delete m.c. *mĕṣûlâ*, v. 4 (var. to the following expression); in v. 6 the last
short colon is lost; for aesthetical reasons the translation veils this; in v. 7a something must be
lacking; *hā'āreṣ*, which must here have the sense of the nether world, has no syntactical connexion; read *'el-taḥtiyyôth hā'āreṣ* and then *misgērû*. Before 7b the parallel bicolon is lacking,
which introduced the description of Yahweh's intervention, for instance, something like *'attâ
šālaḥtā yādhĕkhâ wattiqqāḥēnî mibbôr*, cf. Pss. 18.15; 40.3.

metaphor, but in still more mythological colours; in details and in wording and metaphors derived from the idea of Yahweh's appearance to fight against the powers of the primeval ocean, we get a description of how Yahweh comes 'riding upon the cherub, flying upon the wings of the wind' and 'thundering in the heavens', laying bare the bottom of the ocean and sending out the arrows of his lightnings and scattering the enemies and drawing up out of the depths of the primeval ocean the man who was about to be drowned.

In other cases the account dwells rather upon the mental aspect of the distress. Ps. 30 explicitly mentions the cause of the disaster: the sinful assurance and self-sufficiency which Yahweh had to mortify by hiding his face from the worshipper, so that disaster would overtake him:

> When I was prospering I thought:
>   'I never shall be shaken';
> by thy favour thou hadst set me on strong hills;
>   then didst thou hide thy face—and I was struck by terror.
>
> (30.7-8.)

Or the account may dwell on the importance of humiliating oneself and confessing one's sins, when overtaken by disaster:

> So long as I was silent my body fainted
>   through my roaring all the day;
> for all the day and all the night
>   thy hand was heavy 'pon me;
> my heart dried up and faded away
>   as a meadow in summer heat.
>
> Then did I own my sin to thee,
>   not hiding my sinful guilt;
> I said: 'I will confess my sins
>   to Yahweh, honestly';
> and thou forgavest me my guilt,
>   remittedst my iniquity. (32.3-5.)

Therefore this psalm starts with a testimony to the bliss of having one's sins forgiven, instead of with the usual promise of thanksgiving. And in Ps. 73 the whole story speaks of the trial of faith which the disaster brought about, of the religious problem the worshipper had to face, and how this problem was solved. The underlying disaster is only suggested, yet it is quite evidently there.

The account of the distress is so essential, because as a rule it meant a question of life or death. In the psalms of thanksgiving there re-echoes the intense earnestness of life, as the ancient Israelite might have to face it in all the tribulations and deadly dangers mentioned above. But here we are face to face with the same problem as in the individual psalms of lamentation: the distress is often described in such general phrases that it is not easy to tell what the nature of it was. In some cases it is illness, as in Pss. 30 and 32. In other cases the terms used in the psalm seem to suggest that the worshipper is to be thought of as a person in high position, perhaps the king or the governor, and that the distress had a more or less *political* character, as in Pss. 18 and 138. The underlying reason for the indefinite general wording is probably the fact that these psalms were composed for cultic use and therefore were so modelled as to suit anybody wanting to celebrate a thank-offering festival. Even where we have the healing of illness, the psalm in question *may* of course have been composed for the use of a king, even if it has also been used by ordinary people. So here, too, we find that the boundary line between private and public occasions of distress, and between public (royal) psalms of thanksgiving and private ones, is rather fluid.

Ps. 73 has a character of its own. The worshipper passes lightly over the original distress: though righteous and godly, he has been smitten by some disaster, perhaps illness. What made the distress so bitter is the travail of mind: the resentment at seeing the ungodly prosper, while he himself 'has been plagued all the day long and chastened every morning', and has therefore come to doubt whether there is any sense and righteousness in God's way of ruling the world, and whether being godly is any use at all. As he identifies the 'pure in heart', to whom he himself belongs, with 'Israel', 'the wicked' (*rĕšā'îm*) in all probability refers to pagan overlords, maybe even to fellow-travellers among 'apostate' Jews. The distress is here, as it were, sublimated into religious travail of mind, and when he 'went into the sanctuary of God' and there submitted to the prescribed ritual acts and received the promise of Yahweh's 'justifying' aid—the truth of which was proved later on, when he was actually delivered from his tribulations—the most important aspect of the salvation for which he gives thanks in this psalm seems to be that his doubts were resolved and his temptations conquered, and that faith in the righteousness and favour of God was regained.[13] Just because he had resented the good fortune of the ungodly, he puts the main stress in his confession on the fact that they were

[13] Ringgren too (*VT* III, pp. 265ff.) has seen that the crucial point for the worshipper was his experience at the cultic act with its demonstration of the defeat of the enemies. But this demonstration is scarcely the one given through the rites of the new year drama. The problem of the worshipper is an entirely personal one, and nothing seems to indicate that he is the king at the new year festival, as Ringgren is inclined to think. The problem of Ps. 73 is that of later times, and of psalms like 49 and other 'wisdom psalms' (see Chap. XVI). Würthwein, too, (*Festschrift für Bertholet*, pp. 532ff.), who rightly takes Ps. 73 as a cultic thanksgiving psalm, thinks that it is simply a question of national and political and religious antagonisms, and that the worshipper is the king. But we may not read that much into the parallelism of 'Israel' and 'such as are of a clean heart' in v. 1, see above, II.35, so Würthwein admits that in the psalm the point of view is shifted from Israel to the individual worshipper. But the problem of this particular worshipper is so individual that the shifting cannot be explained by saying that the 'I' is the king speaking on behalf of 'Israel'; if so, it would not mean any real shifting of the problem. Another interpretation of the worshipper's experience, not however convincing, is given by Birkeland, *The Evildoers in the Psalms*, pp. 36ff.

utterly consumed with terror, whereas 'God is good to such as are of a clean heart' (73.1).

In the account of the distress *enemies* sometimes play a part.[14] In the royal psalms, such as Pss. 18 and 138, the case is clear; we have the political enemies of the king, and those probably foreigners, as a rule, as in the royal laments (Chap. VII.2, 3). But even a private individual may be exposed to enemies in war, or to robbers and invaders threatening his life. Sirach complains of slanderers having blackened him in the estimation of the rulers (51.3f.). Even the sick person may feel crushed by enemies, both such as hardly conceal their malicious desire to see him dead and increase his illness through evil wishes and words (30.2; 41.6ff.), and perhaps also those whom he supposes to have caused the illness; this may be the case in 116 and 92. So we again have reason to point out the vague boundary between public and private psalms of thanksgiving. Not infrequently the distress is likened to being hurled into Sheol,[15] as in the psalms of lamentation (Chap. VII.5).

Sometimes the worshipper confesses that the distress is not undeserved; he has sinned against God, for instance through too great assurance (30.7),[16] or through a life lived in gross sins and lack of penitence.[17] The disaster was an instrument in the hands of God for 'educating him through cross and tribulation' and leading him on to the right way (32.3ff.).[18] But we are also assured that Yahweh has saved him on account of his righteousness and blamelessness (18.21f.; 73.13).

In the distress, the worshipper called on Yahweh. When everything seemed hopeless, we are told, he was mindful of Yahweh and called to him for help.[19] Not infrequently the worshipper quotes the words he 'then said' to Yahweh, the reference to the prayer for help taking the form of a miniature psalm of lamentation.[20]

And Yahweh in his mercy heard his prayer[21] and dragged him out of the jaws of death, forgave his sin, healed him.[22] So when we are told that Yahweh drags the godly person out of Sheol or out of the 'pit' (grave), this does not refer to any general conquest of death, nor to life after death, but to deliverance from imminent danger of death (Chap. VII.5).

The second main section of the thanksgiving psalm is the confession to Yahweh as saviour from distress, as already partially indicated in the first words of the psalm. The very object of the thanksgiving psalm is to proclaim the faithfulness of Yahweh before men, not only before the par-

---

[14] Pss. 30.2; 92.8, 10, 12; Isa. 38.13a; Sir. 51.3–9, 11, 15. Cf. Ps. 116.3; Jonah 2.9; and Pss. 18 and 138.6b, 7b.

[15] Pss. 9.14; 30.4, 10; 40.3; 71.20; 103.4; 116.3; Isa. 38.10f., 14; Jonah 2.3ff.

[16] Cf. Ps. 107.11, 17; Isa. 38.17; Job 33.14ff.

[17] Cf. Ps. Solom. 16; Ps. 119.71.

[18] Cf. Ps. 119.67, 71, 75; Ps. Solom. 16.

[19] Ps. 107.5, 18; Jonah 2.8; Sir. 51.7.—Pss. 18.7; 30.3; 107.6, 13, 19, 28.

[20] Pss. 30.10f.; 31.23b; 32.5; 66.18; 73.3–16, and other places; cf. 41.5–11 (by some interpreters considered the psalm of lamentation of a sick person).

[21] Pss. 18.7; 22.25; 34.5, 7; 40.2; 116.1; 138.3; cf. 66.19; 118.5, 21.

[22] Pss. 32.5; 103.3; 107.17ff.—30.3; 107.20.

takers in the festival, but before all men:[23] nobody else can help, neither men nor gods, neither power nor riches, but Yahweh is faithful and merciful, helping a person who puts his confidence in him. From the example of the worshipper himself, everybody else in distress, all pious people, shall learn that it is so! The distressed person of the laments used also to find comfort in the very same thought, and use it before God as a ground for the acceptance of his prayer. This confession, referring to Yahweh in the third person, may sometimes have the character of a hymn and be addressed directly to Yahweh[24]—the dominant note of the thanksgiving psalm being closely related to that of the hymn. Therefore we sometimes find the thanksgiving psalm going on from the individual, from gratitude for God's benefits to *self*, to the unselfish universal, and so becoming a panegyric of God himself and of all his wonderful works in nature and history and human life. The thanksgiving psalm becomes a hymn, like Ps. 103, where the personal experiences only enter as starting-point and motivation.

In the confession somewhat of the desire to win other people for God is always to be heard; it is a testimony in the religious sense of the word: 'do as I have done and turn to Yahweh in distress, then you will be saved! I know it, for I have experienced it myself!' Thus the confession to some extent attains the nature of an admonition, whether it calls the person blessed who confesses his sins and obtains forgiveness and is healed from illness and impurity, or straightway invites others to follow the example of the worshipper.[25]

Here the style and ideas of the 'wisdom poetry' are likely to have made themselves felt; for this wisdom poetry too has for its object admonitory religious and moral instruction, where the teacher (father) often refers to his own experience as a guarantee for the truth of his words. If the experience is expressed in a general sentence, by calling a person blessed, through direct admonition in the imperative, by inviting others to take a lesson from what has been told,[26] this is a result of influence from wisdom poetry. Consequently the thanksgiving psalm may become chiefly instructive, and approach the didactic poem of 'the learned psalmography' (Chap. XVI), as is the case with Ps. 34. In Ps. 73 account and confession approximate to problem poetry, as we find it in the poetry of Job and sometimes in 'the learned psalmography'. The distress of the poet lay in the problem of the justice of God, in view of the good fortune of the ungodly and his own suffering; in his testimony he confesses to the sin and folly of having doubted God and expressed such thoughts before the brethren as would indicate faithlessness to the fellowship of the congre-

---

[23] Pss. 9.15; 22.26; 35.18; 40.10f.; 51.17; 107.32; 116.17ff.

[24] Pss. 30.3f.; 69.3f.; 92.2–6, 10f.; 138.4ff. Direct address: 92.5, 11; 138.3–7; 73.21–27.

[25] Beatification: Pss. 32.1f.; 40.5; cf. 41.2–4. Invitation: 31.24; 32.6f.; 34.6ff.; 124.8.

[26] The universal: Ps. 37.35f.; the beatification: 32.1f.; the exhortation: 34.4ff.; the invitation: 34.4ff.

gation; his message to them will be that God has helped him in spite of this, and that he will help all the 'pure in heart', but will destroy the faithless ones; so that the old belief is right, for he himself has experienced that God is good and righteous, and this experience has solved the problem for him—and to this fact he is now able to testify before the congregation through his psalm of thanksgiving.

The way in which the thanksgiving psalm developed tended to make confession, testimony and admonition the chief points of the psalm, as can be plainly seen from Pss. 32 and 73. Therefore the thanksgiving psalm was the very type of psalm which 'wisdom poetry' and the later 'learned psalmography' would most readily adopt (Chap. XVI.3, 4, 6). Here a mutual interaction takes place, making it natural to interpret many apparent 'didactic psalms' as actually thanksgiving psalms after the experience of salvation (see Chap. XVII.3). In fact the most obvious course may be to look upon an apparently 'objective' and 'instructional' psalm like Ps. 49, teaching about death that puts an end to all the riches and power of a rich person, as a personal psalm of thanksgiving. The personal feature already makes itself felt in the pompous introduction, so curiously out of touch with the sober contents; the poet has found the solution of a 'problem'; the 'wisdom' given to him as inspired knowledge, and yet 'thought out by his heart' is the guided understanding of his mind on the basis of something experienced. The problem itself is again the same as in Ps. 73: why do the rich and mighty people of this world prosper, and why do pious people often live in such poverty, and even have dangers and tribulations overtake them? The answer is the well-known one: the wordly rich people shall sooner or later be overtaken by catastrophe and have to stay in Sheol, once it has opened its jaws against them, whereas the godly shall be saved in distress and deadly danger. But the worshipper does not pronounce this as a general truth, but as something personally experienced: 'God shall (always) redeem my life and take me out of Sheol'. How does he know this? Because he has himself experienced it. God has just done it, and therefore he confesses his faith that He will always do it.[27] Therefore he is also able to say that there is no reason for the godly person to fear in days of disaster, or to be afraid (and tempted) if the wordly-rich man becomes great and mighty, and it may thus look as if the ancient faith in the righteous rule of God with reward and punishment does not hold good: in due season it will happen that the rich man must perish, whereas the godly man shall be saved from distress and danger.

The third main section, sometimes admittedly lacking, is the reference to the thank-offering.[28] The normal form for this section is brought out by the following example, though it is actually taken from a public 'royal psalm of thanksgiving':

[27] Therefore the imperfect of v. 16 is no objection to the interpretation of the psalm as a thanksgiving psalm, as Lindblom (*Horae Soederblomianae* I, p. 24) thinks.
[28] See references in n. 6.

So I enter thy house with sacrifices,
    to pay my vows to thee;
the vows that were poured out by my lips
    and spoken in my distress. (66.13f.)

The worshipper is also thinking of the thank-offering in a literal sense,
when he says:

Now I offer thee the sacrifice of thanksgiving,
    calling on the name of Yahweh;
I pay my vows unto Yahweh now,
    in presence of all his people. (116.17f.)

The worshipper is offering up his thanksgiving for the help, i.e. he is ful-
filling what as a rule he would already have promised while in distress,
in the invocation of the lament.[29] Here the worshipper as a rule addresses
Yahweh himself, but may also speak of him in the third person.

In proportion as pious people came to look upon the sacrifice itself as
a less essential part of the service (Chap. VI.3; VIII.11), the reference to
it became less prominent even in the thanksgiving psalm. Then the thanksgiving psalm itself and especially the testimony contained in it would
come to be considered the real and essential fulfilment of the promise,[30]
the most dignified way of thanking; just as in the laments the vow would
emphasize the thanksgiving psalm more and more,[31] so also the thanking
and praising, 'calling upon the name of Yahweh', would be the proper
answer to the question: 'What shall I render unto Yahweh for all his
benefits toward me?' (116.12.)

In some psalms—laments as well as psalms of thanksgiving—this idea,
as we have already seen, finds a particularly strong and touching expression (see Chap. VIII.11). However, as we have also seen, this does
not imply any rejection of sacrifice, or that these psalms do not belong
to the cult. Even these psalms use expressions indicating that they are
intended to be sung in the sanctuary, before 'the great assembly',[32] i.e.
the cultic congregation. They just give a particularly strong and emotional
expression to the high appreciation of the psalm as a liturgical act and a
pious work, which is characteristic of the Psalter.

So in the third main section of the psalm the worshipper declares that
he is now offering up the ritual psalm of thanksgiving together with other
rites and ceremonies of the thank-offering festival, according to his
promise and in gratitude for Yahweh's benefits to him.

In the introduction to the psalm of thanksgiving—declaring the desire
to thank Yahweh—as well as in the reference to salvation and in the final
confession to Yahweh through the testimony, hymnal motives and forms

---

[29] See references in n. 2.
[30] Pss. 30.13; 32.11; 34.4; 40.10f.; 73.28b; 92.16; Isa. 38.18–20; Job 33.26–28; Sir.
51.16–18.
[31] See above, n. 2 and the references in n. 27 to Chap. VII.
[32] Pss. 40.10; 22.23f., 26; cf. 73.28b; 9.15; 41.13; 43.4; 138.2; Isa. 38.20.

are not infrequently re-echoed. We find here laudatory sayings in general terms as well as descriptions of the great works of Yahweh, and also the participial style: 'he who . . .'.[33]

This is certainly not to be interpreted as comparatively late influence from other species and styles of psalm, but as an original feature. For the psalm of thanksgiving is actually a particular species of the hymn, a doxologizing thanksgiving for some definite benefit, a personally experienced outcome of Yahweh's power, righteousness and mercy. Even here, as in so many other cases, the pure style belongs to a later phase of development.[34]

The experience expressed in the psalm of thanksgiving has established and again confirmed the confidence of the worshipper in Yahweh. That is what he testifies to before the congregation through the 'testimony' of the psalm. So it often contains direct as well as indirect expressions of confidence.[35] Therefore we often find an intrinsic relationship between the psalm of thanksgiving and the 'psalm of confidence' in distress and danger (Chap. VI.4). Considering also the structural unity of prayer life we should find it natural that the detailed hymnal appeal and profession of confidence in Yahweh, which sometimes form a separate introduction to the psalm of lamentation,[36] are there often strongly marked by the style and tone of the psalm of thanksgiving, as in Ps. 27, or actually make up a whole regular psalm of thanksgiving, as in Ps. 40; in this case an earlier independent psalm of thanksgiving has evidently been utilized for this purpose.

Therefore we may really sometimes doubt whether a psalm essentially expressing confidence, and only in general and indefinite phrases referring to a definite occasion, such as Ps. 23 'The Lord is my shepherd', is really meant to be a 'protective psalm' in danger, or a thanksgiving psalm after the experience of salvation. One would like to be able to say something about the occasion for this pearl among the psalms; but perhaps, what gives it a priceless value to all ages may be the very fact that it stands there as a pure expression of confidence in God, unhindered by all special historical circumstances, an adequate expression of the confidence of faith of all sorts of people, and at all times.

This high opinion of the thanksgiving psalm may have resulted in particularly prominent personages occasionally seeking to perpetuate their homage to the deity by having the psalm of thanksgiving inscribed on a memorial stone, or written down on leather or parchment, and set or laid up in the Temple, 'before Yahweh'.

This happened in Egypt, where for instance 'the thanksgiving psalm of the painter Neb-re' (see Chap. XX.4) was written on a memorial

---

[33] See 1 Sam. 2.3–10a; Pss. 18.8ff., 26–28, 31; 30.10f.; 69.33f.; 138.4–6.
[34] Cf. Chap. IV. 4; VI. 4; VII. 5.
[35] Pss. 32.6f., 10f.; 34.8–11, 16ff.; 40.4b, 5a, 12a; 73.1, 23–26; 92.13ff.; 103.3–6, 11, 13, 17ff.; 116.7, 10.
[36] See above, Chap. IV. 5; and n. 9 to Chap. VI.

stone in the Amon-temple at Thebes. The same idea underlies the setting up of votive columns to commemorate the hearing of a prayer—a practice of which many instance are to be found in Syria.[37] Inscribing a whole psalm of thanksgiving on a memorial stone would then have to be considered as a further development of the original short votive inscriptions. The Bible itself refers to such votive memorial columns (Isa. 56.5).

Perhaps the 'writing', 'inscription' (*mikhtābh*) at the head of the thanksgiving psalm of king Hezekiah in Isa. 38.8ff.[38] may refer to such psalms of thanksgiving, written down on votive columns. We have just such a royal inscription of thanksgiving by Birhadad, king of Damascus, consecrated to the god Melkart in gratitude for his hearing of prayers.[39]

3

From Ps. 107 may be inferred that at any rate in later times it became usual to celebrate great communal thank-offering festivals, at which different groups of people who had been saved—released prisoners, returned travellers and seafaring men, sick people who had been healed, would come forth with their sacrifice and say their 'Amen' or 'his mercy endureth for ever', after the part of the common psalm, in which the singers would refer to *their* particular experience.

The psalm starts with a general invitation:

> Give thanks to Yahweh, for he is good,
>   his faithful kindness endures for ever!
> Be this the song of his redeemed,
>   redeemed by him from the power of distress.

Then in four stanzas the different tribulations are described to which the different people have been exposed: 'they that wandered in the lonely wilderness', 'they that lay in darkness and gloom, prisoners in chains and misery', 'they that were afflicted with illness because of their transgressions and iniquities', 'they that went out to sea in ships', who all of them 'cried unto Yahweh in their trouble and were saved by him out of their distresses'. Every stanza ends like this:

> They shall thank Yahweh for his faithful kindness,
>   for the wonders that he doeth for men,

with an explanatory statement, varied according to the different cases, for instance:

> Because he breaketh gates of bronze
>   and cutteth iron bars in sunder.

A corporate general hymn brings the liturgy to a conclusion.

[37] See H. L. Ginsberg in *Louis Ginzberg Jubilee Volume*, pp. 159ff.
[38] See Ginsberg, *loc. cit.*
[39] See Albright in *BASOR* 87, Oct. 1942, pp. 23ff. This typical form of a votive inscription is also the rule in the Punic votive stelae, see Alt in *ZATW* 60, 1944, pp. 156ff.

Probably such common festivals were a result of the cult becoming more 'democratic'; it would be too expensive for many individuals to defray the expenses of the whole sacrifice and the 'fulfilment of the promises'. Perhaps, even, regard for the poor members of the congregation may have played a part; for then they might join in with the sacrifice. In New Testament times we find references to this as well as to such a corporate fulfilment of the promises (Acts 21.23f.). On a definite occasion —just before Easter—Paul took upon himself to pay for the vow and redemption offering for some of the brethren who could not afford to do so. This would naturally take place at one of the great annual festivals, when all adult men according to law were supposed to meet in Jerusalem.

4

The individual private psalms of thanksgiving are the ones in which we find most personal touches and background. Here we find an individual who has been faced with a matter of life or death, but who is now again able to breathe in the 'light of life', in the 'land of the living'. Whether he composed the psalm himself or had it written by a professional psalmist in his name, the occasion and the experience will be so universally applicable, just because it is deeply personal, so that as a matter of course the gravity of life and death and the strong emotions attached to these fundamental experiences will resound strongly, forcibly and personally in the psalms of thanksgiving. Here was a starting-point for a personal individual poetry, even if in formal respects it were to keep to the traditional style.

Yet another possibility of further development in cultic poetry was to be found here. The high estimate of the psalm of thanksgiving as the best sacrifice to God gradually resulted in making it a pious and meritorious work just to compose such a psalm. And—at any rate in later times—this again seems to have resulted in the production of thanksgiving psalms composed by ordinary people who had nothing directly to do with the temple service and singing.

We shall discuss this in other chapters (XVI.4; XVII.3), and we shall also return (Chap. XX.4) to the point that even the private psalms of thanksgiving had alien patterns.

CHAPTER XI

Psalms of Blessing and Cursing

The species of psalms hitherto discussed all belong to the sacrificial acts of the cult (Chap. I.6). But we have seen that psalms of lamentation and of supplication also contain or refer to a sacramental element, namely Yahweh's answer to the prayer through the promise of the cult officiant. And in the more complicated festal psalms belonging to the great complex of the new year festival—which are in some cases to be considered 'liturgies' (Chap. XIII.2) rather than 'psalms'—we also frequently find such a sacramental element. In the group of psalms to be discussed in the following chapters this sacramental element will be more or less the main point.

I

Among the psalms there are some that are formed as—or contain—blessings on the congregation and its individual members (Pss. 118.26; 122.8–9; 115.12–15; 128; 91, and others), and curses against the enemies of the people and against sinners and felons who endanger the security and happiness of community and individual (Pss. 35.26; 40.15; 55.16, 27; 109.6ff.; 119.21; 129.5ff.; 137).[1]

In this form the earliest conception of the cultic words still makes itself felt: the idea of the effectual word, 'creating what it mentions'.

Blessing (bĕrākhâ) is a basic word in the Israelite picture of real life.[2] Put briefly, blessing is identical with the very powers of life and their manifestations in external and internal happiness and welfare: in health, a long life, fertility, power of victory, of happiness, peace and joy and power and integrity of mind in fellowship with the clan, and in a life in conformity to 'justice' and 'law' and 'tradition'. To have 'blessing' includes whatever the Israelite understood by the term šālôm, 'wholeness', 'welfare', 'harmony', or 'peace', as it is usually translated. Every living thing has its particular blessing, which means that life is allowed to expand in 'peace and harmony'. Man's blessing is the joint possession of clan and people: the individual share in it differs with regard to degree and strength and form. It is the mysterious 'potency' and power and strength, immanent in life itself; so that the Israelitic bĕrākhâ in many ways corresponds to the power which the phenomenology of religion has

---

[1] See *Ps.St.* V; Hempel in *ZDMG* 79, 1925, pp. 20ff.; Gunkel-Begrich, *Einl.*, pp. 293ff.
[2] See Johs. Pedersen, *Israel* I–II, pp. 182–212, and *Ps.St.* V, pp. 5ff.

called 'mana'.[3] 'Blessing' belongs to the 'sacred things'; it is a holy power, living in the lives of clan and individual. The word really indicates a health-giving power, creating and promoting life, the power of blessing, 'blessedness'. 'The blessed one' (*bārûkh*) is a person 'having in himself blessing'.

From this blessing, blessing pours out in all sorts of shapes and manifestations. The word not only indicates 'blessedness', but even its visible outcome in happiness and fertility and victory and power and riches. And the power, as well as its outcome, pours out from the one who possesses it. This happens partly unconsciously, as when the presence of the 'luck-bringing' Joseph involuntarily brings happiness into the house of the Egyptian (Gen. 39.2ff.). Where blessing is found in a home it will flow from one to the other (Ps. 133). But in an intensified way the blessing and its outcome are transferred through particular acts and words, filled with effectual blessing and then of course with the character of holy acts and words. In the most usual form of blessing the one who gives the blessing lays his hands on the person who is to receive it, or prays with his hands lifted up above him. The effectual word accompanies—'materializes', and intensifies—the act.[4]

All 'right' (*şaddîq*)—normal, mentally healthy—people have this blessing in themselves, and are able to bless. But not all are equally full of blessing. It all depends on the strength of the spirit power possessed by the person in question, on his 'honour' and 'gravity' (*kābhôdh*). And as blessing is a 'holy' power, it will nowhere attain to greater strength than in the case of persons who in some way or other belong in the sacred sphere: kings, priests, seers, prophets, or the first ancestor in his hour of death, when he is already in touch with the Beyond, and rallies all his will and mental powers in order to transfer it to his sons.[5] But the transferability of the blessing also depends on the receptivity of the one who is being blessed. He must himself be a 'right' man, with a 'right' and healthy soul. It is no use trying to put blessing into a person with a 'crooked' and 'unrighteous' soul, a person who himself is full of 'curse' (see below), just as no curses tell upon a person who is full of blessing.[6] Therefore the phrase of blessing, 'Blessed art thou!' is at the same time the statement of a fact and an effectual word, increasing the blessing of the blessed one, his 'blessedness', as well as his power of transferring it to others.

Blessing appertains to every climax of life, in all important decisions: before a journey, at a wedding, when a dying person takes leave of his people, at the assignment of inheritance.[7] A greeting means a blessing (Ruth 2.4; Ps. 129.8).

[3] See above, Chap. I. 6, and cf. Mowinckel, *Religion und Kultus*, pp. 20ff., 32ff., 64f.

[4] Imposition of hands: Gen. 27.27; 48.14ff.; the word: Gen. 24.60; 27.27–29; 32.1; 48.15f., 20; 49. Num. 6.23–27; Deut. 33.

[5] Gen. 20.7, 17; 27; 48; 49; Lev. 9.22; Num. 6.23ff.; Deut. 33; 1 Sam. 9.13; Sir. 50.26f.

[6] Num. 22.12, cf. Gen. 27.30–40.

[7] See n. 4, and 1 Kgs. 1.31; 2 Kgs. 4.29; Ruth 2.20; 3.10; Tob. 11.17; Ps. 129.8; Jdg. 17.2; 1 Sam. 23.21; 25.33.

As blessing is something holy, and as it possesses creative power, it is obvious to the mind of an Israelite that it must have connexion with the *deity*. In Israelite religion Yahweh more and more became the only mighty one, the only creator. The source of blessing is the strong power to bless, pouring out from Yahweh himself. The holy place where Yahweh 'lives' is the home of all blessing (Ps. 133.3). The prophets see the floods of blessing flowing out from the Temple (Ezk. 48; Ps. 46.5). All the 'good things' pouring out from there may also be called the 'holy things' from the dwelling of Yahweh (Ps. 65.5). The blessed are 'the blessed of Yahweh', 'blessed by Yahweh'.[8] Yahweh's name is mentioned in the word of blessing; the strongest word of blessing is the blessing 'in the name of Yahweh' (Deut. 10.8; Ps. 118.26), including all the power of Yahweh. In very ancient times the blessed person may possibly have created blessing for another person out of his own power and by means of the effectual word; the blessing person is himself the subject of the action (Num. 22.6). But in historical times in Israel the word of blessing more and more took the form of a wish or a prayer for Yahweh to bless: 'may Yahweh bless thee!' Then people would no longer feel that there was any difference of meaning between these terms and 'Blessed art thou!', so that on this point one is justified in speaking of a 'development' from formula into prayer. This does not mean, however, that the idea of the particular effectual power of the word was ever given; but it is Yahweh who puts *his* power into the blessing word of the 'right' person; that is why 'the effectual fervent prayer of a righteous man availeth much'. Yahweh is the subject of the verb of blessing.

The transference of blessing was a holy, a ritual act, revolving round the 'holy' power, and The Holy One; the deity was present somehow through the invocation and mention of his name. Obviously, then, the blessing 'from the very first' had its place in the *cult* itself. To procure, secure and increase 'the blessing', that was the object of the temple services in Israel, put in a nutshell.[9] Through the temple service the congregation got into contact with Yahweh and received his life-creating and life-supporting power, his blessing. Therefore the cultic task of the priests, 'the Levites', may be summed up in the words telling them 'to bear the ark of the covenant of Yahweh and stand before him and minister unto him and bless in his name' (Deut. 10.8).

This intimate connexion between the temple service and the word of blessing is very old and can be traced back in certain expressions and customs which still to some extent betray the earliest conception of the creative power of the act and word of blessing. Through expressions like 'bless Yahweh'—in the traditional texts toned down to mean 'praise and thank him'—and still more when it is said that the doxology 'gives strength unto Yahweh' (Ps. 29.1), there is called to mind an age in which

---

[8] For instance Gen. 14.19; Jdg. 17.2; 1 Sam. 15.13; Ruth 2.20, and many other passages.
[9] Cf. Johs. Pedersen, *Israel* III–IV, p. 299.

the cultic acts and words were supposed even to create and renew the very strength and blessing power of the deity. Conversely it is said about Yahweh, when he puts the inspired song into the mouth of the poet or the cultic singer, that he then also fills him with his own power: 'Yahweh is my song and my strength' (Ex. 15.2; Isa. 12.2). Before the sacrificial feast the 'seer-priest' had to 'bless the sacrifice' so that it might become an effectual, sacramental meal full of blessing (1 Sam. 9.13).

The place of the blessing in the cult is evidenced in many ways. From references in the ritual of Deut. 27.11ff. it may probably be inferred that the people before going to war were lined up in tribes and clans in order to take blessing with them into battle. And as long as the Temple existed the festal service would end in the all-embracing blessing of the priest on the congregation in the well-known words:

> May Yahweh bless you and protect you!
> May Yahweh make his face shine upon you and favour you!
> May Yahweh lift up his eyes upon you and give you peace!

And it is explicitly said that 'when the priests thus put my name on the sons of Israel, I will bless them' (Num. 6.22ff.)—at the same time an evidence of what was said above, that it is Yahweh who adds the power of his blessing to the words, making them effectual. Nor is it to be interpreted differently, when the priests say: 'We bless you with the name of Yahweh' (Ps. 118.26).

Formally we may distinguish between the *blessing word*—'blessed thou!' —and the *blessing wish*—'mayest thou be blessed', or alternatively with explicit mention of the source of blessing: 'blessed thou by Yahweh!'— 'mayest thou be blessed by Yahweh', 'may Yahweh bless thee'. But there is no essential difference of meaning. Nor is there any difference of meaning between the blessing word 'blessed' (*bārûkh*) and the term used in the beatitude, 'blessed is the man who!' (*'ašrê ha'îš 'ăšer*).

Both these terms are used by way of introduction to the word of blessing. Then the person is mentioned to whom the blessing is directed: 'blessed thou!', 'blessed the man who fears Yahweh', and the like. Sometimes an actual individual—or a people—is mentioned, but sometimes the benediction is given in general on all people of such-and-such a character; then more and more characteristic attributes are attached to the name of the person in question. These attributes then indicate the conditions of blessing, for instance, 'he who fears Yahweh'.

The substance of the blessing may be quite general and only just suggested by the word 'blessed'. But the substance, the 'fruits', of the blessing may be mentioned with more or less detail, as for instance in the blessing of the bride on the part of the family:

> Our sister, may you be the mother of myriads,
> may your descendants conquer the gates of their foes!

> (Gen. 27.60.)

Or in the blessing of Isaac by Jacob:

> My son, may God give you
>   (your part) of the dew from heaven,
> of the fatness of the earth
>   and corn and wine in plenty!
> May nations be your servants,
>   and races bow before you!
> Be the master of your kinsmen,
>   may your brethren bow before you! (Gen. 27.28f.)

The benediction may also be bestowed on the individual members of the congregation. It is probably such a cultic benedictory formula which has been handed down to us in Deut. 28.3–6:

> Blessed be you in the town,
>   Blessed be you in the field,
> Blessed be the fruit of your body,
>   Blessed be the fruit of your ground,
> Blessed be the young of your cattle,
>   Blessed be the lambs of your flock,
> Blessed your basket and your store,
>   [Blessed your oil and your wine],
> Blessed be you as you start out,
>   Blessed as you come in!

The examples also show that fertility and display of power were looked upon as essential features of the blessing.

Curse is the very opposite of blessing, it is blessing with a negative sign. It likewise means 'power', though a negative, devastating and destroying power, manifesting itself in 'misconduct', so that the cursed one fails in everything; he is smitten by all sorts of disaster and suffers from want of all that makes life worth living; prematurely he meets with evil and sudden death, and his family and his name are obliterated from earth. A detailed description of the destiny befalling the cursed one is given in the final passage of the 'Law', Deut. 28.15–68.

The curse, 'cursedness', is an operative power, too, spreading from the one who is 'filled with curse' (*'ārûr*) to his family and all his surroundings. It is a 'contagious', disastrous power of the soul, and any intercourse with such a person is bound to bring curse and disaster, so that in this respect it is equal to 'sorcery' (*'āwen*, see Chap. VI.3; VIII.2, 4) and obsession by demonic powers which manifest themselves in illness and all kinds of evil. Like the blessing, it may be 'materialized' in *words* and *rites*, and be inflicted on decent people, who will then have to defend themselves against it by means of purifications and increased blessing and by the help of Yahweh. But 'the evil curse' will not affect a person who is full of blessing and under the protection of God, as long as he keeps close to God. All evil words and wishes of the enemies, all evil thoughts, sneers and mockery, and all outer signs of such demeanour: pointing one's finger, shaking one's head, and so on, are powerful curses. Even the cultic rites and prayers of enemies performed in order to gain victory over Israel, may be considered operative curses, 'sorcery' and 'treachery' directed against Israel. That is why the psalms of lamentation constantly complain of such cursing words and anathematizing acts.

But the curse may also be considered from another angle. The blessing power of an individual and the strong blessing power of Yahweh may be turned into a cursing power against wicked enemies—may become a legitimate defence against wicked people and be made effectual through words and rites. If anybody molests Israel, or the righteous, he will be placed under the ban of Yahweh himself (Gen. 12.3). The same thing will happen to the criminal who breaks the commandments of Yahweh and trespasses against law and religion (Mal. 2.3).

Therefore even the curse has its place in the *cult* and the *rites* of Israel. The ritual curse was used from ancient times against wrongdoers from among the people and congregation, for instance in order to chastise an unknown thief or someone under the suspicion of a secret crime, such as adultery.[10] In the latter case the curse would have a conditional character: it would overtake the person in question if he or she were guilty; if they escaped the consequences, their innocence would be proved. That word and rites belong together can be seen from the law about a woman suspected of marital infidelity. By visible means the priest is to materialize the curse in the 'water of curse' and let her drink it; if she is guilty, she will die from it. The accompanying words prove that at any rate in later times here also the power of Yahweh was invoked and so to speak mobilized against her: 'Yahweh make you a curse (i.e. a cursed thing) and an 'oath' (i.e. an exemplification of cursing words) among your people and make your thigh to rot and your belly to swell!' But alongside of this we find a formula which still brings out the earlier conception about the self-acting power of the 'water of curse': 'This water of curse shall go into your bowels, to make your belly to swell and your thigh to rot!'.

Before a war the enemy was cursed in order to break his power, as we hear in the story of Balaam, Num. 22–24. In the same way a town was cursed if it would not take part in the struggle against the enemies of Yahweh and of Israel (Jdg. 5.23). In Deut. 27.14ff. is handed down a cursing formula in twelve parts, which was used in the temple service on certain occasions against anybody who might have committed or be about to commit any of the crimes therein enumerated—a preventive as well as punitive measure. The curse was pronounced from the altar by priest or seer or prophet before the sacrifice was offered.[11] In the service of the

---

[10] Num. 22–24; Jdg. 17.2; Lev. 5.1; Num. 5.11ff.; Josh. 7.25; 1 Kgs. 8.31.
[11] Lev. 5.1f.; 1 Kgs. 8.31; Deut. 27.14ff.

II, 4

synagogues as well as in the Roman Catholic ritual we find analogies of such curses.[12]

The cursing words generally have the same pattern as the words of blessing: 'Cursed thou!' or 'Cursed be the man who shall do such and such a thing!' Or with explicit mention of Yahweh as fulfilling the curse. Sometimes the effect of the curse is described in detail by way of emphasis. We have had handed down to us a cursing formula exactly corresponding to the blessing formula quoted above:

> 'Cursed be you in the town', etc. (Deut. 28.16ff.)

The explicit denunciation of the crimes to which the curse would be applied of course implies a rather strong element of moral and religious popular education, just like the emphasis on the demeanour upon which the blessing of God would rest, and the enumeration of the good fruits of the blessing.

A formal variety of the curse is the cry of woe: 'Woe (*hôy*) to the man who . . .'. From what was said above of the effect of the evil word, we gather that on the merits of the case there is no essential difference between the cursing word and the cry of woe.

The blessing and the cursing in the name of Yahweh always had their places in the cult of Israel—even the services of the synagogue know both of them very well. In them we have good examples of the sacramental element in the temple service.

2

These important words or formulas accordingly found a place in the psalms —because the psalms are not only 'monologues' but partly 'liturgies' comprising several cultic elements (see Chap. XIII.2). Even in the 'monologue' psalms the power-full words have found a place as modes of composition, expressing some regular element belonging to the species of psalm in question: doxology, testimony, and so on. (See below.)

The word of blessing, inserted between the various voices of the processional psalm, falls upon the ears of the thanksgiving pageant entering the temple court, and seems to concentrate the powerful sanctity of place and moment:

> Blessed by the name of Yahweh be he who enters!
> We bless you from the house of Yahweh. (118.26.)

In the liturgy for a day of penance, Ps. 115, the direct blessing on the congregation by the priest forms a part of the psalm. In Ps. 121 it is addressed to the individual representing the congregation; here the word has a more detailed form describing the substance of the blessing. This is still more prominent in Ps. 128, which is addressed to an individual member of the congregation. In Ps. 91 the priest promises the protection of

[11] Cf. *Ps.St.* V, p. 69.

Yahweh to a person asking for it, in the form of a word of blessing, which by means of a great many concrete features pictures the security of being sheltered by Yahweh and all the good things enjoyed by such a blessed man.

We also find traces of another type of benedictory formula, emphasizing the religious and moral conditions of the blessing.[13] The pageant of Ps. 24 puts questions as to the pre-conditions for visiting the Temple; the answer reads as follows: he who does so-and-so 'shall receive the blessing from Yahweh'.

In substance and aim the blessing word and the intercession (Chap. VI.7) are closely related. When in Ps. 122 the leader of the party of pilgrims (or the pageant) wishes blessing on Jerusalem, it actually means an intercessory prayer for the holy city. It is a matter of personal judgment, whether Ps. 72 is to be called an intercession or a blessing wish. It has this in common with the blessing word that it is addressed to the person who is to receive the blessing, in this case the king. The same thing applies to the wishes for the king in Pss. 20.2–6 and 21.9–13. The homage poem to the king, Ps. 45, which describes itself as an efficacious luck word (*dābhār ṭôbh, 'ōmar*), reaches its climax in the blessing word in v. 17: 'May thy sons come into thy fathers' place, and rise to be princes over all the land!'

Sometimes the benedictory word is used as a mere element of style. In the hymn the eulogy of the people which has Yahweh for its king is an indirect eulogy of Yahweh; see for instance 33.12; 65.5. Thus it may also provide an introductory hymnal motive for confidence in the psalm of lamentation, as in Ps. 41.2ff.—if the latter is to be interpreted in this way In the thanksgiving psalm it serves as a means of instruction and exhortation (testimony), as in 32.1f., or as a hymnal motive for thanksgiving, as possibly in 41.

3

The *curse* (cursing word), introduced by 'cursed be he (the man) who . . .' or by the cry of woe, 'woe be he (the man) who . . .', is less prominent in the psalms. We find it—as we have already seen—most especially in the psalms of lamentation, as an element in the prayers for revenge and punishment of the enemies.[14] The ancient idea and form of the curse is re-echoed especially in the wishing form, which in the personal laments prevails over the prayer form (Chap. VII.4). And sometimes the more or less direct cursing formula appears to be the essential word of the psalm about the enemy, as in Ps. 109.6ff. Here are enumerated all the disasters that will overtake the wicked wretch. Elsewhere the cursing word has usually been replaced by the prayer for Yahweh to crush the enemy. But a prayer like the one in 83.10ff. with its elaborate description of the disaster

---

[13] Pss. 24.3–6; 15. Cf. *Ps.St.* V, pp. 58ff.
[14] See Chap. VI. 3; VII. 4, VIII. 7.

imprecated on the enemies of the people is evidently connected with the ancient cursing formulas, such as seers and other 'divine men' (*'îš 'ĕlōhîm*) and possessors of the effectual word would use against the enemy before the battle; with such words Balak expected Balaam to slay the Israelites for him.

Among the cursing psalms, attention may be drawn to Ps. 137, the prayer for Edom—whom the Jews hated with all their hearts—to be overtaken by all sorts of disasters. The prayer rises out of the background of the bitter memory of the fall of Jerusalem, when the Edomites seized the opportunity of settling in southern Judea. The prayer finally passes into a direct curse in a particularly refined form, namely as a word of blessing on the person who shall inflict the most cruel revenge on Edom.

4

Certain things seem to suggest that in the cultic rituals were used formulas in two parts, containing both blessing and curse. This style pattern was imitated by the wisdom poetry (as in Job 11.13ff., and Sir. 28.13ff.) and from thence even by the admonitions of the prophets; see Jer. 17.5ff. Here it is used to describe 'the two ways', the way of piety and the way of ungodliness, of 'life and death', and the destiny to which they would lead.

Through the learned psalmography (Chap. XVI) this form was also introduced into the latest, private psalmography (Pss. 1; 112) or, to express it more correctly: into the collection of psalms and other poems emanating from the learned 'wise men' (see Chap. XXII.3).

[15] Cf. *Ps.St.* V, pp. 97ff.

CHAPTER XII

The Prophetic Word in the Psalms, and the Prophetic Psalms

Corresponding to the prayers of the congregation and the individual in the cult we have the answer of the deity.

I

As already mentioned (Chap. VI.3) certain things in the structure and style of the laments imply that the priest or some other temple official used to announce to the worshipper Yahweh's merciful promise of hearing his prayer.

In the earliest period in Israel the priest was not originally in the first instance sacrificer but, as with the old Arabs, custodian of the sanctuary, oracle priest, 'seer' and holder of the effectual future-creating and future-interpreting word of power, the blessing and the curse. This earlier system was partly kept up even after the settlement; Samuel in Ramah,[1] for instance, was such a seer priest. A chief or a private individual in doubt how to act in a difficult matter would apply to the seer priest for an oracle, a word from Yahweh about the matter, which the seer priest was supposed to be instrumental in announcing. The same thing was done, for instance, if one wanted to find out the reason why the wrath of Yahweh had smitten the land with disaster.[2] Even in doubtful ritual questions the seers, as later on the priests, would give 'instruction' (tôrâ).[3] That the questions sometimes at any rate were accompanied by a sacrifice may be concluded from the tale about the sacrificial feast celebrated by Solomon at Gibeon (1 Kgs. 3.4ff.), and ending in a revelation of Yahweh with the promise of a special wisdom of judgment; the analogy from the offerings made before the announcement of the effectual words of blessing and curse in the Balaam stories, Num. 22–24, is evidence for the same thing.

From what we know about the oracles of the ancient Israelite seer priests it appears that the answer of the deity was often found by means of so-called technical instruments of oracle, such as casting lots with the holy 'Urim and Thummim'[4] or by means of 'looking' for special 'signs'

---

[1] 1 Sam. 9f.; see Ps.St. III, pp. 9ff.; GTMMM II, pp. 167, 170; III, pp. 11f.; Hölscher, Die Profeten, pp. 121ff.

[2] 1 Sam. 23.2, 4, 10f., 12; 30.7f.; 2 Sam. 5.19.—2 Sam. 21.1ff.

[3] Cf. Hag. 2.10ff.; Zech. 7.1ff. See Begrich 'Die priesterliche Thora' in Werden u. Wesen d.A.T., ed Hempel (BZATW 66); Östborn, Tora in the O.T., pp. 89ff.—Begrich's definition of 'tora' is much too narrow.

[4] See Stade-Bertholet, Bibl. Theologie d. A.T. I, p. 129; GTMMM II, p. 186, note on 1 Sam. 14.37a; cf. 1 Sam. 10.20ff.; Josh. 7.

in the sacrificial animal, and by interpreting them. Casting of lots might be used to learn whom Yahweh had appointed king of Israel, as we can read in the stories of the younger saga about the election of king Saul, and also in order to find out who the unknown culprit might be who on some occasion or other had roused the wrath of Yahweh, as we hear in the stories about Jonathan's breach of the taboo, and about the theft of Achan. It is to some sort of interpretation of signs in connexion with the sacrifice that the term *biqqēr* in Ps. 27.4 refers; it must mean something like 'find out (the tokens)', 'take omens'. Ps. 5.4 explicitly mentions this 'sacrifice for omens' (*bōqēr*).[5] References in some of the psalms seem to show that the so-called oracle of incubation and dreams was also used, oracles being received in their dreams by people passing the night in the Temple or at the sanctuary.[6] Therefore it is quite natural that in the psalms of lamentation we also come across prayer for a 'token for good' (86.17), that is, for a favourable token.[7] But the stories of both Balaam and Samuel prove that ancient Israel did not feel that there was any contrast between such an oracle and real inspiration, as we shall see below.

So in ancient Israel priest and giver of oracles—'seer', 'divine man'—to all appearance meant one and the same person.

When the Israelites settled in Canaan and got to know the Canaanite culture they met with two different types of people interpreting the deity:[8] the temple priests and the ecstatic 'prophets', the *nĕbhî'îm*.[9] In Babylonia the oracle priests, the 'seers' (*barû*) made up a special class of the temple personnel.[10] The *nĕbhî'îm* represented a particular form of religious experience: in a state of ecstacy they experienced the divine presence, and knew themselves to be filled with divine power; whatever they would then do or say would be considered powerful divine signs and words, at once unveiling and influencing the future. People would apply to the *nĕbhî'îm* both as miracle-workers and soothsayers.[11] This ecstatic form of piety was soon adopted by Israel and adapted to Yahwism: the *nĕbhî'îm* became the

---

[5] See *Ps.St.* I, pp. 146f.; *GTMMM* I, p. 8, note on Gen. 4.5a; Gunkel-Begrich, *Einl.*, p. 246. In Nabataean inscriptions the participle *mubaqqiru* is used about a cultic person, probably a vaticinator of the sacrifice (quoted from von Rad in *Festschrift für Bertholet*, p. 430, n. 1 with references to *CIS* II, 2118, 2593, 2661, 2667–2669). In the sect of Damascus *mĕbhaqqēr* is known to indicate the administrative and judicial leader of the sect, corresponding to *episkopos*. Among other things he is to 'instruct (the priest) in the interpretation of the tora' and see to it that the 'casting of lots' (*haggōrāl*, Zadokite Document 13.4; in 13.12 we may have to read *gōrāl hā'ûrîm*, see Hvidberg, *Menigheden af den ny Pagt*, p. 174) was performed in the proper way, when matters of dispute were to be decided. This seems to suggest that *mĕbhaqqēr* originally indicated the person who 'distinguishes', 'discriminates' between the oracular tokens, who gives oracles of some kind or other. Therefore Aalen's interpretation of *biqqēr* as 'officiate at morning prayer' (*Licht u. Finsternis*, p. 61, n. 1) is impossible.

[6] Pss. 3.6ff.; 17.15; and cf. Gen. 28.10ff.; 1 Sam. 3. See *Ps.St.* I, pp. 154ff.

[7] Ps. 86.17; see *Ps.St.* I, pp. 145f.

[8] Cf. *Ps.St.* III, pp. 14ff.; Haldar, *Cult Prophets*, pp. 74ff.; A. R. Johnson, *The Cultic Prophet*.

[9] Canaanite priests and prophets are mentioned, for instance in 1 Kgs. 18.19ff.; 2 Kgs. 10.19; 11.18; 23.5; Jer. 23.13. See Hölscher, *Die Profeten*, pp. 129ff.

[10] See Haldar, *Cult Prophets*, pp. 1ff., Gunkel-Begrich, *Einl.*, pp. 137, 160f., with references to sources and literature; Hooke, *Prophets and Priests*, pp. 11ff.

[11] 1 Sam. 9; 1 Kgs. 17.7ff., 17ff.; 2 Kgs. 1.2ff.; 4–5; 6.1ff., 8ff.; 13.14ff.; 20.1ff.

prophets of Israel announcing words about the future.[12] But at the same time Israel also adopted and remodelled great parts of the Canaanite cultic system with its festivals and its permanent temples and clergy, a well developed and specialized sacrificial system—the daily service in the Temple being a more or less marked element of the cult.[13] The result of this was a distinction between two types of revelation: priestly and prophetic. The *priest*, whose ministry was hereditary and confined to certain families, the 'Levites'; they became more and more pre-occupied with cult and sacrifice, but remained in control of the more technical system of oracles, 'urim and thummim' and so on, dispensing 'guidance' on cultic, ritual, moral and judicial questions, and mediating Yahweh's 'laws' (*tôrôth*) and 'judicial decisions' and 'judgments' (*mišpāṭîm*) and a constantly increasing tradition of such laws,[14] among them such ancient laws as had been taken over from the Canaanites.[15] The *prophets* on the other hand formed looser unions of more or less ecstatically inspired 'divine men'. The call to be a prophet could come to anyone—as with Elisha and Amos—and probably depended on certain psychic predispositions to the ecstatic and visionary state. In new forms they continued the more 'pneumatic' aspect of the character and work of the old 'seers'; instead of oracle tokens and omens there were 'visions' and 'voices' of a psychological nature; the prophets were mediums of the divinely inspired 'word', which was 'whispered to' them[16] or 'came to them', becoming a living and effectual reality in their souls.[17] From these 'prophetic guilds'[18] the classical movement of reform prophets developed, whose names are known to us and whose sayings have been handed down in the books of the prophets.[19] But the boundary between priest and prophet was never an absolute one. Samuel was priest as well as prophet; and both Jeremiah and Ezekiel were members of priestly families.

To understand the prophetic elements in the psalms it is important for us to know that from the very start these prophetic guilds were closely

[11] See Mowinckel in *NTT*, 1909, pp. 185ff., 330ff.; Hölscher, *Die Profeten*, pp. 132ff.; Lindblom, *Profetismen*, pp. 169ff.

[13] See for instance Hölscher, *Gesch. d. isr. u. jüd. Religion*, pp. 69ff.; Lindblom, *Israels religion*,² 1953, pp. 84ff.; Lods, *Israel*, pp. 449ff.; 465ff.; 492ff. [E.T., pp. 387ff.; 401ff.; 424ff.].

[14] Cf. Östborn, *Tora in the O.T.*, pp. 89ff.

[15] As for instance 'the Mishpat collection' in Ex. 21–22 (see *GTMMM* I, pp. 151f.); cf. Alt, *Ursprünge d. isr. Rechts*.

[16] Cf. the set phrase of the oracles, *nᵉ'um* YHWH, '(the word) whispered by Yahweh'.

[17] Cf. Mowinckel in *JBL* 53, 1934, pp. 199ff. = *NTT*, 1935, pp. 1ff.; further [D]*TT*, 1935, pp. 1ff. = *Act. Or.* XIII, pp. 264ff.; id., *Erkenntnis Gottes bei d. alttestam. Propheten*. For the general history of prophetism in Israel see *GTMMM* III, pp. 13f.; Hölscher, *Die Profeten*, pp. 143ff.; 173ff.; Lindblom, *Profetismen*, pp. 112ff.

[18] Literally: 'sons of the prophets'; the expression 'son of such and such a fellowship' is the usual Semitic indication of a member of some sociological unit, a guild, clan or sect. For the prophetic guilds see Hölscher, op. cit., pp. 152ff.; Lindblom, op. cit., pp. 112ff.; Mowinckel in *NTT*, 1909, pp. 198ff.

[19] See Hölscher, op. cit., pp. 181ff., 189ff.; Lindblom, op. cit., pp. 179ff.; Würthwein, 'Amosstudien', *ZATW* 62, 1949–50, pp. 10ff.; cf. Hylander in *Monde Orientale* 25, 1931, pp. 53ff.; Rowley in *Eissfeldtfestschrift*, pp. 191ff.

connected with the temples,[20] just as the 'seers' of Babylonia were reckoned among the temple priests. In Jerusalem, at any rate, an order of 'temple prophets' grew into being. We find evidence of this in Jeremiah, where we hear that the temple prophets were under the jurisdiction of one of the priests (Jer. 29.36); even at the time of Nehemiah (Neh. 6.11ff.)we come across such temple prophets, having the run of the Temple and living under certain religious rules. The stories of Elijah make both Elijah and the prophets of Baal offer sacrifices (1 Kgs. 18.20ff.); so they were connected with the cult. And even if the cultic festivals used to be the occasion on which the free reform prophets, partly hostile to the cult, would appear with their words of doom, as we hear of Amos and others,[21] the promises of the 'loyal', 'state prophets' would certainly also be heard there, and that probably not only by chance, but as a more or less regular element in the liturgies themselves.

In Jewish times we find obvious traces of this development. The Chronicler even speaks of a 'master of the oracles', at his time belonging to the 'Levites', i.e. to the lower temple personnel (1 Chron. 15.22, 27). And when in another place (2 Chron. 20.14ff.) he tells about the prophetic answer given to the prayer of the congregation on a certain day of prayer, and makes one of the Levitical singers present the answer, this may certainly be taken to express what used to take place on such occasions; it shows that prophetically inspired men belonged to the organized temple personnel, subordinate to the priests. It is a pointer in the same direction that the Chronicler considers the Levitical temple singers to be somehow inspired, and uses the term 'prophesy' about their official singing, meaning that their singing arises from an *ex officio* inspiration (1 Chron. 25.1ff.). This means that it was the old prophetic guilds that had been organized into the order of the temple servants (the 'Levites'), and had thus transferred to the latter a show of the inspiration of the old prophets. The statements of the Chronicler show too that it was among these 'singers' that the prophetic guilds were taken up. It is easy to understand this, considering the old conception of the gifts of poets and singers: they were looked upon

[20] See Mowinckel in *NTT*, 1909, pp. 198ff., 224f.; *Ps.St.* III, pp. 14ff.; Johnson, *The Cultic Prophet in Anc. Israel*; Junker, *Prophet u. Seher in Israel*; Welch, *Prophet and Priest in Old Israel*; Hooke, *Prophets and Priests*; Hoschander, *The Priests and Prophets*; Lattey in *JTS* 42, 1919, pp. 155f.; T. H. Robinson in *JTS* 43, 1920, pp. 129ff.; Coleran in *Theol.St.* V, 1944, pp. 411ff.; Scott, *The Relevance of the Prophets*; Pedersen in *Studies in Prophecy*, ed. H. H. Rowley, pp. 127ff.; Plöger in *ZATW* 63, 1951, pp. 157ff.; Hess in *Evang. Kirchenztg.* 7, pp. 129ff.; Kapelrud in *StTh* IV, 1950–51, pp. 5ff.; Würthwein in *ZATW* 62, 1949–50, pp. 10ff.—Haldar's treatment of the cultic prophets of Israel (*Assoc. of Cult. Prophets*, pp. 90ff.) is not very satisfactory, as it has been much too highly adapted to the corresponding Babylonian phenomena, and does not give sufficient consideration to the peculiarities of Israelite religion. The polemics of Begrich (Gunkel-Begrich, *Einl.*, pp. 370ff.) against the demonstration that there were true temple prophets in Israel are mainly irrelevant, leaving unanswered the problems raised by the texts themselves. It is astonishing that M. Schmidt (*Prophet und Tempel*) can devote a whole book to the theme 'prophet and temple' without even touching upon the problem of the organic and sociological relation of the prophets to the Temple and the cult, and without mentioning the problem raised in *Ps.St.* III or in Johnson's *The Cultic Prophet*. It is a quite unhistorical idea that there existed in Israel from the beginning a tension between 'prophetic piety' and temple cult, or even any opposition on the part of the former against the latter.

[21] Am. 7.10ff.; cf. Isa. 28.7ff.; 32.9ff. (cf. *GTMMM* III, pp. 168f.); Jer. 7; 26; 36.

as of divine inspiration, an outcome of supra-normal, inspired 'wisdom'.[22]

Such an institutional organization and incorporation of the prophets in the cultic system does signify a certain distinction between the old prophetic guilds and the great individual prophets with regard to the conception of inspiration. In the earliest prophetic guilds inspiration was something that would come to them time and again as a result of the ecstatic experience, and the latter might be called forth by means of certain 'spiritual exercises', to which for instance would belong dancing and music or deep meditation and contemplation.[23] To the great classical prophets, however, 'the word of Yahweh' would come sometimes unexpectedly, sometimes when they were preparing to receive it through prayer and concentration.[24] With the organized temple prophets inspiration is rather what we should call an official, occupational inspiration, a permanent charismatic equipment belonging to the office itself, just as in Roman Catholic opinion the priest receives such a charismatic official equipment through the act of his ordination. This conception was common enough in ancient Israel. On being anointed, the king was officially equipped with the spirit of Yahweh (Chap. III.3). The ancient Israelite did not feel that there was any contrast between the unconstrained oracle and utterance of a spontaneous inspiration and the oracle that had been won by technical means; for it required a supra-normal equipment to be able to 'see' the 'tokens' rightly, and interpret them rightly, or to be able to handle the casting of lots in such a way that the right oracle would appear. Even at the time of Jesus, Judaism ascribed to the high priest an official prophetic inspiration: he was able to prophesy because of his 'being high priest that year' (John 11.51). Even the technical oracle of the priest, found for instance by the casting of lots, would often have to be given the proper form and style, to be expressed in sensible, intelligible words;[25] this also was an outcome of 'wisdom' and inspiration.

Therefore it is very possible that the ritual of a particular cultic festival would provide that at a certain point the prophet was to announce Yahweh's answer to the prayer, and that the substance of the answer was prescribed by the ritual, whereas wording and composition were left to the free and instantaneous inspiration of the prophet. But it is just as possible that even the wording of the promise would be prescribed by the ritual, as is the case with, for instance, the formula of absolution in present-day divine services.

As we actually come across such prophetic promises in some psalms, and from others we are able to infer that on some occasions they made up a

[22] Pss. 45.1; 49.4f.; 1 Kgs. 5.9ff. See *Ps.St.* III, pp. 26ff., 109f.; IV, pp. 5ff.; VI, pp. 48ff.
[23] See for instance 1 Sam. 10.5ff.; 19.18ff.; 2 Kgs. 3.15; 1 Kgs. 18.42ff.; Isa. 21.6, 8; Hab. 2.1. Cf. Mowinckel in *NTT*, 1909, pp. 204ff.; Hölscher, *Die Profeten*, pp. 143–152; Lindblom, *Profetismen*, pp. 121–132.
[24] Cf. Mowinckel, *Erkenntnis Gottes*, pp. 13ff., 19ff., 26ff.
[25] See *Ps.St.* III, pp. 12ff. See also Jdg. 1.1; 18.6; 20.18, 27f.; 1 Sam. 2.28; 14.18, 36, 41; 23.2, 9ff.; 30.7f.; 2 Sam 2.1; 5.19, 23; 21.1; Ex. 22.7f. Cf. Smend *Alttestam. Religionsgeschichte* pp. 75f.

permanent part of the cultic ritual, we should also like to know whether
it was the task of the priest on duty or of one of the temple prophets to
announce this word. For it by no means follows that it would be the
priest.[26]

The style would be one means of deciding the question. There is no
doubt that the 'guidance' (tôrâ) of the priest from the very first had a
characteristic style of its own: the more or less apodictic instruction or
order: 'thou shalt do (not do) such and such a thing'; or with an introductory sentence stating the particulars of the case: 'when such and such
a thing shall happen, or if such be the case, thou shalt do so and so'.[27]

As far as the psalms are concerned, neither the promises ('oracles') of
Yahweh that have been handed down to us, nor those that may be inferred from different allusions, have this form; they are all of them clearly
and distinctly kept in the usual prophetic style.[28] This seems to show a
likelihood that they arose within the prophetic circles on the basis of
prophetic style and traditional ideas, consequently that they were also
announced by one of the temple prophets in the cult liturgy.

The occasional statements of the Chronicler point in the same direction; the promises of Yahweh at the cultic festival are always put into the
mouth of a singer or a Levite (see above).

But this in no wise implies that in earlier times priest and temple
prophet may not on some occasions have been one and the same person.
We hear that Jeremiah (1.1) as well as Ezekiel (1.1) belonged to priestly
families. And it is a fact that in Jewish times the lower temple servants
in quite large measure consisted of members of ancient priestly families
which had been reduced to a subordinate position.[29] It is therefore quite
possible that in the time of the monarchy Yahweh's promise in the cult
would be announced by one of the priests on duty. But even in this case
it shows how extraordinarily strong was the influence of the prophetic
movement: the priest speaks like a prophet and in the traditional style of
the prophetic speech.

2

In the chapter on the psalms of lamentation and the protective psalms
we saw that Yahweh's merciful answer to laments and prayers was a
permanent element in the acts of offering and purification to which these
psalms belonged (Chap. VI.3). A few of these answers have been preserved
in the national psalms of lamentation as well as in the individual laments.[30]

[26] As Gunkel-Begrich seem to think, Einl., pp. 370ff., cf. ibid., pp. 245ff.; Begrich in ZATW
52, 1934, pp. 81ff.
[27] Cf. Ps.St. III, pp. 12ff; Alt, Urspr. d. isr. Rechts.
[28] For the style of the prophetic statements see GTMMM III, pp. 38ff.; Hylmö, Gml. testam
litteraturhistoria, pp. 72ff.—Even the 'priesterliche Heilsorakel', which Begrich thinks may be
inferred from the allusions of the psalms (see n. 26) has an altogether prophetic style; there is
nothing whatever 'priestly' about either style or substance.
[29] See for instance Bentzen, Stud. zadok. praesteskabs hist.
[30] Pss. 12.6; 60.8-10; 108.8-10; 91.14-16. See Küchler in Baudissinfestschrift, pp. 295f.;
Mowinckel in Ps.St. III, pp. 64ff., 101ff.

Other psalms have direct or indirect references to them.[31] This does not prove that they only occurred as a rare exception; on the contrary, they were certainly a regular feature; a divine answer is certainly to be pre-supposed even in psalms where nothing is said about it. But naturally it would not be included in the actual text of the psalms, since it constituted a more variable feature of the liturgy; that is why the tradition so seldom mentions it.

From Pss. 60 and 108 we can see that the same promise might reappear in different psalms, at different times. Oracles might, in other words, be used over again. This very fact shows that they made up a permanent feature of the liturgy itself, and that the wording would usually be rather stereotyped and according to pattern. This again is another reason why they are so seldom handed down in connexion with the psalms of prayer. It would be a rare exception for the promise to be given a new wording, explicitly based on the concrete historical situation by which the day of prayer was occasioned. This however is evidently the case with Ps. 60, in which the answer has been formulated with reference to a definite historical situation: a war against Edom and other neighbouring peoples. But even such a promise might be used again in a new situation and with a new mode of expression, as will be seen from Ps. 108.

We get an idea of the main contents of these permanent promises through the reference of Ps. 35.3: 'I am thy help'; [32] compare, too, the reference in Ps. 27.14:

> Be strong and make thy soul be brave,
> and wait on Yahweh now!

Several indications suggest that Deutero-Isaiah, who so often clothes his prophecies in the form of the cultic psalm and the cultic ritual,[33] has also several times used the salvation oracle of temple prophet, or priest, as a style pattern of the promise.[34] From these imitations we get an impression of both form and substance. As a rule they start with a 'Be not afraid!' To this was attached the statement that Yahweh has heard the prayer of the wretched one, and then we have the promise of help and salvation, in wordings rather like the ones used in the prayer of the laments: 'I am with thee'; 'I shall deliver thee'; 'thou shalt not be put to shame'; 'I shall answer when thou callest on me'; 'I shall deliver him and make him honoured'; 'thine enemies shall stumble and not prevail against thee' and the like. Even corroboration of the statements of confidence in the psalm belonged to the permanent content of the oracle:

[31] Pss. 20.7; 21.9; 35.3; 62.12; 27.8, 14; Lam. 3.57; etc.
[32] See Begrich in *ZATW* 52, 1934, pp. 81ff.
[33] See *GTMMM* III, pp. 49ff., 190, and above, Chap. V. 5.
[34] So in Isa. 41.8–13, 14–16; 43.1–3a, 5; 48.17–19; 49.7, 14f.; 51.7f.; 54.4–8, and probably also 44.2–5; perhaps also in Jer. 30.10; 46.27; 30.11; 46.28. See Begrich, op. cit. His treatise suffers from the artificial and sharp distinction which he draws between I-psalms and we-psalms; he would have had a richer source of material if he had included the national psalms of lamentation in the I-form.

'Thou art my servant'; 'I shall not leave thee'; 'I am thy redeemer', and so on.[35]

As was the case with cultic words and oracles in general in ancient times, so also these promises had a poetical form. Sometimes they were addressed directly to the worshipper in the second person 'thou', as in Ps. 27.14 (see above). But at other times the promise speaks of the worshipper in the third person as in Pss. 12.6 and 91.14–16. Here evidently the temple prophet (priest) is supposed to be the intermediary and messenger; the deity is supposed to speak to the cultic official about the worshipper, and then the cultic official announces what the deity has said.

All these elements of form are to be found also in the corresponding promises of Babylonian psalms and rituals.[36]

The worshipper again answers this promise through the cultic official on duty by expressing a thanksgiving and laudatory assurance of being heard and receiving help (Chap. VI.3); in fact, the oracle about the hearing of the prayer forms the cultic and style-historical basis of this element in the psalm of lamentation—a good example being afforded by Ps. 12. First comes the lament with invocation, lamentation and prayer (vv. 2–5); then Yahweh's answer through the official of the cult (v. 6):

> For the trouble of the oppressed, the sighing of the needy
>   now will I rise, so saith Yahweh,
> I will set in freedom (the poor oppressed),
>   him that (the wicked) has blown upon.

'Blown upon' is here a form of 'witchcraft' which, as a term for the wickedness of the oppressor,[36a] means nearly the same as: 'has afflicted with "curse"'. And finally we have the anticipatory thanksgiving for the hearing of his prayer on the part of the believer, vv. 7.8, with direct reference to the 'pure words of Yahweh'.

The specimens preserved, as well as the imitations of the style in Deutero-Isaiah, clearly bring out that in these promises we have the normal prophetic style. For all their shortness they are kept in the fuller, more picturesque style of the prophetic word, different from the commanding or didactic style of the *tôrâ*; we have the clear promising note, but also something mysteriously suggesting, which is characteristic of the old seer-oracles. They appear as inspired Yahweh-words, spoken by Yahweh himself ('I'). Sometimes this is made quite clear in the introduction. The speaker introduces himself as an inspired person, 'listening to whatever the deity shall speak through me' and in his ecstasy 'hearing unknown speech' (81.6), which after only a moment of listening he understands to be that of Yahweh himself:

---

[35] For all the details see Begrich, op. cit.
[36] See Begrich, op. cit.
[36a] Cf. Ps. 10.5, and see *Ps.St.* I, pp. 26f., 169f.; Johs. Pedersen, *Israel I–II*, p. 540, n. 2 (to p. 449).

I will listen to what God speaks through me:
certainly, Yahweh is speaking welfare (*šālôm*)
to his people, to his faithful devoted,
and hope to those who turn to him. (85.9.)

Here the forms of free extempore prophetic inspiration have been transferred to the cultic oracle and combined with the announcement of
promises, which perhaps made up a permanent part of the ritual with
regard to both substance and form. We are certainly dealing with true
cultic psalms with real ritual promises, and not private imitations of an
ancient cultic style.

It is not improbable that these oracular answers would sometimes be
supported by certain external 'tokens' or 'omens' of some kind, for instance peculiarities about the sacrificial victim. When Habakkuk, who
undoubtedly was such a temple prophet,[37] declares: 'I will stand upon
my watchtower and will watch to see what He will say unto me' (2.1),
it is most natural to think of some sort of token, which he himself puts into
words.[38] Other references in the prophets as well point in the same
direction.[39] It is natural for us to think that where the wording of the
promise has a particular form and has therefore been handed down in the
text of a psalm, we have promises shaped by the particular temple prophet
himself with reference to the situation, and that it so happened because
some particular 'token' had confirmed the hearing of the prayer.[39a]

3

Promises uttered by temple prophets in the name of Yahweh occur not
only in laments and protective psalms, but also at the regular festivals.
There is a group of royal oracles which were addressed to the king on his
day of anointing and enthronement, or at the festival of harvest and new
year (which was probably also the anniversary of the anointing of the
king[40]) or at some other royal festival, for instance, at his wedding.
Promises occasioned by the anointing of the king are found in Pss. 2 and
110; promises to the royal house in general are given in Ps. 132, and
probably also in the oracle to which the psalm of lamentation, Ps. 89,
refers (vv. 20ff.). Ps. 45 is a promise for the wedding day.

Israel's conception of the ideal king is brought out above all in the
oracles for the installation of the king. Kingship is promised to him by

[37] See *Ps.St.* III, pp. 27ff.; *Jesejadisiplene*, p. 61, cf. p. 146; *GTMMM* III, p. 708; Humbert,
Livre d'Habacuc, p. 293; Mowinckel in *ThZ* 9, pp. 1ff.

[38] Cf. Isa. 21.6ff.—Haldar, *Cult. Prophets*, pp. 101ff., unduly exaggerates his point of view,
and often gives interpretations of the text which are in the nature of arbitrary assertions rather
than sensitive exegesis.

[39] Cf. *Ps.St.* III, pp. 18ff.

[39a] See *Ps.St.* I, pp. 154ff.; Ehrlich, *Der Traum im Alten Testament*, pp. 13ff. Ehrlich denies,
however, that incubation is mentioned or alluded to in the psalms (op. cit., pp. 51ff.); but as
it was evidently in use in Israel, e.g. in 1 Kgs. 3, as Ehrlich himself admits, it may well have
been used in connexion with the ritual use of the psalms of supplication and lamentation too;
Ehrlich does not seem to have proved that this interpretation of Ps. 17.15 is impossible.

[40] See *Ps.St.* III, pp. 78ff.; Lods in *Mélanges Maspero*. I, pp. 91ff.

the prophet by virtue of Yahweh's favour and election, and he points out to him the noble qualities which Yahweh has thereby bestowed on him, as well as the great works he is now going to accomplish in the power of the Lord; he is promised victory and happiness and grandeur and ascendancy over all his enemies. On these royal oracles see above, Chap. III.4.

4

Promise and intercession may easily interchange here. Taking as examples psalms like 20 and 21, probably both uttered before a military expedition and promising to the king Yahweh's help and victory over his enemies, they actually start as an intercession on the part of the congregation (see Chap. VI.7); but the nearer the prophetic poet and singer arrives at an assurance that the prayer will be heard, the more does the prayer change into a promise full of victorious assurance and picturing the coming greatness of king and people; the intercessor becomes the announcer of effectual words of blessing and the inspired promiser of victory. In Ps. 72 it is the blessing wish (Chap. XI.2) that is changed into confident promise. Ps. 20 refers to the real oracle or 'token' on which the assurance is based by saying 'Now know I that Yahweh saveth his anointed'. The psalmist here puts his assurance in his own words, based on what Yahweh has let him know; the oracle itself *may* have been imparted to the king by another cultic official. But even with the psalmist the prophetic element makes itself felt; his declaration of the assurance the oracle has given him gradually assumes the form of a promise.

Therefore the promising notes of psalms like Pss. 21 and 72 are probably not to be looked upon as direct oracles, but as the words of an inspired psalmist, as echoes of such oracles inserted into the intercessions and blessing wishes which the poet-singer puts into the mouth of the congregation. Once more they bring out the close relationship between temple prophet and psalmist, or rather, show that in fact the two would in many cases be one and the same person.

We have pointed out above (p. 224) the close relationship between the blessing and the intercession. But also between the blessing (or cursing) word and the prophetic oracle there existed from the beginning a close relationship. This we may see already in the Balaam legend and the two very old oracles which it includes. Balaam is called for by the king of Moab to curse Israel, but he ends by blessing them, and this blessing is formulated in poems of a definite 'prophetic' style and content; they are efficacious words predicting the future luck and greatness of the people, being in fact artificial *vaticinia ex eventu* on the Davidic kingdom. There is reason to believe that the prophetic style goes back to the efficacious and future-creating blessing and cursing words of the old 'seers', as the ministry of the prophet goes back to that of the seer.

In Israelite opinion the intercessory prayer had the same creating might as the blessing and oracle. It too was an efficacious word with something of the creative might of the other. There is no great difference between the conceptions: 'may this and that blessing happen to you', or 'may Yahweh give you this or that', and 'this or that will happen to you'; all these conceptions are expressed by the same forms of the verb. So there may be cases where it is difficult to decide whether we have a word of blessing, an intercessory prayer, or a prophecy, and therefore we are uncertain how to translate. A psalm like 72 may easily be read as a prophecy of the ideal king, and this has been the traditional explanation; the good wishes for the king in Ps. 21.9ff. have the additional style of a prophecy, and may be translated 'thy hand shall find all thine enemies', etc., as well as 'may thy hand find all thine enemies'. Ps. 45.17 can be translated: 'may thy sons take the place of thy fathers', or 'thy sons shall take. . . .'

This prophetic element in the intercessory prayer has its natural cult-historical explanation. In ancient Israel the prophet was regarded as the right 'prayer man', in whose prayer there was great might (cf. Gen. 20.3, 7; 1 Kgs. 18.41ff.; 2 Kgs. 6.17; Jer. 37.3; 42.2ff.). And what is said above shows us that his might as 'a specialist in prayer' (Johnson) was put at the service of the community in the cult. It was a part of the ministry of the cult prophet to act as an *intercessor*,[41] and that meant in fact also to recite the prayers that had to be recited there. We have seen above that Yahweh's answer to the prayer of the congregation was pronounced by a cult prophet. And so there is reason to think that it was also one of the cult prophets who recited the psalm of lamentation on behalf of the congregation, and this may also often have been the case where the king acted as the official leader of the cult and consequently was considered as the narrator in the national psalms of lamentation; even in the psalms in I-form we may think that the cult prophet often recited the psalm in question on behalf of the king. Not only the cult oracle but also the cultic prayer was the responsibility of the prophet.

5

So it can cause no wonder if by the side of these royal oracles on regular or particular cultic occasions we also find a group of 'prophetic psalms' with promises for the congregation or people. Pre-eminently they belong to the regularly recurring communal festivals, first and foremost the *festival of harvest and new year*. Such promises of victory and happiness and welfare and fertility for land and people and royal family and all classes; of Yahweh's favour and of peace and good crops and of doom and annihilation for the enemies of Israel and all evil powers (89.20ff.; 132.11ff.; 85.9ff.), certainly belonged to the festal cult even of earlier times. They also belong to the epiphany of Yahweh in the new year psalms of later

[41] Cf. A. R. Johnson, *The Cultic Prophet*, pp. 50f.; de Boer, *OTS* III, pp. 31ff.; Wurthwein in *ZATW* 62, 1949–50, pp. 24ff.; Hesse, *Die Fürbitte im A.T.*; Hooke, *Prophets and Priests*; Plöger in *ZATW* 63, 1951. The prophet as intercessor also occurs in the psalm of Habakkuk (Chap. 3), see Mowinckel in *ThZ*, 9, pp. 1ff.

times, as will be seen from Ps. 81. But in later times a new element was added, namely the idea of the *re-establishment of Israel*, the fulfilment of the hope of the congregation for the future; or to put it another way: an eschatological element was added and came to be the most important. From the very beginning, as we have seen, there was always a forward-looking element in the experiences and promises of the new year festival (Chap. V.10), which in Judaism was more and more eschatologically defined (Chap. V.11).

Such psalms as Pss. 75 and 82 announce the coming of Yahweh to judge the pagan world and its unrighteous gods, under whose oppression Israel is now sighing and suffering. They are promises in answer to the prayers of the congregation for the re-establishment of Israel: no doubt they had a permanent place in the festal cult of somewhat later times (Chap. V.13).

Here we are face to face with a peculiar mixing of psalm and oracle, where the oracle is the chief thing but is organically fitted into a short prayer, as in Ps. 82, or into a hymnal invocation and thanksgiving, as in Ps. 75.

Much has been said lately about the 'eschatology of the psalms', and Gunkel and others have sought to interpret quite a number of psalms, particularly 'enthronement psalms', as 'eschatological psalms' (Chap. V.3). This is exegetically not correct, and if the term is supposed to mean that there are psalms in which the poet intends to describe the eschatological age and, so to speak, uses the style of a psalm as the vehicle for such a 'prophecy', it is even misleading; such 'eschatological psalms' do not exist. But there are psalms in which the congregation among other things prays for the great 'turning of the destiny' of Israel to come soon, and there are prophetic psalms, psalm-like elements of the festal rituals, in which the cultic prophet also promises that this turning will take place: he beholds it already, as the extension of the new creation and the salvation which the new year will bring about. Even in comparison with most Protestant hymn-books, the eschatological element in the psalms of Judaism is not very prominent. In fact it is much more prominent in the post-canonical psalmography, for instance in the Psalms of Solomon.

It is therefore misleading to speak of the eschatology of the psalms or psalmists, as has been done by so many since Gunkel advanced his eschatological interpretation.[42] The psalms have no eschatology apart from that of earlier Judaism as a whole. And, to put it shortly, the sum of the matter was the religious, moral, national, and political re-establishment of Israel through the miraculous interference of Yahweh, and a safe and happy future for Israel, including domination of other nations, and with Yahweh

---

[42] For instance, Gunkel-Begrich, *Einl.*, pp. 329ff.; T. H. Robinson in *The Psalmists*, pp. 87ff.; Barnes, *The Psalms* I, pp. XLIIff.; Oesterley, *The Psalms* I, see index. The fundamental mistake of Gunkel-Begrich, in addition to the misinterpretation of the psalms in question themselves, is that they take for granted the existence of an 'eschatology' in Israel even in ancient times *before* the classical period of psalmography.

[43] For details see Mowinckel, *He that Cometh*, Chap. V.

himself living in their midst as King and Protector and maintainer of all 'righteousness' and 'peace' and 'blessing'.[43] The contribution of the psalms to this picture is a testimony to the close relationship still existing between the hope for the future and the cult, and especially the great annual festival, pre-eminently 'Yahweh's day', showing how easy it would be for the congregation, when experiencing the coming of Yahweh at the festival, to experience at the same time in advance by way of a pledge the great re-establishment one day to take place.

And this is not unimportant. It proves that just as the hope for the future had long ago sprung out of the cultic experience of the epiphany of Yahweh—actualized by the great collapse of the year 587, by the fervent promises of the prophets in connexion with the fall of Babylon, and by the restoration of the congregation under Zerubbabel—and had drawn its concrete concepts from the myths and the complexes of ideas of the new year festival,[44] so for a long time it continued to draw new power from the festal cult with its experiences and promises.

6

We have mentioned above that the oracles, which had their permanent place within the ritual framework of the festal cult, not only give expression to the psalmist's evident consciousness of being inspired but partly also take on the forms and conceptions of the free, spontaneous prophetic inspiration. We have also seen that from the point of view of the ancient Israelite there was no essential difference between a free and a more official inspiration, and that being able to interpret a technical oracular token, or some other kind of omen, was itself considered to be an outcome of a charismatic endowment, a prophetic quality.

When looking at the contents of the cultic prophets' words which have been handed down to us, we may perhaps find it strange that these inspired oracular answers should always be positively auspicious, considering the Christian way of looking upon inspiration, and the strong impression received of the prominent part played by threatenings of doom and punishment in classical prophecy; even the oracles of disaster against the enemy are positive promises, from Israel's point of view. Can it possibly be true inspiration, and could the temple prophets always be acting in good faith? For in the reform prophets we find the strongest words of doom pronounced both on the very same cultic congregation to which the oracles of the psalms promise the grace and goodwill of God, and on the whole of their temple service!

Several things may be said in answer to that. In the first place the ancients counted on the effectual creative power of the prophetic word. The word of the deity in the mouth of the prophet not only announced the future, it also had a part in creating it; the prophecy of happiness

[44] See Ps.St. II, 2, pp. 211ff.

II, 5

would also create happiness. In distress and danger or before an important enterprise, in a decisive hour in the life of the people, the prophet was therefore *expected* to prophesy victory and good fortune.[45] In the earliest prophecy the prophet was psychically identified with the whole people; if he felt the word of victory and the wish for victory to be a living power in his own soul, and still more if the violent feelings of ecstasy were added, he would be convinced that the effectual divine word 'was in him'. Only at a later stage of development would the moral and religious consciousness of the prophet be so bound by his personal 'knowledge of God' that it would be able to oppose the collective wishes and ideas of the people. And here we find the 'reform prophets' maintaining such a view in sharp opposition to the great majority of official *nĕbhî'îm*, who were also bona fide, but whose knowledge of God was still on a more primitive collective stage.[46]

Further, we have to point out the part evidently played by the 'tokens' with regard to the cultic-ritual oracles: the oracle was announced as the interpretation of some sort of 'token' (*'ôth, môphēth*),[47] for instance as the result of casting lots with 'urim and thummim'. In the psalms of lamentation, just as in Babylonian psalms, we therefore come across the prayer for a 'favourable token' (actually 'a token for good') :

> Turn unto me and have pity upon me,
>   and make for me a favourable token! (86.17f.)

Such a 'token' was either of good or of evil omen, it would answer either 'yes' or 'no'. If the token turned out to be 'no' this did not mean that the matter was decided; the prayers and offerings might be repeated, one might try over again or try with another kind of oracle, as it is explicitly told of Saul, when Yahweh 'answered him not, neither by dreams, nor by urim and thummim, nor by prophets' (1 Sam. 28.6.; cf. Jdg. 6.36ff.). So Saul tried in all these ways. Only when the omen had given a positive answer,[48] would it be the task of priest or temple prophet to interpret this token in words, and only such positive answers have been handed down in the psalms or imitated by Deutero-Isaiah in his promises. This, then, explains why the oracle with regard to choice of words and contents is so closely related to the prayer (see above, II.59), or that the same wording might be used several times, as in Pss. 60 and 108.

But the true explanation for the fact that the answers of Yahweh through the cultic oracles only contain promises of good omen lies deeper. It has

---

[45] See 1 Kgs. 22. Cf. Mowinckel in *NTT*, 1909, pp. 335ff.

[46] Cf. *GTMMM* III, pp. 16f.; G. von Rad in *ZATW* 51, 1933, pp. 109ff.

[47] See Ps. 86.17; cf. Ezk. 4.3; Isa. 8.18; 20.3; Ex. 3.12; Jdg. 6.17; 1 Sam. 2.34; 10.7, 9; 2 Kgs. 19.29; 20.8f.; Isa. 38.7, 22 (*'ôth*); Ezk. 12.6, 11; 24.24, 27; Deut. 13.2f.; Isa. 8.18; 20.3; Zech. 3.8; 1 Kgs. 13.3, 5; 2 Chron. 32.24 (*môphēth*). Cf. Keller, *Das wort OTH*, pp. 15ff. and 43ff. (for Pss. 86.17 and 74.9). Keller's doubts as to the meaning of 'the tokens' in Ps. 74.9 cannot be based on the corrupt text of v. 4, as the sense of 'sword-knot', 'army standard' (ibid., p. 55) gives no sense here; the enemies do not place their holy standard in a temple which they are just about to plunder and set fire to.

[48] Cf. van der Leeuw, *Phänomenologie* §54, pp. 355ff. (E.T., pp. 379ff.).

to do with the very essence of the cult and with the nature of Israel's faith
in God. The basis of the whole cultic system of Israel is the belief in covenant and election, the belief in Yahweh's own 'faithfulness to the covenant'
and his 'goodwill'—both these meanings being present in the word
ḥesedh. He would not be able to forget his covenant and frustrate it; he
would not fail his people in distress and fail the 'righteous one' on whom
unrighteous enemies had wrought disaster; he would *have to* shape things
so that they might get their due! Relying on the general promise of salvation, involved in election and covenant and Yahweh's coming at the
festival with renewed creation and renewed covenant, those who arranged
the temple service might, *ex officio* and trusting in the inspiration of their
official calling, prescribe that at such and such a point in the ritual the
temple prophet was to promise to the people the merciful help of Yahweh
—just as in some present day forms of divine service the clergyman by
virtue of the fact that the very church has been willed by God, is authorized to announce to the sinner the 'merciful forgiveness of all thy sins'
'on behalf of God and my holy office'.

'The righteous one' we said above. Yes, according to the covenant and
God's merciful election, the people, the congregation as a whole, are 'the
righteous', 'faithful to the covenant' (ḥāsīdhîm), the 'fellow-members of
Yahweh's covenant' ('anšê ḥasdô), and so on; these terms are constantly
used in the psalms[49] for the people and congregation of Israel as a whole.
But did not those who arranged the service know that there might be
sinners, 'unrighteous' people, in the congregation, or that the nation as
a whole had fallen under the wrath of Yahweh because of their sins?
Well, no doubt they did: the psalms often give expression to consciousness
of such sin. But still the congregation, as congregation, is the righteous
people of Yahweh's covenant, even by virtue of his merciful election and
his 'righteousness', which will always maintain the covenant. The cult is
there for the very purpose of restoring and maintaining the congregation's
being 'right' and the 'blessing' to result from it. Therefore any permanent
and valid public worship will always be planned on the basis of the pious
congregation, such as according to its own ideal it ought to be; prayers
and words are not formulated in the way the outsider or the most worthless might be supposed to say them; they express what the congregation
ought to be able to say when it is at its best; they do not presuppose a
minimum, but a maximum level; they seek to raise the congregation
towards its own ideal. Even in the ordering of more modern services the
witnesses at a wedding ceremony are called 'these Christian witnesses';
the wording of the baptismal service cannot be based on the sorry fact
that many sponsors are not very Christian, but prayer, confession and
singing will rather aim at putting them face to face with the Christian
ideal and the responsibility of a sponsor; at a confession the ritual has to

---

[49] Ṣaddîqîm, ḥāsīdhîm, ḥāsīdhēkhā, etc. See above, Chap. VI, pp. 207ff.

take for granted that those who go to it are in a spiritual state making it possible for the priest to absolve them. The words of the cult draw an ideal picture, 'a prototype' of 'the righteous man', of 'righteous people', just because the cult aims at securing such 'righteousness' to them.[50] Likewise the ritual oracular promises of the temple service of Israel are formulated on the assumption that the congregation is what it ought to be, and that it has been sanctified and cleansed through the coming of Yahweh and the ritual acts, so as to make it what it ought to be. They presuppose the proper congregation. Therefore there is no reason for us to doubt that in cases when the wording of the promise was left to the temple prophet himself—and probably this would be the rule—he would have received the merciful promise for the congregation, or its representative through a personal experience of inspiration, in the consciousness of Yahweh's presence and through faith in his mercy, through a prophetic experience at the festal hour.

But *may* the prophet always take for granted that the congregation is 'right'? We can see that in the course of time the men of the temple service themselves became aware of this problem. That is why the liturgies (Chap. XIII.2) enforced the religious and moral demands of Yahweh on those who should come to take part in the blessing of the cult (see Pss. 24. 3–6; 15); the idea evidently seems to be that the individual is to subject himself to these demands; if anybody should take part in the procession who is a sinner, having trespassed against the demands of purity and therefore carrying about with him a 'curse' that may threaten the 'rightness' and blessing of the whole congregation, he is supposed to see the error of his ways and fall back. And at the festival at which the covenant is renewed, the very promise itself reminds the congregation of the demands, the commandments of Yahweh: 'see to it, that the covenant is not going to be broken and the blessing lost again this time as so often before!' (cf. 81.10; 95.7). The condition of the promise is that the congregation is going to keep the commandments of God.

7

Thus the basic tendency of Israel's religion itself makes even the official temple service attach the promises of the congregational festivals to certain religious and moral conditions. As early as the monarchy the promises to the king were given on this condition: '*if* the king (and the people) keep the commandments of Yahweh' (see 89.31ff.; 132.12). Of course the same thing is true of much later times (81; 95). In this way the oracle attains a certain admonitory character; an element of instructive *tôrâ* on the part of the priest is added (see Chap. XIII.2). Probably here two sets of ideas are combined. One is the idea of the new year festival, that Yahweh is coming to renew the covenant: if the people will keep the

---

[50] See above, Chap. VI, pp. 207f.; von Rad in *Festschrift für Bertholet*, pp. 423ff.

commandments of God this time, their happiness will be secured. Here, then, the whole 'decalogical tradition' is attached to the cultic festival (Chap. V.8).

The other is the strong emphasis laid by the reform prophets on the moral pre-condition for the goodwill of God, an idea to which the prophets of re-establishment adhered.[51] But this is certainly not confined to them. That the cult emphasized the commandments of Yahweh as a condition for the renewal of the covenant and of the promise is indeed one of the historical bases of the new understanding on the part of the reform prophets, which was that religion and morality, the commandments of God and the promises of God, are bound up with each other. So we see that a right understanding of the psalms and of the cultic piety connected with them also helps to throw a better light on the religious basis of the *prophetic movement*. It is not to be denied that the earlier critics isolated the prophetic movement too much from its basis in the historically determined religion of Israel, and this led to an exaggerated estimate of what was new in the prophetic movement, and thus made it more difficult to understand. The ground had been better prepared than people were inclined to believe, through the development of revealed history in connexion with the three main factors: the contribution of Moses, the experience of Yahweh's revelation in history, and the fusion of this with the Canaanite cult forms in the temple cult of Jerusalem under David and Solomon. The religion of the cultic psalms is an outcome of this very preparation.[52]

We have seen above how the promises of happiness and blessing at the renewal of the covenant were attached to the condition that Israel should this time keep the commandments of Yahweh better than before; the prophetic psalmists found the explanation of the bad fortune of the people in the sin of the congregation: the promises of the festival did not come true, because Israel was constantly breaking the covenant. And when Yahweh again appears at the festival, and in his mercy is willing to 'make covenant' again, he does so with an earnest admonition that the result shall be better next time.

And we can also see that this admonition was made concrete and urgent through the very words of the cultic ritual. Ps. 50 claims to be a speech by Yahweh, an instructive admonition by Yahweh at his 'appearance' at

[51] See *GTMMM* III, pp. 17, 20f., and 25f.
[52] See above, pp. 88, 233. At present it is almost a dogma among scholars that the religion of the psalms is on the whole younger than the classic prophetic movement and so is dependent on the latter. Wheeler Robinson airs this general opinion in his article 'Psalms' in *EB*, where he uses it as a criterion for dating the psalms (mostly 'post-exilic'). But it is evident that the presentation of the 'prophetic' element in the psalms by Gunkel-Begrich (*Einl.*, pp. 329ff.) is a highly exaggerated one, both in that they take for granted that there is a direct influence of the ideas of the doom and reform prophets, whenever something corresponding occurs in the psalms, and in that they also highly exaggerate the 'eschatological' element in the psalms, and derive even that from 'the prophets'. They have not realized that from the beginning a 'prophetic' element belonged to the cultic order itself, and that it was out of the latter that important ideas in the classical prophetic movement sprang up and grew. Gressmann has already pointed out that the ethic of the prophets is in various respects based on the ethical ideas of the wisdom literature, and that the latter is not an outcome of the former (*ZATW* 42, 1924, pp. 287ff.).

the festival. All through it has the form of a prophetic word, the severe lecture and admonition of a prophet with the emphasis on the commandments and with a conditional promise attached to it. Its cultic basis is the idea of epiphany, of renewal of the covenant, the emphasis on the commandments as commandments of the covenant and conditions of the promise, and finally the prophetic promise as a permanent element of the festal cult's new year. The whole psalm is cast in the mould of prophetic speech, with a hymnal description of the glory of theophany for an introduction.

The commandments enforced by these admonitory prophetic words in the psalms are more or less identical with those of the 'tôrôth of entry' (Chap. XIII.2), which again means: with the commandments which gradually came to be considered the real commandments of the covenant, the commandments of Mount Sinai above all others, the 'decalogical tradition'.[53] In Ps. 50 three sins prevail in the congregation and are even tolerated in their midst, to which the prophet, however, draws attention in the name of Yahweh: theft, adultery and slander (or sorcery). It is not sufficient for the congregation to maintain a lavish sacrificial cult, if they allow such a state of things to continue. We are justified in believing that a psalm like this is not only an outcome of poetical inspiration but of the experience of the prophet himself and of a calling to preach the chastising and admonitory word of Yahweh. And in the psalms there may be a great deal of such experience of the prophetic calling. Even the poet, paying homage to Yahweh as king when he appears, has himself in the holy fellowship of the congregation and in the holy office experienced the presence of the deity, and such experiences have put the poetic and prophetic words into his mouth. We shall return to this element of inspiration in the chapter about the psalmists (Chap. XV).

The influence of the movement of the reform prophets on the temple prophets and their oracles is not limited to mere outward form; it also includes the actual experience and to a certain degree even the content of ideas and the type of piety.

This applies for instance to the critical way in which the prophets looked on the sacrificial cult, and to the claim for a more personal and spiritual temple service, for the offering of heart and personality and feeling and will rather than animals. Here the view of the prophets coincides with one tendency in the psalmists: that of depreciating the sacrificial practices. But there is a basic distinction: the reform prophets emphasize the right fundamental relationship to God in faith and obedience and the social ethic,[54] whereas the psalmists emphasize the offering up of praise and prayer, the thanksgiving psalm and the penitential prayer.[55] As for the emphasis put here on the broken spirit and the contrite heart, it is an out-

[53] See Pss. 81.10; 15.2a, c, 4c; 24.4b; cf. Chaps. XIII.2; V.6.
[54] See *GTMMM* III, pp. 20f.; Mowinckel, *Profeten Jesaja*, pp. 88ff, 94ff; *Jesajadisiplene*, pp. 20–45.
[55] See Chaps. VIII.11; X.2.

come of ideas which might possibly grow out of the soil of cultic religion—out of the spirit prevailing in the *tôrâ*-liturgy—but which are likely to have been stimulated also by the prophetic movement.

But as already mentioned, in the psalms we also meet with the positive emphasis on the religious ethic which is characteristic of the prophets. It is evident in the *tôrôth* of entry as well as in Ps. 50. What interests us about this psalm is just that it combines the view of the sacrificial cult held by the earlier psalmists with that of the reform prophets: the judgment is based on its relationship to morality as well as to doxology. The poet enforces the moral commandments of the 'decalogical tradition' as well as the idea of the psalmists of the cultic doxology as an expression of gratitude. The main stress may be on the first element. At all events not only the earlier temple prophets but also the later prophetic reform movement have influenced it. What distinguishes Ps. 50, for instance, from Hosea, who likewise in accordance with the decalogical tradition declares the moral commandments to be more important than the sacrifice (Hos. 4.1f.; 6.6), is, above all, the moral earnestness, the energy with which Hosea emphasizes the moral commandments as being the demands of a holy God. In Ps. 50 the 'act of judgment', announced in the introduction and prepared through the stately description of the epiphany, passes off in a way rather different from what might have been expected; we are prepared for a real judgment with a purging of the sinners from the congregation, but we merely hear an admonitory scolding with pedagogical instruction. The contents seem to be out of proportion to introduction and framework; to 'judge', to the psalmist, actually here means simply 'rebuke and admonish'—after all, Yahweh is bound by the covenant. To Hosea as well as to the other 'prophets of judgment' the holy demands of God are so earnest and so inseparably bound up with his holy and ardent zeal that the trespasses of the people can but result in annihilating doom. There can be no doubt that between Hosea and his successors on the one side, and Ps. 50 on the other, lies the consolidation of the Jewish congregation in the Persian period, and the toning down of the fiery moral preaching of the prophetic movement which took place during the development of the Jewish 'religion of the law'.

But in the collection Ps. 50 has a rather isolated position. This does not mean that there are not many psalms from a later time than the prophets of doom. But on the whole it was not that particular prophetic movement, inaugurated by Amos and his successors, which put its stamp on the psalms; the prophetic element found is derived from the normal type of prophecy within the circle of 'loyal' temple prophets who actually laid the religious, intellectual and historical basis for the 'prophets of judgment'. Thus there is a difference here between Ps. 50 and the two other psalms (81 and 95) which represent the same part of the festal liturgies: the epiphany of Yahweh for renewal of the covenant and revelation and enforcement of its commandments. These also represent 'the decalogical tradition', but in their case all emphasis is put on the fundamental commandment: that of worshipping Yahweh only. By way of a motivation against breaking the covenant they call to mind the time when Israel at Meribah and Massah 'tempted Yahweh' by 'hardening their hearts', by 'stubbornness' and disobedience. Here the presumptuous and wilful want of confidence in Yahweh's power and promises is set up as the real sin, the reason why Yahweh has rejected the people and punished them by forty years of disaster—the wandering in the desert. This is an idea which altogether agrees with the claim of Isaiah for confidence and faith and with his conception of 'arrogance' as being the real sin, and likewise with the constant admonitions of Deutero-Isaiah to believe and trust in Yahweh's power and willingness to keep the covenant. But the above-mentioned conception of the Meribah tradition is already to be found in the Yahwist, who is certainly older than Amos and Isaiah. So even here the psalmists probably represent 'pre-prophetic' ideas—which is confirmed by the fact that Ps. 81 to all appearance seems to have a North Israelite basis,[56] even if the version before us seems to have been re-modelled in Jerusalem. So this, too, seems to confirm the belief that the 'prophetic element' of the psalms on the whole belongs rather to the presuppositions of the 'prophecy of judgment' than to its consequences.

On the other hand there is one domain in which the influence from the later prophecy, 'the prophecy of re-establishment' from Deutero-Isaiah on,[57] has put its stamp on psalmography, namely as far as the hope for the future is concerned. As we have seen above (Chap. V.3, etc.), the hope of the re-establishment of Israel finds expression in several enthronement psalms and congregational psalms of the festivals. The hope for the future later turned into true eschatology. Some scholars of recent times, and none more than Gunkel, have greatly exaggerated this 'eschatological' element in the psalms. But that it is there in some of the psalms by way of prayers for the re-establishment of Israel with corresponding promises in the oracles of the festival is true enough (see above, II.62f.).

This faith in re-establishment is no original part of the religion of Israel; this is implied in the very word as well as in the content of the hope. It is concerned with the national, religious and moral re-establishment of the realm of David, which was destroyed in 587. It is this hope which in the course of 'post-exilic' days, partly under the influence of Persian ideas, developed into true eschatology; nor is 'eschatology' in the true sense of

[56] In Ps. 81 the people is called 'Jacob' and 'Joseph'; the latter definitely suggests North Israelite origin; cf. Gunkel, *Die Psalmen*, p. 359. On the other hand it is somewhat unlikely that an *official* North Israelite cultic festal psalm would attack the worshipping of other gods, in view of the fact that this was official in the temples of Northern Israel, as long as this kingdom existed —a fact to which Hosea testifies. This seems to suggest that the version at hand must have been influenced by the cult at Jerusalem, which would be much more eager officially to emphasize the dominance of Yahweh. We might conjecture that the present version of Ps. 81 was composed for a new year festival after Josiah had incorporated the southern part of Ephraim with Bethel into his kingdom; it is quite probable that he would then purposely try to adopt the ancient 'Joseph' traditions into the traditions of Jerusalem.

[57] Cf. *GTMMM* III, pp. 23ff.

the word an original or old part of the religion of Israel; it is bound up with Judaism. But this hope and this faith were brought to life by the 'prophets of re-establishment', whose first representative of mark was Deutero-Isaiah, even if he had predecessors.[58] It has its deepest root in the faith in the covenant and to that extent existed in historical Yahwism from the time of Moses onwards; it could only become a hope of re-establishment when the historical experiences centred round the fall of the kingdom and the restoration of the congregation under Cyrus and Darius provided the soil for this new outgrowth of revealed religion.[59] And as pointed out elsewhere,[60] it received its complex of ideas from the experiences and ideas of the festival of new year and enthronement. But its shaping is due to the prophets of re-establishment, the last phase of the great prophetic movement, which was to become the mediator and bearer of the new faith.

To the extent that this hope of re-establishment did put its stamp on some of the later festal psalms and congregational prayers we may speak of the influence of 'prophecy' in the usual sense of the word. It does not apply so much to the basic conceptions—these are older and belong to the festal cult—as to the hope and faith which have found expression in prayers and promises, and which have also gradually made people read and pray the earlier festal psalms and oracles as referring to the hope for the future.

[58] Here may be mentioned such anonymous prophetic sayings and prophetic poems as Isa. 13.2–22; 14.4b–21; 14.24–27; 17.12–14; 21.1–10; 30.27–33; 31.5–9; 33. See Mowinckel, *Jesajadisiplene.*
[59] See Mowinckel, *He That Cometh,* Chap. V.
[60] See *Ps.St.* II, Part II, pp. 213ff., and above, Chap. V.13.

CHAPTER XIII

Mixed Style and Liturgical Compositions

I

Not all the psalms we know are written in a pure unmixed style; from the point of view of form history they often contain elements which must be considered as belonging to different 'species' (types). Thus for instance, as we have mentioned, a hymn or thanksgiving psalm not infrequently ends in a prayer or with a reason for hearing the prayer (84; 103; 104; 125); or a psalm of supplication and lament may start with a hymnal motive so elaborate as to make the introduction a complete hymn (90; 139) or a thanksgiving psalm for previously received benefits (27; 40).

This mixed style is not in itself any evidence of a later origin and a lack of sensitiveness to the laws of art, a poetical decline, or even an absence of any conscious plan on the part of the poet, as has sometimes been maintained.[1] On the contrary, rather, the unmixed species of composition are a product of literary and cultic development. Above we have drawn attention to the fact that a comparison with the old Sumero-Babylonian and Egyptian psalms corroborates the view that the mixture of doxology and lament is older than the unmixed forms of composition.[2]

This mixing of elements has its own practical and psychological reason. It is based on and reflects the fluctuating emotions and thoughts of religious activity, that is, the psychology of the religious life.[3] It is but natural that from the high flights of doxology the mind of the worshipper would return to his own or his congregation's situation and would find expression for this in a short final prayer; or that before the prayer he would bend to God in veneration and homage and, while thanking him, bear in mind his previous benefits. (Cf. the reason for hearing the prayer given in the psalms of lamentation.) It is just as natural that the thanksgiving would be mindful of the future and interpose a word on behalf of the worshipper in times to come.

So we cannot rest content merely with recording and registering this mixture of styles; in each case it has a special reason and intention. In each case we must ask ourselves what the individual psalm is mainly aiming at and explain the mixing of styles from this point of view.

[1] This seems to be the opinion of Gunkel-Begrich, see *Einl.*, pp. 379ff. and cf. the uncomprehending treatment of Ps. 9/10 in the commentary; somewhat similar in Balla, *Das Ich der Psalmen*, pp. 111f. Against such a view: Löhr, *Psalmenstudien*, pp. 2ff.

[2] Stummer in *JSOR* VIII, pp. 123ff., arrives at the same result.

[3] Of course Gunkel-Begrich are not blind to this, but the fact is far from being sufficiently emphasized. See above, n. 1.

As to the way in which the different elements of the whole are to be balanced in relation to each other, the Hebrew had rules of art different from ours. He did not demand that the chief element should always be the most prominent quantitatively speaking. When we say that the Hebrew—in contradistinction to our tendency to analyse conceptions—thought in complete pictures, which he visualized as plastic, but not as abstractions,[4] this includes the corollary that he often visualized the complete picture from a single detail which represented, for him, the whole. To him 'the gate' is identical with 'the city' and the 'community' of that city—but also with what we should call 'the market-place', or the 'court of justice' or 'the head of the state'. We may say that the Hebrew poet can become so obsessed with a detail at the cost of the whole that we moderns may miss his real aim. But he himself saw the whole in this single detail. Thus the main point of Ps. 90 is not the hymn, praising the eternity of Yahweh, nor contemplations of the shortness of human life, but the prayer for the Eternal God not to overlook the short life of a man and let it pass away in misfortune, but to have mercy upon his congregation which consists of such short-lived people. The most important part of Ps. 139 is not the doxologizing meditation on the omniscience and omniprescence of God—that merely supplies a motive in the appeal to God's knowledge of the worshipper—but rather the prayer for the help of God against the 'men of blood'. When modern interpreters often fail to understand the 'mixed composition' of many psalms—such as for instance Ps. 9/10—it is due to a lack of consideration for this difference between Hebrew and modern ways of thinking and poetry and technique of composition.

2

Therefore the question of 'mixed style' is bound up with a proper understanding of the relation of the psalms to the cult and the religious life to which the latter gives expression. This leads to the question of larger liturgical compositions. As was mentioned above (p. 31), the texts of the psalms known to us are not always what we mean by a 'psalm'—a separate, complete cultic poem, expressing one particular feeling and state of mind—but may be larger compositions composed of several independent parts, expressing different emotions and acts within the cultic situation and sometimes, it seems, sung in several parts or by several choirs. That is, we have a liturgical composition, forming (part of) the text for an organically connected series of cultic acts.

Thus the psalms of lamentation with their oracles and final thanksgivings correspond to a series of ritual acts. We must suppose the psalm to be spoken by a man or by a representative of a congregation in actual or threatened distress, and to accompany the sacrifice or the rites of

[4] See Johs. Pedersen, *Israel* I–II, pp. 108f.

purification. The oracle is spoken by the cultic official on duty, the priest or the temple prophet, and it announces that Yahweh has accepted the sacrifice. And then the thanksgiving of the worshipper may follow (see Ps. 12), or the festal hymn may turn back to the oracle and build up the doxology and the expression of confidence in victory on the basis of the oracle, as in Ps. 75.

These varying cultic acts or stages of the cultic act may follow a still more fluctuating course, as in Ps. 60, in which the oracle of promise is followed by another mournful prayer which is finally relieved by the attainment of confidence.

The liturgies of the processions, especially, may in this way take on a dramatic character and thus reflect the progress of the cultic acts themselves, the cult in its essence being a 'holy drama', a changing series of actions and counteractions on the part of deity and congregation.[5] In the chapter about the enthronement festivals we have come across several such festal liturgies. In Ps. 24 we first hear the hymn of the procession to the creator and king, Yahweh; then follows the question to the gate-keepers as to the conditions of admittance to the sanctuary and its blessings, and the answer is given in the form of a 'tôrâ of entry'. And as the structure of the cult always has to take into account the conditions as they ought to be, and thus take for granted that only the pious, 'righteous' congregation will seek the deity—if it were not 'righteous' it would not 'seek God' at all!—so the congregation answers by stating that it fulfils the demands and calls upon the gates to open, for in the procession the king Yahweh himself is now coming. Ps. 132 may be looked upon as the libretto of a holy drama, in which at the annual festival the people present and 'call to mind' the first time that Yahweh entered Zion, led by David; the king 'plays the part' of David, and we hear his men (the priests), who have fetched the ark of Yahweh, calling upon Yahweh represented by the holy ark, to 'arise' and thus give the sign for the procession to start; then comes the prayer that Yahweh may look upon the offspring of David in mercy; and finally the oracle of the prophet announcing happiness and good fortune to him if he will keep Yahweh's commandments. Other complex liturgies are Pss. 66; 81; 95; 118; 121; 126; 134.

The psalms of lamentation are in fact also cultic liturgies containing both the lament and the supplication itself, then Yahweh's promise of help through the temple prophet, and finally the thanksgiving or the confidence of being heard with a reference to the promise. Such psalms are Pss. 12; 60; and 108.

To a certain extent the same thing may be said of such complex psalms as those which start with a thanksgiving psalm for previous benefits, and from this starting-point ask for help in the actual state of distress, such as Pss. 9/10; 27 and 40, which have been mentioned above. But we have now

[5] See *Ps.St.* II, pp. 19ff.; art. 'Drama, religionsgesch.' in RGG[2] I, coll. 2000ff.; and above, Chap. I. 6.

no idea how these two parts were presented within the framework of the ritual, whether they correspond to different liturgical parts accompanied by specific actions, for instance different parts of the sacrificial ritual, and we have no clue to justify any definite guess about it.

Cultic liturgies of this kind often served as patterns for the prophets, when shaping the message they had to announce from Yahweh.[6] Jeremiah for instance not infrequently clothes his prophecies of disaster in the guise of a description of the distress about to befall the people, with a prayer for help and an announcement of Yahweh's refusal. In this reversing of the 'answering oracle' we find ourselves face to face with the prophecy of doom in all its paradoxical pointedness.

3

But the problem of mixed styles in the psalms is not completely solved by a reference to the psychology of religion and to the liturgical compositions of the cult.

It cannot be denied that in the youngest psalmography we sometimes come across a mixing of the formative elements, which must be characterized as a disintegration of the old species of style,[7] a failing of sensibility as to the original connexion between the cultic situation and the true purpose of the psalm on the one hand, and as to form and leitmotivs on the other. The effects of this disintegration is precisely that elements of form and thought from a species of style originally alien to the cultic situation and kind of psalm in question will be mixed up with it and sometimes get the upper hand. In these cases there is very often no question of a new creation in the sphere of style and poetry but simply of deficient liturgical feeling and taste.

Above (Chap. X.2), we have drawn attention to the strong influence of wisdom poetry on the thanksgiving psalms, sometimes threatening to turn the 'testimony', which according to its true nature also seeks to be a confession to Yahweh, into an instructive admonition to the congregation. To a certain extent it may be compared to those of our church hymns which are actually no longer 'psalms', i.e. 'doxology and thanksgiving and prayer' as Luther puts it, but sermons in verse.

In a late psalm like Ps. 119 prayer and lament and hymnal motives so intermingle as to make the interpreters feel at a loss with regard to the character and purpose of the psalm. When a psalm was tied down to an artificial 'alphabetic' pattern—that is to say, every line or stanza starting

---

[6] So for instance Hos. 5.15–6.6; 14.3–9; Mic. 6.1–8; Isa. 33.14–16; Jer. 11.18–23; 15.15–21; 3.21–4.2; 14.2–10; 14.17–15.4; cf. Isa. 63.7–65.25. See Baumgartner, *Die Klagegedichte d. Jeremia* (*BZATW* 32); Mowinckel in *Edda* XXVI, pp. 276ff.; Gunkel in *Zeitschr. f. semitistik* II, 1924, pp. 145ff.; cf. *GTMMM* III, pp. 51ff.

[7] Cf. Gunkel-Begrich, *Einl.*, pp. 308f.

with a new letter according to the sequence of the alphabet[8]—it very otfen resulted in a rambling and obscure train of thought and a loose composition.[9]

But we come to the real disintegration of style only in post-scriptural psalmography, notably in the Psalms of Solomon (see Chap. XVI.5).

[8] Pss. 9–10; 25; 34; 37; 111; 112; 119; 145.
[9] Even this point of view is exaggerated by Gunkel-Begrich, *Einl.*, p. 403; cf. above, n. 1 and 3. Ps. 119 is in fact a (non-cultic) individual psalm of lamentation, its author being a learned scribe and student of the Law; the numerous references to his own faithfulness with respect to the Law are intended as motivations of the prayer. See Mowinckel in *NTT* 61, pp. 95ff., 129ff.

CHAPTER XIV

Psalm Singing and Psalm Singers

I

In the preceding chapter we have tried to give a picture of the different kinds of psalms, from a literary as well as from a religious and cult-historical point of view. It would be of interest here if we could now give a complete picture of the structure and details of the different cultic acts, putting each psalm in its exact place in the whole. But this is not possible; the sources do not afford sufficient direct information. Only on some particular scenes has it been possible to throw gleams of light, so that the psalm can be fitted into its niche in the general framework. We feel for instance that we have some idea what a day of penance in Israel was like, with its invocations and sacrifices and penitential rites, with its laments and the answer of the temple prophets. We also seem to have a rough sketch of the thank-offering festival of an individual. But we have been unable to form any complete picture of the structure of rituals and liturgies and the progress of the temple service at one of the great festivals. Even on the great festal complex of new year we have only been able to throw incidental light; we cannot tell how the details are to be pieced together to make a complete picture, even if we resort to such traditions as are to be found in Mishna or Talmud. The sources do however throw a certain amount of light on the last day, 'that great day of the feast', which is characterized by the idea of Yahweh's enthronement and occupied with the great procession, and all the experiences and ideas attached to this aspect of the festival. But even here we have separate scenes rather than the cultic drama as a whole. With regard to the singing of the psalms however we are able to say at least something definite about the way it was done.

In the preceding chapters we have often alluded to the singers. Sometimes the psalms themselves do so, if only indirectly, by mentioning the instruments on which they accompanied the singing.[1]

A separate *class* or a *guild* of temple servants under the name 'singers' is not explicitly mentioned in the Old Testament in any document older than the census list (Ezra 2) from about 400 B.C. The Chronicler also refers to them by this name and also shows us how they were organized in subdivisions or 'families'.[2] From his reference to them we seem justified

---

[1] See the passages in Quell, *Kult. Probl. d. Pss.*, p. 150. Cf. below, n. 14.

[2] Cf. Büchler in *ZATW* 19, 1899, pp. 96ff., 329ff.; 20, 1900, pp. 97ff.; Köberle, *Die Tempel-sänger im A.T.* None of these papers is aware of the insights afforded by the psalms themselves.

in concluding that some of these 'families' had charge of the singing, while others performed on instruments. In fact a very old psalm, Ps. 68, mentions the temple singers and the players (v. 26). And when Sennacherib king of Assyria mentions 'singing men and singing women' among the 'treasures' which king Hezekiah had to hand over, there is every reason to believe that he is speaking of the temple singers. In Babylonia and Assyria the temples had organized 'singers', who were at the same time the makers of the 'king's musick'.[3] Something similar was the case in Egypt.[4] In Ugarit, too, the singers seem to have made up a special class of the temple personnel,[5] and if so, this must certainly also have been the case in other Canaanite temples of any considerable size.

It is well known that even the semi-nomadic Hebrews were clever musicians;[6] the old south-Judaean traditions regard the musicians as one of the three 'orders' within the semi-nomadic society (Gen. 4.19–21). Thus there is no valid objection to the conjecture that almost from the very first the Temple of Jerusalem had a guild of singers, or that the public cult in Jerusalem was furnished with singing and music as early as the time of David.[7] When the Chronicler proceeds to tell us that David had organized the temple singing with all the divisions and sub-divisions existing at the time of the Chronicler himself (1 Chron. 25), this is certainly a legendary dating-back of conditions as they existed in Jewish times; the census list in Ezra 2 does not seem to know this detailed organization. And yet there is probably a historical nucleus in the tradition which says that the temple music and the singing date back to the time of David. It was David who instituted the cult of Yahweh in Jerusalem and gave it a visible cultic symbol in the shape of the old holy 'shrine', 'the ark' (2 Sam. 6). The general opinion is that at the time of David 'the ark of Yahweh' was standing in a tent ('tabernacle') in the open, just as the later saga-writers—especially the Priestly Document—supposed was the case as early as the time of Joshua at Shiloh (Josh. 18.1). This is not very likely; even if David did not build a special temple we may take for granted that the ark stood in a special room of the royal castle—'David's castle'—some sort of a 'palace chapel'; in fact one passage in the book of Samuel tells us in plain words that when David 'went to the deity' to worship, he 'went into the house of Yahweh' (2 Sam. 12.20, cf. 7.8); so the 'tent' mentioned elsewhere as a cover for the ark (2 Sam. 6.17) must have been standing in this chapel. But at any rate we must assume that when David purposely made the cult performed before the ark the central cult of the realm in his 'Greater Israel', he would also aim at making this cult so magnificant and alluring

[3] See Meissner, *Babyl. u. Ass.* II, p. 67 and index s.v. 'Sänger'; Garstang, *Heritage of Solomon*, p. 73.
[4] See Erman, *Aegypt. Relig.*[2], pp. 61f.; Erman-Ranke, *Aegypten*,[2] pp. 283f.
[5] See Albright, *A.R.I.*, p. 209, n. 93a.
[6] Albright, op. cit., p. 125. Egyptian picture of Palestinian musicians in reproduction in Erman-Ranke, op. cit., p. 285.
[7] Cf. 2 Sam. 6.5, 16, 20ff.; see below, Chap. XV. 5; XVIII. 3, 4.

as to have it outdazzle the other sanctuaries in the country; it was this very allurement that Jeroboam feared (1 Kgs. 12.26ff.). And music and singing especially belonged to such magnificent cults—they were an important element at all the great state temples of the orient. Whether the Chronicler is inventing or elaborating upon an ancient tradition, there may be some truth in what he tells us about David's effort to organize the service of the singers in Jerusalem.[8]

Beyond all doubt the temple singing in Israel can be traced back to Canaanite patterns; tradition itself knows that the (legendary) persons supposed to be the 'ancestors' of the singers were 'native (Canaanites)'.[9] We shall return below to these traditions about the ancestors of the singers (Chap. XV.4).

It is also interesting to take a look at the social status of the temple singers; it may for instance throw some light on the question of the psalmists, to which we shall return below.

In the hierarchic order of Jewish times the singers were supposed to belong to the 'Levites'. This term originally indicated the whole clergy, but in Jewish times it was used only for the lower temple personnel, to a considerable extent consisting of descendants of the priestly families from the earlier sanctuaries in the country, which had been unclassed when all legal cult was centred in the Temple at Jerusalem. In the list in Ezra 2 the singers, together with the door-keepers and the temple slaves, are not yet classed among the true Levites but are placed on a lower rung of the ladder of rank. In the hierarchic system of the Priestly Document, on the other hand, they belong to the Levites, and there seems to be no difference of degree. And the author of the book of the Chronicles seems to put them in the first rank among the Levites. They possessed social aspiration; we have historical evidences of that. The Chronicler distributes them among the three great 'families' of Levites, which were again subdivided, twenty-four in all.[10]

The temple personnel, 'the Levites' in the earlier as well as in the later sense of the word,[11] belonged in a manner of speaking to the property-less. We often hear this in the laws, which therefore enjoin the Israelites to provide for them out of the sacred gifts; they were to receive their livelihood 'from the altar'. And even if the top priests in Jerusalem no doubt had an abundance of this world's goods, the lower cultic personnel—the 'Levites' in the later sense of the word—were socially and economically of inferior standing; they did not belong to the property-owning 'families' but were 'sojourners in the gates of Israel', and not

[8] 1 Chron. 25. See Albright, *ARI*, pp. 125ff., which however, to a certain extent overestimates the historical value of the sources, and is too much inclined to draw conclusions from what *may* have been, to what must have been a fact; cf. Additional Note XXXVI.

[9] *'Ezrahi*, 1 Kgs. 5.11; 1 Chron. 2.6; Ps. 88.1. See Albright, op. cit., pp. 127f.

[10] For details Schürer, *Gesch. d. jüd Volkes* II,⁴ pp. 294ff., 333ff. (E.T. II. i. §24, pp. 226ff. pp. 270ff.).

[11] A short summary by the author in the art. 'Levi und Leviten' in *RGG.*² III, 1601ff. Details, with references to literature, in Hölscher, art. 'Levi' in *RLKlA*.

infrequently they were descendants of former temple slaves or of men 'given unto the temple' (Ezra 2.43ff., 55ff.).

We have evidence also of the existence of strained and antagonistic relations between singers and priests. It seems as if the singers considered their own part in the temple service to be just as important and essential as that of the priests, and claimed that this fact should find expression in the hierarchic precedence code. We find manifestations of this in legends as well as in historical testimonies. In one version of the story about Korah, put together in Num. 16, the priestly story-teller denounces the sons of Korah because they aspired to priesthood and wanted to obtain control of the offering of incense; but, as we shall see below, the sons of Korah represented the temple singers. And from the last days of the Temple we hear that the singers finally achieved the rank of priests and the right to wear the white costumes of the priests.[12] Elsewhere also the psalms show that this rivalry was of long standing. Remarkably seldom do they mention the office of priest,[13] but so much the oftener that of the singers and the temple musicians.[14]

Evidently a close connexion existed between temple singers and temple prophets.

Therefore it is no mere chance that the later temple prophets were classed among 'the Levites' in the later sense of this term, and that in the book of Chronicles a Levite among the singers appears as a cultic prophet;[15] the Chronicler uses the term 'prophesy' about the office of the temple singers and considers singing praise to be an outcome of prophetic inspiration (1 Chron. 25.1ff.).

2

The Jewish tradition in the Mishna has some sparse notes on the appearance of the singers at the temple service, but does not give any complete picture. We are told, for instance, that at the feast of tabernacles (the great annual festival) the singers used to stand on the fifteen steps leading from the court of the people to that of the women, and sing the fifteen 'festal songs' Pss. 120–134, while two priests blew on horns from the gate behind

---

[12] Josephus, *Ant.* XX, 216ff.; see *Ps.St.* VI, pp. 57f.

[13] Pss. 115.10, 12; 118.3; 132.9, 16 and possibly 134.2–4 in all of the 150 psalms.

[14] The horn (šôphār, 'ram's horn'), Pss. 47.6; 81.4; 98.6; 150.3. The trumpet (ḥāṣōṣĕrôth, of metal), 98.6. The lyre (kinnôr, usually translated by 'zither', but see Galling, 'Musik (und Musikinstrumente)' in *BRL*, col. 389ff.; a 'cup-shaped lyre' with a parallel yoke), 33.2; 43.4; 49.5; 57.9; 71.22; 81.3; 92.4; 98.5; 108.3; 137.2; 147.7; 149.3; 150.3. The harp (nebhel, according to traditional translation, actually some kind of lyre, viz. with a sloping yoke, see Galling, op. cit.), 57.9; 71.22; 81.3; 92.4; 108.3; 144.9; 150.3. The ten-stringed harp (nebhel, 'āśôr; likewise a 'sloping lyre'), 32.2; 92.4; 144.9. The long flute ('ûghābh), 150.4. The shawm (ḥālîl), oboe or double shawm, accidentally not mentioned in the psalms. The timbrel (for the hand—tôph), the tambourine, 68.26; 81.3; 149.3; 150.4. The cymbal (ṣilṣāl), 150.4. 'Play (with song)', zāmar occurs 43 times; šîr 'sing', 38 times; 'strike the strings', 4 times, 'rejoice', (referring to the cultic shout accompanying the singing), 11 times, 'praise' very often; 'publish', 'declare', 'show forth', of the cultic song (of thanksgiving), 22.23; 26.7; 79.13; 107.22; 'declare' in the same sense 75.10; 92.3. See Jacob in *ZATW* 17, 1897, pp. 266f.; 273; cf. *Ps.St.* VI, p. 57f.

[15] 2 Chron. 20.14; cf. 1 Chron. 15.22, 27. See Chap. XII.1.

them.[16] As already mentioned, psalms seem to have been sung above all to accompany the sacrificial acts, but at other times as well, for instance in the processions. Then it was the task of the singers to provide the singing at the temple service. When *we* speak of the singing at our own divine services we cannot help thinking of the singing of the congregation. We must not think along those lines with regard to the singing in the Temple.

For in one respect the temple singing was very different from the hymn singing at our divine services. The singing was not congregational; the professional singers alone would sing and play, not the congregation.[17] The congregational part consisted of such 'cultic shouts' as 'amen' or 'hallelujah' or 'for ever and ever', at certain points in the singing.[18] We are explicitly told that at the daily offering in late Jewish times two priests with silver horns would stand behind the singing choir; at every section of the psalm there would be a pause, the priests would blow on their horns and the congregation would fall down in worship[19] and—we may suppose—join in with the answering shouts which were its part in the singing; probably the term 'selah' in the psalm texts refers to this.[20] Something similar must have been the case in earlier times. Probably, as a rule, the precentor intoned and the choir joined in. There is a reminiscence of this in the introit of the hymn, the opening exhortation to praise, which may occur in the first person singular: 'I will praise'. Likewise alternating antiphonic singing between precentor and choir, or between two choirs, occurred, as we may conclude from Ps. 136 (see above, pp. 85f.).

Therefore we have strong reason to assume that even at private sacrifices, for instance the purification or thanksgiving for an individual, one or more official singers would render the psalm supposed to be sung by the sacrificer (the worshipper). The laity had certainly not sufficient knowledge of the subject to do it properly; for as in any old cult, so also in that of Israel and Judaism the greatest importance was attached to doing everything correctly in all details. So, when it says in the psalms 'I (i.e. the worshipper) will sing' or the like, and when it was said in the preceding chapters that the person in question would 'sing' his lament or thanksgiving psalm in the Temple, this means that he did so through one of the temple singers, who would render the psalm in his place.

In another respect also we must realize that temple singing was entirely different from the singing in our churches and meetings, namely with respect to the *tunes*. To us the tune of a song is the chief thing; we can do

---

[16] Tosephta, *Sukka* 4, 7–9.
[17] Josephus, *Ant.* XX, 9, 6. For details see Oesterley, *A Fresh Approach*, pp. 91–122; Eerdmans, *Hebr. Book of Pss.* (*OTS* IV), pp. 51ff.
[18] This seems to be a necessary conclusion from Sir. 50.19: the singers are singing while the people 'rejoice in prayer', i.e. they strike up the shouts of homage and prayer which would emphasize the homage and petitions of the song. Cf. Buhl, *Psalmerne*,[2] p. X. See also Neh. 8.6; 1 Chron. 16.36.
[19] Cf. Num. 10, 8, 10; 2 Chron. 29.26–28; Mishna, *Tamid* VII, 3. See Schürer, *Geschichte* II,[4] pp. 350, 355. (E.T. II, §24, pp. 290, 296).
[20] See below, Chap. XXIII.13.

without the accompaniment. The accompaniment is there for the sake of the tune. In the temple singing of Israel, as in all oriental music, it was the business of the instruments first of all to mark the time.[21] And the singing itself was rather more in the nature of a recitation than of tunes in a modern sense.[22] We do not know on what kind of musical system ancient oriental music was built up; to all appearance it was not at any rate on the octave scales.[23] The 'tunes' to which they would sing were very simple and primitive, probably only covering a single line from the poem and consisting of a couple of notes, perhaps the same note over and over again with a rise or a fall on the last word or syllable of the line. If we are to judge from primitive music elsewhere, we may imagine that what we might call the tune may have consisted in the repetition of the same series of notes, say three times, whereas the fourth line, and thus the close of the 'stanza' or 'tune', was marked by a rise or a fall towards the end.

[21] See above, Chap. I. 4, and the references in n. 36 to Chap I.
[22] See Eerdmans, *Hebr. Book of Pss.* (*OTS* IV), pp. 51ff.
[23] See below, n. 16 to Chap. XXIII. At any rate the contrary opinion cannot be based on the two terms in the psalm headings '*al-'ālāmôth* and '*al-haśśĕmînîth* (against König, *Die Psalmen*, pp. 26f. and Keet, *Liturg. Study of the Psalter*, pp. 48ff.); for this interpretation takes for granted what has to be proved. '*Al-haśśĕmînîth* 'over the eighth' cannot indicate a scale based on eight notes, but must indicate one definite 'thing' or action among several others.

CHAPTER XV

The Psalmists

I

It is among the temple singers that we must look for the authors of the psalms. But we must leave on one side, to begin with, the supposed names of authors in the psalm headings. We shall return to them below and realize that, rightly understood, they do contain information about the authors, but in a way different from that of popular belief.

The original cultic psalmography obviously developed at the temples. This is the case everywhere.[1] So also with the psalmography of Israel, as was suggested above (Chap. I.5; II.1). This conclusion as it applies to psalmography in general and to the origin of the psalm types is generally acknowledged at the present time. On this point the researches and the arguments of Gunkel have prevailed. The same applies to the unquestionably cultic psalms of the Psalter.

On the other hand, scholars partly disagree with regard to the individual psalms handed down to us: are they, or the greater part of them, real cultic psalms, or private imitations of the style and the forms of the ancient cultic poetry, which came into being in surroundings other than those of the temple circles?

When speaking of the different kinds of psalms, we have several times mentioned that Gunkel himself looked upon a great number of the psalms as private imitations; especially was this so as regards laments in the I-form and to a great extent also personal thanksgiving psalms. But we have seen that this conception does not hold good; it is not consistent with the congeniality to the psalmists of cultic piety and its expression in the temple service. And we have also seen that it does not hold good either to maintain, as has been done, that since the psalms often value psalm-singing higher than sacrifice and sometimes seem to manifest aversion to sacrifice, this indicates that we are dealing with the private poetical compositions of laymen.

But the question recurs when we come to speak of the milieu of psalmography and the psalmists. In what circles did the now extant psalms come into being?

The earlier critical view, on the basis of a rather narrow and rigid

---

[1] See for instance Heiler, *Das Gebet*,[4] pp. 165f.

conception of the process of evolution of Israelite religion, maintained that broadly speaking the psalms derive from the age of Judaism, it also supposed them to have developed within certain definite groups of pious laymen and to reflect the division of the congregation into 'the pious' (strictly adhering to the law) and 'the ungodly' (worldly-minded, less strict), known to us from the last two centuries B.C. The terms 'pious' (*hăsîdhîm*, properly, 'faithful to the covenant'), 'righteous' (*ṣaddîqîm*), and so on, were supposed to indicate the 'party' of the pious, later on developing into the 'party' of the Pharisees.[2] This view of the religious and cultic history of Israel is altogether untenable. The 'faithful to the covenant', the 'righteous' of the psalms, actually indicate the whole congregation— 'Israel' as contrasted with the 'pagans' and the downright 'apostates'.

Gunkel also maintained—in conformity with the earlier critical conception—that even if psalmography as such did develop at the temples, and even if there are many actually cultic psalms in the Psalter, still most of them were composed in the conventicle-like circles of pious laymen from the lower classes, 'the poor', 'the quiet in the land', those who suffered most from the oppression of the rich and mighty worldlings or 'ungodly' higher classes. A simple piety is supposed to have existed here, largely detached from the piety of Temple and cult, the people having their own edifying meetings, apart from the synagogues; here they were supposed to deliver the laments and thanksgiving psalms they had composed in illness and distress after having experienced healing and salvation.

It is beyond all doubt that this conception is in fact modern and not at all ancient, and based on a transference from the pietistic 'conventicles' and from the prayer meetings of Christian revivals outside the church in modern times. But this picture applies neither to ancient Israel nor to Judaism.

The very facts, demonstrated above, that the worshipping 'I' of the psalms in many cases must be a leading representative of the congregation and people, and that even in the I-psalms the enemies are not infrequently national and political enemies, and not social oppressors, and that as a rule the state of distress is of a political and national, not of a social nature, knock the ground from under Gunkel's and Begrich's view of the psalmists. After all, the idea of such private, conventicle-like prayer meetings and a 'cult-free' piety in the Judaism of that day is an artificial construction without any basis whatever in the sources. There is no evidence that the divisions within the Jewish congregation resulted in separate private prayer meetings, nor that 'the pious' are simply to be equated with 'the poor' and people of small means. We find separate cultic meetings with sacred meals and rites and rejection of the sacrificial cult only among a definitely sectarian group like the Essenes of the time

---

[2] This is the opinion not only of Rahlfs, Causse, Gelin (see Additional Note XXIX and all the older critical commentaries), but even of one of the latest 'introductions' to the O.T., Pfeiffer's *Introduction*; cf. Additional Notes XXXIV, XXXV. See further above, pp. 243ff.; II.59ff.

of Christ,[3] and their predecessors, the 'sectarians' of the newly-found 'Dead Sea scrolls' and the 'Damascus Document', but never among those who wanted to be loyal to the inherited temple cult order. Among these 'Proto-essenes' there certainly did exist psalmography, as is demonstrated by the new documents; but this psalmography is totally epigonous in relation to the biblical, and has all the marks of the disintegration of the old style mentioned above (Chap. XIV.3); it belongs clearly to the post-biblical 'learned psalmography', of which we shall speak in the following chapter. 'The quiet in the land'—an expression occurring only once in the Old Testament, in Ps. 35.20—does not mean a special social milieu, nor a special pious tendency or pious milieu, but is a poetical term for the congregation or people itself, which wants to live in peace with its neighbours and oppressors, and is not guilty of any such ungodly and arrogant 'noise' as marks its enemies among the pagans and their scheming and rebellious associates.

To support his theory about private conventicles and meetings of pious groups Gunkel quotes the term 'great assembly', to which the psalmists often allude; but this term clearly indicates the regular, or casual, cultic assemblies of the congregation in the Temple. The existence of private assemblies is just an assumption made by Gunkel and others on the basis of their view of the psalms as being essentially private compositions; the sources do not provide any evidence for this assumption. Within orthodox Judaism we know nothing whatever about other religious, 'edifying' meetings apart from the temple and synagogue services. The religious meetings that may have occurred belonged to *sects* which had purposely detached themselves from the main congregation and had their own cultic assemblies, like the Essenes, but then these were themselves in turn real cultic assemblies for the denominational congregation, and no private meetings. But it is completely out of the question that the greater part of the psalms should have come into being or that the collection of the Psalter should have taken place among such a sect. The psalmists testify to their attachment to the Temple, the ancestors and the law in a way much too obvious for that—apart from the fact that it would make it impossible to understand how the psalms could ever have been accepted for use in the temple service of the community itself. This last argument would also apply to the psalms if they were private compositions. The cult was far too bound up with tradition to adopt such poetry; it would have to be consecrated by time in order to be used there.

Certainly, as we shall see below, a private psalmography did finally come into being, namely in the 'wisdom schools' which were closely connected with the Temple, and a few of these poems are also included in the Psalter. But this does not explain the origin of the greater part of the psalms, and still less does it agree with the fact that so many of the psalms were actually used in the cult. The private psalmography known to us as the

[3] See Mosbech, *Essaeismen*, pp. 263ff.

'Psalms of Solomon' from the first century B.C. was never used in the official cult.[4]

Psalm-*singing* certainly did occur more privately. Here we cannot, however, adduce the use of the 'Hallel', i.e. Pss. 113–118 at the paschal repast; after all the paschal repast was something in the nature of cult, and, singing on that occasion was not limited to certain pious groups but prevailed among all Jews, even among the 'wordly-minded'. And it is beyond doubt that the custom of singing these very psalms on that occasion has been adopted from the temple service, and that some of them at any rate were originally really cultic psalms. As to the use of private psalms for recitation in smaller groups, we can only with some probability infer that the productions of the 'learned psalmography' were recited within the 'wisdom school'. However, that is something very different from Gunkel's groups of psalm-singing pious laymen among the lower classes.

When the editors of the sagas and the authors of the later legends time and again make their characters recite a psalm: 'then so-and-so sang this psalm to the Lord'—for instance the so-called Song of Hannah in 1 Sam. 2, or the thanksgiving psalm of king Hezekiah in Isa. 38.9ff.—they certainly mean that this took place on the cultic occasion to which the author was referring or which he had read about in the stories: Hannah's public visit to the Temple after the birth of her son, or that of Hezekiah after having been healed. We cannot even feel sure that the psalm-singing, to which James 5.13 alludes, refers to private singing at home; probably the author has in mind the singing of the congregational assembly after some joyful experience.[5]

Sooner or later the psalms of the Psalter came to be used in the service of the synagogues also, but not as a book of songs nor for singing; they were used as parts of the Holy Scripture, of the authorized and inspired canon, for reading, just like the other biblical books, which were read in the synagogues as holy words of God. From New Testament times we have evidence of their being used as Holy Writ in theological arguments and in lectures and sermons.[6] This does not prove anything about the origin of psalmography and the Psalter or about psalm-singing in the synagogue.[7] It is as Holy Scripture also that the psalms from the second century B.C. have influenced the prayers of the synagogue and the daily prayers prescribed for the pious.[8] But none of the psalms have been purposely composed for singing, or for any other use, in the synagogue.

---

[4] Therefore it is wholly without reason that Kittel thinks that the Psalms of Solomon were used at the service of the synagogues (see Kautzsch, *APAT* II, p. 130). The diapsalma = selah, occurring twice in the manuscripts is no proof of the assertion. In the synagogue there was no singing.

[5] Cf. 1 Cor. 14.26; Ephes. 5.19; Col. 3.16, and see Weizsäcker, *Apostol. Zeitalter*,[3] pp. 557ff. (E.T., *The Apostolic Age*, II, 259ff.). His interpretation of the lyrical sections of the N.T. is nearer to reality than that of Gunkel in *Die Lieder in der Kindheitsgeschichte Jesu*.

[6] Matth. 21.42; 22.41ff.; Mark 12.35f.; Luke 20.41f.; Acts 13.33; *et al.*

[7] Against Quell, *Kult. Probl. d. Pss.*, p. 5.

[8] Mentioned for the first time by the Tannaite Joseph bar Halafta, see Elbogen, *Jüd. Gottesdienst*, p. 82.

2

But if it is true that the great majority of the psalms handed down to us are clearly cultic psalms—and the preceding examination of the species and their settings ought to have proved that much—then the question as to the circles in which these psalms have come into being will find a much simpler answer. For then it is *a priori* most natural to suppose that they also were composed of people who had something to do with the service of the Temple—or, in earlier times, of the temples.

Equally, if indications exist in the psalms that the authors were closely connected with the Temple and temple service, this fact supports the statement that they are really cultic psalms.

What is to be found about this in the psalms themselves?

There can hardly be any doubt that they contain some features showing that most of them were composed at the Temple of Jerusalem—even if there are also some North-Israelite psalms which were probably used at one of the North-Israelite temples, for instance Bethel.

As we have seen,[9] the psalmists time and time again speak of their internal and external relations with the Temple and its orderings and the service there. They are living in the Temple, they are thinking and expressing themselves in the notions of Temple and cult. Very often we are told about the Temple of Zion[10] and the temple mountain,[11] about the temple courts and the holy city,[12] about the altar[13] and about the sacrifices.[14] All these things are mentioned with a feeling of awe, in venerating and rejoicing words, as objects of love and confidence, pride and joy.[15] Through the cult at the sanctuary they have an experience of God, from which flows whatever belongs to the true values of life;[16] there they 'seek Yahweh' in order to 'make their refuge in the shadow of his wings';[17] there flows 'the fountain of life' (36.10) and 'all their springs' are there (87.7). In the Temple the author of Ps. 63 beholds God; to the author of Ps. 73 the problem of life and of the justice of the world order of God is solved there.[18]

[9] See Chap. I. 3–4. Cf. n. 14 to Chap. XIV.
[10] Pss. 5.8; 23.6; 24.7ff.; 26.8; 27.4; 28.2; 29.9; 36.9; 42/43; 55.15; 65.5; 66.13; 69.10; 73.17; 74.3ff.; 76.2; 79.1; 84; 92.14; 100.4; 101.7; 114.2; 116.19; 118.19; 122; 132.7; 134; 135.2; 150.1; *et al.*
[11] Pss. 3.5; 15.1; 24.3; 27.5; 48.3, 12f.
[12] Pss. 31.22; 46.5; 48.2, 3, 9; 50.2; 87.3; 97.8; 101.8; 102; 125; 132.13; 135.21; 137; *et al.*
[13] Pss. 26.6; 43.4; 51.21; 84.4; 118.27; *et al.*
[14] Sacrifice: Pss. 4.6; 27.6; 116.17. Burnt offerings: Pss. 20.4; 52.21; 66.13, 15; 107.22; together with 'full offerings' 66.13. Sacrificial gift: 20.4; 141.2. Performing of vows: 22.26; 50.14; 56.13; 61.9; 65.2; 66.13; 76.12; 116.14. Voluntary sacrifice: 54.8. Thanksgiving sacrifice: 50.14, 23; 56.13; 116.17. Incense offerings: 66.15; 141.2.
[15] Cf. Jacob in *ZATW* 17, 1897, pp. 264–273; Quell, *Kult. Probl. d. Pss.*, pp. 152f. ((*o*) and (*p*)).
[16] Pss. 63.10; 73.17; 84.8; 21.7; 26.8; 27.8; *et al.* Cf. *Ps.St.* II, pp. 19–35, 79f., 130–145, 146–148.
[17] Pss. 17.8; 36.8; 57.2; 61.5; 63.8; 91.4.
[18] This close connexion of the psalmists with the Temple has been rightly claimed and demonstrated by Jacob in *ZATW* 17, 1897, and by Matthes, ibid., 22, 1902, pp. 68ff.; see also Wheeler Robinson in *The Psalmists*, pp. 48ff.

The authors, moreover, even have their daily home in the sacred place. They make the congregation 'visiting' the sanctuary speak as if they were living there, even 'for ever', because it was natural for themselves to use such expressions. If they are to give a concrete picture of the greatest happiness, they do not speak of visiting the Temple, but of staying there for ever. Through good and evil times the longing of the psalmists is for the Temple.[19] Again and again they disclose their knowledge of the cultic life that went on at the Temple, and not infrequently they allude directly to the different ritual functions taking place there.[20]

Broadly speaking the psalms came into being at the Temple, and all the preceding chapters have shown that they were composed for use at the regularly or irregularly recurring cultic functions and situations there, to be recited by or on behalf of persons of such standing that psalms were to be sung for them. That is why they have the uniform and general character to which an analysis of species (types) and style forms testifies.

3

It might therefore be natural to think of the priests as authors of the psalms.[21] If 'the priesthood' is taken in the comprehensive sense as referring to the entire cultic personnel, we are justified in saying that cultic psalmography, broadly speaking, everywhere had its origin among them. But this does not apply to the specialized hierarchy of the Temple of Jerusalem on the one hand, and the extant psalms to be found in the Old Testament on the other.

Very early on, the temple priesthood of Israel—very probably under Canaanite influence—had become primarily sacrificers, to whom the sacrifice and its rituals had become the chief point of the temple service (cf. Chap. XII.1). The psalmists, too, know that sacrifice is a matter of course and necessary,[22] and yet they put a higher value on the psalm-singing, the lament and the thanksgiving psalm; as a rule these are explicitly mentioned in the vow to Yahweh,[23] even if the sacrifice is tacitly implied, as can be seen for instance from 22.23–27, or happens to be explicitly mentioned alongside the thanksgiving psalm.[24] And sometimes we are told in plain words that Yahweh puts more value on the psalm

[19] 'Visit': Pss. 15.1; 61.5; 122; cf. Isa. 33.14. 'Abide': 15.1; 24.4; 84.5. 'For ever': 23.6; 27.4; 84.5, 11; cf. 52.10; 92.13f. Highest bliss: 84.11; 36.9. Longing: 26.8; 27.4, 8; 42.3; 43.3f.; 61.5, 8; 63.2f.; 84.3; 122.1f.

[20] See Quell, Kult. Probl. d. Pss., pp. 150f.; further Ps.St. I, pp. 140ff.; II, pp. 94–130; III, pp. 30–105; V, pp. 33ff.; 82ff.; VI.

[21] So, for instance, Gunkel-Begrich, Einl., p. 30. Bentzen has tried to prove that Ps. 73 was composed by a 'Levite' (see Jahves Gaest, pp. 52ff.); at least his arguments show that the author was connected with the Temple and cult.

[22] Pss. 4.6; 20.4; 22.26; 27.6; 50.14, 23; 52.21; 54.8; 56.13; 61.9; 65.2; 66.13, 15; 76.12; 96.8; 107.23; 116.14, 17; 147.2.

[23] Pss. 7.18; 13.6; 26.12; 27.6; 31.8f.; 35.9f., 27f.; 42.6f.; 43.4f.; 51.15–17; 54.8; 56.13; 57.8f.; 59.17f.; 61.9; 63.3, 6; 69.31ff.; 71.8, 14–18; 86.12; 109.30; 119.7; 140.14; 142.8. Cf. 21.14; Jer. 20.13; Sir. 51.11.

[24] Pss. 27.6; 54.8; 56.13f.; 61.9.

singing and the humble or grateful heart of which it is an expression than on the sacrifice of animals.[25] The latter cannot in itself win the pleasure of Yahweh (see Chap. VIII.11). Much oftener the temple music and the singing are emphasized as something with which the poets are quite familiar.[26]

All this seems to indicate that we have to look for the psalmists among the temple singers.[27]

Other facts seem to point in the same direction: first the expressed sympathy of the psalmists for the poor, the propertyless and those of low social standing.[28] As we have seen above, the 'Levites', and with them the singers, belonged to this class. The attitude of the psalms evidently agrees with this social standing on the part of the singers.

We must admit, however, that this fact was much exaggerated by the older critical investigators of the psalms. Wherever the 'suffering', the 'oppressed', the 'poor', the 'wretched', the 'lowly' ('ăniyyîm, 'ănāwîm, 'ebhyōnîm, etc.) were mentioned, they were taken to refer to social and religious parties within the Jewish congregation itself, and considered to testify to the theory that the psalms had sprung into being among pious but mostly oppressed laymen in the lower strata of society.[29] This conception, however, is not correct. These terms do not indicate 'parties'. As a rule they refer to 'Israel', the people and the congregation themselves, who are 'weak' and 'helpless', and 'poor' and 'wretched' and actually 'suffering' in relation to powerful pagan enemies and oppressors; sometimes the term implies the 'humble', who are patiently waiting for the help of Yahweh.[30] But sometimes the position is that the foreign oppressors have been joined by traitors from within the people and congregation itself, and in some cases these were evidently to be found among the rich and mighty in the land.

Now, as a rule, the adherence of the psalmists to the 'lowly' is not based on social and political but on national and religious grounds. Yet their sympathy for the 'poor' and 'lowly' also shows through. From Ps. 22.27 we can see that the psalmists take an interest in seeing that the poor have their share of the sacrificial meal; references to this may perhaps be found in both 69.33 and 34.3. And in some of the psalms the relation between rich and poor obviously plays a part;[31] the rich are the lofty and ungodly, the poor are the humble and pious having recourse to the Temple.

This social point of view is not just based upon the economic interests of a 'class' but is also an expression of two important religious factors. In

[25] Pss. 40.7; 50.8ff., 23; 51.18f.; 69.31f.—See above, Chap. VI. 3; VIII. 11.
[26] Pss. 49.5; 33.2; 81.3f.; 98.5f.; 147.7; 150; and many other places, see n. 23 to Chap. XIV.
[27] For further details see *Ps.St.* VI.
[28] See *Ps.St.* VI, pp. 59ff.
[29] The classical exposition of this interpretation is Rahlfs, *'Ani und 'Anaw in den Psalmen*; see Additional Note XXIX.
[30] See Birkeland, *'Ani und 'Anaw in den Pss.*; id., *Feinde des Indiv.*, pp. 317ff.
[31] Pss. 37; 49; 52; 62; 73. See Munch in *ZATW* 55, 1937, pp. 36ff. (Cf. Additional Note XXIX.)

the first place the men employed in the cult by virtue of their offices would come to know the pious as being distressed, sick or unclean or suffering from some kind of 'violence'; it was just when the pious person was 'oppressed' or 'suffering' in some way or other that he would have recourse to the Temple in order to receive the help of Yahweh through the sacramental institutions of the cult; such groups of 'suffering ones' we have met in Ps. 107 (Chap. X.3). It would therefore be natural for the cultic officials to write the 'texts' for the liturgies and generally to speak and think from the point of view of these 'oppressed' and 'distressed' people. But, in the second place, we need to be aware that the religious experience, of which the cult was a medium to those who took part in it and lived their lives in it, must also sometimes become such a personal experience of God as the holy, judging and overwhelming one, that a man would become small and humble and 'brought low'. We can see how the prophets, themselves belonging to the common people, would sometimes have such an experience of God through the cult itself; this is evidently the case with the inaugural vision which Isaiah had (Isa. 6); and similarly with Jeremiah (17.12). Holding this point of view, the pious will instinctively react against whatever may be proud and lofty and rich and mighty and self-sufficient; God only is great.[32] The psalmists merged these religious elements connected with the cult with their antagonism to the rich and mighty, and this resulted in a relative evaluation of poverty and riches which tells us something about the circles from which these authors came.

The antagonism based on social position and religious estimation which the attitude of the psalmists to the sacrificial cult (Chap. VIII.11) has proved did exist between themselves and the priests, and their growing self-consciousness in relation to the priests, have also, as we have seen, found expression in legend and tradition (Chap. XIV.1).

Here, too, a truly religious element makes itself felt. The high estimate of temple singing and the psalm, which the authors cherish, is at the same time the outcome of a religious experience, of being 'gripped' by the Holy One, for this feeling will instinctively find expression in rhythm, singing and rejoicings and winged words, but also in the contrite heart and the humble spirit, in the 'lowliness' for which the psalms display such great sympathy.

In this connexion we must also draw attention to the spiritual and personal relationship between psalmists and temple prophets, mentioned above (Chap. XII.1). With the organized guild of temple prophets, the psalmists had a certain spiritual fellowship. In ancient Israel poetry itself was considered to be inspired (see below); the ancient Hebrews as well as Arabs and Hellenes looked upon it as an outcome of divine inspiration, of 'holy excitation';[33] that is why both the songs of the seers and the words

[32] Cf. Isa. 2.9–17, and see *Ps.St.* VI, p. 97.
[33] Cf. Goldziher in *ZDMG* 45, 1891, p. 685; Wellhausen, *Reste arab. Heidentums,*[2] p. 35; van der Leeuw, *Phänomenologie,* §28.1, p. 209. [E.T., *Religion in Essence and Manifestation*, pp. 227f.]

of the prophets appear as poetical works in verse.[34] The prophetesses Miriam and Deborah were also regarded as poetesses in Israel.[35] Just as the prophet who has had his eyes and ears 'opened' beholds visions and hears mysterious divine voices,[36] so the poet hears the adoration of the heavens, which is 'without speech and language, not heard' by normal human ears (19.2-5). Like the prophet (1 Sam. 10.5; 2 Kgs. 3.15) so also the poet (Ps. 49.4f.) is put into a state of inspiration by means of music. In this state he will 'incline his ear to a secret' and have 'wisdom' 'pour forth from his mouth', just like the prophet (49.4f.; 45.2; 78.2). The psalmist too has been listening to the voice of the deity (81.6); through him also 'Yahweh is speaking' (85.9). The poets have seen Yahweh in his heavenly council, turning the leaves of his book—like any other wise scholar—and they have heard him speak of his pious ones and of Zion, or burst into laughter at the idea of the kings of this earth wanting to frustrate his plan (87.6; 2.4). They preach 'revelation' ('instruction' 'guidance', tôrâ), which Yahweh himself has 'whispered to them' (78.1; 110.1; cf. Isa. 8.16; 42.4). They have seen him looking down from his heaven, and they know what counsel he has taken (14.2ff.). They have heard the accusation and the doom he has pronounced against the other gods at his enthronement, and are able to tell the congregation about it (82). They have also seen him 'shining out of Zion' and heard the words of reproof he is going to pronounce to his congregation on a similar occasion because of the sins prevailing in their midst (50.1ff.). Just as the 'heart' of the prophet is able to tell him of things far off and unknown, so the 'heart' of the psalmist speaks divine counsels to him (27.8; cf. 2 Kgs. 5.26).

Reciprocally the temple prophets Nahum and Habakkuk were also psalmists (Nah. 1; Hab. 3). The prophecies of both Habakkuk and Joel give evidence of strong influences from the forms of psalm and cultic liturgy.[37] The same thing applies to Jeremiah[38] and Deutero-Isaiah.[39]

In this way the prophetic element in the psalms, discussed above in a wider context (Chap. XII), also provides evidence that the psalms are derived from the temple singers, who were so closely linked with the temple prophets[40] that the latter were finally organized as belonging to the guilds and 'families' of the singers, as we can see from the Chronicler.

---

[34] Num. 22-24; Gen. 49; Deut. 33. Cf. Lindblom, Profetismen, p. 602.
[35] Ex. 15.20; Jdg. 5.1. Cf. Gunkel in RGG[1] II, col. 1641.
[36] Num. 24.3f., 15; 1 Sam. 9.15; Isa. 22.14.
[37] Cf. Mowinckel, Jesajadisiplene, pp. 133f., 145ff., and for the 'psalms of lamentation' of the prophets, ibid., pp. 62ff., 129. Cf. also Humbert, Livre d'Habacuc, pp. 31ff., 37ff., 280ff., 290ff. See introduction to the book of Joel in GTMMM III; cf. Baumgartner in Festschrift für Budde, pp. 10ff.—The cultic element to be found in the conceptions and metaphors of Joel is also strongly emphasized—sometimes much too strongly—by Kapelrud in Joel Studies, and, in a more cautious and methodical way in StTh IV, pp. 5ff.
[38] Baumgartner, Klagegedichte d. Jeremia; cf. Mowinckel in Edda XXVI, pp. 276ff.
[39] Cf. Gressmann in ZATW 34, 1914, pp. 283ff.; Köhler, Deuterojesaja, pp. 120ff.; see also Ps.St. II, pp. 195ff.
[40] For the above, see Ps.St. VI, pp. 48ff.

On the face of it it is only natural that the temple singers themselves should have the deepest interest in giving expression to the ideas and experiences of the cult through singing, and that it would be their job to provide the psalms needed for the liturgy.

The singers did not recite or sing in the Temple 'at sight'. They had to know the psalms by heart and teach them to their sons. The psalms became the inheritance of the singer families.

It goes almost without saying, therefore, that the singers had the responsibility for copying out the psalms and handing them down. Probably the way they started learning the art of poetry was by copying and studying the old psalms. In other words the singers also had to be 'scribes' or 'sages', and the 'wise scribes' were actually at that time the real 'literary men' and poets. Jesus Ben Sira, for instance, was such a 'sage' and psalmist and, as we shall see, the eponymous ancestors of the singer families were supposed to have been such sages and poets in their day.[41] It is rather suggestive that the best metaphor one of the psalmists can find for his volubility and enthusiastic eulogy is 'the pen of the quick scribe' (45.2); and likewise, that most reflective and rationalistic author of the 'wisdom' and problem psalm, Ps. 49, is able to say,

> My mouth shall now speak words of wisdom,
>> and what my heart has thought is insight;
> I incline my ear to dark parables,
>> and solve my riddle on the lyre.   (49.4f.)

He thus suggests that his wisdom has been received in a state of inspired rapture like the one called forth in the prophets by means of dancing and playing on instruments. The word *maskîl* means a song sprung out of and containing supra-normal insight and effect; it is a term used for a certain kind of psalm (Chap. XXIII.5), and testifies to the connexion between the psalmists and 'wisdom'.

We shall see in the following chapter that in late Jewish times psalmography was taken over by 'wise men' of just the same type as Ben Sira, and also that the poetry of these late authors was included in the Psalter. Evidently the later learned men have taken over an old inheritance from earlier 'wise singers'.

So the production as well as the handing down of the psalms was the business of the 'wise' singers.

Against this view of the psalms as cultic psalms, composed by the professional singers and poets of the Temple, it has been objected that such an interpretation does not agree with the impression of personal emotion and experience brought out so vividly in many of the psalms. In a later chapter (XVII) we shall see that this contrast is unreal; the professional and the

---

[41] I Kgs. 5.9–13. The context shows that the ancient sages mentioned are also supposed to be composers of songs and 'stanzas of wisdom'.

personal do not exclude each other any more than the institutional and the charismatic did, according to the Old Testament way of thinking.

Nor is the fact that the Psalter does contain a few psalms which to all appearance have not been composed for use in the cult, nor by people from the circle of the temple personnel (see Chap. XVI), any objection to the view that the great majority of psalms are derived from the Temple and the temple personnel. For as we shall see below (Chap. XXII), the actual collection of the Psalter is finally the work of 'the wise'; after all, it would be a great deal more strange if some few psalms from their own circle had not been included in the collection.

4

But what about the names of authors given in the headings of the psalms? Do not these headings seem to name actual persons, in particular David?

The answer is that in those cases where the statements contain true tradition they support the view that these psalms have come into being among the temple singers. The secret is to understand them properly, as they were meant by the original tradition.

The headings mention the following names of supposed authors: David, Asaph, 'the sons of Korah', Heman 'the Ezrahite', Ethan 'the Ezrahite', Moses, Solomon. But the term 'Jeduthun', occurring in three headings, is not the name of an author nor even the name of a person, but a liturgical technical term.[42]

In so far as we are here dealing with historical individuals, Solomon is the latest according to the opinion of the later Jewish tradition. The book of the Chronicles dates the others—with the exception of Moses—in the age of David. Accordingly the psalms were supposed to be composed by David and his contemporaries. We shall return below to David and Solomon and Moses, and first discuss some of the headings which do contain real tradition and in a certain sense give real names of authors, namely Asaph, Heman, Ethan and the sons of Korah.

They certainly do not tell us anything about the individual authors of the individual psalms. Pss. 50; 73; 74; 79; and 80 are all ascribed to Asaph. But Ps. 81 is derived from the northern kingdom and can hardly be later than the year 722, when this state was destroyed; in all probability Pss. 74 and 79 were composed after the fall of Jerusalem in 587, whereas Pss. 50 and 73 were composed somewhat later according to their theological attitude and way of setting the problems. So these five psalms cannot possibly have been composed by the same person.

---

[42] David: Pss. 3–9/10; 11–32; 34–41; 51–65; 68–70; 86; 101; 103; 108–110; 122; 124; 131; 133; 138–145, in all, 73 psalms. See further below, n. 52.—Asaph: 50; 73–83; in all, 12 psalms.—Sons of Korah: 42/43; 44–49; 84; 87; 88; in all, 11 psalms.—Heman: Ps. 88 (together with the 'sons of Korah').—Ethan: 89.—Moses: 90.—Solomon: 72 and 127; in the latter it is wanting in G.—Jeduthun: 39 and 62 (together with David), 77 (together with Asaph).—See *Ps.St.* IV, pp. 16f.; Gunkel-Begrich, *Einl.*, p. 458.

But the above-mentioned headings do contain a dependable tradition concerning the circles in which these psalms came into being. What therefore, do these names of authors tell us? In the first place it should be noted that they are the names of such persons—historical or legendary— as were supposed to be the ancestors of the guilds of temple singers.

In the census list in Ezra 2—from about 400 B.C.[43]—Asaph is supposed to be the ancestor of all singers. Granted that he was a historical person, he probably belonged to the temple personnel after the restoration under Zerubbabel, or perhaps in late pre-exilic times.[44] At the time of the list the singers were not yet considered to belong to the 'Levites' but ranked below them, among the lower temple personnel. At the time of the Chronicler, 'Asaph' had become one of the three 'Levitical' families of singers, and the Chronicler makes him a contemporary of David. But this conclusion as to the date is no real historical tradition, it is a later theologico-historical theory; in the opinion of the Chronicler all the orderings of the temple were instituted by David.

In ancient times both Heman (88) and Ethan (89) like Chalcol and Darda', were considered to be famous 'wise men' and veteran authors of 'wisdom', to whom the writer of the saga compares Solomon; they are traditional figures—something like the Æsop of the Greeks or the Bidpai of the Arabs; cf., among the Israelites the wise Daniel and the 'wise man' Agur and 'king Lemuel' as authors of wise proverbs (Prov. 30.1; 31.1). Ethan and Heman were considered to be 'Ezrahites', i.e. 'natives' (Canaanites)[45] as distinguished from the Israelites; this means, in fact, that they are Canaanite representatives of the international, oriental tradition of wisdom and its exponents.[46] But in the tradition these wise men of the past are explicitly identified with the 'guild' of temple musicians; for they are called 'sons of *māḥōl*', which does not mean that they are own sons of a person called Mahol, as it has been misinterpreted until quite lately; *māḥōl* is a collective designation, meaning something like 'dance', 'orchestra'; just as 'sons of the ointments' or 'sons of the goldsmiths' indicate 'members of the guilds of ointment makers' or 'goldsmiths', so 'sons of the orchestra' indicates, as Albright has seen, that they are members of the (temple) guild of musicians.[47] Judging from the type of name, we are here dealing with traditions older than the monarchy in Israel. Such men of the past were considered by the wisdom 'scribes' to be their spiritual—and physical—ancestors. But 'wisdom' and 'prophecy' and 'poetry' and singing all belonged to the same set-up in the ancient orient. We can therefore well understand that the temple musicians and singers and poets also reckoned them as belonging to their circle. In later

[43] See Mowinckel in *NTT*, 1915, pp. 123ff.
[44] The proper name Asaph occurs in the later monarchic period (2 Kgs. 18.18, 37 = Isa. 36.3, 22), and in early Persian times (Neh. 2.8).
[45] See Albright, *ARI*, p. 210, n. 95, and above, n. 9 to Chap. XIV.
[46] 1 Kgs. 5.11 shows that 'the sage' must be more strongly emphasized than is done by Albright: only the younger tradition makes them musicians and singers.
[47] See Albright, op. cit., p. 127.

tradition, therefore, they were considered to be Levites and ancestors of a greater or smaller section of the temple singers. Yet, like poetry, wisdom, too, was considered to be something supernaturally inspired,[48] expressing itself in poetry such as the book of Proverbs, Job or Ps. 49.

According to Ps. 88.1 it is the *sons of Korah* who regarded Heman as one of their great men in days of old; and as Ethan, like Heman, according to Ps. 89.1 was considered an Ezrahite, probably Ethan too was supposed to belong to the sons of Korah. When the headings attribute a good many psalms to the latter, this obviously does not mean that the individual psalm is 'by' the sons of Korah—it could not very well be composed by a whole guild—but it means that this psalm and others with the same heading are 'for' Korah, belong to them, and form part of their repertoire. For Korah also is the name of a 'Levitical family' from the period after the restoration of the Temple. According to Ezra 2.42 the sons of Korah were at that time still door-keepers and so were not yet classed among the real 'Levites';[49] later on they rose to be singers, and were finally, like the latter, classed among the Levites. Like all the other temple families they would then date their pedigree from the time of David and Solomon and include Heman and Ethan among their ancestors. That a psalm belongs to the sons of Korah means that it came into being within this guild and had one of the sons of Korah for its author. In the age of the Chronicler himself (about 300 B.C. or later) the term 'sons of Korah' was no longer used; he speaks of three families of singers, Asaph, Heman and Ethan, each representing the three great Levitical families Gershon, Kohath and Merari—a mixing of tradition and artificial construction, the details of which are rather obscure.

The headings of the psalms represent a somewhat earlier conception than that of the Chronicler. They know but two families of singers, Asaph and the sons of Korah; among the latter we find two wise men of antiquity, Heman and Ethan.

According to the tradition among the collectors of the psalms these three ancestors of the singers were the authors of a great many psalms. Of course this tradition contains a historical kernel, in so far as these psalms—and still others—were composed by members of the guilds of singers. To the members of these guilds of singers it was, in fact, an obvious thing that the old time-honoured and effective songs of the cult should be derived from ancient 'wise men' and ancestors. To whom else could such valuable spiritual inheritance in family and class possibly be attributed? It is therefore a matter of course that the authorship of psalms belonging to the particular official repertoire of individual families would be attributed to one of the ancestors of that family.

---

[48] 1 Chron. 6.18, 22; 15.5, 19, etc.; Ps. 49.4f.; 1 Kgs. 3.4ff.; Prov. 8.22ff.; Job 32.8, 18; 4.12ff.; Dan. 1.17.
[49] For Ezra 2.42 cf. 1 Chron. 9.19ff., and other passages in the book of Chronicles, in which the sons of Korah are not yet 'Levites'.

5

What, then, about *'David'* in the headings of the psalms? We have seen above (Chap. III.6) that the original sense of this note was that the psalm in question was destined and used in the cult 'for David', i.e. for the reigning king. But no doubt also, the collectors and editors of the Psalter understood it to be a bit of information about the author, and no doubt such a note was often added to a psalm on this basis. The question arises therefore whether this is historically possible and correct; the argument implied in the cultic nature of the royal psalms and in the sense of the term *dâwîd* must be supported by an examination of the actual psalms in question.

We then arrive at the result that many, perhaps most of the psalms bearing the name of David must be later than his time. The historical allusions to be found as well as the supposed social and religious conditions, and arguments pertaining to the history of the language, prove that this must be so.[50]

In some of them, for instance, the worshipper clearly is a descendant of David, not David himself (18.51; 89.4, 20, 40, 50; 132.10). Others presuppose that the Temple on Zion, which was built by David's son Solomon, has been erected and stands there 'from of old' (24.7, 9).

In other cases the social conditions reflected in the psalms call for a later dating. Early Israel considered riches, welfare, prosperity and power to be sure evidence of piety, righteousness and the goodwill of God. From one point of view we may look upon the whole of the religious history of Israel in later times as a constant struggle about this problem. Scarcely before the middle and later monarchy did the social displacement occur which, in addition to the priestly and prophetic reaction against Canaanite culture and the disastrous experiences in foreign policy, could lead to a way of thinking like the one we find in Pss. 49; 73; 34; 37; 52 and 62, in which 'rich' and 'mighty' are on the point of being identified with 'violator', 'oppressor', 'sinner'.

The low estimate of the sacrifice of animals mentioned above does not agree with the type of piety we find at the time of David and even later with its perfectly positive view of the sacrifice.[51]

And to add an argument from the history of the language; the marked aramaisms in Ps. 139 or the late Hebrew use of the relative particle *še* and the circumlocution of the genitive construction by means of this particle and the preposition *lě* in Pss. 122 and 146, for instance, prove that in spite of the heading 'by David' in Ps. 122 they must belong to the latest psalms and be dated from a period long after the Exile.

Something similar is the case with a great many psalms.

So this corroborates the view that the 'David' of the headings was not originally meant to indicate the name of the author, but refers to the

[50] Cf. Buhl, *Psalmerne*,[2] pp. XVIIff.; and *Ps.St.* VI, pp. 2f.
[51] See Chap. VIII. 11; X. 2. Cf., for instance, 1 Sam. 26.19; 2 Sam. 6.13, 18; 21.9; 24.18–25.

cultic use of the psalms in the king's Temple, that it was later understood, however, to indicate the author, and by mistake was added to many psalms which cannot be so old. In other words it contains no true informtion or tradition about the psalmists, but is a result of a later interpretation and theory. We can therefore say nothing about the age and author of a psalm on the basis of this note.

On closer text-critical examination we shall find that in many cases the heading 'David' is merely a later addition.[52] It was added in accordance with the *theory* that the psalms were composed by David if nothing was said to the contrary; there is no question here of real tradition. By Jewish scholars 'David' was interpreted as the name of the author, and according to this interpretation the word was added to a great many psalms where it was not originally to be found.

However, if the note 'for David' was understood to mean '(composed) by David', there must be a reason for it. The traditions about the ancestor Asaph, and others, as the authors of the treasured psalms of the guilds of singers, prove that learned men among the later authors and preservers of psalms at a certain point of time began to be interested in this question. Thus it became natural for them to attribute to David the authorship of such psalms as of old used to be called the 'psalms of David', that is psalms composed 'for (and by) David' that is, for and by the king. That David himself had used such a psalm on important occasions of his life and thereby obtained the goodwill and help of Yahweh would naturally mean a strong recommendation for the psalm in question. And in proportion as David was considered the founder of the whole cultic ordering and particularly of the temple singing of Jerusalem (1 Chron. 25), it would also become natural to look upon him as the author of the psalms to which his name was attached. The earlier tradition already considered David a poet and attributed to him for instance the ancient dirge on Saul and Jonathan (2 Sam. 1.17ff.; 3.38f.; cf. 23.1ff.).

In this way a learned interest in the authorship grew into being in the circles in which the psalms were handed down. They began to ask who might have composed such and such a psalm. As a rule they would know nothing about it; it is a characteristic feature of cultic poetry all the world over that it is anonymous. But 'the learned' might 'investigate'—*dāraš*—and draw conclusions. And as David began to be considered the great founder, it would be a ready 'conclusion' that David had composed most of the psalms about which nothing was known to the contrary. In this way

[52] Of the 73 passages in which 'David' occurs in the heading (see above, n. 42) the word is lacking in several manuscripts or translations: Pss. 122 (2 MSS), 124 (3 MSS; Gh), 127 (G), 131 (G, H), 133 (2 MSS, G, T), 138 (Aq, Sexta); in 108 some MSS have *lẹ'āsāph*. The note is lacking in MT, but has been added in G or other translations: Pss. 33; 67; 91; 96; 98; 104; 137. This proves at any rate that in many cases it does not represent old tradition, but secondary theory. Cf. n. 1 to Chap. VIII. From this, as well as from the distribution of the headings among the 5 books of the Psalter (see above, n. 42) we may conclude that the headings of Pss. 90-150 have on the whole been added later and gradually, and that the last two books of the Psalter were originally anonymous in the tradition. Nor does 'of Moses' in Ps. 90 represent an old tradition; see below, §6.

the typical Jewish Midrash or learned legend about David as the author of the psalms came into being. The learned also tried to find things in the psalms which might be interpreted as allusions to experiences and happenings in the life of David. We can see that this was a gradual process; the heading 'by David' occurs several times in the Hebrew text, while wanting in some manuscripts or in the Greek 'Septuagint' or other old translations, and this is certainly not because it was left out by these other witnesses, but because it was not yet to be found in the manuscripts from which they were translated. On the other hand the original of the Septuagint has 'by David' in some cases in which we do not find it in the Hebrew text.[53]

It is due to the same learned interest that several of the headings purport to give information about the situation by referring the psalm in question to a definite incident in the life of David.[54] They do not represent any real tradition, but only later 'learning'. The 'interpretation' of each one is based on particular wordings in the psalm in question, in the usual manner of a true Jewish scholar; they are just typical 'midrash', literally 'investigation', i.e. a learned forming of legends as the result of an 'investigation', which is actually an unhistorical, speculative exegesis of disconnected details. They take the theory for granted that David is the author, and on this basis they try to assign these psalms: a few examples will show how it was done.

According to the heading, Ps. 18 is composed 'by David, who spake it unto Yahweh in the day that Yahweh delivered him from all his enemies and from Saul'. The last words 'and from Saul' may be a later addition, as can be seen from their awkward position in the clause. The heading makes special reference to external enemies, from whom Yahweh has now delivered him. This is evidently based on the words of the psalm about 'peoples' having been conquered by the thanksgiving king, and about the 'enemies' from whom Yahweh has delivered him. 'Accordingly' the psalm must be a recapitulating retrospect over a long chain of conflicts, and must be spoken by a king who had carried on many wars and many kinds of wars, consequently David, and it must be derived from the later part of his life; it must be a thanksgiving psalm for experiences of salvation through a longish period! Actually this psalm is a 'casual' thanksgiving psalm, speaking of an actual incident, a great battle against many foreign enemies ('strangers'), where the king had been in great danger but from which Yahweh had successfully saved him. And the king is not David, but one of David's descendants, as we are explicitly told at the end (v. 50b).

Judging from v. 3, Ps. 63 was used for prayer in the Temple, by a king (v. 12); so when in v. 2 the worshipper says that his 'flesh longeth for God in a dry and thirsty land', this must be meant metaphorically: his distress and danger and thirst for the help of God is like the state of the wayfarer

---

[53] See above, n. 52.
[54] For the situations given in the headings see *Ps.St.* VI, pp. 84ff.

in the desert, where he is on the point of perishing from thirst. This becomes still more obvious if the reading of v. 2 in some manuscripts and the Syriac translation is correct; instead of saying 'in a dry land' they put 'like a dry land'. But the learned scribes interpreted the term literally; they asked themselves, when was David in great danger in a desert, and decided that it must refer to the time 'when David was in the wilderness of Judah' (v. 1) on his flight from Saul, and that the psalm was composed 'by David' on that occasion.

According to the heading, Ps. 52 was composed 'by David, when Doeg the Edomite came and told Saul that David had come to the house of Abimelech'. This is an allusion to the story in 1 Sam. 21.1–8; 22.6–19. But the psalm presupposes the existence of the Temple and must therefore be later than the age of David. Besides, the heading is inaccurate, for 'when Doeg came to Saul' and told him about David and Abimelech, David was already far away in the desert; so that it would need to run: 'when David heard that Doeg had come to Saul'. Nor does the heading agree with the condition of the worshipper in the psalm: the poem complains of 'lying' and 'deceitful words'; but what Doeg told Saul was objective truth: that David had come to Abimelech, who had helped him to escape by giving him food and weapons. In addition to this the psalm only speaks of the evil which 'the man with the tongue' has inflicted on the worshipper *himself*, in this case David; but the evil results of Doeg's denunciations did not fall on David but on Abimelech and his family. How then did the learned men conduct their 'investigation'? They took for granted that 'David' was the name of the author; in the first line they would find that the psalm was directed against a *gibbôr*—which means 'hero', 'giant', and is used, for instance, as the technical term for the guards of the king, but may also imply 'tyrant'; from 1 Sam. 21.8 and 22.17ff. they would see that Doeg belonged to the 'runners' who made up part of the *gibbôrîm*, 'the giants', i.e. the bodyguard of the king. So when 'David' in this psalm complains of a *gibbôr*, it could be no other than Doeg!

6

The last two authors' names, 'Moses' and 'Solomon' are in turn 'interpreted' out of the psalms themselves according to the same 'learned' methods.

Almost unanimously interpreters agree that Ps. 90, attributed to Moses, cannot possibly be so old. The emotions and conditions of the Exodus do not find expression here, nor the primitive collective outlook of those ancient times. It is not a young nation of wandering conquerors speaking here, but a community that knows itself to be under the constant pressure of the wrath of God; a whole people knowing that it has deserved to be punished for its sins, and which no longer asks for political eminence, but only for the simple happiness of being allowed to enjoy in peace the work of their hands; undisturbed, that is, by greedy tax-collectors and moneylenders and armies on the march, and the like. As a motivation for a turning of the destiny the prayer does not plead the promises given to the *people*, as was usual in the earlier national psalms of lamentation, nor a regard for the existence of the people, but suggests the following quite individualistic considerations: since 'we', the generation of individuals living now, cannot reckon with more than seventy years of life at most— exceptionally perhaps eighty—and as we have hitherto experienced only disaster and oppression, therefore we now pray for good fortune, the reward of our sufferings, to come before it is too late for *us* who live now! Those of really ancient times, including Moses, would never have been able to speak in that way. To them the people was everything, the individual by himself nothing. In Ps. 90 individuals appear with their several personal claims for happiness in life, indeed so much so that society recedes into the shade. Obviously the psalm derives from Jewish times, not from the earliest period.

But it is not difficult to see how the learned men were led to think of Moses. In the worshippers whose days and years were passing away in the wrath of God they saw the generation wandering in the desert on account of the judgments of God; these had left Egypt at the age of manhood, and after wandering for forty years they are now facing the end of their lives. The psalm, it will be remembered, complains that the normal limit of human life is seventy years, and one feature of the lament is that this limit is approaching. Thus the learned men have put two and two together: the average age of a generation, the normal age of manhood, is thirty years; thirty plus forty years of roaming in the desert make seventy; the psalm must have been composed by a representative of the people wandering in the desert, i.e. by Moses himself! And in v. 16 they would find the confirmation of this 'result of their investigation' It says here: 'Let thy work appear unto thy servants and thy glory unto their sons'. According to the usual rules of the 'thought rhyme' in Hebrew poetry (Chap. XIX. 7) there is no question here of two different things, as if 'thy servants', i.e. the worshippers of Yahweh, may see his 'work', but 'their sons' see his 'glory'; the two parts express the same thought: let thy servants and their sons see thy work and thy glory, i.e. thy glorious work of salvation; let the present, as well as the coming generation, experience thy grace and thy salvation. But the learned men, busy with literal interpretation, found that Yahweh's 'work' and his 'glory' were two different revelations of the breaking-in of Yahweh, and that the sons alone expect to see the 'glory' of Yahweh; this would have to imply that the generation of those wandering in the desert must die there, whereas only the sons of the emigrants would see the promised land and thus experience the glory of Yahweh!

The same is the case with the headings of Pss. 72 and 127, 'by Solomon'. This ascription is lacking in several manuscripts and old translations, and consequently is sure to belong to the latest additions to the psalm texts. In Ps. 72 we hear of a glorious and mighty king, who will rule over many foreign nations and to whom shall be given of the 'gold of Sheba'! He is called both 'the king' and 'the king's son', so he cannot be David—and on this point the learned men are right. But then, so their argument would run, it can be nobody else but Solomon, known for his riches in gold and his close connexion with the queen of Sheba! The result of this deduction may not be completely out of the question; but the heading is not based on any real, original tradition; it is just a theory, which *may* happen to be right.

We cannot say the same about the heading 'by Solomon' in Ps. 127. This psalm really consists of two 'words of wisdom', pronouncing in general phrases that he who builds a 'house' without Yahweh shall build in vain, for all happiness depends on the blessing of God. These two sayings were used as a psalm for the harvest festival with a view to the consecration of the Temple, which in earlier times used to be celebrated at that season. Judging from all the other cases of influence from 'wisdom poetry', this psalm must belong to a rather late period. None the less the collectors later 'found out' that this psalm about the building of the 'house' must be due to the temple builder Solomon, and so the heading was added—but only in the Massoretic (Hebrew) text.

The headings 'by David', 'by Moses', 'by Solomon' tell us nothing, therefore, of the real authors. The heading 'by David', however, confirms that in days of old the psalms were destined to be used by the *king* when he was representing the community in the cult or taking part in it in some other way (see above, pp. 76f.).

CHAPTER XVI

The Learned Psalmography

I

The temple personnel also included scribes.[1] The historical nucleus of
the tradition about Solomon being the author of 'proverbs' and other
'wisdom poetry',[2] is probably just that he was the one who founded the
school for scribes in Jerusalem and introduced there the international
wisdom poetry of the orient.[3] For along with the teaching of foreign
languages this kind of literature belonged to the special professional education of the 'scribes'. It had its home in the schools for scribes.[4] Here
Solomon was maintaining the tradition of the great empires as well as of
the courts of Canaanite princes.[5] The schools for scribes, and the art and
culture they represented, were an international phenomenon.[6] There is
every reason to believe that the school for scribes in Jerusalem, as elsewhere in the orient, was closely connected with the Temple; this is apparent
by the very fact that the 'wisdom literature' of Israel was reckoned among
the canonical writings.

Scholars have often distinguished too sharply between the different
'classes' of the 'intelligentsia' in ancient Israel: priests, prophets, scribes,
wise men, etc., as if they were sharply defined social and functional
'classes'. In reality there was no hard and fast dividing line between them.
Several prophets are said to have come from priestly families: the majority
of prophets formed, as we have seen above, an official class of cult-
functionaries; the psalmists belonged, as we have also seen, to the temple

[1] See Neh. 13.13; Jer. 36.5f., 10f.—For this chapter see Mowinckel in *NTT*, 1950, pp. 39ff.
and in *Wisdom in Israel* (Rowley Festschrift), pp. 205ff.
[2] 1 Kgs. 3.9; 5.9–14; Prov. 1.1–6; 10.1; 25.1; Eccl. 1.1; 12.9f.
[3] Cf. Mowinckel in *GTMMM* IV, pp. 385ff.—Scott deals at length with this question in the
Rowley Festschrift, pp. 262ff., in my opinion, however, in a too sceptical way and too much
from the viewpoint of literary criticism. It is here more a question of an old scholarly and
legendary tradition than of literary 'influences' from one biblical source upon another. On the
sort of wisdom that in the old tradition was ascribed to Solomon, see Alt., *Kl. Schriften z. Gesch.
Israels* II, pp. 90ff., and further, Noth in the Rowley Festschrift, pp. 225ff.
[4] See Gressmann in *ZATW* 42, 1924, pp. 291ff.
[5] Cf. Gressmann, op. cit., p. 295. 'The ready writer', *sōphēr māhîr* (Ps. 45.2), is an ancient
Canaanite term adopted in Egyptian.
[6] See Gressmann, op. cit., pp. 272ff.; Baumgartner, *Israelit. u. altorient. Weisheit*; Fichtner,
Altorientalische Weisheit; Peet, *A Comp. Study of the Lit. of Egypt, Palest. and Mesopot.*, pp. 99ff.;
Gemser, *Sprüche Salomos*, pp. 5f.; cf. Albright in *The Jewish People, Past and Present* I, p. 36. For
Babylonian religious texts as 'class-books' of language and literature in the Egyptian writing-
schools, see also Gordon, *The Living Past*, p. 133. For writing-schools in Palestine, see Albright
in *BASOR* 86, 1942, pp. 20f., cf. 92, 1943, p. 21. For Sumerian writing-schools, see Falkenstein
in *Die Welt des Orients* I, 3, 1948, pp. 172ff.

singers; Levites gradually became interpreters of the law;[7] the scribes were also the 'wise men' (*hăkhāmîm*).

The guilds of the scribes and of the temple singers and poets were closely connected. A metaphor like the one in Ps. 45.2: 'My tongue is like the pen of a ready writer' (properly: quick writer), seems to indicate that the poet is proudly aware of being a master of the noble art of writing. It is not unreasonable to suppose that the teaching of that part of the professional science of the temple singers which was made up of psalmography would also take the form of learning to copy earlier psalms.

At any rate it was these *learned 'writers'*, who gradually became the 'scribes' of the New Testament, who took in hand the collection and handing down of the Psalter. Even the headings, with their learned interpretations, and their interest in the authors and supposed historical circumstances of the different psalms are indications of this. The fact that the guilds of temple singers have chosen such traditional types of the wise men of old[8] as Heman and Ethan for their 'ancestors', points in the same direction (see Chap. XV.5). The author of the wisdom poem of Job is well aware of the different styles of composition in psalmography.[9] We shall see below that psalmography was cultivated in the circle of learned scribes far down through the ages.

From of old these 'learned' or 'wise' men used to cultivate a special kind of literature, 'wisdom poetry', which was cultivated all over the orient and had a common, markedly international character, both in Egypt and Babylonia and in Canaan. Its characteristic form is the 'saying', the proverb and the exhortation, with moralizing and didactic contents. It aims at practical wisdom in daily living, not least so for the 'scribes' themselves, who have intercourse with kings and great men and are out travelling in foreign countries and have to deal with the affairs of the realm and with all sorts of people. But practical wisdom for day-to-day living— even if it has a utilitarian character—has always a religious basis; the true 'wisdom' is 'the fear of God', that is the deepest motive for morality. As this morality and this poetry are international and related to social position and profession, they also have a general and rational character. What they impress upon people are the—from the point of view of the ancient orient—universal human virtues, and they speak with preference of 'the deity' in general, whereas the more national aspect of religion, expressing itself for instance in the name Yahweh for God, becomes less prominent. This does not prevent it from being adapted to the national religion of Israel, nor preclude the later learned men from finding that the highest 'wisdom' has been revealed in the law of Yahweh.

Now we see that not a few psalms show the influence of wisdom poetry in their content as well as their form. This becomes apparent for instance

[7] See above, II.97ff.
[8] See above, II.92ff.
[9] Cf. Mowinckel, *Diktet om Ijob*, pp. 115ff.; *GTMMM* IV, p. 311.

in the testimonies of the psalms of thanksgiving and their exhortations to the congregation, in which the tone, in the nature of the case, is didactic. Naturally these passages will have the literary form of a 'proverb', a wise saying (*māšāl*). This appears in the psalms in which suffering and the justice of Yahweh are felt to be a problem, one on which the author is pondering and which he is trying to solve; in this case, too, it is especially the psalms of thanksgiving, such as for instance Ps. 73, which take on the character of 'problem psalms'. The psalmists have learnt from the learned men, and the learned men have learnt from the psalmists; when they are speaking of the greatness and wisdom and justice of God they often do so in the form of a hymn, just as their instruction about the 'two roads', the road of virtue and the road of vice, not infrequently takes on the form of the blessing and the curse.

The learned men were also traditionalists; they co-operated in taking care of the ancient holy traditions, both the laws and the sayings of the prophets and the traditions of the Temple, among the latter, that of psalmography. In proportion as the importance of 'Yahweh's law' increased in Judaism, their own importance likewise increased as guardians of the law tradition and law interpretation and of religious life in general. They considered themselves the inheritors both of the prophets and of the psalmists. They became psalmists too, and to the ancient cultic poetry was added a newer, private, learned psalmography.

2

Like everything else in the sphere of mental life, the private psalmography had its roots in the customs of earlier times.

In the first instance, the people of Israel would always sing and compose poetry on the different occasions of life.[10] We have mentioned above the song of victory[11] (Chap. IX.1), sung by the warriors on the battlefield and in the camp, as well as by the women coming to meet them when they returned home. People used to sing while at work, driving their oxen at the plough (Sir. 38.35), and treading the grapes (Isa. 16.9; Jer. 25.30; 48.33). It was an immediate outlet for their emotions and at the same time a practical means of making the work easier and enabling them to work to time as with the ditties sung at the capstan or by quarrymen. But that is why the ancients believed such old stanzas to be 'filled with power' and effectual; the stanza sung when digging a well had the form of an 'exhortative word' inviting the well to 'spring up' (Num. 21.17f.). At weddings and other popular fetes people would dance and sing. At obsequies the 'wailing women' would sing the stereotyped keen (2 Sam. 3.38f.; Jer. 9.10ff.; 22.18f.). At the feasts drinking songs were heard (Isa. 22.13; 56.12). From the wall of the city was heard the watchman's

---

[10] For the following, cf. Hempel, *Althebr. Literatur*, pp. 19ff.
[11] See II.26f.

song (Isa. 21.12); even the prostitute in the street would sing her song to the lyre in order to allure men (Isa. 23.16). At the gathering of grapes in the vineyard or watching the herd at night, songs of love would be sung, like the ones we know from Canticles; even the professional street-minstrel could be heard singing them, when people would gather round him (Isa. 5.1ff.). Several of these steretyped stanzas became the starting-point of a further development of lyric poetry of immediate moment. From the stanza of the funeral wail are derived both a personal lyrical poem like the lament on Saul and Jonathan (2 Sam. 1.19ff.) and the political laments or lampoons, which either in a mournful or in an ironically triumphant way would sing of disasters having befallen tribe, city or people.[12] The lampoon is often mentioned[13]—anyone must be prepared for it, if aiming too high and overtaken by destiny.

The travellers in a caravan would no doubt shorten the journey by singing traditional and universally known stanzas, and also new improvisations, and this might happen whenever several people were travelling in company. We are explicitly told that when the festivals were approaching and people were departing in a body, they would raise the pilgrim's song: 'Let us go to the hill of Yahweh'.[14] In this case, too, a traditional mode of composition was established, of which we can obtain some idea through the allusions found here and there, especially in the prophets. They would start with the invitation 'Let us go up!' or 'We will go up!'. Then the name of the sanctuary would be mentioned, directly or by means of poetical circumlocutions: 'the hill of Yahweh', 'his holy place' and the like. And to this would probably be added both expressions of joy at getting there and laudatory statements about Yahweh and about the sanctuary, picturing the blessings to be expected there.

Here then, right in the midst of the life of the people, 'wordly' and 'religious' poetry meet. And it would be but natural if these pilgrims' songs were strongly influenced by the forms and motifs of the cultic poetry, which so many of the pilgrims had already heard and by which they had been strongly impressed on earlier visits to the sanctuaries. The hymn in particular would put its stamp on the pilgrim's song, more especially in its 'indirect' form in the 'Song of Zion', the eulogy of Yahweh through his glorious sanctuary, from which blessings would pour forth (Chap. IV.2). Conversely, in some cases the temple hymn has adopted elements of composition from the pilgrim's song (cf. Pss. 122.1; 84.2f., 11a).

We may therefore suppose that motifs from the temple songs, and sometimes even some particular psalm, would make their way down to the people and be sung on such occasions. We know that at the time of Jesus it had become a custom at the private paschal repasts in the homes to sing the very psalms that were used at the temple festival, the so-called Egyp-

---

[12] Cf. Am. 4.1f.; Isa. 13; 14; 15; 16; Lamentations, and many other places.
[13] Cf. Num. 21.27–30; Isa. 37; 47; 14.4ff.; Jer. 8.20; Ezk. 12.22, etc.
[14] See Isa. 2.3 = Mic. 4.2; Jer. 31.6; Ps. 122.1. Cf. Gunkel-Begrich, *Einl.*, pp. 309ff.

tian 'Hallel', i.e. Pss. 113–118 (see Chap. XXI.2.j). This does not give us any reason to suppose that any considerable part of our extant psalms originated in private circles or was used there (cf. Chap. XV.1); but it may indicate some of the preludes to the private religious poetry that did arise among the Jews in later times.

3

In spite of the didactic character of the 'learned psalmography', it has one characteristic in common with genuine psalmography: these poems are, and must be considered as, *prayers*. Like every real psalm, they address God, even though they often address men as well. And the origin of this new sort of poetry must be seen against the background of the Jewish view of prayer. Prayer is the most spontaneous outcome of piety—of the relationship to God. In Israel also there always existed more or less free spontaneous prayer, independent of the temple service.[15] And the more the relationship to God became the personal matter of the individual, the more would prayer be a regular part of life in God. We have noticed how a personal relationship of prayer grew into being among the prophets, as a result of the personal problems forced upon them through their calling.[16] The later disciples of the prophets and the learned collectors of the tradition were also pious people. And in proportion as the law and the scriptures became the standard and source of religious life in Judaism, piety was to a certain degree detached from the temple cultus, and found a great part of its nourishment in the synagogue and in the lecture-room (the school) of the learned men. And like the prophets of old, the learned rabbis were considered to be men of prayer. Both synagogue and home developed a prayer life which gradually took set forms. Thus we know that in Jewish times pious people thought it proper to have three fixed hours of prayer daily; this custom is taken for granted in the legends of Daniel.[17]

From the nature of the case, the forms and motifs of free prayer would to a great extent be determined by the fixed traditional style of the regular service. In the psalms the pious would find expressions for what they themselves wished to say, they would learn from them what it was proper to say, and what ought to be said to God. The influence of psalm styles on the 'free' prayers to be found in the Old Testament can be demonstrated step by step. We see it already in the short exclamatory prayers in Amos and Isaiah, and quite distinctly in the lamentations and prayers of Jeremiah;[18] and also in the influence of the hymn style on the sayings of

[15] Cf. Gen. 24.12ff.; 28.20ff.; 32.10ff.; and several other places. See Wendel, *Das freie Laiengebet* (with much material which is really of a ritual nature).

[16] See *GTMMM* III, pp. 21f. Especially to be seen in Jeremiah, see Hertzberg, *Prophet und Gott*; Baumgartner, *Die Klagegedichte des Jeremia*.

[17] Dan. 6.11, 14. Cf. Schürer, *Geschichte* II,⁴ p. 350, n. 40. [E.T. II, i, 290, n. 248.] For prayer in private life and synagogue see ibid., Index, s.v. 'Gebet'. [E.T. Index, s.v. 'Prayer'.]

[18] See *GTMMM* III, pp. 51ff., and below, Chap. XVIII.2.; cf. above, II.93, with references. For Jeremiah, see above, n. 16.

Deutero-Isaiah, and the personal hymnal exclamations sometimes to be found there.[19]

This non-cultic prayer, which was originally free with regard to occasion, time and place, but which gradually attained fixed limits, and which at any rate as far as form and context were concerned was largely dependent on tradition, affords one condition of a non-cultic psalmography. There is another step from this to conscious psalmography. Jeremiah did not compose psalms, but he poured out his heart in guided words, and he imparted these prayers to others, because in addition to the answers received from God they made up a part of his message to his people. Still more obviously the 'hymns' of Deutero-Isaiah are circumlocutions of his message, even if no doubt his own heart is engaged in them; that he sometimes puts the hymn into the mouth of Yahweh himself (Isa. 45.8) testifies to the fact that he did not want it to be looked upon as poetry thought out by his own heart (Ps. 19.15).

On the other hand we find that the latest, anonymous prophets, who were learned collectors rather than original prophets in the old sense of the word, not infrequently burst out into the jubilant hymn to be sung by the saved, when the great 'turning of destiny' has taken place;[20] or they sing it already on their own.[21]

4

So among the learned and inspired collectors of the holy traditions of the ancients a cult-free psalmography also grew into being.

They were men of prayer and they were officially inspired 'pneumatics'. To be able to pray rightly, to make a doxology, or a prayer, with the proper items and in the proper form, was considered not only an evidence of piety but also a proof of the inspiration which the wise claimed for themselves and were conscious of possessing (Sir. 15.10; 39.5f.). It was these wise men who took over and further developed the psalmists' estimate of prayer and psalm as being the true and acceptable sacrifice; a man like Jesus Sirach no longer has any real understanding of animal sacrifice.[22] Thus they started to think it a pious work, acceptable to God, to compose a psalm, especially if a person had been delivered from disaster or danger, and perhaps also to recite it among the circle of disciples; then the latter, too, would learn at the same time something of this pious art ('wisdom'). Evidence for such a custom is found in the narrator's remark about how Tobit recited his poem: 'And Tobit *wrote* a joyful prayer, and said . . . '[23]

[19] Isa. 44.23; 45.8. Cf. *GTMMM* III, p. 52, and preceding note, as well as references in n. 5 to Chap. XVIII.
[20] Isa. 12; 24.15f.; 25.9; 26.1ff.; 27.2f.
[21] Isa. 25.1f.
[22] Sir. 32.6f. See Stade-Bertholet, *Biblische Theologie d. A.T.* II, pp. 178f.
[23] Tob. 13.1. This well attested text is certainly to be preferred to the shorter in Charles's translation.—Philo (*De Vita Contemplativa X*) gives a vivid description of how hymns were sung at the meetings of the Therapeutae.

The esteem in which the learned held the psalm is brought out by their conception of the pious folk of the past. The later writers of sagas and legends every now and then make their characters utter a psalm or a psalm-like prayer when relating both their disasters and their deliverance; this is related about Hannah, king Hezekiah, the prophet Jonah, about Ezra, and Esther, and Daniel and his friends, about king Manasseh, and Tobit, and Judith.[24]

Sometimes the wisdom teachers include such psalms in their writings; this is not infrequently the case with Jesus Sirach, whose mode of composition even otherwise gives evidence of being largely influenced by the psalm style.[25] It aims at teaching and edifying the reader, that is to say at being used for private edification, preferentially in the lecture-room.

Here we are face to face with a learned psalmography which is not derived from the temple singers but is of a truly private nature and has no longer any direct relation to the cult.

Of course this does not exclude the possibility that several of these learned men may have been Levites belonging to the families of singers, nor that among this private poetry there may also have been psalms destined for use in the cult. Perhaps this especially applies to the thanksgiving psalms, which seem to have been the particular favourites of the 'wise'. Among the thanksgiving psalms of the Psalter we find so much personal experience coupled with such manifold varieties of and departures from the old style pattern that we cannot help asking whether this or that psalm was not composed by the individual saved, even though according to the liturgical notes of the heading it has been used on cultic occasions, and so was probably also composed for such use. This applies especially to Ps. 73, the problem and situation of which are certainly typical, and thus universally valid, but in which may be found such personal expressions that there seems to be no reason for a distinction between the 'ego' of the worshipper and that of the author.[26] If Ps. 34 was composed for cultic use, much the same seems to be the case there also. We may suppose, therefore, that it had become accepted among the pious that the person who had been saved had better himself compose the thanksgiving psalm to be recited at the sacrificial feast—if he was at all able to do so, which again means: if he was a 'wise' and 'learned' man. It was both a natural expression of his feelings and considered to be evidence of particular piety to honour Yahweh in such a way.

In addition to the above-mentioned psalms preserved in stories and books of wisdom we also possess from late Jewish times a whole collection of such psalms called the Psalms of Solomon.

The learned psalmist often had a twofold object for his poem. First of all it was meant to be a pious work: to honour God by praising and

---

[24] 1 Sam. 2; Isa. 38; Prayer of Manasses; Tob. 13; Judith 16. See further below, §6.
[25] Sir. 42.15ff.; 39.12ff.; 51.1ff.; etc. See Baumgartner in *ZATW* 34, 1914, pp. 169ff.
[26] See above, Chap. X. 2, and n. 13 to Chap. X, and cf. below, Chap. XVII.

thanking him for his great works and his benefits, and to call upon him similarly when in distress and tribulation—and it was to do so in inspired verses. That is what the author of Ps. 50 makes Yahweh himself impress upon the pious man:

Call upon me in the day of trouble—
I will deliver thee, and thou shalt honour me. (50.15.)

We do not know much about the way this calling upon and thanksgiving were performed. As we have seen, it is just possible that the person who was bringing a thank-offering would also on some occasions recite his private thanksgiving psalm in the circle of relations and friends at the thank-offering feast. And from Sirach's book of Wisdom we may infer that such poems were recited before the students of the schools of wisdom, in the circle gathered round the teacher. And this brings us to the second object: that of teaching young people the art of calling upon and lauding the Lord in inspired 'songs of wisdom'.[27] This is the true religious element: the poet seeks to share his religious experiences with the young people, bear witness to them and through his personal example admonish them to walk in the right way.[28]

5

Some non-cultic poems do appear to have been included in the Psalter; we would suggest Pss. 1; 19B; 34; 37; 49; 78; 105; 106; 111; 112; 127.

One characteristic of this latest psalmography is that broadly speaking it tries to keep to the old paths and adhere to the old rules of composition, but without any real comprehension. As people no longer composed for a definite cultic occasion, the preservation of the specific types of composition was no longer safeguarded by their 'place in life', as it used to be, and the different modes and motives become mixed. We may therefore speak of a disintegration of the style. This is particularly marked in that type of composition which in later Jewish opinion was reckoned amongst the most skilful, namely alphabetic psalms, in which every line or period, ('bicolon', 'distich') starts with a successive letter in alphabetic sequence;

[27] For the connexion between the wisdom psalm and the 'school' see Mowinckel in *Kirke og Folk*, 1934, pp. 27f., and particularly Ludin Jansen, *Spätjüd. Psalmendichtung*. Munch, too, has drawn attention to this connexion and tried to get a clearer insight into it (*Act. Or.* XV. pp. 112ff.), but with rather too many generalizing and unproved assertions. Munch does not distinguish clearly enough between the older and the younger phases, the canonical and post-canonical poetry, and his classification of the material as 'psalms for school prayers' and 'psalms for teaching' is not very happy; the existence of regular 'school prayers' is not proved, but rather disproved, by the fact that the habit of Rabbi Nehemiah of saying a short prayer when he entered or left 'the house of learning' (Jer. Meg. III. 1) is mentioned as something particular. Munch's definition of the individual psalms and their species is not very convincing, and his strong emphasis on the 'polemical' element in many of the Psalms of Solomon does not do full justice to the authors and to the spontaneously religious and witnessing element in the didactic poetry of the men of learning. See further, Mowinckel in *NTT*, 1950, pp. 4ff.
[28] It is the understanding of this personal, primarily religious, element which is missing in Munch, for instance when he suggests that the purpose of the thanksgiving psalm, Sir. 51.13ff., is to 'enlist pupils' (*Act. Or.* XV, p. 135).

here, sometimes, elements of style from nearly all the ancient species of poetry are mixed up, according as the initial letter has called up by association one or other characteristic catchword.

Again, this poetry is more or less influenced by the style and subject-matter of the wisdom poetry. To a greater or lesser degree the psalm becomes a didactic poem. Even the old thanksgiving psalm tended that way (see Chap. X.2). The 'confession of Yahweh's name before the (worshipper's) brethren' is a 'witness' in the religious sense of the word; it includes always a desire to win other people for God. It thus assumes to some extent the nature of an admonition, whether it calls the person blessed who confesses his sins and obtains forgiveness and is healed from illness and impurity, or straightway invites others to follow the example of the worshipper. Here the style and ideas of the wisdom poetry with its exhortatory religious and moral instruction, and its references to the experiences of the teacher, make themselves felt. The thanksgiving psalm may become mainly instructive, and approximate to the didactic poem, as is the case in Ps. 34.

In the learned psalmography this tendency becomes much more prominent. The form becomes that of the admonition or warning of the proverb, and copies the didactic statement of the latter as to how different kinds of people will fare in this world. A favourite subject is the instruction about the destinies of good and evil people, as in Pss. 1 and 112, and more or less successful attempts at proving that the Jewish dogma of retributive justice holds good: that piety will be rewarded and ungodliness punished in this earthly life, even though not until an untimely death has overtaken the ungodly—that is the thought in which the author of Ps. 49 takes comfort.[29]

In this way the psalm receives the character of a theodicy: the author seeks to prove that God has acted rightly. Therefore it often leads to a hymnal element in the style; we get a kind of didactic hymn, like Pss. 78 and 105. The material is then usually derived from the history of Israel,[30] and the intention is to testify to the faithfulness of Yahweh and the breaking of the covenant on the part of the people, proving the justice of punishment and disaster. Such a didactic hymn may develop into a downright 'hymnal legend', a synopsis of sacred history in the style of a hymn, as happens in Pss. 78 and 105. A line may be drawn from the liturgies in connexion with the renewal of the covenant (Pss. 81; 95; see Chap. V.8, pp. 139ff.) via the prophetic exhortation of a psalm like Ps. 50 to a hymnal legend like Ps. 78. But history may also provide the material for a confession of sins and a prayer for restoration on the part of the congregation, and thus result in a historical penitential psalm, like Ps. 106.

As a background to the discussions about the justice of God, we can perceive the religious split in the congregation as a result of the progress of the ideals of the religion of the law. The psalmists side with the strict

---

[29] Cf. Pss. 31.24; 32.1, 6f.; 34.4ff., 12ff.; 37.35ff.; 124.8.
[30] Cf. Lauha, *Die Geschichtsmotive in den alttest. Pss.*; Bückers in *Biblica* 32, 1951, pp. 401ff.

adherents of the law—for they belonged to the 'scribes'—and look upon the others as sinners and apostates. And as it was generally the adherents of the wordly-minded who held power in the Jewish province, the psalmists often put the matter as if it were piety and lowliness on one side, at variance with power and riches and ungodliness on the other; sometimes they seem even to identify the provincial officials with the pagan oppressors. When a pious person was affected by personal tribulations, and particularly such as had to do with the difference between rulers and ruled, 'rich' and 'poor', then the problem about the unequal apportionment of the good things of life and about the 'ungodliness' and 'worldliness' of those in power would become a big issue. Then the pious person might have reason to 'fear', namely that God would fail him, and that the doctrine of retributive justice would not hold good (Ps. 49.6, 16).[31] Then he would comfort himself and his fellow-believers by stating that at all events riches will come to an end in death (Pss. 49; 37); face to face with death, all are alike; but for all that, he will maintain that the ungodly mighty ones will end in disaster, whereas the pious and humble and lowly shall be saved from all dangers (Pss. 34; 37).[32] The experiences of these poets culminate in just such a personal religious confidence' 'As for me, God will redeem my life and deliver me from the hands of She'ol' (49.16). Sometimes a personal experience of the problem and its solution shines clearly through; for instance Ps. 34 is most likely meant to be a thanksgiving psalm on deliverance from some distress; the same thing may apply to Ps. 37; both psalms may have been composed for use in the cult.[33] None of these psalms give expression to the hope of eternal life and the belief in a resurrection and a personal life to follow after death as the solution of the problem and the source of comfort; as yet the belief in resurrection was not part of Jewish religion.[34]

The zeal for the law sometimes finds expression in a hymn to the law of Yahweh (see Chap. IV.3), to which is now attributed nearly all the power-filled and saving qualities, for which the hymn used to praise Yahweh. This is the case in Ps. 19, where the author, in connexion with an ancient hymn to the sun, celebrates the law of Yahweh as the most pro-

[31] Munch (ZATW 55, 1937, pp. 44f.) is not justified in deleting these particular verses (see below, n. 34). Volz (ZATW 55, 1937, pp. 235ff.) is right in saying that the deleting of v. 16 (Staerk, Munch and others) is to delete the whole point of the psalm.

[32] There is nothing to indicate that in these psalms we have simple social antagonisms and 'class strife' between rich and poor, as Munch thinks, in agreement with Lurje (see Additional Note XXIX).

[33] See the personal hymnic introduction in Ps. 34, typical of the thanksgiving psalms, and particularly vv. 5 and 7; cf. also vv. 16–21 and 49.4f. The marks of a thanksgiving psalm are less prevalent in Ps. 37, but see vv. 39f.

[34] It is found neither in Ps. 49—as has been once more maintained by Volz (ZATW 55, 1937)—nor in 16.10f., nor 73.24, 26; see above, pp. 239ff. Lindblom (Horae Soederblomianae I, pp. 21ff.) has tried to prove the meaning of Ps. 49 to be that the rich shall be carried away in the 'final eschatological catastrophe', whereas the pious shall escape; but this seems to me incompatible with the very personal wording of v. 16; the psalm does not speak of an eschatological catastrophe, but of God's judgment on every single man through the end which he suffers, good or evil.

minent work of his creation, the outcome of his 'righteousness' and the truly enlightening and life-giving sun of men, and ends with a prayer that this poem of his may be acceptable to God and secure to himself protection against the designs and temptations of demons.[35] The same love for the law is seen in a great many hymnal motivations of the prayer in Ps. 119. The value of the law, because it enlightens the ignorant and admonishes the faltering, is particularly emphasized. In psalms of prayer and in laments in acute or permanent distress, the author will plead his zeal for the law as a motivation of his prayer, and ask for more enlightenment in order to keep the commandments; this is very conspicuous in Ps. 119.[35a] But otherwise the influence of law religion on psalmography is not very discernible; see below, Chap. XVIII.6.

One may ask what explanation can be given of how such private poetry came to be included in the present collection of cult psalms, and was even used in the official worship of the Temple.

We have already seen how closely the 'scribes' and the 'learned' originally were connected with the temple personnel, especially with the singers and the temple prophets, and how the learned gradually became the guardians of the spiritual and literary traditions of the Temple. In a later chapter (XXII.3) we shall see that they also became the final collectors of the transmitted psalms and the redactors of the canonical Psalter. So at least there remains the possibility that some poems of their own have been included in the collection but were never ritually used, such as Ps. 1 or 127.

As for the thanksgiving psalms, it is easy to show how this may have happened with them. There is evidence for the custom of writing a thanksgiving psalm on a votive stela or on leather and placing it or laying it down 'before Yahweh' in the Temple (see above, II.41). So that personal thanksgiving psalms like Pss. 73 and 49, or 34 and 37, and perhaps also a mixed supplicatory and laudatory psalm like 119, may have been deposited as a votive and memorial gift to Yahweh and a testimony to future generations, and on a later occasion have been included in the treasury of psalms, the transmission of which was the duty of the temple singers and the temple poets. In this way, we can imagine, some of them may have come to be used ritually in the cult.

6

It is this learned, non-cultic psalmography which is continued in the post-canonical, late Jewish psalmography. We meet with two main types: poetry put into the mouths of characters in legendary stories, and free, unattached poetry.

[35] *Zēdhîm*, see *Ps.St.* I, pp. 67ff. (where, however, the interpretation on demons is exaggerated); cf. above. pp. 211ff., 216f.
[35a] See above, n. 9 to Chap. XIII.

The former group, to be found in the additions to Daniel, in Judith and in Tobit,[36] has affinities with the poetry of biblical authors: Hannah's hymn of thanksgiving, the prayer of Jonah, the thanksgiving psalm of king Hezekiah, etc. (pp. 109f.). Even if they are sometimes said to be prayers in danger or distress, they are in fact anthems of praise to the power of God and to his protection of his pious ones, and eulogies of the God of the fathers, who shall one day restore his people. Even in the fiery furnace the three friends of Daniel are said to have recited a hymn of praise.[37] In the main, the old hymnal style has been retained, partly, as we have seen, with inclusion of an eschatological element.

If we ask why the saga-writers put these psalms into the mouths of their heroes, the answer is, because they wanted to enliven their stories with edifying tracts. These are not, of course, free figments of the imagination, they are based on reality—but of course an idealized reality. The biblical authors were no doubt thinking of the normal cultic occasions in the lives of their heroes; so, for example Hannah's psalm in 1 Sam. 2 would obviously be recited at the thank-offering she would bring in connexion with the birth of her son.

When telling us about Tobit, Daniel, etc., among the Diaspora, it is likewise clear that the authors are thinking of the regular prayer hours. In pious circles it was more and more considered a duty, or at least an ideal, to keep these prayer hours. The oldest form of these prayers seems to have consisted of set benediction formulas.[38] But the parable of the Pharisee and the publican shows that the pious used to take the opportunity to bring their personal questions before God in free prayer; the same was done in older times, as we can see from the example of Samuel's mother. Such free prayers might be both supplications and prayers of thanksgiving.

It is this custom which, in more or less idealized form, is reflected in the legendary stories about Daniel, Tobit and others.

That the authors in these cases gave the prayers of their heroes a more or less pure psalm form is of course due to the force of the traditional and conventional literary style. And we all know how strong the influence of the form of the prescribed service prayers is on so-called 'free' prayer. The authors still knew that the psalm was the appropriate form of prayer, and they also knew how a psalm ought to be framed.

As mentioned, almost all these prayers are hymns of praise and thanksgiving. In the triumphs and victories of faith and justice, won in their legends, the Jews saw edifying testimonies to God's action in history for the salvation of his people. Both to the authors and their readers the pious legends were real history.

And so we see that real history might call forth poetry inspired by the traditional psalm literature. That is the case, for example, when the

---

[36] Dan. 2.20–23; Dan. (G) 3.26–45; 3.52–90; Judith 16.2–18; Tob. 13.
[37] Cf. Kuhl, *Die drei Männer im Feuer*, [BZAW 55].
[38] See Schürer, op. cit., II, pp. 539f. [E.T. II, ii §27, pp. 85f.]

author of 1 Maccabees describes the distress of the people under the Syrian oppression in poetical form in the style of the national psalm of lamentation (1 Mac. 2.7ff.). Having told about Simon's victories over the enemies of the people and about the liberation, he ends by describing Simon's just and happy rule (1 Mac. 14.4ff.). Here the historian becomes a poet, his picture becomes a hymn of praise on Simon, in rhythmic form and with consistent use of the thought-rhyme (parallelism), in phrases and metaphors mostly taken from the oracles and blessings on the king in the psalms and from the messianic pictures in the prophets. The author is saying: all this has now been fulfilled in the victories and rule of Simon. His hero becomes the object of a hymn of praise—in the style of the old 'royal psalms'. In this connexion we may also compare Sirach's *Laus Patrum*: 'I will hymn the praises of men of piety, of our fathers in their generations' (Sir. 44.1).

7

Another group of poems, formed of unattached psalms, is found in Sirach and in the so-called Psalms of Solomon.

In addition to the actual 'words of wisdom', and exhortative and didactic poems on the pattern of 'wisdom', Sirach also composed psalms in the traditional psalm style, but with recognizable elements taken from the ideas and forms of 'wisdom'.[39] A great deal of space is taken up by reflections. We find hymns in the I-form, having the greatness of Yahweh in nature for their subject, or speaking of Yahweh's wise and just rule of the world. At other times, to this didactic poem are added hymnal motifs, which in a more or less pure hymnal style speak of God's judgment of the proud-minded, or of his glorious revelation in nature, his wise ordering of the universe and his loving-kindness and mercy in forgiving sins.[40] Sirach avails himself of the hymnal style in a new way when he uses it for a poem of homage to the pious patriarchs and kings and prophets of old. Elements from wisdom poetry sometimes make themselves felt in the style and in the didactic tone. The object is twofold: to give personal expression to the piety of the author and make himself acceptable to God, and to teach the young people the proper fear of God and give them the correct knowledge of the character and the words of God.

The thanksgiving psalm of Sirach, evidently intended for a particular occasion, has a more personal note: that of rendering thanks for the help of God in the dangers to which the calumny of mighty enemies had exposed him. The style is the traditional one, in general terms. The 'promise' of praise with which it ends according to traditional custom has

[39] See Baumgartner in *ZATW* 34, 1914, pp. 161ff.
[40] Hymns and hymnic motives: 42.15–43.23; 39.12–35; 10.14–18; 16.18f.; 16.26–17.24; 17.29f.; 18.1–7; 23.19ff. Laus patrum: 44.1–50.20. Thanksgiving psalm: 51.1–12. Personal prayer: 25.21; 38.9, 14 (Baumgartner, op. cit., p. 181); 22.27–23.6. Restoration of Israel: Sir. (Hebr.) 36.1–17 = Sir. 33.1–13a + 36.16b–22.

evidently been fulfilled by his composing this psalm and reciting it before his colleagues and disciples in the school of wisdom.

It is noteworthy that Sirach shows himself well acquainted with the metrical and strophical rules of classical Hebrew poetry,[41] in striking contrast to the late Jewish Essenian Hodayoth in the Dead Sea Scrolls, or to the Psalms of Solomon.[42]

Sirach also often speaks of prayer; prayer was no doubt part of the daily religious exercise of the 'wise'. He especially mentions prayer for help in illness, for forgiveness of sins, and for healing (25.21; 38.9). It is not quite clear whether he is here thinking of private prayers or of the prescribed liturgical recitation of a psalm of lamentation; the latter is more probable. But sometimes we do meet with personal prayers from him. The prayer aims at securing the power of an appropriate and seemly mode of expression (22.27–23.6), uprightness, humility and purity in thought and wishes, that is to say such virtues as were particularly important in the profession of a teacher of wisdom (34, 1–26 (H)). That he also had the welfare of the people sincerely at heart will be seen from the prayer for the re-establishment of Israel, on the pattern of the national psalm of lamentation and the communal supplications (see Chap. VI). His 'prayer' (těphillâ) for the re-establishment of Israel[43] is written in the correct traditional style of the national psalm of lamentation, with regular strophes, each consisting of two stichs (bicola) and with regular thought rhyme between the two hemistichs (cola).[44] As in the biblical psalms, laments, supplications and motivations of the prayer interchange without any strict order. Even in the circle of the teachers of wisdom the hope for the future was vivid. When Sirach approaches this subject we also become aware of influences from the prophetic style and from the promises of the cultic oracles; here these expressions are used to preach the faith by which the Jewish congregation was living.

That Sirach is not the only 'wise man' of late Judaism occupied with psalm poetry and influenced by the psalm style is seen from the Wisdom of Solomon.[45] Again and again we meet reminiscences of the motifs and forms of psalm poetry. As in the biblical wisdom book of Proverbs also, the late Jewish sage sings the praise of the divine wisdom in hymnic style (6.12ff.; cf. 7.8ff.). Of course the moods and motifs of the hymn of praise appear when the author is speaking about God's grace and charity, his justice and his might (15.1-3; 6.13, 15; 17.1). The hymnic elements become so prevailing in his description of the wonder at the Reed Lake

[41] See Mowinckel, 'Die Metrik bei Jesus Sirach', StTh IX, 1956, pp. 137ff.

[42] Frankenberg's Hebrew retranslation (Die Datierung der Psalmen Salomos, pp. 66ff.) gives at least an approximate impression of the original text. There is no regular balance between the two cola (hemistichs) of the thought-rhyme units.

[43] Sir. (Hebr.) 36.1–17 = Sir. 33.1–13a, 36.16b–22.

[44] See Mowinckel in StTh IX, 1956, pp. 153f.

[45] Translation in Charles, APOT I, pp. 535ff.

(19.6–11) that we get a 'hymnic legend' of the same kind as in Pss. 78 and 105. In Solomon's prayer for wisdom in Wisdom 9 the forms and motifs of the individual (personal) prayer-psalm are imitated.

8

In the Psalms of Solomon[46] we find elements from practically all the old psalm types. These eighteen psalms were composed between the years 63 and 40 B.C. They have an actual historical background in a definite historical situation; it was the fall of the Maccabeans and the conquest of Palestine by Pompey which occasioned most of these prayers and lamentations and confessions of sins and reflections, and evoked the expressions of confident hope which they also contain—in spite of the hard chastening of the Lord, which has fallen even upon the pious, who are co-responsible and have to suffer for the joint sins of leaders and people.

The species of composition are here in the main the old classical ones—no new types have developed—but characteristic of them all is that the elements of reflection and 'wisdom' are much stronger. Another characteristic is that the species of composition are much more intermixed than in the biblical psalms and do not keep to the rules. It is very difficult to classify this late Jewish psalmography according to 'species' ('Gattungen'), and such attempts are apt to become mechanical. But we constantly come across the old primary forms.

As to the form, the two groups, 'I-psalms' and 'We-psalms', are both represented. But as to the content, there is no sharp limit between them. The poets identify themselves with their people, or more correctly with the strict adherents of the law, with the ideal congregation, and speak as its exponents, since they played a leading part within the pious congregation. But often they show their own personal relation to the problems, and speak in their own name, 'I'. They feel the concern of the true congregation as their own concern, and know that all true Israelites agree with them, both in their feeling of being 'just' and in their confession of sins. They feel and express what every true Jew ought to feel and express.

Not all of these eighteen psalms show the same clear connexion with the historical background; some of them may be older than 63 B.C., for example Ps. Sal. 5, a hymn of praise with motifs from the thanksgiving psalm.

The typical mixture of hymn of praise and wisdom poetry is found in Ps. Sal. 10, the benediction of the man 'whom the Lord remembers with reproving, and whom He restrains from the way of evil with strokes'. Cf. Ps. Sal. 6, the benediction on 'the man whose heart is fixed to call upon the name of the Lord', and who experiences the blessings of the

---

[46] The text in Swete's *Old Test. in Greek* III, pp. 765ff. Translation, with introduction and notes by Kittel, in Kautzsch, *APAT* II, pp. 127ff.; Buchanan Gray in Charles, *APOT* II, pp. 625ff.; Norwegian translation by Messel in *NTT*, 1907, pp. 297ff. See Mowinckel, 'Den senjødiske salmediktning', *NTT*, 1950, p. 21.

prayer—possibly meant as a thanksgiving psalm. The well known *māšāl* pattern: the ways of the just and of the ungodly, is the theme of Ps. Sal. 3, cf. Pss. 1 and 112. It begins as a hymn of praise, 'for good is a psalm to God from a glad heart'. But the praise is less direct and soon takes the form of a didactic admonition. When the righteous stumbles, he acknowledges God's righteousness and 'searches His house to remove all iniquity (done) by him in error', and he can do so because he knows that 'they that fear the Lord shall rise to life eternal'. The ungodly 'curses the day of his birth', and 'adds sins to sins'. Of the same type is Ps. Sal. 14.

Pss. Sal. 15 and 16 are private thanksgiving psalms, the latter obviously inspired by the biblical Ps. 32. In the thanksgiving psalm, 13, political events are re-echoed; the poet thanks God because he has been saved from the catastrophe that has befallen the sinners. Contrary to the classical psalms, the poet speaks more of the fall of his antagonists, the 'sinners', than of his own salvation; cf. however, Ps. 73. Here the didactic style is obvious.

Some of the poems, for example, Pss. Sal. 4 and 12, take us into the thick of the strife between the 'ungodly' rulers and the pious circles. Here as a rule the form and style of the psalm of lamentation are used. The 'lament' has the form of a description of the evil deeds and words of the 'sinners', the 'enemies' of the poet and his fellow-believers; thought and expression are influenced both by the rebukes of the prophets and by the description of the wicked in the wisdom literature. The prayer is to the effect that God may remove and destroy the sinners; as in the biblical psalms, this prayer often takes the form of a curse. As in the classical style, the prayer ends by expressing 'the confidence of being heard', for 'the Lord's (word) is salvation for his servant Israel for ever'. For the apostrophe of the wicked man as 'introit' in Ps. Sal. 4.1, we may compare Ps. 52.

In other poems the catastrophe of 63 B.C. is the historical background. Ps. Sal. 1 is a penitential psalm of lamentation. Jerusalem confesses her sins, the sins of the dynasty and the ruling classes, and describes the catastrophe ('the lament'). In Ps. Sal. 7 the poet himself utters the confession on behalf of himself and his people. The description of calamities is mingled with religious reflections. The poem is a mixture of congregational psalm of lamentation in I-form and reflections; the disaster raises the problem of the common responsibility and of God's justice. 'I thought upon the judgments of God since the creation', and have now seen that God is just; the pious have no other escape than God's own mercy, upon which they set their hope.

The poet in Ps. Sal. 2 has already seen the calamitous end of Pompey in 48 B.C., and takes this as the beginning of God's hearing Israel's prayers. This inspires him to a thanksgiving psalm. But still God's hand is heavy upon the people; what has happened is not only a just punishment, but also a profanation of God's own city and Temple. And so he has to utter his lament and pray for salvation. From the point of view of 'Gattung' and style, the poem is a mixture of lament and thanksgiving psalm, with reflections upon the religious problem.

An important element in the ideas of these poets was the eschatological hope, still in the old nationalistic-political, this-worldly form. Ps. Sal. 17 is built up after the pattern of the psalm of lamentation and supplication. It starts with the confession of faith in 'the Lord, our king for ever and ever', 'our hope'. How long shall we still wait upon him and the ful-filling of his promises? 'But for our sins, sinners rose up against us'. Then follows the lament, a description of all the disasters that have befallen the people from the time before the rule of the Maccabees up to the present day, with a confession of their sins. Then the prayer: 'Behold, O Lord, and raise up unto them their king, the son of David, at the time which Thou seest that he may reign over Israel Thy servant'! The prayer includes a long description of the blessings that the Messiah will bring to his people, and ends with the confidence of being heard. Here the influence from prophetic style and ideas is very prominent, and the ex-pression of confidence becomes a confession of the Messianic faith of the poet and his circles.

Ps. Sal. 11 is very interesting. It is composed after the pattern of Pss. 82 and 85: first a description of the expected deliverance in prophetic style, and then the prayer that the deliverance may (soon) come. The original connexion of this pattern with the promises and prayers at the great annual festival is quite clear.[47] The poet is obviously conscious of this liturgical model. But his definite ideas of the deliverance are taken from Deutero-Isaiah. The point of the poem is the prayer for the coming deliverance. The poet has resolved to begin with the description of the deliverance just because these learned and 'wise' poets felt themselves the heirs of the prophets. He wishes to inform the faithful that the deliverance will come. But he also wishes to remind God of his promises; the first part of the poem is also a 'motivation of confidence': may God hear those who trust in him and his promises!

9

Our knowledge of late Jewish psalmography has been immensely extended by the finding of the *Dead Sea Scrolls*, the *Qumran Manuscripts*.[48] As the writer

---

[47] See above, Chap. V, pp. 162ff., cf. *Ps.St.* II, pp. 67ff., 77, 160f.

[48] The standard text editions: *The Dead Sea Scrolls of St. Mark's Monastery*, Vol. I. The Isaiah Manuscript and the Habakkuk Commentary; Vol. I, Fasc. 2, Plates and Transcription of the Manual of Discipline. Edited by Millar Burrows with the Assistance of John C. Trever and William H. Brownlee, New Haven, 1950–51; *The Dead Sea Scrolls of the Hebrew University*, edited by E. L. Sukenik, Jerusalem, 1955. Of the voluminous literature I only mention the excellent book by Millar Burrows, *The Dead Sea Scrolls*, New York, 1955, with bibliography. Especially on the Hodayoth see J. Licht, *megillat hattodayot*, 1957; S. Holm-Nielsen, *Hodayot, Psalms from Qumran*, 1960; and the series of papers (translation and philological notes) published in *JBL* 74, 1955, and 75, 1956, by Joseph Baumgarten and Menahem Mansoor: 'Studies in the New Hodayoth (thanksgiving hymns)' I–III. Cf. the present author's paper in *JBL* 75, 1956, pp. 265ff.

has had no opportunity of studying the matter in detail, he must confine himself to some short, personal reflections.

The manuscripts originate from the library of an Essenian community that lived in the Judaean desert on the north-western shore of the Dead Sea, where the ruins of their community house at Chirbet Qumran have been excavated. The community existed at least in the first, probably in the second century B.C., and the first century A.D.; the building was destroyed by the Roman soldiers in the Jewish War of A.D. 68. Before this catastrophe the members had hidden their literary treasures in different rock caves in the vicinity.

Among the manuscripts is a scroll containing at least fourteen or fifteen, probably more psalms, the *Qumran Hodayoth*, evidently poems originating from this community and, as far as we can see, all beginning with the phrase 'I thank thee, O Lord', '*ôdhěkhā 'ǎdhōnay*. Many of them are very fragmentary.

Apart from these special peculiarities of the songs, they present all the characteristic features of late Jewish psalmody; above all there is a mixture of learned acquaintance with the biblical psalms and other scriptures and the traditional psalm style on one hand, and the disintegration of the style on the other. In contrast to Jesus Sirach there is no regular metre; the hemistichs are often of an unequal length and there are no regular strophes. The thought rhyme (the parallelism) between the two hemistichs is generally, but not always, maintained. All the traditional stylistic elements of the biblical thanksgiving psalm—the introduction, the narrative with its three points, the confession and the witness before the congregation—are as a rule found, but with many repetitions and often without due logical sequence. We also meet the reflections on religious problems, which is so characteristic of the Psalms of Solomon and late Jewish psalmography as a whole.

The 'learned' character of the songs is in accordance with the whole character of the community. They are not just 'popular songs'. The language is Hebrew, and the existence of a big library, the content of the many manuscripts found, and the excavation of the scribe's room of the community prove that it laid weight upon theological scholarship and literary work. A phrase often met with in the songs is, 'Then I understood'. Among the blessings which the poet has won through his experiences is also a better understanding of God's plans, his justice, his 'secrets'. He has eagerly studied the sacred books, God 'has hidden His Law in his heart', he knows it by heart and is in possession of the right understanding and interpretation of the law and the other scriptures.

The background of the songs is always the personal experiences of the poet. He has been in great danger and distress as a result of the aggression of his enemies; he seems to have suffered both false accusations from 'the men of the lie', and imprisonment and torture. His enemies, 'the sons of the darkness' are also the enemies of his community, 'the poor ones', 'the righteous ones', 'the sons of the light'. But God has saved him from his distress, delivered him from the intrigues and the aggressions of his enemies, and therefore he has now to thank and praise him for his wonderful deeds and to bear witness about him before his brethren.

As in the biblical psalms, the descriptions are in very general terms and conventional pictures; very many of the poet's sentences are mere quotations or reminiscences from the biblical texts. It is therefore difficult to say anything definite of his experiences and sufferings.

One has the impression that all these songs are made by one and the same author. And many allusions show that he must have been an important person in the community, one of its leaders. And the songs suggest that the author is the 'Teacher of Righteousness' himself, the man who, according to other texts, has played an important role in the history of the community, whether at its founding or at some later reconstruction.

If this be so, we can the more easily understand why his psalms were copied and handed down within the community. We may go further and conclude that they have been recited or sung at sacral assemblies. That should fit in very well with what Philo tells us about the assemblies of the *Therapeutae*, obviously an Essenian community; 'When the president thinks he has discoursed (some scripture passage) enough ... applause arises showing a general pleasure in the prospect of what is still to follow. Then the president rises and sings a hymn composed as an address to God, either a new one of his own composition, or an old one by poets of an earlier day who have left behind them hymns in many measures and melodies .... After him all the others take their turn ... in proper order while all the rest listen in complete silence except when they have to chant the closing lines or refrains, for then they all lift up their voices, men and women alike'.[49]

I think this picture, at least to some degree, also fits in with the practice of the wisdom schools. In this way Sirach may have ended the discourse of the day with his pupils. And there may be reason to believe that the Psalms of Solomon too were 'published' in this way in some more or less organized 'assembly of the pious'.

10

Finally we must refer to the lingerings of psalmography to be found among the first community of Jewish Christians and mentioned above: the hymns of praise by Zacharias and Mary in the gospel of Luke.[50] Here the rejoicings over the deliverance already experienced through the actual

---

[49] *De Vita Contemplativa X.* I quote the passage from P. Winter (*BJRL* 37, 1954–55, p. 331) who has drawn attention to it in another context.

[50] See Gunkel, *Die Lieder in der Kindheitsgeschichte Jesu*; Sahlin, *Messias und Gottesvolk*, pp. 159ff., 286ff. Further references in Winter, op. cit., pp. 335f., n. 1.

coming of Jesus-Messiah find expression in the ancient epiphany psalm style; the hope for the future is actualized through the new experience that, in Christ, God has again come to his people and has created salvation and established his kingdom for all time. That these two psalms were originally composed in Hebrew (or Aramaic?) and taken over from the tradition by Luke seems quite evident. But they were not made for the context in which they are now embedded. They had originally nothing whatsoever to do with the situation of Mary[51] or Zacharias[52]; they were originally independent psalms.

Nor were these two psalms composed out of the experiences of the individual poets only. The poet is speaking in the name of a congregation— 'we'; what he has experienced is typical for them all.

The 'I' of the poet is here expressing what he and all the others had experienced when accepting and believing the message that the Messiah has come in the person of Jesus; and this salvation is re-experienced whenever the congregation is assembled to pay homage to the Lord in their midst, and it is this experience that breaks out into hymns of thanksgiving. So here again the thoughts and conceptions of the epiphany feast break forth: the Lord has 'hallowed his name', 'done a deed of might' and 'succoured his people Israel'; he has been 'mindful of his mercy— the faithfulness of his covenant (hesedh)'. The promises given to David have become a reality, for the Lord has again established for David a 'horn of salvation'—as in the festal liturgy of Ps. 132. Through the promise of a new Davidic scion the Lord has 'delivered us from the hands of our enemies', and, just as on the day of festival, the people may be 'freed from fear', renewed 'in holiness and uprightness' 'before the Lord' for all time.

In this early Christian psalmography the expectations of the epiphany feast have been fulfilled as an experience in the present; the past marks the realization of that hope for the future which in its turn had grown out of the experiences of the festival.

That the early Christian community saw the new salvation in the form of the eschatologically interpreted psalms of enthronement and their ideology is also corroborated by the hymns of praise to the Lord (and the Lamb) in the Revelation of St John.[53] The heavenly beings 'sing a new song' before the throne of 'the king of the nations', glorifying his 'judgements' and 'salvation':

---

[51] The metrical pattern (see below, n. 54) seems to demonstrate that v. 48a 'for he hath regarded the low estate of his handmaiden' is a later addition, aiming at connecting the psalm with its present context—a connexion, however, that probably had been made already in the oral tradition behind the record of St. Luke. Sahlin, *Messias und Gottesvolk*, pp. 161ff., interprets the line of the abased Zion, which is not very probable. The traditio-historical independence of the Magnificat has been maintained, e.g. by L. Brun, *Lukas evangeliet*, p. 61.

[52] Cf. Gunkel, op. cit.; Klostermann, *Das Lukas-evangelium*, pp. 382f. Winter's attempt (*BJRL* 37, 1954; *JQR* 45, 1954–55) to demonstrate that the Magnificat and the Benedictus are Maccabean psalms is not convincing.

[53] Rev. 5.9; 11.15, 17; 12.10; 14.3; 15.3f.; 19.6.

The kingdom of the world has passed over to our Lord
and his Christ,
and he has become king for ever and ever. . . .
We thank thee, Lord God almighty, who art and wast,
that thou hast taken over by great power and become king . . .
Hallelujah! Now the Lord our God almighty hath become king,
let us rejoice and triumph and give him glory! . . .
Now it has come, the salvation and power,
the kingdom of our God and the power of his Christ.

Here, however, we have no longer the poetry of a learned school, as in Sirach or the Psalms of Solomon. As contrasted with the psalms of Sirach, there does not here seem to be any strict metre;[54] verses and hemistichs are of unequal length; the constituting element of the metrical structure is here in fact the 'thought rhythm', the 'parallelism' between the two hemistichs and the grouping of two by two 'distichs' ('bicola') into short stanzas. What has been preserved of the traditional composition of the psalms is the hymnal style and note and the eschatological content,[55] which are finally grounded in the complex of ideas of the epiphany. That is what has now become new, personally experienced reality to these authors. Therefore these psalms, in a way different from that of the poetry of the Psalms of Solomon as well as of Sirach, practically consist of hymno-eschatological terms from the Old Testament:[56] now the old promises given to the fathers in the Scriptures have turned into reality, and the authors are praising God for it.

The psalm tradition, kept alive by the learned psalmography in certain learned circles, is here reborn—in spite of all dependence on old patterns— in the Christian community, as an expression of something simultaneously experienced in the present, and at the same time an object of faith and hope for the future. In the assembly of the congregation, where anybody who 'hath a psalm' (1 Cor. 14.26; cf. vv. 15–17) recites it to the edification of all, these psalms come to life again. There are good reasons for believing that the spontaneously inspired recitation of hymns, presupposed by St Paul as a normal trait in the life of the Corinthian community, included

[54] Apart from v. 48a, the Magnificat (Luke 1.46–53) consists of 8 stichs (bicola), the two hemistichs (cola) of the stich making a thought rhyme (parallelism); according to form and content each two pairs of stichs makes a small unit or stanza (strophe). These are: I. vv. 46 + 47, 48b + 49; II. vv. 50a + 50b, 51a + 51b; III. vv. 52a + 52b, 53a + 53b; IV. vv. 54a + 54b, 55a + 55b. V. 48a has no parallel and falls outside the scheme. Sahlin's reconstruction of the supposed original Hebrew text as 10 qinah verses often runs contrary to the rule of the thought rhyme and gives unnatural subdivisions. The 'Benedictus' (Luke 1.68–75) is built up of strophes of the same sort: I. vv. 68a + 68b, 69a + 69b; II. vv. 70a + 70b, 71a + 71b; III. vv. 72a + 72b, 73 + 74a; IV. vv. 74ba + bβ, 75a + 75b. The text emendations suggested by Sahlin (op. cit.) are groundless, and the result is not convincing.

[55] That at least is demonstrated by the attempts to retranslate into Hebrew, by Torrey, 'The Translations made from the Original Aramaic Gospels' in Studies in the Hist. of Religion presented to C. H. Toy, pp. 269ff., and 'Outcroppings of Jewish Messianic Hope' in Case, Studies in Early Christianity, pp. 285ff., and by Sahlin, op. cit.

[56] See the synoptic lists in Klostermann, op. cit., pp. 378f., 385f.

such psalms as these, and that this was nothing new in Corinth, but a transplantation of something that had come into existence already in the first congregation in Jerusalem.[57] Psalmography has returned to its original home: in the cultic assembly of the community itself, in the divine service.

[57] Cf. Acts 1.11b; 2.46b; 16.25. See Weizsäcker, *Das apostolische Zeitalter der christlichen Kirche*,³ pp. 557ff. [E.T., *The Apostolic Age* II, 259ff.].

CHAPTER XVII

Traditionalism and Personality in the Psalms

The description of the different types of psalms given in the preceding chapters, has demonstrated to how great an extent the whole of this poetry is bound by tradition. The content, the formal language and the thoughts are determined by purpose and custom. To write poetry was, one may say, to put together the details, thoughts and phrases which were presented by tradition, in the form which, according to custom and tradition, corresponded to the purpose. The personal contribution by the poet consisted in finding new variations of the fixed forms, a new turn in the call to praise, another expression for confidence, a new picture of the fury of the enemy and the hardship of suffering. In this way the poets created many original individual pictures of the noblest kind which later became classical.

The creating of the psalms differs also in another way from what we moderns instinctively expect from poetry. The experiences and emotions to which the psalms give expression were not only those of an individual, but such common events, general experiences and feelings as custom demanded in the particular situation. The poet who wrote a psalm for use, for instance at the purification rites, placed himself in a common situation and expressed what all were expected to feel and accordingly say.

But this does not necessarily imply that the personal element was lacking.[1] In ancient Israel personality with the quality of originality and uniqueness was neither an ideal nor a reality. The personality became conscious of itself through the common experiences and emotions in which the Israelite entirely merged. And the religious experience which lies behind the cult-psalms, behind the enthusiasm and exaltation and adoring surrender, behind the agony of the lamentations and the grateful testimony of the thanksgiving psalms, all this the poets themselves also felt. It is their own, just because it belonged, or ought to belong, to the whole body.[2]

---

[1] Gunkel-Begrich, *Einl.*, pp. 11f.; Oesterley, *A Fresh Approach to the Psalms*, pp. 146ff.; Eissfeldt in *ZATW* 61, 1945–48, pp. 10ff. Here also may be mentioned Gunkel, *Ausgewählte Psalmen*; Leslie, *The Psalms*; James, *Thirty Psalmists*. All these seek to picture the personal religious life of the psalmists on a basis of type-analysis (*Gattungsforschung*).

[2] Oesterley and others are of course wrong in believing that personal piety in a psalm or a prayer proves that these cannot have a cultic or liturgical connexion. Both in books of common prayer and in the hymn books of the various denominations on almost every page we meet with the personal piety and religious experiences of the reformers and of the hymn writers of all ages, although we scarcely ever come across the formal 'I'. That they very often wrote their poems consciously for cultic use, is, however, a matter of plain fact.

For this very reason many of the psalms loudly proclaim what has been personally experienced and accepted, that God had become the poet's own God:

> The Lord is my shepherd, I lack for nothing;
>   he makes me lie in meadows green,
> he leads me to refreshing streams,
>   he revives life in me.
>
> He guides me by true paths,
>   as he himself is true.
> My road may run through a glen of gloom,
>   but I will fear no harm.
>
> For thou art (always) with me, [nay,
>   thou willt protect me, Lord],[3]
> thy shepherd's club, thy (strong) staff—
>   they are my (firm) comfort. (Ps. 23.1-4.)

Here the traditional picture of the shepherd and the sheep is applied to the individual believer, who confidently knows himself to be under the protection of the Lord; and it is completed in realistic detail in a way which is both personally experienced and felt, as well as artistically perfect. The picture of the lamb is not abandoned for a moment, and yet no reader has the slightest doubt that it is the relation between God and the praying poet in his own physical and spiritual everyday existence, which is expressed. The traditional translation 'in the valley of the shadow of death' instead of 'in dark ravines' ('a glen of gloom') is incorrect in so far as it confuses the picture; but behind the picture lies also the thought of God's protection in mortal danger and death agony.

It is a significant fact that this psalm actually breaks all the patterns of 'form history'. Being a pure psalm of confidence, it cannot immediately be classified under any of the 'categories' or 'types' of style history. A real poet using the traditional cultic forms of style has here created a poem which has its own type. It is an expression of the religious traditions of the people of the covenant. It is also an expression of the conception of God with which they were entrusted, and of the personal experiences of God in their own lives and the attitude to life created by these.

When God thus becomes man's safe and only possession and refuge, man may find that everything else disappears and loses its importance. This happened to the writer of the thanksgiving psalm 73, who had gone through hard travail of mind about the apparent arbitrariness and absurdity in the ruling of the world, but who found in the worship in God's sanctuaries that the old faith stood the strain. He now confesses both his sin and the faith he has regained:

---

[3] As the metre (qinah) shows, some words are lacking in v. 4a; rd. *kî 'attâ* [*YHWH*] *'immādhî wĕ 'attâ maḥăsî*, or something similar.

As long as my heart was bitter
    and pain pierced my kidneys
I was a dull, stupid creature,
    no better than a brute before thee.

Yet I am always beside thee,
    thou holdest me by my right hand,
with thy counsel art thou guiding me,
    into glory thou takest me at last.[4]

Whom have I in heaven but thee?
    On earth I care for nothing else.
My body and my soul may fail,
    but God is my portion for evermore. (Ps. 73.21–26.)

The poet has not in mind eternal life beyond death. It is here and now that God is his God, and it is here that he knows it is good to keep near to God (v. 28). For this reason the impression of an unbreakable confidence which can carry one through all life's difficulties becomes still stronger.

These singers have known what it meant to be in the great depths and call on God:

Out of the depths I am crying unto thee,
    O Lord hear my voice!
Let thy ears be listening now
    to the voice of my supplications.

He knows that sin is the cause of unhappiness, and that if God will keep account according to merit no one can stand in his judgment:

If thou shouldest mark iniquities,
    who, Lord, can then stand?

But he knows too that the Lord is a gracious and merciful God, long-suffering and rich in friendliness:

But there is forgiveness with thee,
    that thou mayest be feared.

But it is hard to wait, and many times the question, How long, Lord? has risen to the lips of the god-fearing; with deep longing he is waiting for the Lord and his acquitting and promising word:

I wait for the Lord, my soul doth wait,
    and in his word do I hope,
more than the watchers are waiting for dawn
    my soul is waiting for him.[5]

[4] I.e., thou restorest me to my former glory. 'Glory', 'honour' (*kābhôdh*, pondus) is the normal state of the 'right' man; as struck down by disaster (illness?) the worshipper has been in a state of 'dishonour'. See Additional Note XXX.
[5] V. 5 transp. ante v. 6; del. 6b (dittogr.). Conj. vv. 1c, 2a; del. *'dny* v. 2; transp. *qwth* v. 5 ante v. 6.

But he also knows that he can dare to wait in confidence and assurance for the answer to his prayer:

> For with the Lord there is mercy,
>> and full redemption with him,
> and he will redeem Israel
>> from all their iniquities. (Ps. 130.)

When we know that the worshipper here speaks on behalf of the congregation and about the redemption of Israel, we get a still greater impression of the depth and reality of the poet's strictly personal conviction of sin and of his belief in God, for no-one can speak thus except from personal experience.

These poets also know something about patience, contentment and the self-forgetting sure confidence in God:

> Lord, my heart is not haughty,
>> nor mine eyes lofty,
> I do not undertake matters
>> too wonderful for me.

> Surely I have stilled and silenced my soul
>> like a suckling child with its mother.[6]
> So wait for the Lord, Israel,
>> from henceforth and for ever. (Ps. 131.)

They have perhaps, at least in imagination, tried to lift their eyes to the mountains and the many holy places and powers there, in order to get help:

> I lift mine eyes unto the hills;
>> from whence is help to come?

Such a question might the Jew in the half-pagan environment in which he lived often be tempted to ask. The many sanctuaries 'on the hills' could refer to ancient traditions, and often it might seem as if Yahweh was powerless or would not help, as if Israel's watchman was sleeping. But the poet knows also—and here he builds on the foundation both of what he himself has experienced and the faith of the fathers—that no one can ask these questions in earnest:

> My help comes from the Lord, from him
>> who made both heaven and earth.

And the worshipper gets the answer proclaimed in the very words of the blessings of the cultic liturgy:

[6] V. 2b is an explanatory gloss.

II, 9

> Never will he let thee slip,
>   thy keeper never sleeps.
> Behold the keeper of Israel
>   neither slumbers nor sleeps. . . .
> May the Lord guard thee from all harm,
>   may he preserve thy life.
> May he protect thy going out and coming in
>   from now and for evermore. (Ps. 121.1–2, 4, 7–8.)[6a]

The congregational psalm 137 has a distinctive stamp as compared with the conventional style, and has also sprung out of a genuine poetical ability to identify oneself with the former time of enslavement, with its bitter experiences, burning longings and savage thirst for revenge:

> By the rivers of Babylon yonder
>   we sat down, yea, we wept;
> upon the willows there we left
>   our harps silent hanging.
>
> For there, those who ravaged us required
>   a joyful song from us;
> and those who plundered us asked there:
>   'Sing for us a Zion-song!'[7]

Commentators, more learned than poetical, have asked why they had to sit on the river banks, and why the harps had to hang on the willows: when they did not wish to use them, they might as well have left them hanging on the walls at home. Well, that could indeed be maintained! But just through his conventionalized, not realistic image, the poet has given an incomparably touching expression to the elegiac sentiment which grips him when he pictures to himself the emotions and situation of those who were forcibly evacuated to the land of the enemy. Just so, he himself, the player of harp and composer of psalms in Zion, could imagine that he might have been sitting, if he had been one of them. This is how they must have felt. The poet himself was not among those carried away— the psalm is considerably later than the 'return'—but he identifies himself wholly with his people, both in the past and the present ('we'). For this reason he can also personally re-live the most bitter memories of the people. In his imagination he has been there, and he describes what he then felt, in that fancied situation, just as a man of his occupation would or might have experienced it. He sees himself as a wandering harp-player. In both the ancient and the modern orient it was nothing unusual that both prophets and people connected with the temples should appear as wandering 'men of God', 'on the road'. If the poet had been in Babylon

[6a] On the interpretation of Ps. 121 see *Ps.St.* II, pp. 170f. Similarly Blakeney in *Expos. Times* 59, Jan. 1948, p. 111.

[7] As the metre (qinah) shows, v. 1b is an explanatory gloss, quite unnecessary for the meaning. A new 'colon' begins with *wĕthôlēlēnû* in v. 3; then both metre and parallelism require that *śimḥâ* be placed after *šîr*

he would have been one of the breadless 'Levites' as long as the Temple lay in ruins. And where can wanderers in the orient sit down to rest except by springs and river banks? In arid Palestine one had much to tell about the rivers of Babylon. And one might easily imagine one of the tyrants asking them there to sing to them. But in such a case he knows well what he would have had to rejoin:

> How could we on a strange soil,
>   sing the songs of the Lord!
> If I forget thee, Jerusalem,
>   may my right hand wither!
> May the tongue cleave to the roof of my mouth,
>   if I do not remember thee;
> if Jerusalem be not to me
>   more than my greatest joy. (Ps. 137.1–6.)

Here religion and love of country have melted together into a personal harmony which is unique in ancient oriental poetry. This is also a testimony to the strong historical element in Israelite religion and it carries a note which we now understand particularly well.

If we compare the biblical psalms with the Babylonian, we are struck by the fact that the former are much fresher, more varied and original than the latter, for the monotony of the Babylonian psalms often proves both tedious and dull. And if one has become aware how firm and constant the rules of style are even in the biblical psalm poetry, it comes as a surprise to discover the richness and diversity of the traditional rules. The schematic hymn style which is the rule in the Babylonian psalms is the exception in the Israelite ones. Generally they are fresh, independent poems, like Ps. 8 with the praise of man as God's image; or the mythologically coloured Psalm 19, the 'sun hymn'; or in the living descriptions of Yahweh's coming with victory and salvation in Pss. 46 and 48; or the enthronement hymn with its peculiar character.

The most monotonous impression is produced by the psalms of lamentation, but even here there are many distinctive poems which have made use of the conventional fundamental rules with great personal freedom, for example Ps. 11 with the apostrophizing of the friends as a form of lamentation and expression of confidence; Ps. 36 with all the traditional elements but with a free and rich formulation; Ps. 90, where the 'motif of compassion' (*Mittleidsmotiv*), the shortness of human life, is put in relief against the hymnic contemplation of God's eternity; Ps. 137 where the lamentation which motivates the prayer for revenge is formulated as a historical *peinture de genre*, quivering with love for the homeland; Ps. 139 where the 'motif of innocence', God's knowledge of the worshipper, finds its general background in the contemplation of God's omniscience and omnipresence; or Ps. 62 where the 'motif of confidence' (*Vertrauensmotiv*) is set forth as the exhortation of the worshipper to his own soul about waiting quietly upon God.

The thanksgiving psalms are often richly varied (see below, pp. 143f.). Sometimes it is confession of sin (Ps. 32), at other times the religious problem (Ps. 73), which becomes the main topic, and the fundamental emotion, gratitude, finds many expressions.

The contributions from temple prophecy and the thoughts and forms of the prophetic movement (cf. Chap. XII) also bring a rich variety. In Ps. 2 the oracle of enthronement is attributed to the king himself and connected with the concept of the king's first proclamation to his subjects. In Ps. 110 it has been worked into the pattern of the ritual of anointing.[8] Peculiar is Ps. 82, Yahweh's reproval of the unrighteous rule of the other gods, which is put into the framework of the old oriental cultic conception about an assembly of the gods at new year in order to determine the destiny of the year. In Ps. 50 we see the peculiar prophetic development which the idea of epiphany has had in Israel, namely to become the background for the religio-moral teaching and admonition.

We must admit that many of the psalms can only be characterized as artistic hack-work, or in a few cases perhaps only as hack-work.[9] But the predominant impression is, much more, of a reality which is personally experienced and felt, and which is depicted with genuine poetic inspiration.

For this reason we also see that there have been poets who were on the point of bursting through the old forms, or at least have been able to refashion them in such a way that they really give expression to an individual experience. One has to look very carefully to be able to recognize the conventional stylistic scheme or pattern in the psalm about God's eternity and the brevity of human life (Ps. 90), or in order to perceive that the profound consideration of God's omniscience and omnipresence in Ps. 139 actually is a new form of the motif of innocence: the reference to the fact that the God who knows everything and from whom nobody can flee must also know that the praying worshipper is without guilt in relation to his enemies.[9a]

The psalms of protection and thanksgiving have at times moved so far away from their particular style type that it has been suggested that we ought to separate some of them into a special group of 'psalms of confidence'. To these belong some of the highest ranking ones, regarded from both the religious and the poetic aspect, in the whole collection; for instance Pss. 23; 73; 103.

The exaltation of the hymn writer has sometimes lifted him to heights where the whole universe has revealed its secrets to him, so that he hears the songs of the spheres and the wordless praise of the days:

[8] Widengren, *Psalm 110 och det sakrala kungadömet in Israel*.
[9] Cf. Loehr, *Psalmenstudien*, pp. 3f.
[9a] On Ps. 139 see Chap. III, n. 95.

> The heavens proclaim God's splendour,
>   the firmament speaks of his handiwork.
> Day after day takes up the tale
>   and night after night sheweth (its) knowledge.
>
> Without speech, without words,
>   and yet their voice is (always) heard,[10]
> their order[10a] goeth out through all the world,
>   their words unto the ends of the earth.   (Ps. 19.2–5.)

Or the eye of the poet may be opened to the glory of all that is created, but especially the nobility of man as the lord of creation. But all this serves still more to provide testimony to the majesty of God; and in relation to him man himself, this god on earth, is only dust and ashes. In spite of the fact that the most wonderful song of praise is as little children's babble in relation to the God to whom man lifts his heart, still he must sing about the work of creation, about the stronghold of Heaven which Yahweh raised as an unconquerable protection against his enemies after having overcome them in the struggles of chaos; and also render a grateful song of exaltation about man who, in his wonderful combination of greatness— 'almost a god'—and unworthiness, more than any other created being gives witness to the glory, power and goodness of his creator (Ps. 8).[10b]

2

If, therefore, the psalms have in the main originated among the temple singers and are intended for use by a king, a national leader or a private person, who in connexion with public worship should present a psalm of prayer or praise, it is also evident that we have to distinguish between the poet and the 'I' who prays in the psalm. The psalm has been composed and put into the mouth of the one who has to use it. 'I' is in this respect not the composer himself, but the person for whose use he has made the psalm, and who was to present it in the Temple. We shall probably think that most often, if not always, the individual concerned, for instance the sick person, let the acting temple functionary (the priest, the singer) present the psalm on his behalf.

That a psalm has been used by and for David or another king of course does not mean that it was actually composed by the king concerned. It was not for everybody to be so familiar with the old psalm-style that he could compose the proper cult psalm in the right way. We possess from Babylonia-Assyria copies of one and the same psalm, which has been

---

[10] For this interpretation see Eerdmans, *Heb. Bk. of Pss.*, ad. loc.
[10a] For this interpretation see de Boer in *OTS* X, p. 245.
[10b] On text and interpretation of Ps. 8.2 see Mowinckel in Johs. Pedersen *Festschrift*, pp. 250ff. Stamm's treatment in *ThZ* 13, pp. 470ff., is as unsatisfactory as other attempts to obtain a meaning from the MT.

supplied with different royal names: 'I, Nebukadreṣṣar, pray to thee', or 'I, Ashburbânaplu', etc., according to the king who had made use of the psalm on that specific cultic occasion. The original may perhaps have been composed for use by yet another king, whose name accidentally has not been found on any of the copies that have been thus far discovered, or it may have been made with a blank space for the king's name: 'I, N.N., the son of N.N.', as we sometimes actually find.

In other words the poet has entered into the situation, feelings and needs of the man for whom he composed the psalm. This 'cult-seeking man', in certain cases has been a definite individual, for example that king who on *this* occasion was presenting the psalm of lamentation, as the representative of the congregation (the people). On other occasions the psalm has been composed for use by 'Everyman', one who for instance had to submit to the purification ritual after a sickness. It ought to be self-evident, when we realize that in the Psalter we have royal psalms from very different times, early and late, that not all these kings could have been poets, able to compose the ritual psalms which were to be recited, any more than that it was the oriental kings themselves who 'penned' their inscriptions, even though they appear and speak in the first person.

But this in no wise excludes the really personal element from a palm. A real poet is always personally involved in that which he writes. Even if it was the task of the psalm composer to enter into the situation for which the psalm was composed, in such a way that he could give expression to that which the ill-fated king then felt and ought to feel and say, still the poet was in fact a part of it. The king represented his people, the disaster was also his disaster; and the faith in Yahweh, the god of the covenant, and the relationship to him was also the faith and religious condition of the poet. Here again we must have in mind the ancient Israelite's view of society and of himself. He was a part—in certain cases the fully representative part—of a 'corporate personality'. He is himself only when he is one with his family, his tribe, his people. He has no wish to be 'original'; he wishes to realize Israel's ideal, Israel's human type. It is 'good and pleasant' not only that 'brethren dwell together', but also that they have 'one heart' with each other and feel, think and will the same thing. When the hearts beat in unison then the Israelites are themselves. When he speaks for himself, 'the fact that he is an Israelite, that he is a member of the fellowship, of God's people, that his God is Israel's God is never far below the horizon of the poet's consciousness', to quote one of his modern compatriots.[11] When the Israelite psalm composer speaks in the name of the people or its leader there is room for his own individuality, for his own piety, his own faith, his own conviction of sin, his own gratitude, his own confidence in the God of the fathers, his own thanks for the blessings of

[11] Montefiore, *The Old Testament and After*, pp. 282f. (here cited from H. W. Robinson in *The Psalmists*, p. 83f.).

the past and God's great miracle.[12] The Israelite poet holds exactly the same relationship to his subject as for example the poet who wrote: 'God bless our precious fatherland' or 'God bless the land of Norway'.[13] That the psalms have been written by professional temple-singers, for use in cult activities, in no way implies that they are 'degraded' to 'formulas' as some people have maintained.

But the personal element also appears in another way. Many of the psalms have been composed for use in situations which are so humanly common and familiar—for example, disease—that we can take for granted that many of the professional temple-singers had also had similar experiences. We can safely assume that many of these poets had themselves passed through so much, that they knew what they were talking about. They could of course compose on the basis of a personal experience even if they wrote in the name of someone else. They personally knew both the 'agony of death' and the joy of deliverance. And there is nothing to prevent us from thinking that on such occasions they composed for their own use. That applies perhaps not so much to the psalms of sickness and those in mortal danger; on such occasions the Israelite felt so 'dead', his 'soul' was to such a degree 'emptied', 'poured out on the ground', he was so pressed into the dust, paralysed by the fear of death, thrown into She'ol, swallowed up by the waves and breakers of death, etc.,[14] that it is difficult for us to imagine that he had spiritual power enough left to compose poetry.[15] But he knew what it meant to be thrown into the depths of Hades. For that reason he could write about it when later on he was to compose a psalm to be used by one who was in that situation. But in the thanksgiving psalms he could better express what he spontaneously felt at the time of writing. He may himself once have passed through the agony of death to salvation[16] and for this reason have been able to express his gratitude both in a jubilant hymn to the God of salvation and in personal testimony before the assembled congregation.

But whether the poet wrote about his own experience or that of the congregation or anybody else, he could in any case express his own personal piety, his own view of God and God's relationship to the people and the individual, even though he shared it with most others who belonged to his circle and nation. The fact that, as a rule, he wrote on behalf of somebody else or with a typical, constantly recurring situation in mind,

[12] With the reservation included in the preceding lines, the present writer fully agrees with Eissfeldt (see n. 86 to Chap. IV) in his analysis of the expression 'my God' in the psalms, and of the experience and personal relation which it indicates. But Eissfeldt does not seem to be aware of the necessary differentiation between the poet and the person in whose name he is making his poem; on the other hand he overstresses the 'collective' element in many of the psalms and thinks, as do many others, that 'being bound to the cult' necessarily means something more impersonal than the supposed 'freedom' from it; see op. cit., p. 11.

[13] The first lines of a hymn in the hymnbook of the Norwegian Church, No. 791 (by E. Blix) and of a hymn by the Norwegian poet Arne Garborg, respectively.

[14] See above, Chap. VII. 5; Gunkel-Begrich, *Einl.*, pp. 185ff.

[15] Cf. *Ps.St.* VI, pp. 13f.

[16] Cf. above, Chap. X.4, and below, pp. 141f.

does not exclude the personal elements any more than the prevailing traditions of style could prevent the real poet from showing his true colour.

For this reason we should also be aware of the fact that the distinction between the praying one (the worshipper) and the poet, in reality, is only one which *we* make in order to make clear to ourselves the actual place in life of the psalms, and their function and purpose in the cult. To the ancients themselves the fact was that the poet under no condition appears or should appear. He is completely anonymous and hides behind the worshipper, whether this is the congregation or its representative or the typical individual in a typical universal situation. Modern commentators and preachers often speak of 'the psalmist' and of what he thinks and says and does. What 'the psalmist' does is to lend his word and his art to the praying, praising or thanking congregation or individual. He identifies himself wholly with the one in whose name and for whose use he writes, and he never appears on his own behalf as a cooperator in that which 'happens' in the cult. The commentators speak, for example, of how the 'voices' ought to be distributed in Ps. 2, and find in some cases that first the poet speaks in vv. 1–5, then Yahweh in v. 6, whereupon the king speaks in vv. 7b–9, and the poet finally speaks again in vv. 10–12 (so e.g. Barnes, *The Psalms*). This is a completely modern conception and without any connexion with ancient Israelite mentality or cultic poetry. The poet-prophet in no case appears directly. He has here composed a poem which is to be recited by the king himself or on his behalf at a certain point in the liturgy of anointing, and consequently is supposed to be spoken on behalf of and by the king. It is the king himself, not the poet, who quotes the election and appointment oracle on which he bases his right.[17] The commentator here has the task of realizing the feelings and thoughts of the king, not those of the poet.

When the poet says: 'I will sing', 'I will thank' etc. he does not do so on his own behalf, but on that of the hymn singer or the bringer of thank-offerings or purification offerings.

This of course does not prevent him from underwriting his own words or the sentiments and feelings to which he gives expression. On the contrary, as one who belongs to the congregation, he knows that what he feels and says is what everybody in an ideal and normal way thinks or ought to think and speak in the typical situation before the face of Yahweh. He knows himself to be the normal and typical representative. For that reason he can let the psalms of gratitude and lamentation peal with full register in the way he knows he would have felt in a given situation, or the way he actually has felt when he has happened to be in the same situation, as a sick person seeking purification and help or as the healed one who is bringing his offering of thanksgiving. In the thanksgiving

[17] What has confused modern exegetes is the corruption of MT in v. 6, which makes the verse a word spoken by Yahweh; the correct text, which is warranted by analogous proclamations in the Ugaritic texts, is found in G and partly in Jerome (see BHK³); in this text the king himself speaks, as throughout the psalm.

psalm with its express appeal to the congregation and the people, with witness and admonition based on the personal experience of the worshipper —and that of the poet—it was natural that the worshipper should appear more distinctly as a person:

> I will instruct thee and teach thee
>   in the way which thou shalt go,
> I will fix my eye upon thee,
>   and guide thee with my counsel.[18]
>
>   (Ps. 32.8; cf. 34.12.)

In such cases the poet himself may at times appear and give a glimpse of himself without using the worshipper as his medium.

As we have seen, there is a close connexion between the psalm poets and the temple prophets. The temple prophet had a definite task in the cult liturgy and he was also to a certain extent a psalm poet. He had to form in rhythmic words and stanzas the message from Yahweh which he should proclaim to the congregation at the festivals. Here the poet himself actually appears in the liturgy itself, but strictly speaking only in the introductory formula, not in the content of what he says. He does not appear as an independent character, but as the mouthpiece of Yahweh. He brings a message which he has received, whether it be as an observer and inter-preter of the 'signs' at the sacrifice or through a more or less ecstatic inspiration. He identifies himself wholly with Yahweh—not in the sense of the primitive 'identity-mysticism', but in a moral sense; he makes himself one with Yahweh, surrendering his emotions and his will to him. On the basis of tradition, history and experience, 'he knows Yahweh' to be 'the Lord of the covenant' and the king and watcher over Israel who has revealed his thoughts about his people through the events of history, and now again has pointed to them through the oracles of the festival and the ideas and the religious demands which are expressed through the progress of the liturgy. This 'knowledge' having become actual and living through the experiences of the festival and the idea embodied in the liturgy, he proclaims the message. Then he speaks in the name of Yahweh, and even when he refers to Yahweh in the third person, he actually is speaking with the authority of Yahweh, and it is His message he proclaims or interprets.[19]

Here it happens at times that the person of the prophet-poet appears in a short introductory formula like: 'I will hear what the God says' (Ps. 85.9a). And it may be extended to become an introductory phrase of a more lyrical and personal nature; as in the combined adoration and benediction poem, Ps. 45, where the poet prophet points to the inspired and efficacious words that he is going to proclaim:

---

[18] V. 8 is obviously too short, some words are lacking. For *'î'ásâ* G has *'e'ëseh*, cf. Prov. 16.30; but the context demands *both* conceptions; read as G, and then *we'î'ásâ (ba'asâthî)*.

[19] Cf. G. Hölscher, *Die Profeten*, pp. 147ff. He exaggerates the 'identity' of the prophets with Yahweh and in connexion with that also the ecstatic element; cf. Mowinckel, *Die Erkenntnis Gottes*, pp. 8–28, and *NTT* 49, 1948, pp. 206ff.

> My heart overfloweth with a goodly matter,
> I say a (wonder-working) poem to the king.
> My tongue is the pen of the ready writer.

In spite of the I-form the emphasis here is not on the person of the poet but on the character of the efficacious words he is now going to proclaim, implying that he is charged with this task by Yahweh.

In the latest 'didactic', mostly non-cultic psalm poetry of 'the learned', the ḥăkhāmîm of the type of Sirach, which is continued in the post-canonical times, e.g. in the Psalms of Solomon, the influence from the style of the 'wisdom poetry' (Proverbs, etc.) is strongly felt. It is a didactic poetry, in which the teacher of 'wisdom' also refers to his personal experiences in the school of life. The subject of this poetry is to a great extent the basic religious problem of the Jews: the justice of God in relation to the distribution of happiness and suffering in the world. It becomes problem poetry, in which the individual's reflections, experiences and attempts at solutions play a prominent part.

It is then inevitable that this puts its stamp on the style and that the person of the poet appears more clearly. He becomes the one who through his inspired authority has something to say to those who worry about the same problems. In the wisdom psalms the beginning made in the 'witness' of the thanksgiving psalm and the prophetic psalms (see above) is carried further:

> I have been young and am now old,
> a righteous man I never saw forsaken. . . .
> I once saw a wicked man in great power
> and spreading himself like a green bay-tree;
> When again I[20] went past he was gone;
> I sought him, but he could not be found.
>
> (Ps. 37.25, 35f.)

And then we occasionally come across a personal expression of the problem, as in Ps. 73:

> For I was envious at the foolish
> when I saw the fortune of the wicked. (v. 3);

or in Ps. 49 (according to Moffatt):

> Why should I be afraid in evil times
> when all around I see treacherous foes?

In Ps. 49 we also find an introduction where the motifs and stylistic impulses from the thanksgiving psalm, the prophetic word and the wisdom poem all blend together in a rather bombastic way (vv. 1–2) There is undeniably a certain disproportion between this pretentious introduction and the conventionality of the solution of the 'riddle', which the poet

---

[20] Read wā'e'ĕbhōr, G, Hie, Pesh.

presents in the next lines, namely that all, even the wealthy must die, and that in deadly peril the ungodly rich has not the same assurance that the pious believer has, namely that God frees him from the threatening grip of Hades and lets him live the normal life to its end; accordingly there is no reason for the pious to envy the rich, or fear when ungodly and powerful men rule around him.

The element of reflection and of religious problematics is, however, not necessarily restricted to the late psalm poetry of the 'sages'. The contrast between the promises and permissions of the covenant on the one side and the people's unhappy experiences in history on the other, has relatively early raised a problem. Such a problem, of course, makes itself felt in the soul of the individual. This we can clearly see, e.g. in Ps. 77, a national psalm of lamentation, where the speaking 'I', the worshipper, is the representative of the people, i.e. the king, or another leader of the congregation. On his behalf the poet in the lament in the first part of the psalm expresses his quite personal feelings of perplexity and grief. He compares the present distress with the Lord's promises and deeds of salvation in former days:

> I dwell on days of old,
>   I recall the years gone by;
> thinking to myself by night,
>   musing in my inward quest:
> will the Lord for ever discard us,
>   will he never be kind again?
> Has his love left us for ever,
>   has his faithfulness utterly failed?

One might otherwise, according to modern thought, think that the private psalm poetry of 'the learned', with its 'emancipation from the cult', should have produced more individualistic and new poetic forms. That did not happen. Through the influence of the wisdom style in the psalms of the learned, admonition and reflexion brought about a dissolution of the old styles of writing, because the poets no longer had the support which was offered by the connexion with definite cultic situations. This led to an uncertain and styleless mixture of the old types of composition, which sometimes makes one uncertain about the actual meaning of the writer. Thus it is not immediately clear whether the writer of the artificial product, Ps. 119, intends to write a hymn about the law or a psalm of lamentation and prayer for help, using his love of the law as 'a motive for being heard'. The latter is really the case. The new contribution in the psalm poetry of the learned has essentially been the didactic and problem psalms. A really new type of psalms they have not created. As they no longer had any connexion with the cultic life—the real 'Sitz im Leben' of the psalm poetry—they have failed to realize what a psalm really is. So—at least in my opinion—a 'didactic psalm' is a *contradictio in adjecto*.

As a matter of fact, such exceptions as Pss. 73 and 49 with the other cases of the 'I' of the poet, confirm the observation that the psalm writer is most of all himself and most genuine when he hides wholly behind the worshipper and enters completely into him and his situation, whether the worshipper represents the congregation (the people) or the individual Israelite in the typical situation of sorrow or joy.

When the psalmist then calls in agony out of the deep, or jubilantly gives thanks for experienced deliverance, he is the worshipper. His psalm is completely personal and gives expression to his innermost ego, precisely because he is a representative of a corporate personality, because his innermost soul is united with the congregation and its individual members in sorrow and joy. He knows them, lives in them, and knows what they feel, in their response to the demands of the situation. He feels the same, has perhaps many times felt it on his own behalf. Therefore he reaches the height of his artistic ability when he feels that now it is the soul of Israel and that of the typical Israelite that vibrates in his lamentation or his praise. For this reason we feel the personal heart-beat of this cult poetry not less strongly in the sad melancholic 'we-psalm', Ps. 90, than in the mighty expressions of God's omniscience in Ps. 139. In both cases the poet has identified himself with another, in Ps. 90 with the congregation, in Ps. 139 with someone suffering from illness or struck by another disaster. Thereby he has found the most genuine expressions for his own personality.

Because the poet is most completely himself when he is serving the congregation and its cultic needs, this purely personal element sometimes breaks through into the outward form and makes it natural for him to use the 'I' form even in a congregational hymn:

> O Yahweh, our Lord . . .
> when I consider thy heavens, the work of thy fingers . . .
> (Ps. 8.2, 4.)

Cf. also Pss. 145.1f., 21; 146.1f. Just as naturally 'I' and 'we' occur together in 'the pilgrim psalm', 122:

> *I* rejoice when they say to *me*:
> 'We are going to the house of the Lord'.
> Now stand *our* feet, Jerusalem,
> within thy (holy) gates.

Against the interpretation of the extant 'individual' psalms as cultic psalms, composed among the temple singers, Gunkel raises the objection that they are far too personal to have been 'formulas', 'like other cultic songs'.[21] Gunkel has here failed to realize both what the cultic psalm and what 'the personal' meant to Israel. The commentators who find that the cultic interpretation of the psalms reduces the psalms to

---

[21] Cf. Gunkel-Begrich, *Einl.*, pp. 282, 291.

'formulas' and denies them all personality has not really understood what it is all about. Such views represent an inherited ultraprotestant and rationalistic disregard of the important role of the cultic life in every religion, including Christianity.

3

Yet, in connexion with the thanksgiving psalms the question does arise whether, perhaps, some of them after all may not have been composed by the worshipper himself. This would mean that such a psalm was not composed by the cult personnel for use by another person to celebrate a feast of thanksgiving, and that it had not sprung out of a poetical identification with his situation. Gunkel, with his emphasis on the strongly personal experience behind the psalms of thanksgiving has drawn attention to something which is essentially correct. The facts mentioned above on pp. 135f., one may imagine, *could* point to a private poetry of this nature.

It is a fact that in the latest didactic psalm poetry of the 'learned' we come across several thanksgiving psalms which without doubt were composed by the particular sufferer himself, but which were not intended for ritual use at any feast of thanksgiving in the Temple (cf. Sir. 51.1ff.; 15.2f.; 39.5; 16.24ff.; Pss. Solomon 3; 10; 13; 15; 16). In the book of Psalms we have at least one which is very similar to these learned didactic psalms of thanksgiving, and which it is most natural to look upon as a psalm of thanksgiving, namely Ps. 49 (see above, pp. 138f). As mentioned above, the cause and situation of the thanksgiving are coloured by some of life's own dangers and thrills. The worshipper looks back on vicissitudes involving matters of life and death. He has been all the way down into the jaws of Hades; death had already swallowed him up. At the very last moment Yahweh has drawn him out, and jubilantly he can again breathe freely 'in the land of the living' and feel life and freedom coursing through soul and body. He has been thrust down into doubt and despair, 'his foot was nearly slipping'; he was on the point of losing faith itself; the agony of sin—or the hardening of heart—gripped him; darkness closed in on him—and now God has again led him into the light! Such is life, such is also the life of the pious.

With regard to psalms like 73 and 49 it is very difficult to free oneself from the definite impression that it is the person who himself was tried and saved who has composed the psalm. Here there seems to be no reason, as so often in other cases, to distinguish between the worshipper and the poet.

This personal element rings strongly behind the traditional and conventional form. But it has here, oftener than in the other types of psalms, transformed itself, and been on the point of breaking up the traditional patterns.

It is in the thanksgiving psalms that we perhaps meet with most deviations from the common style. In some of them the suffering and lamentation are very pronounced (Isa. 38.10ff.; Ps. 116.3, 10f.; Jonah 2.3b–7b; Sir. 51.3ff.), in others the hymnic element sounds most strongly (Pss. 103; 138.2b, 4f.), in others the didactic (Pss. 32.1f., 6a, 8–10; 92.8, 13–15). In the royal psalm 18 the story is given with pompous adornment and mythological pictures, almost in a baroque style. In Jonah 2 the picturing of the mythological ocean deep in the nether-world appears very vividly. Ps. 32 voices strong and completely personal views about the happiness in recognizing and confessing one's sin; the traditional basic type is fairly well hidden behind the personal and didactic. That Ps. 73 is, and wishes to be, a thanksgiving psalm is not so easy to see behind the general but personally expressed form of the problem poetry. Ps. 116 is distinguished by the irregular, back and forth treatment of the traditional elements and by its Hebrew, which is anything but classical. Through them all, the terrors of death and the jubilant joy of life ring with the strongest note. All this shows that the poets here have felt personally involved. This does not necessarily imply that the majority of these psalms may not have been composed by the professional temple poets who may very well have written on the basis of a personal experience and about their own case, even if they wrote for ritual use.

But even in these thanksgiving psalms we ought not to overestimate the difference between the personal and the professional elements. The main part of these psalms, 'the story' of the experiences of the worshipper, is as a rule very short, and kept in general or in mythological[22] terms, which does not make it easy to say anything concrete about them. Neither is it here possible to distinguish quite definitely between the psalms which speak about the anguish of the congregation, where the king is speaking, and the psalms in which any private person might be speaking, for instance about healing from sickness. The expressions are usually so general that they may be applied to all cases.

The personal element does not, as we have seen, exclude the possibility that a psalm may be composed by personnel belonging to the temple cult. Suffering and hardship, sickness and mortal danger may be experienced by anybody. In the social organization and the political life of that age they were much more common visitors than we had become accustomed to reckon with in the comparatively idyllic nineteenth century, before the First World War. The 'professional' psalm poets were also able from personal experience to speak about mortal danger and God's miraculous salvation. Great poets who, partly from their own experience, partly from poetic identification, have been able to sing with jubilant and entranced gratitude about the great and glorious deeds of God when he delivers the pious from death, may of course also have been among *them*. That which is personally felt and genuine is not necessarily opposed to the

---

[22] Cf. Ps. 9.14; 30.4, 10; 40.3; 71.20; 103.4; 116.3; Isa. 38.10f., 14; Jonah 2.3ff.

cultic and that which is bounded by and regulated through cult agenda and office. The individual thanksgiving psalms are also mainly ritual psalms and composed by the cult's own staff.

4

When we speak of the personal piety of the psalmists, something must be said about the question of mystical trends in the psalms.[23]

Old Testament religion does not in general favour the growth of typical mystical piety.[24] Primitive cult mysticism, however, was well known even to this religion in its earlier phases: through the cultic functions and sacramental elements there was experienced the participation of divine (holy) power (powerfulness), which gives to soul and body alike the consciousness of an unusual plentitude of power, of renewed vital forces and flowing fullness of life.[25] It is this experience which finds expression in the ecstatic frenzy—or the quiet musing—into which the prophets would fall especially at the cultic festivals or when taking part in the ecstatic exercises at the sanctuary. But the strong emphasis of Yahwism on Yahweh as a personality, as a will superior in power and as the one who is 'wholly other' than anything human, always prevented mysticism from its logical fruition: unity of God and man, and the total absorption of the soul in God.[26] It is characteristic that the Canaanite-Oriental idea that the god himself 'enters' the prophet, has been replaced in Israel by the idea that 'Yahweh's spirit' enters him, and further, that this idea has again been superseded by the concept of Yahweh's 'word' coming to the prophet.[27] The true mysticism of Judaism belongs to later post-canonical times and particularly to the Middle Ages.[28]

But on the other hand, the professional life of prophet and psalmist in intimate connexion with sanctuary and cult would obviously give abundant rise to less extreme mystical experiences. The very experience of

[23] Cf. on this theme Franken, *The Mystical Communion with JHWH in the Book of Psalms.* He finds rather a lot of this in the psalms, but I cannot find that he has really proved his thesis. His definition of the term 'mysticism' is too wide, in so far as he does not distinguish clearly enough betweeen 'mystic' and 'magic', and includes in 'mysticism' both what had better be called 'the magical conception of the world and the things and forces in it' (see Mowinckel, *Religion und Kultus*, pp. 13ff.: 'Das magische Weltbild') and mythological conceptions. But mysticism as a special type of piety and religious experience is independent of the 'magical conception of the world' and of 'mythology'. Another drawback about his treatment of the psalms is that he does not take into account the typological and cult-functional approach, and therefore often misses the right point of context in his interpretation both of the individual terms, as e.g. 'the silence', and of the pertinent psalm as a whole. However, many of his semasiological observations on terminology are of value. See my review of this book in *NTT* 57, 1956, pp. 122f.

[24] For the definition, and a short characterization of 'mysticism', see Micklem, *Religion*, pp. 153ff.

[25] Cf. Eichrodt, *Theologie d. Alten Testaments*, Indexes, s. v. 'Mystische Tendenzen', I, p. 282, III, p. 172. I here refer to Eichrodt just because he has a certain theological tendency to underestimate the importance of cultic mysticism and yet has to mention it quite frequently in his book.

[26] Cf. van der Leeuw, *Phänomenologie*, §43.6, pp. 285ff. [E.T., *Relig. in Essence and Manifest.*, pp. 305ff.]

[27] See Mowinckel, 'The "Spirit" and the "Word" ', *JBL* 53, 1934.

[28] Cf. Bousset-Gressmann, *Religion d. Judentums*,[3] pp. 354, 356, 396, 449ff.

inspiration, as we have dealt with it above in the 'prophetic psalms' (Chap. XII), is a mystical experience of this kind. And when in Ps. 87 the poet undoubtedly includes himself in the body of 'singing and dancing' people and expresses what they all feel in the words: 'all my springs are in thee', he evidently shares the experience of being suffused with 'holy' feelings and divine power. The same thing is implied in a term like 'Yahweh is my power and my song' (Ps. 118.14; Ex. 15.2; Isa. 12.3). The psalmists well knew the ecstatic-mystical experiences attached to the cult.

But both cult life (vita religiosa) and the profession of the prophet give opportunities of meditative absorption in, and concentration on, divine realities, which may lead to mystical experiences. In the psalms we sometimes find allusions to such a meditative and emotional concentration, expressed e.g. by the word śîaḥ. Thus the author of Ps. 119 concentrates on Yahweh's commandments (vv. 15, 22, 48, 78, 97, 99, 148) and his wonders (v. 27). The word always indicates something very emotional, and the sense of it ranges from a more or less enraptured concentration on the exaltation to the ecstatic trance.[29]

We have also reason to believe that the emotional experience of cultic realities and happenings might not infrequently take visionary forms, just as there is every reason to believe that Isaiah had his call vision in connexion with the great new year festival, while kneeling on the threshold of the sanctuary. So, very likely, the psalmist alludes to such visionary experiences in the Temple when using the term 'to behold the beauty of Yahweh' in his palace (Ps. 27.4), originally referring to the unveiling of the image of the god at the festival.[30]

Many places in the psalms speak of the intimate relation of the worshipper to Yahweh: Yahweh is the 'rock' in which he 'takes his refuge' (ḥāsâ), on whom 'he is waiting' (qiwwâ) and on whom he sets his 'hope' (tiqwâ), to whom he 'cleaves' (dābhaq) and is 'firmly tied' (ḥāšaq).[31] This, however, is not the mystical identification, the unio mystica, in the sense of genuine mysticism, but finds its expression in faith, confidence and obedience. The worshipper—and the psalmist—is wholeheartedly willing to subordinate himself to Yahweh's commandments, to 'the fear of God', and surrender to him, and he clings to him in confidence, waiting for him to give all help, in all sorts of distress and danger. So he expects that Yahweh, the Lord of the covenant, the běrîth, will keep his faithfulness, just because 'he has intimate fellowship (sōdh) with those who fear him' (Ps. 25.14). This does not mean that Yahweh has established an unio mystica with his worshippers, but that he has taken them up in his covenant fellowship, and according to his promises will keep his faith to them, will 'be their God' and protector, as a good and mighty 'overlord' is always the pro-

---

[29] Cf. Franken, The Mystical Communion with JHWH in the Book of Psalms, pp. 18ff.
[30] See Bentzen, Fortolkn. t.d.g.t. Salmerne, ad loc.
[31] Cf. Franken, op. cit., pp. 22ff.

tector and refuge of his 'servants'. The words of the psalmist when saying 'I am always with thee' (73.23) has the same meaning.

Therefore the worshipper—and the psalmist—can trust Yahweh to be his 'counsellor'. The true chief and lord is also the 'counsellor' of his community; 'counsellor' is one of the titles of king and chief.[32] To be in the *sōdh* of a great lord[33] involves the lord giving good and luckbringing counsels. So will Yahweh, with his covenant-members, his *ḥăsîdhîm*. They can trust Yahweh to be their counsellor and helper:[34] 'I am always with thee, thou holdest my right hand, guiding me with thy counsel' (73.23). Normally Yahweh gives this 'guidance' through his oracles, in connexion with the cultic rites and through the mouth of priest or prophet, when the worshipper 'seeks' him (*dāraš*) and 'asks' him (*šā'al*). But just as the 'word' might 'come' to the prophet through concentration and openness of mind, in quiet 'watching' and 'listening',[35] even so the psalmists may often have experienced that Yahweh would 'guide' them through the emotions of their souls, through thoughts and words that 'came to them'. In this sense God's guidance has always been a reality to the pious of all religions. It is, perhaps, mysterious, but has nothing to do with mysticism.

Just because this is the relation of the psalmists—and through them of the 'normal' worshipper—to Yahweh, they can say that he is 'the rock of their hearts' (73.26), their good 'portion and cup', their 'goodly inheritance in pleasant places' (16.5f.), that 'a single day within his courts is better than a thousand days outside' (84.11); 'whom have I in heaven but thee? on earth I care for nothing else' (73.25). Words like these must be seen against the background of e.g. Ps. 23; it is not the mystic's extinction of his own personality, his being 'plunged into a vast ocean which is God and again God', which finds expression here, it is the unshakable confidence of those who have experienced the faithful help of God in their own lives, who know that all the fountains of life spring with him (36.10; 87.6).

But not only faith and confidence, even the love of the psalmists speaks in verses like these:

> I love thee, Yahweh, thou my strength,
>   my crag, my stronghold, my deliverer,
> my God, my rock in whom I trust,
>   my shield, my saving horn, my tower! (18.2.)

It is significant that this 'declaration of love' is formulated as an introduction to the king's thanksgiving psalm for deliverance in battle. The religion of the psalm is practical, not mystic in the strict sense of the word.

---

[32] See J. Pedersen, *Israel* I–II, General Index, s.v.
[33] See Köhler, *Der hebräische Mensch*, pp. 89ff. [E.T. *Hebrew Man*, pp. 122ff.]
[34] Cf. J. Pedersen, *Israel* III–IV, pp. 455, 626.
[35] Cf. Mowinckel, *Erkenntnis Gottes b.d.a.t. Profeten*, pp. 19ff.; 'The "Spirit" and the "Word" ', *JBL* 53, 1934.

CHAPTER XVIII

The Antiquity of Psalmography and the Psalms

I

How old, then, is psalmography in Israel, and from what period do the psalms date?

As we have seen, nothing can be concluded from either actual or supposed names of authors in the headings. For the individual psalms we are therefore entirely dependent upon so-called 'internal evidence', i.e. on what we are able to infer from the psalms themselves.

But just because the psalms are cultic psalms, to be used by all and sundry, the terms employed are frequently of such a general nature that they do not tell us much about the time of their historical background. Some date from the monarchy, and others from Jewish times; but that does not take us very far.

In order to make any progress it is of no use to start with the individual psalms; we must ask, rather, whether it is possible to say anything about the age and use of the different psalm types.

Rhythmically formulated cultic words are *per se* almost as old as the cult itself. Cult means repetition, and form and rules; it requires set phrases; the best way to preserve intact words which are to be said over and over again is to put them into rhythmical verse.

The fixed and regular form possessed by the different psalm species of the Bible is an indication of a long history and evolution. Regularity and uniformity are generally later than variety.

Everywhere, even amongst the Hebrews and in ancient Israel, the oldest cultic words are in the nature of self-acting words of power rather than of prayers to a personal God and expressions of definite human feelings towards such a God. But on the whole this is not the case with our extant psalms. These latter are prayers and not magical words. A precisely formulated poetic art has been made a medium of expression for the cultic relationship to a personal, willing and active God.

When did this happen?

2

At the time of Amos (about 750) psalm singing belonged as a matter of course to the temple service (5.23; cf. 6.5). Amos speaks directly only of the temple of Bethel, but there is no reason to doubt that it was just the same at Dan and in Jerusalem.[1]

This is corroborated by the inaugural vision of Isaiah some ten to twenty years later; this vision contains so many elements which are actual features from the Temple and the service there, that we may take for granted that the song of the seraphim in form and substance is an echo of the hymns of the cult; it is therefore quite logical to find it at an early period included in the Christian liturgy of the Holy Communion. It contains the fundamental elements of the hymn of praise in the very shortest wording:

> Holy, holy, holy is the Lord of hosts,
> for the whole earth is full of his glory   (Isa. 6.3.)

Also, we are able to prove that the psalms sung in the Temple—or temples—in the period of the kings represent all the psalm species to be found in the Psalter; but this again means that these species belong to the old literary tradition and are the outcome—or offshoot—of a psalm poetry which is old in Israel.

If we examine the hymns of praise we actually find the first evidence of the traditional style in the earliest dependably datable poem handed down to us in the Old Testament, the Song of Deborah in Jdg. 5. The hymnic element in the introduction and the end of the song is quite obvious.[2] Among the temple prophets of Jerusalem both Nahum and Habakkuk have composed hymns of praise showing fully developed elements of substance and style of this psalm type.[3] Both are connected with the prophetical message and display features from prophetical thought and style; but this very 'mixing' proves that the hymnic form has not been created by the prophet in question; he has adopted an existing and fully developed style and used it to express the message that had been given him to proclaim. The hymn of Habakkuk, so strongly influenced by the ideology of the hymns of epiphany and enthronement, has in all probability really been composed as the prophetical part of an actual temple liturgy and in fact the liturgical notes added prove that it was used in this way.[4] Even Jeremiah was attached to the Temple of Jerusalem, and in him, too, we find hymnic motives and forms used as elements of the prophetic word (5.22, 29)—evidence that he was so familiar with the hymnic style that he would unconsciously have recourse to it, for instance when wanting to motivate the message by pointing to the authority and power of God underlying it.

[1] See Additional Note XXXIII.
[2] Jdg. 5.3–31. On the possible date of the Song of Deborah see Albright in *BASOR* 62, Apr. 1936, 1953, pp. 26ff., although his arguments are not quite conclusive.
[3] Nah. 1; Hab. 3. See *GTMMM* III, pp. 695, 698f., 708, 715ff., and the present author in *ThZ* 9, 1953, pp. 1ff.; cf. above, n. 37 to Chap. XV.
[4] Cf. Mowinckel, *Jesajadisiplene*, pp. 67, 144, 147f.; *ThZ* 9, 1953, pp. 1ff.; Humbert, *Livre d'Habacuc*, pp. 24ff., 58ff., 276, 290ff.

Strong hymnic elements, partly pure hymns, are to be found in Deutero-Isaiah,[5] not least so in his 'disputations', when he argues with his audience in order to make them believe that Yahweh is behind the historical events: Yahweh both can and will save. His is the power, and he had proved his power and his faithfulness to the Covenant before, in creation as well as in his saving works in the history of the people. Here the prophet takes up old traditional subjects for the hymn, working them out in the traditional style. It is particularly interesting to see here that he is also quite familiar with the ideas and forms of the enthronement psalm.[6] Obviously this range of ideas and this mode of expression cannot have been created by Deutero-Isaiah, for he evidently assigns a different sense to them, when using them. The scene which these psalms take for granted and have for their background is the idea of the victorious king in triumph entering his city, which by his help has outfaced all storms, and from whose walls the heralds are proclaiming the appearance of the king in his victorious progress. Deutero-Isaiah uses the picture to describe the coming return of the exiles headed by Yahweh, and the 'holy road'—via sacra—of the processions has become the wonderful road to be built through the desert for the returning people; the call to the heralds on the walls is here addressed to a city now in ruins, but to be re-erected now that the king comes.[7] And Yahweh's victory over the primeval ocean and the dragon has been changed into the victory over the Babylonians by Cyrus, and instead of the drying up of the waters of the primeval ocean, of which the enthronement ideology and the psalms speak, Deutero-Isaiah speaks about the wonderful springs of water which shall well forth in the desert, wherever the exiles shall journey.

From the period of the monarchy we have unmistakable evidence also for the psalm of lamentation, namely in the imitations of its form and substance by the prophets as a vehicle for their message.[8] Sometimes they clothe the actual proclamation of disaster in the trappings of a psalm of lamentation, making the people sing lamentations over the disaster as if it had already taken place, or they themselves intone a lamentation over what is going to happen. Sometimes it is the style of the psalm of lamentation which they use when writing of the sins and oppressions prevailing among the people, and speaking about them in the same terms and forms as the person in the psalm of lamentation when he speaks of the oppressions and persecutions and ungodliness of the evil enemies. The more frequent model is the public psalm of lamentation, though the I-form is sometimes used. This is most clearly seen in Jeremiah.[9] In this

[5] Isa. 42.10–13; 44.23; 49.13; 52.9f. Hymnic motives: Isa. 40.22–24b, 28b–31; 44.25–28; 45.18; 46.10f.
[6] See *Ps.St.* II, pp. 195f.
[7] Cf. Gunkel-Begrich, *Einl.*, p. 420.—For other individual influences on Deutero-Isaiah of the fully developed hymn style, see ibid., pp. 416ff.
[8] Cf. Jer. 3.22b–25; 4.10; 14.2–6, 7, 9, 19–22; 31.18ff.; Hos. 6.1–3; Isa. 40.27; 49.14, 24; 51.9ff.
[9] See Mowinckel in *Edda* XXVI, pp. 233ff.

prophetic poetry we find all the features and formative elements of the psalm of lamentation fully developed: the invocations with a hymnic addition, the lamentation with the question 'why?' and a picturing of the misery, the prayer, the ground for confidence, the confession of sins, the motives of honour and penitence.[10] That Jeremiah is not the originator of this form, as for instance Wellhausen thought, is evident from the fact that it is an unusual element in the prophetic style; its effect on the audience is precisely due to the well-known notes of the lament being sounded in a prophecy: the coming disaster is made concrete and actual: in this very way it is going to happen and to be felt, just as when previously we had reason to complain of disastrous catastrophes. And when Jeremiah for instance composes his dire message as a public psalm of lamentation over the drought and the havoc inflicted by it, and then makes the real message consist of Yahweh's answering oracle having a nature quite contrary to the usual one in the congregational psalms of lamentation, proclaiming: I will *not* hear their prayers, and I will *not* have mercy upon this people, and it is *no* use for you to pray for them— then obviously the crushing weight of this formula is due to the fact that the prophet here reverses what the people were accustomed to hear from Yahweh in answer to psalms of lamentation on the day of penitence.

Even the really individual psalm of lamentation was used by Jeremiah as a model, namely for his purely personal lamentations to God about the heavy burden of his calling, about persecution and hatred on the part of his fellow-countrymen, for his prayer for revenge and salvation, and for the answers God gives him to his prayers.[11] Here again, we find all the elements and forms of the psalm of lamentation and, in contrast to the former group, also the confidence of being heard and rescued, Yahweh's promise of salvation and the anticipatory thanksgiving. Here Jeremiah still more obviously adopts a fully developed literary 'species'. Terms and phrases, which literally and according to their true meaning refer to external disasters, as for instance illness, are used by Jeremiah about his personal religious problems and needs, i.e. in a new meaning. The psalm of lamentation here becomes the pattern for the problem poetry about the success of the ungodly and the sufferings of God's faithful servants, 'heal me' he prays, and means: 'deliver me from all these persecutions and sufferings'. What we find here is not the stylistic origin of the psalm of lamentation, but the first beginnings of an emancipation of its style and type from the cult, and a re-modelling of it for independent, personal poetry.[12]

---

[10] Further details see Gunkel-Begrich, *Einl.*, pp. 422f.

[11] Jer. 11.18–20; 15.15–21; 18.18–23; 20.10–13; 12.1–6; 15.10–12; 20.7–9, 14–18. For these poems see Baumgartner, *Klagegedichte d. Jer.*, in which he has proved their authenticity, as contrasted with the scepticism of earlier critics.

[12] Begrich (*Einl.*, p. 426) is incorrect when he holds that the fact that Jeremiah uses this style of writing is an evidence of the emancipation; this assertion rests on the erroneous opinion that such an emancipation was the rule in the Psalter.

The lament on the evil deeds of the enemies is also echoed in Mic. 7.1–7.[13] Even Habakkuk is clearly influenced by the style of the psalm of lamentation.[14]

The thanksgiving psalm is likewise echoed by Jeremiah. The anticipatory thanksgiving (and the assurance that the prayer will be heard) in the psalms of lamentation in itself presupposes the thanksgiving psalm and the cultic use of it, and as already mentioned Jeremiah's poem of lamentation contains this anticipatory thanksgiving.[15]

Finally we might mention that the prophets also knew and imitated the 'Torah of Entry' as well as the songs of pilgrimage.[16]

In the light of all this, it is not possible to retain the opinion once so common among theologians, that the whole psalmography of the Old Testament must date from a comparatively late period, preferably from the time after the fall of the kingdom and the restoration of the Jewish congregation in the Persian period, or that the origin of psalmography should be attributed to Jeremiah.[17] There can be no doubt that psalmography in Israel dates back to very old times. The Song of Deborah is earlier than the monarchy, and there is every reason to believe that the full development of the most important psalm types, to which the prophetic use of the style forms bears testimony, dates back to the early monarchy.[18]

This conclusion is corroborated by the fact that the language of the psalm poetry has proved to be an archaic one, showing a quite close relation to the language and phraseology of Ugaritic poetry.[19]

3

In a later chapter we shall see that everything seems to indicate that pattern and impulses for psalmography in Israel have come from the Canaanites, who in their turn build on a much older common oriental cultic and literary tradition and style. This fact very much supports the opinion that the psalmography of Israel must be very old. The period most open to influences from the native culture would be the time following close upon the settlement in Canaan, and particularly the early monarchy, when the mingling of the races became an accomplished fact and the kingdom purposely adopted so many earlier political, cultural and religious traditions from the Canaanite kingdoms;[20] the following period was in-

[13] Even Mic. 7.8–20 is strongly influenced by the style and thoughts of the psalm of lamentation: the motive of confidence (the enemy is apostrophized, cf. Pss. 52; 82), vv. 8ff., the promise vv. 11ff., the prayer for deliverance, vv. 14ff. Cf. Gunkel in *Zeitschr. f. Semitistik*, 2, 1924, pp. 145ff., who is hardly justified, however, in considering the poem part of a connected 'prophetical liturgy'. The poem is evidently post-exilic.

[14] See H. Schmidt in *ZATW* 62, 1949–50, pp. 52ff.

[15] Jer. 20.13; cf. the late passage Jer. 33.11.

[16] Mic. 6.6–8; Isa. 33.14–17; Hos. 6.1ff.; Jer. 31.6.

[17] See Additional Note XXXIII.

[18] Davison has already called attention to a great many passages proving the existence of psalmography in pre-exilic times, see *Book of Psalms* I, pp. 20ff.

[19] See M. Tsevat, *A Study of the Language of the Bib. Psalms*, and my review thereof in *ThLtZ*, 1956, 4, coll. 199ff.

[20] See, for instance, Garstang, *The Heritage of Solomon*; Albright, *A.R.I.*

creasingly characterized by the Yahwistic, Levitic and prophetic reaction against everything foreign, and the struggle for what—in adherence to the earlier 'traditions of the desert'—came to be looked upon as true Yahwism.

As already mentioned, psalmography and the rich development of the cult, of which it is a part, are everywhere in the Orient closely connected with the great temples. The temples are the home of psalmography. The same is evidently the case in Israel. We have seen that in the psalms there are innumerable allusions showing the close and intrinsic connexion with the Temple on Mount Zion, and the cult and festivals there.

So there is every reason to believe that a native Israelite psalmography was directly occasioned by the rise of permanent temples and the regular religious services for which they gave opportunity. Such permanent temples as cultic gathering-places for some greater or smaller section of the tribes or for the whole of the old Israelite 'amphictyony of tribes'[21] were something new in the religious life of Israel, and did not come into existence till after the settlement and then—as we know—were directly based on a Canaanite pattern; that the Temple of Solomon was built by Phoenician master builders and on the Phoenician model is stated in plain terms in the Old Testament.[22]

Such a permanent temple existed in Shiloh at the time of the Judges (Jdg. 21.19ff.; 1 Sam. 1). Very possibly there were others, for instance in Dan an idol or cultic symbol of a deity like the one taken by the Danites from Micah in Mount Ephraim (Jdg. 18) presupposes a permanent temple building. But Israel did not possess a 'national temple' of the first rank until they built the royal Temple of Solomon on Mount Zion, and, later on, the North-Israelite temples of Dan and Bethel (1 Kgs. 5f.; 8; 12f., 26ff.).

We may therefore with great probability maintain that when Israel had settled down and built permanent temples, and especially when during the reigns of David and Solomon they had set themselves the task of adopting Canaanite and common oriental culture and science and art,[23] they would also have taken up religious poetry in the international style. The pattern closest to hand would be the Canaanite cultic poetry.

If temple singing and music date back to the age of David or Solomon, it may very well be possible that there is some truth in the tradition linking psalmography to the name of David, even if 'David' in the psalm headings originally just means 'the king' in general. That does not mean that David was personally the originator of psalmography; the earliest tradition does not know him as a poet, but as a minstrel; none of the really old

[21] For this notion and the kind of organization it covers, see Noth, *System d. zwölf Stämme Isr.* pp. 61ff.

[22] 1 Kgs. 5.15ff.; 7.13ff. See Galling, art. 'Temple' in *BRL*, col. 511ff.; Albright, *A.R.I.*, pp. 142ff. Cf. also Cook, *Relig. of Ancient Palestine*, Chap. II. For the scanty evidence of Israelite sanctuaries provided by the excavations, see McCown in *JBL* 69, 1950, pp. 205ff.

[23] 2 Sam. 5.11, 13; 8.7, 17; 10.2; 1 Kgs. 3.1; 5.6, 10–14, 15–22; 7.13; 9.16, 19, 26f.; 10.14–22, 26, 28f. See above, Chap. XVI. 1.

traditions tell us that he was the composer of cultic psalms.[24] But we seem reasonably justified in dating the origin of Israelite cultic poetry back to the time of David. Perhaps it is even older; the Song of Deborah seems to indicate this.

The earliest real temple in Israel seems to have been the one in Shiloh (1 Sam. 1ff.), which existed at least in the period of the later Judges. Even at that period psalm-like prayers to Yahweh *may* have belonged to the regular ritual. Not much later we have the temple of Nob (1 Sam. 21), where the same thing may have been the case.

By far the larger number of the extant psalms originates from the national Temple of Jerusalem, erected by Solomon. Here the Israelite cult was most richly developed. Some of the psalms may derive from some North-Israelite sanctuary, such as Bethel; this might for instance be the case with Ps. 80, where the worshippers are equated with 'Joseph'; the psalm belongs in all probability to the last days of the Northern Kingdom.[25] In Ps. 77, too, the congregation is called 'Jacob' and 'Joseph'. The author of Ps. 89 has included in his poem fragments of an older hymn of praise, vv. 2-4, 6-19, where 'Tabor' and 'Hermon' are mentioned as illustrious Yahweh sanctuaries. It is not impossible that Ps. 68[26] is an old originally North Israelite psalm later adapted for the epiphany festival in Jerusalem,[26a] see, however, below, p. 153.

4

Thus we have the background for the dating of the individual psalms which are still extant.

In the first instance, all the unquestionable royal psalms[27] date from the period of the monarchy, before the fall of Judah in 587. To these unquestionable royal psalms may very likely be added several of the national psalms of lamentation in the I-form, where the praying person is the leading man of the people.

Of course the North-Israelite psalms to be found in the Psalter, such as Ps. 80 (see above), also date from the monarchy. They must have been composed before or shortly after the fall of the Northern Kingdom in 721. To all appearances Ps. 83 dates from the Assyrian period. Pss. 44 and 74 may have been composed shortly after the catastrophe of 587. Even after that disaster some form of the cult was maintained in the temple ruins (Jer. 41.5).

Consequently it is natural for us to ask whether possibly the Jewish

[24] See *Ps.St.* VI, pp. 76-81, and above, Chap. XV. 5.
[25] See Eissfeldt in 'Geschichte u. A.T.' (*Alt-Festschrift*), pp. 65ff.
[26] See Mowinckel, *Der achtundsechzigste Psalm*, pp. 68ff.—Fr. Delitzsch, *Der Prophet Habakkuk*, pp. 118ff., is no doubt right in many of his arguments to prove that Ps. 68 is earlier than Hab. 3; cf. Albright in *Studies in Prophecy* (*Robinson-Festschrift*), p. 9, n. 29.
[26a] See Mowinckel, *Real and Apparent Tricola*, pp. 92ff., where 'Benjamin' v. 28 is interpreted as the ideological name of the king's domain, the old city-state Jerusalem.
[27] Pss. 2; 18; 20; 21; 28; 61; 63; 72; 89; 101; 110; 132; 144 (?); 1 Sam. 2.1-10. See above, Chap. III. 2, and see Additional Note XXXV.

tradition may not be right in speaking of psalms at the time of David. The answer must be that this is in no wise impossible; it is very likely that psalms were composed for the glory of Yahweh as early as the time of David, when he instituted the cult of Yahweh in Jerusalem, and that earlier Canaanite psalms were remodelled in order to suit the Yahweh religion.

But we should also add that hardly any extant psalms are as old as that.[28] In any case we have to realize that if the heading 'for David' originally really meant 'for the king' it affords no true tradition about author or date and consequently there is no reason to think of the time of David in preference to any other.[29]

This means that in each individual case we have to ask for positive evidence proving that probabilities are in favour of dating a psalm from the time of David. The age of an individual psalm must be decided on 'internal grounds', from what may be more or less clearly read out of it, due regard being given to what is otherwise known to us about the spiritual and religious history and state of Israel at different times. And it must be admitted that the vast majority of the psalms can be proved to be later than David, while few, if any of them, can on internal grounds be dated to so early a period. Such an early date can be proved to be probable only for such psalms or portions of psalms as can be shown to be adaptations of older Canaanite psalms; and even then we cannot be certain that the Israelite adaptations were not made later than the time of David. And even though Ps. 104 was probably inspired by the Egyptian hymn to the sun, other things in this psalm seem to indicate that it is rather late; its rather 'de-mythologized' view of Yahweh's 'victory' over the primeval ocean and of the sea dragon Leviathan is more in line with Deutero-Isaiah and the poem of Job. Ps. 110 is very 'old-fashioned'; but as it is concerned with the enthronement of a new king on Mount Zion it cannot very well refer to David who had been anointed and made king a long time before he conquered Jerusalem. But it is not impossible that it may allude to Solomon, who is here enthroned as the legitimate heir of Melchizedek and the old priest-kings of Jerusalem. Quite old, too, is Ps. 68 (see above, p. 152); but it must be admitted that, as its text now runs, it belongs to the Temple of Jerusalem, though this may also be its original form and intention; if this be so, however, it must belong to a time somewhat later than David.[30]

Some scholars have been tempted to find even pre-Davidic psalms in the Psalter. It is prima facie not impossible that some old Canaanite psalm has been adapted to the Yahweh cult (see below); but whether this possible adaptation was made in post- or pre-Davidic times, is of course impossible to decide now.

[28] See *Ps.St.* VI, pp. 75ff., and Additional Note XXXVI.
[29] See Additional Note XXXVI.
[30] See Mowinckel, *Real and Apparent Tricola*, p. 93.

It remains to be said that the psalms seldom contain such clear references to contemporary events that the latter may be used to decide their age.[31] From the point of view of a cultic interpretation of the psalms this is but natural. We may expect to find references to contemporary events most particularly in the national psalms of lamentation, whereas most of the royal psalms of lamentation and the national psalms of lamentation in the I-form refer to such typical and constantly repeated situations and are mostly kept in such general terms that any dating is impossible. And from a religious point of view the psalms give expression to an attitude which in its main features prevailed in the official temple religion of almost all ages, as far as we know.

5

Some psalms, and among them perhaps some of the most profound ones, undoubtedly date from Jewish times.[32] This applies for instance to Pss. 90 and 126; 128; 129; 130 and 131 and many others which presuppose the permanent state of distress of 'Israel' (the Jewish people) under foreign domination and regard the re-establishment of Israel as a subject of prayer and hope. A 'poetical legend' like Ps. 78 is evidently based on the Pentateuch in its present form.

Such pure, liturgical compositions as Pss. 136; 115; 135; 147 to all appearance also belong to a comparatively late period, for as a rule the pure style is later than the more complex one.

The same applies to 'problem poems' like Pss. 49 and 73, which are concerned with the same problem as the poem of Job and the book of Ezekiel.[33]

The strong influence of wisdom poetry in 'the learned psalmography' and the disintegration of the ancient style categories, to which it testifies, are on the whole more especially characteristic of the latest psalmography —such as for instance the Psalms of Solomon, which had no longer any living connexion with cultic poetry,[34] and which can be proved to date from late Jewish times.

6

At one time scholars used to refer a great many psalms to the Maccabean age.[35] There is no need to do this with any single psalm. From the point of view of the history of the canon such a reference is most unlikely; for the Maccabean age the Psalter was a 'canonical' book;[36] already at that time

---

[31] See Additional Note XXXVI.
[32] See above, Chap. V. 11; VI. 5-6.
[33] See above, II. 35f., 38f., 109, 114.
[34] See Chap. XVI. 6.
[35] See Additional Note XXXVII.
[36] For details see Chap. XXI. 8. Buttenwieser would emphasize that (classical) Hebrew had ceased to be a living language long before the time of the Maccabees (op. cit., pp. 10ff.); but that is hardly so very certain, cf. Birkeland, *Sprdk of Religion*, pp. 24ff.

a comparatively finished collection. It is significant that when a new festival was instituted in Maccabean times, namely the temple consecration festival in the year 164, no new festal psalm was composed, but Ps. 30—the existing 'canonical' psalm deemed to be the most suitable—was used as a thanksgiving psalm for the deliverance and the new consecration of the Temple. From this analogy it becomes evident that when for a time under the Maccabees the single verse, Ps. 44.24 was sung at the daily morning offering, this in no way proves that Ps. 44 was composed during the Maccabean period. On the contrary it is just a new example showing how in those days the leaders of the temple cult were on the look-out for suitable parts of the canonical Psalter to be used in a new cultic situation. We may say with certainty that during the Maccabean period no new cultic psalms were composed. By that time the Psalter had been closed, as we shall see below.

A comparison with real Maccabean psalmography, to be found particularly in the so-called Psalms of Solomon and in the psalms scattered about in the non-canonical literature,[37] shows that those of the Bible must be a great deal older. In the latter—namely in the 'wisdom psalms', the 'learned psalmography'—we find only a tendency towards that disintegration and mixing of style types which is characteristic of the Maccabean psalms.

It is significant that no very deep traces can be found in the Psalter of the religion of the law so characteristic of Jewish times. In this connexion we must however mention the two psalms 19B and 119, which certainly allude to the written law, and in addition the representation of the law as God's real benefaction to Israel in Ps. 147.19.[38]

Perhaps the youngest of the psalms are not very much older than the completion of the Psalter, some time before the year 300 B.C. (see below, Chap. XXI.6). But the majority are older; many of them several centuries, or even half a millenium older.

7

To sum up, we may say that the classical time for Israelitic-Jewish psalmography was the monarchy and the earlier Jewish period until about the year 400 B.C.

It very soon becomes evident that there is no essential difference between the psalms of the monarchy and those of earlier Jewish times, whether with regard to basic thought and content, form and style, or poetic power. The catastrophe of 587 was not so epoch-making in psalmography as we might be inclined to think.[39] Not till the later Jewish period

---

[37] See Ludin Jansen, *Spatjüd. Psalmdichtung*, and above, Chap. XVI. 6.
[38] If the term 'nomistic psalms' is—rightly—taken in the sense of psalms chiefly characterized by the typical Jewish form of law religion, then it is an exaggeration, when Birkeland, *Feinde d. Indiv.*, pp. 28off., also reckons Pss. 25; 86; 116; 143, and 32 among the 'nomistic psalms'.
[39] It is rightly emphasized by Gunkel-Begrich, *Einl.*, pp. 416ff.

does it become evident that psalmography is about to decay and become stereotyped, even though, of course, mediocre psalms were composed under the kings as well. In fact the psalms showing the greatest originality and independence, as compared with the traditional style pattern, are not infrequently found amongst those from Jewish times; it will suffice to mention such poems as Pss. 137 and 139. But here, too, the old pattern has been observed, and the main elements are old; only that they have been used in a freer way, with a different emphasis and in a different relationship to one another, so that really original compositions of great effect, profundity and power have resulted.

But within this period it is not possible to write any history of psalmography.[40] Most datings of the individual psalms are too uncertain for that, and we find so many typical, common features recurring in earlier as well as in later psalms that it is not possible to arrange the material so as to produce anything like a clear 'line of development' between the comparatively scarce fixed points. One can only say that a great many of the psalms show the essential features of the official religion of the monarchy both with regard to the idea of God and to the conception of the relationship between God and people, God and man, whereas others display certain features characteristic of the situation and the basic thoughts of earlier Judaism. The picture of God given in the hymns of praise[41] is much the same throughout. In the religious experience reflected and in the prayers addressed to the deity, Yahweh is the only God worth mentioning, absolutely superior to all others, 'righteous, merciful and gracious, slow to anger and plenteous in devotion and in mercy', a helper of the oppressed and an opposer of the haughty-minded. And even the more carefully thought-out monotheism of Judaism takes the existence of other gods for granted and emphasizes how Yahweh, when appearing, will prove himself 'terrible to all (the other) gods'. Everywhere in the psalms, irrespective of their age, the covenant between Yahweh and Israel and the exceptional position of Israel are taken for granted.

On the other hand we may say that the consciousness of sin, the ideal of humility, and the knowledge of total dependence on God, and of the worthlessness of all human aid stand out more clearly in the later than in the earlier psalms, though these thoughts are not lacking in the earlier ones. Likewise, the interest in Yahweh's 'works of righteousness', in the history of the people, and the attachment to the law of Yahweh, stand out more clearly in the later psalms, just as instruction, exhortation and influences from wisdom poetry are much more conspicuous than in the earlier psalms.

Speaking generally, we may also say that the growing appreciation of psalm singing in preference to offerings, and a more symbolic and spiritualizing conception of the sacrificial cult are characteristic of later poems

[40] See Gunkel-Begrich, op. cit., 415ff.
[41] See above, Chap. IV. 6.

rather than of the earlier ones. Here Pss. 50 and 51 are two fairly fixed points, both belonging to earlier Jewish times. This may indicate that Pss. 40 and 69 belong approximately to the same period, whereas Pss. 20 and 66 represent a somewhat earlier type of piety. That Ps. 40 belongs to the later psalms may be concluded from its rather complex character—an earlier psalm has been inserted into it—and from the fact that it puts such emphasis on what is 'written in the book scroll'.

That the psalms which look forward to the restoration of Israel from alien rule and the Diaspora, as for instance Pss. 14 and 53, belong to later times, to Judaism, is very obvious.

We could of course try to write the history of the different psalm types confining ourselves to matters of form and style. But the lack of sufficiently certain datings would make any such attempt follow a pattern of development too schematic and artificial. It would become something in the nature of an abstraction, a conjecture as to how the psalm type in question might have developed. And although in its main features it would probably fit in with reality, we should never be justified in maintaining that the development was always so straightforward. All sorts of influences, for instance from foreign patterns, *may* have made the development anything but plain, and may, for instance, have had the result that peculiarities, which according to an immanent process of style development 'ought' to have come later, have actually been present from the very start. Babylonian-Assyrian and Egyptian, and for all we know even Canaanite psalmography, was fully developed even before it started in Israel, and it is a fact that Israel has used these foreign patterns.

Above all we must beware of imagining that there has always been a 'development' from 'pure' style types to more complicated and 'mixed' ones. On the whole it is probably correct to maintain that the kind of 'style mixing' which manifests itself in a mixing of motifs and formal elements from the most heterogeneous psalm types without any feeling for where they belong, and even letting them be permeated by reflective thoughts and subjectivity and influences from other kinds of poetry—as for instance wisdom poetry — will generally belong to the latest times. This 'style mixing' only became prominent in the post-biblical, late Judaic, 'learned' psalmography, such as the Psalms of Solomon. But even in late times it is not all-pervading; Jesus Sirach still composes psalms in a quite pure, 'classical' style.

Furthermore, it is a general rule in the history of style that compound, undifferentiated style is often older than a homogeneous one. As we have seen earlier, there is consequently no rule that pure we-psalms must be earlier than the mixed I- and we-psalms; all the evidence seems to suggest that the I-style is in itself earlier than the we-style even in the 'national' psalms of lamentation.

In another way, also, such a historical sketch, based on a particular typology of style, would turn out to be a somewhat incomplete and artificial undertaking. For we could not place the supposed phases of development within one particular psalm type in any chronological connexion with the phases of development within the other style types, i.e. of synchronizing the tendencies of development. Thus the 'history' would be just a series of longitudinal sections, which could not with any certainty be put in any chronological relation to one another so as to provide a really many-sided, full, organic picture of the whole.

So the attempt to write a detailed 'history of psalmography' is better avoided.

What can be said is that with regard to its content it follows the course of development in religious history from the national religion of the period of the monarchy, with the prominent part played by the kind in the cult and in religious estimate, to the religion of the Jewish congregation with its deep consciousness of sin, its incipient individualism (cf. Ps. 90), its ideal of humility, its interest in the law and its hope for the future.

From a formal poetic and aesthetic standpoint we may say in the first place that the latest psalms are often inferior to the earlier ones as regards poetic power and originality. They are often based on the latter to the extent of being remodellings of earlier psalms, like Ps. 108, or of adopting parts of earlier psalms, like Ps. 19; sometimes they not only use the old elements and terms, but they repeat unaltered the old metaphors and expressions in a purely cliché-like fashion, or they give the impression of being mere quotations from earlier psalms, as with Ps. 144. The mentioning of Yahweh's benefactions in history may develop into mere prosaic compendiums of the history of Israel, and this motif may be used in the hymn of praise, as in Pss. 105 and 136, as well as in the penitential psalm, as in Ps. 106. Both these psalms, and still more Ps. 119, display a growing tendency towards monotony and unreasonable length.

Further we must admit that the latest psalmography is characterized by the influence of wisdom poetry with its didactic and frequently arid tone, by an excessive alloy of subjective reflection, as well as by a certain disintegration of the classical styles. This has been shown clearly in the chapter on 'the learned psalmography' and the late Jewish psalms (Chap. XVI).

CHAPTER XIX

The Metre of the Psalms

I

The psalms are for singing, and singing implies a constriction of the rhythm called metre.[1]

Even in prose there is a rhythm—the natural rhythm of the language—brought about for instance by an alternation between accented and unaccented, or long and short syllables. A characteristic of the natural prose rhythm is that it is not bound to a regular pattern, it cannot be expressed by means of numerical formulas, it is irrational.

Poetry is originally connected with singing, and characteristic of the rhythm of singing are more fixed rules for the alternation of long and short —or accented and unaccented—syllables. It tends towards expression in a lucid numerical formula, it is rational.[2]

But smaller units of natural prose may have their fixed rhythms. A regular set combination, for instance of a noun and an adjective, has a particular rhythm. And there is a connexion between the natural units of the language and the rhythmical units of poetry. Just as the sentences of a language are based on the smallest units, those logical and grammatical units of a sentence: subject, predicate, object, adjunct, etc., so the poetical rhythm is from the beginning based on the natural units of meaning in the mind. V. Vedel is right when he speaks of a 'rhythm of meaning', a 'sense rhythm', as a fundamental matter in poetry.[3] That is to say that any unit of meaning in the mind makes a rhythmical and musical unity, a 'bar'. We may presume that what is basic about the rhythm of the earliest poetry is the joining of a certain number of such units ('bars', 'metrical feet') into a greater unit of meaning, a sentence, which makes the next metrical unit after the 'bar', viz. the 'line of verse'. Sievers called this smallest unit after the 'bar' (the 'foot'), a 'Reihe' (row); scholars writing in English now mostly call it a 'colon', since ambiguity has crept into the use of the word 'stichos' often used formerly, the colon is what, correctly, should be called a 'hemistichos'.

As a result of the tendency towards regularity and repetition, which is characteristic of a text for singing, the verse line of a poem very soon came

[1] For references to recent literature on the problem of Hebrew metrics, see Additional Note XXXVIII.
[2] Cf. Mowinckel in *Deutsche Ltz.* Vol. 51, 1930, col. 535ff.
[3] See V. Vedel, *Meningsrytme*. In essential matters my conception is based on the fundamental view of Vedel; cf. my paper in *Festschrift für Bertholet*, pp. 379ff.

to consist of a fixed number of the smallest units (metrical feet), which would regularly recur or be varied according to definite rules.

The shortest, so to speak, natural 'row' or 'colon' consists of two parts belonging together logically and metrically (for instance, subject and predicate), the dipod. A very common occurrence in the poetry of all peoples is the double dipod, the four-footed colon—in a poetry of four-footed cola the original dipods may of course resolve, so that we get a 'monopodic' four-footed colon: the feet do not necessarily belong together in pairs logically and rhythmically.

It is inherent in the 'rhythm of meaning' that the number of unaccented syllables is not regular to begin with, because the linguistic units of meaning may consist of a very different number of syllables. What constitutes the metrical foot is the accented syllable in the foot. The number of metrical feet within a colon is originally identical with the number of logically weighty accented syllables.

But from the nature of the case, there will be a limit to the number of unaccented syllables which may rhythmically belong to an accented one. Reasons of thought-expression as well as of euphony tend towards greater regularity, so that certain combinations of accented and unaccented syllables will recur more or less regularly. Words intended to be sung, especially, will tend towards regularity. Even the secondary accents of a polysyllabic word or of the smallest unit of meaning (the sentence) are important as syllables bearing along the rhythm of the line. Not only does the word accent become essential, but the sentence accent and sense accent as well.

These 'natural metrical feet', however, are not the usual classical ones (trochee, dactyl, iambus, anapaest), but rhythmical combinations which in classical metrics are only accepted as exceptions: the amphibrach (x́-x), or its extended variant (xx́-x), the creticus (-́x-́), the coriambus (-́xx-́) and similar rhythmical groups.

But in artistic poetry—we might say, professional poetry—the need for greater regularity may then interfere and establish a fixed regular relationship between accented and unaccented (or long and short) syllables, as is the case in classical Greek and Latin poetry. The artificial metrical feet originating in this way—the trochee, the dactyl, etc., will then find themselves in a certain strained relationship to the original units of meaning, or make themselves wholly independent of the latter.

In the poetry of a particular people intermediate phases of any sort may occur between these two extremes, which are: the original sense rhythm, and the strict classical rhythms.

In the earliest poetry of a people the fundamental and original rhythm will generally be that of meaning. And, more or less, it will assert itself again in a reaction against the strict artificial rhythms. In the poetry of many European and especially of the Scandinavian nations the more spontaneous metrical feet of the sense rhythm have in fact been the actual rhythmical elements of the verse, even if the authors fancied they were writing in the strict classical metres. This has become very evident in modern poetry, and the emancipation from the classical rhythms is intentional.[4]

2

There is every reason to suppose that Hebrew poetry[5] started with the more spontaneous 'sense rhythm'. In old Arabian metrical art the earliest metre—the so-called *saj‘*—seems to be based on cola of four dipodically grouped, unequal feet, in correspondence with the real units of meaning. From the *saj‘* then developed the strict regular metres, in which the metrical feet are no longer identical with the units of meaning.[6]

In Babylonian poetry the usual primary form is a colon of 2 + 2 logical units, with a varying number of unaccented syllables for each accented one, but with an obvious tendency to rank the metrical foot above the unit of meaning, so that a long word, for instance a verb + objective affix, often represents two feet (bars).[7] In most cases the cola are knit together in pairs as 'thought rhymes' (see below).

Of this original Hebrew poetry, however, not much is left, and the little we have—such rhythmic sentences as Gen. 4.23f.; 16.11f.—is not enough to provide a basis for formulating metrical rules.

A difficulty when trying to ascertain the Hebrew metre is the lack of an accurate knowledge of the pronunciation in the different epochs of earlier times. The Massoretic system of pronunciation is partly an artificial systematization based on the recitation in the synagogue (at a time when Hebrew had long been a dead language) and showing traces of grammatical learning and doctrinal consistency. Remnants of earlier systems of vocalization not infrequently indicate a different pronunciation, where the original short vowels had not yet been reduced to indistinct vowels (shewas), or completely lost; and where the original monosyllables (e.g. *qašt*) have not yet been expanded to dissyllables (e.g. *qešeth*).[8] Here we must also bear in mind that the orthography may frequently be older than the actual pronunciation; the relative pronoun for instance is spelt *'ăšer*, but was in many cases pronounced *še*.[9]

[4] Besides the treatise of Vedel (n. 3) cf., e.g., Handagard, *Norsk verslaera*, pp. 241ff.

[5] See Begrich in *ThR*, N.F.4.

[6] See Hölscher in *Budde Festschrift* [*BZAW* 34] and cf. with this his pronouncements in *Th. Ltz.*, 1927, col. 366.

[7] See Zimmern in Gunkel, *Schöpfung und Chaos*, p. 401, n. 1; Meissner, *Babyl. u. Assyr.* II, pp. 153f.; id., *Bab.-assyr. Literatur*, pp. 25ff.; Falkenstein & von Soden, *Sumerische u. Akkadische Hymnen u. Gebete*, pp. 39ff. In Canaanite poetry from Ugarit the 4-footed verse-line—colon—likewise seems to be the main rule. Neither Gordon's scanning of the verse-lines as 3-footed (*Ugaritic Grammar*, p. 79, id., *Ugaritic Manual*, p. 108) nor the attempt of Albright (*Cathol. Bibl. Quarterly*, Jan. 1945, p. 21) is convincing.

[8] Particularly shown by Kahle in his works on the Hebrew text; see the summary in *The Cairo Genizah*, pp. 86–110. Cf. also the works of Brönno and Birkeland on vocality, etc., in Hebrew. According to the period which in Chap. XVIII has been proved to be the classical age of psalmography in Israel, Birkeland's system II will have to be the one that represents vocality and accent in the linguistic structure of the psalms; see *Akzent und Vokalismus*, pp. 53ff.

[9] See Kahle, *Mass. Text d. A.T.*, p. 36.

Even this uncertainty shows the advisability of taking as the starting point the poetry of the classical period, rather than such old poems as the so-called Song of Deborah (Jdg. 5), or the Lament over Saul and Jonathan (2 Sam. 1).

Our insufficient knowledge of the pronunciation in older times also suggests that it is advisable to begin the study of Hebrew metrics with later poems, such as Lamentations, Proverbs, Job and Psalms. Their evidence seems to be unanimous in all essentials, and there is sufficient material to allow us to find out the general rules for the poetry of the classical ages of Hebrew literature.

As for the relation of classical Hebrew metrics to the original, more spontaneous, but prehistoric 'sense rhythm' we shall probably have to distinguish between the popular poetry and improvised prophetic speech on the one hand, and 'professional' poetry on the other. Prophetic speech seems to stick to the more spontaneous rhythms. In professional poetry, on the other hand—and to this latter belong the psalms as well as the wisdom poetry (Proverbs, Job)—there is every indication that a regular rhythm has been carried through. The original sense rhythm frequently shows through, but there is an obvious tendency towards fixed rules for the alternation of stressed and unstressed syllables.

3

The question debated by earlier investigators of Hebrew metrics, whether the rhythm is based on an alternation of long and short, or on accented (stressed) and unaccented (unstressed) syllables, can now be considered as solved. The very structure and spirit of the language indicate that the rhythm is accentual. This is seen *inter alia* by the fact that the accent is relevant for the meaning of a word; there is a difference between *qấmâ*, 'she arose', and *qāmâ*, 'the rising (female being)'. But none of the Hebrew vowel-signs express the quantity of the vowel, and a vowel may be lengthened, as under the pausal tone at the end of a sentence, without any change of the meaning. And on the other hand, there are too many long vowels and syllables in the Hebrew language to make a quantitative rhythm probable.

Since in most Hebrew words the last syllable is stressed, we may also take for granted that the rhythm was rising, i.e. iambic- anapaestic.

There is however another peculiarity of the Hebrew language which must be given due consideration, that is, to give the second syllable before the stressed one (the antipenultimate), a secondary accent, marked by the Massoretes by the so-called metheg accent. A word like *mîrûšālēm*, 'from Jerusalem', is not pronounced *mîrûšālēm*, but *mîrûšālēm*, with two stresses; and a word like *ħăbarbûrōthêhem*, 'their spots' is pronounced with three stresses, *ħăbárbûrôthehém*. The Massoretes have not always expressly marked these secondary accents, but they are deeply rooted in the very system, vocalic and accentual, of the language, and must be reckoned with in a study of metrics.

This means that Hölscher is quite right when he—like others before him—maintains against the system of Sievers, so far held by most Old Testament scholars, that the Hebrew poetic rhythm is in principle iambic. The tendency to make the number of significant words in a line of verse coincide with the number of metrical feet is apparent throughout, from the earliest[10] to the latest psalms.

Hölscher has also mentioned another important point: the possibility of syncopating an unstressed syllable, so that two stressed syllables follow one another; the first of them will then have to be prolonged in reading, or given an extended tonic accent. Instead of the scheme x′x′, we may have, for instance, x ‗ ‗ in each case two feet. This overstressing should, at least ideally, fall on a word that is logically stressed too.[11]

Furthermore, there is no doubt of the existence of verses in which iambic metrical feet alternate with anapaestic ones (xx′). Probably we can here discern a heritage of the old freer 'sense rhythm'. More especially at the end of a colon the amphibrach and its variants (x′x or xx′x) seem to be allowed to replace the iambus and anapaest respectively; this is a consequence of the rule that the accent of a clause or sentence generally falls on the penultimate syllable (the 'pause accent').

We do not yet know anything about the detailed rules for the alternation of 'iambs' and 'anapaests'. A translation of Hebrew verse must often make frequent use of anapaests and amphibrachs, without any definite principle; an English sentence often contains more syllables than the corresponding Hebrew, so that it is often impossible to manage a pure iambic rhythm if one wishes to convey the complete meaning.

In Hebrew Bible MSS. the poetical sections are normally not written stichometrically, i.e. each verse-line making a separate line in the script. True enough, the logical and syntactic units as a rule coincide with the metrical ones, but not always; so, too, the Massoretic verse division and the metrical units often coincide, but again not always, and there are

---

[10] Among these oldest poems, such as Jdg. 5; 2 Sam. 1.19ff., I do not, however, count all four Balaam songs in Num. 23-24, in spite of Albright (*JBL* 63, 1944, pp. 207ff.). The present form of this legend is made up of two recensions ('sources'), the younger no doubt a descendant of the older, not an independent variant to it. The traditional figure of the wise seer Balaam is of course older than the present tale, probably older than Israel. Of the four songs, the two in Chap. 24 are the older; they cannot be older than the Davidic-Solomonic age; the allusion to David in 24.17 is obvious. These two are independent of the tale, which is, so to say, spun out of the songs. The two later songs in Chap. 23 are, on the contrary, made to fit the tale, and belong to a much later time, when the difference between Israel and 'the nations' was felt as its essential characteristic. The two *ex eventu* oracles on Amalek and Cain (24.20, 21), are of course old; after David's days no opportunity would arise for making verses on those dispersed tribes. On 24.23f. I express no opinion: it *may* be the oldest of them all, alluding to the raids of the 'sea-peoples' in the 13th century, as Albright thinks; but the *kittîm* may also be the Macedonians (thus the note in the official Norwegian Bible translation, which is, from the translators' fundamentalist point of view, not incompatible with Mosaic authorship of the Pentateuch).

[11] Cf. Hölscher in *Budde Festschrift*, and in *ThLz.*, 1927, col. 366.

rather many exceptions, even where the Massoretic verse division is clearly wrong.

This means that we cannot always be sure how to group the metrical units merely from the verse feet, or, in other words, how to divide the 'rows' and 'periods'—the cola and bicola (see below)—from one another. But here that 'thought rhyme' mentioned above—the parallelism (see below)—provides us with a fixed starting point. The same service is provided by the alphabetic acrostics which we meet in Lamentations and in several psalms. A section like Lam. 1-4, or a psalm like 25 or 111 and 112 leaves no doubt as to the beginning and end of the verse-line and half-line.

According to still prevalent opinion, the smallest normal metrical unit after the 'foot' is a three-beat verse-line. Considering, however, what has been said above about the 'sense rhythm' and its influence even in later stages of the evolution, we find cause to ponder on seeing how often verse-lines with four words, each indispensable for the meaning, appear in poems which are commonly thought to be written in three-beat (or 3 + 3) lines. Among the numerous cases in Job and Proverbs take Job 3.3, the first verse of the poetical part of the book:

> *yōbhadh yōm 'iwwāledh bô*
> *wĕhallāylā 'āmár hốrâ gắbher.*

Each line consists of four weighty units of meaning, each asking for a particular emphasis when recited. So, in fact, the Massoretes recognize in giving them each a very distinct accent, which in some cases even differs from the usual prose accentuation (*yōbhadh, hốrâ*). A poet ranking as highly as this author may be expected, we might think, to strike the rhythm which is to characterize his poem in the very first lines.

Furthermore, in the assumed 3 + 2 beat verses there often occur 4 and 3 logically indispensable words so that the scanning as 4 + 3 beat verses cannot be doubted, and in addition there are the not infrequent poems where the scanning as 4-beat lines is commonly accepted.

Under all these circumstances it cannot be doubted that the smallest normal metrical unit is the four-footed iambic line,[11a] often with syncope of the light, unstressed part of the foot, e.g.,

> *ta'ăwáth libbố nātháttâ lố* (Ps. 21.3.)
> *rĕṣéh yahwéh lĕháṣṣîlênî* (Ps. 40.14.)
> *sāmúkh libbŏ lố' yîrá'* (Ps. 112.8.)

As a rule the structure of a line is dipodic, i.e., the feet are arranged in pairs as dipods (double feet) both logically and syntactically and thus also metrically.

Three-footed lines also occur, but as far as we can see only in alternation with the four-footed ones. It has therefore to be considered as a brachy-

[11a] See n. 7, above.

catalectic (shortened) line of four feet, the last foot being replaced by a pause (see examples below).

Whether five-footed lines occur is uncertain and rather improbable. Two-footed lines do not occur; Ps. 29 is not written in any 'two-beat metre'; the metre is the normal dipodic four-beat line.

This shortest line, here called a colon, may also be called a half-verse, on the grounds given below.

It is the rule that cola do not occur isolated, but strung together in pairs to make a larger unit called by Sievers *Periode*, but more conveniently called the bicolon, the double colon. This forms the normal 'verse' in Hebrew poetry, and as the colon always forms a half of such a verse it may also be called a 'half-verse'. This bicolon, with its approach and its consolidation or winding up seems to agree with a common physiological and psychological law, which has always played a great role in all forms of art.

As a sample of a normal bicolon may be cited:

> *nĕ'ûm bil'ám bĕnô bhĕ'ôr*
> *nĕ'ûm haggábhr šettám hā'áyn* (Num. 24.3.)
>
> *kî sáḥâ lĕ'āphăr naphšénû*
> *dābhĕqâ lā'árṣ bitnénû* (Ps. 44.26.)

In Hebrew poetry the usual metre is the symmetrical bicolon of two four-footed cola $(4 + 4)$. Since this metre is used throughout the mashal or wisdom poetry, we had best call it the mashal metre.

Besides the mashal metre there quite often occurs an asymmetrical bicolon, one four-footed and the other three-footed $(4 + 3)$. As already mentioned, it is a shortened (brachycatalectic) mashal bicolon. As it was first traced in the poetry of lamentation—qinah poetry[12]—it has been given the name qinah metre.

A few examples of qinah verses are given below:

> *'êkhā yāsĕbhâ bādhádh | hā'îr rabábtî 'ám*
> *hāyĕthá hĕ'álmāná | rabbáthî bhággoyîm* (Lam. 1.1.)
> *'essā' 'ênáy 'el-héhārîm | mē'áyn yābhô' 'ezrî* (Ps. 121.1.)
> *tĕhôm 'él-tĕhóm qōrĕ | lĕqôl ṣinnōrékhā* (Ps. 42.8.)

Much rarer[12a] than the bicolic verse is the tricolic, consisting of three four-footed cola $(4 + 4 + 4)$:

> *miqqōlôth máym rabbîm |*
> *'addîr mimmísbĕrĕ yâm |*
> *'addîr bámmārôm yahwéh* (Ps. 93.4.)

The tricolon may be considered a shortened (brachycatalectic) double bicolon, in fact a 'strophe' (see below).

---

[12] Budde, *Das hebr. Leichenlied*. Like Ley before him, and later Sievers, he was, however, wrong in looking upon the period as a 'fiver' $(3 + 2)$.
[12a] See the author's *Real and Apparent Tricola*, pp. 13ff.

4

The bicolon in Hebrew is linked with a peculiarity of style, viz. the thought rhyme, usually called parallelism or *parallelismus membrorum*,[13] which is characteristic of all ancient oriental poetry. The term indicates that the thought in the first colon is repeated in the second, with the same meaning but expressed in other, synonymous words ('synonymous parallelism'); a certain variation of the thought is not excluded. Instances:

> Why muster the kings of earth,
> and leaders confer together? (Ps. 2.2.)

> Who can be guest in thy tent, Yahweh?
> who can dwell in thy holy mount? (Ps. 15.1.)

But the thought rhyme may also have an antithetical form: the thought of the first colon being elucidated by its antithesis ('antithetic parallelism'):

> For humble folk a saviour art thou,
> But haughty eyes thou bringest low. (Ps. 18.28.)

> For Yahweh doth acknowledge the way of the just;
> But leads the way of the wicked astray. (Ps. 1.6.)

This form is probably to be considered a later development.

Probably still later—but at the same time a witness to the earlier fundamental importance of the thought-rhyme for the poetic style—came the dropping of the thought rhyme, while the formal bicolon, the two cola of which are separated by the metrical caesura, was still retained, the second colon containing a continuation of the thought in the first, or an additional, description with new details, as for instance:

> As an evergreen tree, so shall he be,
> one planted along by water leats,
> that gives its fruit in proper season,
> nor e'er its leaf does wither away. (Ps. 1.3.)

We find this development particularly in the qinah bicolon, in which it is almost a fast rule that the short second colon supplements the first:

> Oh blest be Yahweh who gave us not
> for prey unto their fangs;
> our lives are like a bird that's flit
> from out the fowler's trap. (Ps. 124.6f.)

Commonly this form has been called 'synthetic parallelism', but this term is misleading, since the 'parallelism' in this case is merely of a formal, metrical nature and consists in the binding together of two cola into a bicolon, whereas the thought rhyme within the bicolon has been aband-

[13] On Lowth and the *parallelismus membrorum* see Additional Note XXXVIII.

oned. But even then the law of the thought rhyme may make its influence felt, and lead to what has been called 'repetitive' or 'climactic parallelism': the second colon of the period takes up a leading word from the first and annexes the supplement to it:

> Oh give Yahweh, ye sons of gods,
> oh give Yahweh, honour and might. (Ps. 29.1.)

We find this form developed in its full artistry already in Ugaritic poetry,[14] and it also occurs in Babylonian poetry. The taking up of the leading word may take the form of a comparison elucidating the thought:

> As thirsty hind doth longing feel
> unto the water brooks,
> just so my soul doth thirsty feel
> for thee who art my God. (Ps. 42.2.)

This last example also shows us that though the thought-rhyme within the bicolon has been abandoned, we meet with it again in a more or less complete form as a parallelism between two bicola. Two bicola are used to express the same thought in variant terms:

> Better shelter with Yahweh,
> than on mankind rely;
> better shelter with Yahweh,
> than on noblesse rely. (Ps. 118.8f.)

> All they that seek for thee indeed
> are glad and joy in thee;
> oft, lovers of thy saving help,
> 'Yahweh is great', shall say. (Ps. 40.17.)

The thought rhyme is a fundamental law of style and poetry to such an extent that we often meet with parallel bicola in which the two cola of each bicolon are parallel *inter se*; this means that we get a double thought rhyme within the pair of bicola:

> A(a) For mine is every forest creature,
>   (b)   the beasts upon a thousand hills;
> B(a) I know the mountains' birds, each one,
>   (b)   keep stock of field-bound crawlers. (Ps. 50.10f.)

> A(a) Show me favour, oh God, in accord with thy mercy,
>   (b)   in thy fullness of sympathy wipe out my trespass.
> B(a) Truly wash me free of guilt,
>   (b)   and from my sin do thou me cleanse. (Ps. 51.3f.)

[14] See Albright in *Studies in Prophecy*, ed. Rowley, pp. 3ff., with reference to L. Ginsberg's paper in *Orientalia* V (inaccessible to me).

Here the bicolon A is parallel to the bicolon B, colon Aa parallel to colon Ab, and Ba to Bb.

In such a double bicolon alternate parallelism may also occur:

A(a) As one deaf am I, and do not hear;
  (b) one mute, who opens not his mouth;
B(a) and become as one who cannot hear,
  (b) in whose mouth no repartee is found. (Ps. 38.14f.)

Here A and B are again parallels, but Aa is parallel to Ba and Ab to Bb. There are also other variations.[15]

As already mentioned, the thought rhyme is a peculiarity of style, but very closely connected with a metrical phenomenon, the bicolon. The earliest form is no doubt the 'synonymous' thought rhyme, and the psychological explanation is the same as in the case of the bicolon. The thought rhyme—occurring also in Canaanite, Babylonian-Assyrian and Egyptian poetry[16]—is originally nothing but a repeated line (colon). The earliest, most primitive form of poetry is the repetition of a single line; the simplest form of repetition is the double line: it corresponds to inhaling and exhaling, to the swing of walking and working, of lifting and striking, of tensing and grasping (strain and relief); cf. the stanza for heaving, or the one used at the capstan or in the stone-pit: 'We take a turn—and we heave it up'.[17] Cf. above, on the original hymn as a repetition of a particular sentence or a pair of sentences.[18]

And be it said expressly: first it needs the repetition of a line, or the composition of at least two lines, to make a poem, and to make it possible to speak of a 'metre'. Metre consists of the repetition of the same rhythmical sequence; a single line has its rhythm, as have all clauses of the language, but it has no 'metre'. The oldest poem in the world was a repetition of the same emotionally loaded sentence.

This genetic psychological connexion between the thought rhyme and the bicolon, as well as the fact that the bicolon survives even in cases where the thought rhyme is not used, and finally the wide prevalence of bicola both in lyrical and didactic poetry, allow us to maintain with great probability that the occasional occurrence of detached, isolated single cola without any rhythmical or logical parallel member, at least very often, is due to defective tradition—oral or textual: a colon may have been

---

[15] It is of no particular interest to us here to enter further into the niceties of the varied 'thought rhyme'. We may just mention that they are partly identical with those of Ugaritic poetry, see C. H. Gordon, *Ugaritic Grammar*, pp. 79ff., id., *Ugaritic Manual*, pp. 108ff.; and below, n. 16.

[16] Cf. Gordon, loc. cit. Weber, *Lit. d. Bab. u. Assyr.*, p. 36; Meissner, *Bab.-assyr. Lit.*, pp. 25ff.; Erman, *Lit. d. Aegypter*, pp. 11f. [E.T., p. xxxii]; Pieper, *Aegypt. Lit.*, p. 21. For the Canaanite poetry, see also Hempel's remarks in *ZATW* 55, 1937, pp. 302f. A layman may get an idea of the parallelism through the translation in Hvidberg, *Graad og Latter*, or Ginsberg, *Legend of King Keret*; though Ginsberg divides up the lines the way it is done in the texts, which is not consonant with the true verse lines, but simply determined by the breadth of the tablet columns.

[17] Cf. Handagard, op. cit., pp. 30f., and Hölscher's information about the Arabic metricists, op. cit., p. 93.

[18] See p. 74; cf. also, for the song of victory, Chap. IX, n. 3.

dropped, or a traditional variant or sometimes also an explanatory note ('gloss') may have been inserted in the text.[19] Sometimes such an isolated colon may be a kind of refrain, with which the congregation or another chorus reply to the separate lines or strophes of the psalm, or with which they finish (as in Ps. 2.12b).

5

The importance of the single colon and the single bicolon in Hebrew poetry, as original unit and constitutive element, also explains another poetic peculiarity, namely that the units of rhythm and the units of thought nearly always coincide. The separate colon is a complete thought and sentence, or a comparatively independent unit of meaning within the sentence. As a rule it would be natural to put a comma after each colon, a semicolon or full stop after each bicolon. Thus a Hebrew poem tends to have a somewhat piecemeal and enumerative character, which obviously appears, for instance, in the hymnic style.

In the course of time there were attempts at a more fluent style. Thus the two cola of a bicolon were made into an, at any rate, apparent grammatical unit by leaving out the predicate of the second colon for instance:

> Is, then, thy mercy declared in Grave,
>   thy faithfulness in Hades?
> Is, then, thy wonder known in Darkness,
>   thy righteousness in Oblivia? (Ps. 80.12f.)

Both subjects, 'thy mercy' and 'thy faithfulness', belong to the same predicate: 'is declared'; likewise in the next bicolon, where 'thy wonder' and 'thy righteousness' are the subjects of 'is known'.

But, as mentioned above, the two rhythmical cola may also form a logically coherent bicolon; we find this particularly in the abbreviated qinah verse:

> But for thy great loving-kindness' sake,
>   into thy house I'll come;
> I'll cast myself down in awe of thee,
>   towards thy holy fane. (Ps. 5.8.)

Here the thought rhyme is formed by the two bicola; each of them is a unit of thought and a closed sentence, whereas the two cola of every bicolon are only rhythmically and not logically independent members.

---

[19] Gordon (*Ugaritic Grammar*, pp. 79f., id., *Ugar. Manual*, pp. 108f.) and Albright (in *Studies in Prophecy*, ed. Rowley, pp. 3ff.) refer to the occurrence of irregular 'tricola' in the Ugarit texts as a proof that they must have been original even in Hebrew. To this must be said: 1. the matter will have to be systematically examined as far as the Ugaritic texts are concerned; 2. even behind the latter there is a long history of verbal tradition, which like the last literary formulation of the editors *may* have led to amendments of the original texts; 3. we may not simply transfer the rules of epic literature to lyrics. On the irregularities due to textual corruption see the author's *Real and Apparent Tricola*, pp. 22ff.

In later style one thought or one description may continue through several bicola, as for instance:

> When the Israelites went out of Egypt,
>> Jacob's stock from a stuttering race,
> then Judah became his shrine,
>> Israel his royal domain. (Ps. 114.1f.)

See also Pss. 104.5–9; 107.4–8, 10–15, 17–21, 23–31; 78.1–11. But even here the unit of rhythmical and logical syntactical members is observed; each colon or bicolon constitutes a separate member in the description or the train of ideas.

The true 'enjambement', i.e. the transference of ideas and sentences beyond row or period, so that the logical cæsura does not coincide with the metrical one but falls within a colon, occurs rather seldom. One example:

> Blessed the man / to whom Yahweh
>> does not impute / iniquity. (Ps. 32.2a.)

The logical division (cæsura) is indicated by the vertical line. Even where the bicolon makes one logical unit, the rhythmical cæsura between the cola falls between two comparatively independent units of meaning within the sentence; see example from Ps. 5.8, above, p. 169.[20]

6

Much discussion has centred around the question of strophes (stanzas) in Hebrew poetry. By 'strophes' is meant what is now popularly but erroneously called a 'verse'. The strophe is a rhythmical, or melodic, part of a text including more than one single period (bicolon); in singing it is accompanied by a melody complete in itself and ending in a distinct pausal stop; the thought content also ends with a more or less distinct sense pause. The strophe is not primarily a notional, but a rhythmical and melodic quantity, intrinsically related to the text of the song. When several such strophes having the same form and the same melody are united into one whole, we speak of a strophic poem.[21] The strophe may also be marked off by means of different formal conjunctive elements, such as the end rhyme, the refrain, or a regularly recurring series of metrically heterogeneous lines (cola)—as in the strophes of classical lyrics.

As far as texts for singing are concerned the melody is, as we have seen, the most effective means of marking off and binding together the single

[20] Other instances are Pss. 34.8; 35.27a, b; 40.5a; 55.18b–19a; 69.2; 101.7b; 119.6, 57,88,117; 129.4, etc. In fact Sievers' so-called 'sixers' (according to his system 2 + 2 + 2 feet) are as a rule usual 8-footed mashal periods with an enjambement between the two cola. Sometimes they are regular qinah verses.

[21] See Sievers, *Metr. Studien* I, p. 134. The connexion of the strophe with lyrics and singing is rightly emphasized both by Sievers and Begrich (*ThR* N.F. 4, p. 84), as opposed to all the frequently artificial attempts to base the solution of the strophic problem on criteria of the subject-matter.

strophe. For instance, if the end of a four-line strophe is marked off by letting the first three lines have the same sequence of tones—the same 'melody'—whereas at the end of the fourth line it rises or sinks (as is not infrequently the case in primitive folk-song[22]), neither singer nor audience will be in doubt as to where the strophe ends. In this case the demand for a thought pause after each strophe need not be so stringent; it is quite possible that the logical break within a strophe may sometimes be greater than the one at the end of the strophe.[23] Thus the last part of a strophe may start a comparatively new theme to be further elaborated in the following strophe.

The psalms were texts for singing, and thus possessed the most essential condition for the development of regular strophic structure.

In fact, even from the point of view of content and style Hebrew poetry would naturally tend to develop strophes as a consequence of the thought rhyme. In the great majority of psalms the bicola pair off into units of thought and form either because the bicola are parallel (synonymous or antithetic parallelism), or because their ideas are closely related to one another. The double bicolon is the basic strophe of Hebrew lyrical poetry. In many of the psalms this is so obvious as to leave no room for doubt.[24] In other psalms the palpable double bicolon occurs so often that we may suppose that it is intentional, and that the author meant to carry the arrangement through even where there is no such obvious connexion of thought between the two bicola. In such psalms the strophic division indicates which bicola are intended to belong together; a matter which is sometimes important for the interpretation of the individual bicolon. It is, for example, not unimportant to know that the obscure verse 51.8 strophically, and therefore presumably also logically, is more closely connected with v. 9 than with vv. 6b–7.

In some psalms regular strophic division is marked out by a refrain, as we see in Pss. 42–43; 46; 80; and 99. Even the alphabetic acrostic scheme may be used to mark out strophes when several bicola begin with the same letter.[25]

Consequently we find in the psalms regular strophes of two, three and four bicola each. The strophes of three cola (the 'tricola') in Ps. 93 and others, are, as already mentioned, abbreviated strophes of four cola (two bicola). Of these strophes the one of two bicola is by far the most frequent.

But, as has been mentioned above, the claim that the strophe is rounded off to express one idea must not be overstressed. Ps. 1 consists of three strophes of three bicola, of which the first two speak of the destiny of the righteous, the third of the destiny of the ungodly. This last subject, however, has been touched upon already in the third bicolon of the second strophe: to the summing-up of the saying about the righteous,

[22] See above, Chap. XIV. 2, cf. p. 9.
[23] Cf. Additional Note XXXVIII. 5.
[24] Pss. 3; 8; 16; 19B; 28; 50; 57; 59; 74; 83; 89; 92; 114; 121; 122; 127; 137, et al.
[25] Pss. 9/10; 37; 119; Lam. 1; 2; 3; 4.

'whatsoever he doeth shall prosper', is attached the antithetic parallel colon about the ungodly, 'the ungodly are not so'. Then the following third strophe gives further details. Ps. 18 consists of strophes of four bicola. The strophe vv. 21–24 seeks to show that the escape of the king in battle is a reward for his piety and righteousness, and, to prove this, protests his innocence in different ways. The next strophe, vv. 25–28, first takes up the leading idea of the preceding strophe and states that the escape is 'therefore' the reward of the righteousness of the king, and to this attaches a general statement about the prevailing principle of Yahweh's mode of action: the adequate rewarding of righteousness and punishing of unrighteousness, the principle according to which he has acted in this case also. Logically speaking the break between vv. 25 and 26 is deeper than that between 24 and 25; yet vv. 25–28 make up a connected train of ideas, and there is no reason to suppose that vv. 21–28 do not also consist of regular strophes of four bicola, like the rest of the psalm.

Sometimes even strophes of five (Pss. 44(?); 99; 104) and seven bicola (Pss. 21; 33; 85) occur. Particularly ingenious is the arrangement of Ps. 42–43, which is divided into three main strophes of ten bicola each, these three being again divided into two strophes of four bicola + one refrain strophe of two bicola. The alphabetic psalm 119 consists of twenty-two strophes of eight qinah bicola, one for each letter of the alphabet. Here the division into strophes is perfectly extrinsic; each individual bicolon (qinah verse) is an independent unit, and the bigger sense divisions contain an unequal number of strophes.

In fact, only a minority of psalms are devoid of a regular strophic structure.[26] They belong mainly to the later, 'learned' psalmography, such as Ps. 78, or alphabetic psalms, like Pss. 25 and 34, in which the scheme has divided the psalm into small units of one bicolon. Even here, however, the tendency towards double bicola, logically bound together, frequently makes itself felt. In the alphabetic psalms 111 and 112 the scheme adopted breaks the logical connexion even within the bicolon; here the single cola, not the bicola, are the constitutive units of the metre; only occasionally do the cola form logical bicola with a more or less obvious thought rhyme These rather artificial psalms are, however, the exception that confirm the rule of the constitutive character of the bicolon in Hebrew metrics.

7

The question of single or mixed metre is also disputed. By this we do not here mean whether cola consist of the same or different kinds of metrical feet (for instance iambs and anapaests), but whether the rule is that in one and the same poem only bicola of the same structure are to be used (e.g. only *mashal* bicola, or *qinah* bicola), or if the 'rule' permits an irregular mixing of all lengths of bicola (and cola).

[26] See Additional Note XXXVIII.

According to Sievers' views upon metre, most Hebrew poems must consist of an irregular mixing of all sorts of metrical bicola, arranged indifferently. This would seem, at least to the present author, to be a rather unmetrical 'metre'! But if we were to try to carry through a regular metre according to the metrical system of Sievers, it would lead to such numerous and violent alterations of the text[27] that the system would nullify itself.

There is no denying that texts for singing tend towards regularity of form, not least so in highly finished poetry like the psalms.

There is also no denying that many of the exceptions and irregularities, with which the system of Sievers has to reckon, disappear if we look upon the metre in the way maintained above. With such a history of tradition as that of the psalms, and considering that we are dealing with texts which have been used at the temple service through many centuries under the demands of changing ages, we must obviously take into account the probability that many of the psalms have not reached us in their original form; let us just think of all the revisions and re-writings of our own hymn books. The frequent uncertainty of the tradition is clearly seen if we compare the two versions of the same poem, Ps. 18 and 2 Sam. 22.

This means that a great many irregularities may be due to traditional or textual errors, or to re-writing which no longer adhered to the earlier rules. In many cases exegetic considerations—regardless of the metre—prove that there must be mistakes.

There are many psalms in which the regular metre—mashal metre or qinah metre or the tricolon $(4 + 4 + 4)$—is so evident that there is no need to discuss it.[28] And considering that in the lyric poet Deutero-Isaiah, who is so dependent on the psalm style,[29] there is many a word with the sole purpose of making the line of a verse complete and regular,[30] we are justified in thinking that the regular metre is the basic rule of Hebrew poetry. But of course, even here we have to distinguish between the more strict professional poetry, to which the psalms belong, and for instance the more free, impromptu prophetic speech.[31]

What has been said here does not of course imply that an alternation between, for instance, mashal and qinah bicola is in itself unthinkable. But considering the part played by the double colon and the double bicolon, with thought rhyme and strophic formation, we have a right to expect the bicola to alternate according to definite rules and not indiscriminately.

---

[27] This is the case with Rothstein, *Grundzüge d. hebr. Rhythmus*. See Additional Note XXXVIII.

[28] For instance Pss. 4; 5; 6; 8; 11; 12; 15; 18; 19B; 23; 26; 27; 28; 73; 95; 101; 103; 104; 114; 122; 130; 150.

[29] See *Ps.St.* II, pp. 195ff.; *GTMMM* III, p. 190 (§6a); references in notes 5 and 8 to Chap. XVIII.

[30] See Köhler, *Deuterojesaja*, pp. 56ff., cf. pp. 80, 97.

[31] Therefore we must not draw too positive conclusions with regard to the poetic art of the psalms either from the free irregularity of the Arabic popular poetry in Palestine at the present day or from the Coptic one of Egypt, to which for instance Baethgen alludes, referring to Dalman and Erman (*Die Psalmen,*[3] p. xxvii). The psalms are not popular poetry nor the improvisations of bards (cf. Barnes, *The Psalms* I, pp. 1ff.).

Such regular alternation does not seem to occur. The attempts made to prove that it does are much too speculative and intangible to be convincing.[32]

The evidence for single metres is to be found in the fact that they can be carried through in the individual texts without radical changes. This seems to me to be the case in the psalms. In fact, the alleged irregular mixed metre seems to be the result partly of incorrect tradition, partly of our deficient knowledge of the pronunciation in earlier times as well as of the subtle details of metrical art in Hebrew. There seems to be hardly any doubt that the tricola with climactic parallelism in Ps. 93 are not only dominant but intended, and to be carried out throughout the poem; the exceptions occurring all seem to be the result of the dropping of some words during the textual tradition; the original text may be restored by very simple supplementations.[33]

8

To be distinguished from an irregular mixed metre is the not infrequent alternation of metres in different sections of one and the same psalm. There the alternation is due to a change of contents and emotion. This is the case for instance with Ps. 60, in which the lamentation and the prayer in the first and last sections of the psalm are rendered in strophes of two bicola in the usual mashal metre (4 + 4 metrical feet), whereas the oracle in the central piece consists of short strophes of three cola of four feet each (4 + 4 + 4).

The theophany hymn of Ps. 77.14ff. has the same strophes of three cola in a brief enumerative style, whereas the psalm of lamentation, vv. 1–13, with its reflective thought of a pattern with the poetry of wisdom, displays mashal bicola in a broader, more elaborate style.

Such alternation within the same psalm may also be the result of the poet's incorporation of an earlier psalm in his poem. Thus the first half—the older part—of Ps. 19 is rendered in mashal metre, whereas the later half has the qinah metre. In Ps. 77 the tricolic hymnal part vv. 14ff. seems to be a fragment of an earlier psalm, which the later author of this reflective psalm of lamentation has adopted, and on which he, in a manner,

---

[32] See for instance Sachsse in *ZATW* 43, 1925, cf. also Möller in *ZATW* 50, 1932, Kraft, *The Strophic Structure of Hebrew Poetry.* The same thing applies to E. Lund in *Acta Orientalia* 17, 1939, pp. 249ff., who seeks to put order into the supposed 'mixed metres' by means of a complicated symmetrical system of foot-groups, covering the whole poem; the system is, however, too complicated for the ear to distinguish, and—in so far as it does exist—only perceptible to the eye, if put in figures; cf. Hempel in *ZATW* 57, 1939, pp. 276f. If the system of Sievers is given up, the very premiss—the probability of the existence of 'mixed metres'—disappears.

[33] The metre of Ps. 93 consists of 4-footed tricola, as may be seen from the evident 'feet of meaning' in v. 1; the 'threes' of Sievers in the following verses will therefore also have to be scanned as 'fours'. The tricolic (climactic) thought rhyme is perfectly evident in the tricola 1b + 2 and vv. 3, 4, 5. This entitles us to suppose that in v. 1 some words may have been left out by a homoioteleuton. Before *'ōz* add *hādhār wĕhôdh yhwh*, cf. 96.6; 104.1. In v. 2b one metrical foot is lacking—a predicate—add *kōnantāhû*, cf. the verbs in v. 3. In v. 4 read *'addîr mimmišbĕrê* (*BHK³* a–a). See the author's *Real and Apparent Tricola*, p. 13.

bases his confidence in, and appeal to, Yahweh. The promise to the seed of David, taken up by the author of the psalm of lamentation, Ps. 89 in vv. 20–28, is rendered in a stricter, more syncopated mashal metre than the hymnic section in vv. 2–19, and the final lamentation in vv. 47–52, where moreover the four 'metrical sense feet' and the dipodic structure are much more marked. The tricolic verses in Ps. 97.7–19 *may* mean that at this point the poet has taken up part of an earlier psalm; his own poem is rendered in mashal bicola. On the whole it seems questionable whether isolated tricola (with climactic thought rhymes) occur in psalmography, as Albright, for instance, thinks.[34]

[34] Albright (*Studies in Prophecy*, ed. Rowley, pp. 3ff.) speaks of 'tricola' in **Pss.** 92.10; 67.5; 96.7f.; 118.15f., 25 (besides 93, see the preceding note). The text itself—critical material given in the apparatus in *BHK*³—proves that he is wrong. See on the whole question the author's *Real and Apparent Tricola*.

CHAPTER XX

Israelite and Oriental Psalmography

I

In the preceding chapters we have already touched occasionally upon the relationship between Israelite psalmography and that of the rest of the ancient Near East. The discovery of hundreds of texts through excavations during the last century has proved that a rich cultic psalmography existed among the Sumerians as well as among the Babylonians, Assyrians, Egyptians, Canaanites, Hittites and other nations. Among all these peoples there was a constant cultural intercourse; in fact we are justified in speaking of a common old oriental culture, comprising the material as well as the ideological, the religious as well as the literary aspects of life, and going back originally to the ancient Sumerian culture. Israel, too, absorbed this common oriental culture. And we have now numerous indications that this influence also extended to the religious sphere, particularly in the cultic domain.[1] What has been said about most of the psalm types in the preceding chapters shows that the cultic and ritual 'framework' to which each of them belongs has analogies in all essentials in, for instance, the Babylonian and Assyrian cult; not least so with regard to the great annual festival, Yahweh's festival of epiphany and enthronement—so that we are justified in speaking of a common oriental 'cultic pattern' from which Israel adopted essential elements.

No wonder, then, that what struck people first of all when they got to know the Babylono-Assyrian psalms and cultic prayers and ritual texts, was that they were so much in keeping with biblical psalmography with regard to phraseology, metaphors and standard religious terms.[2] Even early Sumerian psalmography shows many surprising parallels with regard to the types, including their structure and forms, and also the terms and modes of expression. There are hymns to the gods and to the god-king, and 'national' psalms of lamentation occasioned by the enemy's devastation of land and city, etc.[3] On the whole we may say that all the essential characteristic features of the cultic poetry of Babylonia, Assyria and the other peoples of the Near East rest on the tradition created by the Sumerians. But we are still somewhat in the dark as to the relationship

[1] See, for instance, Albright, *A.R.I.* A great many more or less important details are mentioned in all recent presentations of the secular and religious history of Israel.

[2] See, for instance, the collocations in Widengren, *Accad. and Hebr. Pss. of Lament.*, pp. 37ff., 93ff., 197ff., 258ff., 311ff.; Driver in *The Psalmists*, pp. 109ff.

[3] Cf. Kramer in *BASOR* 88, 1942, pp. 10f.; Falkenstein and von Soden, *Sumer. u. Akkad. Hymnen u. Gebete.*

between Sumerian and Egyptian psalmography. There are great likenesses of form and content, but many of them need have no direct connexion. Psalmography everywhere springs from religious experiences and feelings and impulses common to all men, and so will frequently manifest itself in similar ways in different places and at different times. But obviously there was in ancient times an interchange of culture between the valley of the Nile and Mesopotamia, though we are not yet able to account for it. At present we cannot, therefore, say anything with certainty about the question of mutual influence between Egyptian and Mesopotamian religious poetry. The only thing that is certain is that they have both of them strongly influenced Canaan—in this as in most other domains of cultural and spiritual life.

Now there is not the least doubt that this psalm literature[4] is some thousand years or more older than Israelite and Jewish psalmography; nor that Israel in its cultural intercourse with the other peoples of the orient was on the whole the receiving partner. Consequently we must conclude that the psalmography of Israel came into existence under the influence of the earlier oriental one.[5] The most likely conjecture is that it took place with the Canaanites acting as an intermediary. Canaan was the political and commercial sphere of interest of all the empires of the orient, the thoroughfare and battle-ground of migrations and military and trading expeditions throughout the centuries for more than a thousand years. And the culture of Canaan was essentially a mixed culture, with elements from all the surrounding older and bigger nations at the head of the Mediterranean and throughout the Near East.

So the question is not so much whether such and such a psalm or such and such an idea and phrase, such and such a metaphor and term, has been influenced by or derived from Babylonian or Egyptian religious poetry. The question is whether there exists any broad and general connexion between religious poetry and its style-forms throughout the whole of the old orient, and next, what was the relationship of Israel to this earlier poetic culture and its modes of expression.

The answer to the first question is, in fact, quite clear. If we consider the overwhelming number of similarities in composition, metaphors, phrases and expressions, style forms, many basic ideas, we can entertain not a shadow of doubt that there are many and deep historical connexions

---

[4] Among easily accessible selections of translated texts and scientific investigations of oriental psalm literature may be mentioned the following:—selections of Babylonian-Assyrian psalms in translation: Jensen in *KB* VII. 2; Zimmern in *AO* VII. 3, and XIII. 1; Jastrow, *Relig. Bab. u. Ass.* I, pp. 393ff., II, pp. 1ff.; Ebeling in Gressmann, *AOT,²* pp. 241ff.; Ungnad, *Relig. d. Bab. u. Ass.*, pp. 156ff.; Stephens in *ANET*, pp. 383ff. Of more special works: those of Böllenrücher, Hehn, Perry, Schillmeyer and Pinchert. For Sumerian psalmography see Kramer in *BASOR* 88, 1942, pp. 10ff., and in *ANET*, pp. 382, 455; Jacobsen in *BASOR* 102, 1946, pp. 12ff. —and now especially Falkenstein & von Soden, *Sumer u. Akkad. Hymnen und Gebete.* For Egyptian Psalms: Erman, *Lit. d. Aegypter* [E.T., *The Lit. of the Ancient Egyptians*]; Ranke, in Gressmann, *AOT,²* pp. 12ff.; Roeder, *Urkunden;²* Gunkel, *Reden u. Aufsätze*, pp. 136f., 141ff.; Wilson in *ANET*, pp. 365ff. Hittite prayers: Götze in *ANET*, pp. 393ff. For *Old-Arabian* cult lyrics see Grimme in *Orient. Ltz.*, 1925, pp. 13ff.
[5] See Additional Note XXXIX.

between the religious poetry of all these oriental countries. Here as in many other domains we may as justly speak of a common oriental psalmography, as of a Babylonian one, an Egyptian one, etc. Who has influenced whom, it is often impossible to decide in any particular case. What matters is that we have here a great community of culture, which also embraces the style forms, the modes of expression, and the cultic framework and situations to which this poetry belongs. And when compared with Israel, the whole of this common literary culture is prehistoric. It existed throughout the orient, even before Israel entered Canaan and participated in the Canaanite or—as we might in many cases term it—the common oriental culture. A natural consequence of this is that the psalmography presents in a great many examples kinship of style as well as of expressions and ideas both with Sumerian, Babylono-Assyrian and Egyptian psalmography, and likewise Israel is seen to be the one to learn from an earlier literary tradition. This need not mean dependence on any definite model, for instance on some particular Egyptian poem or other, as some people have thought; it means participation in a common literary culture. But of course this does not put out of court the possibility that there may have been direct influences, for instance from the sun hymn of Pharaoh Akhnaton,[6] or that some Israelite psalms may be remodellings of earlier Canaanite ones.

Then the next question is, what has Israel made out of this? It is interesting both to the historian of literature and of religion—and to the historian of revelation—to study more closely what may have been the relationship between Israelite psalmography and that of the rest of the orient; what the Israelites may have learnt from the others; what they have made out of the things they adopted, and how they stamped them with their own religious character.

To make such a literary and religio-historical investigation possible much preparatory work is still needed. Oriental psalm literature has been investigated and systematized from the point of view of form history only to a small extent.[7] On the other hand the real cult-historical investigation is easier here, as the texts often contain information about the ritual framework and ceremonies to which a psalm belongs. As yet only separate motives and the usage of language and metaphors and certain religious ideas in oriental psalmography have been studied in detail. Therefore a

---

[6] Cf. Blackman in *The Psalmists*, pp. 180f. A sober-minded investigation of the relation between the sun hymn and Ps. 104 is given by Nagel in *Festschrift für Bertholet*, pp. 395ff.; he accepts an indirect influence but admits the possibility of its being direct.

[7] We have commencements of such an investigation in Stummer, *Sumerisch-akkadische Parallelen*; Cumming, *Assyr. and Hebr. Hymns of Praise*; Widengren, *Accad. and Hebr. Psalms of Lamentation* (which only in a lesser degree deals with the literary aspect and the composition, and scarcely at all with the form-historical method and point of view). More type-analytical investigation may be found in Castellino, *Le lamentazioni individuali e gli inni in Bab. e Israele*. Several special aspects of the question are dealt with by Gunkel-Begrich in *Einl.*, see index s.v. 'Aegyptisches' and 'Babylonisches'; Begrich in *ZATW* 46, 1928, pp. 212ff.; and more profoundly and systematically in Falkenstein & von Soden, *Sumer. und Akkad. Hymnen u. Gebete*, where many parallels to the biblical psalms in style and composition have been demonstrated.

comparison with regard to composition and 'type' must be content with somewhat general suggestions.

In the following survey it will be most practical to start with the different psalm types. Here the Sumerian and Babylono-Assyrian literatures provide the richest material.

2

Starting with the hymn of praise, we find most of its characteristic peculiarities present in Babylonian, partly also in Egyptian, psalmography.[8] By and large we find the same three main parts: the introductory call to praise, the main body of the hymn with an enumeration of the predicates of honour and great deeds of the god, and the final peroration. But in the introduction there is the difference that the plural and the direct invitation to the congregation do not occur; it is the call to oneself in the singular, which is the rule here: 'I will praise the champion of the gods' or something similar. This points to a difference in the very texture of religious thinking:[9] in Babylonia the person of the king is in a much higher degree the centre of the temple service, whereas in Israel the congregational point of view is much more prominent; besides, as already mentioned (pp. 93, 194), the we-form seems to be later and expresses a view which makes the individual member of the congregation stand out more.

In the Babylonian hymns the main part likewise consists of a reference to the titles of honour and the great deeds of the god, in the same short enumerative style in appositional attributes or relative clauses or a few co-ordinate principal propositions. The bare enumeration is much more prominent than in Israel; frequently the hymn is but an enumeration of the names and titles of the god and other glorifying predicates of a general character,[10] like 'strong hero', 'mighty lord', 'lord without equal' and the like. We also find rhetorical questions such as 'who is like you' or a negative sentence 'nobody is like you' and other ascriptions of praise.[11]

The theme of the hymn is the glorious qualities of the god, his benefactions and his powerful deeds, as a rule the constantly repeated and typical ones—'you who destroy the enemy', and the like—but not infrequently also certain fundamental works of salvation. Foremost among these latter in Babylonia we find the art of creation and the victory over the power of chaos.[12] The whole of the great epic of creation, the *Enuma eliš*, on twelve tablets, is conceived as a mighty hymn to Marduk, and ends with the enumeration of his fifty names of honour. Here the eulogy has been given quite an epic form, with its lengthy narrations and description, elsewhere too the hymns give a detailed description for instance

---

[8] See instances and references to sources in Gunkel-Begrich, *Einl.*, pp. 38, 41, 43, 45f., 48, 49, 53, 54, 55, 56, 58, 59, 68, 70, 72ff., 85.
[9] See Stummer, op. cit., p. 26; Gunkel-Begrich, *Einl.*, p. 38, cf. p. 123.
[10] See Stummer, op. cit., p. 22.
[11] See Gunkel-Begrich, *Einl.*, pp. 54f.
[12] Gunkel-Begrich, *Einl.*, p. 77.

of the overwhelming effect of his appearance or his wrath on gods and men.[13] The subject of the laudatory sentences is generally the god himself; but not infrequently it may be his name, his might, his divinity, his glory, his word.[14] Just as Ps. 29 is a hymn to Yahweh's word and its powerful effect, so the hymn to the moon-god Sin-Nannar describes the destructive as well as the creative and beneficial effects of his word.[15]

A notable form is the 'I-hymn', in which the god appears praising himself. In Israel we find imitations of this in the prophets, as we have seen (p. 92).

Just as the Israelite hymn of praise often ends in a 'wish of blessing' for the deity, such as, 'may the honour of Yahweh last for ever!', so likewise does the Babylonian hymn.[16]

On the whole the Egyptian hymn of praise is built up on the same fundamental pattern. We find the same enumerative style and stereotyped terms.[17] A characteristic feature is that the enumerative eulogy often consists of short references to the mythical deeds and adventures of the god—rather in the nature of a cue—references we generally do not understand, because we do not possess the texts containing the myths themselves.[18] Characteristic of Egypt is the hymn to the king Pharaoh, 'the good god',[19] or to the divine and powerful royal crown.[20] Sometimes the Egyptian hymn becomes more animated and genuine with picturesque and feeling descriptions and a religious fervency, as in the great Amon hymn[21] or the sun hymn of Akhnaton with its vivid little pictures of nature or human life prospering and advancing under the blessing rays of Aton.[22]

So there are numerous parallels between Israelite hymn poetry and that of the rest of the orient, with regard to style, pattern, and details. But at the same time a profound difference makes itself felt. We certainly find the same basic emotions in Israel and in Babylonia, Egypt, etc.: enthusiasm, worship, the desire to give honour and praise to God.[23] In fact these qualities and an intensity of religious feeling are characteristic of an Egyptian poem having many points of resemblance to Ps. 104, namely the sun hymn of King Akhnaton. Nor is this the only evidence of a religion at once intense and exalted in ancient Egypt.[24] But such instances are exceptions. In Babylonian and partly also in Egyptian hymns the eulogy is generally an introduction to a prayer for something one wants.[25] The naive

[13] See, for instance, Zimmern, *AO* VII. 3, pp. 12, 14.
[14] See Stummer, op. cit., pp. 18ff., 23f.; Zimmern, *AO* XIII. 1, pp. 21f.
[15] See Zimmern, *AO* VII. 3, pp. 11f.
[16] See, for instance, the Sin-Nannar hymn in Zimmern, *AO* VII. 3, p. 12.
[17] Cf. Erman, *Aegypt. Relig.*,² pp. 61, 73, and elsewhere.
[18] See Erman, op. cit., p. 32.
[19] Erman, *Lit. d. Aegypt.*, pp. 179ff., 318ff. [E.T., pp. 134ff.; 254ff.]
[20] Erman, op. cit., pp. 35f. [E.T., p. 10f.]
[21] Erman, op. cit., pp. 350ff. [E.T., pp. 281ff.]; Wilson in *ANET*, pp. 365ff.
[22] Erman, op. cit., pp. 358ff. [E.T., pp. 289ff.]; *ANET*, pp. 369ff.
[23] See Gunkel-Begrich, *Einl.*, p. 68.
[24] See Blackman in *The Psalmists*, pp. 177ff.
[25] Gunkel-Begrich, *Einl.*, pp. 85, 249.

idea of flattering the deity by means of ascriptions of honour shows through everywhere. That is why so many of these hymns are a dull and unending enumeration of honorific titles and phrases of homage, often in endless repetition.[26]

Even in Israel we find poetically jejune pieces, such as Pss. 105; 111; 135; 136 and others. And even here we sometimes come across the naïve belief that God enjoys eulogy, or we find eulogy consciously used as a motivation of the prayer, intended to ensure its being heard ('Gebetser-hörungsmotiv').[27] But on the whole this is rare. As a rule the hymn is a true outcome of 'disinterested piety', praising the greatness and glory of God, who is at the same time merciful and terrible, the God who 'is God though every land lie desert'. It is before Him that the authors of the hymns prostrate themselves in worshipping eagerness.

In Babylonia, too, they had the epiphany hymn, describing and praising the glorious appearance of the god at the festival, when he manifested himself for the blessing and salvation of his worshippers and for the destruction of his enemies. In fact, the 'I-hymn' is the outcome of this idea of epiphany. Several hymns actually belong to the festal procession on the festival day of the god and have for their theme his 'exit' from, and 'entry' into the temple.[28] Along with hymnic passages we find here the half 'conjuring' and indefinitely repeated prayer that his 'heart may find its peace and his house rejoice in him', so that he may prove merciful towards his city. On the other hand the tradition does not include any direct prototype of the real 'enthronement hymn'; this particular form seems to be a product peculiar to Israel.

It is also important to note that the true royal hymn is lacking in Israel. This deals with the—oriental—deification of the king. In Egypt it developed into real cult of the king, in which the king and his mighty works and his grace are praised in the style of a hymn to a god; the same style is also used in more secular poems in honour of the king: the line between 'religious' and 'secular', and between a cultic and a non-cultic panegyric is vague.[29] We find the deification of the king and hymns to the king in ancient Sumer and in Babylonia too,[30] though never in such a marked form as in Egypt. Here the hymn style recurs in the titles and ascriptions of honour given to the kings and in the enumeration of their great deeds in the royal inscriptions.[31] Only once do we find an echo of such royal hymns in the psalms of the Old Testament, namely in the description of the king in the nuptial poem, Ps. 45. That the hymn with its attitude and note of worship was appropriate for Yahweh alone was more or less clearly felt by the leading spiritual circles of Israel.

[26] Gunkel-Begrich, Einl., pp. 68f.
[27] See Pss. 104.34; 19.14, and above, pp. 203ff.; 230ff.; II.9ff.
[28] See Meissner, Bab. u. Assyr. II, pp. 160f. Cf. Pss. 44.2-4; 74.12-17; 80.9-12; 144.1f.
[29] See notes 19 and 20, and Erman-Ranke, Aegypten,[2] pp. 58f., 72f., 76, 83, 466; Roeder, Urkunden, pp. 72, 74, 78, 79.
[30] See Kramer in BASOR 88, 1942; cf. Zimmern, AO VIII. 3, p. 8f.
[31] See Mowinckel, Statholderen Nehemia, pp. 124ff.; Eucharisterion I, pp. 278ff.

3

We have already drawn attention to the fact that the Babylonian psalms of lamentation and prayer are generally royal psalms, in which the king as the representative of the people addresses the gods in the I-style. On the whole they belong to the type of 'national psalms of lamentation', and the background is most often political, some national disaster which has befallen king and people and country—defeat, depredation or rebellion. It is this, evidently earlier, I-form, which has also been adopted in many of the Israelite national psalms of lamentation (see above, pp. 92f.). Here we are face to face with the same difference in the religious and the social points of view as with the form of the introduction to the hymn. In the Babylonian autocracy the king himself is the one round whom in the official religion everything revolves; political and national disasters are primarily *his* disasters. In Israel the point of view is more 'democratic'; we find the people, the congregation itself, appearing as a fellowship of individuals, 'we', to complain before the God of Israel. The individual is conscious of being a member of a fellowship, and in the we-psalms the king's person generally recedes into the background.

The Babylono-Assyrian public psalms of lamentation also have their place in the temple cult.[32] On the whole they show the same main features and mode of expression.[33] They start with the invocation, which is generally an enumeration of the great names and ascriptions of honour of the deity and is frequently amplified into a hymnic description of his glory.[34] As a rule the whole of the first part of the psalm is hymnic; then follow the lamentations, generally developing into a monotonous description of the misery and abasement of the suppliant.[35] In the lamentations the enemies play a prominent part;[36] we also hear about the evil words of the enemies, which in addition to the sufferings have made the king ill;[37] likewise the enemies are sometimes simply called and characterized as sorcerers and demons.[38] As in the biblical psalms there is an alternation of lamentations and prayers and 'motives for being heard' without any strict rules, but often with a great many more repetitions and much more monotony than in the Bible. The forms of the prayer are often the same;[39] its subject is deliverance from danger, purification from sin and guilt,[40] guidance into righteousness of conduct and speech. Along with the prayer for revenge and retaliation on the enemy we also find words of cursing against him.[41]

---

[32] See Jastrow, *Relig. Bab. u. Ass.* II, pp. 1ff.
[33] See Widengren, *Accad. and Hebr. Pss. of Lament*, pp. 20ff.; Begrich in *ZATW* 46, 1928, pp. 225ff.
[34] See Gunkel-Begrich, *Einl.*, pp. 213f.
[35] Gunkel-Begrich, op. cit., pp. 363f.
[36] See Birkeland, *Feinde d. Indiv.*, pp. 352ff.
[37] Birkeland, op. cit., pp. 363f.
[38] See *Ps.St.* I, pp. 91ff.; Birkeland, op. cit., p. 377; cf. Mowinckel in *Eucharisterion* I, p. 307 at the bottom.
[39] See Gunkel-Begrich, *Einl.*, pp. 219f., 221, 222f., 225.
[40] Gunkel-Begrich, op. cit., p. 223.
[41] See Widengren, op. cit., pp. 292ff.

The optative mood is more frequent than in the biblical psalms: 'may thy heart find its peace', and the like; we are more apt to find the 'conjuring', 'magic formula' than the more personal prayer in the imperative.[42] On the whole the motivations of the prayer are the same; most prominent is the 'hymnic motive' and the 'motive of honour'. Along with these we also find the 'motive of confidence'.[43] Even the motives of 'penitence' and 'innocence' and, corresponding to them, the two types 'penitential psalms' and 'psalms of innocence' occur in Babylonia. The person praying confesses himself guilty both of the sins he knows and the sins he does not know, and humbles himself before the god.[44] But it may also happen that he finds no sin in himself, and pleads his innocence and his righteousness.[45] In Babylonia the motive of penitence is much more frequent than in Israel, where the suppliant as a rule pleads his innocence. But that is a consequence of the conception of sin being much more arbitrary in Babylonia and less ethically orientated. Behind it lies the idea that the deity is arbitrary: what is right in the eyes of man may be evil in the eyes of the god and vice versa: man can never know what may have outraged the god—or some god—and why he is so angry. That is why he confesses his sinfulness without any attempt at particularization.[46] After all, the Israelite stands more upright before his God. Job is an unthinkable type in Babylonian religion.[47] As a rule the psalms of lamentation end with a promise, of offerings as well as of songs of thanksgiving.[48]

In the Babylonian psalms, much more than in the biblical ones, we find a combination of the psalm of lamentation and the hymn of praise,[49] in consequence of the greater prevalence of the utilitarian idea that one had better flatter the god in order to ensure his goodwill. Repetitions of the different items and even of a whole train of ideas is characteristic of both of them.[50] The individual metaphors and terms are often identical,[51] and the answering oracle as part of the psalm likewise occurs both in Babylono-Assyrian and Egyptian psalms of lamentation.[52]

[42] See Gunkel-Begrich, *Einl.*, p. 224.
[43] See Begrich in *ZATW* 46, 1928, pp. 221ff.
[44] See Widengren, op. cit., pp. 176ff.
[45] Widengren, op. cit., pp. 179ff.
[46] Cf. the penitential psalm in Ungnad, *Relig. Bab. u. Ass.*, pp. 224ff.
[47] In spite of the so-called 'Babylonian Job', as depicted in the text translated by Zimmern in *AO* VII. 3, pp. 28ff., Ungnad, *Relig. d. Babl. u. Assyr.*, pp. 227ff.; *ANET*, pp. 434ff. The type of the 'Righteous Sufferer' is not rare in Mesopotamian literature; a similar text is edited by Lambert and Gurney in *Anatolian Studies* 4, 1954, pp. 65ff. (cf. W. von Soden in *Bibliotheca Orientalis* 10, 1953, pp. 8ff.). A Sumerian parallel is edited and discussed by Kramer in *Wisdom in Israel* (Rowley Festschrift), pp. 170ff. Undoubtedly there are many analogies between the Sumero-Babylonian texts and the book of Job, but more with regard to the outer situation of the Righteous Sufferer than his mental attitude and the 'solution' of the religious problem. In these respects Job is unparalleled in ancient oriental literature.
[48] Gunkel-Begrich, *Einl.*, pp. 247ff., 277. Less one-sided is Widengren, op. cit., pp. 86f., 311ff.
[49] See Gunkel-Begrich, *Einl.*, pp. 85, 213.
[50] Gunkel-Begrich, op. cit., pp. 241, 243.
[51] Gunkel-Begrich, op. cit., pp. 217f. The list of parallels in Widengren, op. cit., provides many instances.
[52] See Gunkel-Begrich, op. cit., pp. 137, 160f.

That there is here a historical connexion is evident. Just as obvious is the fact that the Israelite public psalm of lamentation in one respect at any rate represents a further development of the Babylonian one, namely in the 'we-psalms of lamentation'. But otherwise, they both—and each in its own way—bear the stamp of the different notions of God current in Israelite and Babylonian religion. It is unnecessary to enter into details about the difference caused by the monotheism of Israel, where, on the one hand, the suppliant sometimes declares that he does not expect any help from any powers other than Yahweh, and that he will have nothing to do with them,[53] whereas, on the other hand, in the polytheism of Babylonia we have psalms of lamentation 'to any god whatsoever.'[54] In the Israelite psalms the very qualities characteristic of Yahweh as compared with all other gods are emphasized. As in the hymn of praise, the appeal to the God of history is much more prominent in the Israelite psalm of lamentation. The different ethical orientation of the conceptions of God also makes itself felt.

In Babylonian religion we find another type of the psalm of lamentation, to which there is nothing corresponding in the religion of Israel, namely the psalm of lamentation over the dead god, the god of vegetation, of the Tammuz type.[55] Such laments were looked upon as foreign and idolatrous abominations in Israel.[56] But these laments also contained descriptions of the way the land withered up and became a desert when the god was not there. We sometimes find echoes of these thoughts in the description and the use of metaphors in Israelite psalms of lamentation occasioned by drought and ravaging locusts, etc.,[57] or as a motive for the prophets when describing the way all nature will be thrown out of gear as a result of the sins of the people,[58] or the way Yahweh will punish the fertility cult and its 'whoredom' by barrenness of fields and cattle and people [59]

Along with the national psalm of lamentation in the I-form the Babylonians also had truly individual or 'private' psalms of lamentation, connected with purification from illness, spirit possession or other kinds of impurity,[60] even if it is not easy to draw a line between the two groups. For they are built up in the same style and with the same mode of expression, just as in the Israelite national and individual psalms of lamentation. Common to both Babylonia and Israel is that these psalms have been occasioned by the same kinds of events, such as illness; and by similar cultic and ritual measures against the misfortune, including the use of psalms of lamentation. Here, too, Israel adopted a common 'ritual

---

[53] See Pss. 16.2–4; 115.
[54] See above, n. 46.
[55] See Zimmern, *AO* XII, pp. 11ff.; Witzel, *Tammuz-Liturgien.*
[56] Ezek. 8.14ff.
[57] Jer. 14; Joel 1–2.
[58] Jer. 3.3; 12.4; Hos. 4.3.
[59] Hos. 9.11f.; 4.10f.
[60] See Widengren, *Pss. of Lamentation*, pp. 241f.

pattern' and created a similar religious literature to meet the corresponding ritual need.

But on this point we also find an important difference between Babylonian and Israelite psalms, rising out of the strong emphasis on Yahweh as the only effective God. This had the result that in Israel even disasters and illness are much more firmly traced back to Yahweh himself: 'shall there be evil in a city, and the Lord hath not done it?' says Amos (3.6). Good and evil both come from Yahweh; evil is the punishment resulting from his wrath. We can trace the influence of this on the psalms of lamentation. In Babylonia illness and disasters are generally attributed to demons, sorcerers, and witchcraft.[61] Even the Israelites had the same ideas, but in the psalms of lamentation demons and sorcerers play only a minor part; even where these 'mischievous men' and "*āwen*-doers' are mentioned as 'enemies' and people who bring about illness, it is still Yahweh himself who is at the back of everything and permits them to play their game; his wrath against man's sins is the ultimate cause.[62] As a rule the old terms for sorcery and witchcraft are used in a toned-down and figurative sense for the curses and evil words and intrigues of the national enemies or traitors, and the disasters they have thus brought upon the worshipper.[63] Evidently the language used here in the Israelite psalms is due to a change of the original view, which is still alive in Babylonia.

4

The ritual thanksgiving psalm as a separate psalm species likewise came into existence in Babylonia long before the birth of Israel. There we have the national thanksgiving psalm with a historical and political background, of which we have several examples.[64] But as in the case of the national psalm of lamentation it is kept in the I-form: it is the king who offers thanksgivings for the salvation *he* has experienced. The main elements, the structure and the style-forms, are on the whole the same as in the Bible: an introduction in hymnic form, a (short) account of distress and salvation, and finally a thanksgiving hymn sung by the congregation.[65]

In Egypt we also find royal psalms of thanksgiving with a public, political background. The description of the distress and salvation in the royal psalm, Ps. 18, has so many features in common with the corresponding description in the inscription dedicated to the god Amon in Thebes by Pharaoh Ramses II,[66] that a direct influence has been suggested. The

[61] See Weber, *AO* VII. 4; Meissner, *Bab. u. Ass.* II, pp. 198ff.; Widengren, op. cit., pp. 246ff
[62] See above, Chap. VIII. 2.
[63] See Chap. VI. 3; VIII. 2, 4.
[64] An example, occasioned by the victory over the Elamites, will be found in Zimmern, *AO* XII. 3, pp. 7f.; Gunkel-Begrich, *Einl.*, p. 285. Another example, ibid., p. 286 at the top. The third psalm mentioned by G.-B., the so-called 'Job-psalm', is also a royal psalm with a public background and does not deal with an individual. Cf. also the Assyrian hymn of victory mentioned in n. 67, below.
[65] See Gunkel-Begrich, *Einl.*, p. 287.

relevant portion of the inscription has obviously the same style as the 'recital' of the thanksgiving psalms and proves that the Egyptians, too, had such royal psalms of thanksgiving. Here we might also refer to a victory hymn of the same kind, occasioned by the victory of the Assyrian king Tukulti-Ninurta I (1242–06) over the Kassite king Kashtiliash of Babylon.[67]

There are many clear indications that the royal, that is to say the public, thanksgiving psalm was used among the Phoenicians as well as among the Aramean Syrians.[68] The recital of distress, supplication and hearing of the prayer is also found in its very shortest form in the inscriptions on the votive tablets and columns which kings and magnates used to raise in grateful recognition of the hearing of a prayer, for instance, 'Memorial column raised by Birhadad, son of Tabramman, son of Hezion, king of Aram,[69] in honour of his lord Melkart because he (Birhadad) had prayed to him and he (Melkart) had heard his voice'.[70]

When religion became more 'democratic' all over the orient,[71] it paved the way for the rise of the private thanksgiving psalm. From Babylonia we have no positive evidence, but one of the royal psalms of thanksgiving mentioned above may be of a 'private' character in so far as it is occasioned by illness.[72] More closely related to the biblical psalms are some interesting Egyptian thanksgiving psalms no doubt of private character; the author is an official of the Amon temple at Thebes in Egypt, the painter Nebre, who thanks the god because his son has been cured of serious illness.[73] Here, too, the recovery is described as a deliverance from Sheol. The significant elements here are:

1. an introductory hymn of praise to the merciful god and a profession of faith in him;

2. the recital of the distress—in this case the illness of the son, due to his sin—and of the supplication to the deity, and his hearing the prayer; at this point occurs a rendering of the psalm of lamentation which the suppliant had composed in his distress, with the assurance of being heard which he had expressed, together with the promise which he then gave;

3. finally the thanksgiving, with a repeated profession of faith and testimony that Amon will help anybody who turns to him in trust. The parallels to Ps. 30 are striking.[74]

[66] Translation in Erman, *Lit. d. Aegypt.*, pp. 325ff.; see particularly pp. 329f. [E.T., pp. 260ff., and 263f.].

[67] See Ebeling in *MAOG* 12, 1938. We may also refer to the hymnic-epic texts from the time of the first Babylonian dynasty, see von Soden in *ZA* 40, 1931, pp. 163ff.; 41, 1932, pp. 90ff.

[68] See Gunkel-Begrich, *Einl.*, p. 285.

[69] See 1 Kgs. 15.18.

[70] See Ginsberg in *L. Ginzberg. Jub. Vol.*, pp. 159ff.

[71] See Chap. III. 7.

[72] See Gunkel-Begrich, *Einl.*, p. 287.

[73] See Gunkel, *Reden u. Aufsätze*, pp. 141ff.; *Einl.*, pp. 287ff.

[74] See Ginsberg, op. cit., p. 167.

Nor can there be any doubt as to the harmony of style. Biblical psalmography even here turns out to be a particular Israelite version of a species of religious literature common to the orient.

5

Our knowledge of Canaanite psalmography is much more fragmentary than those of Mesopotamia and Egypt.

From the number of set hymnic phrases which occur in the letters of homage from Canaanite princelings to the Pharaoh of the Amarna age—fifteenth and fourteenth centuries B.C.—scholars have concluded that the writers were using well-known expressions and quotations from the religious hymn literature in order to express their devout submission to their divine overlord, the 'good god' of Egypt.[75] Both expressions and metaphors in many ways agree with the divine hymns from Mesopotamia and Egypt. This proves that the international psalm style was well known in Canaan, so that terms and ideas from the latter would flow easily from the pen of the Canaanite scribes. No doubt they were familiar with them from their own temples and the cult there, which at that very time was strongly influenced by Egyptian religion and style.

Direct sources for our knowledge of Canaanite religious poetry have been furnished by the finds of Ras Shamra, the ancient Ugarit, which is also mentioned in the Amarna letters.[76] Very few real psalms have been found—or as yet deciphered. Two fragments in Akkadian are the best evidence so far;[77] in one of them we have the characteristic hymnic introduction: 'I will sing to Our Lady, the goddess. . . .' Then we have a text in Ugaritic, as yet rather obscure, containing an invocation of the god El or the goddess 'Anat.[78] But there are many epic and mythical cult texts, containing psalm-like features and proving that psalmography was known and practised in Ugarit.

We do not get any detailed picture of the psalm types and their structure in this way. But there is enough to prove that hymns of praise as well as invocations (prayer) in all essentials followed the patterns from Babylonia, which is also to be seen from the fact that texts have been found in Akkadian. The comparisons made by Patton and Coppens between

---

[75] See Böhl in *Theol. Lit. Blatt* 35, 1914, col. 337ff.; id., *De Psalmen* I, pp. 25ff.; Jirku in JBL 52, 1933, pp. 108ff.; Widengren, *Pss. of Lamentation*, pp. 5ff.

[76] Conspectus, with references to the literature, by Baumgartner in *ThR*, N.F. XII, 1940; XIII, 1941; id. *ThZ* III, 1947. The standard works for orientation on these texts are de Langhe, *Les textes de Ras Shamra*, and Gordon, *Ugaritic Manual*; id., *Ugaritic Literature*. A 'hymn to the gods Nikkal and Harḥab' is mentioned by Lods in *Bull. de la Faculté de Theol. Protest.* X, 1937, p. 7; the text in Virolleaud, *Syria* XVII, 1936, pp. 209ff. See further, Obermann in *JBL* 55, 1936, pp. 21ff.; Hempel in *ZATW* 55, 1937, pp. 303f., with references to the edition of texts and to literature. Naturally there is an echo of the psalm style in the addresses to the gods in the epic texts. More detailed investigations in Patton, *Canaanite Parallels to the Psalms*; see also Coppens, *Parallèles du Psautier avec les textes de Ras Shamra*. O'Callaghan, *VT* 4, 1954, pp. 164ff.; Cf. Burrows, *What Mean these Stones?*, pp. 41ff., 235, 268, *et al.*

[77] For the texts RS 94 and RS 95, see de Langhe, op. cit. I, pp. 211f.

[78] RS 13 + 43, see de Langhe, op. cit. I, pp. 173f.

biblical psalmography and Ugaritic religious poetry do not extend to
types of psalms and style of composition.

On the other hand there are many examples of purely linguistic and
'phraseological' conformity. This is also true of religious ideas and notions.
They throw light on many details in Hebrew psalmography and prove a
historical connexion. We may point to such notions as the one about El,
the supreme god, being the 'father' of the gods, the 'eternal' god, the
'father' of years and time, the king and lord, the protector of the poor, of
widows and fatherless; he is enthroned in the heavens, or on the divine
throne in the 'North',[79] on the 'mountain of the North' (ṣāphōn), the 'high
place'; he is 'the one who rides on clouds', 'the Cloud-Rider', or perhaps,
'Cloud-Driver',[80] he who creates and sends thunder and lightning and
rain.[81] We hear of his fight against the monsters of the sea and the dragon;[82]
the thunder is his 'voice'.[83] The words 'house' and 'castle' are both used
of the temple;[84] we hear of the 'courts' of the god and of his abode.[85]
There are allusions to the cedars of Lebanon and Siryon;[86] trees and
stones speak.[87] We hear of the 'blessings' of rain and dew[88] and how the
heavens shall perish as a garment.[89] We also find other instances of partly
literal conformity with the poetic modes of expression in Hebrew.[90] The
psalm of Habakkuk (Hab. 3) might almost be a collection of samples
showing such conformity.[91] In addition the different types of thought
rhyme agree in a striking way.[92]

The Ugaritic texts of which we are speaking were written down in the
fifteenth and fourteenth centuries B.C., but may be traced back to much
earlier originals, the major part of whose currency may have been in oral
tradition. The ideas and the cultural and literary form to which they give
expression were certainly not limited to Ugarit, but are typical of
Canaanite and Phoenician religion and culture as a whole; what little we
previously knew of Canaanite religion fits in excellently with the picture
from Ugarit.[93]

So we can hardly doubt that it was through the Canaanites that the
Israelites got to know the common oriental psalmography with its ideas
and mode of expression, and so received an impulse from without to

[79] Cf. Ps. 89.13 G, which reads ṣāphōn as a proper name, as in Ugarit.
[80] rōkhēbh 'ărābhōth, Ps. 68.5, Ugar. rkb 'rpt.
[81] Cf. Pss. 68.5, 34; 104.3; 10.11.
[82] See above, Chap. V.8.
[83] Cf. Pss. 29; 18.14; 46.7; 68.34; 77.18f.; 104.7.
[84] Ugaritic: byt and hkl—Hebrew bayith and hēkhāl.
[85] Cf. Pss. 116.19; 92.14.
[86] Cf. Ps. 29.5f.
[87] Cf. Ps. 96.12.
[88] Cf. Ps. 133.3.
[89] Cf. Ps. 102.26f.
[90] See the list in Coppens, op. cit., pp. 122ff.
[91] See Cassuto in Annuario di Studi Ebraici, 1935-37.
[92] See references above, Chap. XIX, n. 16.
[93] See Johs. Pedersen in Illustreret Religionshistorie, pp. 191ff.

furnish the cult of Yahweh in a like manner. David, so to speak, substituted Yahweh for El 'Elyon as the god to be worshipped in Jerusalem,
and took possession of the earlier sanctuary there for the new religion, and
eo ipso the Israelite cult entered into a religious form-culture which in all
essentials was common to the Near East, even if the ideas which the forms
were originally supposed to express, and so partly also the mode of
expression itself, underwent radical changes in the Yahweh religion.

6

There is also the possibility of other and more direct impulses and
patterns than those of Canaanite cultic tradition. The fact that David and
Solomon entered into diplomatic contact with other kingdoms, and had
scribes for their correspondence and organized a school for scribes in
Jerusalem, made it necessary to learn foreign languages. The international
diplomatic language of the time was Akkadian written in cuneiform
characters. This is proved by the Amarna letters. The scribes of David and
Solomon certainly had to learn Akkadian and probably also Egyptian
and Hittite. This meant that they had to study texts in those languages,
and that they would become acquainted with the kind of literature which
was particularly cultivated in the 'schools of wisdom' and was an outcome
of the educational and moral ideals of their order, the 'poetry of wisdom'
(the 'proverbs'). In fact, we are now certain that one of the sources of the
so-called 'Proverbs of Solomon' was an Egyptian book of wisdom,
'Amenemope's Wisdom', which has been rediscovered.[94] And just as a
Babylonian mythological poem, the myth of Nergal and Ereshkigal—used
by the scribes of the king as a text for exercises and furnished with marks
for reading—has been found among the texts of Amarna in Egypt, so may
Babylonian and Egyptian psalm texts have existed among the exercise
books used by the scribes of Jerusalem.

In fact the ancient Israelites were not afraid of imitating foreign patterns
in their ways of worshipping. Just as they did not hesitate to worship and
pay homage to Yahweh in a temple built in the usual Phoenician temple
style,[95] they wanted also to pay homage to Yahweh with psalms, as did
the ancient civilized nations, and thus express their relationship to Yahweh
in religious poetry, in cultic psalm singing and music.[96] The style and
forms in which to do so were there ready for use.

So, in principle, it is not a matter of direct influence from Babylonian
psalms particularly, but the adoption of a common oriental cultic and
poetic tradition, a common religious language mould already existing.

The religious literature of the other peoples also provided several
religious points of connexion. Psalmography itself, along with the 'wisdom

[94] See Erman, *Eine aegypt. Quelle d. Spr. Salomos*; Gressmann in *ZATW* 42, 1924, pp. 272ff.;
more detailed index of literature in Gemser, *Sprüche Salomos*, pp. 8ff. Translation of the text in
ANET, pp. 421ff.
[95] See Galling, art. 'Tempel' in *BRL*; Parrot, *Le Temple de Jérusalem*.
[96] See above, II.146ff., 150ff.

literature' of the Babylonians, Egyptians and Canaanites, gives so many indications of lofty ideas about the deity, indeed even of monotheistic trends,[97] and of a truly religious relationship to the deity,[98] that such texts not infrequently require merely a very slight adaptation in order to express what the Israelite believed about Yahweh and felt towards him. So there is nothing to prevent us from thinking that certain Israelite psalms may be directly based on Egyptian and Canaanite ones. As already mentioned, such a thesis has been maintained several times with regard to Ps. 104 and Akhnaton's hymn to the sun.[99] There are also good reasons to suppose that the first part of Ps. 19, which is without doubt a fragment of an earlier poem included by the author in his own psalm,[100] originally belonged to a Canaanite creation hymn to the sun.[101]

The apocalyptic literature affords the best evidence for showing that even Judaism was open to such influences from without. Therefore we may at least mention here the surprising parallelisms both of ideas and of phraseology between Ps. 139 from Jewish times and an Indian hymn. Both start with an elaborate contemplation of the 'omnipresence' of God, and end with a prayer for him to destroy his evil enemies.[102]

7

Whether the historical connexion also includes the metre is harder to say. As already mentioned, the majority of Hebrew psalms are based on a four-footed line (hemistich, colon), strung together by twos into a complete verse which makes a logical metrical unit (the 'thought rhyme').

In Babylonian psalmography the dominating metre is likewise line couplets of two four-footed hemistichs.[103]

According to Erman the short verse line of Egyptian poetry consists of

---

[97] See, for instance, A. Jeremias, *Monotheistische Strömungen*; id., *Handbuch*, pp. 226ff.; Albright, *ARI*, pp. 30f., 33; Eissfeldt, *El im ugaritischen Pantheon*, pp. 69f. Most obvious are the monotheistic reform attempts by Pharaoh Ikhnaton, see Erman, *Aegypt. Relig.*,[2] pp. 77ff. Ikhnaton's well-known sun hymn has been translated among others by Erman, *Lit. d. Aegypt.*, pp. 358ff. [E.T., pp. 288ff.]; Ranke in Gressmann, *AOT*,[2] pp. 15ff.; Wilson in *ANET*, pp. 369ff.

[98] Particularly well brought out by Widengren, *Pss. of Lament.*, p. 42 and elsewhere; cf. also Cumming, *Hymns of Praise*. Gunkel-Begrich *Einleitung in die Pss.*, are inclined somewhat to underestimate the religious efforts of the Babylonians, whereas Widengren can hardly be said to avoid overestimating and equating too nearly with the religion of the biblical psalms (see my review in *NTT* 41, 1940, pp. 155ff.).

[99] See above, notes 66 and 97.

[100] See Additional Note XL.

[101] See Schroeder in *ZATW* 34, 1914; *Ps.St.* VI, p. 76; Morgenstern in *HUCA* XIX, pp. 515ff. It is less likely that Ps. 29 is a slightly remodelled Canaanite psalm, as Ginsberg thinks, *A Phoenician Hymn in the Psalter*; cf. Gaster in *JQR* 37, 1946–47. Nor is the opinion of Albright tenable, that the psalm of Habakkuk, Hab. 3, has been composed out of earlier fragments, directly adopted from Canaanite tradition (*Studies in Prophecy*, ed. Rowley, pp. 1ff.); it is inconsistent with the uniformity of idea pervading the whole poem, see Mowinckel in *GTMMM* III, pp. 715f., id. in *ThZ* 9, 1953, pp. 1ff.

[102] See Hommel in *ZATW* 47, 1929, pp. 110ff.

[103] See Zimmern, *AO* VII. 3, pp. 9f. Falkenstein and von Soden, *Sumer. u. akkad Hymen u. Gebete*, pp. 39ff. The authors allow also for intermingled 3 beat hemistichs (cola); I cannot, however, see why a long word should not be scanned with 2 beats as admittedly happens often in Hebrew (admitted even by followers of Sievers), see, e.g., Gunkel, *Die Psalmen*, pp. 633f.

two to four feet;[104] he then takes for granted that its basis is some kind of 'rhythm of meaning' ('thought rhyme'). He also seems to take for granted that every 'essential word' in the sentence has only one rhythmical accent; but this cannot simply be assumed, nor does it agree with the fact that in most literatures poetry is in an intermediate stage between a pure 'metre of meaning' and a strict metrical system, which is not indissolubly linked to the logical units.[105] I cannot help feeling that the Egyptian examples quoted by Erman are most naturally read in a rhythm of four beats.

Albright has maintained that in Canaanite poetry the double three-footed verse line—the stichos consisting of two hemistichs—is the fundamental one.[106] I do not think that this is correct, either, and it seems to me that here Albright actually starts from the prejudice, to which so many investigators still adhere, that Sievers is right in supposing the fundamental Hebrew metre to be the stichos, or 'bicolon' of 3 + 3 feet. If we start from the principle of a 'rhythm of meaning' and are justified in thinking that the earlier Canaanite-Hebrew language had rules for the secondary accent corresponding to those of biblical Hebrew, we find in the poems from Ugarit a great many hemistichs (cola) which have to be read as four-footed verses, and so many in which the rule of a secondary accent makes it natural to give to a compound word two metrical accents, that we must be right in supposing that here too the line of four feet is dominant. To my mind this applies to the very example given by Albright of his three-feet scansion.[107]

At any rate it is quite certain that Egyptian, Babylonian and Canaanite poetry are all based on the principle of thought rhyme: two hemistichs (cola) make the 'parallel' members of a whole verse. In Egyptian, two such whole verses very often stand in some sort of parallel relationship to each other, making a 'strophe'; strophes of three hemistichs (cola), tricola, also occur.[108] To a great extent the same is the case in Babylonian poetry. Even in Ugaritic poetry we find the law of the thought rhyme. Here, too, we have as a rule stichs (bicola) of two, but sometimes even three, parallel hemistichs.[109] Here, too, the thought rhyme is varied in many ways with great art;[110] most of these types are recognizable in Hebrew poetry; and this also applies to the so-called 'climactic parallelism'.[111] The prophetic psalm of Habakkuk (Hab. 3), describing the

[104] See *Lit. d. Aegypt.*, pp. 10f. [E.T., pp. xxxiff.]. Cf. also Albright's treatise in *JPOS* II, 1922, pp. 69ff.

[105] See above, Chap. XIX. 1.

[106] See 'The North Canaanite Epic', *JPOS* XII, 1932, pp. 185–203; cf. XIV, 1934, p. 248, n. 15; *Cathol. Bibl. Quarterly*, 1945, pp. 19ff.

[107] *Cathol. Bibl. Quarterly*, 1945, p. 21. See above, n. 19 to Chap. XIX.

[108] Erman, *Lit. d. Aegypt.*, pp. 9f. [E.T., pp. xxxff].; Pieper, *Aegypt. Literatur*, pp. 12, 16: as a rule 2 accented syllables. But they often seem to belong together as 2 + 2 (dipodic 4-footed colon). In Coptic poetry the 3-footed verse became the rule.

[109] Albright, op cit., p. 21; Ginsberg in *Orientalia* V, p. 171; Gordon, *Ugar. Grammar*, pp. 80ff., 85ff.; id., *Ugar. Manual*, pp. 109ff., 114ff.

[110] See Gordon, loc. cit.; Albright in *Studies in Prophecy*, ed. Rowley, pp. 3ff. See n. 16 to Chap. XIX.

[111] See Albright, loc. cit.

expected interference of Yahweh against the Assyrians in the style of the hymns of epiphany and enthronement[112] shows how marvellously the style traditions of Canaanite time were kept alive all through the period of the monarchy.[113]

Even with regard to the art-form we may therefore maintain that Canaanite religious poetry was the immediate pattern of Israelite cultic poetry.[114]

What was incompatible with Yahwism was dropped—and this applies above all to the idea of the death and resurrection of the god and to all the sexual rites and the cultic expressions of the fertility cult; the rest of it was imbued with the spirit of the Yahweh religion and used as a mode of expressing the people's feelings when face to face with the Holy One in the cult, for their praise and worship, their lamentations and prayers, and to convey the promise of the deity, and thanksgivings for his word and his help.

[112] See Mowinckel in *GTMMM* III, pp. 715f., and in *ThŽ*. 9, 1953, pp. 1ff.

[113] Cf. Cassuto in *Annuario di Studi Ebraici*, 1935–37, pp. 7ff.; Albright, op. cit., pp. 1ff.

[114] This is of course very important. But it seems an exaggeration when Albright (op. cit., p. 7, n. 24) declares that 'Psalm criticism now stands on the threshold of a new day, in sharp contrast to the situation between 1900 and 1935'. Ugarit has not contributed very much to the understanding of the *essential nature* of biblical psalmography; nor is psalm criticism after the Ugarit findings in a position which is in principle different from the one maintained for instance by the present author in *Psalmenstudien*. See also my paper in *VT* V, 1955, pp. 13ff.

CHAPTER XXI

Earlier Collections
The Compilation of the Psalter

I

The collecting of the psalms did not take place all at one time. The Psalter is quite evidently composed of several earlier, shorter collections.

That such is the case may be seen from the fact that there are several doublets in the collection. Ps. 14 = 53; Ps. 79.2-6 = 40.14-18; Ps. 108 = 57.8-12 + 60.7-14.

In Ps. 72.20 we find a note saying that this is the end of the psalms of David, and yet a whole series of Davidic psalms follows; so Ps. 72.20 was once the concluding note of a separate collection of psalms with the heading 'By (or "for") David'.

In Pss. 2-41 'Yahweh' is nearly always used as the name for God, whereas Pss. 42-83 use 'Elohim' (=God); furthermore we find that Ps. 14 has Yahweh, while the doublet Ps. 53 has Elohim. In other passages the language itself shows that Elohim has been substituted for an original Yahweh; for instance, such combinations of words as 'Elohim, thy (or my) Elohim' instead of an original 'Yahweh, my Elohim' (=God); or the ungrammatical *yahweh 'ĕlōhîm ṣĕbā'ôth* (Ps. 80.5) instead of the correct *yahweh 'ĕlōhê ṣĕbā'ôth*; here the corrected 'Yahweh' has been kept side by side with the correction 'Elohim' which has been made quite mechanically here irrespective of the fact that together with the following *ṣĕbā'ôth* it would have to be *'ĕlōhê ṣĕbā'ôth* (God of hosts).

From these and many similar observations we may infer the existence of the following earlier collections.

2

a. Pss. 3-41, all with the heading 'by David' formed a separate collection, *Psalms of David (I)*, 'the first Davidic Psalter'. The only psalm in which this heading is lacking is Ps. 33, which may have been added to the collection later.

To end the collection we find chosen the psalm which for some reason or other had been furnished with the formula of doxology and the 'amen' of the congregation, features that ended the cultic act for which the psalm was then used (Ps. 41.14). For, as will be seen from a comparison between Ps. 106.48 and 1 Chron. 16.36, the concluding doxologies in Pss. 41; 72; 89; 106 are connected with the use of each psalm in the temple service of post-exilic times, and were not added by the collectors as 'concluding formulas' for the separate collections; it is the collectors who have later used them as concluding doxologies for the psalm collections.

b. Pss. 42–83 once made up a separate collection. This is recognizable from the fact that the original 'Yahweh' has generally been replaced by 'Elohim', God. The reason for the alteration is that later times shrank from pronouncing the name of God, and so the change is linked to the use of this collection in the temple service. As can be seen from the book of Chronicles, there was a period when 'Yahweh' was pronounced 'Elohim' in the service rather than 'Adonai' (The Lord), which became the usual pronunciation at a still later time. This collection is usually referred to as 'The Elohistic Psalter'.

It actually consists of several smaller collections. Among these must be mentioned:

c. A collection of *Korahite Psalms*, Pss. 42–49. It is arranged according to 'types', that is to say, types in the service, indicated by the different technical terms in the headings: first a group of *maschils* ('efficacious songs') Pss. 42–45, then a *šîr* ('song') Ps. 46, and finally a group of *mizmors* ('psalms') Pss. 47–49. For these terms see below, Chap. XXIII.

d. Further, a second collection of *Davidic Psalms (II)*, Pss. 51–72. 'By (or "for") David' is lacking in the title of Pss. 66, 67 and 71 (many manuscripts and the LXX have this note for 67 and 71); this may indicate that the heading was originally put at the head of the whole collection and was only gradually added to each individual psalm; but it may also be that these three psalms have been added to the collection later. Pss. 52–55 are *maschils*, Pss. 56–60 *michtams* ('psalms of atonement'); Pss. 62–65 and 66–68 are *mizmors*; in Pss. 69–71 we find no indication of the type, which may be the reason why they are put last; among these we ought to find Ps. 61, whose present place may be due to alterations of the original sequence; this may also be the reason why a single *mizmor*, Ps. 51, has been put first. The very last is Ps. 72 with the heading *lišĕlōmōh*, which in this case is probably not meant to be 'by Solomon', but '(by David) for the king's son (v. 1) Solomon'. In this case also a psalm which had the liturgical concluding doxology and the 'amen' of the congregation (see Ps. 72.18–19) has been put at the end of the collection, as with Pss. 3–41. Last of all, the collector of 'the second Davidic Psalter' has added a note marking the end of *these* Davidic psalms, namely Ps. 72.20: 'The prayers of David the son of Jesse are ended'.

e. In Pss. 73–78 the collector of the Elohistic Psalter has included a collection of *Psalms of Asaph*, to which probably Ps. 50 once belonged. This psalm is likely to have been transferred to a place immediately before the *Psalms of David (II)* and alongside Ps. 51, because its view of sacrifices and the proper worship of God agreed with Ps. 51 and would supplement what that psalm had to say about the matter.

f. Pss. 84–89 form a separate little collection of *Korahite* psalms, since both Heman (Ps. 88) and Ethan (Ps. 89) were supposed to belong to the sons of Korah (see above, II.97). A solitary Davidic psalm, 86, has been included. In this collection the original 'Yahweh' has usually been retained.

Once again the psalm furnished with a liturgical conclusion has been put last, see Ps. 89.53.

Since in Pss. 84–89 'Yahweh' has not been replaced by 'Elohim', this group was probably not included in the Elohistic Psalter as an extension but was put after Ps. 83 by a collector who combined the 'first Davidic Psalter', the 'Elohistic Psalter' and Pss. 84–89, 'the second Korahite Psalter' into one larger collection—Pss. 3–89. Maybe it was the same man who prefaced the whole collection with Ps. 2.

Within the remaining group, Pss. 90–150, may be distinguished several smaller groups, some of which at some time may have constituted separate small collections:

g. Pss. 120–134, which form a separate collection of 'songs for the procession', as stated in the headings. No doubt most of these psalms were originally composed for use at the festival of harvest and tabernacles, alluding as they do to the complex of ideas characteristic of the latter: mostly likely, too, the group has been arranged with a view to this festival.

The Jews used to call this group, together with Pss. 135 and 136, 'the great Hallel' (see below); probably these two psalms also belonged to the same collection, perhaps as an addition.

h. The *enthronement psalms*, Pss. 93; 95–99 (100), may have constituted a separate collection. Why the national (congregational) psalm of lamentation 94 has been included amongst them is hard to tell: perhaps because it may have been used at the enthronement festival as a psalm of supplication for the coming of God's 'kingdom'.

i. A separate collection or group is made up of Pss. 113–118, the so-called 'Hallel', also called the 'Egyptian Hallel', to distinguish them from Pss. 146–150, called by the same name, and from the 'great Hallel' Pss. 120–136 (see above). The name refers to the term 'Hallelujah' in the superscription to each psalm in the collection and accompanying the singing as a refrain after each strophe or distich. In the time of Jesus, for instance, Pss. 113–118 were sung in the homes at the Passover festival, 113–114 before, and 115–118 after the meal. The origin of this custom is of course that these psalms belonged to the temple liturgy of the Passover festival. Most of them contain references to the Exodus and have indeed been composed as Passover psalms; that is why they have been collected as a group.[1]

j. Pss. 146–150, the 'Hallel psalms' (see above) also make up a special group, sung with 'Hallelujah' as a refrain; cf. headings and endings. The Jews of the time of Jesus and later also used them for morning prayer. The references to Yahweh's kingship and his creation and to the deliverance and restoration of Jerusalem seem to prove that the group was

[1] On the origin and ritual use of the Hallel see Finkelstein in *HUCA* XXIII. 2, pp. 319ff.

arranged for use at the festival of harvest and new year (Tabernacles).

k. Even the three 'hallelujah psalms'; Pss. 105–107, may have constituted a separate collection. Ps. 106 is furnished with a concluding doxology,
v. 48. A comparison with 1 Chron. 16.36 shows that the psalm was already
furnished with this doxology when used in the temple service. So the
formulas of doxology, Pss. 41.14; 72.18f.; 89.53; 106.48, have not been
added by the collectors in order to mark the 'end of a book'; they can be
traced back to the liturgical use of the psalm, and in some cases they are
original, but in others had been added to the text before the collection was
made.

It is doubtful whether separate small collections can be distinguished
within the group Pss. 90–150. It is likewise uncertain whether the whole
of this group ever constituted a separate collection, or whether the smaller
groups and individual psalms were gradually added to the earlier collection, Pss. 2–89; the latter is the more likely.

3

So the Psalter probably came into existence in this way: first several
smaller collections sprang up:

a. 'The first Davidic Psalter', Pss. 3–41, with the final doxology Ps.
41.14; and the three other smaller groups mentioned above: the 'Korahite
Psalter', the 'Second Davidic Psalter', with the final doxology Ps. 72.18–19
and the final note 72.20, and the 'Asaphite Psalter'.

b. Out of the last three above was then formed the large basic collection,
the 'Elohistic Psalter', Pss. 42–83, perhaps with the later addition of Pss.
84–89.

c. The combination of the 'first Davidic Psalter' and the 'Elohistic
Psalter' marks the third stage. Pss. 84–89 may not have been added till
this combination took place. As a counterpart to the concluding royal
psalm, Ps. 89, the collection, Pss. 3–89, has had prefixed the anonymous
royal psalm, Ps. 2, as an introductory psalm. Ps. 89.53 provides the 'concluding doxology' of the whole collection.

d. Then the collection, Pss. 2–89, was gradually extended by means of
other small collections—perhaps both earlier and later ones: Pss. 93–100,
113–118, 120–134 (136) and 146–150, and some individual psalms.
Perhaps the group, Pss. 90–106, had already been formed out of these
psalms and become a separate booklet.

e. No clear principles governing the arrangement of the single psalms
within the smaller collections can be demonstrated; even though scholars
have indicated certain considerations that may have had their influence.[2]

---

[2] Attempts to demonstrate such principles can be found in the commentaries, especially the
older ones (e.g. Hengstenberg, Hitzig, Delitzsch), but also in Bentzen, *Salmerne*, p. 419 (the
arrangement of Pss. 73–82), partly in papers and articles, e.g. by Köster, Jacob (in *ZATW* 18,
1898), Dahse, Snaith, etc. The whole problem is dealt with by Niemeyer, *Het probleem van de
rangschikking der Psalmen*, with a critical review of earlier attempts. But even his own suggestions
do not lead to any convincing positive results.

It follows from what has been said above that the smaller collections have come into existence on different principles: common origin within a guild of singers (Asaph psalms, Korah psalms), supposed authorship (the Davidic Psalters I and II), liturgical use (the maschils, the michtams); often in accordance with literary type (the *ma'ālôth* psalms, the enthronement psalms), sometimes even catch-words (the hallel psalms).

The sequence of the smaller collections within the Psalter seems to have been decided by the *gradual* joining of the single smaller collections into greater units. It may be taken for granted that the Davidic Psalter was deliberately put first. Within the circles of the collectors David was considered the originator and protagonist of psalm poetry.

We have mentioned above (§2e, f) that the last redaction of the Psalter may have displaced this or that psalm from its original place within one of the minor collections.

At the time of the final redaction Ps. 1 was prefixed to the collection as a kind of 'motto' for the aim and use of the whole Psalter.

4

In the manuscripts the Psalter is divided into five books: Pss. 1–41; 42–72; 73–89; 90–106; 107–150: above the last four of these stands 'Second Book', 'Third Book', etc. The form of the letters (a smaller size) shows that these headings do not derive from the actual collectors of the Psalter, but belong to the so-called 'Massoretic marginal notes', and consequently are much later than the emergence of the Psalter.

The division into five, probably in imitation of 'The Law', came last of all. It only partially coincides with the divisions between the original smaller collections, but follows the liturgical doxologies, which happened to occur in the texts from the earlier collections: Pss. 41.14; 72.18f.; 89.53; 106.48.[3] These were taken to be intended divisions and concluding doxologies between 'the books', and then Ps. 150 might be looked upon as the concluding doxology of the fifth section, and of the whole Psalter. Originally, as we have said, these doxologies had nothing to do with the collection, neither with the earlier smaller collections, nor with the composition of the Psalter as a whole.[4]

5

How many psalms are there in the Psalter? The tradition of the scribes allows for 150 psalms in all.

The Greek translation, the Septuagint (LXX), also has the same number, and yet it divides the text in a different way. It supposed Pss. 9

[3] See above, §2a, d, f, h.—Eerdmans, *Hebrew Book of Pss.* (*OTS* IV), pp. 23ff., and Niemeyer, op. cit., pp. 71ff., are evidently right in saying that these 'doxologies' are not meant to be the end of a book but are earlier liturgical additions to the individual psalms concerned.

[4] Snaith (*ZATW* 51, 1933, pp. 302ff.) thinks that the division into five has to do with a supposed cycle of 3 years for the reading of the Psalter in the service of the synagogues.

and 10 to be one psalm, and likewise Pss. 114 and 115. On the other hand, Pss. 116 and 147 are each divided into two psalms.

The division in the Massoretic text is not quite correct. LXX is no doubt right in making Pss. 9 and 10 into one psalm; this is proved by the alphabetic pattern, as well as by the lack of heading to Ps. 10. Pss. 42–43 are likewise one psalm, with the same refrain. On the other hand there is no reason to join 114 and 115 into one.

Whether it is correct to divide Ps. 147 into two parts cannot be decided with certainty. That a division of Ps. 116 is wrong is proved beyond doubt by the homogeneity of form and style history.

Suggestions have also been made to divide Pss. 22, 27, 40 and others into two parts, but without sufficient reason.[5] This means that the Psalter really contains 148 or 149 psalms.

It is clear from 1 Sam. 2; Jonah 2; Isa. 38.1; 1 Chron. 16 and other passages,[6] that other psalms existed, which are not included in the Psalter.

6

When was the Psalter compiled? Or rather: when was the work of collecting completed—for it was a lengthy process.

The Psalter as we know it today is at any rate earlier than *ca.* 130 B.C., when the Greek translator of the book of Jesus Sirach wrote his preface to the book. His words presuppose the existence of a Canon in three parts,[7] and the Psalter has always stood first in the 'Writings', the third part of the Canon. It is also evident from his words that at his time the tripartite Canon already existed in Greek translation, and we may certainly believe that some generations passed between the completion of the Hebrew Canon and the completion of the Greek translation.

But the translator of Sirach also tells us that his grandfather Jeshua ben Sira ('Sirach') living about 190 B.C., had eagerly studied this collection of the Scriptures in three parts, handed down from the fathers. Nor can there be the least doubt about this, for it is quite evident from Sirach's book itself.

Now the objection may be raised that the third part of the Canon, the 'Writings', was not yet quite finished in the age of Sirach. That is quite true; the book of Daniel was written in the year 165 or 164 B.C. But then Daniel was the latest scripture to be included in the Canon. A Canon consisting of 'the Law, the Prophets and the Writings' already existed at the time of Sirach. But to the best of our knowledge the Psalter has always stood first in the 'Writings'; in fact the Canon is sometimes called 'The Law, The Prophets and The Psalms' (Luke 24.44). Even if the third part, the 'Writings', had not yet been finally defined at the time of Sirach, yet it would at any rate contain the Psalter.

[5] For Ps. 27 see Birkeland in *ZATW* 51, 1933, pp. 216ff.
[6] For details Gunkel-Begrich, *Einl.*, pp. 4ff.
[7] See Bentzen, *Introduction to the O.T.* I, pp. 27f.

This is corroborated by Sirach's view of David. When he says about him that 'he ordered stringed instruments for the singing before the altar and an elaborate equipment for the annual celebrations of the feasts' (47.9f.), it is exactly the same view as the one which the Chronicler expresses.[8] But obviously Sirach's view of David has also been determined by the Psalter: 'In all his deeds he offered hymns of thanksgiving and paid homage to the most high God, with all his heart he loved the one who had created him, and with all his soul offered him thanksgiving' (47.8). Evidently Sirach is here thinking of the psalm headings, referring the individual psalms to different events in the life of David, and when using the term 'loved' he is directly referring to Ps. 18.2. And when he further says of David that Yahweh 'has exalted his horn for ever and given unto him the law of the kingdom' (47.11), i.e. the right to the kingdom, he is also referring to psalm passages such as Pss. 89.18; 132.17; 89.29.

I Maccabees, written about the year 100 B.C.,[9] introduces the psalm quotation Ps. 79.2f. as a 'scripture text', and regards the Psalter as a canonical writing.[10]

The same is true in even the earliest Maccabean times. When the festival for the re-consecration of the Temple—the Hanukka festival (feast of dedication)—was instituted after the deliverance of the city from the Syrians, no new festival psalm was composed for that day, but the most suitable psalm from the Psalter was chosen and given a new meaning, namely Ps. 30. The Maccabees felt restricted to the canonical psalm collection.[11]

So the Psalter cannot under any circumstances be later than about 200 B.C. The theoretical possibility that some psalm or other may have been put in later cannot be excluded, but we should need positive evidence for any such theory.

How much older than this it is, is most uncertain. There has been a tendency to conclude from 1 Chron. 16.36 that the Chronicler must have known the quinquepartite Psalter; for here he quotes Ps. 106. 48, and it has been supposed that this verse was only added to the psalm by way of a final doxology to the fourth 'book'. However the odds are that this final verse is not a result of the division into five parts, but rather one of the causes of it, and that it was already added to the psalm for liturgical use.[12] If so, the Chronicler need not have taken the psalm quotation from the completed Psalter, but from one of the earlier collections or from his own knowledge of the temple library and of the liturgical psalms[13]—the Chronicler probably belonged to the Levites, perhaps he himself was a 'singer'.

[8] 1 Chron. 25.1, 3, 6; cf. 16.4.
[9] Cf. Bentzen, op. cit. II, p. 22; Kautzsch, APAT I, p. 31; Charles, APOT I, p. 60.
[10] 1 Macc. 7.17. Cf. reference to Ps. 146.4 in 1 Macc. 2.63.
[11] See above, Chap. XVIII. 6.
[12] This is, for instance, the opinion of Baethgen, Die Psalmen,³ p. XIV.
[13] See above, §§ 2f., and Gunkel-Begrich, Einl., p. 439.

There is still another statement in the book of Chronicles, from which may be gleaned something more. In 1 Chron. 15–16, the Chronicler tells about the institution of the Yahweh cult on Zion under David and the transfer of Yahweh's ark thither; his main source is as usual the earlier record, in this case 2 Sam. 6; but he also introduces several details which obviously do not fit in with the conditions at the time of David; these details are certainly not just free fancies on the part of the Chronicler, but a reflection of the festal cult of his own day or (and) the time immediately preceding. Now even in 2 Sam. 6 the saga-writer has evidently described the festival on the pattern of one of the processions at the festival of harvest and tabernacles, which was also the festival for the consecration of the Temple; he quite simply imagines that just as this festival was celebrated in his own day, so would the inaugural festival at the institution of the cult have been celebrated under David.[14] The same is the case with the Chronicler. He, too, describes the festival after the pattern of a corresponding festival in his own day. He also gives information about the psalm that was sung at the sacrifice. We have every reason to believe that this was no free fancy, but that the psalm really was used in his own day at some point of the ritual on that day during the festival of tabernacles which was especially dedicated to the memory of the transfer of Yahweh's ark; this is corroborated by his story about Solomon's consecration of the Temple, in which he quotes part of Ps. 132, which no doubt belonged to this festal complex.[15] The psalm quoted by the Chronicler in 1 Chron. 16 consists of Pss. 105.1–15; 96.1b–13a; 106.47–48. This means that on one of the days of the harvest festival, or on some festal day on a special historic occasion, a psalm was used consisting of parts of three psalms, which were all of them to be found in the Psalter. The most natural conclusion is that on some special occasion this liturgy was composed by people who felt restricted to an existing 'canonical' book of psalms. They did not think it proper to compose a new psalm for the day, but expressed what they wanted to say by choosing and putting together parts of canonical psalms. So the case is analogous to the use of Ps. 30 for the feast of Dedication.

The question then is, at what time the book of Chronicles came into existence. Nothing can be said about it with absolute certainty. At any rate it can hardly be any earlier than about 350 B.C., and is probably a great deal later, perhaps about 300, or even about 250.[16]

We shall not come much nearer to a solution if we study the different small collections and try to find out how old they may be. We might achieve some results if we were able to say for certain how old the latest psalm of each collection is. But that is hardly possible. And even if it were,

[14] See *Ps.St.* II, pp. 109ff.
[15] See above, Chap. V.9.
[16] Cf. Bentzen, *Intro. to the O.T.* II, pp. 215f. Noth, *Überlief. gesch. Stud.* I, pp. 159ff.

the collection of, for instance, Asaph might have been started much earlier, and gradually have had later psalms added to it.

If it is correct that the name 'sons of Asaph' was in use for the guild of temple singers before 587, then the nucleus of the Asaph collection *may* date from pre-exilic times, and have been gradually extended. As it now stands it doubtless contains psalms later than the restoration under Cyrus or Darius.

The nucleus of the two Davidic collections may likewise be older. A statement by Amos (6.15) alludes to David as the inventor of stringed instruments. But this need not refer to the idea that the temple music was instituted by David. There is no positive evidence of this idea until the book of Chronicles. But there it is an undisputed fact, and it is certainly older than, the age of the Chronicler himself. But the title 'Davidic psalms' need not have anything to do with this idea. As we have seen, 'Davidic psalms' originally has the same meaning as 'royal psalms'. The nucleus of the two Davidic collections may very well date back to the period of the monarchy. If so, a great many later psalms have been added even here in the course of time.

The Korah collection can hardly have come into being as a separate collection till after the time when 'the sons of Korah' had become the name of a section of the guild of singers, which happened, as we have seen (II.97) in Judaic (post-exilic) times. But that does not mean that all the psalms of this collection date from this period; several of them, as for instance Pss. 45; 84; 89 (Ethan), are no doubt older.

From the above we may arrive at some conclusion as to the time when the Psalter was completed.

The Korahite collection (§2e) and the Psalter both know the sons of Korah to be a 'family' of temple singers. They have this rank in some of the genealogical lists and notes about the temple service included in the book of Chronicles,[17] whereas in other lists they belong to the doorkeepers or inferior classes of 'Levites'.[18] From this we may probably conclude that their rank as singers was still of comparatively recent origin at the time of the Chronicler,[19] i.e. some time between the years 300 and 200 B.C.

So we should probably be justified in dating the compilation of the Psalter to a time somewhat earlier than the book of Chronicles, perhaps some time before the year 300 B.C., maybe even fifty years earlier.[20]

[17] 2 Chron. 20.19; 1 Chron. 6.18ff.
[18] 1 Chron. 9.31; 26.1ff., compared with 9.17ff.
[19] Cf. Gunkel-Begrich, *Einl.*, pp. 440ff.
[20] Eerdmans, *Hebr. Book of Pss.*, pp. 14f., thinks that from 2 Macc. 2.13 we may conclude that the Psalter was compiled by Nehemiah. But there is no reason for placing any reliance on this apocryphal statement. If Nehemiah had undertaken such a pious work, he would have mentioned it among all his other good works *in piam memoriam sui*. What we have in 2 Macc. 2.13, is just an earlier version of the unhistorical legend about 'Ezra and the Great Synagogue', who reproduced the holy writings that were lost.

CHAPTER XXII

The Purpose of the Psalter

I

This subject has been touched upon several times in the preceding chapter.

It is a fact that the great majority of psalms are truly cultic psalms which were also composed to be used in the temple service.

It is also a fact that the collection as we know it really was used in the service by the later Jewish community; this can be seen from what the tradition tells us about a great many individual psalms (Chap. I). Now we may object that this evidence merely proves the cultic use of some particular psalms, but that it does not say anything definite about whether the whole book was meant to be 'the hymn book of the Second Temple'. There is some truth in this objection. So we had better express our thesis in this way: there came a time when every psalm used in the temple service had to be from the Psalter. Firstly, this means that the psalms which had from early times established themselves by regular use in the temple service would all be included in the Psalter. But secondly it must be added that in later Jewish times no psalms were used at the temple service which were not found in the book. The Psalter attained such canonical authority and 'monopoly' that when a new festival was instituted and there was need of a special psalm for the festal offering, a new psalm would no longer be composed, but one of the psalms of the Psalter was chosen and interpreted in a way which would fit in with the festival. This can be seen from the fact that according to its heading Ps. 30 was used at the feast of dedication, which was instituted in the year 161 (1 Macc. 4.25) while the contents of the psalm prove beyond doubt that it had not been composed for such use; it is, in fact, the thanksgiving psalm of an individual for restoration to health.

That the Psalter was being used as a song-book for the temple service is seen not only from such headings as the ones in Pss. 30.1; 92.1; 100.1; to which must be added corresponding notes in the Greek translation of Pss. 24.1; 29.1; 48.1; 93.1; 94.1; and from the traditions of the Mishna and Talmud (see Chap. I.2), but also from a great many technical terms in the headings and elsewhere, which without doubt refer to the liturgical use of the psalms (see Chap. XXIII).

On the other hand, the collection also includes a few psalms which were certainly not composed for cultic use (see Chap. XVI).

Even these psalms may of course have been used in the cult later on. This might for instance be the case with Ps. 127. But psalms like 1, 111, 112 are not very likely to have been used as cultic psalms—though it is not quite out of the question.

2

We had better approach the question as to the purpose of the whole collection by studying the purpose of the separate small collections.[1] That is a comparatively simple matter. Obviously the small booklets with the psalms of Asaph and the psalms of the Korahites[2] were prepared in order to collect the psalms sung by the sons of Asaph and the sons of Korah.

Much the same is the case with the second group of Davidic psalms Pss. 51–71. They all have the heading lamĕnaṣṣēaḥ and often other liturgical and musical notes as well.[3] Here the intention was to collect in one booklet the so-called 'Davidic psalms' used in the temple service for some special purpose.

This also explains the purpose of the 'Elohistic Psalter'.[4] This is a combination of psalm booklets which were actually being used by the singers at the temple service, and had been composed for this very purpose, and had been selected by the temple officials themselves, including the guilds of singers.

The same thing may apply to the 'songs of the festal procession'[5] and the enthronement psalms,[6] if we are right in considering them to be cultic psalms.[7] They are booklets of psalms used at definite festivals or sections of a festival as are the 'Hallel psalms'.[8]

The Davidic psalms group I[9] are perhaps in a somewhat different position. It certainly does not prove anything that nine of them[10] have no liturgical notes in the headings, for these were added in a rather casual way, since manifestly cultic psalms like Pss. 118 and 150 have none. But it is significant that amongst them we find not a few psalms apparently belonging to the later private psalmography,[11] such as Pss. 25; 34; 37; 49.

The case of Books 4 and 5 is somewhat similar—cf. Pss. 105; 106; 111; 112—and so, consequently, is that of the Psalter as a whole. These collections cannot without more ado be designated song-books for temple worship, collected for that purpose.

---

[1] This has been rightly maintained by Begrich, see Gunkel-Begrich, Einl., p. 447.
[2] See Chap. XXI. 2c, e, f.
[3] Pss. 53; 54; 55; 56; 57; 58; 59; 60; 61; 62; 67; 69; for these notes see Chap. XXIII.
[4] See Chap. XXI. 2b, f.
[5] See Chap. XXI. 2g.
[6] See Chap. XXI. 2h.
[7] See above, pp. 113ff., 139f., 184f., and Additional Note XXIV.
[8] See Chap. XXI. 2i, j.
[9] See Chap. XXI. 2a.
[10] Pss. 17; 25; 26; 27; 28; 33; 34; 35; 37.
[11] See Chap. XVI.

3

It will be more fruitful to approach the question of 'purpose' by asking: in what circles was the Psalter, and before that the Davidic group I, collected?

After all that has been said about private psalmography, there can be no doubt about the answer: in the 'learned' circles. The psalm collection as a whole came into existence through a combination of the earlier cultic collections and other individual cultic psalms together with some private psalms, composed in the learned circles and with obvious traces of the thoughts and style forms of 'wisdom'.

This means that while the earlier small collections came into existence among the singers, the Psalter as a whole, and probably even the Davidic psalms group I (Pss. 3–41) were collected by the learned, 'the scribes', 'the wise'. Their interest in psalmography along with their interest in the ancient sacred tradition and all matters of religion led them to create out of the earlier cultic booklets the larger Psalter, mostly containing earlier cultic psalms, but also some of the learned psalmography.

4

Now it should also be possible for us to tell *why* the collection was made. Perhaps not directly in order to have a book of psalms for the cult; that was not necessary, for at the time there was probably a settled tradition as to which psalms were to be sung on different occasions—as can be seen from Ps. 92.1 and the Septuagint.[12] Nor was it made in order to have a book of songs for the private edification of the general public; they could not read, and so were in no need of *books* for their edification.

Yet to a certain extent both these considerations have played a part. But the leitmotif was the theological and religious interest of the learned in sacred traditions of an authoritative character. We may put it in this way: the learned 'traditionalists' wanted to collect and keep whatever they could find of sacred inspired poetry from the time of the fathers; it was sacred just because it was supposed to derive from 'the wise of the past'[13] and to have been used in the cult ever since the days of 'David'.[14] Being ancient, sacred poetry it ought to have its place in the temple service and serve as a pattern for the prayers of the pious, or even be used as models for prayers in the wisdom schools and in the private devotions of the individual pious—i.e. learned—person.

This psalm prayer was primarily regarded as a poetry of praise in honour of God; hence the name of the book, 'Hymns'.[15] What the book contained of prayers and supplications was looked upon by the collectors as 'praise', singing in honour of God; confession of sin, penitence and

[12] See Chap. I. 2.
[13] See Chap. XV. 4.
[14] For the way later Judaism looked upon David as the institutor of all details in the cult on Mount Zion, and particularly so of the temple songs and music, see 1 Chron. 25; 2 Chron. 8.14. Cf. above, Chaps. XV. 5, XVIII. 4.
[15] See above, p. 89, and n. 2 to Chap. I.

prayer were supposed to indicate that one 'gives honour to God'. This conception agrees with the late Jewish view of the cult in general: cult is 'divine service', the congregation submitting to the orderings of God and acknowledging him as Lord and God, expressing their willingness to obey all his laws and in return receiving his blessings through the sacral performances he himself has instituted; it all happens in order 'that God in all things may be glorified' (cf. 1 Pet. 4.11). By the term 'praises', the collectors as well as the transmitters thought of the directly cultic use of the psalms to be found in the book, and also of the more private cultic use, as for instance the use the learned themselves made of their own and earlier psalms as prayers in the school of learning.

From the standpoint of the wise the psalms as inspired poetry would also contain instruction—exhortation, admonition, chastisement, comfort—for the religious life, and also give expression to the hope for, and the promises of, the restoration of Israel. It could and ought to teach a pious and righteous man the 'way of life', so that he might become wise and lead a godly life, but it also ought to point out the kind of destiny that would befall the ungodly and unrighteous, 'who walketh in the counsel of the ungodly and sitteth in the seat of the scornful'. It would help a man to fear Yahweh, 'to delight in the law of Yahweh and meditate in his law'—theoretically and practically—'day and night', as it is expressed in the prefatory poem.

To the collectors themselves the cultic point of view appeared to be of minor importance. They were therefore ready to look upon the different psalms as a product of the life of an individual, just as the statements of the situations in the headings[16] tell us. It is the same as when the saga-writers make the pious people of the past utter a psalm[17] on all sorts of occasions.

5

But the very collection of the psalms and their canonicity, which it presupposes and again in its turn strengthens, also resulted in making the collection *the* book of psalms for the temple service. The existence of a canonical book of psalms, the majority of which were truly cultic psalms, would have as its first result that even those psalms in the book which had not been composed for cultic use would gradually be used in such a way—as may be concluded from the liturgical notes with which even such 'theoretical' psalms as Ps. 49 or Ps. 127 have been furnished. And secondly, it also resulted in making it almost impossible to think of taking a cultic psalm from any other source. As the development of the cultic liturgy of Judaism—for instance the institution of new festivals, such as the feast of dedication and the Purim festival—called for psalms for the new situations, one had recourse to the canonical psalms and tried to find something

[16] See Chap. XVI. 5.
[17] See Chap. XVI. 4.

suitable. In this way Ps. 30 became a sacrificial psalm at the feast of dedication, and in the Maccabean period Ps. 44.23 was used for some time as a daily morning prayer at the morning sacrifice;[18] the thanksgiving psalm, Ps. 92, was used at the morning sacrifice on the Sabbath, the enthronement psalm Ps. 93 according to the Septuagint as a psalm for Friday and so on; but originally none of the psalms for the different days of the week[19] had anything to do with those days.[20]

This new interpretation of earlier psalms, to which the existence of a canonical and exclusive book of psalms necessarily led, also resulted in additions to earlier 'I-psalms', so that these were explicitly referred to the situation of 'Israel', the Jewish congregation.[21] Thus these additions are indirect evidence telling us that the Psalter actually did become *the* book of psalms for the worship of the congregation, even though in origin it did not directly and explicitly have this aim.

On the other hand the very existence of such an inspired holy book would react on the private use of psalm singing. Along with the influences from the learned circles it would for instance probably lead to the custom of singing the 'doxology'—the Hallel—at the Passover festival in the homes.

The emergence of the canonical Psalter also definitely put an end to any new cultic psalmography. Therefore it is quite out of the question that late Jewish poetry would have been included in the Psalter. To late Judaism, the Psalter was a work of the 'prophets of the past', singing 'inspired songs' at the temple service.[22]

---

[18] Bab. Sota 40a.

[19] Pss. 92 (Sabbath), 24, 48, 82, 94, 81, 93. See p. 3.

[20] Just as Snaith (*Studies in the Psalter*) has not been able to give any evidence whatever to prove that the enthronement psalms are psalms for the Sabbath.

[21] Pss. 25.22; 34.23; 131.3.

[22] Cf. 1 Chron. 25.1–3.

CHAPTER XXIII

Technical Terms in the Psalm Headings

It is generally accepted that the technical terms occurring in the psalm headings—or in the margin (e.g. *Selah*)—have something to do with the liturgical use of the psalms. But in many cases their real sense is most uncertain; some of them are almost unintelligible. Nor had the translators of the ancient versions any sure knowledge of what they meant.[1] Consequently the translation will often be of the nature of a more or less probable conjecture. To put it negatively, we may say that the usual interpretation of some of them, for instance Nos. 19, 22 and 23 below, as indications of the 'melody' to which the psalm is to be sung, is an untenable modernism which agrees neither with our knowledge of oriental 'melodies' nor with the way the psalms were used in the Jewish cult.[2]

A. Some of the terms which indicate the type of psalm in question.

1. *Šîr*, 'song'. *Šîr* is the usual word for a song, and is used of religious (cultic) as well as of secular songs. And it may be taken for granted that in Israel the singing was always accompanied by some kind of music.[3] *Šîr* as an indication of cultic singing (and music) is most likely to have had a more specialized, technical meaning; there would be no point in stating in a heading that the text for cultic singing was a 'song' in a general sense. However, we do not know what special type of cultic song the use of the word in the headings indicates.

As a heading by itself the word is found only twice (Pss. 18 and 46). Beyond that it occurs together with *mizmōr* 'psalm'; five times it stands before *mizmōr* (Pss. 48, 66, 83, 88, 108), three times after *mizmōr* (Pss. 67, 68, 87). In addition, it occurs five times together with *mizmōr* but separated from it by one or two words (Pss. 65, 75, 76, 30, 92). This means that a psalm can be at once a *šîr* and a *mizmōr*, which shows that both words have a more or less specialized technical sense. When Ps. 92 is called a '*šîr* for the sabbath', this undoubtedly means that it was used at the daily morning sacrifice (the *tāmîdh* offering) on that day. Then this may also be

---

[1] For these technical terms see *Ps.St.* IV, and besides, Jacob in *ZATW* 16, 1896, pp. 129ff.: 17, 1897, pp. 48ff., 263ff.; Buhl, *Psalmerne*,[2] pp. XLIff.; Baethgen, *Die Psalmen*,[3] p. XXXIV; Peters, *The Psalms as Liturgies*; Bentzen, *Indl. til Salmerne*, pp. 65ff.; Eerdmans, *Hebr. Book of Pss.*, pp. 51ff. What Gunkel-Begrich, *Einl.*, pp. 455ff., have to say about these terms is mostly worthless fancy, in some measure based on groundless alterations of the text and—apparently—on a certain unwillingness seriously to adopt the cultic point of view in psalm interpretation. Explanatory statements of most of the interpretations given in this chapter will be found in *Ps.St.* IV; the cases in which my opinion has changed will be mentioned in the notes below.

[2] See Eerdmans, op. cit., pp. 51f.

[3] Cf. Eerdmans, op. cit., pp. 52f.; Oesterley, *A Fresh Approach*, pp. 91–122.

the sense in Ps. 30: 'a *šîr* for the re-consecration of the House'. Of the psalms with the indication *šîr*, Pss. 48, 49, 67 and 68 certainly belong to the festival of harvest and tabernacles, as probably does Ps. 87. Pss. 18, 66 and 92 are thank-offering psalms, whereas Pss. 83, 88 and 108 are lamentation psalms and psalms for a day of humiliation and prayer. So the term *šîr* is hardly to be referred to the contents or to be connected with a definite kind of cultic festival. Perhaps it alludes to the connexion with the act of sacrifice in the ritual in question; but it is more likely to indicate the mode of presentation or the musical accompaniment.

2. *Mizmōr*, 'psalm'. This term occurs fifty-seven times in all, forty-four times alone, thirteen times together with *šîr*—'song' (see above, no. 1). In the Old Testament the word is used only in the psalms; in Sir. 49.1 it indicates (song and) music at a non-cultic festival. So it seems to have been chiefly used of religious song and music. The translation 'psalm' can be traced back to the Greek translation, *psalmós*, indicating a song with stringed instruments. The primary sense of the verb *zmr* seems to be 'pick'; in a musical sense it would mean 'thrumming' on a stringed instrument, and from that, 'make music'.[4] It has the same meaning in Akkadian. But singing is always included; the verb indicates singing to a stringed instrument, or playing a stringed instrument accompanied by singing or a recitative text. *Mizmōr* then indicates a (religious) song accompanied by stringed instrument(s). Whether it had a still more specialized sense in the psalms cannot be ascertained, but it is likely, considering what was said above of *šîr*.

3. *Šîr hamma'ǎlôth*, 'The songs of the festal processions', Pss. 120–134, in the strict sense of the word 'songs of ascension'.[5] The 'Ascensions' (in the plural) seems to have been the term for the festal procession at the festival of harvest and new year, and thence perhaps for the festival itself

---

[4] Cf. Eerdmans, op. cit., p. 52.

[5] Besides *šîr hamma'ǎlôth* occurs *šîr lamma'ǎlôth*, 'a song to (be used at) the ascents', Ps. 121. The term *šîr hamma'ǎlôth* is probably best explained in the way Cheyne has suggested, as a determined plural of a compound *šîr-ma'ǎlâ* 'a song for the ascent,' pl. *šîr-ma'ǎlôth*, or determined, *šîr-hamma'ǎlôth* instead of the usual construction *šîrê hamm*. The term was actually the title of the whole collection, but it has then been placed at the head of every individual psalm (Cheyne). The noun *ma'ǎlâ* by itself means 'ascent'. In the psalm headings it must have a special technical, i.e. cultic and liturgical sense, cf. 123.1: a song for (or at) the ascent(s)—the plural may have an 'amplificative' sense. The starting point of the interpretation must be that the verb '*ālâ* 'ascend' is a term used of the 'ascent' of Yahweh in a festal procession to the Temple in Ps. 47.6, and in general for the 'marching up' of the festal procession, Ps. 24.3. From this it may be concluded that *ma'ǎlâ*, and then eventually the amplificative plural *hamma'ǎlôth*, became a term for the festal procession itself. This is confirmed by Ps. 84.6 'Blessed are the men whose strength is in thee (i.e. Yahweh), in whose heart are *mĕsillôth*'; *mĕsillâ* means a paved road; in the context it must mean a road leading up to the Temple, the *via sacra* referred to in Isa. 35.8 which has been the archetype of Deutero-Isaiah's idea about the wonderful road through the desert, on which Yahweh shall go 'home' in triumphal procession at the head of the exiled; that is to say, the road of procession which the Temple of Jerusalem must have had like all other cultic metropolises of the orient. See above, pp. 169f. As *mĕsillâ* indicates the physical, material, road, the term of Ps. 84.6 is evidently a metaphor. So when G paraphrases *ma'ǎlôth*, it is to the point, and at the same time shows that the translators were aware that *ma'ǎlâ* indicated the holy 'festal procession' by the *via sacra* to the Temple. In Christian terminology we might express the term in Ps. 84.6 by 'church-going'.

(see Chap. XXI. 2g). The translation 'the festal journeys' (the pilgrimages) is misleading; most of the fifteen psalms have nothing to do with pilgrimages but belong in the Temple and were evidently used at the festival of harvest and tabernacles.

4. *Mikhtām*, 'Psalms of atonement', Pss. 16; 56–60; possibly also Isa. 38.9 (corrected text), cf. Akkadian *katamu*—'cover' (atone for); the word is probably transferred to the psalm from its object in connexion with the sacrifices and ceremonies of atonement and purification on a day of prayer and humiliation, and so is only used for psalms of lamentation; even an expression of confidence in Yahweh, as in Ps. 16, is such an act of 'atonement', which would 'cover' sin in the eyes of Yahweh.[6] The only exception is Isa. 38.9, if here we replace the MT heading *mikhtābh*— 'scripture', 'inscription' by *mikhtām* (cf. note on Isa. 38.9 in *GTMMM* III), for this psalm is a psalm of thanksgiving after illness; however, this makes the correction improbable (cf. above, Chap. X. 2).

5. *Maśkîl*, Pss. 32, 42, 52–55, 74, 78, 88, 89, 142; 2 Chron. 30.22, as well as Ps. 47.8, is used about psalms of different types. The root SKL includes the notion of wisdom, cunning, and success; the verb *hiśkîl* means to know how to reach one's aims and succeed in reaching them, and thus be justified as a wise man. But 'wisdom' in all these cases is considered something more than 'natural'; the 'wisdom' is related to 'mana', the supra-normal power. A *maśkîl* thus probably indicates the cultic poem as the outcome of a supra-normal 'wisdom' and 'insight' as to the way in which the deity ought to be worshipped and influenced; originally the word probably also sought to express that the song was filled with active power and was particularly 'effective' in use. Cf. the ancient Indian offering-songs, the 'vedas', derived from the same root as 'wit', 'wisdom', etc. It is impossible to tell whether in later times the word got a more 'rationalized' and 'technico-liturgical' sense. It does not mean a 'doctrinal' psalm—a contradiction in terms. The word may thus be translated 'efficacious song'.

6. *Šiggāyōn*, Ps. 7, probably means a 'psalm of lamentation', cf. Akkadian *šegu*, 'psalm of lamentation' (vb. = 'howl, lament'). It probably indicates a lamentation psalm of a special character or for a particular purpose and perhaps therefore accompanied by special ceremonies, *šigyōnôth*, to which Hab. 3.1 alludes. Both Ps. 7 and Hab. 3 belong to some act by which king and people prepare themselves to meet 'the nations' and urge Yahweh to 'judge' them.

7. *Tĕhillâ*, 'doxology', 'praise', Ps. 145, elsewhere used about praising God and paying 'homage' to him in general. In Ps. 145, a late heading, it

---

[6] The objection of Eerdmans, that 'atonement was made by sacrifice and confession of sins (Lev. v5)' (op. cit., p. 76), is of no importance; atonement was made through the whole series of ritual functions, of which sacrifice was a part; as has been shown in Chaps. VI–VIII, confession of sin also took place for instance through the penitential psalm. The laws of P only give fragmental information about the rituals of atonement, so we cannot infer much from what they do not say.

probably has quite a general sense: 'a (cultic) doxology by David'. Cf. also Additional Note I.

8. *Tĕphillâ*, 'prayer', Pss. 17, 86, 90, 102, 142, Hab. 3, is likewise quite a comprehensive term, which is not only used of psalms of lamentation and prayer, but sometimes of any kind of prayer, even the doxologizing one, Ps. 72.20. In the headings it probably indicates the psalm as a (cultic) psalm of lamentation and prayer in general.

B. A few technical musical terms also occur.

9. *Binĕghînōth*, 'with stringed instruments', always follows after the indication *lamĕnaṣṣēaḥ* ('to dispose to mercy', cf. below, no. 17), Pss. 4, 6, 54, 55, (61), 67, 76, Hab. 3.19. It thus indicates the means of attaining such an aim: accompanying the singing with (harp and) lyre (1 Chron. 15.21) probably, as distinguished from the more noisy music of percussion instruments, with which the cultic act was opened 'in order to make (the deity) hear', 1 Chron. 15.19–22. Such cultic terms are as a rule old, and to be referred to an age in which the ideas about the deity were more anthropomorphic than in the prophetic religion of later times (cf. 1 Kgs. 18.26f.). Later times did not ponder on the original sense, but in the music found a means of emphasizing the prayer in general, a demonstration of respect that would please the deity.

10. *'Al-hannĕḥîlôth*, 'to the flute playing', Ps. 5, may actually mean 'to the flutes', but the translation is very uncertain.[7] If correct, it is an indication of the same kind as the preceding one. The Babylonians had a special kind of lamentation psalms called 'flute psalms of lamentation'.

11. *'Al-maḥălath*, Pss. 53 and 88, perhaps has the same sense; cf. Ethiopic *maḥalat* = song, playing, instrument (flute); i.e. 'to the flute'.[8] Or perhaps in both cases: 'over (i.e. together with) the ceremony called "the flute playing".' The type of the three psalms and the analogy from the Babylonian seem to indicate that the flute belonged to the rites of the psalms of lamentation, cf. Jer. 48.36; Matt. 9.23.

What special kind of flute the two terms may indicate is unknown to us. One difficulty about the interpretation suggested here is that the usual words for 'flute' in the Old Testament are quite different ones: *'ûgābh* and *ḥālîl*; but of course that may be a mere accident, and if the above interpretation is correct both words will be derived from the same root as *ḥālîl*. Besides, it is quite possible that there were several kinds of flutes, and that the cultic instruments were called by names different from the ordinary secular ones. Oriental pictures prove that the long flute, the cross-flute and the double shawm or oboe were known;[9] possibly also the pan-pipes with several (five or seven) tubes.

---

[7] This interpretation is in agreement with Peters, op. cit., p. 44. It differs from that of *Ps.St.* IV, p. 35.
[8] Here differently from *Ps.St.* IV, see preceding note.
[9] Cf. above, n. 36 to Chap. I.

The most natural translation of 'al-maḥălāth is, however, 'in connexion with (properly "over") illness', i.e. at the purification from illness.[10] This translation fits in very well in Ps. 88, but not in Ps. 53. But there is just a chance that Ps. 53 was later used for a ritual situation different from the one for which it was originally composed; cf. Ps. 30.

12. Higgāyôn, 'pealing', Pss. 9.17; 92.4 probably indicates the places in which the music ought to emphasize the singing in a special way, some kind of 'musical flourish'.

13. Selāh occurs seventy-one times (more in LXX), and in Hab. 3. The word evidently indicates a point where a pause of some kind is to be made in the recitation of the psalm, thus, for instance, where it stands at the end of the separate strophes, as in Ps. 46. It is natural to combine this with the information about the 'sections' (pārāq) of the recitation mentioned above (II.80). In late Jewish and Rabbinic times this was supposed to mean that at such a point the congregation was to join in with some shout of homage, namely 'for ever' (neṣaḥ); that is why most ancient translators render selāh by 'for ever', and that is what the M.T. means by the vowel signs (qĕrê) with which the consonants have been furnished, but which do not fit in with the form and tone of the word. If this were the original sense, one might consider the word to be derived from the verb SLL, which means 'lift up', and translate it by 'lifting up' (the voice), 'call'; 'for ever' would then indicate the concrete noun 'call', 'shout', with which the congregation were to join in.[11]

But this does not agree with the comparatively numerous passages in which the word follows immediately on the mentioning of disasters or judgments from God, which have fallen upon the suppliant.[12] Therefore it is more natural to think of some sort of 'neutral' homage paid to the deity and indicating either honouring and grateful homage or humble and repentant submission to him. Eerdmans is likely to be right in deriving the word from a verb SLH, corresponding to Aramaic SL', 'bend'. It would indicate the points at which the congregation 'bends', i.e. falls prostrate, touching the ground with their foreheads in token of respectful homage and submission to God, corresponding to the rak'at of the Mohammedans in their ceremony of prayer (sala'at).

C. Other terms indicate the liturgical aim and use of the psalms.

14. Lĕthôdhâ, 'for thanksgiving', Ps. 100, probably indicates that the psalm was used at the 'thank-offering' tôdhâ. Here this offering is not taken

[10] Thus in Ps.St. IV, p. 33, and Eerdmans, op. cit., p. 65.

[11] Thus in Ps.St. IV, pp. 1off. For selah cf. also Stieb in ZATW 57, 1939, pp. 102ff., and Gyllenberg in ZATW 58, 1940–41, pp. 153ff.; Scott, The Meaning and the Use of 'Selah'. The objection of Eerdmans (op. cit., p. 85) that the verb sll 'make high' is only used about the building of roads, is not correct; Ps. 68.5 does not speak of Yahweh's journey through the desert, as Eerdmans thinks, but of his 'ride on the cloud', as will be seen from the parallel expression in the Ugaritic texts; cf. Ps. 18.11.

[12] Eerdmans (op. cit., p. 84) is right with regard to this objection to my former interpretation. Related to the interpretation of Eerdmans is that of Snaith in VT II, 1952, pp. 43ff., with reference to Taanit VII. 3: the day psalm was divided into 3 sections, and after each section a trumpet gave a signal for the congregation to prostrate themselves.

in the sense of private or casual thank-offering (voluntary, or in consequence of a promise, see Chap. IX. 2; X. 1), but as a kind of congregational festal offering, cf. 2 Chron. 29.31; 33.16. Ps. 100 most likely
alludes to this offering at the festival of tabernacles.[13]

15. *Lĕʿannôth*, 'for penance', Ps. 88, properly 'to humiliate', namely one's
soul, indicates the purpose of the psalm as a psalm of lamentation and
penitence. Had perhaps the ritual for purification from illness a special
part called 'penance' or '(self) humiliation'?

16. *Lĕhazkîr*, 'for reminder', Pss. 38, 78, means that the psalm will
'remind' Yahweh of the distress with which the cultic act in question is
concerned, whether it be the individual sin of the suppliant (the people),
or the wrongs of the enemy. So the psalm probably has to do with the
so-called *'azkārâ* sacrifice, the 'memorial sacrifice' ('memorial gift'), Lev.
2.2; 5.12; Numbers 5.18, which had the same purpose.

17. *Lamĕnaṣṣēaḥ* is used fifty-five times, and in addition in Hab. 3.19.
The usual translation (AV) 'to the chief Musician' (the conductor) is
certainly wrong and is not known to any of the early translations, most of
which look upon the term as a verbal noun, indicating an act and not used
about the acting person. Put before such a noun the preposition *lĕ* is
generally used to indicate the aim of the act in question.   In 1 Chron.
15.20–22 the infinitive is used with the preposition *lĕ* —*lĕnaṣṣēaḥ*—about
music with (harps and) lyres (and song accompaniment), in order to
indicate the aim of this musical performance, as distinguished from that
with percussion instruments which were used in order to 'make (Yahweh)
hear' (see above, no. 9). The primary sense of the verb is: 'beam, shine,
light'. It is therefore most natural to interpret the term in 1 Chron. 15.21
after the analogy of such ancient cult terms as 'smooth the countenance of
Yahweh', that is mollify Yahweh; cf. the formula of blessing: 'Yahweh
make his face *shine* upon thee, and be gracious unto thee'. The sense of
the term would then be: to recite such psalms to such music as would be
likely to make Yahweh's face shine with grace and goodness,[14] i.e. to
dispose Yahweh to mercy. Accordingly it would be most natural to
interpret the psalm heading as follows: 'for the merciful disposition (of
Yahweh)', 'to dispose (Yahweh) to mercy', in a toned-down sense perhaps:
'for homage' (of Yahweh). This can be said of the psalm of supplication
as well as of praise, cf. the way the Targum renders it: 'for praise'. Perhaps
some special part of the manifold liturgy of the temple service had this
particular aim and effect, and then the psalms in question would be used

---

[13] Lev. 7.12ff. does not refer to such congregational offerings (against note in *GTMMM ad
loc.*); the term 'he who offers it up' shows that we have the offering of an individual. What
distinguishes it from the promised and the voluntary *tôdhâ* of 7.16ff. is not clear.

[14] To this Eerdmans objects (op. cit., p. 61) that the usual term for this idea is *hā 'ir pānîm*,
occurring in Pss. 31.17; 67.2; 80.4; 8.20; 119.135; Num. 6.25, and that it would be rather
strange if in the heading a verb was used in a sense in which it did not occur in any other place
in the O.T. But such technical terms are often very old, and may have been preserved, even if
everyday language would later use other expressions; archaic technical terminology is not
infrequent, least so in the cult.

on these occasions, according to detailed rules 'unknown to us to-day.

18. *Lîdhûthûn* or *'al-yĕdhûthûn*, Pss. 39, 62, 77 is often taken as a personal name: 'by (or for) Jeduthun' (AV: '[to the chief musician] even to Jeduthun'), Jeduthun being supposedly a by-form of Ethan. But this is incompatible with the preposition *'al* in Pss. 62, 77. *Yĕdhûthûn* in the psalm headings must be a cultic term indicating either the action 'over' which (*'al*, see below, D) the psalm was sung, or the purpose 'to' which (*lĕ*) it is aimed. The word seems to be derived from the verb *yādhâ* and must then mean something like 'confession'; the psalm was sung 'at (the) confession' or 'for confession'. This seems to allude to a definite part of the liturgy, which was particularly supposed to express the humble or penitent 'confession to the name of Yahweh' (1 Kgs. 8.33, 35; cf. Ps. 32.5; Prov. 28.13. All three psalms mentioned here contain such a confession, the first of them of the sins of the suppliant, all three of them of his (their) lowliness and helplessness and dependence on the mighty aid of God.

Thus in the psalm headings the word has nothing to do with the personal names Jedithun or Jeduthun, used several times in the book of Chronicles for a guild of singers and their ancestor (1 Chron. 9.16; 16.37, 41f.; 25.1, 3, 6; 2 Chron. 5.12; 29.14; 35.15; Neh. 11.17) instead of, as elsewhere, Ethan.[15]

This may be a mis-interpretation on the part of the Chronicler or in the later tradition of the text. The word may, however, at a later time actually have been used as a proper name and have been confused with Ethan. Cf. such proper names as Haggai, Shabbetai, Hoduyah(u) (Qere: Hoda-wyah), Hodiyyah, all derived from some cultic situation or action.

D. Another group of technical terms must be referred to the cultic act to which the psalm belonged and 'over' which it was sung.

19. *'Al yônath 'ēlîm rĕḥōqîm*, Ps. 56. The traditional translation 'to the speechless dove in the distant places' (literally 'to the dove of speechlessness —or silence—of distant places—or of distance') gives no sense; instead of 'speechlessness', 'silence' (*'ēlem*), LXX rightly interprets and pronounces the word as 'gods' *'ēlîm* (freely translated 'holy ones'), and so we should translate 'over the dove to the distant gods'.[16] This probably alludes to a cultic act like the one prescribed in Lev. 14.2ff.; there we hear of a dove which during a purificatory rite was dipped into the water with the blood of the sacrifice and then let loose 'into the open field'; cf. the scapegoat

---

[15] See Chap. XV. 4.

[16] This term, and likewise the ones in notes 20, 21 and 22 below, are usually considered the opening words of familiar songs, to the tune of which the psalm in question is to be sung, cf. the way the melody is indicated in our hymnbooks. This view is supported neither by the text nor by tradition; nor do the supposed opening words agree with any of the characteristic openings of any of the species of Hebrew poetic composition known to us. For the refutation of the whole of this un-oriental idea of 'melodies' in a modern sense of the word, see Eerdmans, *Hebr. Book of Psalms*, pp. 51ff. Keet's arguments about temple music, *Liturg. Study of the Psalter*, pp. 47ff., are—unconsciously—partly based on the assumption that the tune is indicated in the headings; that the heading *'al tašḥeth* (no. 22) refers to 'a popular tune' is by him declared to be 'doubtless' (op. cit., p. 53).

'for Azazel', Lev. 16, on which the sins of the people were laid, and which was then chased into the desert to the demons. In the Bible the word 'god', '*ēl*, '*ĕlōhîm*, may also indicate inferior supernatural beings, even ghosts and demons. The expression 'the distant gods' is now known from the Ugarit texts.[17] The heading, then, says that this 'psalm of atonement' (see no. 4) accompanied a ritual act in which a dove (cf. Lev. 1.14ff.; 5.6–10) was let loose to 'the distant gods', i.e. to the demons far away in the desert outside the 'world', with the 'guilt' of the suppliant, and thus with the impurity and disaster which had befallen him; cf. for this idea, in addition to the 'scapegoat' for Azazel, also the ceremony behind the metaphor in Zech. 5.11.

20. '*Al-'ayyeleth haššahar*, Ps. 22, also alludes to an animal offered in sacrifice, and to an act of sacrifice at the early dawn, one feature in the rites of purification to which the psalm belonged.[17a] At the sacrifice of purification ('sin offering') the animal had to be a female, Lev. 5.1–4. In contrast to Deut. 12.15, the earlier practice—as in Babylonia and Phoenicia—allowed the sacrifice of red deer and gazelles, see Gen. 27, cf. Isa. 40.16; Ps. 50.10–12. As a rule the offering took place at or before sunrise (Job 1.5); from Assyria we know of sacrificial rituals starting in the evening and lasting all through the night and reaching their climax a short time before sunrise.[18]

21. '*Al-šôšannîm*, 'over the lilies', Pss. 45, 69; '*al šûšan 'ēdûth*, 'over the lily of revelation', Pss. 60, 80. Possibly these may refer to a rite in which oracles, 'revelation', 'witness', 'omens' were taken from lilies. Concerning oracles as part of the festal service as well as of the liturgies on the day of humiliation and prayer see above, Chap. XII. 2–5. From the legend of the blossoming rod of Aaron, Num. 17.6ff., we may conclude that on certain occasions omens were taken from the way flowers did or did not bud. Ps. 60 is a prayer during danger from war, and contains an oracle; the whole of Ps. 45 is an (effective) wish of blessing with promises for the marriage of the king; Pss. 80 and 69 are prayers for help after defeat and against dangerous enemies. All four—of Ps. 60 the first part—may have been sung 'over the lilies', before the oracle was taken, which, it was then hoped, would confirm the prayer or the good wishes. This conception would also agree with Ps. 45, the wedding psalm of the king; here it might allude to the taking of oracles with regard to the fertility of the king's marriage; see the wish for sons in v. 17. The red lilies were also a symbol of love and fertility, cf. Canticles 2.1f., 16; 4.5; 5.13; 6.2f.; 7.3.

22. '*Al-tašhēth*, 'destroy it not', stands in the headings of Pss. 57, 58, 59 and 75. All four psalms have this in common, that they speak of the lasting contrast between Israel and the pagan peoples oppressing the

---

[17] See Eissfeldt, *El im ugarit. Pantheon*, p. 12; possibly 'Unterweltsgötter'.
[17a] Jirku (*ZATW*, 65 1953, pp. 85f.) finds here the divine name Shahar, that is, however, gainsaid by the article before the word. The presupposition of Jirku's interpretation is the false idea that the terms indicate the melody (see n. 16).
[18] After Bentzen, *Indl. til Salmerne*, p. 75; cf. Meissner, *Bab. u. Assyr.* II, pp. 238f.

nation, and that they look back to an explicit word from Yahweh (an oracle) about help, or even quote such a word (Ps. 75). They probably allude to an acute danger, a threatening attack or the like; this is least certain in the case of Ps. 75; but even here the disaster is seen in the image of an acute danger. So the heading probably indicates a ritual act to which the psalm in question belonged. A main point of this act may have been the symbolical rite, to which Isa. 65.8 evidently alludes: the cluster of grapes is a symbol of Israel; the prayer, 'destroy it not', has as its motivation that there is still 'blessing' in the grape, and Israel has still a nucleus of righteous people, and is kept alive by the grace of Yahweh's blessing. Cf. for this, the prayer of the suffering sinner in Ps. 51.13: 'Take not thy holy spirit from me!'

E. Finally there is a group of terms of which we hardly yet know the literal sense.

23. '*Al-haggitttth*, Pss. 8, 81 and 84 may have something to do with the 'Gittite' Obed-edom in 2 Sam. 6.10f., in whose house Yahweh's ark stayed till it was brought to the citadel of Jerusalem. For this story hardly deals with something that happened just once, but rather with a 'legend', reflecting a fixed cultic custom, the rite of a festal day: from a house outside the temple precincts the festal procession with Yahweh's ark probably used to proceed at the festival of harvest, new year and enthronement, which was also the festival for the consecration of the Temple (see Chap. V. 9). The contents of the three psalms fit in well with the idea of the festival: the homage to Yahweh as king and creator and ruler of the world, the allusion to the making of the Covenant and to the origin of the people, the prayer for and the promise to king and people. Does *haggitttth* perhaps indicate the place from which the procession with the ark proceeded? Or the ark itself? Or the ritual act when it was lifted up at the start of the procession? Or perhaps a special instrument, 'the Gittite (lyre)' used in the festal procession with the ark?

24. '*Al-'ālāmôth*, Ps. 46.1, and in 1 Chron. 15.20, and

25. '*Al-'hāššeminith*, Pss. 6, 12; 1 Chron. 15.21, are somehow related to one another.[19] The first term is combined with playing on harps, the second with playing on lyres. From the description in 1 Chron. 15 we may perhaps infer that the terms indicate something in connexion with the festival of temple consecration in earlier times, i.e. the festival of harvest, new year and enthronement. At any rate this would agree with

[19] The usual opinion is that these two terms indicate the soprano ('after [the way of] women') and the men's voice one octave deeper ('after the eighth'). But there is not the slightest reason to believe that the music of the Israelites was based on the octave scale; Keet's attempt to maintain the usual interpretation (*Liturg. Study of the Psalter*, pp. 47ff.) is not convincing; if '*ālāmôth* means 'young women' it cannot possibly indicate instruments with (only) high tones, as Keet thinks, agreeing with Delitzsch; nor can we imagine harps and lyres which can only produce high tones. Eerdmans (*Hebr. Book of Psalms*, pp. 61ff.) thinks that the term means 'sung by young women' (in the festal procession); but this disagrees with the statement in 1 Chron. 15.20f.

Ps. 46. Ps. 12, too, a prayer and a promise about the rescue of Israel from the pressure of alien rule, may have belonged to this festival. It does not agree quite so well with Ps. 6, a psalm of illness; but it is quite possible that later times may have interpreted this psalm as speaking of the state of distress of the people, and the promise, pre-supposed by vv. 9ff., about the destruction of the pagans and the restoration of Israel. The two terms might then indicate some prominent elements of the festal ritual. But it is also possible that 1 Chron. 15.20f. tells us what the Levites, mentioned there, would regularly do at the cult, not just what they did on this particular festal occasion, so that the two terms would rather indicate regular ritual acts or facts in connexion with the cult music.

'al-'alāmôth has sometimes been supposed to occur at the end of Ps. 48, the last two words of v. 15, *'al-mûth*, being interpreted as a scribal error for this term; that is most uncertain and not necessary. As to the meaning of the word, any connexion with *'almâ* 'young woman' is impossible. G translates *ὑπέρ τῶν κρυφίων* making it a derivative from the root 'LM 'be hidden, be concealed', and there may be some tradition behind this translation. If this derivation is correct, we have a cultic notion: 'hidden things, secrets, mysteries', or the like. In Egyptian religion the 'secrets' (mysteries) indicated the dramatic presentation of the fate of the deity from death to life, unveiled to the believers through the festal cult and imparting to them the life of the deity;[20] in Babylonian religion the 'secrets of the gods' likewise indicated the revelation and knowledge of the life-giving and saving rites, their origin and use and effects;[21] 'the secret of Esagila' (i.e. the Marduk temple) is the name of one part of the festal liturgy of the Babylonian festival drama of new year.[22] Both Pss. 46 and 48 allude to dramatic presentations of Yahweh's work of salvation, which the believers have been permitted to 'see', and which *eo ipso* contain revelations full of promises of the salvation in which they are now about to share. Is *'alāmôth* perhaps the term for this religious 'mystery', to which the two psalms belonged?

Haššemînîth literally means 'the eighth' (feminine). The number eight plays an important part in many ritual acts: the eighth act of purification is the decisive one, etc.[23] If this term has something to do with the festival of harvest and new year (see above), it may allude to the conclusive 'eighth' ritual act, immediately preceding the announcement of Yahweh's answer and promise—which is given in plain words in Ps. 12.6, and is quite obviously supposed to have been announced before Ps. 6.9–10.

26. *'al-mûth labbēn*, Ps. 9.1, traditionally translated by 'after (or, for, on the occasion of) death for the son (or, death of the son)', which gives no sense in connexion with Pss. 9/10. It has been supposed to be a scribal error

[20] See Erman, *Aegypt. Relig.*,² pp. 272ff.
[21] See Meissner, *Babyl. u. Assyr.* II, pp. 139f.
[22] See Frankfort, *Kingship*, p. 318.
[23] See Lev. 12.3, 15.13f., 19.28f.; Num. 6.9–11; Lev. 14.

for 'al-'ălāmôth, just as the last two words of Ps. 48.15, 'al-mûth, were supposed to be a mistake for the same term; all the ancient translations actually read (or interpret) 'al-'ălāmûth in Ps. 9.1 instead of 'al-mûth. It is not impossible that Pss. 9/10 was used in the festal drama at the festival of new year (the 'myth of the fight of the nations'). The consonants of the following word *lbn* mean 'be white'; perhaps we should read it as *lĕbhēnâ* 'the full moon', indicating the date of the festal act?

27. *lĕlammēdh*, Ps. 60.1, is perhaps not a liturgical term. The Norwegian translation renders it by 'to be learnt', but it cannot mean that; the verb is in the active voice and so would have to mean 'to teach' (so AV). But the verb also—and really—means 'prick, prod, goad on'.[24] In 2 Sam. 1.18 the word occurs by way of editorial information about the aim of the lamentation over Saul and Jonathan, and there it probably ought to be translated: 'and he (David) recited it in order to goad the sons of Judah on to (the use of, or protection against) the bow' (cf. v. 6).[25] The compilers of the Psalter may have meant something like this: David composed the psalm in order to encourage the people or goad them on to fight. Or is the expression perhaps actually a ritual term with the sense: 'to goad on' Yahweh to intervene against the enemies of his people? That would fit in very well with the content of Ps. 60.

[24] Cf. *malmādh* or *malmēdh*, a goad-stick with which to goad the oxen; the iron spike itself is called *darbōn*.
[25] *GTMMM* II, p. 234, note on 2 Sam. 1.18a is wrong; there is no reason to omit the remark; it belongs to the text, but of course it is the remark of the compiler or the saga writer and it must be put down to his account.

Additional Notes

NOTE I (p. 2, n. 2; II, 210, n.7)

The cultic meaning of the words *těhillâ* and *hillēl* appears in passages like Pss. 22.26;48. 11;100.4; 149.1; Neh. 12.46; 2 Chron. 20.22. And it is in the light of these passages where the meaning is obvious that the others will have to be interpreted; in fact the word is practically always used in connexion with cultic functions. The Hebrew *těhillîm* in the title of the Psalter is a later (post-biblical) plural for the older *těhillôth*. The word *těhillâ* 'doxology', 'hymn', is derived from the verb *hillēl*, indicating the utterance of shouts of joy and exultation arising from an overwhelming feeling of exaltation and strength and pride (cf. the hithpael *hithhallēl*, to glory in, give expression to one's feeling of elevation and pride): most often it implies shouting in honour of somebody. Probably it refers to a definite succession of sounds or tones, something like yodelling. The verb is almost exclusively used about the cultic shouts of joy and salutation 'before' and in honour of Yahweh (or some other god), and has received the technical sense of praising (the deity) with joy and singing; historically, indeed, the song of homage has been developed out of the shouts of joy. The noun *těhillâ* means honour, pride in the sense of fame as well as of psychical feelings; and, objectively speaking: what a man glories in and takes a pride in and finds his strength in, whether it be his own great achievements or his god. When used about God it indicates his works of glory and greatness, and the fame and glory he shall win and may claim on account of them. To mention, to enumerate with praise, these *těhillôth* is a *těhillâ*, a tribute of praise and homage; hence the technical, cultic sense: anthem of praise, hymn. Duhm's interpretation of the title of the Psalter (*Die Psalmen* p. X) and Quell's scepticism (*Kult. Probl. d. Pss.*, p. 4, note 1) are therefore illegitimate.

NOTE II (p. 12, n. 52)

See de Wette, *Commentar über die Psalmen*; Ewald, *Die Dichter des alten Bundes* I.2; Frants Buhl, *Psalmerne*. Other representatives of the earlier historico-critical school are Hitzig, Olshausen, Hupfeldt, Baethgen and Briggs. In a class by himself stands Cheyne with his subjective remodelling of the texts almost beyond identification, because of his view of the dominant part played by the Negeb tribes in earlier Judaic times. Eerdmans—who likewise has his own view of the religious history of Israel, and looks upon the Psalms as a kind of Yahwistic partisan poetry—takes an analogous attitude, though he carries it out in an altogether different way. As traditionalistic as can well be, even to the literal understanding of the supposed names of authors in the headings, we have Hengstenberg's *Kommentar*. Delitzsch in his *Commentar* shows a moderate standpoint with an increasing tendency to allow for the historical point of view. Much the same may be said about König's *Die Psalmen*—so unaccommodating and averse to all later view points is it, that it may be said to have appeared at least ten years too late. The 'time-historical' interpretation was pushed to its extreme consequences in Buttenwieser, *The Psalms*. He claims to be able to date accurately practically every single psalm in the collection, and even to tell which psalms were composed by Deutero-Isaiah, or by the author of the poem of Job; though he certainly does not shrink from a radical dividing-up of the individual psalms, and sometimes even rearranging the parts, basing this on purely formal and logical deductions from details, without making allowances for the power of a fixed tradition of style. A method akin to that of Buttenwieser is shown by Morgenstern in his essays on a great many individual psalms (in *HUCA*).

NOTE III (p. 23, n. 1)

'On the classification of the Psalms according to their contents much labour has been spent', says Baethgen (*Die Psalmen* ³ p. IV). Most of this painstaking work, however, has been in vain, because it has been done in a modernizing spirit and from the point of view of modern literary categories and definitions. Thus modern commentators speak of 'nature lyrics', as if 'nature' were a source of poetical inspiration to men of ancient cultures, as it has been to the European 'romantic school'; or we hear of a 'psalm of conversion' (Nyberg, *Studien z. Hoseabuche*, pp. 118ff; something of the same kind in Eerdmans, *Hebr. Book of Psalms*, p. 41), as if the ancient Israelites had special services for converts, or perhaps revival meetings with corresponding types of psalms. Baethgen acquiesces in Hengstenberg's classification (*Commentar ü. d. Psalmen*) according to the prevailing emotional note of the individual poem: psalms born out of a prevailingly joyful and rejoicing emotion, psalms born out of a prevailing feeling of sadness and sorrow and low spirits, and psalms born out of a quiet contemplative state of mind, such as religious and moral 'didactic psalms'. But even Baethgen must own to the difficulty that many psalms bear witness to two quite different states of mind, e.g., Ps.22.

Other commentators try to give a classification that takes into consideration both contents and emotion ('Stimmung'). So e.g. König (*Die Psalmen*, pp. 33f.): (*a*) epic-lyrical psalms as e.g., Ex. 15.1b–18, or such psalms as give some 'reflection of the history of salvation' ('Heilsgeschichte'), God's deeds in creation, nature and history, as Ps. 19 or 'the beginning of His special kingship in Israel', as Ps. 99, *et al.*;(*b*) descriptive poems like Pss. 95; 97;(*c*) didactic psalms;(*d*) 'lyric poems', expressing emotions of joy, like thanksgiving psalms, or of sorrow and sadness, like the penitential psalms;(*e*) psalms 'trying to influence the sphere of will', including prayers in misfortune and distress, or 'benedictions' like Ps. 1. The inadequacy of this skeleton-like system will be seen clearly enough from the fact that, e.g., kindred psalms like 99; 95 and 97 are referred to different categories, whereas thanksgiving psalms and penitential psalms are supposed to belong to the same class; what has been given here is obviously no real typology, either from the point of view of contents or from that of form or emotion.

Other scholars give other mixtures of heterogeneous principles and points of view. So e.g. Bertholet in Kautzsch, *HSAT* II,³ p. 106; Steuernagel's classification in his *Einleitung i. d. A. T.* has also been partially orientated according to (supposed) religious types of piety and sorts of ideas, and entirely neglects the form-historical point of view, which might have provided objective facts. Partly influenced by Gunkel's typological method, but still without any consistent principles, are the classifications by Staerk (*SATA* III 1) and Kittel (*Die Psalmen*); the latter divides into (a) congregational and individual hymns of praise, (b) poems of thanksgiving and of prayer, (c) didactic poems, (d) spiritual songs. The classification of Barnes (*The Psalms*, XVf.) is likewise heterogeneous and unsystematic; between his groups 1. 'prayers' and 3. 'petitions for deliverance', there is no actual difference; his group 4. 'confessions of faith' has not been distinguished as to matter and form from group 2. 'hymns'; his 'confessions of sin' also include psalms which are not psalms of confession or penitence. Pfeiffer's *Introduction* does not even make attempts at a classification based on an examination of forms *and* contents in their relation to each other. The same applies to Eerdmans, *Hebr. Book of Pss.* and to Steinmann, *Les Psaumes*, who distinguishes between royal psalms and Messianic psalms and regards 'the psalm of immortality' (Ps. 16) as a specific 'type' besides 'cries of suffering' and 'lamentations and imprecations'.

What is lacking in all these classifications is, in short, the cult-functional point of view, the only one that can lead to a satisfactory result.

NOTE IV (p. 29, n. 6)

Gunkel's 'form historical' method, and with it the assertion that psalmography was originally connected with the cult, has been adopted among others by Balla (*Das Ich der Psalmen*); H. Schmidt (*Thronfahrt Jahves; HBAT* 16); Causse (*HRPhR* VI, pp. 155ff.); Gressmann (in Simpson's *The Psalmists*); Hylmö (*Gml. Test. litt. historie*, pp. 23ff.); Eissfeldt (*Einleitung*, pp. 138ff.); Ballscheit (*Der Gottesbund*, pp. 147ff.); Bentzen (*Indledn. til Salm.; Fortolkning av Salm.*); Hempel (*Althebr. Lit.*, pp. 30ff.); Hylander (*G.T.s psalmbok*, pp. 31ff.); Cosgrave (*Canadian Soc. of Bibl. Studies Bul.* no. 5, pp. 3ff.); Leslie (*The Psalms . . . in Light of Hebrew Life and Worship*); Muilenburg ('Psalm 47' in *JBL* 63, 1944, pp. 235ff.); T. H. Robinson (*The Poetry of the O.T.*); Paterson (*The Praises of Israel*); Ridderboos (*Psalmen en Cult*), Terrien (*The Psalms and their Meaning for To-day*); Montgomery (*The Bible*, pp. 74ff.); Würthwein (in *Festschrift für Bertholet*, pp. 532ff.); as well as the present author (*Ps.St.* I–VI). Staerk (*SATA* III 1) and Kittel (*Die Pss.*) likewise in a great measure agree, though they do not always succeed in maintaining this viewpoint. A cultic and liturgic interpretation is also maintained by Peters, *The Pss. as Liturgies*; the Psalms are not 'occasional poems, celebrating some historical event', but 'hymns composed or used for liturgic ends' (op. cit., p. 63). But Peters has invalidated his thesis by referring the *Elohim-psalter* (Pss. 42–84) to the sanctuary of Dan, without giving sufficient reasons for it, and by assuming a connexion between the Yahwistic and the Elohistic sections of the Psalter and the sources of the Pentateuch J and E, respectively; the common but erroneous theory that 'E' belonged to the Northern Kingdom has contributed to this Dan-theory of Peters. Nor has Peters based his argument on the safe foundation of form-history; he has therefore laid too much weight on details which are illuminated by the conventional forms of the traditional style; so for instance, when in Ps. 42 he finds clear references to the wells of Dan (instead of the rivers of the underworld, Sheol), or argues against Jerusalem being the city of Yahweh in Ps. 46 on topographical grounds: by Jerusalem there is no 'river'—but see Isa. 33! In Keet (*A Liturg. Stud. of the Pss.*) the thesis—in itself correct and with many good details—has not been sufficiently well founded. Even the Catholic investigator Podechard has been influenced by Gunkel's method; likewise Paterson, *The Praises of Israel*. In principle even Baumann's 'Struktur-Untersuchungen im Psalter' I, *ZATW*, 61, 1945/48, pp. 114ff.) is based on the foundation of *Gattungsforschung*, though one does not notice it much because of his rationalistic and logistically determined treatment of the texts and—from the very point of view of type investigation—unjustifiable dividing-up of the individual psalms and rearranging of the parts. (Baumann does make many exegetically valuable contributions, but this is another matter). The sensitive book of Welch, *The Psalter*, bears evidence of a clear understanding of the connexion between cult and psalmography. See also, for instance, von Rad's pronouncement in *Festschrift für Bertholet*, pp. 427f.; likewise the article by Weiser, ibid., pp. 513ff. I hope the present book may prove that I myself am perfectly aware that Weiser is partly justified in the reservations made by him (ibid., p. 515, n. 2.).

König (*Die Pss.*, pp. 45ff.) absolutely rejects form analysis and the cultic point of view, and the same must be said of Kaminka (*MGWJ* LXXI, p. 289) and Eerdmans (*Hebr. Book of Pss.*, pp. 6ff.) and of some Catholic psalm commentators like Herkenne and Calès. Nor does Barnes understand it (*The Psalms* I, pp. 1ff.). He certainly disagrees with the 'time historians' and maintains that the psalms contain very few clear references to contemporary historical events, yet he considers the psalms to be private poems, based on the pious reactions of individuals to personal or public events in their own lives. He will hear nothing of a religious and sociological situation of life being the background of psalmography; 'in these early days the singer did not sing for the congregation, nor compose "hymns" for temple worship', he says (p. XI), though all analogies from the literature of the world prove the contrary. The reader of the commentary looks in vain for any attempt to arrange the material according to form historical points of view, or to see the concrete background of the origin of the psalm types; in some instances Barnes even rejects such an explanation, for instance with regard to the enthronement psalms (op. cit., pp. LXXIVf.). When we consider the year of publication, 1931, the whole commentary seems strangely *passé*; much space is given to a discussion of Duhm's 'Maccabean hypothesis', and under the heading 'Recent theories' he examines—besides the problems from *Ps.St.* I and II—Smend's 'collective ego' without even mentioning Gunkel or Balla and the form and cult historical method, which alone is able to solve this old problem.

Neither does Buttenwieser realize the necessity and value of the cult historical point of view. He is aware that not a few psalms have some relation to the cult (*The Psalms*, pp. 4ff.), but he does not realize that it is a relation in principle and essence, nor does he see the value of form history in our attempts to get a correct picture of the relationship. The interest in arranging the individual psalms into groups and species of one set and style entirely disappears in the pursuit of illusory references to contemporary history and a chronology. Buttenwieser's arbitrary dividing-up of a psalm text is made possible by his contempt for form and cult history; a typical example is his treatment of Ps. 107, which from a form and cult historical point of view is quite clearly a unity, but in which Buttenwieser detaches vv. 23-31, making them a fragment of a lyrical description of a 'storm at sea', whereas the rest are supposed to be a poem by Deutero-Isaiah on the deliverance of Israel from the Exile (op. cit., pp. 303ff.). His ability to ascribe the authorship of a great many psalms to Deut.-Isa. is explained by his contempt for form history. Form history shows up clearly the conventionalism of style in the psalm's phraseology and metaphor, and makes it quite impossible to talk about priority regarding their use, or to assume a common author on the basis of such phraseological elements.

Even Pfeiffer (*Introduction*, pp. 632f.) shows very little understanding of the form and cult historical point of view. No more than the two preceding authors does he give a full description or examination of it, and yet he rejects it after a short discussion which fails to get to the bottom of the matter; occasionally he argues against the view of the present author in *Ps.St.*, which, however, he seems to know mostly from quotations (see reference on p. 643, note 20 to *Ps.St.* II instead of VI). When Pfeiffer fails to see the genetic and organic relations between psalmography and cult, it is due to his untenably late dating of the psalms. A little more understanding is shown by Nötscher (*Die Psalmen*, p. 4). But Bonkamp (*Die Psalmen*) does not take advantage of the aid afforded by type investigation. Among the antagonists of *Gattungsforschung*, Eerdmans finds that Gunkel's method makes all the psalms become 'like scrambled eggs' (*Hebrew Book of Psalms*, pp. 6ff.). Even Tur-Sinai (*OTS* VIII, pp. 263ff.) denies that the psalms have a cultic origin; he believes them to be excerpts from historical books (!). Haller's summary of the investigation in *ThR*, N.F. 1 gives his impression of the situation, cf. Baumgartner in *ARW* XXVI, pp. 74ff.; most instructive is A. R. Johnson's article in *The Old Testament and Modern Study*, pp. 162ff.

NOTE V (p. 78, n. 111)

The tendency towards the 'democratization' of the cultic rituals seems to be a common feature in religions; cf. Widengren, *Relig. värld*, pp. 192f. In the case of Babylonia this fact was first pointed out by Jastrow, *Relig. Babyl. u. Ass.* II, pp. 106f., 117. For

Israel see Mowinckel, *Ps.St.* VI, p. 74; *id. NTT* 1934, pp. 14ff. Bentzen, *Sacrale Kongedömme*, pp. 52, 58ff., 61; Birkeland, *Feinde d. Indiv.*, pp. 114ff. The idea and the term have also been adopted by English and other 'myth and ritual' investigators, cf. Engnell, *Div. Kingship*, pp. 50f., and index s.v. 'Democratization'. Riesenfeld, *Jesus transfiguré*, pp. 11f., seems to be taking the term in a too restricted sense when he apparently thinks only of the transfer of the part played by the king to other cultic officials. Riesenfeld, too, here seems to put the king too much in the place of Yahweh; the Israelite new year festival is first of all concerned with the enthronement of Yahweh, not with that of the earthly king. In Egypt the democratization is quite obvious; originally it was only the king, who, through death and the death ritual, was made one with the god, Osiris; later it was extended to include the nobles, and finally any individual Egyptian; see Frankfort, *Kingship*, pp. 120, 197ff., 257f.; Albright, *FSAC*, pp. 138f.; Steindorff-Seele, *When Egypt Ruled the East*, pp. 148, 150.

NOTE VI (p. 107, n. 1)

The old translation of this expression is 'The Lord is king' (Luther; the Bible of the Dano-Norwegian King Christian III; Moffatt), 'The Lord reigneth' (Engl. ARV); and this translation is still upheld by Eissfeldt (*ZATW* 46, 1928, pp. 81ff.), Barnes, Buttenwieser, Eerdmans ('Jahu reigns as king'), Nötscher, Ridderboos (*VT.* 4, 1954, pp. 87ff.), amongst others. In fact, the question of translating by the present or by the perfect is no purely grammatical problem to be considered by itself, but it has to be solved from the point of view of a total conception of the psalm(s) in question. In the first place we may take for granted that the Massoretes had a definite intention and gave expression to a traditional interpretation when they vocalized the word as a verb in the perfect, *mālakh*, and not a noun *melekh*, which would make a nominal clause, but which would no doubt be the most likely interpretation of the consonantal text to come to mind, because of the rare occurrence of the verb *mālakh*, as well as from the point of view of any unreflecting dogmatism. The MT would suggest activity, not a state. Secondly it is well known that a great many Hebrew verbs have a meaning at once ingressive and durative: sit down and sit, become great and be great, and so on; so, too, *mālakh*, become a king and be a king. From the point of view of Hebrew psychology and way of thinking the 'ingressive', or perhaps rather, the active sense is always superior; a man *is* great just because or as long as he proves himself great and makes himself great, and so on; a man 'is sitting', because he has 'sat down'. The context must decide whether in a given case the emphasis has to be put on the ingressive or on the durative element. Thirdly it is a fact that the linguistically quite analogous '*ābhšālôm mālakh, šělōmōh mālakh*, etc., as well as the analogous Akkadian *mardukma šarru* are shouts of homage hailing the king at his enthronement, and stating the fact that now he 'is king' because he 'has just become king'; being shouts of enthronement, they do not in the first place emphasize that from now on he 'reigns' (and shall reign), but that he has now 'become king' and therefore hereafter reigns. If therefore we may take for granted that the expression is really a shout of homage at the enthronement, it is of secondary importance whether we *translate* 'reigns as king' or 'has become king', for in any case the attention is turned towards the 'ingressive' element. This is certainly what MT wants to express through the vocalization *mālakh*. If the intention was only to express 'an existing and enduring state' (Buttenwieser, op. cit., p. 340), why did they not vocalize *melekh* taking the sentence as a regular nominal clause?

Now there is no denying that the imaginary picture appearing to the authors of these psalms and being conjured into being by them before their audience, by their poetic vision, is the picture of an enthronement; all the parallelisms with features from the enthronement of the earthly king prove this; Yahweh is seen and described as sitting on his throne, not because he is supposed to have been there, throned, from before the creation of the world, but because from a definite point of time he has laid hold of, or, (if one interprets eschatologically) will lay hold of, regal power. This is unreservedly admitted as a matter of course in eschatological interpretation: as the End approaches Yahweh will manifest himself as the one who rises and performs great works and seizes power and (after that) sits 'enthroned' and 'reigns' and 'is king'; cf. the way Barnes expresses it: 'Jehovah will manifest himself as king' (*The Psalms* II, p. 461); it was not manifest before that he was really king, but now something happens to reveal him as king, that is, a royal epiphany and at least a 'virtual enthronement'. This is *de facto* admitted by all adherents of the 'time historical' interpretation (see above, pp. 109f): the psalms refer to some historical event at which Yahweh has manifested himself as king, and, to the minds of men, that means that he has 'seized power', has made his kingdom an actuality to the mind, he has taken possession of his kingdom. Of quite vital importance therefore is the interpretation of the imagined situation of a particular psalm. Nor is it easy to understand how one can possibly get away from the connexion between the phrase 'NN *mālakh*' and the concept of an enthronement, which the use of the phrase would otherwise indicate.

That even (late) Jewish and early Christian apocalyptic tradition interpreted the matter in this way, will be seen from Rev. 11. 15–17, in which the phraseological and conceptual echoes of the enthronement psalms are obvious; here the theme of the anthem is that 'the rule of kingship of the world has passed to (aorist ἐγένετο) our Lord and His Anointed,' 'because Thou has assumed Thy great power and hast become king' (aor. ἐβασίλευσας): i.e., assumption of power—enthronement—homage to the king.

Eissfeldt (*ZATW* 46, 1928) tries to deny that an act of enthronement is described in the psalms. He maintains that the use of the epithet 'king' about Yahweh never implies the idea of an act of enthronement, mythically conceived (or experienced through the cult); the psalms (and the festival serving as their basis) 'apply to the very Yahweh who is here as otherwise imagined and praised as a king. The mere fact that the epithet "king" is used about Yahweh does not allow us to draw conclusions as to the nature of the festival, but the latter has to be interpreted by means of more obvious characteristics, and these do not point towards an enthronement festival' (op. cit., pp. 99f.). So, he would have us believe, the set of terms and conceptions in the enthronement psalms simply mean what is not infrequently expressed in other places: that Yahweh is pictured as king and hailed by this name even in the hymns of the festival. Further, Eissfeldt thinks, there is an unacceptable logical contrast between the idea that Yahweh always *is* king and that at a definite point of time He *becomes* king; he will not admit that this contrast only exists to the modern rationalistic way of thinking and disappears as soon as the nature of the cult reveals itself to us. Eissfeldt has justly pointed out that the title of king is in constant use for oriental gods, and he has collected very valuable material, to which may now be added the Ugaritic texts, where *mlk* is used about El as well as about other gods (see Eissfeldt, *El im Ugarit. Pantheon*, pp. 30, 46f.). This is valuable as a background for the use of this title about Yahweh, and it strengthens the conjecture that it has been adopted from the Canaanites. But at the same time it indicates that Israel may probably also have adopted other conceptions and cultic usages attached to the title, not least so the conceptions of the enthronement.

Of course Eissfeldt is right in saying that not all the *mlk* passages speak of an enthronement, but if it is true that the idea of a mythically conceived enthronement of Yahweh did actually exist and found expression in a particular festival, any allusion to the epithet 'king' would *eo ipso* easily contain and call forth by way of association the idea of enthronement, and such an association may be intended. Then the question is whether the idea of enthronement can be discerned in the 'enthronement psalms'. Eissfeldt's mode of proceeding is to take every passage in isolation, and maintain that when considered by themselves they cannot with mathematical certainty be claimed as referring to an enthronement or an enthronement festival; characteristic of his method is his comment on 1 Kings 22.19, where we are told that Yahweh is sitting on his throne: 'freilich ist damit nicht *notwendig* (the italics are mine) die Vorste lung Jahwes als König verbunden' (op. cit., p. 104, n. 3). No, not with mathematical 'necessity'; it probably does happen sometimes, at any rate in fairy-tales, that page-boys may amuse themselves by sitting on the royal throne, when the throne room is empty for a while! In point of principle Eissfeldt's isolating method, also used by Nötscher, must be pronounced an error. No abstracted consideration of isolated details, but only a comprehensive interpretation of all traces, can afford a truly representative total picture, which will throw light on all the details. Eissfeldt cannot deny that Ps. 47 describes an act, and not a state, but he will just not admit that it has to be an act of enthronement. However, if one considers the act which the author of Ps. 47 has in mind (but to which he only refers through some characteristic details), in connexion with the characteristic terms and allusions in the other enthronement psalms and with the picture of the enthronement of the king as depicted elsewhere in the O.T., one has to be very blind not to realize that the authors of these psalms do have the act of enthronement in mind. Their poems are based on the idea of an act in which Yahweh takes part and is acting—a stirring drama. In opposition to Eissfeldt see the conclusive arguments of Kraus, *Königsherrschaft Gottes*, pp. 3ff. With this method, based on a wide consideration of the entire material, Eissfeldt's exegetical procedure about details can bear no comparison. In this connexion there is no need for me to detail Gunkel's objections (*Einl.* pp. 100ff.), urged by Eissfeldt, as Gunkel himself admits that I have proved the existence of the idea of enthronement in the psalms, as well as of a cultic and mythical act forming a background for them, i.e. the existence of such a festival of enthronement as the one with which this species of psalms is connected.

NOTE VII (p. 111, n. 12)

The eschatological interpretation is, in fact, a revival of the earlier exegesis of the Church, always in pursuit of 'messianic' 'prophecies', and this not only in the enthronement psalms. The earlier messianic interpretation is distinguished from the newer, historically minded one by taking for granted that prophecy is the leading subject of the O.T., and that a great many psalms are prophecies in the dogmatic sense of soterio-history, for their authors sought not only to express their reactions to the events of life, but also to 'prophesy' concerning things to come. This basic idea is in itself wrong. Certainly a psalm may—though only as part of the cult liturgy—contain a prophetic element, a promise from God to the congregation (see Chap. XII). But on the whole the psalm is a 'sacrificial' part of the cult (see my *Religion u. Kultus*, pp. 100ff.); the congregation or the individual is addressing God in prayer, and therefore it is no 'prophecy'.

In a somewhat modified version we find this interpretation of the psalms in Delitzsch (*Comm. ü. d. Psalmen*); he speaks of a group of psalms 'in the spirit of Deutero-Isaiah', Pss. 91–100, which he calls 'theocratic' psalms, as distinguished from the 'christocratic', the downright 'messianic' ones; that is to say: they describe, in imperfect Old Testament fashion, the final state as the kingship of God, not of Christ. Baethgen (*Die Psalmen³*) shares the time historical interpretation of his age, and thinks that the true enthrone-ment psalms refer to a comparatively recent experience of Yahweh's universal kingship in a historical event; Baethgen is thinking of the fall of Babylon and the return from the Exile. But he combines this with an eschatological interpretation: the congregation see the guarantee of the fulfilment of their eschatological hope in Yahweh's powerful deed in history, and now celebrate Yahweh as the one who has proved and will prove himself saviour and king of the world. Here the eschatological element is taken in its true his-torical sense, namely as the hope by which Judaism lived; the dogmatic theory of prophecy is gone, and the problems are based on modern science. From the point of view of methodical principle, Baethgen's interpretation cannot be rejected. But its drawback is the impossibility of referring the experience of the poet to the sphere of history and politics.

This was realized by Gunkel, and therefore—in consequence of his opinion of the age of eschatology and of the psalms—he arrived at the purely eschatological interpretation. Gunkel cannot find any other explanation of the close relationship between the con-ceptions contained in the psalms and the eschatological conceptions of the prophets, other than a dependence on the prophets on the part of the psalmists. And because the prophets sometimes describe the coming salvation 'indirectly' by acting as lyrical singers, voicing in advance the exultation of the congregation over the final salvation, as if it has already taken place, he would interpret these psalms in the same way also. For what purpose, then, these poets may have composed their eschatological poems is not really apparent in Gunkel; it would be most natural to interpret his expressions in *Isr. Literatur* and *Ausgew. Psalmen* (on Pss. 46 and 97) to the effect that the psalmists sought to describe the things to come in order to strengthen their own faith and that of their contemporaries. On Gunkel's modified interpretation in *Einleitung* see, Additional Note VIII. Gunkel's eschatological interpretation has been adopted, among others, by Balla, *Ich der Pss.*, p. 36, n. 3; Staerk *SATA* III. 1, pp. 51ff.; Kittel, *Die Psalmen*, on Ps. 47; Feuillet in *Nouvelle Revue Théologique* 73, without new arguments. Kraus, op. cit., pp. 15f., has declared himself against the eschatological interpretation, in all essentials for the same reasons as the present author.

Note VIII (p. 111, n. 16; p. 191, n. 216)

The answer to the question whether the Psalter includes eschatological psalms or not, depends of course to a certain degree on the definition of the word 'eschatology.' The present author cannot approve the diffuse definitions of many scholars, according to which eschatology includes nearly every sort of national aspirations and wishes and beliefs about a splendid and lucky, but quite intramundane future. The Israelite belief founded upon the belief in the election and the covenant, which is expressed in sentences such as, 'Who is like unto thee, a people saved by Yahweh' (Deut. 33.29); or, 'Blessed the people that knows tĕrû'â, i.e. whose King is Yahweh' (Ps. 89.16), or 'Yahweh will not cast off his people nor forsake his inheritance' (Ps. 94.14), in short: the belief that there always will be a 'future' for Yahweh's elected people is no eschatology. It is, at most, to use Toynbee's expression, 'futurism'. What the present writer means by eschatology, he has said in *He that Cometh*, pp. 125ff.

The answer depends, however, also on what is meant by an 'eschatological psalm'. This term seems commonly to mean a poem with the expressed purpose of describing 'the last things'—a literary 'prophecy' or a contemplation on the final catastrophe, as for instance, '*Dies illa, dies irae*,' or Brorson's 'Den store hvite flokk vi se' (Norwegian Church

Hymnbook no. 619); or a poem in which the author imagines himself living in the eschatological age, as if it had already arrived, and gives vent to his own feelings and those of the congregation at this experience. When talking of eschatological psalms Gunkel is thinking of the latter category, and he is right in saying that it does exist, namely in the prophets, where it serves as impressive clothing for the prophecy. But in spite of the arguments in Gunkel-Begrich, *Einl.* p. 81, we must insist that in such cases the prophets are quite evidently speaking of the future; this is indicated either by an introductory formula or must be taken for granted because such a 'song' is plainly part of an oracle, or, as in Deutero-Isaiah, because it is proved by the actual situation: at this very moment the 'coming thing' is being experienced; even his jubilant hymns are attached to the prophecies. In the psalms, on the other hand, there is no indication whatever that the authors wish them to be interpreted as prophecies. This does not mean that there are not psalms in the proper sense of the word which contain eschatological motifs or some outlook to the more remote future. On this point see Chap. V. 12–13, where the forward looking aspect of the festival and its psalm is dealt with, but some words may also be added here.

That the forward-pointing aspect of the experiences and psalms of the enthronement festival has been a point of connexion for the later eschatological ideas, and that these therefore found their way into the complex of ideas connected with the feast, was realized by Volz (*Neujahrsfest Jahwes*). In *Ps. St.*II I failed to make this not unimportant point clear, which may, however, be due to an over-reaction against the vagueness of many scholars' definition of 'eschatology'. Cf. now however, *He that Cometh*, pp. 96ff., 138ff., and above, Chap. V.13.

The same vagueness may also be the reason for unclear and somewhat unmethodical treatment of the question 'psalms and eschatology' by many psalm commentators. I cite only two instances.

Th. H. Robinson, in *The Psalmists*, has shown awareness of the forward-pointing aspect of the festival and psalms, but the matter is vaguely envisaged and presented. This is due to two facts: (1) Robinson still adheres to the theory of Gressmann about a 'pre-prophetic eschatology', used by prophets and psalmists as 'raw material' for the descriptions of the future as well as of the ideal (historical) king; and (2) he has not quite grasped the intentions of the investigation of different literary types (*Gattungsforschung*), and therefore does not treat in the same way things that are of one set; it will not do, for instance, to discuss Ps. 47 from another point of view than 96 and 97 and 98; if Pss. 20 and 21 refer to the actual king we cannot find expectations of a future descendant of David in Ps. 132, etc. Robinson does not use the term 'eschatological' with a distinct meaning, and does not clearly distinguish between 'forward-pointing' and 'eschatological'. But even Robinson admits that there are very few eschatological traits to be found in the psalms.

Even Oesterley's conception is vague (*The Psalms*). He accepts the theory that the enthronement psalms are real cultic psalms belonging to the festival of new year and enthronement, but all the same maintains that they are all of them eschatological. We are not really told what is the relation of 'the eschatological element' to the festival, and how it came to form such an essential part of the substance of the idea of the latter. According to Oesterley even Ps. 93 treats of 'the eschatological drama'; but the real and only subject of this psalm is creation, and victory over the ocean as the basis of Yahweh's kingship; it is not correct to say that the victory over the primeval ocean is here nothing but a 'symbol' of Yahweh's victory over his enemies in general; in the psalm itself there is not the least hint that this victory is meant to be taken in an eschatological sense.

NOTE IX (p. 112, n. 17)

The first approach to a cultic interpretation of the enthronement psalms is the emphasis of Olshausen and Duhm on the purely 'liturgical' character of several of them. But the idea of a special cultic situation and a corresponding mythical performance of a particular enthronement festival is not really apparent. However, Duhm took the first step by acknowledging Ps. 47 as a cultic liturgical psalm for the new year festival, but he did not realize the consequences of such a correct interpretation; this is because he did not follow out the 'liturgical' interpretation but chose to consider some of the enthronement psalms from the time historical point of view, and thus tore asunder a group making a consistent whole. Gressmann approaches very near the right interpretation in his *Ursprung d. Eschat.*, pp. 294ff. Here he regards the style of the enthronement hymns as a half-understood imitation of such psalms as may be supposed to have been sung in Babylonia-Assyria at the enthronement of a *new* god and on his entering into possession of the empire of the world; the performance is supposed to imply that the new god in question has not previously been king and governor of the world. In the background stands the theory of Winckler and the pan-Babylonians about the alternating world periods, whenever the sun as a result of precession enters into a new sign of the zodiac; then the god of the sign in question takes over supreme rule. Gressmann is aware of the fact that in Babylonia and elsewhere a particular day was celebrated as the enthronement day of the new god. He has further realized that in Israel an entire plexus of concepts is grouped round the idea of the enthronement of Yahweh, complementing each other and serving to make up a picture of such a mythical performance as a whole. When Yahweh seats himself on his throne and becomes king of the world, then, says Gressmann, this idea literally implies that until then he is not king; but as this is a completely un-Israelite and actually polytheistic way of thinking, the whole idea of enthronement must be of foreign, in fact of Babylonian, origin. With this Babylonian conception Israel also, according to Gunkel, adopted the custom of celebrating a certain day as the enthronement day of Yahweh—how and to what extent and with what religious substance he does not tell us—and they expressed the connexion between enthronement and new year festival in Ps. 47. 'Wie man in Babylonien oder sonstwo bei den Nachbarvölkern am Neujahrstage—und ebenso beim Anfang einer neuen Welt—die Thronbesteigung eines neuen (sic!) Gottes feierte, so ward dieses Beispiel in Israel nachgeahmt, weil es so zum Stil gehörte (!). Während anderswo natürlich (!!) verschiedene Götter nacheinander den Thron bestiegen (!) so musste man sich in Israel wohl oder übel mit dem einen Gott begnügen' (!).

If Gunkel had known at that time what we know to-day of the enthronement festivals of Marduk, Anu and other gods in Babylonia, he would certainly not have written like this. We know now that the conception of the enthronement of the god does not mean that a new god, who has not been king before, becomes the ruler of the world; evidently this conception is related to Winckler's theory of world periods and the ancient oriental view of the world ('*altorientalische Weltanschauung*') which takes for granted that at the beginning of every new period (when the sun enters into a new sign in the zodiac) a new deity was made the supreme god; as a matter of fact the idea of the enthronement of the god involves the idea of a repetition of what has been, of a return to the origin, and is but a special version of the epiphany of the god; at the annual cultic festival the same god becomes king anew each time.

Gunkel does not make clear what has really been imitated in Israel; whether the conception of the enthronement of the god, or its realization in a corresponding cultic act. However, as he suggests that festal processions, in which Yahweh 'in his palladium' passes up to the Temple as a king (op. cit., p. 295, n. 1), were known to Israel, he seems to allow for a real cultic enthronement evidently related to the new year festival, as in Babylonia. So much the stranger does it appear, therefore, that he did not realize the cultic character of the enthronement psalms, nor infer from them the existence of a corresponding enthronement festival. It looks as if Gunkel's eschatological interpretation of the psalms must have prevented him from seeing the true consequences of his indications; a lack of insight into the real nature of the cult and its significance even in ancient Israel may have tended in the same direction. Yet it was these very indications, in addition to the information given by Zimmern in *KAT*[3] about the Babylonian idea of enthronement and festival, as well as Duhm's interpretation of Ps. 47, which put the present author on the track of the Israelite enthronement festival, see *Ps.St.* II, pp. XIff.

NOTE X (p. 113, n. 18)

Even Gunkel had suggested that the image of a real festival lay behind the poetic vision of these psalms; for the authors were supposed to have derived their picture of the enthronement of Yahweh from the enthronement festivals of the earthly king, and to a certain extent, of course, this is correct: the enthronement of the god is naturally imagined after the analogy of that of the earthly king. Gunkel maintains that the enthronement psalms are religious, eschatological poems, imitating the poetical vision and style of supposed 'wordly' enthronement poems, and he uses the allusions in the psalms to the ritual of anointing as material for a description of these hypothetical songs. But we know nothing about such 'worldly enthronement hymns.' What the psalmists— and before them the actual ritual of Yahweh's enthronement festival—have imitated, were not 'worldly' royal hymns, but the poetical picture of the enthronement of the earthly king. In fact Gunkel himself seems to admit that the existence of 'worldly' enthronement hymns is rather problematic, see *Einl.*, p. 106. His maintenance of this theory is inconsistent, so long as he finds himself forced to admit the existence of an enthronement festival of Yahweh, and to derive the origin of the psalm species from it, see Additional Note XIII.

NOTE XI (p. 113, n. 20)

The cultic interpretation of the enthronement psalms and, in consequence thereof, the acknowledgment that one of the chief festivals of Israel really did bear the character of an enthronement festival of Yahweh was first advanced by the present author in the volume of *NTT* published in connexion with the Reformation Jubilee of 1917 (pp. 13ff.), and substantiated at greater length in *Ps.St.* II. It has been adopted by an increasing number of later investigators, for instance L. Dürr, *Ursprung u. Ausbau*; Hölscher, *Urspr. d. jüd. Eschatol.*; Schmidt, *Th Ltz* 1929, col. 77ff.; id., *Die Thronfahrt Jahves*; Böhl, *Nieuwejaarfeest en Koningsdag*; v. Gall, *Basileia*, pp. 20ff.; Gunkel, *Einl.*, pp. 105ff.; Sellin, *Einleitung*[4]; Hempel, *Gott u. Mensch*,[2] pp. 16, 180 et ser.; Meinhold, *Einführung*,[2] p. 310; Causse, *Les plus vieux chants de la Bible*, pp. 97ff.; Quell, *Kult. Probl. d. Pss.*, p. 77; Volz, *Theol. Blätter*, 1924; Loisy in *RCritHR*, 1923, pp. 122ff.; Lods in *RHR*, 1925, pp. 15ff.; Bellas in *Theologia*, 1930; Humbert in *RHPhR* 15, 1935, pp. 1ff.; Bentzen, *Indl. t. Salm.*, pp. 126ff., and in *Fortolk. t. d. gmltstm. salmer*; Hooke in *Myth and Ritual*, p. 13; Oesterley ibid., pp. 122ff. (which only refers to H. Schmidt, see however Oesterley, *A Fresh Approach*, pp. 142ff.); Johnson in *The Labyrinth*, pp. 71ff.; Hooke, ibid., p. 230; Hylmö, *G.T. lit. hist.*, pp. 25f.; Engnell, *G. T.* I, pp. 54ff.; Hvidberg, *Graad og Latter*; Kapelrud in *NTT*, 1940, pp. 38ff.; Widengren, *Relig. värld*, pp. 198f.; Johs. Pedersen,

Israel III–IV, pp. 431ff.; Lindblom, *Israels religion*, pp. 82f., 110; Eichrodt, *Theol. d. a. T.*, pp. 56f.; Leslie, *The Psalms . . . in the Light of Hebrew Life and Worship*; Muilenburg in *JBL* 63, 1944, pp. 235ff.; in principle even Aubert (*RThPh*, 1927), in spite of many reservations and an ample use of 'atomizing' procedure about details; G. von Rad, *Formgesch. Problem d. Hexateuchs*, pp. 18ff.; idem., *Festschrift für Bertholet*, pp. 427ff., passim; A. Weiser, ibid., pp. 513ff. Gaster, *Thespis*, too, finds that the harvest and new year festival of Israel (feast of tabernacles) has many important features, in all essentials identical with those of my 'enthronement festival'.

Opposed to the theory of an enthronement festival, among others, is König who writes from a modern Lutheran, but actually rationalistic, point of view, with a now strangely antiquated conception of the psalms, and with no understanding whatsoever for the form-historical and cult-functional point of view which enables us to understand the psalms correctly. Opposed also are Eissfeldt (see Additional Note VI), and Steuernagel (in *Preuss, Kirchenzeitung*, 1928), Pap (*Isr. Neujahrsfest*) maintains the eschatological interpretation without any new arguments and without invalidating any evidence against it. The reason why he opposes it is his insistence that there existed no new year *festival* in pre-exilic times; but the sources prove the opposite, see Chap. V, n. 35.

Snaith (*Stud. in the Psalter*; idem., *Jewish New Year Festival*) does his utmost to restore the time historical interpretation of the psalms and rather overestimates the possibility of ascertaining the historical dating and use of individual psalms; he concludes that the enthronement psalms are sabbath psalms. But it will not do to ignore the analogies of the surrounding religions as Snaith does. He insists that the Babylonian *akîtu* festival was no new year festival until the sixth century B.C. (op. cit., pp. 214ff.); but in no way has he been able to invalidate the evidence produced by Zimmern, Pallis, Labat and Frankfort, nor has he allowed for the fact that the ancient civilizations had many 'new year times' and festivals with the characteristics of a 'new beginning'. That the *akîtu* festival was a new year festival culminating in the renewed enthronement of the god is plainly seen from the idea of *Enuma êliš* with its *marduk-ma šarru*, and from the fact that this epic was the 'festival legend' of the feast long before the sixth century. Snaith has not even discussed the evidence brought forward by Hvidberg (*Graad og Latter*) and others to prove that the Ugaritic Baal myth belonged to a new year and enthronement festival of Baal. For his dating of the connexion of the kingship idea with the new year festival, see Chap. V.4. The existence of an 'enthronement aspect' of the harvest and new year festival of Israel, as argued in *Ps.St.* II, was not derived from the ideas of Volz (*Neujahrsfest Jahwes*), as is claimed by Snaith (op. cit., p. 195); on the contrary it was discovered by Volz and myself independently, as may be seen from the preface to *Ps.St.* II; nor has it been inferred from the Babylonian analogy, as may also be read in the same place; on the contrary it is the result of the application of the cultic principle of interpretation to the psalms themselves. (Even Kraus unduly exaggerates the importance of the Babylonian new year festival for my argument in *Ps.St.* II).

Also opposed to the idea of enthronement festivals are Synave in the article 'Psaumes' in *Dict. Theol. Catholique* XII, and Eerdmans (*Hebr. Book of Pss.*). Eerdmans, again, has no understanding of the form and cult historical point of view—quite apart from the fact that his original conception of the psalms as partisan poetry actually places him outside the whole modern discussion of the problems. Cf. my review in *NTT* 1949,pp. 205ff., and see also Ridderboos, *Psalmen en Cultus*, which, against Eerdmans, points out a number of pieces of evidence from outside the Psalter for the use of psalms in the cult. Nötscher (*Die Psalmen*) has a better appreciation of the cultic nature of the psalms, but rejects a special enthronement festival—though without any real arguments, and basing his case on a consideration of the individual psalms in complete isolation, without trying to see what is common to a group and then finding the explanation for it; cf. his remark on the matter in connexion with Ps. 47: 'Von einem Thronbesteigungsfest Jahves sagt der Dichter nichts' (cf. on Ps. 93). As if the author of a Christian Easter hymn must always put in a remark about the feast of Easter!

Albright (*Cath. Bibl. Quartl.*, Jan. 1945, pp. 28f., cf. *JBL* 61, 1942, pp. 122f.) admits that the authors of the enthronement psalms have seen a vision of Yahweh's enthronement, but rejects the existence of any real cultic enthronement festival; the Israelites are supposed to have adopted the idea of an enthronement from the Canaanites, not as a cultic reality, but only as a poetic 'literary' performance; it is supposed to have happened in connexion with the adoption of original Canaanite psalms containing the idea of the enthronement of the god. But even if psalms like 29; 68; 82 and the enthronement psalms 93ff. should be Israelitic remodellings of original Canaanite Baal-psalms, as maintained by Albright, this does not prove that the idea of an enthronement must have been just 'literary' in Israel; in the first place, an eventual adoption must be supposed to be motivated by the existence or the adoption of a corresponding cultic reality in Israel; in the second place, there are to be found even in late Jewish tradition too many features of kingship and enthronement in connexion with the cult of the harvest and new year festival for us to think that they are due to 'literary' influence.

Even Barnes (*The Psalms* I, pp. LXXIV ff.) is very sceptical, although he admits that the theory seems to fit in very well with, for instance, Ps. 47. His two arguments against it do not hold good; it is not correct to say that the main point of the new year festival in Babylon was the renewal of the earthly king, not the enthronement of the god; see the description of the festival, e.g. in Frankfort, *Kingship*, pp. 313ff.; nor is it correct to say that we find no allusions to such a festival in the O.T.; as has been emphasized in *Ps.St.* II we are not dealing with a new, as yet unknown and just postulated festival, but with a hitherto unnoticed aspect of the well-known main festival of the year (see above, pp. 151ff. and my *Zum israelitischen Neujahr*, p. 46), that of harvest and new year. Whether the enthronement of the earthly king was also celebrated by an anniversary feast, as is doubted by Barnes on the grounds of 1 Sam. 10.1, is of secondary interest in this connexion. On the whole, Barnes does not seem to have fully realized what the religious experience of the cultic festival meant to the ancient Israelites. For instance, if one has realized the important part played by the 'judgment' of Yahweh in the plexus of ideas of the whole festival (see above, pp. 189ff.), a statement like the following: 'These psalms contain too much about an approaching judgment to be considered as merely ritual exercises [sic!] for yearly use' (op cit., p. 461) seems rather strange, to say the least.

There is no reason for me to discuss Buttenwieser's critique of my discovery (*The Psalms*, pp. 321ff.), as he contents himself with a repetition of the arguments of Eissfeldt and Gunkel, partly of course because he fails to understand a form and cult historical point of view (cf. Additional Note IV).

Kraus, *Die Königsherrschaft Gottes im A.T.*, tries to mix a cultic and an eschatological interpretation. On the basis of 2 Sam. 6 and 1 Kings 8 he seeks to prove that even from the age of David and Solomon a 'royal Zion festival' was celebrated in commemoration of the divine legitimation of David's family as the chosen royal race, and the choice of Jerusalem as the future centre of the cult; this festival was celebrated simultaneously with—and probably as part of—the annual feast in the month of Ethanim; a certain number of psalms belonged to it, particularly Ps. 132. First of all it was centred round the covenant with David, round the king and the future 'Heilskönig aus Davids Geschlecht', and Jerusalem. Its most important cultic feature was the great entry of the king, accompanied by the Ark of Yahweh. It did not contain any form of an 'enthronement of Yahweh'. After the downfall of state and kingdom it lost the basis of its existence, but with Deutero-Isaiah a new idea emerged: the kingship of Yahweh superseded that of David's family, and Israel as a nation took over the promises to David; therefore the entry of Yahweh is now forthcoming as, at the head of the people carried away, he returns through the desert to Jerusalem, where his enthronement takes place in the re-erected Temple. After the Exile the new 'new year's day' (*rō'š haššanâ*, 1st of Tishri) came into existence, and now the prophecies of Deutero-Isaiah about the entry of Yahweh as king are supposed to have made such an impression on the Jews, that a corresponding cultic custom was introduced, an enthronement procession of Yahweh with the rites belonging to it as a main feature of the new year festival; to this new festival with its new ideology is supposed to have been transmitted the idea of the 'royal Zion festival' about a renewal of the covenant; only now no longer as a renewal of the covenant with David, but as a renewal of the Sinai covenant with all Israel; the new year psalm 81 testifies to this. To this post-exilic 'enthronement festival of Yahweh' then belong the 'enthronement psalms' properly so called, dependent on Deutero-Isaiah and expressing the actualization of the 'eschatological' expectation of the latter, revived by the festival. To this hypothesis we would raise the following objections: (1) Kraus is repeating Gunkel's fundamental mistake with regard to a purely *gattungsgeschichtlich* definition of the material, without taking into account the fact that a festival of such complicated substance may also have included psalms of different types, but all more or less defined by the enthronement ideas; thus for instance Ps. 95 is detached without pertinent reasons, and so we are cut off from part of the relevant material to which Ps. 81 leads the way (see p. 142, and see below, Additional Note XXIV). (2) The 'royal Zion festival' rests on a perfectly untenable interpretation of 2 Sam. 6–7 and 1 Kgs. 8 (see Additional Note XIX). (3) The conception of Deutero-Isaiah's relationship to the kingship of the Davidic family in the re-established Israel rests on an evident, even though to a certain extent traditional (see for instance Buhl's *Jesajakommentar*), mis-interpretation of Isa. 55.3b–5, reversing the meaning into its opposite. (4) It is not correct to say that the enthronement psalms are dependent on Deutero-Isaiah; the opposite is the case, and the psalm species as such is older than Deutero-Isaiah; see above, pp. 154ff. (5) Kraus does not discuss the question of a 'new year's day' in pre-exilic times, and the proofs of such. (6) His reasoning is often mixed up with dogmatic pre-judices, preventing him from realizing what 'the mythical' really is, and also from utilizing oriental analogies; even the claim—in itself right—for an interpretation of the Old Testament texts on the basis of the O.T. itself may be exaggerated into one-sidedness. In spite of certain valuable details and views worth consideration, the re-construction offered by Kraus must on the whole be considered a failure.

Note XII (p. 113, n. 21)

It is interesting to note how Gunkel felt compelled to modify his original eschatological interpretation in the direction of a cultic one. In his earlier works (*Isr. Literatur*; the article '*Psalmen*' in RGG;[1] *Ausgew. Pss.*[4] pp. 201f.; *Red. u. Aufs.*, pp. 123ff.) he rather appears to think that the enthronement psalms are private (literary) 'prophecies,' poetic prophecies or eschatological descriptions, or expressions of the eschatological belief, put in the style of a psalm; the analogies from the 'prophets' to which he refers seem to confirm that this was how he meant it. In the *Einl.* he has felt the weight of the impression of actual experience made by these psalms, and of the arguments for the connexion with the cult, and therefore has to admit that at a certain period in Israel—during the late monarchy—a real cultic enthronement festival of Yahweh was celebrated on a Babylonian pattern, and that enthronement hymns made up part of this festival. Only, the latter proved rather ephemeral; the enthronement hymns handed down to us have all an eschatological meaning and are limitations—no longer of 'worldly royal hymns', as Gunkel used to think, but—of cultic hymns for Yahweh's enthronement festival, now lost to us; they are no longer supposed to be due to direct transcriptions of eschatology into verse, but to an eschatological re-reading of the idea of the enthronement of the god. Gunkel even goes so far as to admit that these (eschatological) psalms belonged to certain cult festivals, characterized by the presence of eschatological ideas; he is evidently thinking of the harvest and new year festivals; then the congregation would experience in faith the coming age, as if it were present, and identify itself with the emotions that would fill it then (*Einl.*, p. 80). However, by all these concessions Gunkel has in fact knocked the ground from under the feet of the eschatological interpretation. What prevented Gunkel from seeing this was his unproved and unprovable theory about the great age of eschatology, and his postulate as to the priority of the prophets in spiritual history all along.

The only 'argument' left is the very starting-point: that the enthronement psalms have a lot of ideas in common with eschatology. But from where are these ideas derived? Is it not possible that eschatology may have received them from the cult? And are these psalms *in need of* eschatology for an explanation? My discussion of the problem in *Ps.St.* II has proved at least that they *may* be explained out of the very nature of the cult and the festival and the kind of experience they would give. In the religions of the surrounding nations, though they contained no eschatology, all the main ideas and conceptions of the enthronement festival are present—even as cultic ideas, and to be explained from the idea of the coming of the god for re-creation and enthronement. Why, then, should the same ideas in Israel have to use the roundabout way of eschatology? Gunkel's last argument is the supposed dependence of the enthronement psalms on Deutero-Isaiah (*Einl.*, p. 116; repeated by Kraus, op. cit., p. 20). For an answer to this argument see Chap. V.11, 12. The Ugaritic texts have now thrown completely new light on the question of an ancient Yahweh enthronement festival, for these texts show us the religious milieu found by Israel on entering Canaan, and from which they took over their main cultic festivals—the three agrarian ones (see Kapelrud in *NTT*, 1940, pp. 388ff.). In these texts the yearly enthronement of the god is a central idea. A date as late as the Babylonian period for Israel to have adopted a Babylonian festival, for which there was no point of connexion beforehand, is not at all likely.

Yet the eschatological interpretation of Gunkel has some truth in it, to which I have not done justice in my statement in *Ps.St.* II. I have tried to make amends for that in the presentation in Chap. V.11.

NOTE XIII (p. 114 n. 27)

As has been pointed out by Eissfeldt the idea of the god as king is a general oriental (Semitic), one but of course related to definite political circumstances, and dates from the Sumerian period on, cf. *Lugal*, 'The King', as the name of a god. Of course the Arabian divine epithet *malik* has a meaning different from that of the Hebrew *melekh* or the Akkadian *šarru*. Now the meaning of the Hebr. *melekh* will obviously have to be decided not from the eventual etymology of the term, but from a historical interpretation of the texts themselves, as seen in connexion with the political and social circumstances of Israel in the period of the monarchy and of the other ancient oriental peoples. Therefore Buber (*Königtum Gottes*, pp. 63ff.) is quite unjustified in explaining *melekh* as '(mitziehender) Berater' on the grounds of etymology and conditions among the Bedouins—and so dating the idea of Yahweh as 'king' back to the desert period.

NOTE XIV (p. 120, n. 45; p. 147, n. 124)

Pap, *Das israelitische Neujahrsfest* holds that 'even in the earliest times' there existed 'two new-years, one of them finishing off and starting the agrarian year, in the autumn, the other one more ecclesiastical and official, in spring'. Quite evidently this last statement is not correct; none of the pre-exilic sources testify to a year beginning in spring. The spring new year is obviously due to the introduction of the Babylonian calendar in exilic and post-exilic times with new, Babylonian names for the months, and with new year's day at the vernal equinox, and Nisan (formerly the month of Abib) as the first month. In the Deuteronomistic saga at the end of the book of Kings the dates of the earlier sources have obviously been recalculated according to the new Babylonian year (see Mowinckel, *Die Chronologie d. isr. u. jüd. Könige*, pp. 199ff.). This new year beginning in spring never had an ecclesiastical character; the religious, cultic new year to this day has always started in the autumn. On the other hand Pap maintains that in pre-exilic times there never existed any new year festival (of a cultic nature). Against Pap, Snaith, *The Jewish New Year Festival*, pp. 9ff., rightly claims that Passover never had the character of new year, that in pre-exilic times a double new year did not exist; and with convincing reasons he arrives at the result that a pre-exilic new year festival did exist, and that it coincided with the great harvest festival, simply '*the* feast'. He is without doubt fully justified in maintaining that this new year festival had a double character: it both marked the expiration of the year, and expressed gratitude for the crop of the year (op. cit., p. 58), and it also had the character of a cult at the beginning of a new year to express 'the anxiety for the rains' (ibid., p. 62). The climax of the art of exegetic interpreting away is represented by Aalen, *Die Begriffe 'Licht' und 'Finsternis'*, pp. 43ff., who maintains that ancient Israel and earlier Judaism had no 'new year' and no 'new year festival' at all; they were merely interested in the fact that the 'cycle' of the natural year had somehow come to an end, whereas they did not pay attention to the rather natural conclusion that consequently a new year would be starting; neither in their daily way of thinking and speaking nor in the organization of their cult did they ever emphasize the beginning of the year. Aalen's main positive proof of this strange thesis is the (to other scholars obvious) fact that in spoken language, in poetry and religious symbolics the alternation of day and night plays the dominant part; from this fact he draws his antithetic conclusion, and then tries to interpret away such evidence from the text as tends in the reverse direction. According to Aalen the Jews are not supposed to have adopted any new year festival until the second century B.C., and then only under the influence of the Seleucid calendar, that is to say, at a time when Judaism was already making conscious efforts to consolidate and draw a line of demarcation against foreign, 'pagan' influences. I shall not further discuss here the arguments of Aalen, but refer to my critique in *Zum israelitischen Neujahr u. z. Deutung d. Thronbes-teigungs-psalmen*, pp. 10ff., cf. N. A. Dahl in *NTT* 53, 1952, pp. 61ff.

That the notion of the beginning of the new year existed in pre-exilic Israel is proved in a very unambiguous manner by the t rm *bĕṣē'th haššānâ*, Ex. 23.16, which does not mean 'at the end of the year', as it is traditionally taken, and as is still maintained by Snaith and Aalen, but, as has long since been pointed out by Buchanan Gray (*Sacrifice in the O.T.*, pp. 300f.): 'the beginning of the year'. Hebrew *yāṣā* 'go out' does not indicate the end but the beginning of an action; cf. the expression 'go out—go in'—begin and finish off the daily job, and the Akkadian *ṣît šamši* 'the exit of the sun' = sunrise, *ṣît arḫi*

= 'the beginning of the month'; see further my discussion of the arguments of Snaith and Aalen in *Zum isr. Neujahr.*, pp. 11ff. That the annual cycle was then supposed to end and start anew, that is to say that the year formed a cycle returning to its starting-point, is brought out by the parallel term in the earlier 'Yahwistic' festival calendar, Ex. 34.22 *thĕqûphath haššānâ*; cf. the expression used by Isaiah in 29.1, 'add ye year to year; let the feasts go round', *haggîm yinqōphu*; so the round of the feasts is repeated year after year; cf. too, Isa. 32.10 *yamîm 'al šānâ*, which evidently means, 'to-day within a year', i.e. within the next feast in a year's time—the passage is addressed to the women celebrating the feast. Pre-exilic is also the so-called 'peasant calendar' from Gezer, in which *yrhw 'sp* is the first of the months; see Albright in *BASOR* 92, 1943, pp. 16ff. From earlier post-exilic times we have the set phrase *rō'š haššānâ* for 1st Tishri, Ezk. 40.1, and from P in Ex. 12.2 the explicit provision that *Nisan* is to be considered *rō'š hŏđhāšîm*, the first month of the year; the (comparatively) new thing enforced here is not that there is to exist such a 'first month', but that now, as contrasted with earlier (and still prevailing) practice, Abib-Nisan is to be considered the *rō'š haššānâ*, cf. *Zum isr. Neujahr*, pp. 18ff., 28ff.

That this beginning of the year had also a *cultic* meaning is brought out by the simple fact that both pre-exilic sources, Ex. 34.22 and 23.16, regulate the time of the harvest festival (*hag hā'āsîph, hag haqqāṣîr*) according to this juncture; it is to be celebrated when 'the year turns', 'when the year begins'. 1 Sam. 1.20f., and Judges 21.19 evidently refer to this yearly festival. The cultic rites belonging to it not only had the nature of a thanksgiving feast for the passing year, as maintained by Gunkel (*Einl.*, p. 110), but also the nature of a foundation festival for the new year, as has been seen both by Volz and Snaith. The green branches, the pouring of water, as well as other features according to their origin are plain and obvious fertility rites meant to secure rain and crops for the coming year (see Chap. V, n. 77). Cf. *Zum isr. Neujahr*, pp. 31f.

We know now from the calendar systems of many primitive peoples that 'new year' need not cover just one single day: a 'new year's time' is often older than a new year's day (see Chap. V,n. 46). Consequently the 'new year festival' celebrated in the cult did not necessarily have to fall on the first day of the first month. Also, in point of principle, it is of no account whether in the calendar this 'festival time' is to be looked upon as the end of the old year or the beginning of the new; its nature of 'foundation festival' for the time to come is quite independent of this. For the fundamental question as to the age and cultic nature of the new year festival, it is really of no account which day of the calendar may have been considered the new year's day of Israel in different periods. Snaith's attempts to fix these days are of course valuable in themselves, but mean nothing for the fundamental problem about the 'enthronement psalms' and the 'enthronement festival'. A change of the date need not alter the religious nature or the cultic rites of day or festival; the reader may compare the transition from the Julian to the Gregorian calendar. In the Middle Ages for quite a long time the new year was supposed to begin at Easter, before it was changed to Christmas time, and later to the 1st of January. However, we know that the pre-exilic festival of harvest and new year began on the 15th of the month of Tishri. When we are told in 1 Kgs. 12.32 that Jeroboam celebrated the new year festival on the 15th day of 'the eighth month' (post-exilic terminology), i.e. the old month of Bul, as distinguished from the ordering of Jerusalem, what is different is not the date but the month, and the latter was in Jerusalem Ethanim, in post-exilic terminology 'the seventh month'; the date was evidently the same in both places. That means, the day when the moon was at its full. This date obtained even in post-exilic time, Lev. 23.34 (H and P). We do not know whether in earlier times the month was astronomically fixed in relation to the autumnal equinox; even this is fundamentally of no consequence for the problem of the new year festival and 'enthronement festival'.

Note XV (p. 123, n. 57)

Snaith (*Studies in the Psalter*), accepting the information of G and Talmud to the effect that Ps. 93 was used as a sabbath psalm, namely at the morning sacrifice, considers the enthronement psalms to be sabbath psalms. Aalen (*Licht und Finsternis*, pp. 60ff.) thinks they are 'morning psalms', which must be supposed to mean that they have been composed as psalms for the daily morning sacrifice (*tāmîdh*) in the Temple. Both theories are impossible, though some of these psalms may later have been *used* in such a way. But this obviously means a re-orientation of their original purpose just as much as in the use of Ps. 30 as a Hanukkah psalm. In the enthronement psalms not the least trace is to be found of references to the sabbath or to ideas connected therewith, nor is there to be found a single term or a single idea pointing to the morning. Aalen considers the mention of creation to be such a reference, and makes great efforts to construct an Israelitic conception which saw every morning as a repetition of creation. The only passage in the whole of the Old Testament which might possibly be interpreted in this way is Job 38.12–15; see, however, my discussion of the passage in *Zum isr. Neujahr*, p. 65. The theory of Snaith suffers from an internal contradiction in so far as he admits that the dragon fight and the creation motive—certainly in a 'symbolic' re-interpretation as an expression of Yahweh's victory over evil as such in the past—is a leit-motif in the enthronement psalms; but why should psalms made for the day of rest be wholly and solely concerned with the active deeds of Yahweh? These psalms do not present Yahweh just sitting enthroned now after his finished deed, but as having taken possession of an active kingship, by which he shall also exercise active 'government' (*mišpāṭ*); he is not only described as the one who has carried through the fight, but also as the one who comes to take up the fight against his enemies, who are now anxious witnesses to his fear-inspiring epiphany, see for instance Ps. 97—see also my detailed discussion of Snaith's theory in *Zum isr. Neujahr*, pp. 39ff.

Note XVI (p. 123, n. 59; p. 124, n. 62; p. 175, n. 177)

The most natural interpretation here would be to take *kēseh*, Ps. 81.4, to be a synonym to *hōdheš* 'the new moon', and Targum has understood the term to mean '(the new moon of) the new year'. But the corresponding Akkadian *kus'eu* as well as the context of Job 26.9 prove that the word must mean 'full moon'; see the detailed evidence in Snaith, *Jewish New Year*, pp. 99f. To that extent Snaith is right. But what of *hōdheš*? Does the psalm here mention two different festivals in 'antithetic parallelism'? Snaith tries to solve the problem in opposition to Targum and earlier Jewish interpreters by supposing that both terms indicate the day when the moon is at its full (in the month of Tishri), and he seeks to prove that *hōdheš* originally did actually indicate 'the new month day' and not till the post-exilic change of calendar did it get the sense of 'new moon day'. He takes for granted, then, that in Israel in earlier times the month began when the moon was at its full. This has not infrequently been maintained before, and no doubt it is right; it is seen from the simple fact that the old word for 'month' is *yērāh*, which is certainly closely related to *yārēah*—'(full) moon'. But Snaith cannot be right in thinking that throughout the pre-exilic period the month was reckoned to begin at full moon. This is disproved for instance by 1 Kgs. 12.32, where the date of Jeroboam's harvest festival is said to be the 15th of the month (Bul), and the festival was doubtless celebrated when the moon was at its full, just as in Jerusalem. The semasiological development of the word *ḥōdheš* 'the new', as Snaith reconstructs it, is most unlikely. In the nature of the case it must have indicated the new moon, before it was used about the more developed and artificial notion of 'month'. So there is no getting away from the fact that *ḥōdheš* in Ps. 81 means the 'day of the new moon.' The psalm actually mentions both days, the day of the full moon and the day of the new moon. The former is at the same time *yôm haggēnû*, i.e. no doubt the day when the moon is at its full in the month of Tishri. So the day of the full moon can only be the 1st of Tishri, which is consequently supposed to exist as a separate cultic day. But right from the beginning the psalm was meant to be used on one of these days, and so probably on the one mentioned first, the day of the full moon. So Targum and Talmud are right in referring it to the day of *šôphār*. But the way the 'festival' is mentioned shows that the two days are looked upon as being closely connected with one another, as parts of the very same plexus of festivals. In consequence the psalm shows that (certain of) the ideas originally belonging to the complex festival of harvest and new year have here been transferred to the special new year's day.

NOTE XVII (p. 125, n. 67)

On the basis of a purely literary and source-critical argumentation Eissfeldt (*ZATW* 46, 1928) claims that the conception of Yahweh as a king is not older than Isaiah, Isa. 6 being in his opinion the oldest proof text. But of course it is quite impossible to fix the historical date of such an idea merely on the basis of the accidental and fragmentary source material handed down in the Old Testament. Nevertheless even Gunkel (*Einl.*, pp. 110f.) with similar arguments tried to maintain that an enthronement festival only came into existence on the Babylonian pattern during the later monarchy. At any rate we may certainly take for granted that Isaiah gives expression to the prevailing conception of Yahweh, when he sees him as the enthroned king in the Temple, and gives him the usual cultic title: 'The King, Yahweh Zebaoth'. Against Eissfeldt's late dating see also Porteous, *The Kingdom of God in Pre-Exilic Hebrew Religion*, cf. Buber, *Königtum Gottes* (see below).

Morgenstern (*HUCA* XVI, 1941, pp. 40ff.) agrees so far as to say that the idea of Yahweh as the king of Israel probably came into existence (on a Canaanite pattern) as early as the ages of David or Solomon, but thinks that it was not 'universalistic' until the time of the prophets (here he adopts the arguments of Eissfeldt, based on literary criticism). But if we take for granted, as he does, that the idea of Yahweh as king has something to do with the cult, and particularly so with the new year festival—actually the festival for the creation of the world—there is no real difference between Yahweh as king of Israel and as king of 'the world', just as there is no difference in Hebrew between 'land' and 'world' (both are *'ereṣ*, and the 'world' which is being created in the cult is always the 'world' of that particular congregation); 'universalism' is virtually there as a result of the idea of creation, organically connected with the new year festival. But of course Morgenstern is right in saying that the idea of Yahweh's kingship had no anti-dynastic sting in it to begin with, nor any theocratical one, if this word be taken in a political sense. That is the mistake of Buber (*Königtum Gottes*) among others, that he interprets the kingship of Yahweh in a theocratic way, and so seeks to date the anti-dynastic and theocratic criticism of, for instance, 1 Sam. 7–8; 10–12, back into the past of Israel. The representation of the earthly king as the 'vassal' or 'regent' of the divine king is—from a political standpoint—really a way of laying a foundation for an earthly kingdom, and in the orient actually had that effect. In Ps. 84.4 the praying king himself addresses Yahweh as 'my king'; in Ps. 44.5 the speaker is probably again the king, and he uses the same expression there and in 68.25; cf. also the heart-felt relationship in Ps. 89 between the universal God of the world, Yahweh, and *'our* king', David's seed.

Snaith (*Jewish New Year*) on the contrary thinks he has proved that the 'king motive' as part of Jewish new year ideology does not date further back than from the second century B.C., and his line of argument seems to have been accepted by Rowley (review of Snaith's book in *Theol. Ltz.*, 1948, no. 9, col. 535). But this possibility exists only if one can also prove: (1) that Ps. 47 is no older than the second century B.C.; (2) that *tĕrû'ath melekh*, Nu. 23.21, does *not* refer to the cultic homage to Yahweh as king (see Chap. V, n. 4); and (3) that the cultic epiphany festival for the king Yahweh—no doubt the background of Isa.6—*cannot* be the feast of tabernacles and new year.

Buber gets an ideological basis for the supposed ancient opposition to the earthly kingdom by postulating that as early as the age of Moses Yahweh was already considered the (only) 'king'—*melekh*—in Israel. But he is only able to maintain this by explaining the term from the Arabic, which is out of harmony with its meaning in Old Testament Hebrew (see above, Additional Note XIV). Furthermore, Buber here seems to be contradicting himself: if the title *melekh* used about Yahweh did not originally mean 'king', but something else, how, then, could it give rise to an anti-royalist attitude to the earthly king? In the really old sources in the Old Testament there is not the slightest trace of any fundamental opposition to the earthly kingdom. Buber is right in criticizing Eissfeldt's late dating of the idea of Yahweh's 'kingship', but his own early dating is still more out of the question.

NOTE XVIII (p. 127 n. 71; p. 175, n. 176)

For the solution of this problem it is of no consequence whether 2 Sam. 6 is supposed to give an accurate account of the course of the festival, or whether the saga-writer and tradition before him are supposed to have adapted the descriptions to the festal customs of their own times. Therefore Kraus (op. cit., pp. 30ff.) is wrong in putting the problem as if the question were, whether we have to do with *either* a 'once only' festival, *or* one that was celebrated repeatedly. Nor should he therefore assign to me the idea of using 2 Sam. 6 and 1 Kgs. 8 as accounts of a repeated festival, on the ground that they only received the character of festivals celebrated once through the editorial framing. In both cases the author of course intends to describe one particular festival once celebrated; what I have asserted is that he *moulds* this particular event on the pattern of a regularly repeated festival, just as it was celebrated in his own time. After all, Kraus finally arrives at the same result: the festival of 1 Kgs. 8 was and was intended to be a 'repetition' of that of 2 Sam. 6, and both are identical with a later regularly repeated 'royal Zion festival.' I am blamed by Kraus because my interpretation 'rests on a false estimate of the date of the chapter, 2 Sam. 6, as well as of the pre-deuteronomistic basis of 1 Kgs. 8' (op. cit., p. 30), and on 'the lack of any profound penetration into the literary origin, the age and the peculiarities of the texts' (ibid., p. 32). That is not so. I never maintained that 2 Sam. 6 was derived from 'the exilic deuteronomist' (ibid., p. 31). Hypothetically I am quite willing to accept the theory of Rost that the chapter (incl. 1 Sam. 4–6) is derived from 'der Überlieferung von der Thronnachfolge Davids' (see his work under the same title). But I do not agree to the out-of-date interpretation to the effect that we have here a literary product, a 'written source' from the ages of David or Solomon; and I cannot admit that Rost has provided evidence *proving* that the 'stories about the ark' belonged to the 'enthronement traditions', just as I cannot find that Bentzen has proved the direct cultic use of these stories (*JBL* 67, 1948, pp. 37ff.); he himself admits his idea to be rather hypothetical. Here, as in the book of Samuel as a whole, we have a plexus of oral traditions, subjected to the laws of alteration applicable to all oral tradition. Such changes will take different effect upon different materials according to their characters; the tendency to form legends and insert definite ideas is stronger when religious than when purely historical traditions are concerned, and therefore decidedly more recognizable in the 'stories of the ark' than in the tales from David's last years, though even there it is perceptible. The fact that, for instance, 2 Sam. 12–20 contain reliable historical tradition does not prove of course that their tradition complex was written down at the time of David or Solomon. Obviously neither 2 Sam. 6 nor 1 Kgs. 8 rests on contemporary reports; who would at that time be interested in writing down such 'social news'? The old oriental chronicles (*dibhĕrê hayyāmîm*) did not contain such detailed material. Therefore it goes without saying that when narrative tradition and saga writing sought to relate *how* a festival, about which the official annals might have a short note, took place when the ark was transferred, and the Temple consecrated, the story would unconsciously be moulded on the model of well-known corresponding festivals from their own time. I do not think that 2 Sam. 6 rests on any contemporary or exact tradition or knowledge about the ceremonies at David's enthronement as king of Jerusalem and heir of the old Jebusite kings (against Porter in *JTS* 5, 1954, pp. 161ff.); but I think that, in as far as the account is moulded on the pattern of *every* repeated enthronement festival at Jerusalem, it does contain traits which may have been there since David's time. To this extent I can agree with the main idea in Porter's paper, although I think that he goes much too far in finding allusions to Canaanite enthronement rites and ideas in 2 Sam. 6.

Kraus thinks he has proved that 2 Sam. 6 is really the *hieros logos* of the new cultic metropolis of Jerusalem, furnished to provide the religious justification of the new ordering of the central cultic sanctuary by David, and that 2 Sam.7 is the actual sequel of Chap. 6. I cannot admit that Chap. 6 is such a *hieros logos*. The story certainly has a traditio-historical—Rost and Kraus use the term 'literary'—connexion with 1 Sam. 4–6, tending to show that the ark of Jerusalem was identical with the old amphictyonic sactuary of Shiloh, which was lost during the wars with the Philistines. To this extent the catena of stories is a 'cultic legend', but no *hieros logos* of the sanctuary—Jerusalem would find this in the old tale of Gen. 22. An Israelite *hieros logos* would seek to justify the choice of a particular sanctuary by marking it out through a theophany; such is not to be found in the stories about the ark, and even if one agrees with Kraus in considering Chap. 7 to be the original sequel, on the merits of the case even this chapter says nothing about any legitimating theophany; a prophetic oracle is no theophany. But the arguments of Kraus to prove that Chap. 7 is the sequel of Chap. 6 fail completely; they are based on a perfectly arbitrary and modernizing settlement of a great many questions (op. cit., p. 34), of which not the slightest hint is to be found in the text, and the logical connexion between the chapters supposed by Kraus is a mere supposition. If Chap. 7 was intended to provide the justifying basis of Chap. 6 any normal author would surely have placed this motive before Chap. 6; as a legitimation of Chap. 6, Chap. 7 in every respect comes *post festum*. As I claim to have proved in *SEÅ* 12, 1947, pp. 228ff., 2 Sam. 7 is a perfectly independent tradition, a 'theological legend' attempting to give an answer to an entirely different question: why did not the great David build a temple? It takes in the traditional cultic promises to 'David' (cf. Pss. 89.20ff.; 132) as an edifying element in the story.

Kraus, however, arrives at one useful result. He finds evidence in 2 Sam. 6 and 1 Kgs. 8 of a yearly repeated festival in Jerusalem, a feature of the feast of tabernacles, in which the great procession with the ark of Yahweh played an essential part, and where the king has a central place as the leader of the cult (cf. Porter, op. cit.). But he is wrong in calling this festival 'das königliche Zionfest' and maintaining that the king whom Yahweh has chosen is the central figure. In so far as we may draw conclusions from the above texts, the religious focus is decidedly the personal presence of Yahweh as represented by his ark (so, rightly, Porter, op. cit., too). The king plays a prominent part in the cult, but nothing more. And the psalm texts referred by Kraus to this festival are chosen in an arbitrary way. For if Pss. 2 and 72 do belong to it, it must be identical with the (repeated) royal initiation festival; both these psalms are no doubt texts of anointing and initiation; but in this case Ps. 110, for instance, also belongs here. Arbitrary and unjustifiable also—in spite of Gunkel—is the separation of part of Ps. 24, likewise of Ps. 78. Certainly a connexion exists between Pss. 84, 87, 122 and the feast of tabernacles (for instance, the choice of the sanctuary), but it is quite different from the one supposed by Kraus. Neither these psalms nor Ps. 24 are centred round the earthly king. Therefore the 'royal Zion festival' of Kraus is an invention, the result of his singling out one particular aspect of the ideology of the festival of tabernacles and new year, and interpreting an arbitrary number of texts partially according to this construction of his. The feast of tabernacles and new year was certainly a *Zionfest*, and it was also the 'festival of the royal house', but it was first of all something much more.

NOTE XIX (p. 132, n. 81, 82; p. 182, n. 194)

When compared with Ps. 132 this passage shows that the recital of the 'stanza of departure' for the ark of Yahweh was not only a custom practised during the wandering in the desert, but a regular custom belonging to the cultic procession with the ark; cf. likewise Weiser in *Festschrift für Bertholet*, pp. 520ff. The same thing may be concluded from the legend about the fall of Jericho, Josh. 6; when here the walls of the town fall because of the power of Yahweh's ark, carried seven times round the town, and because of the sound of *těrû'â* from the trumpets, it is a motive which owes its existence to a reverse interpretation of an actual ritual custom: a wall was consecrated and made strong by such a holy circumambulation (cf. Neh. 12.31ff.); therefore, says the legend, the same divine power in the ark (cf. 2 Sam. 6.6f.) could make the town walls of the enemy break down. The official theory about the material identity of the ark of Shiloh with that of Jerusalem is hardly correct, and the historical kernel with regard to the legends of 1 Sam. 4–6 is probably that it was lost to the Philistines. For ancient thought the matter is of little account; the identity does not depend on the material ark in itself, but on the fact that it has the proper shape and has been consecrated for its use; therefore the Israelites would not hesitate to make a new ark on the model of the old, if the latter had been lost. This was doubtless done later on also, e.g. when we are told about the plundering of the Temple of Jerusalem by Pharaoh Shishak 'that he took away the treasures of the Temple of Yahweh as well as of the king's house; he even took away all' (1 Kgs. 14.25), he evidently did not spare the symbol of Yahweh, decorated with gold; on the contrary, in the orient they used to take away the symbols of the gods in triumph; but all the same, Pss. 132 and 24, as well as the statement of Jer. 3.16f., take for granted that Yahweh's 'ark of the covenant' existed in Jerusalem right up to the destruction of the Temple in 587.

NOTE XX (p. 41, n. 32; p. 50, n. 19; p. 134, n. 88).

The idea of a uniform pattern of religion and cult, dominating in all essentials the whole civilization of the ancient east, actually dates from the so-called 'pan-Babylonian school' active at the commencement of this century, with H. Winckler and A. Jeremias as its leading representatives. In general we may refer to Winckler's discussion of religion and cult in *KAT*,[3] and in his *Geschichte Israels in Einzeldarstellungen*, and to A. Jeremias, *Die Altorientalische Geisteskultur*, and *Das Alte Testament in Lichte d. Alten Orients*, whereas H. Zimmern's treatment of the importance of Babylonian religion for the Old Testament and the New Testament in *KAT*[3] is a good deal more sober. According to the pan-Babylonians it was the supposed old-Babylonian *Weltanschauung* and culture developed on an astronomical and scientific basis which always underlay religious and cultic 'symbolism'; cf. the characteristic title of one of Winckler's essays: *Himmels- und Weltenbild der Babylonier als Grundlage der Weltanschauung und Mythologie aller Völker*. Since the appearance of this school, however, a series of detailed investigations have partly undermined the very foundation of the theory which was based on the highly developed nature of Babylonian astronomy—see the work of Fr. X. Kugler, *Im Bannkreis Babels*—and also have made clear the one-sidedness and unreality of their consistent astral interpretation of the myths (as expressed for instance in Stucken's *Astralmythen*). Furthermore it has been shown that ancient oriental culture presents a much more varied picture than the pan-Babylonians realized. On the other hand, the latter were no doubt right in maintaining that in antiquity the Near Eastern cultures had many important and fundamental features in common, and that the mutual influences were just as intimate as those of the Hellenism of the Roman Empire or of the Christendom of the Middle Ages. Lately archaeology has largely corroborated this (cf. n. 54 to Chap. 1). One of the things the pan-Babylonians lacked was sufficient knowledge of general comparative history of religions and ethnology and of the different branches of these subjects. Based on such wider knowledge, and deriving in the last instance probably from Frazer and other leading English and American historians of religion and ethnologists, we find the idea of a common 'ritual pattern' in the ancient East taken up by Hooke and others, from the point of view of Myth and Ritual; the two collective works edited by Hooke: *Myth and Ritual* and *The Labyrinth* may be considered to present the programme of this school. The ideas expressed here have been adopted by several Swedish investigators among others (Engnell, Widengren, Haldar, Riesenfeld), so that we may perhaps be justified in speaking of a 'myth-and-ritual school'; cf. the comparatively cautious summing-up of their ideas by Riesenfeld, *Jésus transfiguré*, pp. 9ff. Perhaps the most important contribution of this school has been the acknowledgement of the close relationship between myth and cult, but—as contrasted with the pan-Babylonians—with an emphasis on the priority of cult and rites; and an understanding of the important part played by the vegetation and fertility cult in the religions of the old orient. Added to this, as already mentioned, we have the broad general religio-historical and ethnological background. There was, however, no lack of preparatory works providing a basis for the myth and ritual ideas. Even the so-called 'religio-historical school' under Gunkel, Bousset, Gressmann and others (cf. Gressmann's *Albert Eichhorn und die religionsgeschichtliche Schule*) had drawn important religio-historical conclusions from the acknowledgment of the strong mutual cultural influences among the peoples of the orient, and of the dominant part played in this respect by the Sumero-Babylonians; and they had drawn attention to the importance of Syria and Canaan in this cultural exchange as transit-lands, where all the material and spiritual roads of intercommunication crisscross. From his form historical standpoint Gunkel had, in principle, recognized the connexion between religious poetry and cult, and had seen that, just as cult and rites may explain forms and types, so forms and types may be used to reconstruct cultic situations and conceptions. In his *Ps.St.* II the present author has demonstrated the connexion with regard to ideas between rites and myths of the anniversary new year feast of Israel and the corresponding Babylonian ones, and indicated Canaan as the intermediary; he has also pointed out that the Babylonian sources—the Canaanite ones were not sufficiently known at that time—might be cautiously used to support and supplement the reconstructions of Israelite festal cults indicated by the psalms. Likewise he has emphasized the connexion between cult and rites on the one hand, and myth on the other, and maintained that the myth is the accompanying epic-lyrical expression of the realities taking place and being experienced through the cult.

The myth-and-ritual school was built on the foundation laid by these and similar investigations. The two books edited by Hooke and mentioned above should be looked upon as programme writings, laying before us new problems to be solved, rather than as accomplished and decisive proofs of the idea of an oriental ritual pattern prevailing everywhere. It is a significant fact that Hooke in *Myth and Ritual* starts by outlining the elements of the supposed universally valid pattern (p. 8), though there is no evidence to prove what is rather decisive, namely that the 'pattern' does exist everywhere and always and with the fundamental features supposed to belong to it. In the following detailed investigations from different areas the existence of the pattern is simply taken for granted; though surely this ought to be what the detailed investigations were to prove, modify, or disprove. Little is seen, therefore, of the modifications of the 'pattern' which must have taken place, as the elements melted into the particular structure of the different religions, though the 'pattern' is admitted to have been disintegrated and the separate elements to have been adopted without any clear understanding of their real and original sense. But in view of the way in which the idea has been taken up by certain investigators, for instance Haldar, and partly by Engnell and others, there is a danger of drifting into a 'pan-patternism' at least as one-sided and unreal as pan-Babylonianism used to be. This applies not least to the king 'ideology', for it belongs to the theory that the king was everywhere considered 'identical with' the god, and that in the cult he appeared as the suffering, dying, rising, fighting, victorious and enthroned god. On this, see below, pp. 136ff., 241ff.

NOTE XXI (p. 135, n. 91)

See Baumgartner in *ThZ* III, 1947, p. 95. In Ugarit there was also an oceanic god Yam, 'the Ocean' (Bauer in *ZATW* 51, 1933, p. 92, reads Yaum—'the Day'), see Albright in *JPOS* XVI, pp. 17ff.; Virolleaud, *Le dieu de la mer dans Ras Shamra*, J. Gray, 'Canaanite Mythology and Hebrew Tradition', *Transactions of the Glasgow University Oriental Society*, 1954, pp. 47ff. In one of the myths we are told about a fight between Yam and Baal, in which Baal is finally victorious. The myth is difficult to interpret, as the text is very fragmentary. But it does not seem to have anything to do with creation. The Ugaritic god of creation was El (see Eissfeldt, *El im Ugar. Pantheon*, pp. 53ff.); he is probably to be looked upon as one of the typical 'High Gods', whose origin is partly due to the desire for an explanation of the origin of existence, and so he has become god of creation. Baal was too much the god of natural fertility to attract to himself the idea of creation, and supersede El in the cosmological part he was playing. In the texts Baal is never seen to have anything to do with the creation of the world (see Kapelrud, *Ba'al in the Ras-Shamra Texts*). The religious and cultic requirements were satisfied, because fertility as the foundation of life was secured through the resurrection of Ba'al. The relationship between El and Baal is a refutation of the theory that the 'High God' must at the same time *eo ipso* be the god of fertility (Engnell, *Div. Kingship*, Index s. v. 'High God'; id., *Gamla Testm.* I, pp. 110ff.; Widengren, *Relig. värld*, pp. 57ff.; id., *Hochgottglaube i. a. Iran*, pp. 5–93).

II, 16

NOTE XXII (p. 135, n. 92)

The earlier interpretations of the primeval ocean in Babylonian cosmogony as an expression for spring flood (for instance Zimmern in *AO* II, 3; Driver, *Book of Genesis*, p. 28; Jastrow in *JAOS* XXXVI, pp. 277, 296) used to emphasize too much that the god of creation was also the god of the spring sun, putting an end to the rainy season and the flood. Against this Clay, has pointed out that in Babylonia the rainy season and the flood season do not coincide; the flood is not a result of the scanty rain in winter, but of the melting of the snow in the mountains of Armenia, and it lasts from March till June; see Heidel, *Babylonian Genesis*, pp. 83f. This is certainly true. On the other hand, it was inherent in the Babylonian conception of creation that in the beginning the water—the flood—was there, but the ordered world—the earth to be cultivated—was not there till the water had gone; creation would mean that somebody made the world rise (again) out of the flood; the flood is 'cloven' and the earth emerges. It is just possible that the Babylonians imagined this to be the work of the (summer) sun god; as a sun god Marduk is not only the god of spring. But Marduk was hardly a sun god originally; he has too many chthonic features for that, not the least being that he dies and rises again. And apart from this, Enlil and Enki or Ninurta are older than Marduk as gods of creation, and none of these was originally a sun god; see Kramer, *Sumerian Mythology*. It would be natural for the epic-mythical version of the idea of creation to regard the creation of the 'world' out of the flood as a result of the victorious struggle of a god against the flood. The Sumerians also knew other versions of the idea, see Kramer, op. cit.

NOTE XXIII (p. 139, n. 109)

Volz (*Neujahrsfest Jahwes*, p. 16) declares that not the 'agrarian material' but the 'historical spiritual' aspect of the Yahweh festival is the original one. This, however, means doing violence to the sources; it goes against (*a*) the fact that the feast was first celebrated as an agrarian (Ba'al) festival by the Canaanites, (*b*) its name of 'harvest feast' or 'feast of tabernacles', as well as (*c*) the references to be found in the earliest sources. Cf. the description of the festival—evidently the new year festival—in Shiloh, 1 Sam. 1 and Jdg 21.19f., pointing to a purely agrarian cultic festival; cf. also the Canaanite festival in Shechem, Jdg. 9.27. Cf. p. 125, and p. 187.

Similar objections must be made against von Rad, when he tries to prove that it was not the idea of the enthronement of the God, but the Sinai tradition that formed the original cult myth of the harvest festival (*Das formgeschichtliche Problem d. Hexateuchs*; see also Rohland, *Bedeutung der Erwählungstraditionen für die Eschatologie*, p. 11). The idea of the enthronement was connected with the festival already in its Canaanite stage—which von Rad could not know in 1926, before the Ugaritic finds. It is improbable that the Israelites would have taken over the feast as, so to say, only an empty shell, without its myth; or that they would immediately have changed the myth for another, historical one. The age of the Sinai tradition as such is not affected by this statement (against Rohland, op. cit., pp. 11f.); in Israel's own faith, as Israelite traditions, they are of course the older ones—this fact I have never denied—but in their connexion with the enthronement festival they are the younger ones.

This being so, it is a mistake when Porteous (*Kingship of God in Pre-exilic Hebr. Relig.*, pp. 6f.) ascribes to me the opinion that the 'cult was the origin of the story of the Exodus'. The festal myth is an integral aspect of the cult; it has also—and that relatively early—adopted the historical traditions, which existed in Israel since the days of the Exodus, of course, however, in a more and more developed legendary form. Their connexion with the feast has also furthered this development, and to a certain degree recast the traditions according to the pattern of the myth. Lauha, *Die Geschichtsmotive in den alttest. Psalmen*, deals with the historical motifs in the Psalms. Cf. also Bückers, in *Biblica* 32, pp. 401ff.

NOTE XXIV (p. 142, n. 111; p. 167, n. 157; II. 203, n. 7)

Here we deal with the question, which psalms are pertinent to our inquiry into Yahweh's enthronement festival. Gunkel, uncritically followed by Kraus and Rohland, would restrict the number to the enthronement hymns proper, the stylistically defined group of *yhwh mālakh* hymns, 47; 93; 96; 97; 98; 99. From a merely style historical, style typological (*gattungsgeschichtlich*) point of view this may seem justified. It is also justified to take this group as the point of departure when seeking the cultic setting of hymns of this sort. But here the weakness of Gunkel's one-sided style typological method becomes evident. A cultic feast always includes a great complex of ideas pertinent to its main central *kerygma*. It seems justified by a great many religio-phenomenological parallels to maintain that on such an occasion all the chords of religious experience and emotions are sounded. To a festival of this sort belong not only hymns of praise, but, e.g., supplications and prayers as well. The picture of such a feast cannot be reconstructed by means of a single stylistic type of psalm. For example it would be quite illegitimate to reconstruct the religious contents and rituals of the Christmas festival from such hymns only where the words 'A Saviour is born to us', or the like, are found; or to restrict the description 'paschal hymns' to such hymns only where the kerygma 'Christ is risen' *expressis verbis* is used within a definite literary pattern. We are obliged to take into consideration hymns and texts where we find the basic ideas of the festival in question expressed, often as the main theme of the hymn, even if the style forms and expressions may not be the same. To the present author it seems astonishing that the above-mentioned scholars have not realized this self-evident truth.

Thus, in reconstructing the 'ideological' content and rituals of the enthronement feast, we cannot restrict ourselves to the small group of *yhwh mālakh* psalms alone.

The idea of the feast may also have found expression in a divine oracle, consistent with the consequences of the enthronement of the god, or in prayer for the empirical experience of those consequences, or in other forms of 'composite liturgies' (Chap. XIII). We must look for other psalms as well, where the ideas and experiences and emotions of the said group are prominent, and which fit in with the festal pattern, the main lines of which are expressed or sketched within the narrower group.

Here we begin with Ps. 95, which Gunkel (*Einl.*, pp. 94ff.; commentary to the psalm), followed by Kraus (op. cit., pp. 1f., 117), excludes from the enthronement psalms. Ps. 95, however, is a 'liturgy' where the hymn of praise is followed by a divine proclamation. And the hymn in the first part is, in its ideas and to a great extent also its forms, a clear-cut enthronement psalm. It is not difficult to understand why Gunkel felt obliged to exclude Ps. 95; for it does not contain—as Gunkel himself in his commentary tacitly admits—the least trace of the eschatological aspect, which at all costs, so to say *ex definitione*, he wants to find in the enthronement psalms. But Ps. 95 unmistakably belongs to the above-mentioned psalms and thus adds a new argument to the many others against Gunkel's eschatological interpretation. We certainly do not find in Ps. 95 the usual distinguishing term 'Yahweh has become king'; but it is difficult to understand by what right we should claim that this very term had to be used in all enthronement hymns, as long as the *enthronement situation* is quite evident. The psalm has the idea of Yahweh as king in common with the other psalms of the group, and consequently also his elevation above all other gods, v. 3, cf. 96.4; 97.7; 99.2; further, the connexion between his kingship and creation, vv. 3–5, cf. 93.1–4; 96.1–6, 10; the invitation to kneel before the king and pay homage to him with songs and stringed instruments, vv. 1f., 6, cf. 96.1–3, 7–10; 97.1; 98.1, 4–8; 99.5, 9. Whereas in the other psalms the invitation is mostly addressed to all nations and to the whole universe, it is here addressed to the congregation of Israel; but this feature it has in common with 97.8–12; 98.1–3a; 99.5–9; the reference to Yahweh's (royal) commandment it has in common with 99.7.

Now if Ps. 95 belongs to the group of enthronement psalms and to the festival which they imply, this fact will have consequences for the understanding of these psalms and of the cultic festival—consequences fatal to the interpretation of Gunkel. First: Ps. 95 involves Ps. 81, for the latter is in every respect a (more detailed) parallel psalm to 95; in the Talmud tradition it is referred to the same festival as the enthronement hymn 47, namely to the new year festival, which was also considered to be the enthronement day of Yahweh; in the text we find obvious allusions to the customs characteristic of new year's day, and from which it received its name: the cry of *tĕrû'â* and the blowing of *šôphār*. It is illogical that Gunkel accepts the evidence of the Talmud about new year's day as far as Ps. 47 is concerned but rejects it in the case of Ps. 81.

The fact that all the enthronement hymns with the exception of 47 are to be found in the same place, quite definitely suggests that here a separate collection must have been included in the Psalter, a 'booklet' of psalms grouped for some definite use, i.e. to be used on one and the same cultic occasion (some festal day or part of it). This booklet must have started not later than 93 and must have comprised the succeeding psalms up to 99 inclusive, so that it is direct evidence of how the temple clergy looked upon and used Ps. 95. There can be hardly any doubt, however, that the booklet also contained the little hymn *Ps. 100*; cf. the invitation to the whole world to praise Yahweh, v. 1, with 96.1–3, 7–10; 97.1; 98.4; 99.1–3; the invitation to enter into his gates and come before his presence (the procession!) with singing, vv. 2b, 4 with 95.1f., 6f.; 99.5, 9; the motive that he has created his people, v. 3, with the almost identical wording of 95.7. The thank-offering mentioned in the heading and referred to in characteristic terms in v. 5 (cf. 107.1) is therefore not the thank-offering festival of an individual but a thank-offering of the congregation at one of the great feasts (against Gunkel, *Einl.*, p. 102).

Now if Pss. 93–100 make a 'booklet' for a special festival, *Ps. 94* must be included. This is a congregational psalm of lamentation with a prayer for deliverance from the permanent heathen supremacy under which Israel was living after the Exile. According to the Talmud (Bab. Sukka 53a) it was used at the feast of tabernacles. It has the idea of epiphany, v. 1, in common with the enthronement psalms (and festival), and of Yahweh as the 'judge', *šôphēṭ* of the earth, v. 2.

In addition to these psalms there are also a great many others which are evidently connected with the plexus of ideas of epiphany and enthronement. The wording of *Ps. 48* (v. 12) is in verbatim accordance with the enthronement hymn 97.8; further, the former psalm praises Yahweh as the king (v. 3), who has now appeared (*nôdhā'*, v. 4, cf. 98.2) and is enthroned on Zion, vv. 3f., 9, cf. 99.2; it is a question of a mythical victory won by Yahweh, and this thought is also the background of the rejoicings of the enthronement hymns 93.3f.; 96.2, 4; 97.6ff.; 98.1ff.; 99.4. The connexion, therefore, with the ideas and expressions of the enthronement festival is perfectly evident, and compared to this fact it is of secondary importance that the procession mentioned is probably different from the one of the kingly entry of Yahweh: the harvest festival had many processions.

Morgenstern has tried to revive the historical interpretation of Ps. 48, see *HUCA* XVI, pp. 1ff. By pressing the details not very convincingly, he finds it necessary to distinguish vv. 5–8 as a fragment having come in from somewhere else (why? and how?), a fragment which, by taking literally the 'east wind breaking the ships of Tarshish', he dates at 480, the date of the destruction of the Persian fleet before the battle of Artemisium, while the rest of the psalm is supposed to date from the period between 516 and 485 and to be an expression of certain highly strung Messianic expectations which came to an end abruptly through that national catastrophe of 485 which is supposed to underlie the documents in Ezra 4. Morgenstern greatly overestimates the possibility of dating the origin and development of religious ideas and terms; thus the idea and expression 'for the sake of his name' is supposed to have been created by Ezekiel—a theory that the casual and desultory nature of the tradition in the Old Testament puts out of court. In regard to substance and emotions Ps. 46 is a parallel psalm to 48; so it is hardly without consequence that these two psalms have been handed down side by side with the enthronement hymn Ps. 47. It is very likely that the heading of Ps. 46 has something to do with the festival of harvest and epiphany, see below, Chap. XXIII. 24; it probably refers to the very things 'seen' by the congregation of Ps. 48.9. Rohland (*Bedeutung der Erwählungstraditionen*, pp. 123ff.) strangely takes the jubilant hymn of praise, Ps. 46, as a 'liturgy' for a day of lamentation and supplication in a definite historical danger!

Parallel to these two psalms as to subject and emotions we have Ps. 76. All three have in common with the enthronement psalms the idea that Yahweh has just appeared, 'become known' (*nôdha'*, v. 2), as king after having performed great works (48.3ff.); Yahweh has now raised his tabernacle in Zion (76.2)—a result of the great works which he has performed in v. 2, and which have made him 'known' in Judah v. 1. Notice too the parallelism between the revolt of the primeval ocean and the raging enemies of 46.2–8, and between Zion and the paradise surrounded by streams in 46.5. All three psalms contribute much to our knowledge of the substance of the festival; we get concrete information of Yahweh's victory, and a hint as to the dramatic presentation of it through the festal liturgy (the 'sham fight'); we also learn a little more about the feelings evoked by the epiphany of Yahweh and the confidence of Zion's safety in all storms because Yahweh himself has come to reside there.

Psalm 33 probably echoes the same ideas and the same cultic situation—for whatever cultic use this regular hymn may have been composed. Notice the invitation of the enthronement hymn to 'sing a new song', v. 3; the description of Yahweh as creator, vv. 4, 7, 9, 15; as the one who is superior to the counsels of all earthly powers, vv. 10f., who protects his people from the horses and chariots of others (the Exodus motive)—all features to be found in the enthronement hymns, or connected with the plexus of ideas of this festival.

Psalm 149 is essentially of the same character; the new song, v. 1; the invitation to praise Yahweh with singing and playing, v. 3, in wording strongly reminiscent of the enthronement hymns, cf. 95.2; 47.7f.; 98.5f.; Yahweh as the saviour of his people, giving them victory and the power to slay all other kings and peoples; the celebration of it in the Temple, vv. 1, 5f.

Psalm 24 combines the characteristic ideas of the kingship of Yahweh, his work of creation and his solemn entry into the Temple; there can hardly be any doubt that the personal presence of Yahweh is symbolized by his ark, as in Ps. 132 (see below). So there is every reason to believe that the procession for which it was composed must be the procession of enthronement, as even Gunkel seems willing to admit (*Einl.*, p. 107). In favour of this very probable conjecture is the fact that the emphasis on Yahweh's commandments and the necessity of keeping them, which is the thought of vv. 3–6, has much in common with the idea of covenant and the emphasis on the commandments in Pss. 95 and 81, evidently a regular feature of the ritual of the harvest festival. In consequence of this, Ps. 15, the parallel of 24.3–6, at any rate with regard to style and substance, must be derived from the enthronement and new year festival, for whatever use the psalm may originally have been composed.

It is from the ideas and cultic customs to be found in Pss. 95 and 81 that Ps. 50 gets its true explanation: the union of Yahweh's epiphany and his overwhelming appearance with the idea of his *mišpāṭ* and *dīn*, which in this case, however, under the influence of the thought that Yahweh's coming means the destruction of the evil powers among the people, and under the influence of the preaching of the prophets, is considered in the light of punitive judgment.

That the festal procession, supposed to be the triumphal entry of the king Yahweh, made an essential part of the ritual of the festival is evident from Ps. 47.6; in this festal procession—we may say, as a matter of course—Yahweh's presence would be represented by some cultic symbol and indeed—again as a matter of course—by his holy ark. From a cultic mythological standpoint the entry with the ark is a repetition of the first entry under David. Evidently Ps. 132, which gives the dramatic text for the singing at such a procession, must have belonged to the same festival. The centre of the procession is Yahweh's ark now about to be placed as his 'footstool' before his throne; Yahweh is imagined to be the enthroned king. This is corroborated by the fact that it belongs to the 'songs of the festal procession' (see below), and by the use the Chronicler has made of it in 2 Chron. 6.41f., (see p. 127). The same is true of Ps. 118, which has the character of a public thanksgiving festival; but the victory for which thanks are offered is not an individual event, but all the saving victories won by the people with the help of Yahweh throughout its history; the psalm considers them by the light of the 'myth about the fight of nations'. It also contains other references to the festival of harvest and new year (the symbol of fertility, the green branches, the allusion to the festival of lights, v. 27).

In Ps. 82 Yahweh's accession to kingship is supposed to mean the destruction of the other gods, as in the enthronement hymns (96.4f.; 97.7; cf. 99.2f.), or, more precisely, an act of judgment with the passing of the sentence of death (cf. the idea of judgment in Ps. 50). As we have now clear evidence that Ps. 82 was used at the feast of tabernacles (Bab. Sukka 53a), so too this psalm shows what kind of ideas were attached to the harvest festival, and as Gunkel's eschatological interpretation in this case, as elsewhere, is not supported by form or substance, there is at any rate nothing to prevent us from supposing that it was also composed for this use.

Closely related to Ps. 82 is Ps. 75, starting as a hymn to Yahweh, who then himself appears as the God who reveals his judgment (the idea and style of epiphany); he is the judge destroying the wicked, whose rage is paralleled with that of the primeval ocean (v. 4), and he is the protector and saviour of his righteous ones—all forming ideas and conceptions characteristic of the enthronement and harvest festival and its psalms; compared with this its original purpose is less important; like Pss. 50 and 82 it throws light on some of the thoughts of the festival, because it adds new details to the ideas otherwise known from the festal psalms.

As proved in detail in the text, the thought of the Exodus from Egypt, of the miracle of the Reed Lake, of the Covenant of Mount Sinai, and the entry into Canaan, in short of the creation of Israel as the people of Yahweh, even in the enthronement psalms appears to be the base of Yahweh's kingship, though only by way of reference; and no doubt these saving events were soon referred to the harvest festival of which the enthronement festival is a special aspect. In the hymn used by the author of the Blessing of Moses as a frame for his poem (Deut. 33.2–5, 26–29), these very events are looked upon as Yahweh's first epiphany, and the basis of his enthronement as king of Israel; I have not the slightest doubt that we have here (a fragment of) an enthronement hymn, which certainly does not have the particular and characteristic style of the hymns, Pss. 93–99, but is all the same quite dominated by some of the main ideas of the festival. Cf. the author's *Der achtundsechzigste Psalm*, pp. 75ff.

Neither have we, therefore, any reason to doubt that the psalm, Ex. 15.1b–18—in which the Exodus, the miracle of the Reed Lake, and the entry, parallel with creation, culminate with the erection of the sanctuary in Jerusalem—is meant to be a hymn of the festival of harvest or enthronement. In like manner the creation of the cultic metropolis and the temple of Esagila makes the keystone of the work of creation of the king-god in the Babylonian epic of creation and enthronement, *Enuma êliš*. It seems to have been a widespread idea that creation culminates with the creation of the sanctuary; in Ugarit the enthronement of Baal is likewise combined with the erection and consecration of his temple; the temple has a cosmic meaning. That Ex. 15.1b–18 does not date from the time of Moses, as some investigators still think, is seen from the fact that it takes for granted the first settlement as well as the election of the sanctuary on 'the mountain of Yahweh's inheritance', i.e. in Zion, and the temple building there, see v. 17. The fact that the expression 'mount of his (i.e. the god's) inheritance' for 'the god's holy mountain and temple,' has been taken over from Canaanite terminology, where it (i. a.) is used about the mountain of Baal, does not of course prove that it could not be applied to Mount Zion in Ex. 15; nor does it prove that the hymn must be a very old one (against Albright, *Archaeology of Palestine*, p. 233). See my *Der achtundsechzigste Psalm*, pp. 73f. H. Schmidt (*ZATW* 49, 1931, pp. 59ff.) would cut off v. 1b and thereby get rid of the clear thematic connexion of the psalm with the miracle of the Reed Lake, but the latter is not simply a side motif, but the very theme of the psalm. Schmidt's interpretation of the psalm as a 'collective' thanksgiving psalm has no foundation whatever in the style of the psalm. To suppose that the two lines of v. 21 should be the original 'song of Miriam', to which the poem, vv. 1b–18, is to be considered a later addition (Gunkel and many others) is a poor way out of the difficulty; it is unmistakable from the description of the scene in Ex. 15 that v. 21 (= v. 1) is meant to give the theme of the song in vv. 1b–18, in which the precentress leads, whereas the other women take it up as a 'refrain' (after each stanza?).

Nor have we any reason to look upon Ps. 114—in which the Exodus and the immigration are mentioned together with Yahweh's accession to his kingship over Israel ('then Israel became his *mamlākōh*, his dominion')—as a psalm for the Passover; it gives expression to the ideas which were attached to the harvest festival a long time before the Passover became one of the main festivals.

Even Ps. 29 is derived from the same sphere of ideas, with its description of Yahweh's great work when fighting against the primeval ocean, and of his enthronement when he seated himself on his throne over the defeated ocean, and from then on sits enthroned for ever (v. 10), and imparts to his people blessing and power and victory (v. 11). For the fight against the ocean as the base of kingship, cf. Ps. 93. That even the 'creation psalm', Ps. 104, belonged to the liturgies of the new year festival has been maintained by Humbert (*RHPhR*, 1935); he is probably right.

Were Pss. 8 and 84 among the psalms used, perhaps even composed for the enthronement festival, or the harvest feast (tabernacles) in general? In favour of this hypothesis may be mentioned the heading *'al haggittîth* found also at the head of Ps. 81. Though we do not know what it means (see *Ps.St.* IV, pp. 43ff. and below, Chap. XXIII. 23), it is very likely that it indicated some cultic ritual regulation and not a melody or an instrument or the like; as we find it at the head of Ps. 81, we have considerable reason to believe that it has to do with new year's day. If so, it would indicate a similar use of Pss. 8 and 84. Ps. 8 speaks of Yahweh as the creator, which would suit the new year festival; Ps. 84 strikes the note of a thanksgiving psalm and was evidently used during the procession to the Temple, in which the king of the people ('thine anointed') played a prominent part, cf. Ps. 132; the reason why it was used in this way, seems to be the mention of Yahweh as king, v. 4. The psalm then testifies to the love for the Temple and to the feeling of safety in its shelter, because Yahweh dwells there, a feeling which would naturally soar particularly high on the day of his epiphany, and thus it contributes to the characteristic tone of the day.

The first part of the congregational thanksgiving psalm, Ps. 66.1–12, is also strongly influenced by the ideas and emotions of the enthronement festival; notice first of all the invitation to all the world and to all nations to praise Yahweh, vv. 1, 4, 8, cf. 47.1; 96.7–9; 97.1; 98.4f.; his saving works for Israel as the motivation of the praise, v. 9, cf. 96.2; 97.7–12; 98.2f.; the references to Yahweh's 'terrible' (*nôrā'*, cf. 99.3) works, vv. 3, 5ff., cf. 96.2f., 5; 97.7f.; 98.1–4; 99.4, with the verbatim accordance of v. 5a with 46.9a; further, the reference to the miracle of the Reed Lake and the entry as the great work, vv. 4, 8–12, cf. Deut. 33.2–5, 26–29; Ex. 15.1–18; the reference to the great afflictions laid upon Israel by other nations, from which Yahweh, however, has delivered her, vv. 8–12 (see pp. 152ff. about the 'myth of the fight of nations' and the 'time of afflictions', and cf. 81.7f.; 118.10–14); and finally the reference to his eternal dominion over the nations on account of his victory over them, v. 7 (it should matter little that the verb *māšal* is used here instead of *mālakh*).

H. Schmidt would interpret Ps. 68 as a liturgy at the festal procession on the entry of Yahweh as king; and there is hardly any doubt that this is the only interpretation by which this difficult and much disputed psalm finds its proper explanation—as already suggested by myself in *Ps.St.* II, pp. 141, 332; VI, p. 31,n. 3), and now dealt with at length in my *Der achtundsechzigste Psalm* (against Albright in *HUCA* XXIII, 1, pp. 1ff.).

That the very ideas characteristic of the enthronement psalms and festival have also influenced many of the psalms of the harvest feast (tabernacles) in the *ma'ălâ* booklet of psalms, 120–134, will be easily seen: creation in 121.2; 124.8; 134.3; Yahweh enthroned in the heavens, 123.1, in Zion, 125.2; 134.2; cf. 132.7; Jerusalem as the city never to be shaken, but safe in all storms, 121; 125; 127.1. To this must be added the particular thought of the harvest feast: blessing and fertility and good crops, in 128; 121.7f.; 122.7–9; 126.5f.; 134.3; 132.15; a thought which can be traced in the real festal psalm of enthronement, 81.17. There is also every reason to believe that the actual heading 'psalms of ascent' (AV 'songs of degrees') is an allusion to the procession, see Chap. XXIII. 3.

It has to be emphasized, however, that it is not necessary to presume that the above-mentioned psalms were all composed for the enthronement or harvest festival; but we may certainly maintain that they bear the stamp of the ideas, experiences and hopes characteristic of this festival, and that they cannot be explained unless we take into account this circle of ideas; while these psalms for their part throw a clearer light on many details within the circle.

NOTE XXV (p. 147, n. 122)

That the kingship and enthronement of Yahweh are based on and include the covenant with Abraham and Isaac and Jacob, and the entry of the people into Canaan, is also seen from the enthronement psalm which the Chronicler makes the temple singers sing at the transfer of Yahweh's ark to Jerusalem, 1 Chron. 16.8–36. The psalm has been pieced together out of Pss. 105.1–15 (vv. 8–22), 96.1–13b (vv. 23–33), and 106.1, 47f. (vv. 34–36). Incidentally, that shows that at the time of the Chronicler these psalms belonged to the same festival, and is an indication that the booklet, of which the enthronement psalms make the beginning and are the determining element (see Additional Note XXXIII), included Pss. 93–106 (perhaps even 90–92, that is to say, the whole of the fourth book of the Psalter?). Stylistically the psalm of the Chronicler is no strict enthronement hymn, in the sense that the exclamation 'Yahweh has become king' is lacking, nor does the word 'king' occur in it; but the insertion of Ps. 96 speaks plainly enough: at the festival of which the Chronicler is thinking, these psalms were heard, and by the light of the thought expressed in Ps. 96 he wants us to read, too, the hymn with the reference to the covenant, which he has placed in front of it (Ps. 105.1–15); it is to 'Yahweh of the ark' that psalms like 96, i.e. the enthronement psalms, are sung, as the ark is carried in procession, and it is this God who remembers the covenant and the entry, and upholds it, and who will therefore even now save his people, and some day gather its scattered members (v. 35).

Note XXVI (p. 151, n. 133)

That Ps. 82 belongs to the new year festival (see Additional Note XXIV) has also been realized by Morgenstern from a different starting-point, see *HUCA* XIV, pp. 29ff. On the ground of formal logical considerations Morgenstern understands vv. 2–5a about human judges, and therefore declares these verses to be an interpolation; in that way there is no longer any motive for the condemnation of the 'gods', and so he has to postulate that there was originally another crime, for which they were sentenced to death, and finds such a one in Gen. 6.1–4. The latter, however, does not look upon the sexual intercourse of 'the sons of god' with the daughters of men as a mortal sin and does not mention that Yahweh took any action against the 'gods'; he merely prevented the disastrous consequences of the connexion by limiting the lifetime of men and so also of the 'giants', to 120 years. The task of exegesis is to explain the text, in the case in hand: how could the 'gods' be considered the responsible unrighteous judges on earth in the societies of men? That the 'gods' were (sometimes) imagined to be the (subordinate) governors (of Yahweh) on earth will be seen from Deut. 32.8, as well as from Ps. 58.2. Ps. 82 obtains internal unity and consistency as soon as we realize that its 'mythological background' is the Yahwistic change of 'the myth of the assembly of gods' ('the doom myth', see *Ps.St.* II, pp. 65ff.) of the (Babylonian) new year ritual and myth of creation, in accordance with the change of 'the myth of the fight with chaos' (*Ps.St.* II, pp. 45ff.) into a 'myth of the fight of gods' (*Ps.St.* II, pp. 50ff.).

Note XXVII (p. 146, n. 121; p. 157, n. 141); II. 3, n. 6)

By MT *šĕbhûth* is considered a derivation of *šābhâ* = lead into captivity; and the term *šûbh šĕbhûth*, read as *š. šĕbhîth* = turn the captivity, put an end to the captivity, i.e. lead home the exiles and dispersed. But the newer interpretation of it as a 'figura etymologica' of the verb *šûbh*—'turn the turning', is no doubt correct. Preuschen (*ZATW* 15, 1895, pp. 1ff.) tried to restore the traditional interpretation, but has been convincingly refuted by Dietrich, *BZATW* 40, and by Baumann in *ZATW* 47, 1929, pp. 17ff. On the other hand Baumann is wrong when he thinks that the expression does not involve the idea of a *restitutio in integrum*; a return to the original starting-point is indicated by the verb *šûbh*. Baumann's own interpretation: 'repeal the bond or claim' is untenable, because it takes no notice of the connexion of the term with the new year, a connexion which in spite of the protests of Gunkel (in his psalm commentary) is quite obvious from Pss. 85 and 126, in which 'the turning' is focused on abundance of water, seed sown, and harvest. Why the vocalization of MT in Ps. 126.1, 4—and to the latter naturally also belongs the vowel letter *y* in *šibhath*, v. 1—is to be more conclusive here than elsewhere has not been explained by Eerdmans (*Hebr. Book of Pss.*, pp. 408, 558).

Dietrich, however, is wrong in maintaining with Gunkel and others that the term *per se* has an eschatological meaning. That the expression in itself is not eschatological is seen from Job 42.10; Lam. 2.14. Dietrich's book was written without any knowledge of my cultic interpretation, he has therefore been unable to take up any stand about it. But it strikes one that Gunkel as a matter of course takes the term to be proof of an eschatological interpretation of every psalm in which it occurs, even if a cultic interpretation would be much more natural, as in Pss. 85 and 126. At any rate the very occurrence of the term in such psalms ought to raise the question whether it has not originally had a non-eschatological meaning; for even a specifically eschatological expression like 'the kingship of Yahweh' originally had a non-eschatological sense.

NOTE XXVIII (p. 198, n. 15; p. 199, n. 19; p. 227, n. 4; II. 9, n. 20).

On the original and technical meaning of the word *'āwen* see *Ps.St.* I (cf. V, p. 14ff., n. 1; VI, p. 17, n. 3), where, however, the original meaning 'evil force, sorcery', has been maintained in a too one-sided way, and carried out with too great consistency. For the sense: evil mischievous use of 'power' = 'sorcery' see also Johs. Pedersen, *Israel* I–II, pp. 320ff.; Bentzen in *Salmerne fortolkede*; Guillaume in *JRAS* 1942, pp. 111ff., and his discussion with Driver ibid. 1943, pp. 6ff., 251ff.; 1944, pp. 165ff.; 1946, pp. 79ff. Gunkel (*Einl.*, pp. 196ff.), is certainly right when saying that the interpretation has been carried out in too one-sided a way in *Ps.St.* I, and several of his arguments are of value; but they cannot be conclusive as long as he abides by the same view of the individual psalms of lamentation as *Ps.St.* I, namely that practically all of them are psalms of illness and 'the enemies' are the fellow-countrymen of the sick person himself; for, as proved in *Ps.St.* I and by Birkeland in *Feinde d. Indiv.*, the consequence of this interpretation must be that *'āwen* is everywhere used in its 'technical' sense and that the enemies have caused the illness, and are therefore 'sorcerers'. In fact, Gunkel has to admit that the earliest and true sense of the word is something like '(evil) power, and its use and result'. The proper corrective of the one-sidedness of *Ps.St.* I has been provided by Birkeland, op. cit., with evidence that the enemies in a great many I-psalms are the foreign political enemies of the king, and that consequently *'āwen*, much oftener than was supposed in *Ps.St.* I, is used in a toned-down sense as a 'characterizing abusive term' about destructive activity and devilry and disaster, and is often used also of the evil intrigues and words and attacks of the national enemies, 'the heathen'. Birkeland certainly goes too far in *his* direction, and reduces too much the number of the psalms of illness, as well as the real use of *'āwen*. Against this one-sidedness, see my critique of his book in *NTT* 1934, pp. 1ff. The necessary revision of the one-sidedness of *Ps.St.* I has already been made there, as in the present book. To this extent the critique of Ridderboos (*De 'Werkers der Ongerechtigheid'*) comes a little *post festum*. Ridderboos is no less one-sided in his 'conservative' and traditionalistic interpretation of the I-psalms, and his critique distinguishes itself invidiously from that of Gunkel and of Birkeland because of his unwillingness to understand at all the 'primitive' senses of the word, and his lack of a clear perception of the psalms as a whole. He has planned the whole investigation polemically around certain individual passages, and so prevents the material from appealing to him on its own merits.

NOTE XXIX (p. 210, n. 43; p. 233, n. 73; p. 229, n. 8, 9; II. 18, n. 52; 93, n. 31; 113, n. 32)

Of fundamental importance for the interpretation of 'the oppressed' (*'ānî*) as the 'party'—or even the 'organization'—of the poor, humble and pious 'that are quiet in the land', we had the book by Rahlfs: *'Ani und 'Anaw in den Psalmen. I.* His theory has dominated nearly all modern commentaries on the psalms (e.g. Baethgen, Briggs, Buhl, Duhm, etc.) right up to the victory of the cultic interpretation. It was accepted without any doubts and reservations even by Gunkel (*Einleitung; Die Psalmen*); and by Causse (*Les pauvres d'Israël*) who speaks about 'la communauté des pauvres' (op. cit., pp. 140ff.). See the review by Birkeland, op. cit., pp. 23ff. The thesis of Causse is held by Gelin, *Les pauvres de Yahvé*, who fancies that even the psalmists belong to 'the poor' as a spiritual community of righteous persons; it is remarkable that Gelin takes no account of Birkeland's inquiry (see below).

The first attack on the principle behind the theory of Rahlfs is probably *Ps.St.* I, pp. 113ff.; the decisive corrective to the party theory however was given by Birkeland in *'Ani und 'Anaw*; with the positive verification, showing that many of these I-psalms are really national royal psalms, in his *Feinde d. Indiv.* Munch has tried to restore the old party theory, this time as a theory about class warfare. Joining Lurje (*BZATW* 45) he seeks to find in the Old Testament a class warfare à la Marx, supposed to be reflected in the preaching of the prophets (*ThStKr* 107, pp. 217ff.) as well as in the psalms (*Monde Orientale* XXX, 1936, pp. 13ff.; *ZATW* 55, 1937, pp. 36f.); he arrives at the conclusion that *'ani* and *'anaw* indicate classes. Munch has drawn attention to some weak points in *Ps.St.* I, where the interpretation of these words has been wrongly bound up too closely with the one-sided interpretation of the I-psalms as psalms of illness. But Munch's argumentation in favour of the theory of class warfare is rather subjective, and unduly presses the sources; his interpretation of the psalms is incompatible with the acknowledgement of even these psalms as public psalms of the cult, and it becomes unnecessary, as soon as one has grasped the national character of most of the I-psalms.

NOTE XXX (p. 241, n. 58)

More detailed arguments for the interpretation of the psalm passages 16.10; 17.15; 49.16; 73.23ff. and possibly 17 belong in a commentary. Here we can only enumerate a few points. Modern investigators in general admit to-day that when we read of deliverance from Sheol it is usually a question of deliverance from acute danger of death; the faith in resurrection is only more or less vaguely perceptible in the following few psalms: 16, 49, 73, and possibly 17. This fact should make us very careful when reading another meaning into the supposed exceptions, and make us insist on a scrupulous use of the exegetical evidence. First of all, stress has been laid on the verb *lāqaḥ*, which is used about the saving interference of Yahweh in 49.16 and 73.24, and which is also used in Gen. 5.24 and in 2 Kgs.2.3ff. about God, who 'carried away' Enoch, and Elijah. But if the word were to have this sense in Pss. 49 and 73, then 73.24 at any rate would imply the doctrine that the pious person—or just the suppliant himself?—was carried away directly when dying, or without dying, and that would be something quite different from the Jewish faith in resurrection. The conception to be found behind the stories about the rich man and Lazarus—that a righteous person passes directly from death into Paradise—is at any rate not the usual Jewish conception (cf. Billerbeck IV, pp. 1017, 1020; Bousset, *Relig.*,[3] pp. 293f.). But if we do not here give *lāqaḥ* the 'technical' sense of 'carrying away', but let it have the usual sense of 'taking', that is to say, from Sheol, as in 49.15, the analogy with Gen. 5.24 likewise vanishes, and with it the argument based on the verb *lāqah*.

It ought to be obvious that 16.10 cannot be interpreted about rising from the dead, i.e. from Sheol; for we are told in plain words that Yahweh 'will not leave my (i.e. the suppliant's) soul in Sheol, and will not suffer a fellow of his covenant to see the grave' (i.e. he will not go to his grave and to Sheol). If this is to have another sense than the usual one: 'as long as I live on earth Yahweh will deliver me from danger of death and not let me go to my grave (too early)'—then it must mean that the suppliant is not going to die at all; but such a meaning would be opposed to all Jewish ideas of death and resurrection. So in Ps. 16 we must needs have the usual conception of the psalms that Yahweh will save the pious one from sudden death and untimely danger of death— as long as his life on this earth shall last—whereas sooner or later some such catastrophe shall befall the ungodly person.

In Ps. 17.15 the matter is also quite simple; here we are told that while Yahweh is going to slay the ungodly and destroy them and their families, the suppliant during the lifetime allotted to him shall be satisfied at the sight of Yahweh, 'when I awake', that is to say, either each morning after the sleep of the night, or after a special sleep, namely in the Temple, in order to receive an oracle of incubation. The text in no case speaks of an 'awakening' from the 'sleep of death'. Lindblom (*ZATW* 59, 1942–43, p. 11) rightly says that every eschatological point of view lies beyond the scope of this psalm. Volz has tried to interpret Ps. 49 as if the author meant to announce a newly revealed insight to the effect that the (worldly) rich would have to *stay* in Sheol for ever, whereas God would deliver the pious thence, which would mean preaching life after death (*ZATW* 55, 1937). But if this were so, we should decidedly expect the positive aspect of the new doctrine—the deliverance of the pious from Sheol—to have been expressed and emphasized; in general this is not so, however; v. 16 bears the same quite personal character as the assurance of the pious praying person in other places: that he for his part may rest satisfied that Yahweh shall deliver him from sudden death and danger of death as long as he is going to live on earth. Volz is right when saying that the text strongly emphasizes that the rich shall *stay* in Sheol; but this gets its explanation from the Israelite view of mortal danger and illness: a person in danger of death *is* already in Sheol; the suppliant says: the ungodly rich shall stay there, I myself shall be snatched from there by Yahweh, i.e. he will make me healthy and safe again. The most probable interpretation of Ps. 49 is therefore that it is meant to be a thanksgiving psalm on having experienced deliverance; it is on a basis of personal experience that the suppliant expresses his personal assurance in v. 16, and bears testimony, and admonishes all other people.

That there is a personal experience underlying Ps. 73 is perfectly evident, and told in plain words; the intention of the psalm is to be a thanksgiving psalm bearing testimony to salvation and assurance of future personal safety in communion with God (in 'the presence of God'), cf. n. 11b to Chap. X. And as long as *lāqah* in v. 24 does not give us any reason to think of being 'carried away' (see above), and as 49.16 does not allow us to refer it in a special way to a 'resurrection', and as the suppliant can hardly mean to say that he has been 'taken' by God in a way different from other people, the most natural thing is to interpret Ps. 73 in the same way as Pss. 16 and 49: disaster and death shall suddenly befall the ungodly, I myself and all God's pious people (v. 1) who trust in God and live in communion with him shall be guided safely on our ways in life by his 'counsel', and 'afterward' 'received' to 'glory' again, viz. the glory of health and happiness belonging to the pious person, as contrasted with the state of 'dishonour' that illness and disaster are supposed to involve. Birkeland's interpretation of Ps. 73 as an exception to the main rule (*StTh* 3, p. 70) is therefore unnecessary. In *Festschrift für Bertholet*, pp. 426ff. von Rad seeks to prove that among the temple personnel there were certain circles with mystical tendencies; here the cultic elements and conceptions were being spiritualized, and even the conception of 'life' itself was spiritualized, with an emphasis on the spiritual communion with the deity. It is possible that such tendencies existed; Ps. 73 at any rate seems influenced by them; but this does not suffice to prove that that and other psalms express the idea of such a life after death. Even von Rad bases his arguments on the erroneous theory that *lāqaḥ* as a matter of course is a technical term for 'being carried away (to the beyond)' (ib., p. 434).

NOTE XXXI (p. 197, n. 11; p. 243, n. 61, 62; p. 245, n. 68, 69, 70)

For the conception that the 'psalms of suffering' deal with the king's cultic death and resurrection in identity with Yahweh as a dying and again rising god, see Engnell, *Div. Kingship*, p. 170, n. 4; p. 210 (cf. index s.vv. 'Passion', 'Penitence' and 'death' of the king), and *SEÅ* X, pp. 31ff.; Widengren in *SEÅ* X, pp. 66ff.; Riesenfeld (see below), and in an extreme form Haldar, *Studies on the Book of Nahum*.

This interpretation of the ideological and style historical background of the conception of the descent into the underworld (Sheol) is not new; it will be found in A. Jeremias and von Baudissin, see Chap. VII, n. 55. Widengren has been able to reinforce the hypothesis by means of a great many details based on the latest texts and sources. But these do not prove anything beyond the fact that the idea that the suffering person was 'threatened by death' was expressed in the usual terms of being in the power of Sheol, and that such conceptions and descriptions found some of their typical expressions in the descriptions of the descent of the dead deity into Sheol; thus, the *form* of the description of the state of the sufferer has been borrowed from the myth of the dead god. To the Israelite, illness and other forms of mortal danger were already death; the sick person or the person in mortal danger 'had death within himself', he was in the power of Sheol (see Johs. Pedersen, *Israel* I–II, p. 153, cf. p. 462). To describe danger of death and menace of death as a state of death, as a sojourn in the realm of death, is a quite widespread idea, as Gunkel-Begrich have proved by a great many examples, see *Einl.*, pp. 185ff. Riesenfeld (*Resurrection in Ezek. XXXVIII*, pp. 5ff.) seems to take the theory for granted that in Israel the king was supposed to 'die' and 'rise again' in the cult of the new year festival, and is then able to read it into texts like Hos. 4.2; Micah 7.8; Ps. 16.5. None of these, however, involves any references to king or 'resurrection'. The background of the originally Canaanite proverbial term in Hos. 4.2 is evidently the death and resurrection not of the king but of the god of vegetation himself, an idea which according to several testimonies was well known to the half pagan Israelites of the north. As for Mic. 7.8 it is impossible to find the king's death and resurrection in it, if this theory is not taken for granted beforehand. On Pss. 16.5; 17.15 see above, Additional Note XXX. Against the conclusions of Widengren and Engnell, based on the presentation of the psalms, see also Bentzen in *Eissfeldt-Festschrift*, pp. 57ff.

A more modest version of the theory of the king's cultic suffering and the interpretation of many psalms as belonging to the ritual drama is represented by A. R. Johnson (*The Labyrinth*, ed. S. H. Hooke): the king acts as the representative of Yahweh in the ritual fight against the 'enemies'; his 'ritual tribulations' are his hard struggle in the ritual 'sham fight' (see also his *Sacral Kingship*, pp. 102ff., 108, 112, 119). The one-sided and unproved assertions of Engnell and others represent an exaggeration of Johnson's hypothesis. So here it may suffice to answer Johnson's arguments. As mentioned in the above text, Johnson is perfectly right in saying that the dramatic presentation of Yahweh's victory over the 'nations' in the cult played a part in the Israelite new year festival. But there is nothing to prove that the king was looked upon as the leader of the struggle on behalf of Yahweh, nor that Israel had anything corresponding to the Babylonian rite with the atoning humiliation of the king (see above, p. 243). Johnson bases his conjecture as to the cultic suffering of the king as part of the ritual 'sham fight' on his interpretation of Ps. 89, which he considers to be a psalm of the new year festival. But this interpretation is not right; Ps. 89 is a casual psalm of lamentation for a fast day of humiliation and prayer, occasioned by a real defeat in war; the suppliant (the king), here as a motive for being heard, calls to mind the divine promises, which were given to the ancestor David and would be repeated to the king at every new year festival, and the works of Yahweh, the 'fight of the primeval ocean' and the creation, which are likewise motives of the new year festival; but *here*, in Ps. 89, they are being used to express the actual situation; the king alludes to these earlier evidences of power and blessing in order to motivate his prayer for help and his confidence in Yahweh and in order to make him interfere even in the actual historical distress. See above, Chap. VII. 1.

But if Ps. 89 has been occasioned by a historical event and not by a cultic myth, there is no longer any reason to interpret Ps. 118 as if it were referring to the king's 'suffering in the cult'. In fact, Ps. 118 really belongs to the new year festival, and the speaker is the king or the leader of the people, but the 'fight' he mentions here on behalf of the people, a fight which Yahweh has brought to a happy end, must be referred—as in Ps. 129—to all the various historical disasters which had befallen Israel throughout her history, illustrated by a single compressed picture, and thus conventionalized on the pattern of 'the myth about the fight of nations'; there is no question of acute suffering as in the psalms of lamentation, and consequently no occasion for any theory about 'the king as suffering in the cult'.

Finally as regards Ps. 18—the third psalm on which Johnson bases his theory—it is the thanksgiving psalm of a king for deliverance from distress; the distress is described as a sojourn in Sheol, in the waves and breakers of the underworld. But here no more than elsewhere is this idea to be understood 'literally'; this is a 'picture' of the distress brought upon the king by his enemies during the battle, more realistically described in vv. 36–43, a real battle on an earthly battlefield, not a 'ritual fight' or a martial game; the enemies are 'people's, 'nations', 'strangers' (vv. 44, 45, 48, 50), and the result of the battle is that they are conquered by the king. The victory over the 'nations' is not a result of the deliverance from the 'underworld', but identical with it; already in v. 15: 'he sent out his arrows, and scattered them; and he shot out lightnings, and discomfited them', there is an allusion to these human enemies, who are directly mentioned, without any metaphors, later on in the psalm. The psalm itself is a thanksgiving psalm, belonging to the thank-offering festival after the victory has been won on the battlefield, see Chap. IX. 4; the cultic element does not come in till the deed, of which the psalm is retrospectively telling us, has been fulfilled. The same thing applies to the thanksgiving psalm 116; a ritual suffering is not hinted at in a single word. And let it be said in this connexion that there seems to be no special reason to interpret Ps. 2 as an annual re-adoption of the king after his supposed sufferings under the attacks of 'death' in a ritual sham combat, as Johnson thinks (*Sacral Kingship*, pp. 118ff.); true enough, the situation is poetically and mythologically conventionalized, but is yet a real historical situation; the enemies are the surrounding 'kings', not demonic powers.

So none of these psalms gives us any reason to interpret the distress of which the psalms of lamentation are speaking—not even when they describe it as a sojourn in Sheol—as a distress experienced only in the cult. Certainly these psalms belong to the cult, but what is laid before God in the liturgies of the day of humiliation and prayer, are real human historical conditions, and real human historical distress and affliction and suffering, and no ritual sham suffering. Beyond the supposed fundamental evidence of Pss. 18; 89 and 118, to which Johnson has drawn attention (op. cit.), and Ps. 116, Engnell has not been able to provide any proofs of the 'cultic suffering' of the king, see *SEÅ* X, p. 32, n. 4; p. 34, n. 10 and 11. Without giving any grounds whatever he adds Pss. 22; 49; Isa. 38.9ff. and—apparently joining Widengren (see Chap. VII, n. 92)—Ps. 88; see *Div. Kingship*, p. 176,n. 4; *SEÅ* X, p. 32,n. 4. As for Ps. 88, see above, pp. 237f. What has been said there applies also to Pss. 22; 49 and Isa. 38.9ff.: they speak of real urgent distress. In Ps. 49, moreover, the internal social and religious antagonisms of Judaism form the tangible background; when the very basis supposed to be there fails to substantiate itself—in this case Engnell's interpretation of Pss. 18; 89; 118 and 116—there is no longer any reason to read the thought of a 'ritual suffering' into the other royal psalms of lamentation—ard most particularly not if, like Engnell, one holds that the king in the supposed cultic act represents the god of vegetation, 'that the Tammuz line and the king line of the cult are in fact nothing but two aspects of one and the same thing' (!) and seeks to 'maintain their "identity"' (*SEÅ* X, p. 33, n. 45). To Bentzen's well-aimed objection that 'the suffering of the king' forms no part of the ritual of the Israelite new year festival (*Jesaja* I, p. 100, cf. also *Sakrale Kongedömme*), Engnell answers by repeating that such evidence does exist, namely in the said royal psalms of suffering (*SEÅ* X, p. 34)! But as long as the 'sufferings' of the king in a majority of psalms must be referred to actual historical distress, or to real prosaic illness, strong positive arguments are needed in order to prove that the suffering in other psalms, in which it is described in a perfectly analogous way, have to be referred to ritual sham suffering. However— and I repeat it—we may admit that the *form* in which the description of the suffering is frequently conveyed to us as a sojourn in Sheol may have been strongly influenced by the form in which death is described in the cultic conceptions of the descent into the nether world by the god Tammuz (see above, p. 240, and Chap. VII, n. 64).

NOTE XXXII (II. 6, n. 15*a*; 8, n. 19*a*)

In *The Evildoers in the Book of Psalms* Birkeland goes still further than in *Feinde d. Indiv.* in interpreting all the psalms of lamentation as royal psalms, the distress as a national and political one, and consequently the enemies mentioned as foreigners. His main argument seems to be the great similarity in the description of the distress and the enemies found in all the psalms in question (see e.g. *Evildoers*, p. 45). But when these descriptions admittedly are given in very general and conventional terms, with very few allusions to the definite factual circumstances, then it is only to be expected that they have a very stereotyped form and content. Whether the evildoers are political enemies or sorcerers, they are described after the traditional 'pattern' of a *rāšā'*, a 'rascal'.

Birkeland (see Chap. VIII, n. 15a) admits that there *are* real psalms of illness (op. cit., pp. 40ff.), but even so he thinks that the enemies are foreign political potentates, who take the illness of the king as an opportunity to attack him. But see above, p. 199. It seems to me impossible to avoid the interpretation according to which the enemies are the persons who have *caused* the illness, or at least whom the sufferer suspects to have caused it. Birkeland's statement (op. cit., p. 41): 'As long as it is not proved we are not entitled to assume the existence of *Laiengebete* within the book of Psalms', seems to me to be begging the question. '*Laiengebete*' (laymen's prayers) is used here not in the usual sense of this word, for non-cultic and non-ritual prayers, but for ritual prayers destined for the cultic performance of Everyman in his private affairs. The 'democratiza-tion' of religion in Judaism should not be denied.

NOTE XXXIII (II. 147, n. 1; 150, n. 17)

These words quoted from Wellhausen, *Isr. u. jüd. Gesch.*[6], p. 147, are typical of those supporting the post-exilic dating of the psalms. See also the commentaries of Buhl, Briggs, Duhm, and many others, who practically all date the psalms to Jewish times; likewise Pfeiffer's *Introduction*. Kennet in *Old Testament Essays*, pp. 119ff. makes a belated attempt at a late dating, generally in the age of the Maccabees, and without discussing the evidence to the contrary implied in the cult-functional point of view as a whole. The reaction against the late dating is not only based on our extensive knowledge of the cultic poetry of the orient, and especially of Canaan, at the time of Israel's entry, but also on the deeper insight into cultic history which is a result of the cult-historical method itself; see the present author in *VT* V, pp. 13ff. It is also evident, however, that the dating of the psalms must be undertaken from a critical viewpoint of the internal process of evolution in the spiritual history of Israel. No sound interpretation can be based on such an individual conception of religious conditions in ancient Israel as that of Eerdmans (*The Religion of Israel*, Leiden, 1947).

But the reaction against earlier psalm criticism may also be exaggerated. A pronounce-ment like that of Engnell, *Div. Kingship*, p. 176,n. 2, that there does not exist more than one single 'post-exilic' psalm, viz. Ps. 137, can only rest on a superficial study of the texts and their *spiritual* substance, and on a juvenile inclination towards sweeping antithetical assertions. Even Eerdmans, *Hebr. Book of Pss.*, pp. 41ff., is very sparing with post-exilic ('Judaic') psalms; he seems to rest content with some 4 or 5: Ps. 147, supposed to allude to the building of walls under Nehemiah; 137, according to Eerdmans, 'exilic'; 103, which 'seems to have been composed under the fresh impression of the edict of Cyrus'; 107, supposed to treat of the home journey of the exiles through the desert; 135 which is 'a post-exilic version of Ps. 115', and 134 which is of the same type. These precise datings also go far beyond the limits of justifiable exegesis and often rest on a misconception of the nature and intention of the psalm in question; there can be no doubt that Ps. 107 deals with a general thank-offering festival, and that Ps. 103 is a thanksgiving psalm on recovery from illness. But when Eerdmans dates all the other psalms from the period of the monarchy, the reason—apart from his constant over-interpretation, finding historical allusions even in conventional metaphors—is a total view of the religious conditions of ancient Israel, which the present author cannot share, and which is not sufficiently supported by the sources. For my views see my critique in *NTT* 1949; cf. Rowley's review of Eerdmans, *Religion of Israel* in *Bibliotheca Orientalis* IV, 1947, No. 6, pp. 152ff.

NOTE XXXIV (II. 86, n. 2)

Pfeiffer, *Introduction*, p. 624, thinks there is no evidence of psalm singing in the Temple of Jerusalem until about the year 400 B.C., and that consequently most of the psalms must date from post-exilic times. He then builds on the fact that the earliest documentary mention of the temple singers is to be found in the census list of Ezra 2, which indeed dates from that time. But then he completely overlooks the arguments provided by form and style history, and also the imitations of psalm style in Jeremiah and in Deutero-Isaiah and as early as Isa. 6.3 (and in the Song of Deborah, Jdg. 5!) which indirectly prove that cultic psalm-singing must have been much older even in Jerusalem. The Sennacherib cylinder is direct evidence (see above, II. 80) of the existence of temple singers in Jerusalem long before 400. Further, Pfeiffer urges that Am. 5.23 refers to the cult of the Northern kingdom, but that the cultic singing was denounced by Amos, who was from Judah, because such a thing did not occur in Jerusalem. Am. 5.23 certainly refers to Bethel, but from this we should not conclude that psalm-singing did not occur in Jerusalem. Nor is it correct to say that Amos denounces psalm-singing as such; if so we should also have to maintain that Isaiah denounced prayer *per se* (Isa. 1.15). Now it is probably generally acknowledged that the sharp attacks of the prophets on the cult and the arrangements belonging to it do not involve any rejection of the cult *per se*; neither does the attack of Amos on 'the noise of the songs' in the ungodly Bethel. The attitude of Amos was not determined by what was to be found or not to be found in Jerusalem, but by his religious and moral knowledge of Yahweh.

NOTE XXXV (II.86, n. 2; 152, n. 27).

The commentator's alternatives to the king have been (*a*) a foreign king as the overlord of the Jews; (*b*) a Maccabean king or prince; (*c*) a 'personification' of the congregation of Israel. But (*a*) is excluded by the fact that the anointed king is too often described as reigning on Zion and being in a very close connexion with Yahweh; (*b*) is impossible because the whole hypothesis of the Maccabean origin of a greater or lesser part of the Psalter is untenable, see Chap. XVIII. 6; and (*c*) falls together with Smend's 'collective' hypothesis.

Pfeiffer in his *Introduction*, pp. 629ff., still tries to insist that the king in these psalms is a foreign or Maccabean prince or a 'personification' of Israel. In fact, such an interpretation could *a priori* only receive consideration as a final alternative if the most natural and likely interpretation were to meet with insuperable difficulties, or if it were a fact beyond contradiction that all the psalms were post-exilic; but neither is the case. The standpoint of Pfeiffer is literary and dogmatic. (See pp. 46ff.; and for the supposed reference to Simon the Maccabee in Ps. 110, see n. 31 to Chap. XVIII. All the arguments adduced by Pfeiffer in the discussion with Gunkel against a natural interpretation of the royal psalms vanish as soon as due allowance is made for type analysis and its results; but Pfeiffer does not even consider this essential aspect of Gunkel's argument. Pfeiffer thinks that only two psalms are pre-exilic: 24.7–10 (so he is not aware of the liturgical unity of this psalm) and 45. One cannot help regretting that an investigator so critical and otherwise well orientated as Pfeiffer has been able to abide by such an antiquated view of the psalms without realizing how far beyond the point of view of earlier criticism psalm investigation has actually passed by utilizing form history and cult history. Cf. the author's review of the present state of our knowledge in *VT V*, 1955, pp. 15ff.

NOTE XXXVI (II.81, n. 8; 153, n. 28, 29; 154, n. 31).

Among more recent psalm commentators Böhl (*De Psalmen* I, p. 30) maintains the *pre-Davidic* origin of Pss. 8; 19A; 29; 'great parts of 68'; 82; 90; 'and particularly 104'. Böhl thinks that in some of these cases we have Israelite adaptations of older Canaanite poems; H. L. Ginsberg believes he has proved the 'Phoenician' origin of Ps. 29 (*Atti del XIX Congresso Internat. d. Orientalisti 1935*). The possibility of this may be admitted (see II.188). As for Pss. 19A and 29 I admit the possibility, in the former case the probability, that they are Israelite adaptations of older Canaanite psalms (see II.190). Ps. 29, however, in its present form is based on the conception of Yahweh as king and victor over the primeval ocean (*mabbûl*) and so probably presupposes the developed ideology of the enthronement festival of Jerusalem; it can therefore hardly be earlier than the kingdom and the Yahweh cult in Jerusalem.

When Böhl, however, thinks he has found a proof of his thesis in the fact that such psalms 'glorify in an archaistic form God's deeds in nature and history', his argument fails. In a traditional literary style so conventionalized as the psalm style, archaisms are no proof of antiquity (see below on the psalm, Hab. 3). For Ps. 104 see II. 153. For 68 see the author's *Der achtundsechzigste Psalm*. If this psalm represents a Jerusalemite redaction of an older north Israelitic psalm, at all events this redaction has been a very slight one, to be traced in one or two verses only; there is no reason for dividing the psalm through any sort of source criticism; apart from the two or three rather hypothetical Jerusalemite additions (see the author's *Real and Apparent Tricola in Hebrew Psalm Poetry*, pp. 92ff.) the psalm makes a coherent and organic unity, as demonstrated in my *Der achtundsechzigste Psalm*. For Ps. 90 see above, II. 105f.; Gemser (*De Psalmen* III) does not insist on the authorship of Moses. According to its substance and the presupposed political conditions of Israel in Ps. 82, this psalm cannot be separated from Pss. 12, 14 and 58, which are all of them much later than the age of David; see Birkeland, *Feinde d. Individuums*, pp. 44f. Böhl does not give any positive reasons for dating Ps. 8 to pre-Davidic times, and only mentions that J. de Groot has maintained the possibility of 'pre-Davidic parts in Pss. 6, 38, 40, 46, 65, 78, 136, 145 and 149'. I must confess that I am quite unable to see any such possibility; every attempt to disentangle such 'parts' is nothing but mere arbitrariness.

Turning to the question of Davidic psalms it is significant that Böhl does not with certainty date any particular psalm to the age of David. From archaeological quarters it has been maintained (for instance by Albright, *A.R.I.*, pp. 125f.) that the finds of the Ugaritic texts and other archaeological data have refuted the objections made against Davidic authorship of at any rate some of the psalms. This is, however, a premature conclusion. What has been added to our knowledge with regard to these matters by the archaeological investigation of the last decades is a more definite picture of religious poetry, cultic psalms as well as music, writings and literature, etc., even in pre-Israelite Canaan, so that *a priori* from *this* point of view no objections can be made to the possibility of temple music and psalmography at the time of David. This was, however, an insight to which type analytical and cult functional psalm exegesis had attained already in the works of Gunkel and his followers even though there was little practical knowledge of these things—see the author's paper 'Psalm Criticism between 1900 and 1935' in *VT* V, pp. 13ff. The existence of Canaanite psalmography had been inferred already from the Amarna letters (see n. 65 to Chap. XXI), and more than 25 years ago I considered the possibility of dating Ps. 68 to the time of Saul, and Ps. 60 to the time of David or Solomon (cf. *Ps.St.* III, pp. 65ff.; VI, p. 38, n. 9). Even the new archaeological matter has not been able to give anything more than such a *possibility*. When considering the Davidic date or authorship of this or that definite psalm, everything depends on the internal evidence of each individual psalm. As for the heading *lĕdhāwīdh* it proves *per se* absolutely nothing in this respect; as it was originally not meant to be a real statement of the author's name (see above, pp. 77f., II. 98ff.), the probability that a psalm with this heading should date from David is *a priori* no greater than the probability of its dating from any other time. There is no denying that the formula *lĕdhāwīdh* has been added to a great many psalms which on internal grounds must be dated to much later, even post-exilic times; clear instances are Pss. 56; 57; 59, the background of which is the disastrous wars with the neighbouring peoples after the 'disruption'; cf. Pss. 124 and 126, praising Yahweh for the restoration of Jerusalem and the return of the exiles: cf. also Ps. 51 from the times of Nehemiah or a little earlier.

When Albright (op. cit., p. 126) alleges that 'the short psalm' 2 Sam. 23. 1ff. is certainly a Davidic poem, his argument is not very convincing; 2 Sam. 23.11 is neither a 'psalm' nor a true prophecy but a *māšāl* in mixed wisdom and prophetic style suggesting a prophecy *post eventu*, like Gen. 49 and Deut. 33, put into the mouth of the dying ancestor; as literary genre it has its analogies within the comparatively late poetry of the Old Testament. See my paper in *ZATW* 45, 1927, pp. 30ff., the argument of which A. R. Johnson's remarks (*Sacral Kingship in Ancient Israel*, p. 15) in my opinion have not been able to invalidate. That the poem opens with the archaic formula *nĕ'um dāwīdh* like the no doubt ancient songs of Balaam in Num. 24, is of course no proof of high age, as Albright supposes; artificial archaisms are no rare phenomena in any literature, including that of Israel; we find the same archaisms in Prov. 30.1, cf. also *nĕ'um peša'*, Ps. 36.2, a psalm which belongs to the age of national disasters, after the division of the realm. That literary archaisms do not necessarily prove the antiquity of a poem is seen, e.g. from the numerous archaisms of style and matter in Hab. 3, which certainly is to be dated from the last years of the monarchy.

As this very psalm shows, mythological and stylistic archaisms are no reason to postulate an old 'nucleus' in the text at hand; see the present author's treatment of Hab. 3 in *ThZ* 9, pp. 1ff.

Böhl, de Groot, Albright and others have talked about Davidic 'nuclei' in this or that psalm (see above), but none of them have ever tried to extract the definite 'nucleus', or to give clear criteria for such a literary critical operation. The main reason for the theories about Davidic 'nuclei' seems to be the commentator's subjective evaluation of the poetical and religious value of this or that psalm, which he therefore wants to reserve for his beloved St. David. It must, however, be stressed that before putting out a theory about an older 'nucleus' in a psalm, one must demonstrate objective criteria and material traces in the psalm, which seem to *demand* as a solution the theory of an older stratum being taken up and altered and enlarged by a younger poet. Literary criticism is a methodical science, not wishful thinking. It is an unsound method to try to find ancient psalms by leaving out such parts as obviously point to later times and thus postulating an old 'nucleus'. So e.g. when Albright (*Studies in Prophecy*, ed. Rowley, p. 6) postulates an old 'nucleus' in Ps. 67, supposed to refer to the 'cult of the tabernacle'; this theory is against the uniform structure of the psalm, envisaging the thanksgiving for the crop of the earth in vv. 7f. Nor will it do to maintain that the song of Miriam in Ex. 15 'is substantially Mosaic in date' (ibid., p. 5) by leaving out the last verses which actually give the scope of the whole psalm; see the present author's *Der achtundsechzigste Psalm*, pp. 73f. Of course that does not rule out the existence of psalms which have been composed on the basis of an earlier poem or have simply incorporated (a fragment of) such a poem, like Pss. 19 and 77 (see pp. 411, 435, 451). But in this case one has positive formal, style historical and ideological instances to refer to, not just random individual conjectures. As for Ps. 77, the theory—sound in itself—that an earlier poem has been used in vv. 14ff. is not supported by the heading, as Albright supposes (op. cit., p. 9); for 'Jeduthun' is no proper name corresponding to the Canaanite Ethan, but a musical term in the liturgy, see Chap. XXIII. 18; and even if it were, it does not matter more than does the heading 'by Ethan' in Ps. 89.1.

Other scholars still maintain the Davidic authorship of certain psalms. Ps. 18 is considered as Davidic by König and others; Pss. 60 and 108 by König and Buttenwieser; Ps. 68 by Eerdmans (or possibly Solomonic), etc. To this the following short remarks may be made.

Ps. 18 has, in a somewhat different recension, been taken up as an addition to the deuteronomistic saga, from the time after 520; there is no reason to suppose a 'pre-exilic' deuteronomistic saga, see Hölscher (in Gunkel Festschrift, *Eucharisterion*, pp. 158ff.). This fact is, however, of course no guarantee for the opinion that the 'tradition' about David as author is more correct in this case than elsewhere; for the theory of David as an author of psalms is at any rate earlier than the Deuteronomist; so 2 Sam. 22.1 gives no evidence in addition to that of Ps. 18.1. In fact Ps. 18 was made for the use of a descendant of David, see v. 51. A more accurate dating of Ps. 18 is very uncertain; Cross and Freedman (*JBL* 72, 1953, pp. 15ff.) think that the orthography allows a dating to the ninth or eighth century. In my opinion the available matter for writing a detailed history of Hebrew orthography is much too scanty.

When Eerdmans, *Hebr. Book of Psalms*, pp. 40, 199ff., considers Ps. 30 to be Davidic, he bases his argument on an untenable interpretation of its matter and aim. He also seeks to ascribe Ps. 51 to David; that not only conflicts with vv. 20f. (omitted by Eerdmans), but also with the individual self-testimony of the praying person, that he has only sinned against God, that is to say against no human being, which is quite incompatible with the story about the wife of Uriah.

That Ps. 68 is one of the oldest psalms is also the opinion of the present author, who has tried to prove the possibility of a Benjaminitic origin in the times of Saul (see Chap. XVIII, n. 26a). In its present form it is connected with the cult in the Temple of Jerusalem, and now I am most inclined to think that this was its original intention. It most certainly belongs to the new year and enthronement festival (see above, p. 172), which again means that it can scarcely have been made before the erection of Solomon's Temple, probably somewhat later.

Ps. 60 also is one of the older psalms. But the content of the oracle in vv. 8–10 seems to show that the historical background is the attempt of one of the Judaean kings to *regain* the countries that had formerly belonged to the realm and its anointed king; the stressing of his claimed sovereignty over Ephraim, Manasseh and Gilead seems to point to a time after the disruption. A part of this psalm has, together with 57.8–12, been used for the new composition Ps. 108, which then of course must have been made for an analogous situation at a somewhat later time. Buttenwieser's dating of the two psalms to the age of David is due to an over-eclectic interpretation of the historical allusions.

A number of psalms are accepted as genuinely Davidic also by Kissane (*The Book of Psalms*, I), but his arguments are in no way more convincing that those of the above-mentioned scholars, and must be met by the same refutations.

NOTE XXXVII (II.154, n. 35).

The Maccabean dating has been carried through most consistently by Duhm (*Die Psalmen*, pp. xviff.); only in the cases of Pss. 137; 8; 19A; 46; 48; 76; 84A and possibly also 87; 16; 51; 3; 4; 11 and 62 is he willing to admit the probability or possibility of pre-Maccabean origin. Even Cornill, who is much more cautious, claims at any rate 4–5 Maccabean psalms and declares: 'all honest exegesis must recognize that there are Maccabean psalms' (*Intro. to the Canonical Books of the O.T.*, p. 408). According to Duhm the psalms mostly refer to controversies or warfare between the 'parties' of 'the Pharisees' and the 'Hasmoneans' or 'Sadducees'—a view already refuted by Gunkel's explanation of 'the enemies' in the psalms of lamentation (cf. also *Ps.St.* I), and definitively by Birkeland's pointing out that these enemies were mostly foreign. Baethgen (*Die Psalmen*,[3] pp. xiiiff.) has already proved in a very thorough-going and sober investigation that for canon-historical and other reasons the existence of any considerable number of Maccabean psalms is most unlikely; after Baethgen's discussion of the matter, very strong positive evidence is needed in order to allow us to interpret any psalm as **Macca-bean**. Gunkel's comparative style-historical investigation has corroborated this result; cf. also Gressmann in *The Psalmists*. Likewise against the Maccabean theory are Barnes (*The Psalms*, pp. xxiiiff.)—though he sticks to the hypothesis of party warfare (ibid. p. xxx)—and Buttenwieser (*The Psalms*, pp. 10ff.). When we consider the perspectives revealed by the style and cult historical method we may safely say that Kennet's attempt to maintain that psalmography originated in the age of the Maccabees (*Old Test. Essays*, pp. 219ff.), is sadly out of date; he thinks all psalms were composed between the years 168 and 141 B.C.

If we look at those individual psalms which even Cornill considers to be definitely Maccabean, namely, 44; 74; 79 and 83, and which Pfeiffer (*Introduction*, p. 628) still looks upon as the pillars of the hypothesis, we must admit that they do not contain a single convincing feature. The disasters over which all these psalms are lamenting may just as well be those of 598 or 587, or any other, unknown, historical calamities. The consciousness that Israel herself is righteous and guiltless (Ps. 44) is much more charac-teristic of the view of the official cult religion in earlier times than in the age of the Maccabees—which is also corroborated by the Psalms of Solomon; cf. the royal psalm 18.21ff. There is no reason to interpret '(the house of) the festal assembly of God' in 74.8 as referring to synagogues, even if, for instance, Menes (*ZATW* 50, 1932, p. 269) thinks it obvious; the ancient cult term *mô'ādhîm* is never used of them; on the contrary, the psalm is earlier than the centralization of the cult in Jerusalem (after 520). The mention of 'Asshur' in 89.9 excludes any dating earlier than 612. Attention has been called to the initials of the verse lines 110.1–4a, supposed to form the acrostic *sm'n* for the Maccabee 'Sim'on'; but the initials of the really metrical verse lines are *nmrbn;* besides we may say that an acrostic covering only part of a poem and taking no notice of the last part, as is the case here, does not really exist. The same may be said of the supposed acrostic in 2.1–10: *lyny w'štw* 'to Jannay and his wife', with an allusion to the Maccabee Jannai; the actual initials are *lyt['] ny'w[']stw + 'p[']* in vv. 11, 12.

NOTE XXXVIII (II.159, n. 1; 166, n. 13; 171, n. 23; 172, n. 26; 173, n. 27).

1. Surveys of the history of the problem of Hebrew metrics are to be found in most of the bigger introductions to the Old Testament or to the psalms; see, for instance, Eissfeldt, *Einl.*, pp. 62ff.; Cornill, *Einl.*,[6] pp. 11ff. [E.T. *Intro.*, pp. 15ff.]; and particularly Begrich in *ThR*, N.F. 4, 1932. Cf. also Albright in *JPOS* II, pp. 6ff., and T. H. Robinson, *The Poetry of the O.T.*, with many fine observations. Of the theories which have been important to the investigation and have met with more or less sympathy may be men-tioned the works of Ley, Bickel, Budde, and particularly Sievers.

The first investigators of the problem were bound to the classic ideas about metrics and their teminology, which were based on the classical quantitative metres.

Since Ley it is commonly agreed that the Hebrew metre is *accentual*. Bickel's attempt to prove a strongly alternating metre, iambic or trochaic, with alternating short and long syllables, has found no approval and is easily refuted. Gábor (*Der hebräische Urrhythmus*) has tried to show that the Hebrew metre is based on alliteration, but in order to carry through this theory he has to postulate an accenting of the Hebrew words different from the traditional one, and maintain that in the period to which most of the poetry belongs, Hebrew had a penultimate accent instead of an ultimate; but that is at variance with all we know and can reasonably conclude about the structure of the historical Hebrew language itself; cf. H. Birkeland, *Akzent und Vokalismus im Hebräischen*; against Gábor see also Begrich in *ThR* N.F. 4, pp. 79f. Byington's attempt in *JBL* 66,

1947, pp. 63ff. at a solution of the problem on a mathematical basis is much too complicated to be convincing, and also suffers from the fact that due allowance is not made
for linguistic development.

2. The first secured result was found by Budde with his discovery of the qinah metre,
the a-symmetric bicolic verse of the funerary rites, used also in the song of lamentation,
as in the book of Lamentations. Budde, however, scanned the qinah wrongly as a
'fiver', a bicolic verse of 3 + 2 'feet' (beats, metrical accents). One reason for this
mistake was that he took into account the primary word accent only and thus was bound
to find too many irregularities in his 'Fünfer'.

In the footsteps of Ley and Budde followed Sievers with his noteworthy *Metrische Studien.*
His system has been accepted by the great majority of Old Testament scholars up to
the present time.

According to Sievers the fundamental form is the *Doppeldreier*, the 'double three', a
rising bicolon (3 + 3) with an in principle anapaestic rhythm, but frequently even iambs
and monosyllabic feet, or with a 'dissolution of the thesis', so that we get three (or more)
unaccented syllables between two accented ones. As the second main form, with Budde,
he reckons the qinah bicolon. And as the third, a 4 + 4 bicolon, the *Doppelvierer* (the
'double four'), as in Ps. 29.

Besides these three basic metres Sievers also finds a great many variants. As variants
of the 'double threes' and 'double fours' he finds the 'sevens' (4 + 3), the 'reversed
sevens' (3 + 4), and the 'sixers' (2 + 2 + 2), and as variants of the 'fivers' he finds the
'reversed fivers' (2 + 3) and the 'double twos' (2 + 2). Characteristic for his system is
that these variants almost never appear as the regular and consistent metre of any whole
poem, but always as quite irregularly intermingled exceptions within a poem in 'double
threes', 'double fours' and qinah metre.

To this theory Hölscher (*Budde-Festschrift*, pp. 93ff.) most justly has objected that the
long syllables are too predominant in Hebrew for a waltz rhythm like that of Sievers to
be natural. But above all we object that the rules of accentuation suggested by the
Massoretic system of vocalization and punctuation do not agree with such a mincing
rhythm. This is seen from the rules about the secondary accent (*metheg*) on the second
next syllable after the accented syllable of a word, as well as from the accentuation
actually used sometimes by the Massoretes in verse—both of them pointing to a marked
iambic rhythm of the language itself, which cannot have been without its dominant
influence even on the poetical rhythm and metres. In a language with so many long
vowels as the Hebrew it is very improbable that only the syllable with the primary
stress should have a metrical accent, and that the many other long or accented syllables
should be rhythmically as unaccented as is required by Sievers' system, although he of
course is aware that the syllable with secondary stress *may* get the metrical accent: he
has not realized, however, that it not only may, but very often *must*. Similar critical
remarks have also been made by Gray.

The intermingling of all sorts of variant bicola without any definite rules, is another
stumbling-block to Sievers's system. Fatal, likewise, is Rothstein's attempt to save the
system by giving it real rules and regularity; for this can only be done by a rearrange-
ment of the text in such an arbitrary way that the system is doomed. In fact Sievers's
system leads to an effacement of the difference between verse and prose rhythm, as is
seen by his attempt to put Genesis into metre (and even make this the basis of a literary
source critique).

When Sievers finds the anapaestic metre to be the fundamental form of Hebrew
metrics, he has in fact, be it consciously or unconsciously, been led by some idea of the

'sense metre' (see above, II.159). He has started from the fact that in Hebrew poetry most cola seem to consist of three words (units of meaning). But this is only apparent: an overwhelming number of these 'words' consist of a verb or a noun + postfix, i.e. of a verb and an object, or a noun with a possessive pronoun, that is to say two logical units.

Hölscher has also pointed out that the Massoretes not infrequently give four accents to cola consisting of only three units of meaning. For instance:

> lámma rágešú goyím
> úle' ummĭm yéhgu—ríq (Ps. 2.1a).

See also Pss. 2.2a, 5a, 7a, 10b, 12a; 3.2a, 4, 5b, 6a, b; 5.6a, 8a; 6.6b, 10b; 7.13b, 14b, 16a, 18b; 8.5a; 9.4b, 20b; 15.1b, 4b; 22.5a, b, 6b, 7b, 9b, 10a, 11b, 24a, 27a; 23.4a; 24.1b, 5a, 7a, 9a; 25.3a, etc.

And here we must note that the Massoretic system does not mark all accented syllables; the marks are first of all punctuation marks or conjunctional marks, which, when wanted, are put on the accented syllable; consequently there are even accented syllables (accent of word or sentence) which are not emphasized by any accentual mark.

On the basis of all these observations Hölscher has given a short outline of his opinion on Hebrew metrics. According to him the supposed 3 + 3 bicolon is in fact a 4 + 4 bicolon, mostly dipodic; thus the basic difference between Sievers's *Doppeldreier* and his *Doppelvierer* disappears. The qinah bicolon is likewise no *Fünfer*, but a 4 + 3 bicolon. At any rate in later Hebrew metrical art a primary form is, according to Hölscher, the four-footed—dipodic—colon of one light and one heavy syllable alternately (iambic metre), in which the light syllable, however, is often syncopated, so that two heavy syllables adjoin; the first of them will then have to be prolonged in reading or given a circumflected tonic accent. The difference between the scanning of Sievers and that of Hölscher will be seen from the following example, according to Sievers a three beat colon and a two beat colon, according to Hölscher a four beat colon and a three beat colon:

according to Sievers:

> 'eká yašebá badád
> ha'ír rabbati-'ám

but according to Hölscher:

> 'eká yašebá badád
> ha'ír rabbáti 'ám (Lam. 1.1),

and in this case the latter accentuation is directly supported by the Massoretes.

Hölscher's suggestions have been followed up by the present author in his investigations of the qinah metre and the regular symmetric bicolon in Proverbs, Job and the majority of the psalms. Among the qinah verses in Lamentations—which by general consent and without any doubt is an asymmetric verse, where the latter colon is a 'foot' shorter than the former—there are so many former cola which according to the principle of the 'sense metre' *must* be scanned as four beat cola, and so many latter cola, that *must* be scanned as three beat cola, that there can be no doubt that the qinah is really a 4 + 3 bicolon (not a 3 + 2). And likewise in the wisdom poetry, among the supposed three beat cola there are a great many which definitely consist of four logical units and accordingly demand to be considered as four beat cola. Out of seventy cola in Proverbs at the first glance twenty-eight are seen to contain four units of meaning; in Chap. 4 there are twenty-one quite obvious cola of four words out of a total number of fifty-four; in Job Chap. 3 there are twenty-seven out of fifty-one. And if we pay regard to postfixes or negations and the like the great majority are cola of four words. That means that the supposed 'double threes' are actually 4 + 4 bicola.

By this interpretation of the basic Hebrew metre Sievers's irregularities disappear, his 'sevens' and 'reversed sevens' and 'sixers' are regular, 4 + 4 bicola, which have been wrongly scanned by Sievers and his followers. Some of the supposed 'sixers' are wrongly scanned qinah verses. The 'reversed fivers' and the 'double twos' also disappear: they are but wrongly scanned qinah verses.

Pfeiffer (*Introduction to the O.T.*, pp. 271f.) also seems to be of the same opinion; he speaks of the 4 + 3 accents in the metre of Lam. 1–4, and declares: 'The most common Hebrew verse has four accents in each half-line (4 : 4)'. He is, however, scarcely right in speaking of 'two and three feet' verses.

3. The iambic metre is to Hölscher and the present author the inevitable consequence of the vocalic and accentual system of the Hebrew language. When he (op. cit., pp. 99f.) rejects the 'constantly accentuated' system of Sievers and joins Bickel's *Silbenalternation*— modified by syncope—this does not mean that he accepts a system of 'quantities', but that he also allows the accents to decide; his syncopized metrical feet with one unstressed and one stressed syllable may therefore in the usual modern terms be called 'iambic'.

Sievers based his system on the main stresses of the single words only. Bruno, *Rhythmus d. alttestam. Dichtung*, thinks that only the syllable with the main stress is rhythmically relevant, that this syllable always must hold its natural accent, and that practically all the particles are rhythmically irrelevant. This is contrary to the rules of Hebrew accents as well as to all analogies—and to the sense of poetry. A metrical system leading to so many inversions of the verse parts as that of Bruno, and, for instance, to the dividing up of Ps. 50 into two psalms, is doomed. That Bruno has repeated the experiment of Sievers and recognized his system in historical prose texts like the books of Samuel or Kings (*Das hebräische Epos*) does not strengthen our belief in it.

Poetical rhythm, however, is always a sort of compromise between the natural 'irrational' rhythm of the prose language and a strong metrical system. In almost all modern European languages the metrical accent in principle *can* fall on almost every full vowel in the line of verse. The metrical accents are not limited to the accented syllables of a word or a combination of words (a sentence). Even a lighter syllable in a word may in verse get a rhythmical accent, become a heavy syllable. But of course this must not lead to unnatural accentuations in a word.

In Hebrew metrics due allowances must be made both for the secondary accent (the *metheg*) and for the retraction of the word-accent in closely connected words, as e.g. the construct connexion; see the above quoted instances from the Massoretic accentuation. The result is that even short syllables and words and syllables which are unaccented in prose rhythm may take the metrical accent—with the same restriction as mentioned above.

To what extent the short 'murmured vowels' (*šĕwā'*) in Hebrew may become rhythmically accented syllables we do not know exactly. But we have to remember that in earlier developmental stages of the language most of them were full vowels. And we can be sure that they must be accounted for in the metrical system, just as in Arabic poetry, and in principle, therefore, there is no reason why they should not occasionally take a ·metrical accent.

4. In the above considerations it has been taken for granted that in Hebrew poetry the shortest verse-line, the colon, as a rule does not appear as a single colon, but in close metrical connexion with another colon, the two thus making a bicolon, sometimes a tricolon. In fact, the colon is normally a 'hemistich', and the bicolon or tricolon, a

'stich'. This phenomenon is connected with the stylistic rule of the *parallelismus membrorum*, the 'thought rhyme', for the first time methodically observed and studied by Lowth. Gray (op. cit.) again emphasizes the importance of the law of parallelism for the understanding of Hebrew verse, against the neglect of it on the part of Sievers, especially as manifested in his unsuccessful attempt at a metrical conception of Genesis. The law of parallelism as a constitutive feature, preventing the isolated colon from appearing as a metrical unity, is also strongly emphasized by Th. H. Robinson in *ZATW* 54, 1936, pp. 28ff. See also his paper in *Festschrift für Bertholet*, pp. 438ff. Cf. also my review of König, *Das Buch Hiob*, 1929, in *Deutsche Ltz.*, 1930, col. 535ff.

Besides the normal metres, mashal and qinah, G. Fohrer (*Die Hauptprobleme des Buches Ezechiel*, pp. 63ff.) has tried to demonstrate the existence of what he calls 'short verses' (*Kurzverse*), i.e. 'strophes' of an irregular number (mostly 5 and 7) short lines of irregular metrical structure (mostly with 2–4 beats + primary accents) without any parallelism between any of the cola. A metrical structure such as this would be against all known rules of Hebrew poetry; it means an effacement of the difference between poetry and prose, and is won—as Fohrer's treatment of Ezekiel demonstrates—by a perfectly arbitrary literary criticism of the texts. Against Fohrer see the present author in *ZATW* 65, 1953–54, pp. 167ff.; 68, 1956, pp. 97ff.

5. The most redoubtable champion of regular *strophes* (stanzas) in Hebrew poetry was B. Duhm, both in his *Die Psalmen*, and in his commentaries on the prophets. The usual opinion—against strophic regularity—is expressed among others by Barnes (*The Psalms*, pp. livf.), Th. H. Robinson (in Oesterley and Robinson, *Introduction to the O. T.*, pp. 147f.), and Oesterley (*A Fresh Approach*, pp. 131f.). Barnes sums up his sober view in this way: 'The Psalmist is feeling after strophical form, but he does not bind himself to it. . . . For the psalmist's strophes are occasional luxuries, not rigid necessities' (op. cit., p. lv). The error of these investigators seems to me to be that they approach the problem from a wrong quarter, starting with the question of more complicated strophic forms instead of starting from the simplest main rules of Hebrew poetry, namely the law of thought rhyme; as seen from the text this law almost automatically tends towards what I have called the 'simple basic strophe', consisting of two parallel bicola.

Normally the strophical and the logical division of a poem coincide. But the poetry of almost every literature and language shows that this coincidence very often is only a relative one; it may often happen that a new thought element is touched on at the end of one stanza and gets its more detailed exposition in the next stanza.

We cannot but attribute to the Hebrew poets a similar liberty with regard to the correspondence between logical and strophic intervals. We have no right therefore to decree, as for instance Th. H. Robinson does, that 'neither between two lines nor between two strophes, can there be any enjambement' (in Oesterley and Robinson, op. cit., p. 147). Occasional enjambement between two lines is a fact; see Pss. 78.2–11; 32.5b; 35.27b, etc.; then something similar may also occur between two strophes. If we admit this and are content to maintain that the strophe makes a *relatively* logical unity within the totality (see Chap. XIX, n. 25), it is easy to point out the fundamental strophe of two bicola (stichs) practically throughout the whole Psalter. A sober summary of the obvious material with regard to strophes in Hebrew poetry is given by Montgomery in *JBL* 64, 1945, pp. 379ff. Cf. also Condamin, *Les Poèmes de la Bible*.

6. As for the question of regular or irregular metres within the same poem, the adherents of the non-regular—in my opinion, unmetrical—metre seem to form the majority. Their opinion seems often to be based on a sort of miraculous belief that MT represents the original wording of the poems, as, for instance, König. But non-regular

metres are upheld by text-critically more radical scholars like H. Schmidt, Staerk (in *BATW* 13), Gunkel, and to a great extent also Bentzen; the same must be said of Barnes (*The Psalms* I, pp. 1ff.), who imagines the psalmist to be a kind of romantic Ossian, 'as he sat under the shadow of a great rock, harp in hand, extemporizing his words to fit his music' (ibid., p. liv)—an idea just as far from reality as 'Ossian' himself was. In their extenuation may be mentioned the fact that these scholars mostly also adhere to the system of Sievers.

More detailed arguments for the present author's opinion on Hebrew metrics are given in 'Zur hebräischen Metrik I' in the *Festschrift für Bertholet*, pp. 379ff. (on the qinah verse); 'Zur hebräischen Metrik II', in *StTH* VII, pp. 54ff.; 'Metrischer Aufbau und Textkritik, an Ps. 8 illustriert', in the *Johs. Pedersen-Festschrift*, pp. 250; 'Der metrische Aufbau von Hes. 62.1–2 und die neuen sogen. "Kurzverse",' *ZATW* 65, 1953–54, pp. 167ff.; 'Marginalien zur hebräischen Metrik', ibid. 68, 1956, pp. 97ff.; 'Die Metrik bei Jesus Sirach', *StTh* IX, pp. 137ff.; and *Real and Apparent Tricola in Hebrew Psalm Poetry*. His view has found at least partial adherents in Horst, *ThR*, N.F. 21, pp. 97ff., and Segert in *Archiv Orientalní* XXI, 1953, pp. 481ff., 511ff.

Joseph Scaliger (*Thesaurus Temporum*, Lugd. Batav., 1606) had already realized that the main Hebrew metre is 4 × 4 stichoi, each of the parallel hemistichs consisting of two iambic dipodies (2 + 2 ‖ 2 + 2), the consequent rythm being thus normally 'alternating'. But since he was bound by vocalization and interpunction of the Massoretic text, Scaliger had to admit many exceptions to the rule. Scaliger's ideas were taken up and developed by the Copenhagen professor Niels Pedersen ('Nicolaus Petraeus Aurilesius') in his Hebrew Grammar, Copenhagen, 1633 (see A. Bentzen, 'Niels Pedersens hebraiske Metrik', [D]TT, 1933, pp. 81ff.

NOTE XXXIX (II . 177, n. 5).

Driver (*The Psalmists*, pp. 109ff.) claims that the influence of Babylonian psalmography on that of Israel has been 'negligible'. But the interesting parallel material, to which he draws attention, as clearly as possible proves the opposite. Driver simplifies the matter too much by planning his investigation as a discussion of Gressmann's opinion that the influence from Babylonia-Assyria was direct during the later monarchy. In each case of common phraseology and ideas, Driver pleads that the similarities *may* have come into existence independently in both places, or that they are of such a general nature that there is no need for a special explanation. But we may not limit the investigation in this way to individual cases, and overlook the cumulation of striking conformities. Driver's own material shows that there is here a common oriental religio-poetical style, the background of which is in all essentials a common view of the world and of reality. It is not a question of a relationship of races and peoples and languages, as Driver argues, but of a common culture; nor of an eventual 'proto-Semitic' literature and world of ideas, on which both Babylonians and Hebrews may have been dependent, but of a pre-Semitic and, as far as we can see, in its main features Sumerian, literary culture, which in the course of time became common oriental, and was in time adopted also by Israel. Obviously, then, the younger nation must have come into the inheritance of the older ones. The problem is not whether in these cases Israelite poets have studied and imitated individual Babylonian psalms—that has probably never occurred—but whether Israelite psalmography has any historical connexion with the common oriental one, which is many centuries earlier. In other words it is not a question of 'direct' influence on individual authors, but of a fellowship in culture, of a sharing in a literary style. These factors faced Israel as soon as they began the task of forming their cult in the new cultural conditions in Canaan, conditions from which Israel has learnt something at all points, partly positively through adoption, partly negatively by rejection. Driver defeats his own argument by allowing for an 'indirect' influence from Babylonian poetry through the Canaanites. That is just it. But this influence is certainly of greater extent than Driver is willing to admit. If it is a fact that Israel shares the common oriental literary culture, the question of 'direct' or 'indirect' influence loses a great deal of interest. On the other hand, it is indisputable that in this common literary inheritance the essentials have been derived from Babylonia. It is therefore perfectly correct to speak of Babylonian 'influence', even if it has mostly taken place via the Canaanites, and even if no Israelite psalmist ever heard or read a Babylonian psalm. Such indirect influence via Canaan is also admitted by Castellino, *Le lamentazioni individuali e gli inni en Bab. e in Israel.* Therefore Driver's conclusion misses the mark, when he says: 'We cannot therefore believe that the Babylonian hymns and psalms exercised any real influence on the work of the Hebrew psalmists' (op. cit., p. 172).

NOTE XL (p. 91, n. 36; II.190, n. 100).

That the two parts of Ps. 19 do not originally belong together is the general opinion to-day. In favour of this opinion are the different themes, the different metres, and the different style—19A is a description with richly coloured, mythologically formative pictures; 19B lists in aphoristic enumeration all the commendatory terms that may be used about the Law—to say nothing of the different view of religion: in 19A the supreme god El and the divine 'hero' the Sun, in 19B Yahweh, the revealer of the saving 'law'. But it is not, as some people have thought, a question of two originally independent poems, which accidentally became united; 19B has been composed as a sequel to 19A and with a definite motive: Yahweh is at once the God of creation and of the sun and of the law. That 'sun' and 'justice' belong together is an old oriental idea, as has been proved by Schroeder (*ZATW* 34, 1914, pp. 69f.) and Dürr (*Sellin-Festschrift*, pp. 38ff.). Consequently Dürr thinks that the same author must have composed the whole of Ps. 19; but the very fact that Ps. 19 is a fragment makes this impossible: at least one half verse is lacking before v. 5b as well as after v. 7; the extended description of the sun seems to presuppose that other great works of God in the firmament should also have been mentioned; against Dürr's theory is also the fact that 'justice' and 'righteousness', which in the orient and in the Old Testament are elsewhere identified with the sun-god and the sun, are not as a matter of course identical with Yahweh's 'law'; 19B does not talk of 'righteousness', but of 'the law'. Nor has the remark of Aalen about Ps. 19 (*Licht und Finsternis*, p. 28) 'solved the problem about the composition of the psalm'. To Aalen the leit-motiv of the psalm is the idea that sun, moon and stars proclaim the creative glory of God through their obedience to God's *huqqîm*, i.e. the system of laws to which they have been subjected, and he refers to Pss. 148.3ff.; 104.19. But the first part of the psalm nowhere mentions Yahweh's *huqqîm*, 'the laws of nature'; nor does it 'deal with day and night'; it deals with the celestial bodies and especially with the sun, because all in their own way proclaim the glory of God both by day and by night; the alternation of days and nights is only one element of vv. 2-7. So the author must be supposed to have incorporated part of an earlier psalm—possibly a fragment he has come across among the temple records—and used it as an introduction to his own hymn to the law.

Act Or = Acta Orientalia, Leiden.

AfO = Archiv für Orientforschung, Berlin.

AKML = Abhandlungen für die Kunde des Morgenlandes, herausgeg. von der *DMG*, Leipzig.

AnalOr = Analecta Orientalia, Commentationes scientificae de rebus Orientis antiqui, Roma.

ANET = Ancient Near Eastern Texts Relating to the Old Testament, ed. by James E. Pritchard, Princeton 1950, ²1955.

ANVAO = Avhandlinger utgitt av Det Norske Videnskaps-Akademi i Oslo.

AO = Der alte Orient, herausgeg. v. d. Vorderasiatisch-ägyptischen Gesellschaft, Leipzig.

AOB², *AOT²*, *AOTB*, see Bibliography under Gressmann.

APAT = see Bibliography under Kautzsch.

APOT, see Bibliography under Charles.

ARW = Archiv für Religionswissenschaft, Berlin—Leipzig.

ASGW = Abhandlungen der Sächssischen Gesellsch. d. Wissenschaften, Berlin.

ANVAO = Avhandlinger utgitt av Det Norske Videnskaps-Akademi i Oslo. II. Hist. Filos. Klasse.

BA = Beiträge zur Assyrologie, Leipzig.

Basileia, see Bibliography under von Gall.

BASOR = Bulletin of the American Schools of Oriental Research, New Haven, Conn.

Bertholetfestschrift = Festschrift Alfred Bertholet zum 80. Geburtstag, herausgeg. von W. Baumgartner, O. Eissfeldt, K. Elliger, L. Rost, Tübingen 1950.

BH² = Biblia Hebraica³ edited by R. Kittel, Stuttgart, 1937.

BHEAT = Bulletin d'Histoire et Exegèse de l'Ancien Testament, Louvain.

BJRL = Bulletin of the John Rylands Library, Manchester.

BRL = Biblisches Reallexikon, see Galling.

BSGW = Berichte über die Verhandl. d. Sächssischen Gesellsch. d. Wissensch., Berlin.

Buddefestschrift = *BZATW* 34, 1920.

BWANT = Beiträge zur Wissenschaft vom Alten und Neuen Testament, Stuttgart.

BZATW = Beihefte zum *ZATW*, Giessen.

DMG = Deutsche Morgenländische Gesellschaft.

[D]TT = Theologisk Tidsskrift, København.

EB = Encyclopaedia Britannica.

Eissfeldtfestschrift = Festschrift Otto Eissfeldt zum 60. Geburtstage, Halle 1948.

Eucharisterion = Ευχαριστηριον. Studien zur Religion u. Literatur d. Alt. u. Neu. Testaments, H. Gunkel zum 60. Geburtstage . . . dargebr. *FRLANT* 36, 1923.

FRLANT = Forschungen zur Religion und Literatur d. Alten u. Neuen Testaments, Göttingen.

Fr.Rel.-Urk. = Främmande Religionsurkunder i urval och översättning I–III, utg. af N. Söderblom, Stockholm 1908.

GTMMM = Det Gamle Testament, oversatt av S. Michelet, Sigmund Mowinckel og N. Messel, I–III, Oslo 1929ff.

HBAT = Handbuch zum Alten Testament, herausgeg. v. Otto Eissfeldt, Tübingen.

HKAT = Handkommentar z. Alten Testament, herausgeg. v. W. Nowack, Göttingen.

HSAT = see Bibliography under Kautzsch.

HUCA = Hebrew Union College Annual, Cincinnati, Ohio.

ICC = International Critical Commentary, Edinburgh.

JAOS = Journal of the American Oriental Society, New Haven.

JBL = Journal of Biblical Literature, Philadelphia, Pa.

JE = Jewish Encyclopaedia.

JPOS = Journal of the Palestine Oriental Society, Jerusalem.

JQR = The Jewish Quarterly Review, London.

JRAS = Journal of the Royal Asiatic Society, London.

JSOR = Journal of the Society for Oriental Research.

JThS = Journal of Theological Studies, London.

KAT³ = E. Schrader, Die Keilinschriften und das Alte Testament, 3. Aufl. neu bearb. von H. Zimmern u. H. Winckler, Berlin 1903.

KATSl = Kommentar zum Alten Testament, herausgeb. v. E. Sellin, Erlangen—Leipzig.

KB = Keilinschriftliche Bibliothek, Berlin.

KHCAT = Kurzer Handcommentar zum Alten Testament, herausgeg. v. K. Marti, Freiburg—Tübingen—Leipzig.

MAOG = Mitteilungen der altorientalischen Gesellschaft, Leipzig.

Martifestschrift = B*Z*ATW 41, 1925.

MGWJ = Monatschrift für Geschichte u. Wissenschaft d. Judentums, Frankfurt a. M.

MO = Le Monde Oriental, Uppsala.

NGWG = Nachrichten der Gesellschaft der Wissenschaften zu Göttingen.

NTT = Norsk Teologisk Tidsskrift, Kristiania—Oslo.

OTS = Oudtestamentische Studiën, uitgegev. d. P. A. H. de Boer, Leiden.

Ps.St. I–VI = Mowinckel, Psalmenstudien I–VI, see Bibliography.

REKlA = Real-Encyclopädie der klassischen Altertumswisenschaft, herausgeg. von Pauly-Wissowa-Kroll, Stuttgart.

RGG = Religion in Geschichte und Gegenwart I–V, Tübingen 1909–13; *RGG²* = 2. Aufl. 1927–32.

RHPhR = Revue de l'Histoire et des Philosophies Religieuses, Strasbourg.

RHR = Revue de l'Histoire des Religions, Paris.

RoB = Religion och Bibel. Nathan Söderblom-sällskapets Årsbok, Stockholm.

Robinson Festschrift = Studies in Old Testament Prophecy, Presented to Professor Theodore H. Robinson by the Society for Old Testament Study, ed H. H. Rowley, Edinburgh 1950.

RThPh = Revue de Theologie et de Philosophie, Lausanne.

SATA = Die Schriften des Alten Testaments in Auswahl, neu übersetzt und für die Gegenwart erklärt, von H. Gressmann, H. Gunkel, M. Haller, H. Schmidt, W. Staerk und P. Volz, I–III, Göttingen. 2. Aufl. 1921ff.

SbBAW = Sitzungsberichte der Berliner Akademie der Wissenschaften.

SBOT = The Sacred Books of the Old Testament, ed. P. Haupt, Leipzig—Baltimore—London ('The Polychrome Bible').

SbPAW = Sitzungsberichte der Preussischen Academie der Wissenschaften, phil.-hist.-Kl., Berlin.

Sellinfestschrift = *BWAT* 13, 1913.

SEÅ = Svensk Exegetisk Årsbok, Uppsala.

SNVAO = Skrifter utgitt av Det Norske Videnskaps-Akademi i Oslo, II. Hist.-Filos. Kl.

StTh = Studia theologica cura ordinum theologorum Scandinavorum edita.

ThLtz = Theologische Literaturzeitung.

ThR = Theologische Rundschau, Tübingen.

ThZ = Theologische Zeitschrift, Basel.

TTK = Tidsskrift for Teologi og Kirke, Oslo.

TU = Text en Uitleg, Groningen–Batavia.

UUÅ = Uppsala Universitets Årsbok.

VAB = Vorderasiatische Bibliothek, Leipzig.

VT = Vetus Testamentum, Leiden.

Wellhausenfestschrift = *BZATW* 27, 1914.

ZATW = Zeitschrift für die Alttestamentliche Wissenschaft, Giessen.

ZDMG = Zeitschrift der Deutschen Morgenländischen Gesellschaft, Leipzig.

ZDPV = Zeitschrift des Deutschen Palästina-Vereins, Leipzig.

ZTK = Zeitschrift für Theologie und Kirche.

BIBLIOGRAPHY

(See also *List of Abbreviations*)

ALBRIGHT, W. F., 'The Earliest Forms of Hebrew Verse', *JPOS*, 2, 1922, pp. 69ff.

'Zabûl Yam and Thâpit Nahar in the Combat between Ba'al and the Sea', *JPOS*, 16, 1936, pp. 17ff.

'The Song of Deborah in the Light of Archaeology', *BASOR*, 62, Apr. 1936, pp. 26ff.

Review of Mowinckel, 'The two Sources of Predeuteronomic Primeval History (JE) in Gen. 1–11', *JBL*, 57, 1938, pp. 230ff.

'The Babylonian Matter in the Predeuteronomic Primeval History (JE) in Gen. 1–11', *JBL*, 58, 1939, pp. 91ff.

'A Teacher to a Man of Shechem about 1400 B.C.', *BASOR*, 86, Apr. 1942, pp. 28ff.

'A Votive Stele Erected by Ben-Hadad I of Damascus to the God Melcarth', *BASOR*, 87, Oct. 1942, pp. 23ff.

'A Tablet of the Amarna Age from Gezer', *BASOR*, 92, Feb. 1943, pp. 28ff.

Archaeology and the Religion of Israel. Baltimore, 1943.

'The Gezer Calendar', *BASOR*, 92, Dec. 1943, pp. 16ff.

'The Old Testament and the Canaanite Language and Literature', *Catholic Biblical Quarterly*, Jan. 1945.

'Israel in the Framework of the Ancient Near East', in *The Jewish People, Past and Present*, Vol. I, New York, 1946, pp. 27ff.

'The Psalm of Habakkuk', Robinson Festschrift, pp. 1ff.

ALT, A., *Die Ursprünge des israelitischen Rechts*, Leipzig, 1934.

'Zu den Schlussformeln der punischen Weihinschriften', *ZATW*, 59, 1944, pp. 156ff.

Kleine Schriften zur Geschichte des Volkes Israel I–II, Munich, 1953.

AUBERT, L., 'Les Psaumes dans le culte d'Israël'. Extrait de la *RThPh*, N.S. XV, 1927.

BAETHGEN, FR., *Die Psalmen* (*HKAT* II, 2), 3. Aufl. 1904.

BALLA, E., *Das Ich der Psalmen* (*FRLANT* 16), 1912.

'Das Problem des Leides in der israelitisch-jüdischen Religion', *Eucharisterion*, I, pp. 214ff.

BALSCHEIT, BR., *Der Gottesbund. Einführung in das Alte Testament*, Zürich, 1943.

BARNES, W. E., *The Psalms* I–II (Westminster Commentaries), London, 1931.

BARTH, CHRISTOPHER, *Die Errettung vom Tode in den individuellen Klage und Dankliedern des Alten Testaments*, Basel, 1947.

BASTIAN, A., *Die Völker des östlichen Asiens*, I–III, Leipzig–Jena, 1866–67.

BAUDISSIN, W. VON, *Adonis und Esmun*, Leipzig, 1911.

Kyrios als Gottesname, I–III, Giessen, 1929.

BAUER, H., 'Ein aramäischer Staatsvertrag aus dem. 8. Jahrhundert v. Chr. Die Inschrift der Stele von Sudschin', *AfO*, 7, 1932, pp. 1ff.

'Die Gottheiten von Ras Schamra', *ZATW*, 51, 1933, pp. 81ff; 53, 1935, pp. 54ff.

BAUMANN, E., '*Šub šebut*. Eine exegetische Untersuchung', *ZATW*, 47, 1929, pp. 17ff.
'Strukturuntersuchungen zu den Psalmen I', *ZATW*, 61, 1945–48, pp. 114ff.
'Alttestamentliche Religion', *ARW*, 1917–27.
'Struckturuntersuchungen im Psalter II', *ZATW*, 62, 1950, pp. 115ff.
BAUMGARTNER, W., *Die Klagegedichte des Jeremia* (*BZATW*, 32), 1917.
'Die literarischen Gattungen in der Weisheit des Jesus Sirach', *ZATW*, 34, 1914, pp. 169ff.
'Joel 1 und 2', in *Buddefestschrift*, pp. 10ff.
Israelitische und altorientalische Weisheit, Tübingen, 1933.
'Ras Schamra und das Alte Testament', *ThR*, N.F., 12, 1940, pp. 163ff.; 13, 1941, pp. 1ff.; 85ff.; 157ff.
'Das Nachleben der Adonisgärten auf Sardinien und im übrigen Mittelmeergebiet', *Archiv für Volkskunde*, 43, 1946, pp. 122ff. = *Zum A.T. u.s. Umwelt*, 1959, pp. 247ff.
'Ugaritische Probleme und ihre Tragweite für das Alte Testament', *ThZ*, N.F., 3, 1947, pp. 81ff.
BEGRICH, J., 'Die Vertrauensäusserungen im israelitischen Klagelied des Einzelnen und in seinem babylonischen Gegenstück', *ZATW*, 46, 1928, pp. 221ff.
'Zur hebräischen Metrik', *ThR*, N.F., 4, 1932.
Die priesterliche Tora, *BZATW*, 66, 1936, pp. 63ff.
'Das priesterliche Heilsorakel', *ZATW*, 52, 1934, pp. 81ff.
Review of Ludin Jansen, *Die Spätjüdische Psalmendichtung* in *SEÅ*, III, pp. 126ff.
See Gunkel.
BENTZEN, AAGE, *Jahves Gæst*, Copenhagen, 1926.
'I Anledning af Gunkels Kommentar og Indledning til Salmerne', [*D*]*TT*, 1928, pp. 99ff, 177ff.
Studier over det zadokidiske præsteskabs historie, Copenhagen, 1931.
Indledning til de gammeltestamentlige salmer, Copenhagen, 1932.
Fortolkning til de gammeltestamentlige salmer, Copenhagen, 1939.
Jesaja fortolket, I–II, Copenhagen, 1943–44.
Det sakrale kongedømme, Copenhagen, 1945.
'Der Tod des Beters in den Psalmen', *Eissfeldtfestschrift*, pp. 57ff.
Messias—Moses redivivus — Menschensohn, Zürich, 1948. [E. T. *King and Messiah*, London, 1955.]
'The Cultic Use of the Story of the Ark in Samuel', *JBL*, 67, 1948, pp. 37ff.
BENZINGER, I., *Hebräische Archaeologie*, Tübingen, ²1907.
BERTHOLET, A., *Das Buch der Psalmen*, HSAT, II⁴.
BEWER, J., 'The Textcritical Value of the Hebrew MS. Ken. 96 of Isaiah 49, 3', *Jewish Studies. Kohut Memorial Volume*, 1935, pp. 86ff.
BICKEL, G., *Carmina Veteris Testamenti metrice*, Oeniponte, 1882.
Dichtungen der Hebräer, zum ersten Male nach den Versmassen des Urtextes übersetzt, I–III, Innsbruck, 1882–83.
BILLERBECK, P., *Kommentar zum Neuen Testament aus dem Talmud und Midrasch*, I–IV, Munich, 1922–28.

BIRKELAND, H., *Grunnriss av hebraisk syntaks*, Oslo, 1932.
' '*Ani und 'anaw in den Psalmen*' (*SNVAO*, 1932, II, 4), 1933.
'Die Einheitlichkeit von Ps. 27', *ZATW*, 51, 1933, pp. 216ff.
Die Feinde des Individuums in der israelitischen Psalmenliteratur, Oslo, 1933.
Akzent und Vokalismus im Althebräischen (*SNVAO*, 1940, II, 3), 1940.
'Opstandelsestroen i Det Gamle Testament', *SEÅ*, XIII, 1948, pp. 22ff.
Språk og religion hos jøder og arabere, Oslo, 1949.
'The Belief in Resurrection of the Dead in the O.T.', *StTh*, III, 1949, pp. 60ff.
The Evildoers in the Book of Psalms (*ANVAO*, II, 1955), 1955.
BLACKMAN, A. M., 'Myth and Ritual in Ancient Egypt', in *Myth and Ritual*, pp. 15ff.
'The Psalms in the Light of Egyptian Research', in *The Psalmists*, ed. Simpson, pp. 177ff.
BLAKENEY, E. H., 'Psalm CXXI', *Expos. Times*, 59, 1947–48, p. 111.
BLESSING DAHLE, P., 'Eine Siegeshymne der Ama-zulu', *Festschrift Meinhof*, Hamburg, 1927, pp. 174ff.
BÖHL, FR., *Nieuwejaarsfeest en konigsdag in Babylon en in Israel*, Groningen, 1927.
'Hymnisches und Rhythmisches in den Amarnabriefen aus Kanaan', *Theol. Ltr.blatt*, 1914, No. 15, cols. 137ff.
De Psalmen, I–II (*Text en Uitleg*), Groningen—Batavia, 1946–47.
BÖLLENRÜCHER, J., *Gebete und Hymnen an Nergal* (*Leipz. Sem. Stud.*, I, 6), Leipzig, 1904.
DE BOER, P. A. H., 'De Vorbede in het Oude Testament', *OTS*, III, 1943.
'Etude sur le sens de la racine QWH', *OTS*, X, 1954, pp. 225ff.
BOMAN, TH., *Das hebräischen Denken im Vergleich mit dem Griechischen*, Göttingen, 1952.
BOUT, H., *Het Zondebesef in het Boek der Psalmen*, Utrecht, 1952.
BRÄUN"ICH, E., 'Beiträge zur Gesellschaftsordnung der arabischen Beduin-Stämme', *Islamica*, 1933, 1–2.
BRIGGS, C. A., *The Book of Psalms*, I–II (*ICC*), 1906.
BRØNNO, E., *Studien über hebräische Morphologie und Vokalismus* (*AKML*, 48), 1943.
BRUN, L., *Jesu evangelium*, Oslo, ²1926.
BUBER, M., *Königtum Gottes*, Berlin, 1932.
BUDDE, K., 'Das hebräische Klagelied', *ZATW*, 2, 1882, pp. 1ff.; cf. ib. 3, 11, 12; *ZDPV*, 6, 1883.
BÜCHLER, A., 'Zur Geschichte der Tempelmusik und der Tempelpsalmen', *ZATW*, 19, 1899, pp. 96ff.; 20, 1900, pp. 17ff.
BÜCKERS, G. H., 'Zur Verwertung der Sinaitraditionen in den Psalmen', *Biblica*, 32, 1951, pp. 401ff.
BUHL, FR., *Psalmerne oversatte og fortolkede*, Copenhagen, 1900; ²1918.
BURROWS, MILLAR, *What Mean these Stones?* New Haven, Conn., 1941.
BUTTENWIESER, M., *The Psalms, Chronologically Treated with a New Translation*, Chicago, 1938.
BYINGTON, S. T., 'Mathematical Approach to Hebrew Metres', *JBL*, 66, 1947, pp. 63ff.
CASSUTO, U., 'Il capitule 3 di Abaquq e i testi di Ras Šamra', in *Annuario di Studi Ebraici*, 1935–37, Roma, pp. 9ff.

II, 18

CAUSSE, A., *Les 'pauvres' d'Israël* (*Prophètes, psalmistes, Messianistes*), Strasbourg—Paris, 1922.
Les plus vieux chants de la Bible, Paris, 1926.
'L'ancienne poésie cultuelle d'Israël et les origines du Psautier', *RHPhR*, 6, 1926, pp. 1ff.
CHARLES, R. H., ed., *The Apocrypha and Pseudepigrapha of the Old Testament*, I–II, Oxford, 1913.
CHEYNE, T. K., *The Book of Psalms*, London, 1888; in revised form, 2 vols., 1904.
COOK, S. A., *The Religion of Ancient Palestine in the Light of Archaeology*, London, 1930 (Schweich Lectures, 1925).
The 'Evolution' of Biblical Religion. Reprint from *The Modern Churchman*, Nov. 1934, Oxford, 1934.
COLEMAN, J. E., 'The Prophet and Sacrifice', *Theological Studies*, V, 1947, pp. 411ff.
COPPENS, J., *Les Parallèles du Psautier avec les Textes de Ras-Shamra-Ougarit* (*BHEAT*, 18), 1946.
'La portée messianique du Psaume CX', Extrait des *Ephemerides Theologicae Lovanienses*, XXXII.
CORNILL, C. H., *Einleitung in das Alte Testament*, 6. Aufl. Tübingen, 1913.
'Psalm 130', *Buddefestschrift*, pp. 38ff.
COSGRAVE, F. H., 'Recent Studies on the Psalms', *Canadian Soc. of Bibl. St. Bull.*, No. 5, Toronto, July 1939, pp. 3ff.
CRIADO, R., *El valor dinamico del nombre divino en el Antiquo Testamento*, Granada, 1950.
CROSS, F. M. and FREEDMAN, D. N., 'A Royal Song of Thanksgiving: 2 Sam. 22 = Ps. 18', *JBL* 72, 1953, pp. 15ff.
CUMMING, CH. G., *The Assyrian and the Hebrew Hymns of Praise* (*Columbia Univers. Orient. Studies* 12), New York, 1934.
DAICHES, S., *Studies in the Psalms*, Oxford, 1930.
DANELL, G. A., *Psalm 139* (*UUÅ*, 1951, 1), Uppsala—Leipzig, 1951.
DAVISON, W. T. and DAVIES, T. W., *The Book of Psalms*, I–II (The Century Bible), Edinburgh.
DELITZSCH, F., *Der Prophet Habakkuk*, 1843.
Biblischer Commentar über die Psalmen, I–II, Leipzig, 1859–60, 4. Aufl. 1883.
Der Prophet Habakuk, Leipzig, 1893.
DEURSEN, A. v., *De Achtergrond der Psalmen*, 1947.
DIETRICH, E. L., *Šub šebut. Die endzeitliche Wiederherstellung bei den Propheten* (*BZATW*, 40), 1925.
DITTENBERGER, *Sylloge inscriptionum Graecorum*, 3. ed. III, Lipsiae.
DOSSIN, G., 'Les archives epistolaires du palais de Mari', *Syria*, 19, 1938, pp. 105ff.
DRIVER, G. R., 'The Psalms in the Light of Babylonian Research', in *The Psalmists*, ed. Simpson, pp. 109ff.
'Witchcraft in the Old Testament', *JRAS*, 1943, pp. 6ff.; see also 'Hebrew Notes', *ib.*, 1944, pp. 165ff.
DRIVER, S. R., *The Book of Genesis* (Westminster Commentaries), London, 1904.
DUHM, B., *Die Psalmen* (*KHCAT*, 14), 1899; 2. Aufl., 1922.
Das Buch Hiob (*KHCAT*, 16), 1897.

DUHM, H., *Die bösen Geister im Alten Testament*, Tübingen, 1904.

DÜRR, L., *Ursprung und Ausbau der israelitisch-jüdischen Heilandserwartung*, Berlin, 1925.
Psalm 110 *im Lichte der neueren altorientalischen Forschungen*, Münster, 1929.
'Reichsgründungsfeiern im Alten Orient', *Theologie u. Glaube*, 20, pp. 305ff.
'Zur Frage nach der Einheit von Ps. 19', *Sellinfestschrift*, pp. 37ff.

DUSSAUD, R., *Les origines cananéennes du sacrifice Israelite*, Paris, 1921.

EBELING, E., 'Babylonisch-assyrische Texte', in *AOB*[2].
'Bruchstücke eines politischen Propagandagedichtes aus einer assyrischen Kanzlei', *MAOG*, 12, 2, 1938.

EDSMAN, C.-M., 'Gammal och ny typologisk tolkning av G. T.', *SEÅ*, 12, 1947, pp. 85ff.

EERDMANS, B. D., *The Hebrew Book of Psalms (OTS*, 4), 1947.
'Essays on Masoretic Psalms', *OTS*, 1, 1942, pp. 1–16, 105–296.

EHRENZWEIG, A., 'Biblische und klassische Urgeschichte', *ZATW*, 38, 1919–20, pp. 65ff.

EHRLICH, E. H., *Der Traum im Alten Testament (BZATW*, 73), Berlin, 1953.

EICHRODT, W., *Theologie des Alten Testaments*, I[2]–II, Leipzig, 1935–39.

EISSFELDT, O., 'Jahwe als König', *ZATW*, 46, 1928, pp. 81ff.
Ba'al Zaphon, Zeus Kasios und der Durchzug der Israeliten durchs Meer, Halle, 1932.
' "Mein Gott" im Alten Testament', *ZATW*, 61, 1945–48, pp. 1ff.; see also *The Evangelical Quarterly*, XIX, 1 Jan. 1947, pp. 7ff.
Einleitung in das Alte Testament, Tübingen, 1934.
'Psalm 80', *Geschichte und Altes Testament* (Alt Festschrift, *BHTh*, 16), 1955, pp. 65ff.

ELBOGEN, I., *Der jüdische Gottesdienst in seiner geschichtlichen Entwickelung*, Frankfurt, [3]1931.

ELLIGER, K., 'Das Christuszeugnis des Alten Testaments', *Zeitschr. f. System. Theologie*, 19, 1937, pp. 377ff.
Die Bedeutung der Geschichte Israels für die Kirche Jesu Christi. Reprinted from *Für Arbeit und Besinnung*, 2, 1948, Stuttgart.

ENGNELL, I., *Studies in Divine Kingship in the Ancient Near East*, Uppsala, 1943.
'The Text K II from Ras Shamra', *Horae Soederblomianae*, I. Mèlanges Johs. Pedersen, I. Stockholm, 1944, pp. 1ff.
Gamla Testamentet I. En traditionshistorisk inledning, Stockholm, 1945.
'Till frågan om Ebed Jahve-sångerna och den lidande Messias hos "Deutero-jesaja" ', *SEÅ*, 10, pp. 31ff.

ERMAN, A., *Die aegyptische Religion*, 2. Aufl. Berlin, 1909.
Die Literatur der Aegypter, Leipzig, 1923. [E.T. *The Literature of the Ancient Egyptians*, tr. A. M. Blackman.]
'Eine aegyptische Quelle der Sprüche Salomos', *SbPAW*, 15, 1924, pp. 86ff.

ERMAN, A. and RANKE, H., *Aegypten und aegyptisches Leben im Altertum*, Tübingen 1923.

EWALD, H., *Die Dichter des Alten Bundes*, I, 2, Göttingen, 1839; 3. Ausg., 1866.

FALKENSTEIN, A. and von SODEN, W., *Sumerische und Akkadische Hymnen und Gebete*, Zurich—Stuttgart, 1953.

FEUCHTWANG, D., 'Das Wasseropfer und die damit verbundenen Zeremonien', *MGWJ*, 54, 1910, pp. 541ff.; 55, 1911, pp. 55ff.

FICHTNER, J., *Die Altorientalische Weisheit in ihrer israelitisch-jüdischen Ausprägung (BZATW*, 62), 1933.

FISH, T., *Some Aspects of Kingship in the Sumerian City and Kingdom of Ur* (reprinted from *BJRL*, 34), Manchester, 1951.

FOHRER, G., *Die Hauptprobleme des Buches Ezechiel* (*BZATW*, 72), 1952.

'Ueber den Kurzvers', *ZATW*, 66, 1954, pp. 119ff.

FOLLET, R. and Nober, P., 'Zur orientalischen Musik', *Biblica*, 35, 1954, pp. 230ff.

FRANKEN, H. J., *The Mystical Communion with JHWH in the Book of Psalms*, Leiden, 1954.

FRANKENBERG, W., *Die Datierung der Psalmen Salomos* (*BZATW*, 1), 1896.

FRANKFORT, H., *Kingship and the Gods. A Study of Ancient Near Eastern Religion as the Integration of Society and Nature*, Chicago, 1948.

FRAZER, J., *The Golden Bough: A Study in Magic and Religion*, I–XII, London, 1911–15.

GÁBOR, I., *Der hebräische Urrhythmus* (*BZATW*, 52), 1929.

GADD, C. J., 'Babylonian Myth and Ritual', *Myth and Ritual*, ed. Hooke, pp. 40ff.

Ideas of Divine Rule in the Ancient East (Schweich Lectures, 1945), London 1948.

GALL, A. VON, 'Ueber die Herkunft der Bezeichnung Jahwes als König, *Well-hausenfestschrift*, pp. 147ff.

Βασιλεια του Θεου. *Eine religionsgeschichtliche Studie zur vorkirchlichen Eschato-logie*, Heidelberg, 1926.

GALLING, K., *Die Erwählungstraditionen Israels* (*BZATW*, 48), 1928.

Biblisches Reallexikon (*HBAT*, 1), 1937.

'Der Beichtspiegel. Eine gattungsgeschichtliche Studie', *ZATW*, 47, 1929, pp. 125ff.

GARSTANG, J., *The Heritage of Solomon*, London, 1934.

GASTER, TH. H., 'Psalm 29', *JQR*, 37, 1946–47, pp. 55–56.

GELIN, A., *Les pauvres de Yahvé*, Paris, 1953.

GEMSER, B., *Sprüche Salomos* (*HBAT*, 16), 1937.

De Psalmen III (Text en Uitleg), Groningen—Batavia, 1949.

GENNEP, A. VAN, *Les rites de passage*, Paris, 1909.

GESENIUS-BUHL, *Hebräisches und aramäisches Handwörterbuch über das Alte Testament*, 16. Aufl. (= Gesenius-Buhl[16]), Leipzig, 1915.

GIERLICH, A. M., *Der Lichtgedanke in den Psalmen. (Freib. Theol. St.56)*, Freibg. im Breisgau, 1940.

GINSBERG, H. L., *The Legend of King Keret, a Canaanite Epic of the Bronze Age* (*BASOR* Supplementary Studies, 2–3), 1946.

'A Phoenician Hymn of the Psalter', *Atti del XIX. Congresso Internat. d. Orientalisti*, 1935, pp. 472ff.

'Psalms and Inscriptions of Petition and Acknowledgement', *Louis Ginzberg Jubilee Volume*, American Academy for Jewish Research, New York, 1945, pp. 159ff.

'The Hebrew University Scrolls from the Sectarian Cache', *BASOR*, 112, Dec. 1948, pp. 19ff.

GORDON, C., *The Living Past*, New York, 1941.

Ugaritic Grammar (Anal. Orient., 20), 1940.

Ugaritic Handbook, Rome, 1947.

Ugaritic Literature, Rome, 1949.

Ugaritic Manual, Rome, 1955.

GRAPOW, H., 'Vergleiche und andere bildliche Ausdrücke im Aegyptischen', *AO*, 21, 1–2, 1920.

GRAY, G. B., *Forms of Hebrew Poetry*, London, 1915.
'The References to the "King" in the Psalter, in their Bearing on Questions of Date and Messianic Belief', *JQR*, 7, 1894, pp. 658ff.

GRAY, J., 'The Desert Sojourn of the Hebrews and the Sinai-Horeb Tradition', *VT*, 4, 1954, pp. 148ff.
'Canaanite Mythology and Hebrew Tradition', *Glasgow University Oriental Society Transactions*, 1954.

GRESSMANN, H., *Musik und Musikinstrumente im Alten Testament*, Giessen, 1903.
Ursprung der israelitisch-jüdischen Eschatologie (FRLANT, 6), 1905.
Altorientalische Texte und Bilder zum Alten Testament, Tübingen, 1909 (=*AOTB*); 2. Aufl., 1926, I. Texte (=*AOT*²); II Bilder (=*AOB*²).
'Die literarische Analyse Deuterojesajas', *ZATW*, 34, 1914, pp. 254ff.
'Die neugefundene Lehre des Amenemope und die vorexilische Spruch-dichtung Israels', *ZATW*, 42, 1924, pp. 272ff.
'The Development of Hebrew Psalmody', *The Psalmists*, ed. Simpson, pp. 1ff.

GRIMME, H., 'Ein Festpsalm aus altarabischer Heidenzeit', *Orient. Ltz.*, 1925, pp. 13ff.

GROOT, J. DE, *De Psalmen*, Baarn, 1932.

GUILLAUME, A., 'Magical Terms in the Old Testament', *JRAS*, 1942, pp. 111f.; *ib.*, 1943, pp. 251ff.; *ib.*, 1946, pp. 79ff.

GUNKEL, H., *Schöpfung und Chaos in Urzeit und Endzeit*, Göttingen, 1895.
'Die israelitische Literaturgeschichte', in *Die Orientalischen Literaturen (Kultur der Gegenwart*, herausgeg. v. P. Hinneberg, I, 7), Berlin—Leipzig, 1906.
'Die Lieder in der Kindheitsgeschichte Jesu bei Lukas', *Festgabe für A. v. Harnack*, 1911, pp. 43ff.
'Die Königspsalmen', *Preuss. Jahrbücher*, 158, 1914, pp. 42ff.
'Psalmen' in *RGG*¹ and *RGG*².
Reden und Aufsätze, Göttingen, 1913.
Genesis (HKAT, I, 1), 4. Aufl., 1917.
Ausgewählte Psalmen, 4. Aufl., Göttingen, 1917.
Die Psalmen (HKAT, II, 2), 1926.

GUNKEL, H. and BEGRICH, J., *Einleitung in die Psalmen (HKAT*, Ergänzungs-band), 1933.

GYLLENBERG, R., 'Die Bedeutung des Wortes Sela', *ZATW*, 58, 1940, pp. 153ff.

HALDAR, A., *Associations of Cult Prophets among the Ancient Semites*, Uppsala, 1945.
Studies in the Book of Nahum (UUÅ, 1946, 7), Uppsala—Leipzig, 1947.

HALL, H. R., 'Israel and the Surrounding Nations', in *The People and the Book*, ed. Peake, pp. 1ff.

HALLER, M., 'Ein Jahrzehnt Psalmenforschung', *ThR*, N.F., 1, p. 377.

HANDAGARD, I., *Norsk verslæra*, 2. utg., Oslo, 1942.

HEHN, J., *Hymnen und Gebete an Marduk (BA*, 5, 3), 1907.

HEIDEL, A., *The Babylonian Genesis*, Chicago, 1941.

HEILER, FR., *Das Gebet. Eine religionsgeschichtliche und religionspsychologische Untersuchung*, 4. Aufl., München, 1921. [E.T. *Prayer, A Study in the History and Psychology of Religion*, London, 1932.]

HELBING, R., *Auswahl aus griechischen Inschriften* (*Saml. Göschen*, 754), Leipzig.

HEMPEL, J., 'Die israelitischen Anschauungen von Segen und Fluch im Lichte altorientalischer Parallelen', *ZDMG*, 79, 1925, pp. 22ff.
Gott und Mensch im Alten Testament, Stuttgart, 1926.
Die althebräische Literatur und ihr hellenistisches Nachleben, Wildpark—Potzdam, 1930.
'Chronik', *ZATW*, 55, 1937, pp. 298ff.
Heilung als Symbol und Wirklichkeit im biblischen Schrifttum (*NGWG*, I, 1958, 3).

HENGSTENBERG, E. W., *Commentar über die Psalmen*, I–IV, Berlin, 1842ff.

HERZBERG, H. W., *Prophet und Gott. Eine Studie zur Religiosität des vorexilischen Prophetentums*, *BFChTh*, 28, 3, Gütersloh, 1923.

HESSE, FR., *Die Fürbitte im Alten Testament* (Dissertation), Erlangen, 1951.
'Würzelt die prophetische Gerichtsrede im israelitischen Kult?', *ZATW*, 65, 1953, pp. 45ff.
'Das Kultprophetentum in Israel', *Evang.-Lutherische Kirchenzeitung*, 7, 1953, pp. 129ff.

HIRSCH, E. G., Art. 'Psalms' in *JE*, 10, pp. 241ff.

HJELT, A., *Sjukdomslidandet och fienderna i psalmerna. (Ett bidrag til bedömande af S. Mowinckels teori)*, *Buhlfestskrift*, pp. 64ff.

HOCART, A. M., *Kingship*, London, 1927.

HÖLSCHER, G., *Die Profeten*, Leipzig, 1914.
Geschichte der israelitischen und jüdischen Religion, Giessen, 1922.
Art. 'Levi' in *RLKlA*.
'Elemente arabischer, syrischer und hebräischer Metrik', *Buddefestschrift*, pp. 93ff.
Die Ursprünge der jüdischen Eschatologie, Giessen, 1925.
Review of E. Morbeck, *Profeten Jesaja, stil och äkthet*, I, *Theol. Ltz.*, 1927, cols., 366f.

HOMMEL, H., 'Das religionsgeschichtliche Problem des 139. Psalms', *ZATW*, 47, 1929, pp. 110ff.

HONEYMAN, A. M., 'The Evidence for Regnal Names among the Hebrews', *JBL*, 67, 1948, pp. 13ff.

HOOKE, S. H., ed. *Myth and Ritual. Essays on the Myth and Ritual of the Hebrews in Relation to the Cultic Pattern of the Ancient East*, Oxford, 1933.
ed., *The Labyrinth. Further Studies in the Relation between Myth and Ritual in the Ancient World*, London, 1935.
Prophets and Priests, London, 1936.
The Origins of Early Semitic Ritual, London, 1938.

HORST, F., 'Die Kennzeichen der hebräischen Poesie', *ThR*, NF, 21, 1953, pp. 97ff.

HOSCHANDER, J., *The Priests and Prophets*, 1938.

HUGHES, E. R., ed., *The Individual in East and West*, Oxford, 1937.

HULST, A. R., *Belijden en loven*, Nijkerk, 1948.

HUMBERT, P., review of *PsSt* II, in *RHPhR*, 1936, pp. 1ff.
'La relation de Genése I et du Psaum 104 avec la liturgie du Nouvel-An Israëlite', *RHPhR*, 1935.
Problèmes du Livre d'Habacuc, Neuchatel, 1944.
La 'Terou'a'. Analyse d'un rite Biblique, Neuchatel, 1946.

HVIDBERG, FL. FR., *Graad og Latter i Det gamle Testamente*, Copenhagen, 1938.
Den israelitiske Religions Historie, Copenhagen, 1944.
HYLANDER, I., 'Sions' älv', *NTT*, 1931, pp. 1ff.
Gamla testamentets psalmbok, Stockholm, 1937.
HYLMÖ, G., *Gamla testamentets litteraturhistoria*, Lund, 1938.
'De s. k. vallfartssångerna i Psaltaren', *LUÅ*, N.F., I, bd. 21: 2, Lund, 1925.
JACOB, B., 'Beiträge zu einer Einleitung in die Psalmen', *ZATW*, 16, 1896,
pp. 129ff., 265ff.; 17, 1897, pp. 48ff., 263ff.; 18, 1898, pp. 99ff.; 20, 1900,
pp. 49ff.
JACOBSEN, TH., 'New Sumerian Literary Texts', *BASOR*, 102, Apr. 1946, pp.
12ff.
JAHNOW, HEDVIG, *Das hebräische Leichenlied im Rahmen der Völkerdichtung*
(*BZATW*, 36), 1923.
JANSEN, H. LUDIN, *Die spätjüdische Psalmdichtung* (*SNVAO*, II, 1937, No. 3),
1937.
'Typologien i Johannesevangeliet', *NTT*, 1948, pp. 144ff.
JASTROW, M., *Die Religion Babyloniens und Assyriens*, I–II, Giessen, 1905–12.
'The Sumerian View of Beginnings', *JAOS*, 36, 1917, pp. 122ff., 274ff.
JEFFERSON, H. C., 'Psalm 93', *JBL*, 71, 1952, pp. 155ff.
JENSEN, P., *Babylonische Epen und Mythen*, *KB*, VI, 2, 1916.
JEREMIAS, A., *Monotheistische Strömungen innerhalb der babylonischen Religion*,
Leipzig, 1904.
Handbuch der altorientalischen Geisteskultur, Leipzig, 1913.
Die ausserbiblische Erlösererwartung, Berlin, 1927.
Das Alte Testament im Lichte des Alten Orients, 4. Aufl., Leipzig, 1930.
JIRKU, A., *Die Dämonen und ihre Abwehr im Alten Testament*, Leipzig, 1912.
'Kana'anäische Psalmenfragmente in der vorisraelitischen Zeit Palästinas
und Syriens', *JBL*, 52, 1933, p. 108.
'Ajjelet haš-Šahar (Ps. 22, 1)', *ZATW*, 65, 1953, pp. 85f.
JOHNSON, A. R., 'The Rôle of the King in the Jerusalem Cultus', *The Labyrinth*,
pp. 71ff.
The Cultic Prophet in Ancient Israel, Cardiff, 1944. Second Edition, 1962.
The Vitality of the Individual in the Thought of Ancient Israel, Cardiff, 1949.
'Jonah II. 3–10: A Study of Cultic Phantasy'. *Studies in Prophecy*, ed. H. H.
Rowley, 1950, pp. 82ff.
'HESED and HASID', *Interpretationes ad Vetus Testamentum pertinentes Sigmundo
Mowinckel septuagenario missae*, Oslo, 1955, pp. 100ff.
JUNKER, H., *Prophet und Seher in Israel*, 1927.
KAMINKA, A., 'Neueste Literatur zu den Hagiographen', *MGWJ*, 71, 1927,
pp. 289ff.
KAHLE, P., *Der massoretische Text des Alten Testaments nach der Ueberlieferung
der babylonischen Juden*, Leipzig, 1902.
Die Massoreten des Ostens, Leipzig, 1913.
Die Massoreten des Westens, I–II, Stuttgart, 1927–30.
The Cairo Geniza (Schweich Lectures 1941), London, 1948, ²1959.
KAPELRUD, A., 'Jahves tronstigningsfest og funnene i Ras Sjamra', *NTT*, 1940,
pp. 38ff.
Review of Chr. Barth, *Die Errettung vom Tode*, *SEÅ*, 13, 1947, pp. 55ff.

KAUTZSCH, E., *Die Apokryphen und Pseudepigraphen des Alten Testaments*, I–II, Tübingen, 1900 (= *APAT*).

Die Heilige Schrift des Alten Testaments, I–II, übersetzt von . . . 4. Aufl. herausegeg. v. A. Bertholet, Tübingen, 1927 (*HSAT*).

KEET, C. C., *A Liturgical Study of the Psalter*, London, 1928.

KELLER, C. A., *Das Wort OTH als 'Offenbarungszeichen Gottes'*, Dissert., Basel, 1946.

KENNET, R. H., *Old Testament Essays*, Cambridge, 1928.

KISSANE, E. J., *The Book of Psalms*, I, Dublin, 1953.

KITTEL, R., *Die Psalmen Salomos*, *APAT*, II, pp. 127ff.

Die Psalmen (*KATSl*, 13), 3.–4. Aufl., Leipzig, 1922.

KLAUBER, E., *Assyrisches Beamtentum nach den Briefen aus der Sargonidenzeit* (*Leipz. Sem. Stud.*, V, 3), 1910.

KLOSTERMANN, E., *Das Lukas evangelium* (*Hdb. z. N.T.*, II, 1), Tübingen, 1953.

KÖBERLE, J., *Die Tempelsänger im Alten Testament*, Erlangen, 1899.

KÖHLER, L., *Deuterojesaja stilkritisch untersucht* (*BZATW*, 37), 1933.

Der Hebräische Mensch, Tübingen, 1953. [E.T. *Hebrew Man*, London, 1956.]

KÖNIG, E. *Die Psalmen eingeleitet, übersetzt und erklärt*, Gütersloh, 1927.

KOLARI, E., *Musikinstrumente und ihre Verwendung im Alten Testament. Eine lexikalische und kulturgeschichtliche Untersuchung*, Helsinki, 1947.

KOLDEWEY, R., *Das wiedererstehende Babylon*, Leipzig, 1913. 4. Aufl., 1925.

KRAFT, CH. F., 'Some Further Observations Concerning the Strophic Structure of Hebrew Poetry', *A Stubborn Faith, Papers on Old Testament Subjects*, ed. by Edward C. Hobbs, Dallas, 1956, pp. 62ff.

KRAMER, S. N., 'The Oldest Literary Catalogue', *BASOR*, 88, Dec. 1942, pp. 10ff.

Sumerian Mythology, Philadelphia, Pa., 1944.

'Man and his God. A Sumerian Variation of the "Job" Motif', *Wisdom in Israel and in the Ancient Near East* (Rowley Festschrift,) ed. M. Noth and D. W. Thomas (*Suppl. VT*, III), Leiden, 1955, pp. 140ff.

KÜCHLER, FR., 'Das priesterliche Orakel in Israel und Juda', *Baudissinfestschrift*, pp. 285ff.

KÜMMEL, W. G., review of Riesenfeld: *Jésus transfiguré*, in Symbolae Biblicae Upsalienses 11, suppl. to *SEÅ*, 13, pp. 49ff.

KUHL, C., *Die drei Männer im Feuer* (*Daniel 3 und seine Zusätze*), (*BZATW*, 55) 1930.

LABAT, R., *Le caractère religieux de la royauté assyro-babylonienne*, Paris, 1939.

LABYRINTH, see Hooke.

LAMBERT, W. G. and GURNEY, O. R., *Anatolian Studies*, 4, 1954, pp. 65ff.

LANDSTAD, M. B., *Kirkesalmebok, revidert og forøket*, Oslo.

DE LANGHE, R., *Les Textes de Ras Shamra-Ugarit et leurs Rapports avec le Milieu Biblique de l'Ancien Testament* I–II, Gembloux—Paris, 1945.

Review of Engnell, *Studies in Divine Kingship in the Ancient Near East*, Biblica, 10, 1953, pp. 18ff.

LANGTON, E., *Essentials of Demonology*, London, 1949.

LATTEY, C. J., 'The Prophets and Sacrifice', *JThS*, 42, 1941, pp. 155ff.

LAUHA, A., *Die Geschichtsmotive in den alttestamentlichen Psalmen*, Helsinki, 1945.

VAN DER LEEUW, G., *Phänomenologie der Religion*, Tübingen, 1933. [E.T. *Religion in Essence and Manifestation*, London, 1938.]

LESLIE, E. A., *The Psalms Translated and Interpreted in Light of Hebrew Life and Worship*, New York—Nashville, 1949.

LEY, J., *Grundzüge des Rhythmus, des Vers- und Strophenbaus in der hebräischen Poesie*, Halle, 1875.

Leitfaden der Metrik der hebräischen Poesie, Halle, 1887.

LIDZBARSKI, M., *Handbuch der nordsemitischen Epigraphik*, I–III, Weimar, 1898.

LINDBLOM, J., *Micha, literarisch untersucht*, Åbo, 1929.

Profetismen i Israel, Stockholm, 1934.

Israels religion i gammaltestamentlig tid, Stockholm, 1936.

'Bemerkungen zu den Psalmen I', *ZATW*, 58, 1942–43, pp. 1ff.

'Die "Eschatologie" des 49. Psalms', *Horae Soederblomianae*, I, 1, 1944, pp. 21ff.

Senjudiskt fromhetslif enligt Salomos Psaltare, Akad. avh. Uppsala, IX, 23, 1909.

LINDER, SV., 'Individuella och kollektiva psalmer', *Kristendomen och vår tid*, 1928, pp. 45ff.

LODS, A., 'Les idées des Israélites sur la maladie, ses causes et ses remèdes', *Martifestschrift*, pp. 181ff.

'Recherches récentes sur le Livre des Psaumes. Les idées de M. Mowinckel', *RHR*, 1925, pp. 15ff.

'Éléments anciens et éléments modernes dans le rituel du sacrifice israélite', *RHPhR*, 8, 1928, pp. 399ff.

Israël des origines au milieu du VIIIᵉ siècle, Paris, 1930. [E.T. *Israel from its Origins to the Middle of the Eighth Century*, London, 1932.]

'Le rôle des oracles dans la nomination des rois, des prêtres et des magistrats chez les Israélites, les Egyptiens et les Grecs', *Memoires de l'Institut Francais*. LXVI: *Mélanges Maspero*, Vol. I, pp. 91ff.

'Poèmes phéniciens du XIVᵉ siècle avant J.-C.', *Bull. de la Fac. Libre de Théol. Protest. de Paris, III*, 10, May 1937, pp. 2ff.

LÖHR, M., *Psalmenstudien (BWAT, N.F., 3)*, 1922.

LOISY, A., review of *PsSt.*, II, in *Rev. Crit. Hist. Relig.*, 1923, pp. 122ff.

LOWTH, R., *De sacra poësi Hebraeorum praelectiones academicae Oxonii habitae*, 1753.

LUND, E., 'Eine metrische Form im Alten Testament', *Acta Orientalia*, 17, 1939, pp. 294ff.

LURJE, M., *Studien zur Geschichte der wirtschaftlichen und sozialen Verhältnisse im israelitisch-jüdischen Reiche (BZATW, 45)*, 1927.

McCOWN, C. C., 'Hebrew High Places and Cult Remains', *JBL*, 69, 1950, pp. 205ff.

McCULLOUGH, W. S., 'The "Enthronement of Yahweh" Psalms', *A Stubborn Faith*, ed. E. C. Hobbs, Dallas, 1956, pp. 53ff.

MATTHES, J. C., 'Die Psalmen und der Tempeldienst', *ZATW*, 22, 1902, pp. 65ff.

MEINHOLD, K., *Einführung in das Alte Testament*, 2. Aufl., Giessen, 1926.

MEISSNER, BR., *Babylonien und Assyrien*, I–II, Heidelberg, 1920–25.

Die babylonisch-assyrische Literatur, Wildpark—Potzdam, 1930.

MENES, A., 'Tempel und Synagoge', *ZATW*, 50, 1932, pp. 268ff.

MESSEL, N., 'Salomos salmer. Oversættelse og indledning', *NTT*, 1907, pp. 297ff.

MEYER, ED., 'Die Mosesagen und die Lewiten', *SbBAW*, 1905, pp. 651ff.

Die Israeliten und ihre Nachbarstämme, Halle, 1906.

MICKLEM, N., *Religion*, Oxford, 1948.
MÖLLER, H., 'Strophenbau der Psalmen', *ZATW*, 50, 1932, pp. 240ff.
MOORE, G. F., *Judaism in the First Centuries of the Christian Era, the Age of the Tannaim*, I–III, Cambridge, Mass., 1927–30.
MONTGOMERY, J. A., 'Stanza-Formation in Hebrew Poetry', *JBL*, 64, 1945, pp. 379ff.
  The Bible. The Book of God and Man, Ventnor, N. J., 1948, see 'The Ego of the Psalms', pp. 74ff.
MORGENSTERN, J., 'The three Calendars of Ancient Israel', *HUCA*, I, 1924, pp. 13ff.
  'Additional Notes', *ib.*, 3, 1926, pp. 77ff.; 'Supplementary Studies', *ib.*, 10, 1935, pp. 1ff.; 'The Chanukkah Festival and the Calendar of Ancient Israel', *ib.*, 20, 1947, pp. 1ff.; 21, 1948, pp. 365ff.
  'The Gates of Righteousness', *HUCA*, 6, 1929, pp. 1ff.
  'The Mythological Background of Psalm 82', *HUCA*, 14, 1939, pp. 29ff.
  'Psalm 48', *HUCA*, 16, 1941, pp. 1ff.
  'našequ bar . . .', *JQR*, 32, 4, 1942, pp. 371ff.
  'Psalms 8 and 19A', *HUCA*, 19, 1946, pp. 494ff.
  'The Origin of the Synagogue', *Studi orientalistici in onore di Giorgio Levi della Vida*, II, Rome, 1956, pp. 192ff.
MOSBECH, H., *Essæismen*, Copenhagen, 1916.
MOWINCKEL, S., 'Om nebiisme og profeti', *NTT*, 1909, pp. 185ff., 330ff.
  'Om den jødiske menighets og provinsen Judeas organisasjon ca. 400 f. Kr.', *NTT*, 1915, pp. 123ff., 226ff.
  Kongesalmerne i Det Gamle Testament, Kristiania (Oslo), 1916.
  Statholderen Nehemia, Kri.a., 1916.
  Ezra den skriftlærde, Kri.a., 1916.
  'Die vorderasiatischen Königs- und Fürsteninschriften', *Eucharisterion*, I, pp. 278ff.
  'Tronstigningssalmerne og Jahves tronstigningsfest', *Norsk teologi til reformationsjubileet*, 1917, spesialhefte til *NTT*, 1917, pp. 13ff.
  Psalmenstudien, I. 'Äwän und die individuellen Klagepsalmen, 1921; II. Das Thronbesteigungsfest Jahwäs und der Ursprung der Eschatologie, 1922; III. Kultusprophetie und prophetische Psalmen, 1923; IV. Die technischen Termini in den Psalmenüberschriften, 1923; V. Segen und Fluch in Israels Kult und Psalmdichtung, 1924; VI. Die Psalmdichter, 1924. (*SNVAO*, 1921–24.)
  'Det kultiske synspunkt som forskningsprinsipp i den gammeltestamentlige videnskap', *NTT*, 1924, pp. 1ff.
  Diktet om Ijob og hans tre venner, Kristiania, 1924.
  Art. 'Drama, religionsgeschichtlisches', *RGG²*.
  Art. 'Levi und Leviten', *RGG²*.
  'I porten', *Studier tilegnede Frans Buhl*, Copenhagen, 1925.
  Profeten Jesajah, Oslo, 1925.
  Jesajadisiplene. Profetien fra Jesaja til Jeremia, Oslo, 1926.
  'Stilformer og motiver i profeten Jeremias diktning', *Edda*, 36, 1926, pp. 276ff.
  'Salmeboken og gudstjenestesalmen', *NTT*, 1927, pp. 153ff.

Mowinckel, S., 2. Mos. 18–34; 4. Mos. 20–25; 32–33; 5. Mosebok; Josva-
boken; Samuelsboken; Kongeboken; Jesaja; Jeremia; Tolvprofetboken
in *GTMMM*, I–III.
'Die letzten Worte Davids', in II Sam. 23, 1–7, *ZATW*, 45, 1927, pp. 30ff.
Le Décalogue, Paris, 1927.
'A quelle moment le culte de Jahwé à Jerusalem est il officiellement devenu
un culte sans images?' *RHPhR*, 9, 1929, pp. 197ff.
Review of E. König, *Das Buch Hiob* in *Deutsche Ltz.* 3. Folge, 1. Jahrg. 12,
1930, cols. 529ff.
'Die Komposition des Deuterojesajanischen Buches', *ZATW*, 44, 1931,
pp. 87ff., 242ff.
'Die Chronologie der israelitischen und judäischen Könige', *Act. Or.*, 10,
1932, pp. 161ff.
'Fiendene i de individuelle klagesalmer', *NTT*, 1934, pp. 1ff.
'The "Spirit" and the "Word" in the Preexilic Reforming Prophets', *JBL*,
53, 1934, pp. 199ff.
' "Ånden" og "Ordet" hos de føreksilske reformprofeter', *NTT*, 1935,
pp. 1ff.
'Ekstatisk oplevelse og rasjonal bearbeidelse hos de gammeltestamentlige
profeter', [*D*]*TT*, 1935, pp. 1ff.
'Extatic Experience and Rational Elaboration in Old Testament Prophecy',
Act. Or., 13, pp. 264ff.
'Hat es ein israelitisches Nationalepos gegeben?', *ZATW*, 53, 1935, pp.
130ff.
'Zur Geschichte der Dekaloge', *ZATW*, 55, 1937, pp. 218ff.
Det Gamle Testament som Guds ord, Oslo, 1938.
Gamla testamentet som Guds ord, Stockholm, 1938.
Review of Widengren, *Accadian and Hebr. Psalms of Lamentation*, *NTT*, 1940,
pp. 155.
'Die Erkentnis Gottes bei den alttestamentlichen Propheten', Supplement
to *NTT*, 1941.
'Oppkomsten av profetlitteraturen', *NTT*, 1942, pp. 65ff.
'Kadesj, Sinai og Jahve', *Norsk Geografisk Tidsskrift*, 9, 1942, pp. 21ff.
'Nathanprofetien i 2. Sam. 7', *SEÅ*, 12, pp. 220ff.
'Zum Problem der hebräischen Metrik', *Bertholetfestschrift*, pp. 379ff.
'Den senjødiske salmediktning', *NTT*, 1950, pp. 1–54.
Der achtundsechsigste Psalm (*ANVAO*, II, 1953, 1), Oslo, 1953.
'Zur hebräischen Metrik II', *StTh*, VII, 1953, pp. 54ff.
'Metrischer Aufbau und Textcritik, an Ps. 8 illustriert', *Studia Orientalia
Johanno Pedersen Septuagenario ... dicata*, Havniae, 1953, pp. 250ff.
'Der metrische Aufbau von Jes. 62, 1–12 und die neuen sog. kurzverse',
ZATW, 65, 1953, pp. 167ff.
'Marginalien zur hebräischen Metrik', *ZATW*, 67, 1956, pp. 97ff.
'Psalm Criticism between 1900 and 1935 (Ugarit and Psalm Exegesis)',
VT, 5, 1955, pp. 13ff.
Real and Apparent Tricola in Hebrew Psalm Poetry (*ANVAO*, II, 1957), Oslo, 1958.
'Zum Psalm des Habakuk', *ThZ*, 9, 1953, pp. 1ff.
'Zu Psalm 16, 3–4', *Theol. Ltz.*, 1957, cols. 649ff.
'Notes on the Psalms', *StTh*, XIII, 1959, pp. 134ff.

MUILENBURG, J., 'Psalm 47', *JBL*, 63, 1944, pp. 379ff.

MUNCH, P. A., 'Einige Bemerkungen zu den *'anåwim* und den *rešå'im* in den Psalmen', *MO*, 30, 1936, pp. 13ff.

'Die Stellung Jesajas zu den sozialen Fragen seiner Zeit', *ThStKr*, 107, 1936, pp. 217ff.

'Das Problem des Reichtums in den Psalmen 37, 49, 73', *ZATW*, 55, 1937, pp. 36ff.

'Salme 37, 49, 73', *TTK*, 1937, pp. 52ff.

'Die jüdischen "Weisheitpsalmen" und ihr Platz im Leben', *Act. Or.*, 15, 1937.

MURRAY, J., 'Instrumenta musica S. Scripturae', *Verbum Domini*, 32, 1954, pp. 84ff.

Myth and Ritual, see Hooke.

NAGEL, GEORGES, 'A propos des rapports du Psaum 104 avec les textes égyptiennes', *Bertholetfestschrift*, pp. 395ff.

NICOLSKY, N., *Spuren magischer Formeln in den Psalmen* (*BZATW*, 46), 1927.

NIEMEYER, C. TH., *Het problem van de rang-schikking der Psalmen*, Leiden, 1950.

NILSSON, M. P., *Primitive Religion*, Tübingen, 1911.

Primitive Time-Reckoning, Lund, 1920.

NOETSCHER, FR., *Die Psalmen* (Echterbibel, 1), Würzberg, 1947.

NORDEN, EDU., *Agnostos Theos. Untersuchungen zur Formengeschichte religiöser Rede*, Leipzig, 1913.

NORTH, C. R., 'The Religious Aspect of Hebrew Kingship', *ZATW*, 50, 1932, pp. 8ff.

NOTH, M., *Das System der zwölf Stämme Israels* (*BWANT*, 52), Stuttgart, 1930.

'Die Heiligen des Höchsten', *Interpretationes ad Vetus Testamentum . . . Sigmundo Mowinckel missae*, Oslo, 1955, pp. 146ff.

NYBERG, H. S., *Studien zum Hoseabuche*, Uppsala, 1935.

NYSTRÖM, S., *Beduinentum und Jahwismus. Eine soziologisch-religionsgeschichtliche Untersuchung z. Alten Testament*, Lund, 1946.

OBERMANN, J., 'An Antiphonical Psalm from Ras Shamra', *JBL*, 55, 1936, pp. 21ff.

O'CALLAGHAN, R. T., 'Echoes of Canaanite Literature in the Psalms', *VT*, 4, 1954, pp. 164ff.

ÖSTBORN, G., *Tora in the Old Testament*, Lund, 1945.

OESTERLEY, W. O. E., *The Sacred Dance. A Study in Comparative Folklore*, Cambridge, 1923.

'Early Hebrew Festival Rituals', *Myth and Ritual*, pp. 111ff.

A Fresh Approach to the Psalms, London, 1937.

The Psalms Translated with Texcritical and Exegetical Notes, I–II, London, 1939.

OLSHAUSEN, J., *Die Psalmen erklärt*, Leipzig, 1853.

OPPENHEIMER, L., 'Assyriological Glimpses, IV', *BASOR*, 107, Oct. 1947, pp. 7ff.

PAP, L. I., *Das israelitische Neujahrsfest*, Kampen, 1933.

PALLIS, SV. AAGE, *The Babylonian Akîtu Festival*, Copenhagen, 1926.

PARROT, A., *Le temple de Jérusalem* (*Cahiers d'archéologie biblique*, 5), Neuchatel—Paris, 1947.

PATAI, R., *Man and Temple*, London, 1947.

PATERSON, J., *The Praises of Israel: Studies literary and religious in the Psalms*, New York, 1950.

PATTON, J. H., *Canaanite Parallels to the Book of Psalms*, Baltimore, 1944.

PEDERSEN, JOHS., *Israel*, I–II. Sjæleliv og Samfundsliv; III–IV. Hellighed og Guddommelighed, Copenhagen. 1920–34. = Israel, its Life and Culture, London–Copenhagen, I–II, 1926, III–IV, 1940.
'Passahfest und Passahlegende', *ZATW*, 52, 1934, pp. 161ff.
'Canaanite and Israelite Cultus', *Act. Or.*, XVIII, 1940, pp. 1ff.
Illustreret Religionshistorie, (Editor), Copenhagen, 1948.
'The Rôle Played by Inspired Persons Among the Israelites and the Arabs', *Studies in Prophecy* (Robinson Festschrift), ed. H. H. Rowley, Edinburgh, 1950.

PEAKE, A. S., Editor, *The People and the Book*, London, 1925.

PEET, T. E., *A Comparative Study in the Literatures of Egypt, Palestine and Mesopotamia* (Schweich Lectures, 1929), London, 1931.

PERRY, E. G., *Hymnen und Gebete an Sin* (*Leipz. Sem. Stud.*, II, 4), 1907.

PETERS, J. B., *The Psalms as Liturgies*, Paddock Lectures, 1922, New York, 1922.

PFEIFFER, R., *Introduction to the Old Testament*, New York—London, 1941.

PFISTER, F., art. 'Epiphanie', in *RLKlA*, Suppl. Bd. IV, cols. 277ff.

PHILIPS, G. E., *The Old Testament in the World Churches*, London, 1942.

PIEPER, M., *Die ägyptische Literatur*, Wildpark—Potzdam, 1928.

PINCKERT, J., *Hymnen und Gebete an Nebo* (*Leipz. Sem. Stud.*, III, 4), 1920.

PORTEOUS, N. W., *The Kingship of God in Pre-Exilic Hebrew Religion* (Paper read at Oxford, 1938), London (n.d.)

PORTER, J. R., 'The Interpretations of 2 Sam. VI and Psalm CXXXII', *JThS*, 1954, pp. 161ff.

PRESS, R., 'Das Ordal im alten Israel', *ZATW*, 51, 1933, pp. 121ff., 227ff.

PREUSCHEN, E., 'Die Bedeutung von *šub šebut* im Alten Testament', *ZATW*, 15, 1895, pp. 1ff.

PROHT, J. DE and ZIEHEN, L., Editors, *Leges Graecorum, sacrae*, Fasc. 1–2, Lipsiae, 1896–1906.

PUUKO, A., 'The "Enemy" in the Psalms', *OTS*, VIII, 1950.

QUELL, G., *Das kultische Problem der Psalmen* (*BWAT*, N.F., 11), 1926.

RAD, G. VON, *Das formgeschichtliche Problem des Hexateuchs* (*BWANT*, 78), 1938.
'Das judäische Königsritual', *Theol. Ltz.*, 1947, cols. 211ff.
'Erwägungen zu den Königspsalmen', *ZATW*, 57, 1940–41, pp. 216ff.
' "Gerechtigkeit" und "Leben" in der Kultsprache der Psalmen', *Bertholet-festschrift*, 1950, pp. 418ff.

RAHLFS, A., '*Ani und 'anāw in den Psalmen*, Göttingen, 1892.

RANKE, H., see Erman.
Aegyptische Texte, AOTB and AOT².

RAVN, O. E., *Herodots Beskrivelse af Babylon*, Copenhagen, 1939.

RIDDERBOS, N. H., *De 'Werkers van Ongerechtigheid' in de individuelle Psalmen*, Kampen, 1939.
Psalms en Kult, Kampen, 1950.
'Yahwäh Malak', *VT*, 4, 1954, pp. 87ff.

RIEHM, E. C. A., *Handwörterbuch des biblischen Altertums*, 2. Aufl., Bielefeld, 1893–94.

RIESENFELD, H., *Jésus transfiguré, l'arrière-plan du récit évangelique de la transfiguration de Notre-Seigneur*, Copenhagen, 1947.
The Resurrection in Ezekiel XXXVII and the Dura-Europos Paintings (UUA, 1948 : 11), 1948.
RINGGREN, H., 'Är den bibelska skapelsesberättelsen en kulttext?' *SEÅ*, 13, 1948, pp. 9ff.
Psaltarens fromhet, Stockholm, 1957.
ROBINSON, H. WHEELER, 'The Inner Life of the Psalmists', *The Psalmists*, ed. Simpson, pp. 45ff.
'The Social Life of the Psalmists', *ib.*, pp. 67ff.
Art. 'Psalms' in *EB*, vol. 18, pp. 662ff.
'The Group and the Individual in Israel', *The Indiv. in East and West*, ed. Hughes.
'The Hebrew Conception of Corporative Personality', *Werden und Wesen des A. T.*, pp. 49ff.
ROBINSON, TH. H., 'The God of the Psalmists', *The Psalmists*, ed. Simpson, pp. 23ff.
'The Eschatology of the Psalmists', *ib.*, pp. 87ff.
'Some Principles of Hebrew Metrics', *ZATW*, 54, 1936, pp. 28ff.
'Anacrusis in Hebrew Poetry', *Werden u. Wesen d. A. T.*, pp. 37ff.
'Basic Principles in Hebrew Poetic Form', *Bertholetfestschrift*, pp. 438ff.
The Poetry of the Old Testament, London, 1947.
'Hebrew Sacrifice and Prophetic Symbolism', *JThS*, 43, 1942, pp. 429ff.
ROEDER, G., *Urkunden zur Religion des alten Aegypten*, Jena, ²1933.
ROHLAND, E., *Die Bedeutung der Erwählungstraditionen Israels für die Eschatologie der alttestamentlichen Propheten* (Dissertation), Heidelberg, 1956.
ROTHSTEIN, J. W., *Grundzüge des hebräischen Rhythmus*, Leipzig, 1909.
ROWLEY, H. H., review of Snaith, *The Jewish New Year Festival* in *ThLtz.*, 1948, cols. 533ff.
The Re-Discovery of the Old Testament, London, 1945.
'Was Amos a Nabi?', *Eissfeldtfestschrift*, pp. 191ff.
The Meaning of Sacrifice in the Old Testament (reprint from *BJRL*, 33, 1), Manchester, 1950.
'The Religious Value of Sacrifice', *Expos. Times*, 56, 1944–45, pp. 69ff.
'The Prophets and Sacrifice', *Expos. Times*, 56, 1944–45, pp. 305ff.
Review of B. D. Eerdmans, *Religion of Israel*, *Bibliotheca Orientalis*, IV, 1947, pp. 152ff.
SACHSSE, E., 'Untersuchungen zur hebräischen Metrik', *ZATW*, 43, 1925, pp. 173ff.
'Palästinische Musikinstrumente', *ZDPV*, 50, 1927, pp. 19ff., 167ff.
SAHLIN, H., *Der Messias und das Gottesvolk. Studien zur protolukanischen Theologie*, Uppsala, 1945.
SCHEFTELOWITZ, J., *Altpalästinischer Bauernglaube*, Hannover, 1925.
SCHMIDT, H., *Die Thronfahrt Jahves*, Tübingen, 1927.
Die Psalmen (HBAT, 15), 1934.
Das Gebet des Angeklagten im Alten Testament (BZATW, 49), 1928.
'Das Meerlied', Ex. 15, 2–18, *ZATW*, 49, 1931, pp. 59ff.
Der Mythus vom wiederkehrenden König im Alten Testament, Giessen, 1925.
SCHMIDT, M., *Prophet und Tempel. Eine Studie zum Problem der Gottes Nähe im Alten Testament*, Zollikon-Zürich, 1948.

Schollmeyer, A., *Sumerisch-babylonische Hymnen und Gebete an Šamaš*, Paderborn, 1912.

Schönbächler, V., *Die Stellung der Psalmen zum alttestamentlichen Opferkultus*, Freiburg, 1941.

Schroeder, O., 'Zu Psalm 19', *ZATW*, 34, 1914, pp. 69f.

Schubart, W., 'Die religiöse Haltung des früheren Hellenismus', *AO*, 35, 2, 1927.

Schürer, E., *Geschichte des jüdischen Volkes im Zeitalter Jesu Christi*, I–III, 3.–4. Aufl. Leipzig, 1901–09. [E.T. *History of the Jewish People in the Time of Jesus Christ*, Edinburgh, 1899.]

Schulz, A., *Psalmenfragen*, 1940.

Scott, R. B. Y., 'The Meaning and the Use of "Selah" in the Psalter', *Canadian Soc. of Bibl. Stud. Bull.*, No. 5, July 1939, pp. 17ff.
The Relevance of the Prophets, 1947.
'Solomon and the Beginning of Wisdom in Israel', *Wisdom in Israel and in the Ancient Near East* (Rowley Festschrift), ed. M. Noth and D. W. Thomas, (*Suppl. VT*, III), Leiden, 1955, pp. 262ff.

Segert, S., 'Vorarbeiten zur hebräischen Metrik', *Archiv Orientalni*, XXI, 1953, pp. 481ff., 511ff.

Seierstad, I. P., *Die Offenbarungserlebnisse der Propheten Amos, Jesaja und Jeremia* (*SNVAO*, 1946, No. 2), 1946.

Sellin, E., *Das Zwölfprophetenbuch* (*KATSl*, 12), ²1922.
Einleitung in das Alte Testament, Leipzig, 1910; 7. Aufl., 1935.

Sievers, E., *Metrische Studien*, I–III, *ASGW*, 1904–05, 1907.

Simpson D. C., (Editor) *The Psalmists* Oxford, 1926.

Sjöberg, E., *Gott und die Sünder im palästinischen Judentum* (*BWANT*, 4, 27), 1939.

Slotki, P. I. W., 'Typographic Arrangement of Ancient Hebrew Poetry', *ZATW*, 49, 1931, pp. 211ff.

Smend, R., 'Ueber das Ich der Psalmen', *ZATW*, 8, 1888, pp. 56f.
Lehrbuch der Alttestamentlichen Religionsgeschichte, Freiburg, 1899.

Snaith, N. H., *Studies in the Psalter*, London, 1934.
Jewish New Year Festival, its Origins and Development, London, 1948.
'The Triennial Cycle and the Psalter', *ZATW*, 51, 1933, pp. 302ff.
Hymns of the Temple, London, 1951.

Snijdelar, E. A. A., *De Psalmen bewerkt uit de grondtekst*, 1949.

Soden, W. von, 'Der hymnisch-epische Dialekt des Akkadischen', *ZA*, 40, 1931, pp. 163ff.; 41, 1933, pp. 90ff.
'Zur ersten Tafel von *Ludlul bēl nēmeqi*', *Bibliotheca Orientalis*, 1953, pp. 8–12.

Söderblom, N., *Gudstrons uppkomst*, Stockholm, 1914.

Stade, B. and Bertholet, A., *Biblische Theologie des Alten Testaments*, I–II, Tübingen, 1905–11.

Staerk, W., *Lyrik* = *SATA*, III, 1, ²1920.
'Ein Hauptproblem der hebräischen Metrik', *Sellinfestschrift*, pp. 193ff.

Stamm, J. J., 'Eine Bemerkung zum Anfang des achten Psalms', *ThZ*, 13, 1957, pp. 470ff.

Steindorff, G. and Seele, K., *When Egypt Ruled the East*, Chicago, 1942.

Steinmann, J., *Les Psaumes*, Paris, 1951.

STENDAHL, KR., 'Gamla Testamentets förestållningar om helandet. Rafa' = utsagorna i kontext och ideologi', *SEÅ*, 15, pp. 5ff.

STEUERNAGEL, C., *Lehrbuch der Einleitung in das Alte Testament*, Tübingen, 1912. 'Psalmen zu einem Thronbesteigungsfest Jahwes?' *Preuss. Kirchenzeitung*, 1928, No. 22–24.

STIEB, R., 'Die Versdoubletten des Psalters', *ZATW*, 57, 1939, pp. 102ff.

STRECK, M., *Asurbanipal* (*VAB*, VII, 1–3), 1916.

STUMMER, FR., *Sumerisch-akkadische Parallelen zum Aufbau alttestamentlicher Psalmen*, Paderborn, 1922.
'Die Psalmengattungen im Lichte der altorientalischen Hymnenlitteratur', *JSOR*, 8, 1924, pp. 123ff.

TERRIEN, S., *The Psalms and their Meaning for To-day*, Indianapolis—New York, 1952.

THORNTON, E. A. G., 'The Hebrew Conception of the Speech as a Creative Energy', *Hibbert Journal*, 44, 1945–46, pp. 132f.

TORREY, C. C., 'Outcroppings of the Jewish Messianic Hope', in *Studies in Early Christianity*, ed. S. J. Case, New York—London, 1928, pp. 285ff.

TSEVAT, M., *A Study in the Language of the Biblical Psalms* (*JBL Monograph Series*, Vol. IX), Philadelphia, 1955.

TUR-SINAI, N. H., 'The Literary Character of the Book of Psalms', *OTS*, VIII, 1950, pp. 263ff.

UNGNAD, A., 'Babylonisch-assyrische Texte', *AOTB*.
Aramäische Papyrus aus Elephantine, Leipzig, 1911.
Die Religion der Babylonier und Assyrer, Jena, 1921.

VEDEL, VALD., 'Meningsrytme', *Edda*, 12, 1919, pp. 268ff.

VIROLLAUD, CH., 'Hymne phénicien au Nikal et aux déesses Kosarot provenant de Ras Shamra', *Syria*, 16, 1936, pp. 209ff.
'Le dieu de la mer dans la mythologie de Ras Shamra', *Acad. Inscr. Belles-Lettr.*, 1946, pp. 498ff.

VOLZ, P., *Das Neujahrsfest Jahwes*, Tübingen, 1912.
Review of PsSt II, *Theol. Blätter*, 1924.
'Psalm 49', *ZATW*, 55, 1937, pp. 235ff.

WEBER, O., *Die Literatur der Babylonier und Assyrer*, AO, Erg.-heft. 2, Leipzig, 1907.
Dämonenbeschwörung bei den Babyloniern und Assyrern, AO, 7, 4, 1906.

WEGENER, M. *Die Musikinstrumente des alten Orients* (*Orbis Antiquus* 2) Münster i.W. 1950.

WEISER A., *Die Psalmen*, I–II (*Das Alte Testament Deutsch*, 14–15), Göttingen, 1939, [5]1959.
'Zur Frage nach den Beziehungen der Psalmen zum Kult: Die Darstellung der Theophanie in den Psalmen und im Festkult', *Bertholetfestschrift*, pp. 513ff.

WEISSBACH, FR. H., *Das Stadtbild von Babylon*, AO, 5, 4, 1904.

WEIZÄCKER, C., *Das apostolische Zeitalter der christlichen Kirche*, 3. Aufl., Tübingen, 1902. [E.T. *The Apostolic Age*, I–II, Edinburgh, 1894–5.]

WELCH, A. C., *The Psalter in Life, Worship and History*, Oxford, 1926.
Prophet and Priest in Old Israel, London, 1936.

WELLHAUSEN, J., *Prolegomena zur Geschichte Israels*, 5. Ausg., Berlin, 1899.
'Bemerkungen zu den Psalmen', in *Skizzen und Vorarbeiten*, VI, Berlin, 1899.
The Book of Psalms (SBOT, 14), 1895.
Israelitische und jüdische Geschichte, 6. Aufl., Berlin, 1907.
Reste arabischen Heidentums, 2. Ausg., Berlin, 1927.
WENDEL, A., *Das freie Laiengebet im vorexilischen Israel*, Leipzig, 1931.
Das israelitische Gelübde, Leipzig, 1931.
WENSINCK, A. J., 'The Semitic New Year and the Origin of Eschatology',
Act. Or., I, 1922, pp. 158ff.
The Arabic New Year and the Feast of Tabernacles, Amsterdam, 1925.
Werden und Wesen des Alten Testaments = BZATW, 66, 1936.
WESTERMANN, C., *Das Loben Gottes in den Psalmen*, Berlin, 1953.
'Struktur und Geschichte der Klage im Alten Testament', *ZATW*, 66,
1954, pp. 44ff.
DE WETTE, W. M. L., *Commentar über die Psalmen*, Heidelberg, 1811; 2. Aufl., 1823.
WIDE, SAM., 'Ur Greklands religionslitteratur', *Fr. Relig. Urk.*, III, pp. 199ff.
WIDENGREN, G., *The Accadian and the Hebrew Psalms of Lamentation as Religious
Documents*, Stockholm, 1937.
Hochgottglaube im alten Iran (UUÅ, 1938, 6), 1938.
Psalm 110 och det sakrala kungadömet i Israel (UUÅ, 1941, 7, 1).
'Det sakrala kungadömet bland öst- och väst-semiter', *RoB*, II, 1943, pp. 49 ff.
Religionens värld, Stockholm, 1945.
Religionens ursprung, Stockholm, 1946.
'Konungens vistelse i dödsriket. En studie til Psalm 88, *SEÅ*, 10, pp. 66ff.
'Till det sakrala kungadömets historia i Israel', *Horae Soederblomianae*, I, III,
1947, pp. 1ff.
WIEDEMANN, A., *Die Unterhaltungsliteratur der alten Aegypter*, *AO*, 3, 4, 1903.
WIJDEN, A. H. VAN DER, *Die 'Gerechtigkeit' in den Psalmen*, Nijmegen, 1952.
WILLESEN, F., 'The Cultic Situation of Ps. LXXIV', *VT*, 2, 1952, pp. 289ff.
WINTER, P., *Magnificat and Benedictus—Maccabean Psalms* (reprint from *BJRL*,
37, pp. 328ff.), Manchester, 1954.
'The Cultural Background of the Narrative in Luke I and II', *JQR*, NS,
45, 1954–55, pp. 159ff., 239ff.
WITZEL, M., *Tamuz-Liturgien und Verwandtes (Anal. Orient.*, 10), 1935.
WÜRTHWEIN, E., 'Erwägungen zu Psalm 73', *Bertholetfestschrift*, pp. 532ff.
'Amosstudien', *ZATW*, 62, 1950, pp. 10ff.
'Absprung der prophetischen Gerichtsrede', *ZTK*, 49, 1952, pp. 1ff.
ZIMMERLI, W., 'Ich bin Jahwe', *Geschichte und Altes Testament* (Alt Festschrift
= *Beitr. z. Hist. Theol.*, 16), Tübingen, 1953, pp. 179ff.
ZIMMERN, H., *Biblische und babylonische Urgeschichte*, *AO*, 2, 3, 1903.
'Beilagen', in Gunkels *Schöpfung und Chaos*, pp. 399ff.
See *KAT³*.
Babylonische Hymnen und Gebete in Auswahl, *AO*, 7, 3, 1905: II. Ausw., *AO*,
13, 1, 1911.
König Lipit-Ištars Vergöttlichung (BSGW, 68, 5), 1916.
Zum babylonischen Neujahrsfest, I–II (*BSGW*, 58, 1906, pp. 126ff.; 70, 5, 1918).
'Babylonische Vorstufen der vorderasiatischen Mysterienreligionen?'
ZDMG, 76, 1922, pp. 36ff.
Das babylonische Neujahrsfest, *AO*, 25, 3, 1926.

Subject Index

To be used in conjunction with the Table of Contents.
Note: **page** numbers referring to Vol II are *italicized*.

Index of Scripture Passages Treated

For references to Rabbinical writings, see Talmud, in Subject Index.
Minor Scripture references, especially in the Psalms, have not been indexed.
Note: page numbers referring to Vol. II are italicized.

Index of Authors

Note: page numbers referring to Volume II are *italicized*.